DISCARD

NEURAL NETWORK FUNDAMENTALS WITH GRAPHS, ALGORITHMS, AND APPLICATIONS

McGraw-Hill Series in Electrical and Computer Engineering

Senior Consulting Editor
Stephen W. Director, *Carnegie Mellon University*

Circuits and Systems
Communications and Signal Processing
Computer Engineering
Control Theory
Electromagnetics
Electronics and VLSI Circuits
Introductory
Power and Energy
Radar and Antennas

Previous Consulting Editors
Ronald N. Bracewell, Colin Cherry, James F. Gibbons, Willis W. Harman,
Hubert Heffner, Edward W. Herold, John G. Linvill, Simon Ramo,
Ronald A. Rohrer, Anthony E. Siegman, Charles Susskind, Frederick E. Terman,
John G. Truxal, Ernst Weber, and John R. Whinnery

Communications and Signal Processing

Senior Consulting Editor
Stephen W. Director, *Carnegie Mellon University*

Antoniou: *Digital Filters: Analysis, Design, and Applications*
Bose and Liang: *Neural Network Fundamentals with Graphs, Algorithms, and Applications*
Candy: *Signal Processing: The Model-Based Approach*
Candy: *Signal Processing: The Modern Approach*
Carlson: *Communications Systems: An Introduction to Signals and Noise in Electrical Communication*
Cherin: *An Introduction to Optical Fibers*
Collin: *Antennas and Radiowave Propagation*
Collin: *Foundations for Microwave Engineering*
Cooper and McGillem: *Modern Communications and Spread Spectrum*
Davenport: *Probability and Random Processes: An Introduction for Applied Scientists and Engineers*
Drake: *Fundamentals of Applied Probability Theory*
Huelsman and Allen: *Introduction to the Theory and Design of Active Filters*
Jong: *Method of Discrete Signal and System Analysis*
Keiser: *Local Area Networks*
Keiser: *Optical Fiber Communications*
Kraus: *Antennas*
Kuc: *Introduction to Digital Signal Processing*
Papoulis: *Probability, Random Variables, and Stochastic Processes*
Papoulis: *Signal Analysis*
Papoulis: *The Fourier Integral and Its Applications*
Peebles: *Probability, Random Variables, and Random Signal Principles*
Proakis: *Digital Communications*
Schwartz: *Information Transmission, Modulation, and Noise*
Schwartz and Shaw: *Signal Processing*
Smith: *Modern Communication Circuits*
Taub and Schilling: *Principles of Communication Systems*
Taylor: *Principles of Signals and Systems*

NEURAL NETWORK FUNDAMENTALS WITH GRAPHS, ALGORITHMS, AND APPLICATIONS

N. K. Bose

HRB-Systems Professor of Electrical Engineering
The Pennsylvania State University, University Park

P. Liang

Associate Professor of Electrical Engineering
University of California, Riverside

McGraw-Hill, Inc.

New York   St. Louis   San Francisco   Auckland   Bogotá
Caracas   Lisbon   London   Madrid   Mexico City   Milan   Montreal
New Delhi   San Juan   Singapore   Sydney   Tokyo   Toronto

This book was set in Times Roman by Publication Services, Inc.
The editors were Lynn Cox and John M. Morriss;
the production supervisor was Richard A. Ausburn.
The cover was designed by Joseph Gillians.
Project supervision was done by Publication Services, Inc.
R. R. Donnelley & Sons Company was printer and binder.

**NEURAL NETWORK FUNDAMENTALS WITH
GRAPHS, ALGORITHMS, AND APPLICATIONS**

This book is printed on acid-free paper.

1 2 3 4 5 6 7 8 9 0 DOC DOC 9 0 9 8 7 6 5

ISBN 0-07-006618-3

Library of Congress Cataloging-in-Publication Data

Bose, N. K. (Nirmal K.), (date).
    Neural network fundamentals with graphs, algorithms, and
applications / Nirmal K. Bose, Ping Liang.
        p.   cm. — (McGraw-Hill series in electrical and computer
engineering. Communications and signal processing)
    Includes bibliographical references and index.
    ISBN 0-07-006618-3
    1. Neural networks (Computer science)   I. Liang, Ping, (date).
II. Title.   III. Series.
QA76.87.B68   1996   95-169
006.3—dc20

ABOUT THE AUTHORS

N. K. Bose is the HRB-Systems Professor of Electrical Engineering at the Pennsylvania State University, University Park. He received the M.S. and Ph.D. degrees in Electrical Engineering at Cornell University and Syracuse University, respectively. He is the author of *Applied Multidimensional Systems Theory* (Van Nostrand Reinhold; 1982), *Digital Filters* (Elsevier Science, 1985; Krieger, 1993), and main author as well as editor of *Multidimensional Systems: Progress, Directions, and Open Problems* (Reidel, 1985). He edited several special Issues, contributed to many handbooks, and coedited *The Handbook of Statistics* volume on *Signal Processing and its Applications* (North-Holland, 1993). He is the founding editor-in-chief of the *International Journal on Multidimensional Systems and Signal Processing* and serves on the editorial boards of several other journals. Professor Bose has written numerous research papers in the areas of circuits, control, signal processing, image processing, graph theory, multidimensional systems theory, and neural networks. He was elected to be a Fellow of the Institute of Electrical and Electronics Engineers (IEEE) in 1981 for his contributions to multidimensional systems and circuits and systems education. Dr. Bose has served as visiting faculty at several institutions, including the American University of Beirut, the University of Maryland, and the University of California, Berkeley.

P. Liang received the M.S. and Ph.D. degrees in electrical engineering from the University of Pittsburgh. He was a researcher at the University of California, Santa Barbara, and from 1988 to 1992 he was an Associate Professor of Computer Science at the Technical University of Nova Scotia, Halifax, Canada. Since 1992, he has been with the faculty of the College of Engineering at the University of California, Riverside. He has published many refereed journal and conference papers in image processing, computer vision, robotics, and neural networks. Dr. Liang is a senior member of the Institute of Electrical and Electronics Engineers and an associate editor of two leading research journals.

To those who struggled in spite of obstacles to promote a better understanding of what we are and to those who might continue that trend.

With love to our families, especially Enakshi Bose for her early exposure to neural networks and Lusha Liang for her wisdom about learning and life.

There is "true" Knowledge. Learn thou it is this:
To see one changeless Life in all the Lives
And in the Separate, One Inseparable.

THE SONG CELESTIAL (BHAGAVAD-GITA)
TRANSLATED FROM THE SANSKRIT TEXT
BY SIR EDWIN ARNOLD

CONTENTS

I Fundamentals

III Recurrent Networks

IV Applications of Neural Networks

LIST OF FIGURES

LIST OF TABLES

PREFACE

There has been a proliferation of literature from scientists in several disciplines on the topic of neural networks since its resurgence in the early 1980s. The need for presenting the diverse results under a unified format motivates the writing of this book, which should be suitable for use in senior- and first-year-graduate-level courses as well as for self-study by professionals. The authors believe that the imposition of specific prerequisites will be futile in a subject that covers so many fields. Instead, a reasonable maturity acquired in the undergraduate curricula in electrical engineering, computer engineering, computer science, mathematics, physics, and related disciplines is satisfactory for an adequate comprehension of most of the material in the book. Ability, willingness, creativity, and motivation are the key characteristics for success here as in almost all human endeavors. Therefore, though the book is intended primarily for first-year graduates and professionals, talented seniors—for example, those selected in the university scholars or similar programs—will benefit from exposure to the topic in the selected format for presentation.

Any network, neural or electronic, is characterized by a *topology* and has *components*. The study of topological relationships is facilitated through the use of graph theory whereas the characteristics of components are needed for completing either the analysis or realization of a specified input-output description. This book differs from all other books that have appeared on the subject by its consistent use of graph theory for topological classification of various neural network structures. Graph theory is also useful for analyzing and designing large-scale networks such as neural networks. For example, a proof of the fact that the problem of training is NP-complete is motivated by concepts in graph theory. Many problems that are tackled by neural networks can be best described by axioms in graph theory. Graphs have been used to facilitate analysis of node and edge failures in reliability and fault tolerance studies of a variety of large-scale networks including electrical networks, communication and transportation networks, and switching networks. Similar usage is being witnessed in neural networks, and adoption is expected on a wider scale. Synthesis of neural networks, with simultaneous training of connection weights and structure, has been shown to be systematically feasible by employing Voronoi diagrams and Delaunay tessellations, which can be constructed with increasing efficiency, as recent research in computer science, computational geometry, and parallel computational geometry shows.

The role of neurocomputing in providing an alternative approach to tackling hard combinatorial problems can be better appreciated not only from a presentation of some of those key problems but also from an exposure to the classical algorithms and their modern variants that have contributed to their solutions. Neurocomputing complements rule-based computing but cannot replace it. Since neurocomputing depends on the development of associations between excitation-response pairs through learning rather than on an *if-then* mode of logic, its domain of successful application is expected to be different from that of programmed computation. It is believed that this feature of learning provides the key to some, albeit not all, of the decision-making processes of the mind and brain in comparison with computers. Neurocomputing, therefore, is much less restrictive than traditional rule-based computing because it is not constrained by the shattering implications of the theory of incompleteness concerning the undecidability of certain propositions in any formal mathematical system of axioms and rules. However, neurocomputing is not a panacea for all problems (otherwise, humans would never have needed to invent rule-based computers), and its full capabilities are yet to be assessed. Since an artificial neural network mimics the behavior of a biological system, it shares many of the advantages that living systems have over computers. Some of the future challenges lie in the establishing of the extent to which it can acquire the neurobiological properties of thought and consciousness. In addition to learning, the complexity of size and connections that provide the important and indispensable structural aspects also need to be better appreciated and more fully understood. The contents of this text will provide the tools that enhance the understanding of those and other key issues to enable the reader to participate in the exciting developments in this flourishing as well as promising area.

Part One, consisting of three chapters on the elements of neuroscience, graph theory, and algorithms, contains the important fundamentals, which the readers will find useful for comprehending the contents of the remaining three parts. Since artificial neural networks (ANNs) attempt to mimic the biological brain and the central nervous system, the nature and characteristics of ANN systems will be better appreciated after some understanding of neuroscience, illustrated typically by the models developed and used to explain the functioning of the human brain. The reader is subsequently introduced in Chapter 2 to the rudiments of graph theory that will be useful in the characterization of the topologies of various neural network structures. Graph theory originated about two centuries ago; the benefit reaped from a judicious blend of the old and the new is aptly illustrated by the impact of modern computational geometry in the solution of many problems that have been formulated in the theory of graphs. The expected useful joint role of graphs and computational geometry in neural network design is substantiated by the proven use of Voronoi diagrams in a systematic approach to designing multilayer feedforward neural networks. The potentials for exploiting very recent developments in parallel computational geometry toward the solution of hard combinatorial problems, and the possibilities for generalization of the design approach just cited to recurrent neural networks, illustrate how this book aims at stimulating and challenging the reader to tackle open problems after digesting the fundamentals expounded in depth with sufficient clarity in the text.

Algorithms and complexity theory are briefly introduced in Chapter 3 for the following reasons. First, existing algorithms for hard problems provide insight into approaches toward the design of neural networks, whose performance may subsequently be evaluated using the classical algorithms as benchmarks. The application of neural networks has been hampered on the one hand, and unjustifiably hyped on the other, because of the lack of adequate performance comparisons with mature algorithms. To promote such comparison we present some mature algorithms for a set of well-known problems with a wide range of applications. Second, complexity theory for neural networks is itself a topic that merits further investigation; appropriate measures of complexity for neural networks have been the subject of debate.

In Chapter 3 the reader is also exposed to typical problems of great utilitarian value, for which efficient algorithms are available, as well as to developments in computer science that concern the NP-complete and NP-hard classification concepts. Hard problems such as Steiner's problem and several others encountered in the distinct but interlinked stages of partitioning, placement, and routing of very large-scale circuits, have been subjects of intensive investigations. Because neural networks provide an alternate approach of attack for those hard problems, it is important that the reader gain at least a passing familiarity with the nature of some of those problems and the context in which they occur. These objectives are attained in the later portions of Chapter 3, where the basic differences between serial and parallel processing are also highlighted.

The title of the book, therefore, correctly reflects the philosophy behind its mode of exposition; the authors hope that it will bring out more clearly than in previous treatments not only the differences between neural and rule-based computing, but also some of the common objectives. In the early 1980s, the role of neural networks in providing an alternative approach for obtaining solutions (though suboptimal) of hard problems in combinatorial optimization theory was realized. For instance, in the design automation of large-scale circuits the problems of optimal partitioning, placement, and interconnection, which belong to the distinguished class of NP-complete problems, were tackled with some success at IBM by the method of simulated annealing.

Part Two consists of four chapters, starting with the descriptions of perceptrons, Adalines, and Madalines, which were among the earliest neural networks to incorporate learning by supervision. In spite of the shortcomings of perceptrons, the associated training algorithms for the class of linearly separable patterns is endowed with the convergence property, which is proved in Chapter 4. The LMS algorithm has also been widely used, especially before the popularization of the backpropagation method. The concept of order has proved to be significant in the understanding of limitations of perceptronlike machines and is discussed in a complete but simple manner in the latter parts of Chapter 4.

Multilayer feedforward structures, which are characterized by directed layered graphs and are generalizations of those earlier structures, are studied in Chapter 5, not only when the structures are fixed but also when those are allowed to vary and grow. In the case of fixed structures, the method of backpropagation based on supervisory training has been widely used to train multilayer ANNs. In spite of continued improvements, many of which are discussed in the text, the limitations of the fixed structure have prompted investigations into the need for structural training. This possibility is introduced in the second half of Chapter 5 and continued in Chapter 7 with descriptions of growth networks. The scope of applying unsupervised learning to train multilayer networks is also considered through principal component analysis networks as well as a method for self-organization of ANNs characterized by the layered topology. Another multilayer feedforward neural network considered is the Probabilistic Neural Network, which is characterized by a statistically derived activation function and a method of training that is quite different from the one associated with the backpropagation algorithm.

Issues regarding complexity are considered in Chapter 6. The size of a network is investigated in terms of the number of learning exemplars and valid generalization. Computability, intractability, and learnability issues in a neural network are addressed. The concept of capacity, as exemplified by the VC-dimension, conveys useful information about the problem size computable by a neural network to provide estimates on the number of exemplars needed for learning and, very importantly, generalization. Chapter 6 is for advanced readers, and total familiarity of all concepts expounded there is not mandatory for adequate comprehension of what follows in Chapter 7.

Exposure in Chapter 5 to a type of design in which the structure is not fixed a priori, and appreciation of (if not total familiarity with) computability and learnability issues in Chapter 6, position the reader for comprehending the need for the so-called growth algorithms, presented in Chapter 7. A trend toward training for structural variables and parameters, in addition to thresholds and connection weights, is increasingly observed in research, where the conflicting factors of size and versatility are also being addressed. Another concern that is attracting the attention of researchers and is discussed in Chapter 7 is the properties of neural networks that have nonlinear and adaptive synapses between the neurons.

The versatility of a neural network is considerably increased by the incorporation of feedback. Part Three begins with a detailed analysis of symmetric and asymmetric neural networks in Chapter 8, where the characterizing graph is, in general, not layered. The differences from the networks in Part Two are noticeable, not only in the topology, but also in the manner in which weights are assigned to the connections. The concept of the energy function, its construction in a particular problem of interest, and the goal of minimizing this energy function are ubiquitous factors in the Hopfield network and the Bidirectional Associative Memory network. These types of networks are useful in retrieving complete data from keys that carry noisy or incomplete data, and they can also serve as content-addressable associative memories. These characteristics mimic those in the human brain and cannot be readily replicated by conventional computers. Improvements and improvisations in minimizing the energy function lead to other types of neural networks such as the Boltzmann machine, which is also described in Chapter 8.

Competitive and self-organizing networks are introduced in Chapter 9, where Hamming nets, MAXNETs, Adaptive Resonance Theory (ART) networks, Kohonen's self-organizing maps, counterpropagation networks, radial basis function networks, and Fukushima's neocognitron are covered. Many of these networks, such as the neocognitron, require a large number of units and connections but have been used for sophisticated tasks such as handwritten character recognition. The counterpropagation network is an example of a network that incorporates both supervised and unsupervised learning schemes. Many of these networks and their variants employ different learning rules from those previously covered and have topologies characterized by distinct classes of graphs.

In Chapter 10, selected key applications of the theory presented earlier are discussed in sufficient detail. These applications include well-studied ones, such as the traveling salesperson problem, and more recent ones such as the tracking of multiple targets in clutter by Hopfield nets. From perusal of this chapter the reader will be able to infer the scopes as well as limitations of neural networks. These promises and perils substantiate the need for understanding the fundamentals of neurocomputing so that the areas of potentially successful applications can be selected, bottlenecks and limitations realized, and obstacles overcome by resort to scientific procedures or guidelines as opposed to brute-force or trial-and-error strategies. The purpose of this book will be well served if it contributes to that understanding and to the realization of the problems as well as the potentials of this novel avenue that the collective computational capability of neural networks opens up toward tackling classical problems. The authors also hope that this text, through its unified premise of presentation that dwells on the topological foundation of structures, will relieve the reader somewhat from the sense of bewilderment and frustration caused by the abundance of scattered literature on the subject. The bottom line in the authors' philosophy behind the writing of this text has been the exposition of sound theory for sound practice, to the extent they believe is currently feasible. Their attempts will be amply rewarded by further developments, refinements, and amalgamations of concepts and ideas that may ultimately evolve into a cohesive and unified realizability theory for neural networks, just as the classical realizability theory of various classes of electrical networks witnessed four or five decades of intense research activity.

While writing this text, the authors have benefited considerably from the use of some of the many software made available. The reader is encouraged to use a software package only after the underlying concepts and guidelines have been understood. This book does not indicate a strong preference for one or the other of the name-brand software packages available in the market; however, the Neural Network Toolbox accompanying MATLAB® (The MathWorks, Inc., Natick, MA) was extensively used to solve examples, some of which are documented in the text. Since such a facility is now readily available at low cost, the reader is encouraged to acquire one and use it to solve not only some of the examples that are assigned in the text but also those that might arise in professional experience and that may be amenable to attack with the resources derived from this text.

In addition to use by professionals, the text is suitable for use in classroom settings in a variety of ways. The authors hope that all users will read Chapter 1 so that they acquire an understanding of a biological neural network, which an artificial neural network seeks to replicate. Chapters 2 and 3 are for the serious student who wishes to identify common topological properties in several different neurocomputing architectures and to evaluate the performance of algorithms to solve a particular problem by neurocomputing as well as by classical computing. Those wishing to venture immediately into the topic of artificial neural networks, distinguished by the property of learning, may go directly to Chapter 4 and then to Chapter 5. For a deeper understanding of the capabilities of a perceptron, it is important to understand the concept of order, which is described in the later part of Chapter 4. Otherwise, one may proceed to Chapter 5 following the perusal of the subject matter concerning the perceptron and the Widrow-Hoff rule. The discussion of the backpropagation algorithm in Chapter 5 should be read by everyone, because other procedures in that as well as other chapters use this popular algorithm as a benchmark for comparison. Chapters 6 and 7 are for advanced readers. In particular, Chapter 6 provides insights into theoretical developments in computational learning theory, whereas the growth networks described in Chapter 7 satisfy the curiosity roused in a reader following exposure to structural training exemplified by the Voronoi diagram–based procedure in Chapter 5. Chapter 8 should be read by all, because of the importance of the feedback model as a content-addressable memory and also for its use in attempts to tackle hard combinatorial optimization problems, albeit with varying degrees of success. Chapter 9 contains descriptions and analysis of performance of a variety of other neural network architectures; the reader may study it in its entirety or pursue it selectively. This comment also applies to Chapter 10, which alerts the reader to the immense scope of applications of neural network principles.

The whole book can be covered thoroughly either in a two-semester sequence or in one semester devoted to fundamentals followed by a period of self-study. For a one-semester course, exclusively devoted to neural networks, Chapter 1 may be followed by Chapters 4, 5, 8, and 9. Another variant of a one-semester offering, with students in computer science and mathematics in the audience, would include Chapter 1; selected portions of Chapters 2, 3, and 6; and Chapters 4, 5, and 8. For an undergraduate course, some of the sections requiring more mathematical sophistication, such as Section 4.3, on order; Section 5.1, on function representation; Section 5.4, on unsupervised learning; and Sections 8.1.2 and 8.1.4, can be skipped without affecting the presentation of the other materials. In any course the ample set of exercise problems and projects motivated by the sampling of applications should be of value. The flowchart in Fig. PRE.1 will provide a quick guide to some of the various paths that could be traversed to realize different objectives in the classroom usage of this book. The attention to fundamentals, leading up to the cutting edge of research, is expected to quench the thirst of both the student, contemplating entering research, and the professional, already involved with some aspects of the topic.

The first author introduced a course on the subject matter of this book in 1990 at The Pennsylvania State University, University Park. The second author introduced a graduate course in neural networks at the Technical University of Nova Scotia in the same year. The second author also visited University Park for a couple of weeks that year, and the possibility of developing a text centered around the syllabus and class notes was discussed. Considerable momentum toward that goal was generated after the second offering of the course at The Pennsylvania State University, University Park, in 1992 and the increasing research activities of both authors in the area of neural networks. Several graduate and undergraduate students as well as postdoctoral scholars worked with the authors on various projects that required knowledge of neural network fundamentals. They carried on extensive simulations in the labora-

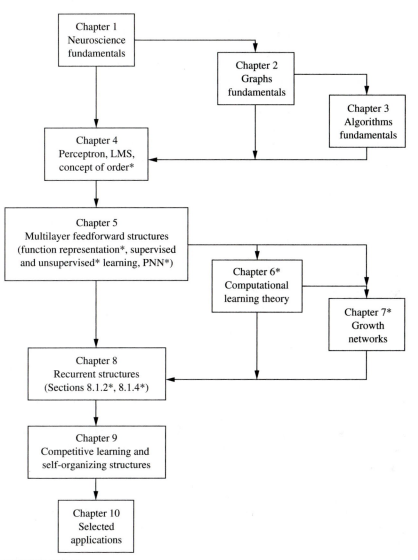

FIGURE PRE.1
Flowchart of relationships among chapters. The star (*) superscript implies an advanced topic.

tories, which contributed to a greater appreciation of the techniques presented in this book. Singled out for special mention is A. K. Garga, who completed a Ph.D. dissertation on structure-trained neural networks. His enthusiasm for the subject matter is noteworthy and his insights into computer processing were helpful in the construction of some nontrivial examples. Thanks are also due to Dr. B. Zhou, who worked out some examples; Dr. H. C. Kim, who did some of the figures; and J. Chun, who, besides doing many of the remaining figures, also worked out most of the examples in the accompanying solutions manual. This manual is available to course instructors and professionals. Among those who showed special interest in the topic and went on to prepare their theses or conduct research on a variety of related problems under the direct supervision of the authors are G. Babich, W. Eggert, M. Pechanec, W. Prehl, and M. Revay at The Pennsylvania State University, University Park; N. Jamali and H. F. Yin at the Technical University of Nova Scotia; plus Dr. F. M. Song and K. Jin at The University of California, Riverside. The authors are very grateful to the numerous reviewers of this manuscript for their encouraging and constructive comments. These reviewers include Professors Rafael M. Iñigo, University of Virginia; Haniph A. Latchman, University of Florida; Satish S. Nair, University of Missouri–Columbia; Yun Peng, University of Maryland, Baltimore County, Fathi Salam, Michigan State University; Edgar Sánchez-Sinencio, Texas A&M University; and Jennie Si, Arizona State University. The first author is very grateful to HRB-Systems for continued support that allowed him to pursue many novel and challenging avenues of research at Penn State. He also wishes to thank the Office of Naval Research and the National Science Foundation for supporting some of his research activities in the area of neural networks.

The second author acknowledges the support for research extended to him by the Natural Science and Engineering Research Council of Canada, the National Science Foundation, and the University of California, through the internal research grants.

Though plans for writing this book were hatched in 1990, some of the tools used were acquired years ago. The first author was fortunate to have conducted research in graph theory and combinatorics in the 1970s. Both authors benefited from their earlier exposure and involvement with computational complexity theory. Several torches helped light the path to the fascinating terrain of neural networks, where exploration led the authors a step closer to understanding themselves as living systems, such as artificial neural networks attempt to model or replicate. During that journey and after arrival at the destination they were exposed to the voluminous literature associated with the subject matter. The task of citing all is futile, because a mere compilation of those references will fill several volumes of this size. The authors tried to be just in the selection of references but apologize in advance for any pertinent item that was inadvertently omitted.

This book was sought by many publishers. The authors' choice of publisher was a matter of optimization based on the criteria of care and concern for excellence, without sacrificing timeliness and speed. Certainly, McGraw-Hill lived up to the authors' expectations, and they hope that the readers agree.

We wish to convey our sincere thanks to Jerome Colburn and Marguerite Torrey for their excellent copy editing. Lynn Cox, Kris Engberg, John Morriss, and Jeff Topham extended all cooperation necessary to keep the production of this book on schedule. Last but not least, the book could not be completed without the influence, motivation, and patience over the years of our families, both immediate and extended.

N. K. Bose,
P. Liang

LIST OF ACRONYMS

3NX	three-node XOR network
Adaline	adaptive linear element
ALVINN	autonomous land vehicle in neural networks
ANN	artificial neural network
ART	adaptive resonance theory
ASIC	application-specific integrated circuit
BAM	bidirectional associative memory
BM	Boltzmann machine
BPA	backpropagation algorithm
CAN	crossbar associative network
CAT	computer-assisted tomography
CC	cascade correlation
CLN	competitive learning network
CMAC	cerebellar model arithmetic computer
CMOS	complementary metal-oxide-semiconductor (technology)
CNF	conjunctive normal form
CNN	cellular neural network
CNS	central nervous system
CPG	central pattern generators
CPN	counterpropagation network
CPU	central processing unit
CXOR	complementary XOR
DT	Delaunay tessellation
DAP	data association problem
DCT	discrete cosine transform
DSP	digital signal processing
DTM	deterministic Turing machine

EEG	electroencephalograph
FFT	fast Fourier transform
FIR	finite impulse response
HBF	hyper basis function
HD	Hamming distance
HMM	hidden Markov model
HN	Hamming network
IC	integrated circuit
ID	instantaneous description
IIR	infinite impulse response
JPDAF	joint probabilistic data association filter
LMS	least mean square
LSI	large-scale integration
LTF	linear threshold function
LVQ	learning vector quantization
Madaline	multiple adaptive linear element
MC	minimum cut
MFT	minimal Fermat tree
MOSFET	metal-oxide-semiconductor field-effect transistor
MST	minimal spanning tree
NAND	not AND
NC	polylogarithmic time algorithms
NDTM	nondeterministic Turing machine
NMRI	nuclear magnetic resonance imaging
NP	nondeterministic polynomial (algorithm)
P	deterministic polynomial (algorithm)
P-RAM	parallel random access memory
PC	personal computer
PCB	printed circuit board
PDAF	probabilistic data association filter
PDF	probability density function
PDP	parallel distributed processing
PSP	postsynaptic potential
PET	positron emission tomography
PNN	probabilistic neural network
RAM	random access memory
RBF	radial basis function
RBP	recurrent backpropagation
RC	resistance capacitance
SA	simulated annealing
SMT	Steiner minimal tree
SOFM	self-organizing feature map

TLU	threshold logic unit
TSP	traveling salesperson problem
UCL	unsupervised competitive learning
ULSI	ultralarge-scale integration
VC dimension	Vapnik-Chervonenkis dimension
VLSI	very large-scale integration
VoD	Voronoi diagram
VONNET	Voronoi (diagram) neural network
XOR	exclusive OR

GLOSSARY OF NOTATIONS

$\mathbf{a}^{\mathrm{T}}$	transpose of vector $\mathbf{a}$
$\mathbf{A}^{\mathrm{T}}$	transpose of matrix $\mathbf{A}$
$\mathbf{a} \cdot \mathbf{b}$	$\mathbf{a}^{\mathrm{T}}\mathbf{b}$, the inner product of vectors $\mathbf{a}$ and $\mathbf{b}$
$a + b$	boolean sum of a and b
$a \odot b$	boolean product of a and b
$a \oplus b$	exclusive OR of a and b
$a \oplus b \oplus c$	parity function for three variables a, b, and c
$a \in A$	element a belongs to set A
$a \notin A$	element a does not belong to set A
$\|\mathbf{a}\|$	Euclidean norm, unless specified otherwise, of vector $\mathbf{a}$
$[a, b]$	closed interval $a \le \lambda \le b$
(a, b)	open interval $a < \lambda < b$
$(a, b]$	semiopen interval $a < \lambda \le b$
$\lceil x \rceil$	ceiling function, giving the smallest integer not less than real number x
$\lfloor x \rfloor$	floor function, giving the integer part of real number x
$\|x\|$	absolute value of real number x
$\mathbf{A}^{+}$	the unique Moore-Penrose inverse of matrix $\mathbf{A}$
$\mathbf{A}^{\mathrm{H}}$	Hermitian conjugate of matrix $\mathbf{A}$
$X \subset Y$	set X is a proper subset of set Y
$X \supset Y$	set X contains set Y
$\|V\|$	cardinality of set V
$\ln$	natural (base e) logarithm
$T \times T$	Cartesian or direct product of set T with itself
T^k	Cartesian or direct product of T, k times
$\mathbb{R}^n$	n-dimensional real Euclidean space
$\operatorname{sgn} x$	signum function in variable x

sup	supremum (least upper bound)
$T_b(x)$	threshold function, which equals 1 for $x > 0$ and α for $x \leq 0$, where α is 0 or -1 or a small positive number
β	momentum parameter
η	learning parameter
θ_i	threshold parameter for ith neuron
$-\theta_i$	bias parameter for ith neuron
∇	gradient operator
ΔD	small change in D
$\wedge$	logical AND
$\vee$	logical OR
$\cup$	set union
$\cap$	set intersection
$\{0, 1\}$	set of unipolar binary elements 0 and 1
$\{-1, 1\}$	set of bipolar binary elements -1 and 1
$\{0, 1\}^n$	n-fold Cartesian product of $\{0, 1\}$
$\{-1, 1\}^n$	n-fold Cartesian product of $\{-1, 1\}$
$O(g(n))$	growth no faster than the growth of $g(n)$
$k!$	factorial of k
$\binom{n}{k}$	$\dfrac{n!}{k!(n-k)!}$
$\mathbb{R}^n \longrightarrow \{0, 1\}$	mapping from $\mathbb{R}^n$ to set $\{0, 1\}$
$k \leftarrow (k+1)$	replace k by $(k+1)$
$k+1 \rightarrow k$	set k to the value $(k+1)$
$\approx$	approximately equals
$\triangleq$	is defined to be
$P(x \mid y)$	probability of x conditioned on y
$T \setminus I$	set difference of sets T and I

PART
I

FUNDAMENTALS

$\mathbf{A}$*rtificial neural networks* (ANNs), also called *parallel distributed process-ing systems* (PDPs) and *connectionist systems,* are intended for modeling the organizational principles of the central nervous system, with the hope that the bio-logically inspired computing capabilities of the ANN will allow the cognitive and sensory tasks to be performed more easily and more satisfactorily than with conven-tional serial processors. Because of the limitations of serial computers, much effort has been devoted to parallel processing architectures, also described in this part. In the extreme case of fine-grained parallel processing architecture, the function of a single processor is at a level comparable to that of a neuron. If the interconnections between the simple fine-grained processors are made adaptive, a neural network results.

ANN structures, broadly classified as *recurrent* (involving feedback) or *non-recurrent* (without feedback), have numerous processing elements (also dubbed *neurons*, neurodes, *units*, or *cells*) and connections (forward and backward *interlayer connections* between neurons in different layers, forward and backward *intralayer connections* or *lateral connections* between neurons in the same layer, and *self-connections* between the input and output of the same neuron). Neural networks may not only have differing structures or topology but are also distinguished from

1

one another by the way they learn, the manner in which computations are performed (rule-based, fuzzy, even nonalgorithmic), and the component characteristics (transfer characteristics of the neurons or the input/output description of the synaptic dynamics). These networks are required to perform significant processing tasks through collective local interaction that produces significant global properties. Therefore, the necessary fundamentals for a serious study of neural networks include the elements of neuroscience, to illustrate the biological principles that an ANN attempts to mimic; the elements of graph theory, to extract the essence of the architecture of structures; and the rudiments of algorithms, to derive an appreciation for the science of computing (serial or parallel, classical or neurocomputing) and the types of problems or applications that are efficiently tackled.

Part I therefore consists of three chapters devoted to the topics of neuroscience, graphs, and algorithms. Wherever possible, discernible building blocks that are replicated in the system under study are identified and highlighted so that the behavior or composition of an apparently complex whole may be understood or inferred from a knowledge of the simpler part. For example, each neuron, irrespective of its size, shape, and variety, is an important building block of the central nervous system. Its general features and properties convey an understanding about the nature and mechanism of signal transmission in complex biological systems consisting of billions of neurons. Similarly, very simple but distinguished classes of graphs, such as complete graphs and bipartite graphs, serve as important building blocks for a variety of artificial neural network topologies encountered throughout the book. The study of algorithms and algorithmic learning is itself facilitated by a knowledge of graph theory.

The initial difficulty with the word *nonalgorithmic* can be realistically addressed by understanding what the complementary word *algorithm* stands for. In the subject of neural networks, the universe of discourse, consisting of the set of algorithms and its complement, is essential; whereas in classical optimization and decision-making problems, one is essentially concerned with algorithms only. ANNs are implemented by algorithms that, in certain cases, can be constrained to exhibit convergence. However, some believe that the seat of consciousness and thought for decision making in the biological neural network is nonalgorithmic, a feature that casts serious doubt on the ultimate capability of ANNs to simulate a biological neural network precisely. The goal therefore should be to find means for approximating the property and functions of a real neural network with an ANN. The implications of algorithmic computing, as opposed to nonalgorithmic computing, are expected to provide proper distinction between the performance of an ANN and of a biological network.

The fundamentals in this section are useful not only in the analysis and design of ANNs but also in their layout prior to fabrication. Since the myriad components and connections and their packaging under stringent spatial constraints make the system large-scale, the role of graph theory, algorithms, and neuroscience is pervasive. Our presentation of these fundamentals, though necessarily terse, should be adequate for preparing the reader to undertake a serious study of neural networks and their applications, described subsequently in this text.

CHAPTER

1

BASICS OF NEUROSCIENCE AND ARTIFICIAL NEURON MODELS

The human brain is made up of a vast network of computing elements, called *neurons,* coupled with sensory receptors (affectors) and effectors. The average human brain, roughly three pounds in weight and 90 cubic inches in volume, is estimated to contain about 100 billion cells of various types. A neuron is a special cell that conducts an electrical signal, and there are about 10 billion neurons in the human brain. The remaining 90 billion cells are called *glial* or glue cells, and these serve as support cells for the neurons. Each neuron is about one-hundredth the size of the period at the end of this sentence. Neurons interact through contacts called *synapses.* Each synapse spans a gap about a millionth of an inch wide. On the average each neuron receives signals via thousands of synapses.

The brain organizes this huge number of neurons (also referred to as *cells* because glial cells are not of interest here, or *units*), each with weak computing power, into a massively parallel complex network in which these neurons interact with each other dynamically to produce a powerful information processor. Neurons are five to six orders of magnitude slower than current silicon gates. The modern computer easily outperforms the human in preprogrammable, repetitive computations. However, real-time speech understanding and visual perception, which a human being almost effortlessly implements, are still beyond the reach of serial digital computers even after allowing for an increase of speed by several orders of magnitude. Many of the tasks are difficult for the serial digital computers, either because the computational load requires speed and storage not realizable with existing technology or because of

3

the possible inherent intractability of some problems, including their complete and accurate symbolic descriptions.

Human beings, as well as many other living creatures, tackle practical problems almost effortlessly in comparison with a serial digital computer. The motivation for artificial neural network (ANN) research is the belief that a human's capabilities, particularly in real-time visual perception, speech understanding, and sensory information processing and in adaptivity as well as intelligent decision making in general, come from the organizational and computational principles exhibited in the highly complex neural network of the human brain. Expectations of faster and better solutions provide us with the challenge to build machines using the same computational and organizational principles, simplified and abstracted from neurobiological studies of the brain.

To comprehend how the brain works, neurobiologists want to understand the stimulus-response characteristics of a single neuron and the interconnections of neurons that form either subregions of the brain or smaller subdivisions of the nervous system. This approach is a bottom-up one. Such lower-level models not only help us understand what properties of neurons are likely to be important for higher-level functions, but also suggest better ways for extracting these properties for possible inclusion in higher-level models. Psychologists attempt to understand the brain function from the cognitive and behavioral levels. This approach is a top-down one. Some favor a compromise between the two extreme positions of bottom-up and top-down.

To understand the brain functions completely in terms of neural activities, it is necessary to model multiple levels of the system equipped with the receptors and effectors, the phenotype (genetically and environmentally determined physical appearance, especially as considered with respect to all possible genetically influenced expressions of one specific character), and the environment the models interact with. This approach is exemplified by the work of Nobel laureate Gerald Edelman and his school [310]. Their approach, called synthetic neural modeling, closely resembles the neurobiological bottom-up approach. However, it goes beyond other neurobiological models because here bottom-up processing is viewed as a combination of elementary forms. The ultimate goal of research in neural networks is to provide a bridge between the preceding two approaches and to understand human brain functions and intelligence through models of networks of neurons. We believe that this goal is not even close to realization.

In this chapter, we are interested in promoting qualitative understanding of the dynamics, complexity, and functions of networks of neuronlike elements in the analysis, synthesis, and development of artificial neural networks to solve practical problems. Our perspective is the building of useful machines through learning rather than through our copying the organizational and functional features of the brain. This perspective is useful because our knowledge of nervous system functions is far from complete. The optimal implementation of a principle depends on the technology available to implement it as well as on the intended applications. Note as an analogy that though airplanes do not flap their wings, the same aerodynamic principles that govern the flight of birds apply to airplanes as well. Mathematical analysis of neural networks based on simplified models of actual biological neural networks helps us to infer the computational principles employed in the massively parallel machine, since those models are simple in comparison to the actual nervous system, where the principles may be buried inside too many interwoven factors. This analysis in turn can provide neurophysiologists with ideas of what to look for and how better to interpret their laboratory findings.

An important issue in neural networks is size, together with the associated *scaling property.* Very small, simple networks have extremely limited capability. Therefore, it is desirable to investigate how to analyze and synthesize large neural networks so that any interesting behavior or capability might become evident. This requires mathematical understanding of the dynamic behavior, convergence, time, size, and space complexity issues of large networks. Large networks are difficult to analyze. A prevailing notion is that in order to understand something complex, one must determine whether it can be replicated with simpler components, each of which can then be studied in depth. Knowledge gained from smaller networks is therefore useful for understanding larger networks. These smaller networks may either be approximations to or serve as components in larger, more complex ones. One must bear in mind that there may be qualitative changes of behavior as one proceeds from small, simple networks to large, complex networks. These qualitative changes can be identified and understood if it is possible to trace the evolution from the former to the latter category. At present, even the algorithmic implementations of the characteristics of many small networks are either not well understood or not well developed. Therefore, tall claims and naïve generalizations made from the use of small, simple networks without knowledge of their scaling properties and limitations should be viewed with suspicion.

Following is a list of some of the areas where research efforts should be focused from the perspective of building computationally useful machines:

1. To gain thorough mathematical understanding of existing neural networks and their algorithms, including dynamics, convergence, space, size, and time complexities.
2. To develop more robust and faster algorithms for existing networks.
3. To design new networks and accompanying algorithms with useful capabilities.
4. To develop realizability theory for building large networks using small networks.
5. To design large networks, consisting of sparsely connected assemblies of densely connected subnetworks, that allow serial and integrative processing of outputs of the subnetworks.
6. To search for greater applications, well-matched to the organizational and computational styles of neural networks, in engineering problems.

1.1   THE BRAIN AS A NEURAL NETWORK

The brain is made up of a vast network of neurons, which are coupled with receptors and effectors. It is subdivided anatomically into three major parts: the cerebrum, the cerebellum, and the brainstem. The large, convoluted *cerebrum* at the top consists of two hemispheres, called cerebral hemispheres, one on the right side and the other on the left side of the skull. On the front of the cerebrum are the frontal lobes, which are primarily responsible for the brain's output, whereas the parietal, temporal, and occipital lobes at the back register input of sensory signals to the brain. Below and at the back of the cerebrum is the *cerebellum,* which resembles two spheres. The cerebellum provides precise coordination and control of the body. Inside and partially hidden under the cerebrum are a variety of structures including the *brainstem.* Figure 1.1 shows two views of a human brain. The input is provided to the brain by millions of receptors via *afferent* neurons. The surface membranes of the receptors receive incoming signals and constantly monitor changes in the body's internal and external environments. Received signals flow from the receptors via afferent neurons to the brain, where processing takes place, following which efferent neurons transfer the plan of action to the effectors. The receptors serve as transducers for sensed energy, from interaction with the environment and other parts of the body, to neural signals. The neurons in the brain continuously combine signals from receptors with encoded past experiences to generate signals used by the effectors for adaptive interactions with the environment. The brain affects the body and the environment through the effectors. The effectors convert the neural signals from the brain to other forms of energy, enabling actions or responses to the receptor signals. The neural network consisting of the brain and the spinal cord is the *central nervous system* (CNS).

Within the spinal cord itself are simple stimulus-response reflex paths. However, receptor signals entering the brain interact with the multitudinous signals already in the network, which is composed of billions of neurons with complex feedforward as well as feedback connections. Such interactions not only modify the activities of the neurons but also generate signals to control the effectors. In this way, the CNS makes the current state of the organism depend on its current excitations as well as on its memory of past experiences. Past experience is represented by the activities of the neurons, the topology of the connections, and their strengths. Such a representation of experience is constantly updated through receptor signals.

The mammalian brain is characterized by a large *neocortex* (new cortex) with a surface layer of *gray matter,* where computational chores are performed. In a human brain, the neocortex dominates the rest of the brain in size as well as in processing capabilities for sensory and cognitive functions. The human cerebral cortex, which constitutes the surface layer of the cerebrum, is a thin sheet; however, it contains so many billions of neurons that it must fold and refold to fit within the volume of the skull. *Neuron cell bodies tend to occur in layers.* The interior of a cerebral hemisphere consists of white matter, which is largely made up of connecting fibers (axons), and separated regions of gray matter. Gray and white matter occur both in the large cerebrum and in the smaller cerebellum. It is worth noting that the connecting fibers occupy more space in the brain than the cell bodies do.

Different parts of the brain have different functions. However, a given function may require interaction among many parts of the brain. When an area involved with a specific function is damaged, cooperation between other areas may restore some or all of the impaired function. Recent research has revealed that the number of dendritic connections may be increased by exercising the brain, except in the case of

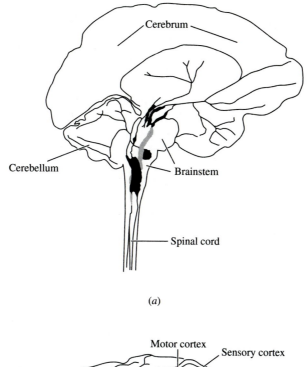

(a)

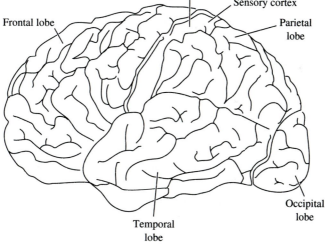

(b)

FIGURE 1.1
Two views of the human brain: (a) cross-sectional side view showing the
major parts: cerebrum, cerebellum, and brainstem; (b) view showing cortex
and lobes.

massive destructions such as those caused by stroke.[1] Some areas of the cortex are called *sensory,* since they primarily process information from one sensory modality. These include the somatosensory (related to tactile, pressure, and temperature information received from the body surface, joints, and muscles of the limbs via the spinal cord), visual, auditory, taste, and olfactory areas.

Some organizational and computational principles of the brain. The following is a list of some of the dominant organizational and computational principles that seem to be employed by the brain, as inferred from existing anatomical and physiological data:

1. *Massive parallelism.* A large number of simple, slow units are organized to solve problems independently but collectively.
2. *High degree of connection complexity.* Neurons have a large number of connections to other neurons and have complex interconnection patterns; consequently, the brain has a huge number of variables.
3. *Trainability.* Interneuron interaction parameters (connection pattern and strength) are changeable as a result of accumulated sensory experience.
4. *Binary states and continuous variables.* The action potential (see subsection 1.2.3) of a neuron is an all-or-none process. Each neuron has only two states: resting and depolarization. Though exceptions to this can occur (for example, in preganglion retinal neurons), it is fair to assert that the majority of neurons have a binary output response. However, the variables of the brain are continuous (potentials, synaptic areas, ion and chemical density, etc.) and vary continuously in time and space.
5. *Numerous types of neurons and signals.* The brain uses many different types of neurons with different signal types.
6. *Intricate signal interaction.* The interaction of impulses received at a single neuron is highly nonlinear and depends on many factors.
7. *Physical decomposition.* The brain is organized as a mosaic of assemblies or, in other words, subnetworks. Each subnetwork consists of several thousand densely connected neurons. These subnetworks are the basic processing modules of the brain. Connections to distant neurons are assumed to be much sparser and with much less feedback, allowing for autonomous local collective processing in parallel followed by a more serial and integrative processing of those local collective outcomes.
8. *Functional decomposition.* From a functional point of view, the brain is also decomposed into a collection of areas. Each area, or subnetwork, is responsible for specific functions.

---

[1]E. Ubell, "The Brain Reveals Its Powers," *Parade*, September 13, 1992, pp. 20–23.

The last two decomposition principles seem to be nature's way of dealing with the complexities of the brain itself and the environment it must cope with. In the next section, we look at the basic properties of the building elements of this amazing network.

1.2 BASIC PROPERTIES OF NEURONS

The mechanisms that describe the transfer characteristic of a typical neuron are complex. However, it is believed that individual neurons do not transmit large amounts of information. Rather, the collective behavior of groups of neurons operating in a massively parallel mode is responsible for signal transmission through and processing in a neural network. To simplify the analysis of such activity through the construction of models called *neuromimes,* which mimic the behavior of an actual neurophysiological system, one makes several assumptions. With reference to the structure of a neuron described in the following subsection, let us assume that the transmission of electrical signals through the dendrites is unidirectional, that all interactions between neurons are by chemical synaptic activation only, and that all synapses are either excitatory or inhibitory. None of these assumptions holds universally, but, nevertheless, they have been widely adopted.

1.2.1 Structure of a Neuron

There are many different types of neurons or cells. This section presents the basic properties shared by many neurons. From a neuron (Fig. 1.2) body (*soma*) many fine branching fibers, called *dendrites,* protrude. The dendrites conduct signals to the

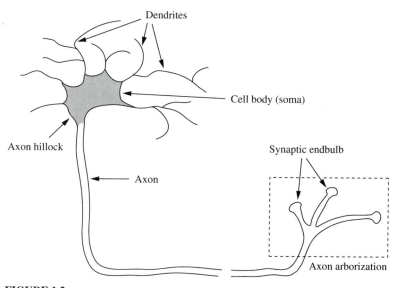

FIGURE 1.2
Schematic of a neuron.

soma or cell body. Extending from a neuron's soma, at a point called *axon hillock* (initial segment), is a long fiber called an *axon,* which generally splits into smaller branches constituting the *axonal arborization.* The tips of these axon branches (also called *nerve terminals, endbulbs, telodendria*) impinge either upon the dendrites, somas, or axons of other neurons or upon effectors. The axon-dendrite (axon-soma, axon-axon) contact between an endbulb and the cell it impinges upon is called a *synapse.* The signal flow in the neuron is (with some exceptions when the flow could be bidirectional) from the dendrites through the soma converging at the axon hillock and then down the axon to the endbulbs. A neuron typically has many dendrites but only a single axon. Some neurons lack axons, such as the *amacrine* cells.

1.2.2   Dendritic Tree

The branching structure composed of dendrites is called the dendritic tree. This has a large spread with a surface area usually greater than 80 percent of the cell membrane area. In the unidirectional model of signal flow popularly adopted, the dendrites and soma receive signals via either synaptic or electrical gap junctions. In dendrites (as well as in axons) electric current tends to flow longitudinally, i.e., parallel to the axis with very little transverse flow. Consequently, the mathematical formulation of transmission of electric signals through cables has been applied to dendritic trees as a means to understand the signal and information processing characteristics of dendrites. Digital computers have greatly facilitated numerical solutions to the partial differential equations, involving space and time variables, that characterize the signal flow, especially when the membrane conductance in dendrites requires modeling with variable-parameter active rather than fixed-parameter passive devices. The analysis of the transmission-line model of the dendrite leads to the exact or approximate computation, depending on the situation, of the dendritic delay. The occurrence of this delay can be exploited; for instance, see the example illustrating the use of a neuron as a direction-of-motion detector later in this chapter. For a mathematical analysis of the dendrite as a cable network, see ref. [92].

The importance of dendrites as the basis for complex information processing came to be appreciated after the earlier modeling (McCulloch-Pitts model, to be described later in this chapter) of a neuron as a summing node; such models ignored the *dendritic computations,* which are critical in any such analysis. Nerve impulses arriving at the synapses between neurons generate dendritic microprocesses, which contribute to the computational power of the brain. Thus, these junctions influence processing besides being involved with transmission of signals. The dendritic trees of many neurons are studded with a large number of short appendages called *dendritic spines,* each ending as a bulbous head. These must be incorporated in an accurate neuron model. The spines can receive either direct synaptic inputs or no such inputs. In the latter case, the spines may be incorporated into the membrane of the parent dendrite. Otherwise, the membranes of the dendritic spines and parent dendrites are different, and both contribute to dendritic delay because of their associated time constants in the lumped-element electric circuit model. Incorporation of the role of dendritic computation in neuron modeling has paved the path to viewing a neuron as a network of processors with variable degrees of interdependence. For a detailed treatment of the important role of dendrites in neuron modeling see the articles in ref. [252].

1.2.3   Action Potential and Its Propagation

In most mammals an electrical charge difference across the membrane of a neuron at rest causes a (transmembrane) *resting potential* of approximately -70 mV (positive exterior, negative interior). At the synapses, *graded potentials* are generated in the dendrites of the postsynaptic neuron by stimuli that cause ion movements across the cell membrane. The amplitude of a graded potential is proportional to the strength of the stimulus, and it decreases with distance from the point of generation. When the ion movements cause an increase of membrane resting potential by about 15 mV (from, say, -70 mV to -55 mV), the graded potentials trigger the *firing* of the neuron. That is, if the aggregation within a short period of time of all potential differences across the membrane at the axon hillock exceeds a threshold, an electrical impulse is generated. This impulse, called an *action potential,* is propagated along the axon. (Axonless neurons, such as the amacrine cells, function without action potential; they operate only with the graded potential, which is a local potential and not transmitted.) Most neurons have both the graded and action potentials. A sum of graded potentials below the threshold fades away quickly. The short time period during which summation of graded potentials at the axon hillock takes place is called the *period of latent summation.*

The action potential, or *spike,* results from a change in ion concentrations, especially of sodium and potassium ions, inside and outside of the cell membrane, as propounded by Hodgkin and Huxley in 1952 [160]. They theorized its occurrence because of the pumping of such ions into and out of the cell through specialized channels in the membrane. The rate and pattern of occurrence of action potentials in a neuron are believed to encode information that is communicated to other neurons. The action potential, an all-or-none process, is only generated if the membrane potential exceeds a certain threshold. For the same neuron, no matter what kind or how large the stimulus, as long as it results in a membrane potential difference that exceeds a threshold, an action potential of the same form and amplitude is generated. The action potential signals strength of stimuli by frequency rather than by amplitude.

An action potential is propagated without decay along the axon. Therefore, an axon can be viewed as an active transmission line. The action potential at one part of the axon causes the ion concentrations to change, leading to the activation of another action potential at another point down the axon. Thus, the transmission of a spike is characterized by a process of regeneration along an axon, which keeps the spike unattenuated.

An example of action potential is illustrated in Fig. 1.3. When a stimulus is applied either to a part of the soma or to a part of the axon of a neuron, the potential

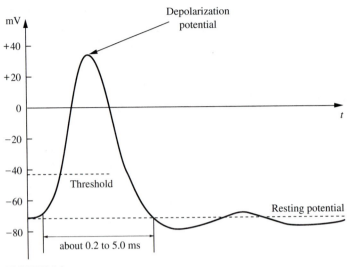

FIGURE 1.3
An action potential.

across the membrane at the point of stimulation is driven from the resting potential of -70 mV to exceed the threshold potential of approximately -55 mV, followed by a jump to a depolarization potential of about $+35$ mV. This is due to a large flow of the positively charged sodium ions from outside the cell to its inside. This phenomenon is called *depolarization* (*activation* or *excitation*) and can last from about 0.2 ms to 5.0 ms. The latent period from stimulation to depolarization is about 0.06 ms. After depolarization, the potential changes back to resting potential. However, before reverting to resting potential, there is a postdepolarization period of small and slow oscillation, called the *period of afterpotential*. The length and amplitude at the postdepolarization period vary widely in different neurons.

   Immediately after depolarization, a neuron cannot be excited again by any stimulus; this time interval is called the *absolute refractory period*. An action potential cannot propagate through an axon during the refractory period. Then there is a period called the *relative refractory period*, when the neuron can be activated again, but only with a stimulus that is much larger than the normal threshold. The absolute refractory period determines the minimum separation between two successive activations. The interval between two successive spikes (action potentials), called the *interspike interval*, is greater than this separation. This interval is actually a random variable, and the train of spikes generates a random process. Different refractory periods correlate with the time durations of the polarities of the postdepolarization potentials. In a human some neurons can generate 500 action potentials per second.

   There are two types of axons: *myelinated* and *unmyelinated*. A myelinated axon is wrapped in a sheath of *myelin* (insulating cells wrapped tightly around the axon), with small gaps, called *Ranvier nodes*, between successive segments. In an unmyelinated axon, the impulse is propagated as local current. When one part of an axon is polarized, it becomes positive inside and negative outside. Its unpolarized neighbor is negative inside and positive outside. Therefore, the potential difference between polarized and unpolarized neighboring segments causes a flow of ions, resulting in a local current (Fig. 1.4). This local current activates the unpolarized neighboring segment, and the impulse is propagated. A myelinated axon is insulated except at Ranvier nodes. Therefore, the local current can only flow between Ranvier nodes. Activation is then propagated from node to node by a process known as *saltatory conduction,* which speeds up the passage of the impulse and saves energy.

The speed with which an impulse propagates along an axon varies widely, depending on the diameter of the axon and the thickness of the sheath of myelin, in the case of a myelinated axon. The speed of axonal propagation can be as low as 1 m/s (meters per second) for an unmyelinated axon and well over 100 m/s for a myelinated axon.

Characteristics of action potential propagation along axons.

1. An action potential is propagated without decay.
2. The propagation of an action potential along one axon does not interfere with other neighboring nerve fibers.
3. Excitation of an axon at any point on a nerve fiber by an injected signal causes this signal to propagate along both directions.
4. An axon is not easily exhausted; it can propagate many impulses for a long period of time.

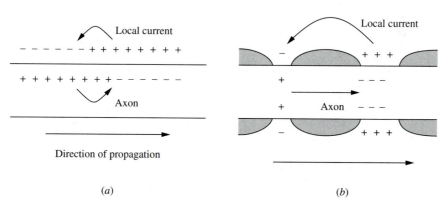

(a) (b)

FIGURE 1.4
Local currents in an axon. During the generation of an action potential, the cell membrane becomes very permeable to Na^+ (positively charged sodium) ions, which flow inside, causing the membrane potential to rise. After a short while, the membrane becomes impermeable to Na^+ ions but permeable to K^+ (positively charged potassium) ions, which move outside to restore the membrane to its resting potential. (a) Unmyelinated axon; (b) myelinated axon.

1.2.4 Synapses

A neuron is totally enclosed by its membrane. The excitation of a neuron affects other neurons through contacts of its endbulbs with membranes of other neurons. Such contacts are called synapses (Fig. 1.5). The membrane on the endbulb is called the *presynaptic membrane*. The membrane upon which the endbulb impinges is called the *postsynaptic membrane*. The small space between the presynaptic and postsynaptic membranes is called the *synaptic cleft*. Communication between neurons is facilitated by the release of small packets of chemicals into this gap. One particular neuron may communicate with over 100,000 other neurons.

When an action potential reaches the endbulb of the presynaptic membrane, it causes a potential change across the postsynaptic membrane. The direct cause of the change in the electrical potential of the postsynaptic membrane is primarily chemical and not electrical. The electrical impulse transmitted across each synaptic gap is chemically induced and controlled.[2]

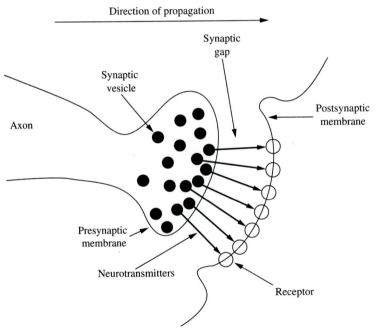

FIGURE 1.5
Transmission of presynaptic axon signal across synaptic gap (cleft) to postsynaptic neuron.

---

[2]*Electric gap synapses,* found particularly in prevertebrate systems, are an exception to this statement; however, they are not of interest for this discussion.

An action potential propagated to the endbulb causes the release of chemical substances called *neurotransmitters* from little packets (*synaptic vesicles*) in the presynaptic membrane. Neurotransmitters diffuse across the synaptic cleft to the postsynaptic membrane and cause a change of electrical potential across the postsynaptic membrane. About 100 different neurotransmitters have been found in the human brain. These include dopamine (lack of which results in Parkinson's disease), serotonin, and acetylcholine (involved in memory and learning; lack of the latter two has been suspected to be involved in Alzheimer's disease). The following list summarizes the important characteristics of synapses:

1. An impulse that arrives at an endbulb generally generates a subthreshold change in the postsynaptic membrane. Potential changes across postsynaptic membranes cause signals to propagate along the dendrites and cell bodies of neighboring neurons almost without decay. All postsynaptic potential changes are transmitted to the axon hillock. If a sequence of impulses reaches a synapse in a short period of time, or if many impulses reach multiple synapses of a neuron, the collective effect of many subthreshold changes may yield a potential change at the axon hillock that exceeds the threshold.

2. Signal flow is unidirectional from presynaptic neuron to postsynaptic neuron, although exception to this can occur when the synaptic cleft junction conducts in both directions, depending on which cell is at a higher potential. Bidirectional chemical synapses have also been observed in the vertebrate central nervous system, though their properties are not well known. The unidirectional property is important for mediating the direction of flow of information in the central nervous system.

3. The delay from the time a propagating impulse is incident at the presynaptic membrane to the time the potential changes across the postsynaptic membrane is relatively long. This occurs because the mechanism of transmission across the synaptic cleft involves release, diffusion, and reception of neurotransmitters. This delay is approximately 0.5 to 2 ms.

4. The functioning of the synapse is very sensitive to overall physiological conditions of the body and to drugs. Synapses are most likely to become exhausted. This phenomenon could lead to a type of *synaptic plasticity*, which is described next.

5. A significant and widespread characteristic of chemical synaptic transmission is *plasticity*. Synaptic plasticity either facilitates or inhibits chemical synapses during repetitive firing. It is known to influence the transfer and processing of signals to a very great extent in the CNS [241].

6. Synapses differ in shape, size, form, and effectiveness. Synapses can be classified according to place of contact (Fig. 1.6).

    (*a*) *Axon-dendrite synapse.* An endbulb of one neuron impinges upon a dendrite of another neuron.

    (*b*) *Axon-soma synapse.* An endbulb of one neuron impinges upon the cell body of another neuron.

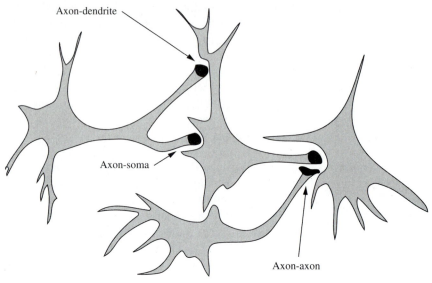

Axon-dendrite

Axon-soma

Axon-axon

FIGURE 1.6
Different types of synaptic contacts.

(*c*) *Axon-axon synapse.* An endbulb of one neuron impinges upon an endbulb of another neuron.

The axon-dendrite and axon-soma synapses are most common. Dendrodendritic synapses between dendrites of neighboring neurons are also possible. However, their characteristics and functional significance are not well known [241]. Electric gap synapses have also been observed in the vertebrate retina. Those have been modeled according to the passive coupling resulting from current driven into the receiving neuron as a result of the potential difference between pre- and postsynaptic elements [241].

7. Synapses can also be classified according to effect of contact.
   (*a*) Excitatory synapse: Excitation of the presynaptic neuron contributes to the depolarization of the postsynaptic neuron, or in other words, makes it easier to be depolarized.
   (*b*) Inhibitory synapse: Excitation of the presynaptic neuron moves the potential of the postsynaptic neuron away from the threshold or, in other words, makes it harder to be depolarized (hyperpolarization).

   Whether a synapse is excitatory or inhibitory depends not only on the type of neurotransmitter the presynaptic membrane releases but also on the types of receptors in the postsynaptic membrane. There are two types of inhibitory synapses.
   Presynaptic inhibition exists at axon-axon synapses. As shown in Fig. 1.7*a*, there is an axon-soma excitatory synapse between axon 1 and soma of neuron 3, and an axon-axon synapse between axon 1 and axon 2. Axon 2 and neuron 3 have no

direct contact. Excitation of axon 2 alone has no effect on neuron 3. Excitation of
axon 1, say, causes a 10 mV excitatory postsynaptic potential (Fig. 1.7*b*). However,
if axon 2 is first excited before axon 1 is excited, the excitatory postsynaptic potential in neuron 3 is reduced to about only 5 mV (Fig. 1.7*c*). That is, the excitatory
postsynaptic potential in neuron 3 is inhibited because the impulse in axon 2 reduces
the amount of excitatory transmitter released by axon 1. The postsynaptic potential
in neuron 3 is still excitatory. The inhibitory effect of axon 1 is on axon 2 and not
directly on neuron 3. Therefore, it is called presynaptic inhibition.

Postsynaptic inhibition is caused by inhibitory neurons. There are a large number of inhibitory neurons in the brain. These types of neurons form only inhibitory
synapses with other neurons. Because the inhibition in a neuron is caused by an inhibitory (hyperpolarizing) postsynaptic potential, it is called postsynaptic inhibition.
An affected neuron does not fire so long as the inhibitory input is active, irrespective of excitatory inputs that may be present. Only after the inhibitory input ceases

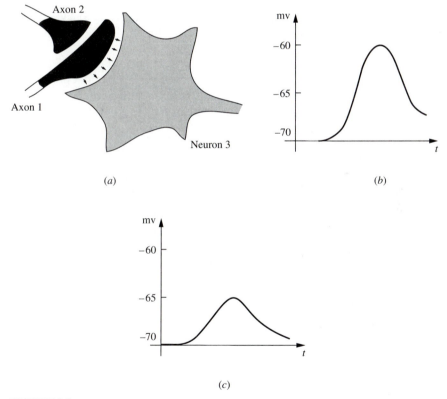

FIGURE 1.7
Presynaptic inhibition. (*a*) Axon-axon synapse and its effect on signal transmission; (*b*) postsynaptic potential in neuron 3 due only to excitation by axon 1; (*c*) effect of initial excitation of
axon 2 on the postsynaptic potential in neuron 3.

can the neuron again depolarize and fire an action potential. This phenomenon of *absolute inhibition*, resulting from only one inhibitory input no matter how many excitatory inputs are present, is replicated by the McCulloch-Pitts cell discussed in Section 1.3.1. See also Problem 1.7 at the end of this chapter.

1.2.5 Connection Patterns between Neurons

There are many different and complex connection patterns in the central nervous system. The following are three major connection patterns.

1. *Divergent connections.* A neuron may be linked through synapses to many other neurons using its axon arborization (Fig. 1.8). This type of connection pattern enables the signal from one neuron to be passed on to many other neurons.
2. *Convergent connections.* Many neurons may be linked through synapses to one common neuron (Fig. 1.9).
3. *Chains and loops.* These types of connections may involve many neurons and many subloops. Loops enable positive and negative feedbacks in a network. Examples of chains and loops are shown in Fig. 1.10 with only a few neurons.

In general, afferent neurons, which send signals into the brain, mainly use divergent connections to pass the information to many neurons for parallel processing; efferent neurons, on the other hand, which send signals to the effectors, mainly use convergent connections. Neurons in the brain, responsible for processing the incoming signals, use many types of complex connections, including chains and loops.

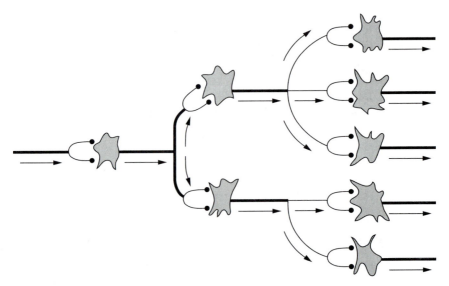

FIGURE 1.8
Divergent connections.

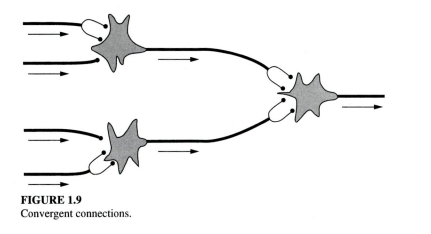

FIGURE 1.9
Convergent connections.

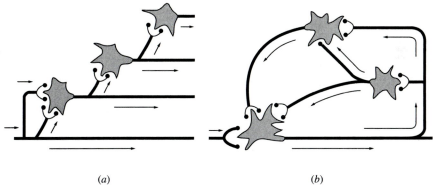

(a)   (b)

FIGURE 1.10
(<i>a</i>) Chain and (<i>b</i>) loop connections.

1.2.6   An Example: A Motion Detection Neuron

We show in this section how a simple neuron can detect motion in a given direction
as a result of the geometric arrangement of its dendrites. Consider a neuron with
four dendrites, each receiving a signal via a single synapse from a visual receptor
(Fig. 1.11a). The four synapses A, B, C, and D are at increasing distances from
the axon hillock. Assume that each receptor yields a presynaptic potential when
it is stimulated by a spot of light. The presynaptic potentials cause postsynaptic
potentials to converge and to be summed at the axon hillock. Because of propagation
delay and decay, the changes in potential at the axon hillock caused by simultaneous
postsynaptic potentials from A, B, C, and D are different, as shown in Fig. 1.11b.
The farther a synapse is away from the axon hillock, the lower is its peak value and
the greater the delay in its occurrence. If the four receptors are stimulated simultaneously causing postsynaptic potentials simultaneously at the four synapses, their
value following summation at the axon hillock may be less than the threshold and

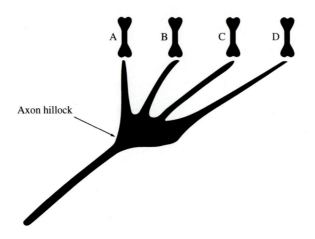

(a)

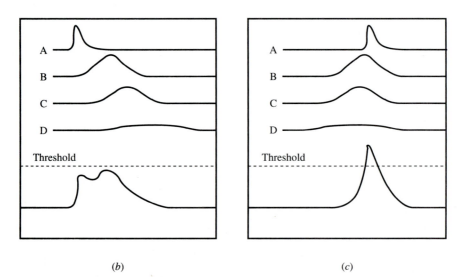

(b)   (c)

FIGURE 1.11

Neuron as a motion detector. (a) This neuron functions as a motion detector because of its dendritic geometry. "Maximal" stimulation (b), exciting A, B, C, and D simultaneously, does not excite the neuron; but (c) if the synapses are activated in the order D-C-B-A so that the four peaks reach the axon hillock nearly simultaneously, the combined effect will exceed the threshold. (*Source:* Adapted from M. Arbib, *The Metaphorical Brain: Neural Networks and Beyond,* ©1989 John Wiley & Sons, Inc. Adapted by permission of John Wiley & Sons, Inc.)

not sufficient for exciting the neuron. However, if the four receptors are stimulated in the order D, C, B, A, so that the peaks of the four postsynaptic potentials reach the axon hillock at approximately the same time, then their combined effect may exceed the threshold, yielding a response of the neuron (Fig. 1.11c). The four peaks will approximately coincide only if a spot of light travels from right to left at a speed within a given range such that postsynaptic potentials are caused in the order D, C, B, A, and with appropriate intervals between them. Therefore, this simple neuron can detect the direction and speed of motion across the four receptors. It will not respond to stationary objects or to objects traveling from left to right. Neither will it respond to objects traveling from right to left but with a speed outside of the range it is capable of detecting. This lack of response occurs because, when the speed is too low or too high, the peaks will arrive at the axon hillock at different instances such that the summation at any instant or, more accurately, within any period of latent summation, is less than the threshold.

This example shows that the geometry, or connection pattern, may have a great impact on the function of neurons. By realizing that a neuron in the brain can have 100,000 synapses and complex connection patterns, it is not surprising to see the wide range of complex tasks the brain can perform, even disregarding its dynamics.

1.3 NEURON MODELS

Neural network models, even neurobiological ones, assume many simplifications over actual biological neural networks. Such simplifications are necessary to understand the intended properties and to attempt any mathematical analysis. Even if all the properties of neurons were known, simplification would still be necessary for analytical tractability. A few models of neurons will be presented in this section.

1.3.1 McCulloch-Pitts Model

McCulloch and Pitts [250] modeled simple logical units called cells (or "neurons") so as to represent and analyze the logic of situations that arise in any discrete process, be it in a brain, in a computer, or anywhere else. Accordingly, the automata made up of these elementary units are usually called neural networks. We follow here closely the exposition in ref. [260]. A McCulloch-Pitts cell is a very simple two-state machine. From each cell emerges a single line or wire, called the *output fiber of the cell.* This output fiber may branch out after leaving the cell. Output fibers from different cells are not allowed to fuse together. Each branch must ultimately terminate as an input connection to another (or perhaps the same) cell. Two types of terminations are allowed. One provides an excitatory input, the other an inhibitory input. Any number of input connections to a cell is permitted. The flow of information through a cell may be controlled by gates, which could be either of the excitatory or of the inhibitory type. The former is said to fire or activate the cell, whereas the latter is associated with the complementary function.

Each cell is a finite-state machine and accordingly operates in discrete time instants, which are assumed synchronous among all cells. At each moment, a cell is either *firing* or *quiet,* the two possible states of the cell. For each state there is an associated output signal, transmitted along the fiber branch of the cell. Since each cell has only two possible states, it is convenient to think of the firing state as producing a pulse whereas one may think of *no pulse* as the name of the signal associated with the quiet state.

Cells change state as a consequence of the pulses received at their inputs. Each cell has a number associated with it, called the *threshold* of the cell. This threshold determines the state transition properties of a cell C in the following manner. At any time index k there will be a certain distribution of activities in the fibers terminating upon C. We ignore all fibers that are quiet at this time and look to see if any inhibitory inputs are present. In the presence of one or more such inputs the cell C will not fire at time index $(k + 1)$. This type of inhibition is referred to as *absolute inhibition* because a cell will fire at time index $(k + 1)$ if and only if, at time index k, the number of active excitatory inputs equals or exceeds the threshold and *no inhibitor is active*.

The McCulloch-Pitts *network* (called *net* for the sake of brevity) model is based on several simplifying assumptions. First, the state of a cell at time index $(k + 1)$ is assumed to depend on its state at time index k and on any input at that same instant of time. Second, the inhibition is taken to be absolute in the sense that a single inhibitory signal can block response of a cell to any amount of excitation. This assumption can be replaced by one in which a cell fires if the difference between the amounts of excitation and inhibition exceeds the threshold. In fact the reader is advised to solve the relevant problems at the end of this chapter using this last assumption. Finally, a standard delay between the input and output of each cell is assumed. Since the individual cells or neurons operate on the same time scale, the overall network operation is synchronous. Biological neurons, however, operate on different time scales and therefore function asynchronously.

In this type of network, any kind of more or less permanent memory must depend on the existence of closed or feedback paths. Otherwise, in the absence of external stimulation, all activity must soon die out, leaving all cells in the quiet state. A *feedback fiber* runs from the output fiber of a cell back to an excitatory termination at the input of the very same cell. Once this cell has been fired (by a signal from the *start* fiber), it will continue to fire at all successive time instants until it is halted by a signal on the inhibitory *stop* fiber. Throughout this interval of activity, it will send pulses to the *gate* cell and permit the passage of information.

The internal state of a net without any *loops* or *cycles* (see Chapter 2 for their precise definitions) in a graph can depend only on the stimulation that has occurred in a bounded portion of the immediate past. The bound is set by the length of the longest path (see Chapter 2 for definition of path in a graph) in the net. In a net with cycles, the length of possible paths within the net may be unbounded; so there is no limit to the duration of information storage. This form of storage is called *dynamic recirculating* form. In the human brain not all information is stored in this form. Short-term memory is dynamic and stored in the form of pulses reverberating around closed chains of neurons. Long-term memory is static and stored in the form of changes in connections, thresholds, and microanatomy [260].

Each neural network built from McCulloch-Pitts cells is a finite-state machine, and every finite-state machine is equivalent to and can be simulated by some neural network. At any moment, the global state of the net is given by the firing pattern of its cells. Let $\mathbf{x}(k)$, $\mathbf{u}(k)$, and $\mathbf{y}(k)$ denote, respectively, the state, input, and output vectors at time index k. The state vector is composed of the state of each neuron at a certain time index as given by its last output. For suitable functions, $\mathbf{F}(\cdot)$ and $\mathbf{G}(\cdot)$, the state-transition equation

$$\mathbf{x}(k + 1) = \mathbf{F}(\mathbf{x}(k), \mathbf{u}(k))$$

is determined by the connection structure of the network, and the output vector

$$\mathbf{y}(k + 1) = \mathbf{G}(\mathbf{x}(k), \mathbf{u}(k))$$

is determined by the fibers that carry output signals.

A further development of the work of McCulloch and Pitts led to threshold logic units (TLUs) with adjustable weights. A TLU is a device with n inputs, $x_1, x_2, \ldots, x_n$, and an output y. There are $n + 1$ parameters, namely the weights $(w_1, w_2, \ldots, w_n)$ and a threshold θ. The TLU computes an output value at discrete time indices $k = 1, 2, \ldots$, according to

$$y(k + 1) = \begin{cases} 1 & \text{if } \sum_{i=1}^{n} w_i x_i(k) \geq \theta, \\ 0 & \text{otherwise.} \end{cases} \tag{1.1}$$

Positive weights $w_i > 0$ represent excitatory synapses, whereas negative weights $w_i < 0$ represent inhibitory ones. Note the unit time index delay occurring between the instants when the inputs are applied and the output appears. A TLU is sketched in Fig. 1.12. A McCulloch-Pitts neuron is governed by the threshold decision rule of a TLU, shown in Eq. (1.1), or of its bipolar variant (in which case the output state 0 is replaced by -1). Equation (1.1) and its variants are popular because of their mathematical tractability. They fail, however, to capture the stochastic spatial and temporal complexities inherent in neuronal information processing. The reader is referred to ref. [252] for further details on this matter. In applying this model, the

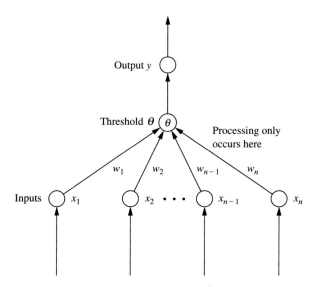

FIGURE 1.12
A threshold logic unit (TLU), whose transfer characteristics are described in Eq. (1.1). Processing takes place in the unit whose threshold is shown. The other units are shown only for completeness and are really not needed in the model of a TLU.

output of a TLU is often assumed to belong to the set $\{\alpha, 1\}$, which represents the binary states of a neuron, where α is a nonzero number. The value of α may be either -1, in the bipolar case, or a small positive number, e.g., 0.1, in the modified unipolar case. This choice will lead to faster convergence in almost all learning algorithms, because if $\alpha = 0$ (the strict unipolar case), the updates of a weight connected to the output of a neuron will become zero, whereas making α nonzero ensures that a weight will be updated whenever it is required.

This model of a neuron is highly simplified (see Problem 1.1, asking readers to list the simplifications made in deriving this model). A network of these very simple neurons can compute any logical (Boolean) function (consult Problem 1.7 in particular). Indeed, with properly chosen weights any digital computer can be simulated by a network of TLUs. That is, a network of simple neurons can do at least what a modern digital computer can.

1.3.2   Neuron Models with Continuous Transfer Characteristics

The action potential or spike of a biological neuron is a continuous variable. The time instant at which a postsynaptic potential change occurs affects its interaction with other potential changes. Information is not encoded only by the excitation and resting states of neurons; the rate at which a neuron is excited also carries information. Real neurons have integrative time delays due to capacitance. The time evolution of a real neuron is better described by differential equations instead of the discrete time transition equations for TLUs. Let us examine a widely used neuron model that includes some of the foregoing considerations.

Instantaneous input x_i to the ith neuron is defined to approximate the mean soma potential from the effects of its excitatory and inhibitory synapses as well as its threshold. If there are no external inputs and leakage current is ignored, then with the outputs y_j for $j = 1, 2, \ldots, n$ from n neurons used as inputs to the ith neuron (having a threshold θ_i) after multiplication by connection weights w_{ij}, the value of x_i is

$$x_i = \sum_{j=1}^{n} w_{ij} y_j - \theta_i. \tag{1.2}$$

The output y_j of a neuron represents the short-term average of the firing rate of neuron j and is given by

$$y_j = f(\lambda x_j), \tag{1.3}$$

where λ is a positive number. The unipolar or *logsigmoid* form of the input/output (transfer) characteristic $f(\cdot)$ is described by

$$y_i = \frac{1}{1 + \exp(-\lambda x_i)} = \frac{1}{1 + \exp\left[-\lambda\left(\sum_{j=1}^{n} w_{ij} y_j - \theta_i\right)\right]}, \tag{1.4}$$

and it approaches the characteristic of a unipolar TLU as λ tends to ∞.

The transfer characteristic may also be defined (for the bipolar case) through

$$y_i = \frac{2}{1 + \exp(-\lambda x_i)} - 1 = \frac{2}{1 + \exp\left[-\lambda\left(\sum_{j=1}^{n} w_{ij} y_j - \theta_i\right)\right]} - 1. \quad (1.5)$$

In Eq. (1.5), the limiting values of y_i as λ approaches ∞ are either $+1$ or -1, depending upon whether x_i is positive or negative. This characteristic is referred to as *tansigmoid*.

A more realistic model includes the time delay due to membrane capacitance C_i and leakage current through the transmembrane resistance R_i. The dynamics of such a neuron model are described by the following equations:

$$C_i \frac{dx_i}{dt} = \sum_j w_{ij} y_j - \frac{x_i}{R_i} + I_i,$$

$$x_i = f_i^{-1}(y_i), \quad (1.6)$$

where I_i is the external current stimulus to neuron i. Note that the weight w_{ij} has the dimension of transconductance, which is realizable by an active device. Therefore, synapses are modeled by active devices in this case.

Figure 1.13 illustrates the parameters of this model superimposed on a neuron. An electrical circuit simulating Eq. (1.6) is shown in Fig. 1.14. The weights w_{ij} are realized as transconductances. Each operational amplifier has two outputs, y_i and $-y_i$, to avoid negative weights for inhibitory links. An inhibitory input to neuron i from neuron j is linked by a positive weight to the $-y$ output of neuron j.

1.3.3 Other Neuron Models

The importance of the McCulloch-Pitts model is its applicability in the construction of sequential machines to perform logical operations of any degree of complexity. The model focused on logical and macroscopic cognitive operations, not detailed physiological modeling of the electrical activity of the nervous system. In fact, this deterministic model with its discretization of time and summation rules does not reveal the manner in which biological neurons integrate their inputs. For an excellent comprehensive account of other modeling schemes, see ref. [241].

At a more detailed level, the modeling of the average rate at which a neuron generates impulses may not be sufficient. It may be desirable to model the spike of an action potential. Doing so enables one to model the timing of spike generation and the temporal interactions between spikes arriving at different time instances. Loeb [237] and Sejnowski [345] have shown that submillisecond timing information can be important in the cerebral cortex. The modeling of spikes also enables a network to encode information conveyed in the temporal patterns of spikes. The magnitudes of stimuli that a neuron receives are coded by the frequency of impulses the neuron generates. This phenomenon is better described by a spike-based model than an average firing rate–based model.

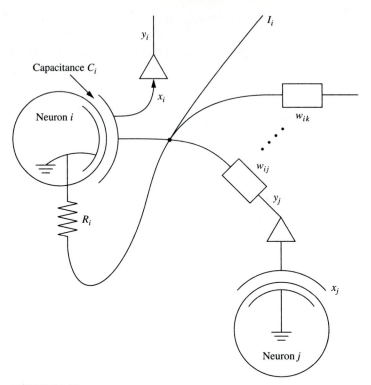

FIGURE 1.13
Model showing how the dynamics of the ith neuron are coupled with the output y_j from the jth neuron through the connection weight w_{ij}, external current I_i, etc.

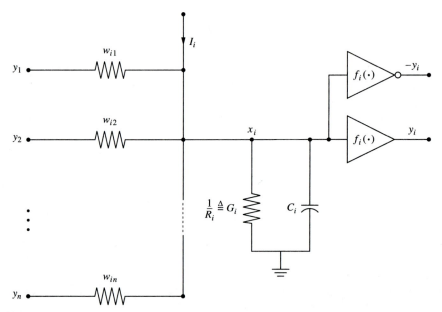

FIGURE 1.14
The electrical circuit simulating Eq. (1.6).

The theory of stochastic processes has played an important role in the modeling of biological neurons for the purpose of comprehending the underlying principles in cognition and perception. The transmission of the action potential from one neuron to another is a stochastic phenomenon; and stochastic partial differential equations have been introduced to allow for the spatial extent of neurons, with special reference to dendrites [378]. The voltage across a nerve cell membrane, the threshold, and the interspike interval in a biological neural network are all random variables. The amplitude of the response in the postsynaptic cell and the timing of the postsynaptic potentials are stochastic features of synaptic transmission, a process whose structure and properties are still not fully understood. The problem of modeling the stochastic activities of an aggregate of even a million neurons that may define a neural network might easily become analytically intractable.

Therefore, some simplifications need to be made when modeling, say, the spike of an action potential. For example, the afterpotentials and the different refractory periods should be simplified. Such simplifications are necessary for performing theoretical analysis on the resulting model. Spike-based models are less popular at present. However, some examples of use of such models occur in the work by von der Malsburg and Schneider [392] and in the frequency modulation neural network [376].

Finally, note that a key challenge in neurocomputing with ANNs continues to be the development of powerful, general-purpose learning algorithms [49]. Learning in neural networks is the process of adjusting connection weights with the objective of getting a better response. Some of the learning rules to be encountered later in networks like learnmatrix (Section 3.6.3) depend on Hebb's contribution to neuroscience [152]. Hebb modeled the collective behavior of biological neurons by enunciating an organizational principle at the cellular level following detailed and painstaking neurophysiological experimentation and studies. He hypothesized that when a neuron i repeatedly and persistently excites a neuron j, some growth process or metabolic change takes place in one or both neurons such that the efficiency of i as one of the units firing j is increased. Mathematically, this principle translates to an updating scheme, described next, for the connection weight w_{ij} linking neurons i and j. Let x_i and y_j be, respectively, the input to neuron j from neuron i and the output from neuron j. Then, the update equation given next constitutes the *Hebbian learning rule:*

$$w_{ij}^{\text{new}} = w_{ij}^{\text{old}} + \alpha x_i y_j. \tag{1.7}$$

This learning rule is local; that is, updating a weight requires information on the states of only the neurons involved in the connection. The coefficient α is a positive number called the *learning rate* parameter. Note that x_i could also be an external input to unit j, and that the output y_j could be replaced by a signal that is a function of y_j and an external signal in order to generate more varied and versatile learning rules. See Problems 1.14 and 1.15 for applications of the Hebbian learning rule to realize logic functions. There are some limitations of this simple learning rule, and more powerful learning rules will be encountered later. In Chapter 4 the reader will be exposed to the *perceptron* learning rule with guaranteed convergence [in the case of the so-called separable patterns in feature space, where application of the rule in Eq. (1.7) does not always lead to a similar property] and the *LMS* (least mean squares)-based *delta* rule (performance-based, because it seeks to minimize a certain error function). The generalized delta rule for training a broader class of structures is presented in Chapter 5. In addition to learning associated with supervised training, the topics of reinforcement learning and competitive learning along with their ramifications are presented in the later chapters of this text.

1.4   CONCLUSIONS AND SUGGESTIONS

The mechanisms governing the functioning of the CNS, composed of billions of interconnected neurons, are now understood sufficiently to permit meaningful modeling. The objective here has been to provide a balanced presentation of the similarities and differences between the physiological system and the connectionist models. To achieve this goal, biological neurons have been described in sufficient detail to motivate the material in subsequent chapters, whereas the topic of modeling has been so far characterized by important representative samples. The reader undoubtedly will realize that this choice is due to restrictions of space and also the availability of extensive documentations elsewhere [241].

Neurons, the basic computational elements in the brain, are interconnected to produce its computational power. Therefore, the brain can be viewed as a network of billions of simple computing devices, each operating on its own set of inputs and transmitting its output to specific sets of other computing devices in the network. A neuron, being a cell, is the anatomical unit of the CNS. Maturana and Varela [248] refer to the neuron as a basic *living system* and claim that it is completely characterized by the property of *autopoiesis.* A closed system that is autopoietic is autonomous, self-referring, and self-constructing. The property of autopoiesis is necessary and sufficient to characterize a system as a living system in physical space. According to ref. [248], an autopoietic system is a network that produces, transforms, and destroys its own components. Its structure must change so that it generates appropriate changes of state in response to changes in its environment in order to live and not disintegrate or die. This structural coupling is crucial for changes in the living system during its lifespan (learning) as well as for changes carried through reproduction (evolution). An artificial neural net tries to model a living system by attempting to replicate its description from observation of the input/output behavior. Many different internal descriptions can capture the input/output behavior (provided through exemplars in a training set in supervised learning, for example) over the domain of observation, but the property of autopoiesis can be satisfied only by the internal states and intricate connections and dynamics of a living system. For this to happen in an ANN, the system must incorporate the feature of structural adaptation, as will be seen in Chapters 5 and 7. Even an organism as small as a worm, with only a few hundred neurons, is highly structured, and much of its behavior is believed to be the consequence of built-in structure and not learning [420]. This belief contrasts with past assumptions of fixed simple structures for ANN models, where complexity was injected only through a large number of learned interconnections. Work over the years in neuroanatomy and neurophysiology has demonstrated that living organisms do not fit this image [420]. The property of autopoiesis encompasses the power to learn and the power to reproduce, which were used by Wiener to characterize a living system [412].

The CNS is an autopoietic system. It is a closed network of interconnecting neurons such that any change in the state of activity or structure of a collection of neurons leads to a change in the state of activity or structure of either another or the same collection of neurons. This collective computational capability of a set of neurons is a key distinguishing feature of neurocomputing, in contrast to the classical Von Neumann computer with one central processor operating in a serial rule-based mode. The characteristics of a neural network are compared to those of a Von Neumann computer in Table 1.1.

Modeling of the brain has been facilitated by the emergence of high-tech equipment for performing computer-assisted tomography (CAT), nuclear magnetic resonance imaging (NMRI or MRI), and positron emission tomography (PET). CAT scan machines transmit *x-rays* through the brain; a computer creates images of the cross sections of the brain; and the computer uses mathematical analysis, based on the Radon transform, to reconstruct the three-dimensional (3-D) brain from its 2-D projections. An MRI machine employs a computer to read data from *radio signals* sent into the brain and then construct a 3-D picture of the brain. A PET apparatus detects the positions of *injected radioactive substances* to reveal where in the

TABLE 1.1
Similarities and differences between neural net and Von Neumann computer

Neural net	Von Neumann computer
1. Trained (learning by example) by adjusting the connection strengths, thresholds, and structure	Programmed with instructions (if-then analysis based on logic)
2. Memory and processing elements are collocated	Memory and processing separate
3. Parallel (discrete or continuous), and asynchronous	Sequential or serial, digital, synchronous (with a clock)
4. May be fault-tolerant because of distributed representation and large-scale redundancy	Not fault-tolerant
5. Self-organization during learning	Software-dependent
6. Knowledge stored is adaptable; information is stored in the interconnection between neurons	Knowledge stored in an addressed memory location is strictly replaceable
7. Processing is anarchic	Processing is autocratic
8. Cycle time, which governs processing speed, occurs in millisecond range	Cycle time, corresponding to processing one step of a program in the CPU during one clock cycle, occurs in nanosecond range

brain the chemical reactions occur in response to particular types of sensory stimuli. The interaction between medicine and technology is providing new understanding of the causes of many ailments and possible cures. For example, Parkinson's disease occurs when, for reasons unknown, the neurons responsible for the release of the neurotransmitter *dopamine* shrivel and die. Their death causes the failure of signal transmission, which leads to loss of muscular control. A remedy based on the implantation of fetal cells deep into the brain to stimulate production of dopamine has been suggested; both the ethics and the efficacy of such a treatment are currently under intense debate. Another neurotransmitter, *serotonin,* is believed to be linked with behavioral disorders such as depression and mood swings.

The nature of signal transmission between neurons has been a topic of intense research and controversy for over 50 years. First, chemicals called neurotransmitters were shown to carry signals between neurons. For example, glutamate and aspartate are excitatory, whereas glycine is inhibitory. Synaptic transmission via neurotransmitters is being studied in conjunction with the mechanism of *volume transmission.* Volume transmission is believed to occur in much larger time scales than does communication through synapses and involves information flow in the extracellular spaces in the brain, somewhat akin to wireless propagation of *radio waves* through space [6]. Acupuncture is thought to depend on volume transmission, as do the changes in the activity of the brain during slumber and wakefulness and the varying levels of alertness, mood, and sensitivity. More recently, it was demonstrated [106] that the underlying mechanism of transmission could also be electrical. That finding led to the discovery of certain channels, dubbed *gap junctions,* between cells. Each such channel pierces the membranes of two adjoining cells. The cell-to-cell junctions formed by rings of proteins, called *connexons,* in the walls of the channel allow ions and small molecules to pass between two cells. A connexon is shaped like a hexagonal doughnut, formed by a cluster of six proteins called *connexins.* Unanswered questions about gap junctions include how they are structured, how they open and close, how they influence the development of a living system, how they function in cell metabolism, and what their complete role is in the central nervous system [106].

The layers of interconnections in a mammalian brain [128], which are responsible for various sensory-motor functions in response to particular types of sensory stimuli, are also present in other classes of living creatures. For example, the cross section of retinal tissue from a bird's eye shows layered organization [395]. The presence of elaborate interconnections among several layers of interneurons (neurons that are interposed between sensory and motor neurons) suggests that a considerable amount of image processing occurs at the level of the retina in birds.

Whether attempts to simulate the biological brain will succeed is unknown. The developing technologies of very large scale integration (VLSI) and ultra large scale integration (ULSI), which make possible the building of entire computers or even arrays of computers on a single chip of silicon, have a much more challenging task in the replication of even a nonmammalian brain [9]. As far as synthetic emulation of the human brain is concerned, it is believed that there are facets of human thinking that can never be emulated by a machine [291].

PROBLEMS

1.1. Summarize the simplifications made in the McCulloch-Pitts model of a neuron, on the basis of the introduction to brains and neurons given in Sections 1.1 and 1.2.

1.2. By using data on cat spinal neurons, the number density of synapses per unit length as a function of distance x from the soma in μm is estimated as [378]

$$n(x) = 70 - 0.10x \qquad 0 < x < 500.$$

Estimate the total number of synapses per neuron from these data.

1.3. The interspike interval distribution in terms of the threshold parameter θ and the parameter β associated with the difference in rate between excitatory and inhibitory postsynaptic potentials (PSPs) is approximated by

$$I(\theta, \beta, t) = \frac{\exp[-(\theta/t) - \beta t]}{t^{3/2}}$$

where t is the temporal variable. Plot $I(\theta, \beta, t)$ over a conveniently chosen time interval for various choices of the parameters θ and β. Infer the qualitative behavior of the shape of the distribution over different ranges of parameters.

1.4. The postsynaptic conductance change due to chemical synaptic transmission is sometimes modeled by the equation

$$g(k, \alpha, t) = kt \exp(-\alpha t),$$

where the parameter α determines its time course and the parameter k scales its amplitude. How realistic is it to approximate $g(k, \alpha, t)$ as a pulse function, being 1 at some specified level during the occurrence of presynaptic action potentials and 0 otherwise? To answer the question, you may decide to perform numerical simulation for various choices of the parameters, especially α.

1.5. One of the earliest and simplest models of a neuron [378] is a lumped time-invariant resistance/capacitance (RC) circuit driven by a current source I representing synapses or experimental electrodes and modeled by the differential equation

$$C\frac{dV}{dt} + \frac{V}{R} = I \qquad V < \theta$$

where V is the voltage across nerve cell membranes and θ is the threshold below which the equation is valid. Justify whether or not the imposition of the threshold makes the model nonlinear, and reconcile your answer with the input/output characteristics of a biological neuron.

1.6. It was mentioned in the text that neurons within the cerebral cortex occur in layers. Suppose bands of fibers along the layers and also perpendicular to the layers form a slablike or modular arrangement of the neocortex. Further, suppose that the area of each slab is 250 μm^2 and let there be five million such slabs, each containing 2000 neurons. Feel free to make reasonable assumptions, if needed, to answer these questions:

(*a*) Estimate the total number of neurons in the cerebral cortex.

(*b*) Estimate the thickness of the cerebral cortex.

(*c*) What would be the resulting area if the slabs were laid adjacent to each other on a plane without gaps?

1.7. Consider a TLU that models Eq. (1.1) with n inputs $x_1, x_1, \ldots, x_n$. Each input may be assumed to be unipolar binary, i.e., a value of either 1 or 0. Suppose that the input x_i is multiplied by weight w_i, where $w_i > 0$ for $i = 1, 2, \ldots, p$; and $w_i < 0$ for $i = p+1, \ldots, p+q$, with $p+q = n$. The situation when either $p = 0$ or $q = 0$ is permitted.

(a) Suppose that $w_1 = w_2 = \cdots = w_p \triangleq w_E$ and $w_{p+1} = w_{p+2} = \cdots = w_{p+q} \triangleq w_I$. Show that the inhibition is absolute, i.e., the TLU produces 0 as output, irrespective of the input (as long as there is at least one nonzero inhibitory input), for any value of q in the interval $1 \le q \le n$, provided the threshold θ satisfies the inequality

$$\theta > pw_E - |w_I|.$$

(b) For the weight distribution in part (a), show that the TLU will produce 1 as output for r or more nonzero inputs when $1 \le r \le p \le n$ and $w_I = 0$ if and only if

$$rw_E \ge \theta > (r-1)w_E.$$

(c) Suppose that $\theta = 3$, $n = p = 3$, and $w_1 = w_2 = w_3 = 1$. Construct a truth table to show that in this case the TLU realizes the logical AND function.

(d) Suppose that $\theta = 1$, $n = p = 2$, and $w_1 = w_2 = 1$. Construct a truth table to show that in this case the TLU realizes the logical OR function.

(e) Study the logical function realized in the case when $\theta = 2$, $n = p = 3$ and $w_1 = w_2 = w_3 = 1$.

(f) Show that the universal logic function NAND is realized in the case when $\theta = -1$, $n = q = 2$, and $w_1 = w_2 = -1$.

1.8. Argue for or against the truth of the following statement: The brain can be modeled as a nonlinear dynamic system, and therefore its behavior can be understood by using a state-space approach if the transition equation $\dot{x} = f(x, \alpha)$ is known, where x is a state vector for the brain and α is the external input vector.

1.9. Design a simple TLU circuit to compute the exclusive OR (XOR) function, $x \oplus y$, where x and y are binary variables.

1.10. Suppose there are eight binary inputs $x = (x_7 x_6 x_5 \cdots x_0)$, where $x_7 x_6 x_5 \cdots x_0$ can be considered as a binary representation of a number. For example, 00100011 is the binary (radix 2) representation of the decimal (radix 10) number 35. Let $D(x)$ denote the decimal number represented by x. Design the simplest TLU circuit to compute the following predicate function:

$$\Psi_1(x) = \begin{cases} 1 & D(x) \ge 8; \\ 0 & \text{otherwise.} \end{cases}$$

1.11. Repeat Problem 10 with Ψ_1 replaced by the predicate function

$$\Psi_1(x) = \begin{cases} 1 & D(x) \ge 8 \text{ and } D(x) \text{ is odd}; \\ 0 & \text{otherwise.} \end{cases}$$

1.12. A basic property of a biological neuron is the refractory period, during which firing on two successive closely spaced time instants is not permitted [260]. The TLU with an inhibitory feedback from the output can model this phenomenon. Study this possibility by considering four binary-valued excitatory inputs to a TLU with its threshold set at $\theta = 2$ and an inhibitory feedback from the output.

1.13. Plot the transfer characteristics, described in Eqs. (1.4) and (1.5), for various choices of the parameter λ. The plots of y_i versus x_i for any finite value of λ are called the unipolar and bipolar *sigmoid* (logsigmoid and tansigmoid) characteristics and are used in the popular back propagation algorithm, which you will study in Chapter 5. With reference to the plots of the functions obtained, answer the following questions:

(a) Are the functions you plotted continuous, smooth, differentiable, monotone increasing, and bounded?

(b) Are the functions you plotted invertible? If so, find the inverse map $g(\cdot)$ that makes the composite map, $f(g(\cdot))$ an identity map.

(c) Investigate the limiting case when the parameter λ approaches ∞. The characteristics generated in the limit are called unipolar and bipolar *hard-limiters*.

1.14. Suppose that x_1 and x_2 are two bipolar binary variables assuming values from the set, $\{-1, 1\}$. A TLU is described by the equation

$$w_1 x_1 + w_2 x_2 + w_3 = 0,$$

where w_1, w_2, and w_3 are parameter values to be determined that will allow the realization of the logical OR gate. The bias w_3 may be viewed as multiplying a fixed unity-valued input. You may assume that the output of the OR gate is -1 when the input vector $\mathbf{x} \triangleq (x_1\ x_2)^T$ is $(-1\ -1)^T$ and, it is $+1$ for each of the other cases when the input vector is, successively, $(1\ 1)^T$, $(1\ -1)^T$, and $(-1\ 1)^T$. The authors suggest that the Hebbian rule be applied to realize the objective. The unity-valued fixed input vector is used to form the augmented input vector, $\mathbf{x}_a \triangleq (x_1\ x_2\ 1)^T$. After fixing the parameter α at a suitable value, like 1, apply the weight update rule in Eq. (1.7) successively to each of the input vectors and the corresponding target output to arrive at the final weight vector. You may choose the initial weight vector to be the null vector.

1.15. Repeat the preceding problem in the case of the logical AND gate and then answer the following questions.

(a) What happens if the binary variables are unipolar, i.e., they assume values from the set $\{0, 1\}$?

(b) What happens if the binary output is unipolar, i.e., it assumes values from the set $\{0, 1\}$?

(c) Summarize the limitation of the learning rule you used.

CHAPTER
2

GRAPHS

The origin of graphs can be traced to 1736, when Leonhard Euler published a paper that solved a problem posed to him on the layout of bridges in the city of Koenigsberg, Germany. The interested reader might refer to the exposition in Seshu and Reed [350, p. 19] regarding this. The elegant solution provided by Euler paved the way for the development of the theory of graphs, which has found applications in diverse disciplines including electrical network theory, transportation, sociology, layout design of circuits, and logic-circuit representation of Boolean functions. As early as 1961, Seshu and Reed [350, p. 7] remarked in their survey of applications of graph theory, "Still another application is to neural networks." Although it is natural to use graphs for describing and categorizing the topology of various neural network structures, the power of graphs has not been fully exploited in the study of neural networks as it has been, for example, in the analysis and synthesis of classical analog electrical networks. To remedy the problem and to keep the presentation compact and self-contained, we introduce those portions of the subject of graphs that are relevant to our task of studying the connectivity properties of neural network structures.

In Section 2.1, terminologies and preliminaries in graph theory that are applicable in the topological characterization of artificial neural network (ANN) structures are introduced. In Section 2.2, some particular classes of graphs, such as complete, multipartite, and layered, which will be encountered at various places in the text, are described. Section 2.3 is devoted to the topic of directed graphs, because they are required to describe such ANN structures as the multilayer feedforward structure. Matrix descriptions of graphs, relevant in connectivity studies, are briefly considered in Section 2.4. Some topological invariants, such as thickness and crossing number of graphs, are considered in Section 2.5 in anticipation of their potential use in the layout design of ANN. Voronoi diagrams and Delaunay tessellations are briefly introduced in Section 2.6 because of their proven as well as potential applications in the design of neural networks, especially in structural training of such networks. Finally, some concluding remarks are made.

2.1 TERMINOLOGY AND PRELIMINARIES

A *graph G* is an ordered 2-tuple, $(V(G), E(G))$, consisting of a set $V(G)$ of *vertices* (a vertex is alternately referred to as a *point,* a *node,* or a *0-simplex*) and a set $E(G)$ of *edges* (an edge is also referred to as a *line,* an *arc,* or a *1-simplex*). When each edge is assigned an orientation, the graph is *directed* (see Section 2.3) and is called a *digraph.* Otherwise, the graph is *undirected.* Undirected graphs, the focus of our discussion in this section, are referred to just as graphs. Each edge is a line or arc whose endpoints, which may or may not be distinct, must be from the set $V(G)$. $E(G)$ could be a null set, in which case the graph is referred to as a *vertex graph.* $V(G)$ is usually assumed to be nonempty and will be treated so here. Note, however, that a few authors have used the term *null graph* to describe the situation when $V(G)$ is allowed to be a null set. Here we restrict attention to finite graphs only, where $V(G)$ and $E(G)$ are finite sets. The cardinalities $|V|$ and $|E|$ of $V(G)$ and $E(G)$ are the number of vertices and edges in G. To avoid notational clutter, it is standard practice to replace $|V|$ and $|E|$ by appropriate declared symbols. This is done throughout except in Section 2.5, when discussing the graphical representation of space structures, where cells of higher dimensionality besides 0-cell (vertex) or 1-cell (edge) occur. An edge with nondistinct endpoints is called a *self-loop.* When more than one edge exists between two endpoints, the graph is said to contain parallel edges. Such a graph is referred to as a *multigraph.* A graph that is devoid of self-loops and parallel edges is called *simple.* What we have called a graph is sometimes referred to as a *linear graph* in order to distinguish from situations involving, for example, hypergraphs. However, when the adjective *linear* does not serve such discriminatory purpose, its usage is redundant.

Since graph theory owes its foundation to the classical paper of Euler, we digress to describe the class of *Euler graphs.* A graph in which every vertex is of even degree belongs to this class. The number of edges having a particular vertex for one of their endpoints is the *degree* of that vertex. If the edges of a graph or a subgraph can be ordered such that each edge, excluding the initial edge and the final edge, has a vertex in common with the preceding edge in the ordered sequence and the other vertex in common with the succeeding edge, the subgraph is an *edge sequence.* The number of times an edge appears in an edge sequence is the *multiplicity* of an edge in that edge sequence. An edge sequence is called an *edge train* (or *walk*) if the multiplicity of each edge in the sequence is 1. The initial and final vertices are the *terminal vertices* of the edge sequence or edge train. If the terminal vertices of an edge train coincide, it is a *closed edge train;* otherwise, it is open. If the degree of each nonterminal vertex of an edge train is 2 and the degree of each terminal vertex is 1, the edge train is a *path.* A graph is *connected* if there is a path between any two distinct vertices of the graph. A graph that is not connected has two or more separate parts. A graph with one vertex and no edges is defined to be connected. If an edge train that contains more than one edge is closed and each vertex is of degree 2, the edge train is a *loop* or *circuit*. A closed edge train having only one edge is a self-loop. A *subgraph H* of a graph *G* consists of subsets of vertices and edges of *G* such that the endpoints of every edge in *H* are also in *H*. Any connected subgraph of a graph over the same set of nodes that is devoid of loops is a *spanning tree*.

> **Example 2.1.** Consider the graph G_1 in Fig. 2.1, where the vertices and edges are labeled by positive integers and lowercase letters, respectively. This mode of labeling facilitates discrimination between the two types of entities: vertices and edges.
> The graph G_1 has four vertices and seven edges. It has one self-loop formed by edge f at vertex 1 and one set of parallel edges formed by edges c and g, each of which has as endpoints the vertices 2 and 3. The degrees of vertices 1, 2, 3, and 4, are, respectively, 4, 4, 3, and 3. Since every vertex is not of even degree, G_1 is not an Euler graph. The alternating sequence of vertices and edges described by 4 a 1 b 2 b 1 is an open edge sequence where the multiplicities of edges a and b are, respectively, 1 and 2. The sequence of vertices and edges described by 4 a 1 b 2 b 1 f 1 a 4 is an example of a closed edge sequence. The sequences of vertices and edges described by 4 a 1 b 2, 4 a 1 b 2 g 3 c 2, and 4 a 1 b 2 g 3 c 2 e 4 are examples of a path, an open edge train, and a closed edge train, respectively. The closed edge train described by 4 a 1 b 2 e 4 traces a loop. The graph G_1 is connected, because there is at least one path between any two vertices. G_1 has several spanning trees. You may wish to identify a couple of such spanning trees.

The importance of connected Euler graphs originates from the fact that this class and a simple variant completely determine whether or not an arbitrary specified graph can be drawn as a closed edge train or an open edge train. Specifically, a graph is a closed edge train if and only if it is a connected Euler graph. Furthermore, a graph is an open edge train if and only if it can be obtained by removing one edge (that is not a self-loop) from a connected Euler graph. It is easy to conclude that such a graph must have exactly two vertices of odd degree. The initial and terminal vertices of the open edge train are these two odd-degree vertices. Proofs for these results are not difficult to construct and can be found in ref. [350, pp. 20–22].

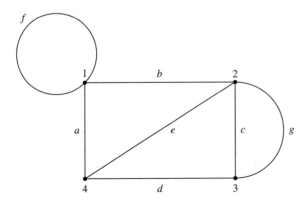

FIGURE 2.1
An undirected graph G_1 having four vertices labeled 1, 2, 3, and 4 and seven edges labeled a, b, c, d, e, f, and g. This graph is used in Example 2.1 to illustrate the various terminologies in the theory of graphs.

It is trivial to determine whether or not a graph is an Euler graph, and therefore it is equally simple to establish if a specified graph is an open edge train or a closed edge train. The edge train requires traversal of each edge once and only once, though the vertices may be visited more than once. A variant of the problem solved by means of Euler graphs is characterized by the Hamiltonian class of graphs. Here, the objective is to determine whether a connected graph contains a subgraph that is either a closed edge train or an open edge train and in which each vertex of the original graph occurs only once (except, of course, the terminal vertices, which coincide in the case of a closed edge train). Such a constrained closed edge train, each of whose vertices is of degree 2, in the specified graph is called a *Hamiltonian loop;* whereas a similarly constrained open edge train, where all vertices except the initial and terminal ones are of degree 2, in the same graph is called a *Hamiltonian path.* The imposition of the constraint changes an easy problem to a very complicated one. Indeed, a set of necessary and sufficient conditions for a graph to contain a Hamiltonian circuit (or a Hamiltonian path) is not yet known. The concept of the Hamiltonian loop is useful in the construction of neural network solutions to the traveling salesperson problem, which is discussed in Chapters 3 and 10.

Certain basic general results for graphs are useful in the analysis of connectivity properties of neural networks. We introduce here two results that will find application in this text.

Theorem 2.1. In any graph, the sum of the degrees of the vertices is equal to twice the number of edges.

Proof. This follows from the fact that each edge is associated with two endpoints, each of which contributes to the vertex degrees. (In the case of a self-loop, the endpoints are not distinct, but a value of 2 is added to the sum of vertex degrees.)

Theorem 2.2. The number of vertices of odd degree is either even or zero.

Proof. Let the number of edges be e, and let δ_k be the number of vertices of degree k, for $k = 1, 2, \ldots, m$. Then, by Theorem 2.1,

$$\delta_1 + 2\delta_2 + 3\delta_3 + \cdots + m\delta_m = 2e.$$

Therefore,

$$\delta_1 + \delta_3 + \delta_5 + \cdots = 2e - 2\delta_2 - 2\delta_3 - 4\delta_4 - 4\delta_5 - \cdots,$$

which proves the result, since only odd integers occur as subscripts on the left and either an even integer or zero results on the right side of the foregoing equation.

The reader may wish to verify that both Theorems 1 and 2 are satisfied by the graph G_1 in Example 2.1. The number of edges in a spanning tree associated with a connected graph over n nodes is $(n - 1)$. A graph that has no loops or circuits is called *acyclic,* and a spanning tree belongs to this class of graphs. A connected graph has many distinct spanning trees. The number of such distinct spanning trees can easily be evaluated [350]. An explicit formula for the number of spanning trees in K_n (defined in Section 2.2) was given by Cayley as early as 1889 [73], and more recent results on other classes of graphs are available, for example, in ref. [50]. The edges of the graph that do not belong to a particular spanning tree are called *chords* or *links* associated with the spanning tree. The number of chords or links is $e - n + 1$, where e is the number of edges in the connected graph having n nodes. When a chord is added to a spanning tree, a loop results. Since the addition of each chord results in a new independent loop, the number of independent loops in any connected graph having e edges and n nodes is $e - n + 1$. When a graph has p separate connected components, the subgraph consisting of the p spanning trees (one over each of the p connected parts) is called a *spanning forest*. The number of edges in a spanning forest over a graph having n vertices, e edges, and p connected components is $n - p$, and the number of independent loops is $e - n + p$.

2.2   SPECIAL TYPES OF GRAPHS

We will encounter certain graphs quite frequently later in the text. For instance, a graph without self-loops and having exactly one edge between any two distinct nodes is called *complete*. A complete graph over n nodes is denoted by K_n and is, necessarily, simple. A graph whose node set $V(G)$ is the union of two disjoint subsets (having, respectively, n_1 and n_2 nodes), such that each edge has endpoints in both of the different subsets of nodes is called *bipartite*. A simple bipartite graph over a specified 2-tuple (n_1, n_2) of nodes in the two parts that has the maximum possible number of edges is called complete, and this *complete bipartite graph* is denoted by K_{n_1,n_2}. If the node set of a graph is decomposed into three mutually disjoint subsets having, respectively, n_1, n_2, and n_3 nodes, and if each edge of the graph has endpoints in two distinct subsets of this grouping, then the graph is referred to as *tripartite*. A simple tripartite graph over a fixed 3-tuple (n_1, n_2, n_3) of nodes is complete when it contains the maximum number of edges. This *complete tripartite graph* is denoted by K_{n_1,n_2,n_3}, and the reader may wish to verify that it has $n_1 n_2 + n_2 n_3 + n_3 n_1$ edges. It is straightforward to generalize the preceding descriptions for K_{n_1,n_2} and K_{n_1,n_2,n_3} to the case of complete l-partite (multipartite) graphs, denoted by $K_{n_1,n_2,\dots,n_l}$. The graphs K_4, $K_{2,5}$, and $K_{2,1,3}$ are shown in Fig. 2.2.

> **Example 2.2.** Consider the graphs in Fig. 2.2. The graph K_4 has 4 nodes and 6 edges. The graph $K_{2,5}$ has 7 nodes and 10 edges. The graph $K_{2,1,3}$ has 6 nodes and 11 edges. Note that the edges of a graph need not be represented by straight lines. K_4, $K_{2,5}$, and $K_{2,1,3}$ have, respectively, 3, 4, and 6 independent loops.

> **Example 2.3.** Let n be an even number. What is the maximum number of edges possible in a simple bipartite graph over n vertices?
> Let the number of vertices in the two parts be n_1 and n_2, so that
> $$n_1 + n_2 = n.$$
> It is only necessary to consider complete bipartite graphs. The number e of edges in K_{n_1,n_2} is
> $$e = n_1 n_2 = n_1(n - n_1).$$

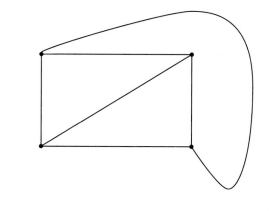

(a)

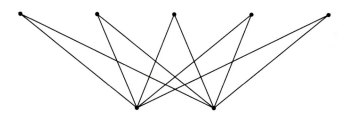

(b)

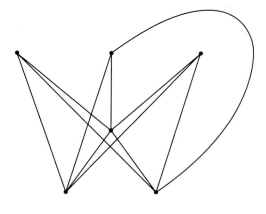

(c)

FIGURE 2.2
Special types of undirected graphs: (a) the complete graph K_4 over four vertices; (b) the complete bipartite graph $K_{2,5}$, where edges connect a set of two vertices in one part to a set of five vertices in another part; (c) the complete tripartite graph $K_{2,1,3}$.

Temporarily treating n_1 and n_2 as continuous variables, we see that the derivatives,

$$\frac{de}{dn_1} = n - 2n_1 = 0, \qquad \frac{d^2e}{dn_1^2} = -2,$$

imply that e is maximum for $n_1 = n/2$. Since $n_1 = n/2$ and $n_2 = n/2$ are integers, the maximum is attained for values of n_1 and n_2 that satisfy the physical constraints of the problem. Therefore, $K_{n/2,n/2}$ contains the maximum number of edges among all simple bipartite graphs over n nodes. This number is $n^2/4$.

The foregoing simple example illustrates the use of graphs for designing feedforward layered networks which will be introduced in Chapter 5. A variant of the problem in Example 2.3 is to keep the number of edges constant and minimize the total number of nodes. Such an approach would be useful for optimizing the probability of *valid generalization* in neural network learning, a topic to be introduced in Chapter 6.

We say that two graphs G_1 and G_2 are *isomorphic* if there exists a one-to-one correspondence between their vertex sets and a one-to-one correspondence between their edge sets so that the corresponding edges of G_1 and G_2 are incident on the corresponding vertices of G_1 and G_2. The operations of removal and additions of vertices of degree 2 lead to the concept of *graph homeomorphism*. The removal operation of a vertex v results in the replacement of two edges, say (v_1, v) and (v, v_2), that are connected at v by a single edge (v_1, v_2). The vertex addition operation, on the other hand, implies the addition of vertex v so that an edge (v_1, v_2) is replaced by two edges (v_1, v) and (v, v_2) that are node-coalesced at v. We say that two graphs G_1 and G_2 are graph homeomorphic if they either are isomorphic or can be made isomorphic by a sequence of vertex removal or vertex addition operations as just described.

An important class of graphs that will be useful in the characterization of a popular type of neural network structure called the feedforward structure is the class of *layered graphs*. A *complete layered graph* may be viewed as concatenations or node-coalesced cascades of compatible complete bipartite graphs. The process of node coalescence for $K_{3,4}$ and $K_{4,2}$ is illustrated in Fig. 2.3, where the resulting complete layered graph is also shown. Note that the compatibility condition required on K_{n_1,n_2} and K_{n_3,n_4} for node coalescence to take place is that $n_2 = n_3$. In the analysis of failure due to either neurons or interconnections of neural networks, the concepts of vertex connectivity and edge connectivity are relevant. The *vertex connectivity* of a connected graph G is the minimum number of vertices whose removal from G results in either a disconnected graph or a graph with a single vertex. The *edge connectivity* of a connected graph G is the minimum number of edges whose removal from G results in either a disconnected graph or a graph with a single vertex. Removal of a vertex implies the removal of all the edges incident on that vertex. A removal of an edge keeps intact the terminal vertices of the edge in the graph. Therefore, vertex connectivity of G can never exceed its edge connectivity, which in turn is less than or equal to the degree of a vertex in G having smallest degree. The reader may wish to confirm that both the vertex and edge connectivities of any tree equal unity.

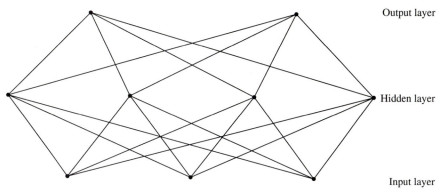

Output layer

Hidden layer

Input layer

FIGURE 2.3
Graphical representation of a layered neural network formed by node-coalescing a cascade of $K_{3,4}$ and $K_{4,2}$. The graph, which is undirected, has loops. If the graph is directed, with arrows in the edges running from the bottom toward the top of this page, then the graph is acyclic.

2.3 DIRECTED GRAPHS

So far, we have dealt with *undirected graphs,* where the edges are not assigned any orientation. In a *directed graph,* consisting of a set $V(G) = \{v_1, v_2, \ldots\}$ of vertices and a set $E(G) = \{e_1, e_2, \ldots\}$ of edges, there exists a mapping of every edge onto some *ordered* pair of vertices (v_i, v_j). Directed graphs bear significance in the study of neural networks because the signal is constrained to flow in a particular direction in some artificial neural networks. For example, in multilayer feedforward networks the signal flow along each edge is unidirectional. An undirected graph can be converted to a directed graph (referred to for brevity as a *digraph*) by replacing each edge with two edges having opposite orientations, as shown in Fig. 2.4. On the other hand, a digraph has an *underlying undirected graph,* which is defined as the graph obtained by deleting the arrows (orientation or ordering information) from the digraph. Note that if a digraph is derived from an underlying undirected graph by replacing each undirected edge by two directed edges, as shown in Fig. 2.4, this new digraph will not be identical to the original digraph from which the underlying undirected graph was obtained.

Many of the results for undirected graphs have appropriate counterparts in the case of directed graphs. For example, the counterpart of Theorem 2.1 is Theorem 2.3

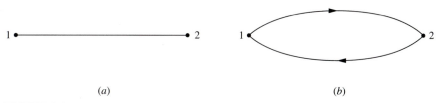

(a)   (b)

FIGURE 2.4
Replacing an undirected edge by two directed edges. (*a*) Undirected edge. (*b*) Directed edges.

in the case of directed graphs. Since the proof is trivial, it is omitted. We refer to an edge as contributing to the *in-degree* if it is entering a vertex and as contributing to the *out-degree* if it is exiting a vertex.

Theorem 2.3. In any digraph G, the sum of all in-degrees is equal to the sum of all out-degrees, and each sum is equal to the number of edges in G.

Example 2.4. Consider the directed graph G_2 shown in Fig. 2.5. G_2 has one directed self-loop, formed at node 4 by the edge f, which is incident at that node and also exits from it. The only set of directed parallel edges is formed by g and d. Note that b and h do not form a set of directed parallel edges, because their orientations with respect to nodes 1 and 2 are different. The in-degrees of vertices labeled 1, 2, 3, 4, and 5 are 2, 2, 4, 1, and 0, respectively, whereas their out-degrees are 1, 3, 0, 4, and 1. Clearly, Theorem 2.3 is satisfied by G_2. Furthermore, edges c and g form a directed path from node 4 to node 3. Edges h and b form a directed loop. Note that there is no directed path from, for example, node 3 to node 4, and edges c, d, and e do not form a directed loop, though they do form a loop in the underlying undirected graph.

A digraph devoid of directed loops is called *acyclic*. In the preceding example, the graph G_2 is not acyclic because there is a directed self-loop and a directed loop,

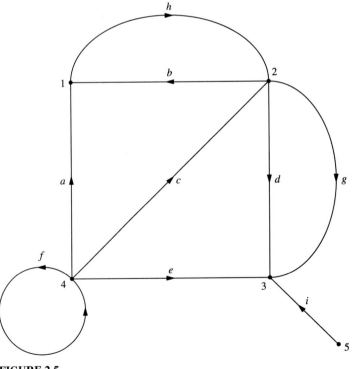

FIGURE 2.5
Directed graph G_2 in Example 2.4.

neither of which can be present in an acyclic digraph. Only by removing edge f and either edge b or h can G_2 be made acyclic. Paths, edge trains, edge sequences, and loops, in addition to being what they are in the underlying undirected graph obtained from the digraph by deletion of the arrows, also possess orientation in the case of a digraph. A directed edge train, for example, from a vertex v_i to v_j is an alternating sequence of vertices and edges, beginning with v_i and ending with v_j such that each edge is oriented from the vertex preceding it to the vertex following it, subject to the constraint that no edge is repeated. When that constraint is eliminated, the sequence is called a directed edge sequence. When a directed edge train is further constrained so that the degree, defined to be the sum of in- and out-degrees, of each vertex is either one or two, a directed path results; when this path closes on itself, a directed loop is formed, as was illustrated in Example 2.5 for the special digraph G_2. A digraph is said to be *strongly connected* if there is at least one directed path from every vertex to every other vertex. A digraph is *weakly connected* if the underlying undirected graph is connected. Obviously, the digraph G_2 in Fig. 2.5 is weakly connected but not strongly connected. A comment on an edge like edge i in Fig. 2.5 is necessary with respect to its relevance in neural networks. Such an edge may be used to describe the connection from an external input to a neuron when the threshold as well as the connection weight must be trained. (See Problem 4.5.) In graph theory, a vertex that, like the one labeled 3 in Fig. 2.5, is one endpoint of a *pendant* edge such as i (the other endpoint of a pendant edge must be of degree 1) is called a *cut-vertex* or *articulation point*. A *cut-set* is a set of edges whose removal splits a weakly connected directed graph into two separate parts. For example, for the weakly connected digraph (call it G) in Fig. 2.6, the edges (v_1, v_2), (v_2, v_4), and (v_3, v_2) constitute a cut-set because their removal splits G into two subgraphs G_0 and $\tilde{G}_0$, where G_0 is a vertex graph consisting of vertex v_2 and $\tilde{G}_0$ consists of the remaining vertices in G along with the edges (v_1, v_4), (v_3, v_4), and the self-loop at v_4. In a flow network (see Chapter 3), if G_0 and $\tilde{G}_0$ contain the source and destination nodes, respectively, then the subset of edges in the cut-set that are incident from the vertices in G_0 to vertices in $\tilde{G}_0$ define a *cut*. The cut associated with the cut-set just described consists only of the directed edge (v_2, v_4).

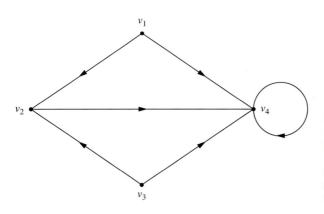

FIGURE 2.6
A directed graph with one self-loop and no parallel edges whose adjacency matrix representation is given in Example 2.5. This directed graph also has no loops and therefore is acyclic.

2.4 MATRIX REPRESENTATION OF GRAPHS

The power of graphs becomes very clear when the network to be analyzed is large. Since such analysis is done through powerful computers, it becomes necessary to represent the graph to a computer. Matrices over the 2-element (0, 1) *Boolean ring* are very suitable for such representations, because manipulations on the digital computer become convenient to implement because of modulo-2 operations. The 2-element Boolean ring is also a field, because all the postulates for a field, including the existence of a multiplicative inverse, are satisfied in this case.

There are a variety of matrix representations. The reader may already have encountered incident matrices, cut-set matrices, tie-set matrices, and mesh matrices in electrical circuit analysis [350]. In connectivity studies of the brain models employing a digital computer, the adjacency matrix X or its variant, the interconnection matrix C, is relevant. Such matrices also find use in interconnection and routing problems in the layout design of large-scale integrated circuits [56]. If artificial neural networks are to be fabricated on chips, packaging and layout design considerations are expected to outweigh other factors from the standpoints of cost, size, and reliability. Therefore, the need for some knowledge of matrix representations applicable to such situations motivates the brief presentation next.

2.4.1 Adjacency Matrix

Let G be a directed graph with n vertices and no parallel edges. Then the adjacency matrix $X = [x_{ij}]$ of the digraph G is an $n \times n$ binary-valued (0, 1) matrix whose element $x_{ij} = 1$ if there is an edge directed from the ith vertex to the jth vertex and $x_{ij} = 0$ otherwise. Thus, a diagonal element is nonzero if and only if there is a self-loop at the relevant node.

2.4.2 Interconnection Matrix

This is similar to the adjacency matrix except that each diagonal element is 1. This matrix may be denoted by $C = [c_{ij}]$.

> **Theorem 2.4.** The (i, j)th entry in X^r equals the number of different directed edge sequences of r edges from the ith vertex to the jth.

> **Proof.** By induction, we see that the (i, j)th entry of $X^r = X^{r-1}X$ is
>
> $$\sum_{k=1}^{n} [(i, k)\text{th entry in } X^{r-1}]x_{kj}$$
>
> $$= \sum_{k=1}^{n} (\text{number of directed edge sequences of length } (r-1) \text{ from vertex } i \text{ to } k)x_{kj}.$$

> **Comment.** If one is not interested in the *number* but only in the feature of connectivity, then one may replace arithmetic summation with logical summation (see Section 3.6.3).

Example 2.5. Consider the directed graph in Fig. 2.6. There is one self-loop but no parallel edges. The adjacency matrix $\mathbf{X}$ is easily determined to be

$$
\mathbf{X} = \begin{bmatrix} 0 & 1 & 0 & 1 \\ 0 & 0 & 0 & 1 \\ 0 & 1 & 0 & 1 \\ 0 & 0 & 0 & 1 \end{bmatrix}.
$$

The sum of the elements in the ith row of $\mathbf{X}$ is the number of edges exiting from vertex v_i, or the out-degree of vertex v_i. Therefore, the sum of all out-degrees is equal to the sum of the elements in $\mathbf{X}$. The sum of the elements in the jth column of $\mathbf{X}$ is the number of edges incident on vertex v_j, or the in-degree of vertex v_j. The sum of the elements of $\mathbf{X}$ therefore also equals the sum of all in-degrees. Clearly, these observations justify the validity of Theorem 2.3. Some powers of $\mathbf{X}$ are calculated next:

$$
\mathbf{X}^2 = \begin{bmatrix} 0 & 0 & 0 & 2 \\ 0 & 0 & 0 & 1 \\ 0 & 0 & 0 & 2 \\ 0 & 0 & 0 & 1 \end{bmatrix} \qquad \mathbf{X}^3 = \begin{bmatrix} 0 & 0 & 0 & 2 \\ 0 & 0 & 0 & 1 \\ 0 & 0 & 0 & 2 \\ 0 & 0 & 0 & 1 \end{bmatrix}.
$$

Furthermore, $\mathbf{X}^2 = \mathbf{X}^3 = \mathbf{X}^4 = \mathbf{X}^5 \cdots$. The reader should verify that Theorem 2.4 is satisfied.

2.5 TOPOLOGICAL INVARIANTS

This section summarizes certain properties in graphs that provide graphical representations of structures, such as polyhedra, that remain invariant under a topological transformation. These results indicate the problems faced in the layout of a brain model and suggest the need to investigate three-dimensional (3-D) wiring in integrated circuits (ICs) as well as the truly 3-D layout of the neurons and their interconnections in the real brain. Counterparts of the results on the thickness and the like presented here for complete graphs and complete bipartite graphs are not available for layered graphs, and such results are worth investigating as a means for obtaining theoretically tight bounds on the number of layers or slabs needed in the standard approach to layout of a brain model. In this section, only an undirected graph is of concern. If an ANN is characterized by a directed graph, the results in this section apply to the underlying undirected graph.

A mapping ϕ of one geometrical figure or structure A into another structure B is a *topological transformation* or a structure homeomorphism if the mapping is one-to-one and bicontinuous. *One-to-one (bijective, biunique)* mapping ϕ means that for any two points v_i, v_j in the structure, $\phi(v_i) = \phi(v_j)$ if and only if $v_i = v_j$; this implies that there exists an inverse transformation ϕ^{-1} such that $\phi^{-1}(v_k) = v_i$ if and only if $\phi(v_i) = v_k$. *Bicontinuity* in the map ϕ means that both ϕ and ϕ^{-1} are continuous, and it allows $\phi(v_i)$ and $\phi(v_j)$ to be arbitrarily close if v_i and v_j are sufficiently close. Topological transformation naturally leads to loss of metric and projective properties.

2.5.1 Euler and Schlaefli Invariants

A result credited to Euler, but first obtained by René Descartes in 1640, states that a polyhedron (a solid whose surface has only polygonal faces) without holes having $|V|$ vertices, $|E|$ edges, and $|F|$ bounded faces satisfies the constraint

$$|V| - |E| + |F| = 2. \tag{2.1}$$

The invariant, $|V| - |E| + |F|$, is referred to as the *Euler characteristic*. Note that each vertex is zero-dimensional, each edge is one-dimensional, and each face is two-dimensional. The validity of Eq. (2.1) may be justified as follows. Imagine the polyhedron without holes to be hollow [this does not interfere with the conditions on which Eq. (2.1) dwells], with a surface made of thin rubber. Cut one face, and deform the remaining surface until it stretches *flat* on a plane. Then the resulting graph G will have the same number of vertices and edges as the polyhedron, but one less bounded face. Of course, it also has an unbounded face. For G then, it will be shown that

$$|V| - |E| + |F_1| = 1, \tag{2.2}$$

where F_1 equals the number of bounded faces of G. "Triangulate" G to get G_1; in other words, in some polygon of G that is not already a triangle, draw a diagonal. It can be easily confirmed that the Euler characteristic of G_1 is the same as that of G. Form G_2 by taking any boundary triangle in G_1 and deleting that part of the boundary triangle that does not belong to some other triangle. The reader may check that the Euler characteristics of G_2 and G_1 are invariant. The procedure is continued until one triangle remains, for which $|V| - |E| + |F_1| = 1$. Therefore, Eq. (2.2), and hence Eq. (2.1), must be true.

A century after Euler published his result described in Eq. (2.1), Schlaefli [236, pp. 11–38] generalized the relationship between the number of elements of different dimensionality in a structure, as described in Eq. (2.3). Let N_i represent the number of elements of dimensionality i so that $N_0 = |V|$, $N_1 = |E|$, $N_2 = |F|$, N_3 is the number $|C|$ of cells, and so on. Then the relationship between the elements of dimensionalities from 0 to d is

$$\sum_{i=0}^{d} (-1)^i N_i = 1 + (-1)^d. \tag{2.3}$$

Clearly, for $d = 2$, Eq. (2.3) specializes to Eq. (2.1). For $d = 3$, Eq. (2.3) specializes to the constraint in Eq (2.4):

$$|V| - |E| + |F| - |C| = 0. \tag{2.4}$$

Example 2.6. Consider a tetrahedron. Draw it and verify that is has four vertices, six edges, and four faces. It may be viewed in 3-D as consisting of two cells, resulting from the fact that it divides space into two cells (inside and outside the singly connected closed surface). Therefore, Eq. (2.4) is satisfied. The planar graph associated with a tetrahedron may also be drawn in 2-D, where it has four vertices, six edges, and three bounded faces. Therefore, Eq. (2.2) is satisfied. Note that the planar graph also has an unbounded face, which, if taken into account when counting the number of faces, leads to satisfaction of the constraint in Eq. (2.1). Also see Problem 2.13.

2.5.2   Genus

A property that remains invariant under a topological transformation is that of *genus,* defined next.

> **Definition 2.1   Genus.** The genus of a surface is the largest number of nonintersecting simple closed curves (*Jordan curves*) that can be drawn on the surface without separating it.

The genus of the Euclidean plane, denoted by $\mathbb{R}^2$, is zero. The points on the surface of a sphere can be mapped to the points on $\mathbb{R}^2$ bijectively, with the property of bicontinuity satisfied. Therefore, the genus of a sphere, like the genus of $\mathbb{R}^2$, is zero. Note that the sphere is bounded, but its topological equivalent $\mathbb{R}^2$ is not. The genus of the surface of a doughnut-shaped structure is 1, and since a sphere with one handle is its topological equivalent, the unity genus remains invariant. The genus of the surface of a sphere with two handles is 2, and so on. For a surface S, of genus p, that is divided into a number $|F|$ of regions or faces by marking a number $|V|$ of vertices on S and joining them by, say, $|E|$ curved arcs or edges, the Euler characteristic is given by

$$|V| - |E| + |F| = 2 - 2p. \tag{2.5}$$

The equality in Eq. (2.5) can be justified from the following considerations. A surface S of genus p is topologically equivalent to the surface of a sphere with p handles. The process of cutting one end of each handle, straightening each handle out, and then flattening out each of the projecting handles results in a spherical surface with $2p$ regions or faces removed, but with the same number of vertices and edges as S. Therefore, Eq. (2.5) follows, because application of Eq. (2.1) yields

$$|V| - |E| + (|F| + 2p) = 2.$$

The genus $\gamma(G)$ of a graph G is the smallest genus of all surfaces on which G can be *embedded* (drawn). The graphs of genus 0 are the *planar* graphs. A planar graph, having a finite number of vertices and edges, can be embedded (drawn) on the plane $\mathbb{R}^2$ without edges intersecting except at vertices. Certain useful results follow when a finite connected graph is restricted to be planar. A planar graph always has one unbounded face. If this face is included in the set F of faces, then Eq. (2.1) also applies to the planar graph. The concepts of a *dual* graph and a planar graph are related. A celebrated theorem, due to Hassler Whitney, states that a graph has a dual (geometric or combinatorial) if and only if it is planar [350, p. 45]. There is an isomorphism between the edges of a graph G and its dual graph G_D. G_D can be constructed very easily from G. Since such construction is only of peripheral interest in this book, the interested reader is referred to any elementary text on graph theory or electrical network theory, where the constructive procedures are illustrated [350].

Definition 2.2. A planar graph to which no edges other than parallel edges or self-loops can be added without destroying the planar property is called a *maximal planar graph.*

A maximal planar graph is said to be *triangulated* if each of its faces, including the unbounded face, has three edges, which implies that

$$3|F| = 2|E|. \tag{2.6}$$

Remember that $|F|$ in Eq. (2.6) is the total number of faces including the unbounded face. By substituting Eq. (2.6) into Eq. (2.1), it follows that for a maximal planar graph

$$|E| = 3|V| - 6. \tag{2.7}$$

It readily follows, then, that for any finite connected planar graph

$$|E| \leq 3|V| - 6. \tag{2.8}$$

Theorem 2.5. The complete graph, K_5, is nonplanar.

Proof. In K_5, $|V| = 5$, $|E| = 10$, and therefore Eq. (2.8) is not satisfied, thus violating the necessary condition for planarity.

Theorem 2.6. The bipartite graph $K_{3,3}$ is nonplanar.

Proof. In a bipartite graph, there cannot be loops with an odd number of edges. In $K_{3,3}$, therefore, no region can be bounded with fewer than four edges. Hence, if this graph were planar, we would have

$$2|E| \geq 4|F|. \tag{2.9}$$

Substituting for $|F|$ from Eq. (2.1) into Eq. (2.9), one infers that the inequality

$$|E| \leq 2|V| - 4 \tag{2.10}$$

must hold for $K_{3,3}$ to be planar. However, for $K_{3,3}$, $|V| = 6$, $|E| = 9$, implying that $K_{3,3}$ is nonplanar because the necessary condition in Eq. (2.10) for planarity is not satisfied. However, note that $K_{3,3}$ does satisfy the other necessary condition for planarity as given in Eq. (2.8).

K_5 and $K_{3,3}$ are in fact the basic nonplanar graphs and are referred to in the literature as *Kuratowski graphs* after C. Kuratowski, who established in 1930 that a necessary and sufficient condition for a graph to be planar is that it contains as a subgraph neither K_5, nor $K_{3,3}$, nor any graph homeomorphic to K_5 or $K_{3,3}$. Note that the condition in Eq. (2.10) is necessary and sufficient for a complete bipartite graph to be planar except in the trivial case when $n_1 = n_2 = 1$. The reason is that K_{n_1,n_2} is known to be planar provided either n_1 or n_2 is less than or equal to 2 or each is equal to 2 (otherwise, it contains $K_{3,3}$ as a subgraph). The reader can easily draw K_{n_1,n_2} as a planar graph when either n_1 or n_2 is less than or equal to 2 or when each is equal to 2, and can also verify that Eq. (2.10) is satisfied in that type of situation, except, of course, in the trivial case just cited. (Try this!) It can then be verified that Eq. (2.10) is violated when both n_1 and n_2 are greater than or equal to 3. (Again, try to prove this by applying elementary calculus.) Note, however, that the condition in Eq. (2.10) may not be sufficient for a bipartite graph that is not complete to be planar.

Results on genus and other topological invariants to be discussed are known in the literature mostly for complete graphs and complete bipartite graphs. To describe such results, it is necessary to introduce the notations $\lfloor x \rfloor$ for the integer part, or *floor*, of x, and $\lceil x \rceil$ for the smallest integer not less than x, or the *ceiling* of x.

For $n \geq 3$, the genus $\gamma(K_n)$ of a complete graph K_n is given by

$$\gamma(K_n) = \left\lceil \frac{(n-3)(n-4)}{12} \right\rceil. \tag{2.11}$$

For $m, n \geq 2$, the genus $\gamma(K_{m,n})$ of a complete bipartite graph $K_{m,n}$ is

$$\gamma(K_{m,n}) = \left\lceil \frac{(m-2)(n-2)}{4} \right\rceil. \tag{2.12}$$

Thus, $K_{3,3}$, K_5, and K_7 are not embeddable either on a plane or on a sphere (each of which has genus 0) but are embeddable on a doughnut-shaped torus (whose genus is 1).

2.5.3 Thickness

Thickness is another topological invariant.

Definition 2.3 Thickness. The thickness of a graph G is the minimum number of pairwise edge-disjoint planar subgraphs whose union is G, each of which is over the same number of vertices present in G without constraining their locations.

The notion of thickness finds applications in the design of printed and integrated circuits where, to minimize costly junctions, it becomes necessary to use 2 or more layers, connected through holes (such holes are called *via holes*).

The thickness for complete and most complete bipartite graphs is now known. A planar graph, of course, has unit thickness, and a graph is biplanar if its thickness is 2. Using Eq. (2.10), one can easily show that $K_{7,7}$ is not biplanar. No simple, elegant proof is known of the simple fact that K_9 is not biplanar. The procedures in refs. [32] and [379] for proving the preceding fact are primarily enumerative and of brute force type.

Theorem 2.7. The thickness $t(K_p)$ of a complete graph K_p, whenever $p \neq 10$, or $p \neq 9$, is

$$t(K_p) = \left\lfloor \frac{p+7}{6} \right\rfloor. \tag{2.13}$$

Proof. The exceptions noted are due to the fact that K_9 is known to have a thickness greater than 2; and when $p = 10$, $t(K_{10}) = 3 \neq \lfloor \frac{17}{6} \rfloor$. To carry on with the remainder of the proof, note that the number of edges in K_p is $p(p-1)/2$ and that the maximal planar graph over p nodes has $(3p - 6)$ edges. One may conclude that

$$t(K_p) \geq \left\lceil \frac{\frac{1}{2} p(p-1)}{3(p-2)} \right\rceil. \tag{2.14}$$

For positive integers a and b, the following holds:

$$\left\lceil \frac{a}{b} \right\rceil = \left\lfloor \frac{a+b-1}{b} \right\rfloor. \tag{2.15}$$

By setting $a = \frac{1}{2} p(p-1)$ and $b = 3(p-2)$ in Eq. (2.15) and then simplifying, it follows from Eq. (2.14) that

$$t(K_p) \geq \left\lfloor \frac{p+7}{6} \right\rfloor. \tag{2.16}$$

To prove equality in Eq. (2.16) with the exceptions noted for p, and other cases when $p \neq 4 \bmod 6$, the interested reader is referred to a constructive procedure [37], which is beyond the scope of this text. The remaining cases were also successfully tackled by 1976.[1]

As of 1972, the only value of $p \leq 45$ for which $t(K_p)$ was not precisely known was $p = 16$ [37, 149]. Of course, since $t(K_{15}) = 3$ and $t(K_{17}) = 4$, by straightforward applications of Theorem 2.7 it follows that $t(K_{16})$ must be either 3 or 4. The fact that K_{16} is decomposable into three planar graphs was shown in ref. [249].

It has been shown [38] that the thickness of the complete bipartite graph $K_{m,n}$, if $m \leq n$, is

$$t(K_{m,n}) = \left\lceil \frac{mn}{2(m+n-2)} \right\rceil \tag{2.17}$$

except, possibly, when m and n are both odd and there exists an integer k such that

$$n = \left\lfloor \frac{2k(m-2)}{(m-2k)} \right\rfloor.$$

Problems often call for graphs that have a given property that is critical in the sense that no proper subgraph has the same property. In the context of thickness, such graphs are called thickness-minimal, or *t-minimal*. The results of research on determining which graphs are *t*-minimal were summarized by Arthur M. Hobbs of the University of Waterloo in a survey of thickness that he conducted. An updated

---

[1]V.B. Aleksev and V.S. Gonchakov. Thickness of arbitrary complete graphs. *Mat. Sbornik,* 101(143): 212–230. 1976.

version of his summary, influenced by later developments described in this section, is as follows:

1. All homeomorphs of K_5 and $K_{3,3}$ are 2-minimal, and these graphs constitute the complete set of 2-minimal graphs.
2. K_9, $K_{7,7}$, and $K_{5,13}$ are 3-minimal, but there are an infinite number of nonisomorphic 3-minimal graphs.
3. K_{17} is 4-minimal.
4. $K_{2m-1,4m^2-10m+7}$ and $K_{4m-5,4m-5}$ are m-minimal for $m \geq 2$.

2.5.4 Some Other Topological Invariants

Other topological invariants, *n-thickness, coarseness, crossing number*, and *rectilinear crossing number*, are briefly discussed in this section.

Definition 2.4 n-Thickness. The n-thickness of a graph G is the minimum number of subgraphs of genus at most n whose union is G. The n-thickness of a graph G will be denoted by $t_n(G)$.

It is known that

$$t_1(K_p) = \left\lceil \frac{p+4}{6} \right\rceil \tag{2.18}$$

$$t_2(K_p) = \left\lceil \frac{p+3}{6} \right\rceil \tag{2.19}$$

It is interesting to note that the ordinary thickness of all complete graphs became known *after* the 1-thickness and 2-thickness of all such graphs had been found.

Definition 2.5   Coarseness. The coarseness $c(G)$ of a graph G is the maximum number of edge-disjoint nonplanar subgraphs into which G may be decomposed.

The coarseness $c(G)$ of complete graphs is given by

$$c(K_{3n}) = \begin{cases} \dbinom{n}{2} & p = 3n \leq 15 \\[2ex] \dbinom{n}{2} + \left\lfloor \dfrac{n}{5} \right\rfloor & p = 3n \geq 30 \end{cases}$$

$$c(K_{3n+1}) = \binom{n}{2} + 2\left\lfloor \frac{n}{3} \right\rfloor \qquad p = 3n+1 \geq 19 \quad \text{and} \quad p \neq 9n+7$$

$$c(K_{3n+2}) = \binom{n}{2} + \left\lfloor \frac{14n+1}{15} \right\rfloor$$

The coarseness of the complete bipartite graph $K_{m,m}$ is

$$c(K_{m,m}) = \left\lfloor \left\lfloor \frac{m}{3} \right\rfloor \frac{m}{3} \right\rfloor \tag{2.20}$$

and furthermore

$$c(K_{m,n}) \geq \min\left(\left\lfloor \left(\left\lfloor \frac{m}{3} \right\rfloor \frac{n}{3} \right) \right\rfloor, \left\lfloor \left(\left\lfloor \frac{n}{3} \right\rfloor \frac{m}{3} \right) \right\rfloor \right). \tag{2.21}$$

Definition 2.6   Crossing number. The crossing number, $\nu(G)$, of a graph G is the minimum number of pairwise intersections (excluding those at the vertices of G) of its edges when G is drawn in the plane.

Clearly, $\nu(G) = 0$ if and only if G is planar. The crossing number $\nu(K_p)$ of the complete graph satisfies the inequality

$$\nu(K_p) \leq \frac{1}{4} \left\lfloor \frac{p}{2} \right\rfloor \left\lfloor \frac{p-1}{2} \right\rfloor \left\lfloor \frac{p-2}{2} \right\rfloor \left\lfloor \frac{p-3}{2} \right\rfloor. \tag{2.22}$$

For $p \leq 10$, it has been shown [144] that Eq. (2.22) is an equality, yielding values of $\nu(K_p)$ as given next. For $p > 10$, Eq. (2.22) is *conjectured* to be an equality.

p	2	3	4	5	6	7	8	9	10
$\nu(K_p)$	0	0	0	1	3	8	18	36	60

The crossing number of the complete bipartite graph, $K_{m,n}$, satisfies

$$\nu(K_{m,n}) \leq \left\lfloor \frac{m}{2} \right\rfloor \left\lfloor \frac{m-1}{2} \right\rfloor \left\lfloor \frac{n}{2} \right\rfloor \left\lfloor \frac{n-1}{2} \right\rfloor. \tag{2.23}$$

For $\min(m, n) \leq 6$, Eq. (2.23) has been proved to be an equality [193]. For arbitrary m, n, Eq. (2.23) is conjectured to be an equality.

When the edges in Definition 2.6 are restricted to horizontal and vertical straight line segments, we have the concept of *rectilinear crossing number, $\bar{\nu}(G)$*. Evidently,

$$\bar{\nu}(G) \geq \nu(G). \tag{2.24}$$

For any simple graph G, $\nu(G) = 0$ if and only if $\bar{\nu}(G) = 0$, because if a simple graph is embeddable in a plane, then it can be drawn using straight line segments (Fary's theorem [111]) provided the locations of the vertices are not fixed a priori. Note that Fary's theorem allows the vertices of the graph to be moved as long as the edge incidence relationships are preserved. For $p \leq 7$, and $p = 9$,

$\nu(K_p) = \bar{\nu}(K_p)$, but $\bar{\nu}(K_8) = 19$, whereas $\nu(K_8) = 18$ [144]. It has also been shown that[2]

$$\bar{\nu}(K_p) > \nu(K_p) \qquad p \geq 10. \tag{2.25}$$

It has been conjectured that $\bar{\nu}(K_{10}) = 63$.

The rectilinear crossing number $\bar{\nu}(K_p)$ of a complete graph K_p satisfies Eq. (2.26) [177],

$$\bar{\nu}(K_p) \leq \left\lfloor \left(7p^4 - 56p^3 + 128p^2 + 48p \left\lfloor \frac{p-7}{3} \right\rfloor + \frac{108}{432}\right)\right\rfloor, \tag{2.26}$$

and equality is *conjectured*. It is suspected that

$$\bar{\nu}(K_{m,n}) = \nu(K_{m,n}) = \left\lfloor \frac{1}{2}m \right\rfloor \left\lfloor \frac{1}{2}(m-1) \right\rfloor \left\lfloor \frac{1}{2}n \right\rfloor \left\lfloor \frac{1}{2}(n-1) \right\rfloor.$$

2.6   VORONOI DIAGRAMS AND DELAUNAY TESSELLATION

The *Voronoi diagram* (VoD) of a set of specified points—sometimes referred to as sites—is a partition of the d-dimensional Euclidean space $\mathbb{R}^d$ that assigns a surrounding region, or *Voronoi cell* (representable as the intersection of a finite number of closed half-spaces), of "nearby" points to each of the sites. The Voronoi cell around a chosen site describes a region that contains, in its interior, points that are nearer to this site than any other site. Let us formally define the VoD.

> **Definition 2.7   Voronoi diagram.** Let $\mathbf{x}$ and $\mathbf{y}$ denote points in $\mathbb{R}^d$, and suppose that $d(\mathbf{x}, \mathbf{y})$ is the Euclidean distance (other metrics also possible) between $\mathbf{x}$ and $\mathbf{y}$. The Voronoi diagram over a finite set $\{\mathbf{x}_1, \mathbf{x}_2, \ldots, \mathbf{x}_n\}$, of points in $\mathbb{R}^d$ is the set of n convex regions $R_i = \{\mathbf{x} \mid d(\mathbf{x}, \mathbf{x}_i) \leq d(\mathbf{x}, \mathbf{x}_j)$ for all j in the index set $\{1, 2, \ldots, n\}\}$, for $i = 1, 2, \ldots, n$.

The Voronoi diagram just defined is sometimes referred to as the *closest-point* VoD; when the inequality in the preceding definition of R_i is reversed, the *farthest-point* VoD results, but we will not make this distinction here. The Voronoi diagram can be used to define *nearest neighbors* in a finite set of specified points: nearest neighbor points are only those points whose Voronoi cells share a boundary. In the plane, the graph, over the same set of points, whose edges have only nearest neighbors as endpoints is the geometric *dual* of the Voronoi diagram. In the plane $\mathbb{R}^2$, the VoD has a straight line dual, called the *Delaunay triangulation*. The counterpart of this in higher dimensions is called the *Delaunay tessellation* (DT).

---

[2]R.K. Guy. The decline and fall of Zarankiewicz's theorem. In F. Harary, editor, *Proof Techniques in Graph Theory*, pp. 63–69, Academic Press, Inc., New York, 1969.

An example of a VoD over a specified set of marked points is shown in Fig 2.7, where each Voronoi cell is a polygon. The majority of vertices are degree 3 vertices because an arbitrary set of three points in a plane falls on a circumcircle, whose center becomes a vertex in the VoD. Higher-degree vertices occur when a subset of four or more specified points, over which a VoD is desired, falls on a circle. Such a distribution of points is called *degenerate*. Note that the cells could be unbounded. Since Voronoi diagrams are useful in the design of neural network structures, as will be explained later, it is encouraging to note the emergence in computational geometry of fast algorithms for constructing higher-dimensional Voronoi diagrams. It has been shown recently that such constructions are possible in linear expected (average) time [104] for random points in a d-dimensional ball under certain assumptions on the distribution of points in the ball. Software packages for constructing Voronoi diagrams are becoming available. The package *Mathematica*®(Wolfram Research Inc., Champaign, IL) is very convenient for drawing the VoD over a specified set of points in a plane. The Delaunay tessellation is also useful in the design of neural networks, and fast methods for its construction are being developed. Such a tessella-

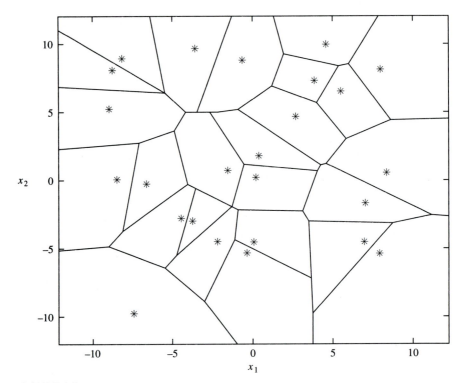

FIGURE 2.7
Voronoi diagram over a set of points (sites, represented by stars) on a plane. With one exception, the degree of each vertex is 3. Only one vertex is of degree 4, which is a degenerate case. The outer bounding rectangle is artificial and is not a part of the VoD.

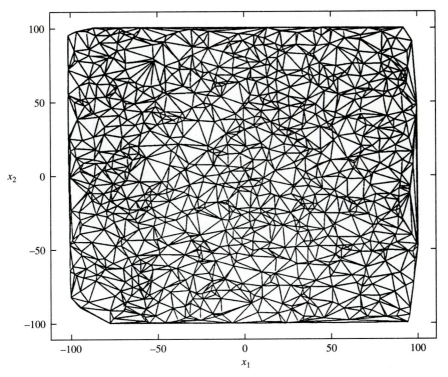

FIGURE 2.8
The Delaunay tessellation over a specified set of 1000 points on the plane. In the plane, this tessellation is called a triangulation, for obvious reasons.

tion, which reduces to a triangulation in the 2-D case, is shown in Fig 2.8 when the number of points is 1000. It was already noted that when the distribution of points in a plane is not degenerate (that is, four or more specified points are not on the same circle), then each of the vertices of the VoD over the specified points is of degree 3. It readily follows that the geometric dual of such a VoD must have each of its bounded faces consist of three edges, justifying the name Delaunay *triangulation*.

2.7 CONCLUSIONS AND SUGGESTIONS

Graphs are useful for studying topological and structural properties of neural networks. Since different neural networks have different underlying topologies, which facilitate their classification and study, it is natural to utilize graph theory when analyzing and designing neural networks. Only the bare essentials in graph theory are presented here. Some additional material is included in anticipation of future applications to topological invariants. In particular, the notion of thickness has proved to be useful for establishing lower bounds on the number of layers needed for embedding a network, subject to the planarity constraint in each layer. Other constraints are also important. One practical constraint is the limitation on the degree of the vertices in the graph due to hardware realizability restrictions such as fan-in or fan-out. The reader's attention is drawn to results on thickness for K_n and K_{n_1,n_2}, when the vertices are degree-constrained [53].

Voronoi diagrams, variously referred to as Dirichlet domains, Wigner-Seitz cells, and Thiessen diagrams, have found wide applications in diverse problems such as packing and covering problems, spatial data analysis, and interpolation [141]. For a comprehensive survey of the theory and applications of VoD, consult ref. [277]. Since the applicability of VoDs to the topic of neural networks has recently been proven [51], the reader is alerted to the rapid developments in computational and combinatorial geometry [105] that make it feasible to construct such diagrams in higher-dimensional space very efficiently. Although VoDs have been defined here over Euclidean metric, they are not so restricted. VoDs may be used to advantage over other metrics, particularly the rectilinear or Manhattan metric, in the design of neural networks.

Some of the material in this chapter will lead the reader to an appreciation of the difficulty in the solution of "apparently simple" problems. K_{16} is a reasonably small graph. However, it was not known for a long time whether the thickness of K_{16} is three or four (for a solution, without the fixed-vertex or homologous constraint described in the following paragraph, see ref. [249]), though the thickness of larger-sized complete graphs had been established. Similarly, the map coloring problem on surfaces of genus greater than zero was tackled before the resolution, albeit in a very cumbersome form (which appears to be difficult to verify), of the four-color conjecture for planar maps. In the layout design of neural networks, the combinatorial graph-theoretical results are intended to provide guidelines and bounds rapidly rather than precise uncompromising solutions.

The development of printed and integrated circuit technologies raised many topological problems concerning the layout of a circuit on a plane. A low-cost layout, for example, is obtainable if the number of crossings between the conducting paths on the same layer is minimized. This problem translates to the drawing of a graph on a plane with the minimum number of crossings. The generalization of this problem involves the drawing, say of K_n, in k planes so that the total number of crossings in the k planes is minimized, subject possibly to the additional constraint (due to technological convenience) that all homologous vertices coincide when the k planes are superimposed (*fixed-vertex constraint*). Let $\text{Cr}(n, k)$ denote the minimum number of crossings required for drawing K_n in k planes, either with or without the fixed-vertex constraint. The value of $\text{Cr}(n, k)$ in both cases is known only for a small number of values of n and k. For example, $\text{Cr}(9, 2) = 1$ even if the fixed-vertex constraint is present [279]. In particular, $\text{Cr}(n, t) = 0$ where t denotes the thickness of K_n. Since the modeling of neural networks in VLSI is likely to involve several layers, the combinatorial results involving topological invariants find another fertile arena for potential application besides satisfying the need for sharpening and reshaping of old results and the derivation of new ones.

PROBLEMS

2.1. Let n be an even number. What is the maximum number of edges possible in a three-layer simple graph having n vertices formed from a node-coalesced cascade of K_{n_1, n_2} and K_{n_2, n_3}, where $n = n_1 + n_2 + n_3$? Is your answer unique? Identify your solution (or solutions).

2.2. The central nervous system of a particular mammal is hypothesized to have about 10^{12} neurons with 10^3–10^4 synapses at the input per neuron and 10^3–10^4 output synapses per neuron. Make any assumption you feel is necessary to estimate the number of connections in the central nervous system.

2.3. What is the maximum number of edges possible in a tripartite graph over $6l$ nodes, where l is an integer? Identify a tripartite graph that has this property when $l = 11$.

2.4. A complete layered graph may be viewed as concatenations or node-coalesced cascades of certain complete bipartite graphs. For example, a particular six-layer graph could arise from a node-coalesced cascade of $K_{10,9}$, $K_{9,4}$, $K_{4,10}$, $K_{10,20}$, and $K_{20,3}$. For this complete six-layer graph calculate the following:

(a) The total number of nodes.

(b) The total number of edges, using Theorem 2.1.

(c) The total number of paths from the nodes in the first layer to the nodes in the top layer, such that each such path has only the smallest possible number of edges.

(d) The number of independent loops.

Furthermore, investigate the situation when the constraint of *smallest number of edges* in (c) is removed.

2.5. Generalize each of the results in Problem 2.4 to an l-layered net formed from a node-coalesced cascade of K_{n_1, n_2}, K_{n_2, n_3}, K_{n_3, n_4}, $\ldots$, and K_{n_{l-1}, n_l}.

2.6. What is the number of edges in (a) K_n, (b) K_{n_1, n_2}, (c) $K_{n_1, n_2, \ldots, n_l}$?

2.7. Find the number of nodes and edges in the graph of a cubical grid having n nodes on each of the lines along each of the three dimensions in three-dimensional space. Write down the expression for the number of independent loops in this graph characterizing the topology of the cubical grid. Verify your answer by enumerating the degrees of the various vertices and then applying Theorem 2.1 to get the number of edges.

2.8. Consider the graph of a planar grid that has $(m + 1)(n + 1)$ vertices and $2mn + m + n$ edges, each running either horizontally or vertically and of unit length. Therefore, the coordinates of the vertices, following a row-by-row scan from left to right and bottom to top, are $(0, 0), (1, 0), \ldots, (m, 0), (0, 1), (1, 1), \ldots, (m, 1), \ldots, (0, n), (1, n), \ldots, (m, n)$. Let $T(m, n)$ denote the number of shortest paths from $(0, 0)$ to (m, n).

(a) Write a difference equation whose solution with proper boundary conditions would yield $T(m, n)$.

(b) Solve your difference equation to get $T(m, n)$ explicitly in terms of m, n.

(c) Can you extend your results from parts (a) and (b) to the cubical grid? If so, find the number of shortest paths from $(0, 0, 0)$ to (m, n, r) in the graph of a cubical grid having $(m + 1)(n + 1)(r + 1)$ vertices and the appropriate number of edges, each of unit length.

2.9. The edges of the graph shown in Fig. P2.9 represent streets, and the vertices represent intersection of streets. A police station is located at point A. A patrol car is to start at the station, cover each street at least once, and return to the station. The car should not stop or turn around at any point.

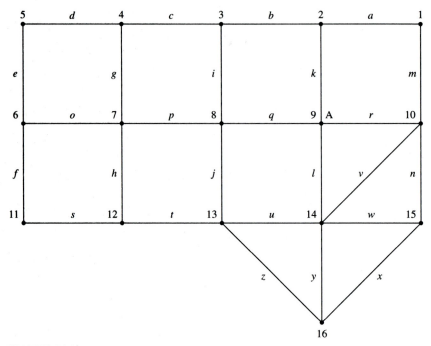

FIGURE P2.9

    (*a*) Find a path so that a minimum number of streets is traversed more than once in a patrol of all streets.

    (*b*) If the patrol car is to start at *A*, is to cover each street at least once, but is not required to return to *A*, find a path so that a minimum number of streets is traversed more than once in this case.

2.10. Consider a connected graph that is devoid of loops or circuits. The graph has no vertex whose degree is greater than 4. In the graph, there are two vertices each of degree 2, one vertex of degree 3, and three vertices each of degree 4. How many vertices, each of degree 1, does the graph have?

2.11. Calculate the number of independent loops in (*a*) K_{10}, (*b*) $K_{7,6}$, and (*c*) $K_{7,6,5}$.

2.12. (*a*) Calculate the number of independent loops in the complete tripartite graph $K_{3,4,3}$.

    (*b*) Calculate the number of independent loops in the three-layer graph formed from the node-coalescence of $K_{4,6}$ and $K_{6,2}$.

2.13. A regular polyhedron is a polyhedron on whose surface all the polygons are congruent and all the angles at vertices are equal. Some examples of regular polyhedra are the cube and the tetrahedron. (For a cube, $|V| = 8$, $|E| = 12$, $|F| = 6$; and for the tetrahedron, $|V| = 4$, $|E| = 6$, $|F| = 4$.) Use Euler's formula in Eq. (2.1) to prove that there are exactly five regular polyhedra; and determine $|V|$, $|E|$, and $|F|$ for each of the three remaining polyhedra. *Hint:* Use the fact that if each polygonal face has sides, with edges meeting at each vertex for a regular polyhedron, then $n|F| = 2|E|$, $r|V| = 2|E|$.

2.14. Prove that the thickness of $K_{7,7}$ must be greater than 2.

2.15. Find the thickness of the graph representing a layered neural network in Fig. 2.3.

2.16. Find the minimum number of crossings required for drawing $K_{7,7}$ in two planes under the fixed-vertex constraint.

2.17. A set of n points is prescribed on a plane, and a Voronoi diagram over this set of points is constructed. Show that the geometric dual (see Section 2.6) of the Voronoi diagram has triangulated faces provided no circle can be drawn with four or more of the prescribed points on its boundary.

2.18. The number of different colors necessary and sufficient to paint all vertices in a given graph such that no edge in the graph has both of its end vertices of the same color is defined to be the *chromatic number* of the graph (see Chapter 6 for its applicability in proving certain important results on the intractability of loading and training problems). Calculate the chromatic numbers of (a) K_n, (b) K_{n_1,n_2}, and (c) K_{n_1,n_2,n_3}.

2.19. Prove or disprove that a continuous line (or curve) such as the dashed line (or curve) attempted in Fig. P2.19 can be drawn by cutting every line segment once and only once. If it can be done, provide relevant reasons and construct one such line (or curve). If it cannot be done, indicate relevant reasons.

2.20. Indicate whether each of the statements below is true or false. If you are able to answer all parts correctly, then most probably you have many of the facts described in this chapter well in hand.

  (a) The graph in Fig. 2.1 can be drawn as a closed edge train.

  (b) A simple graph with 10 vertices and 26 edges cannot be bipartite.

  (c) A tripartite graph is also a layered graph, but a layered graph need not be tripartite.

  (d) The thickness of $K_{7,7}$ is 2.

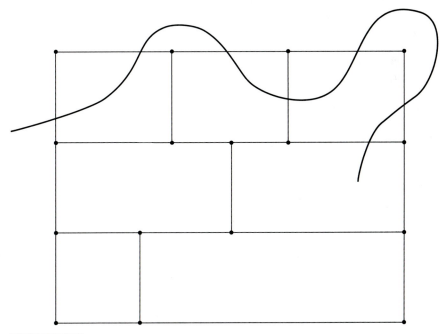

FIGURE P2.19

(e) The thickness of K_9 is 3.

(f) There are 729 nodes in a simple tripartite graph. Each part must have the same number of nodes so that the number of edges is maximized.

(g) There are 800 nodes in a three-layer simple graph. So as to maximize the number of edges, the middle layer must contain the smallest number of nodes.

(h) A graph with no parallel edges and no self-loops is a simple graph. The sum of the degrees of the vertices in a graph is equal to two times the number of edges only if the graph is simple.

(i) Any loop or circuit in a simple bipartite graph must have an even number of edges.

(j) A simple maximally planar graph is known to have 60 edges. The graph cannot have less than 32 nodes.

(k) A maximally planar simple bipartite graph has 15 vertices. The maximum number of edges possible in this graph is 26.

(l) The adjacency matrix representation for a graph is valid only if the graph is devoid of self-loops and parallel edges.

(m) The sum of the degrees of vertices in any graph must be an even positive integer.

(n) A connected graph may be drawn as an open edge train if and only if the number of vertices of odd degree is zero.

(o) A graph with one node and one edge does not exist.

(p) In any directed graph, a cut is a proper subset of a cut-set.

(q) A complete multipartite graph $K_{n_1,n_2,\ldots,n_k}$ is planar if and only if $n_i \leq 2$, for $i = 1, 2, \ldots, k$.

(r) Any Voronoi diagram over a finite number of points in a plane is always a planar graph.

(s) A connected graph with n nodes cannot have each of its vertices of degree 1 when $n \geq 2$.

2.21. If every face (including the unbounded face) of a simple connected planar graph with 100 edges, embedded in a plane, is bounded by four edges, determine the total number of vertices in the graph. Also identify a special type of graph that has this property.

CHAPTER
3

ALGORITHMS

Large-scale problems, represented by graphs, are solved on the computer with the help of detailed step-by-step methods. Therefore, algorithms and their analysis are important topics. Though neurocomputing provides an alternate approach for tackling hard problems, a neural net's performance may subsequently be evaluated using the classical algorithms as benchmarks. To promote such a comparison, an understanding of some mature algorithms, for a set of well-known problems with a wide range of applications, is essential. Similarly, the crucial role of complexity theory in neural networks can be better understood and appreciated with knowledge of models for computation, of the problem-solving capability of a serial or parallel computer, and of how a problem is classified according to difficulty under accepted measures of performance evaluation. This chapter prepares the reader for such tasks.

An *effective procedure* is a finite, unambiguous description of a finite set of operations and is used for such purposes as computing a function or performing a sequence of unrelated operations. An effective procedure can be implemented on simple machines that are devoid of intelligence and innovative capabilities. Computer programs and recipes in a cookbook are examples of effective procedures. An effective procedure that specifies a sequence of operations that always halts is called an *algorithm.* Effective procedures and algorithms are represented by languages with syntactic properties like finiteness of symbols or alphabets and statements.

In Section 3.1, the concepts of languages and of deterministic and nondeterministic Turing machines are very briefly stated. The Turing machine is a model for expressing arbitrary algorithms. When viewed as a programming language, it has a string of symbols for its data structure. To analyze an algorithm one must assess the computational complexity in its implementation. To facilitate this, the classes P and NP of languages are defined (in terms of Turing machines), and the concept of

NP-completeness is introduced and its implications are mentioned. In Section 3.2, the reader is introduced to examples of actual algorithms used for solving common problems. The algorithms chosen are simple but representative and illustrate the notions of labeling as well as backtracking. In Section 3.3, the fundamentals behind interconnection and routing algorithms are described in some detail, starting with the simple minimum spanning tree construction algorithms and leading up to the NP-complete problem of Steiner tree construction. Since neural networks have been used during the last decade to provide suboptimal solutions to hard combinatorial optimization problems encountered in the layout design of large-scale circuits, the classical approaches taken for tackling partitioning and placement problems, which are linked to routing in overall packaging and layout design, are described in Section 3.4. The broad aim of the layout procedure is to be able to build, with a given set of components and with the given interconnection techniques, a system specified by the logic design and possible additional constraints. Whereas the logic design depends on the electronic properties of the circuits, layout design is concerned with physical properties, physical implementation, and manufacturing techniques, including the problem areas of partitioning, placement, and interconnection. It must be borne in mind that the layout problem radically changes with manufacturing techniques, as with the transitions from the vacuum tube to the discrete transistor and then to the medium- and large-scale integrated circuit (IC). Now, in the very-large-scale integration (VLSI) era, new concepts of system construction based on automated design techniques are being developed. As a result, computationally feasible algorithms are being sought, and in their absence heuristic algorithms have been the sources for meeting the utilitarian demands. The promises and limitations of polynomial-time deterministic algorithms, with regard to their suitability for parallelization, are briefly examined in Section 3.5. Associative memory algorithms, based on a behavioral learning law as well as on the mathematics of the generalized inverse to solve for a linear associator, are examined in Section 3.6, to complete the readers' preparation for entering into a serious study of neural networks. Conclusions are drawn and suggestions for additional reading are made in Section 3.7. The reader is urged to attempt several problems provided at the end of the chapter to test his or her comprehension of classical algorithms, in order to better appreciate the role of neural networks for tackling identical problems.

3.1 COMPUTATIONAL COMPLEXITY: P- AND NP-COMPLETE PROBLEMS

To evaluate the computational complexity of an algorithm to solve a specified problem, one needs a model for the computing machine. Various models are possible, but the k-tape Turing machine shown in Fig. 3.1 is ideal for its power as well as simplicity. A one-tape Turing machine is essentially a finite-state machine associated with an external storage or memory medium that has the form of a sequence of squares (cells) marked off on a linear tape, which is of infinite extent along both directions. A k-tape Turing machine [8] consists of k pages (tapes), each marked off into an infinite number of cells. Each cell contains one of a finite number of tape symbols.

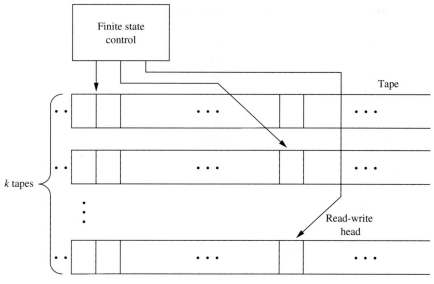

FIGURE 3.1
A *k*-tape Turing machine.

Each tape is scanned by a tape head capable of reading or writing. The operation of a Turing machine is determined by a primitive program, called *finite state control,* which is in one of a finite number of states that can be regarded as a position in a program. According to the symbols read from the tape cells under the heads and the current state of the finite state control, a Turing machine may do any of the following:

1. Change the state of the finite state control.
2. Print a new symbol on the cell under a tape head.
3. Move a tape head one cell left (L) or right (R) or keep it stationary (S).

Formally, a *k*-tape Turing machine is a 7-tuple, $(Q, T, I, \delta, b, q_0, Q_f)$, where Q is the set of states; T is the set of tape symbols; I, a subset of T, is the set of input symbols; $b \in T \backslash I$ ($T \backslash I$ denotes the set difference of T and I) is a blank; q_0 is the initial state; Q_f is the set of final states; and δ, the *next-move function,* maps a subset of $Q \times T^k$ ($T^k = T \times T \cdots \times T$, k times, where $\times$ denotes Cartesian product) to $Q \times (T \times \{L, R, S\})^k$. In the *initial state* of a Turing machine, all the tape heads are at the left end of their tapes, and the first tape holds a string of input symbols, with one symbol per cell, starting with the leftmost cell; all the other tapes are blank. A string of input symbols is *accepted* by a Turing machine if and only if the machine, when started in the initial state with that string on its first tape, makes a series of moves during which it reads all of the symbols in the string and subsequently enters an *accepting state.*

An *alphabet*, such as T or I, is a nonempty finite set of symbols. A *word* in an alphabet is any finite string of symbols from that alphabet. A *language* is a set of words over some set of alphabets. The language accepted by a Turing machine is the set of strings of input symbols that it accepts. An *instantaneous description* (ID) of a k-tape Turing machine M is a k-tuple $(\alpha_1, \alpha_2, \ldots, \alpha_k)$, where each α_i is a string of the form xqy, where xy is the string on the ith tape of M and q is the current state of M. The symbol immediately to the right of the q is the symbol being scanned on the ith tape. The *time complexity* $T(n)$ of a Turing machine M is the maximum number of moves made by M in processing any input of length n, taken over all inputs of length n. If M does not halt, then $T(n)$ is undefined. An algorithm may be viewed as a Turing machine that is guaranteed to halt for all input strings.

For a given input x, one can think of a *nondeterministic Turing machine* (NDTM) M as executing either several or all possible sequences of moves in parallel until either an accepting ID is reached or no more moves are possible; i.e., after i moves, one can think of a number of copies of M to be in existence. Each copy represents an ID in which M can be after i moves. On the $(i + 1)$st move, a copy of C replicates into j copies if the Turing machine has j choices for a next move when in ID C. Thus, the possible sequence of moves that M can make on input x can be arranged into a *rooted tree* (this is a spanning tree where a certain vertex called the *root* is distinguished from the other vertices of the tree) of IDs. Each path from the root to a leaf in the tree represents a possible sequence of moves. If σ is a shortest sequence of moves that terminates in an accepting ID, then as soon as M makes those moves, it halts and accepts the string x. The time spent in processing x is the length, $|\sigma|$, of σ. Nondeterministic machines should not be construed as implementing algorithms that are either probabilistic or random; rather, the algorithms are allowed to be in many states simultaneously. This permits *choice* among a finite set of alternatives by exploring the elements of that set *simultaneously*.

A *deterministic* simulation of the Turing machine M would require tracing out the tree for all possible sequences of moves on x, in some order until a shortest sequence that terminates in an accepting ID is found. If no sequence of moves leads to acceptance, then a deterministic simulation can run forever. Thus, a NDTM can perform tasks that deterministic machines of equal time complexity cannot do. Formally, one defines a k-tape NDTM, M, as a 7-tuple $(Q, T, I, \delta, b, q_0, Q_f)$, where all components have the same meaning as for a deterministic Turing machine (DTM) except that here δ is a mapping from $Q \times T^k$ to subsets of $Q \times (T \times \{L, R, S\})^k$.

We define *P-time* to be the set of all languages L (or problems that are represented by the languages, as described shortly) that can be accepted by DTMs of polynomial time complexity. We define *NP-time* to be the set of all languages (or problems) that can be accepted by a NDTM of polynomial time complexity. The terms *P-time* and *NP-time* are usually abbreviated to P and NP, respectively. In view of the previous discussions, one can conclude that P should be a subset of NP. A problem is *NP-hard* if every problem in NP is reducible to it in P-time; it may not be in NP. The question whether or not P = NP is unresolved. However, one can show that a certain subset of languages in NP are as hard as NP, i.e., if a deterministic polynomial-time bounded algorithm exists to recognize any one of these languages, then there exist deterministic polynomial-time bounded algorithms to recognize any language in NP. This subset of languages constitutes the *NP-complete* class. One way to prove that a language L_0 is NP-complete is to show that $L_0 \in$ NP and that every language $L \in$ NP is polynomially transformable to L_0. It is possible to conclude that either all NP-complete problems are in P or none are. The former holds if and only if P $=$ NP. Therefore, a problem is *NP-complete* if it is *NP-hard* and also belongs to the set NP. Although P and NP usually apply to worst-case time complexity, more recently the less pessimistic and practically more useful average-case time complexity performance measures have also been classified under P and NP.

We have defined P and NP in terms of languages. A wide variety of problems from different disciplines can be translated into language recognition problems by means of suitable encoding. The language-problem relationship may be set up through the following assumptions regarding encoding:

1. Integers will be represented in decimal radix.
2. For graphs $G = (V(G), E(G))$, with $|V| = n$, vertices $v_1, \ldots, v_n$ will be represented by decimal numbers $1, 2, \ldots, n$ and edges by strings of the form $(i_1, i_2, \ldots)$, where i_k is the decimal representation of corresponding edges.
3. Boolean expressions with n propositional variables will be represented by strings in which the symbol $*$ represents AND, $+$ represents OR, $-$ represents NOT, and integers $1, 2, \ldots, n$ represent propositional variables.
4. Parentheses are used whenever necessary.

We will say that a problem is in P or NP if and only if the described encoding of the problem, as in Example 3.1, is in P or NP.

> **Example 3.1.** The Boolean expression $(P_1$ OR $P_2)$ AND P_3 is represented as $(1 + 2) * 3$.

Consider the language L representing *satisfiable* Boolean expressions (those for which some assignment of 0s and 1s to the variables gives the expression the value 1). We claim $L \in$ NP. A nondeterministic algorithm begins by guessing a satisfying assignment of 0s and 1s to the propositional variables in an input string. Then the values (0 or 1) are substituted and the resulting expression is evaluated to verify that it has a value 1. The evaluation can be done in a time proportional to the length by using what are called *parsing* algorithms. Even the existence of the most inefficient, but polynomial-time, algorithm will show that. Thus, the *satisfiability* problem is in NP. A Boolean expression is in *conjunctive normal* form (CNF) if it is a product of sums of *literals,* where a literal is either a variable like x or its complement $\bar{x}$. Thus, $(x_1 + x_2) * (x_2 + \bar{x}_1 + x_3)$ is in CNF, whereas $(x_1 + x_2 * x_3)$ is not. It has been shown via complicated arguments [82], which are beyond the scope of this presentation, that the satisfiability problem for Boolean expressions in CNF is NP-complete. With the NP-completeness of the satisfiability problem for Boolean expressions in CNF as hypothesis, and by using a chain of *polynomial transformations,* it is possible to show that some other problems are also NP-complete. This strategy is very powerful for proving NP-completeness. Several problems in graphs, such as the *clique* problem (a k-clique of a graph G is a complete subgraph of G with k-vertices, and the clique problem poses the question whether an undirected graph having a clique of size k exists in G), can be shown to be NP-complete by first showing that those problems are in NP and then polynomially transforming the satisfiability problem for Boolean expression in CNF to each of those problems. The process can then be continued with other problems to which proven NP-complete problems such as the clique problem can be polynomially transformed. This strategy will be used in Chapter 6 to prove Theorem 6.1, concerning the NP-completeness of the problem of training a three-node neural network, from a known result regarding another problem.

In Chapter 1 we saw that McCulloch and Pitts described structures that are built up from very simple components, so only these components are defined axiomatically and their combination can be extremely complex. Turing, on the other hand, started top-down by axiomatically describing the whole machine without specifying what its elements are, just by describing how it is supposed to function.

3.2 SHORTEST-PATH AND MAX-FLOW MIN-CUT PROBLEMS

Here we discuss the solution to two standard problems. Both problems and their solutions are extensively documented in the literature [76, 311], and the algorithms used to solve these problems have been analyzed. Both problems illustrate the use of a class of algorithms called *labeling algorithms*. Dijkstra's algorithm to solve the shortest-path problem and the Ford-Fulkerson algorithm to solve the max-flow min-cut problem are described next. Both of these problems illustrate computational problems that are solved by graphs.

3.2.1 Dijkstra's Shortest-Path Algorithm

Consider a connected directed graph with a finite number of vertices $v_i, i = 1, 2, \ldots, |V|$, where $|V|$ denotes the number of elements in the set V of vertices, and in which the edge that exits from vertex v_i and enters into vertex v_j has an associated *weight* d_{ij}, which equals some cost assigned to the edge (v^i, v^j) joining vertex v_i to vertex v_j. We make the assumption that $d_{ij} \geq 0$, for all $j \in \{1, 2, \ldots, |V|\}$. (A variant of the algorithm, to be discussed shortly, is available to handle negative costs, but when the sum of the edge costs in a directed loop is a negative number, the problem becomes meaningless.) Without loss of generality and for the sake of simplicity, we assume the graph to be simple. The graph G may also be considered to be directed, because any undirected edge, for which $d_{ij} = d_{ji}$, may be replaced by two directed edges from vertex v_i to v_j and from v_j to v_i. For the problem to be challenging, $d_{ij} \neq d_{ji}$, in general, and the triangle inequality in a metric space (see Section 3.3) need not be satisfied; i.e., it is possible for $d_{ik} + d_{kj}$ to be less than d_{ij}. Therefore, it may be more appropriate to associate d_{ij} with a positive cost rather than a metric in a metric space.

Let $l(v_i)$ denote the *label* on vertex v_i, and for the sake of convenience let $v_1 = s$ and $v_{|V|} = t$ denote, respectively, the source and terminal vertices. Dijkstra's algorithm involves updating the labels from the *temporary* to the *permanent* categories until the terminal vertex attains a permanent label. Denote the set of vertices that have directed edges from a vertex v_i (i.e., the set of edges adjacent to v_i) by $A(v_i)$. The various steps in Dijkstra's algorithm are as follows:

1. *Initialization:* Set $l(s) = 0$ and mark the label of s as permanent. Let $l(v_j) = \infty$ (or a sufficiently large integer in comparison with the distances involved, given or estimated, between any pair of vertices), for all $v_j \neq s$, and mark each of these labels as temporary. Set $v_i \longleftarrow s$.
2. *Updating of labels:* For all $v_j \in A(v_i)$ that have temporary labels, update the labels according to

$$l(v_j) = \min[l(v_j), l(v_i) + d_{ij}].$$

3. *Marking a label permanent:* Among all vertices v_k belonging to the set T of vertices having temporary labels, find one or more vertices $\{\hat{v}_l\}$ for which

$$l(\hat{v}_l) = \min_{v_k \in T}[l(v_k)].$$

If there is only one such vertex $\hat{v}_l$, mark its label as permanent. Otherwise, choose any one of the vertices $\hat{v}_l$ and label it as permanent. Set $v_i \longleftarrow \hat{v}_l$.
4. a. *If only the shortest path from s to t is desired:* If $v_i \neq t$, go to step 2. If $v_i = t$, $l(v_i)$ is the length of the shortest path from s to t. Stop.
   b. *If the shortest path from s to every other vertex is required:* If some labels are temporary, go to step 2. If all the vertices are permanently labeled, then the labels are the lengths of the shortest paths. Stop.

Example 3.2. Find the length of the shortest path from vertex v_1 to vertex v_{10} in the directed graph with associated edge weights shown in Fig. 3.2.
The various steps in Dijkstra's algorithm described above may be carried out to generate the following tabular form, leading to the solution. The permanent labelings are identified by circumflexes.

v_1	v_2	v_3	v_4	v_5	v_6	v_7	v_8	v_9	v_{10}
$\hat{0}$	∞	∞	∞	∞	∞	∞	∞	∞	∞
$\hat{0}$	5	4	$\hat{3}$	∞	∞	∞	∞	∞	∞
$\hat{0}$	5	$\hat{4}$	$\hat{3}$	∞	8	10	∞	∞	∞
$\hat{0}$	$\hat{5}$	$\hat{4}$	$\hat{3}$	8	8	10	∞	∞	∞
$\hat{0}$	$\hat{5}$	$\hat{4}$	$\hat{3}$	$\hat{8}$	8	10	15	∞	∞
$\hat{0}$	$\hat{5}$	$\hat{4}$	$\hat{3}$	$\hat{8}$	8	10	15	∞	∞
$\hat{0}$	$\hat{5}$	$\hat{4}$	$\hat{3}$	$\hat{8}$	$\hat{8}$	10	$\hat{9}$	10	∞
$\hat{0}$	$\hat{5}$	$\hat{4}$	$\hat{3}$	$\hat{8}$	$\hat{8}$	10	$\hat{9}$	$\hat{10}$	13
$\hat{0}$	$\hat{5}$	$\hat{4}$	$\hat{3}$	$\hat{8}$	$\hat{8}$	$\hat{10}$	$\hat{9}$	$\hat{10}$	13
$\hat{0}$	$\hat{5}$	$\hat{4}$	$\hat{3}$	$\hat{8}$	$\hat{8}$	$\hat{10}$	$\hat{9}$	$\hat{10}$	$\hat{13}$

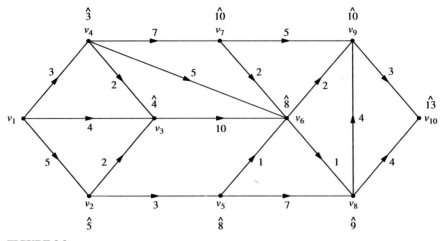

FIGURE 3.2
Directed graph with associated edge weights showing the implementation of Dijkstra's algorithm in Example 3.2.

Note that by implementing the algorithm on the specified problem, all the vertices became permanently labeled. Therefore, the lengths of the shortest paths from vertex v_1 to the other vertices are the numbers at the bottom row, excluding, of course, the $\hat{0}$ element. The union of all the shortest paths from $v_1 = s$ to the other vertices is called an *arborescence* rooted at vertex s.

To list the shortest path or, eventually, the arborescence rooted at s, backtracking is necessary. For example, to construct the shortest path from s to t, we must backtrack from the terminal vertex t such that we go to the preceding vertex whose label differs from the label of t by exactly the weight of the joining edge. A shortest path is nonunique when there are two or more such preceding vertices. The backtracking is continued until the source vertex s is reached, leading to the construction of one or more shortest paths. The types of operations required for implementing this algorithm are additions and comparisons. For a complete directed graph over $|V|$ vertices, there are $|V|(|V|-1)$ directed edges. In this worst case, the computation time for implementing the algorithm is proportional to $|V|^2$, since $|V|(|V|-1)/2$ additions and $2|V|(|V|-1)$ comparisons suffice. Check whether the preceding statement is true.

3.2.2 Max-Flow Min-Cut Algorithm

Consider a directed connected graph $G = (V(G), E(G))$. The directed edge (v_i, v_j) that is incident on vertex v_j from vertex v_i has a *capacity* c_{ij}. This capacity constrains the flow along edge (v_i, v_j) to a nonnegative value that is either less than or equal to c_{ij} volumetric units. For the sake of convenience, the source and terminal vertices are labeled $v_1 = s$ and $v_{|V|} = t$, respectively. As before, $A(v_i)$ denotes the set of those vertices $v_j \in V$ for which a directed edge (v_i, v_j) exists in G, and $A^{-1}(v_i)$ denotes the set of vertices $v_k \in V$ for which a directed edge (v_k, v_i) exists in G. A set of numbers q_{ij} defined on the directed edges $(v_i, v_j) \in G$ constitutes a valid *flow* when they satisfy the conditions in Eq. (3.1):

$$\sum_{v_j \in A(v_i)} q_{ij} - \sum_{v_k \in A^{-1}(v_i)} q_{ki} = \begin{cases} w & \text{if } v_i = s \\ -w & \text{if } v_i = t \\ 0 & \text{if } v_i \neq s, t \end{cases} \qquad (3.1)$$

where w volumetric units are the total flow from source to the sink t. Recall from Section 2.3 that a cut-set is a set of edges whose removal splits the connected graph G into two separate parts, G_0 and $\tilde{G}_0$. Also, recall the definition of a cut, which has an important role in the ensuing discussion.

Definition 3.1. A cut-set, $G_0 \longrightarrow \tilde{G}_0$, of directed edges linking the separate parts G_0 and $\tilde{G}_0$ in G separates s from t if $s \in V_0$ and $t \in \tilde{V}_0$, where V_0 and $\tilde{V}_0$ are, respectively, the vertex sets in G_0 and $\tilde{G}_0$. The value of such a cut-set is the sum $\sum_{i,j} c_{ij}$, for $(v_i, v_j) \in G_0 \longrightarrow \tilde{G}_0$, of the capacities of all edges of the *associated cut* (that is, edges of the cut-set whose initial vertices are in G_0 and final vertices are in $\tilde{G}_0$); and the minimum cut-set, $G_m \longrightarrow \tilde{G}_m$, $s \in V_m$, $t \in \tilde{V}_m$, is then the cut-set with the smallest such value, where V_m and $\tilde{V}_m$ are, respectively, the vertex sets in G_m and $\tilde{G}_m$.

Next, the maximum-flow minimum-cut (max-flow min-cut) theorem is stated with proof, and the various steps in its implementation are described via the labeling algorithm, which allows for the construction of the valid maximum flow.

Theorem 3.1   Max-flow min-cut. The value of the maximum flow from the source vertex s to the terminal vertex t equals the minimum value over all the cut-sets separating s from t.

Proof. The maximum flow from s to t cannot exceed the value of the minimum cut-set, $G_m \longrightarrow \tilde{G}_m$, because each edge, directed from G_m toward $\tilde{G}_m$ in the cut that is associated with this cut-set, connects the two separate parts G_m, containing s, and $\tilde{G}_m$, containing t; and the flow along each such edge is nonnegative.

The following steps indicate how the value of this minimum cut-set is attained.

1. Set $V_0 \longleftarrow \{s\}$.
2. If $v_i \in V_0$ and either $0 \leq q_{ij} < c_{ij}$, for $v_j \in A(v_i)$, or $q_{ji} > 0$, for $v_j \in A^{-1}(v_i)$, then place v_j in the set V_0.
3. Go to step 2 unless $q_{ij} = c_{ij}$, for all $v_j \in A(v_i)$, and $q_{ji} = 0$, for all $v_j \in A^{-1}(v_i)$, in which case $|V_0|$ cannot be increased; that is, $V_0 = V_m$.
4. Stop.

After the implementation of the preceding steps, with step 2 being repeated until $|V_0|$ cannot be further increased, one of two possibilities must occur.

Case (*i*). $t \in V_0$. In this case the set of edges along the path from s to t will be called a *flow-augmenting set*, because the value of the flow can be increased as follows. Define

$$\delta_f = \min_{(v_i,v_j)}[c_{ij} - q_{ij}] \qquad v_j \in A(v_i), \qquad v_i \in V_0$$

$$\delta_b = \min_{(v_k,v_i)}[q_{ki}] \qquad\qquad v_k \in A^{-1}(v_i), \qquad v_i \in V_0$$

$$\delta = \min[\delta_f, \delta_b].$$

Add δ to the flows in the "forward" edges (v_i, v_j) from s to t and subtract δ from the flows in the "backward" edges (v_k, v_i) from t to s, as just defined. These operations continue to satisfy the constraints in Eq. (3.1) and also result in an increased flow from s to t.

Case (ii). $t \in \tilde{V}_0$. In this case

$$\sum_{(v_i,v_j)\in G_0 \to \tilde{G}_0} q_{ij} = \sum_{(v_i,v_j)\in G_0 \to \tilde{G}_0} c_{ij}$$

and

$$\sum_{(v_k,v_i)\in \tilde{G}_0 \to G_0} q_{ki} = 0,$$

implying that the value of the flow equals the value of the cut-set, $G_0 \to \tilde{G}_0$, where $G_0 = G_m$. If the capacities, c_{ij}'s, are integer-valued, the maximum flow is attained in a finite number of steps. The minimum cut has its forward edges from s to t saturated, whereas the flows in its backward edges are reduced to zero.

A labeling algorithm has been developed to realize the maximum flow, subject to the capacity constraints on edges and the conditions in Eq. (3.1). In this algorithm, each vertex can only be in one of three possible states:

1. Labeled and scanned; i.e., it has a label, and all vertices adjacent to it have been processed.
2. Labeled and unscanned; i.e., it has a label, but not all its adjacent vertices have been processed.
3. Unlabeled.

A label on a vertex v_i is of the form $(+v_j, \delta(v_i))$ or $(-v_j, \delta(v_i))$. In $(+v_j, \delta(v_i))$, the component $+v_j$ implies that flow along the directed edge (v_j, v_i) can be increased, whereas $-v_j$ in the label $(-v_j, \delta(v_i))$ implies that the flow along edge (v_i, v_j) can be decreased. In both types of labels, the component $\delta(v_i)$ represents the maximum amount of additional flow that can be sent from the source vertex s to v_i along the flow-augmenting path from s to t under construction. The various steps in the labeling algorithm are summarized as follows.

Labeling algorithm for realizing maximum flow.

1. *Initialization:* All vertices are unlabeled.
2. Label s by $(+s, \infty)$ so that s is labeled and unscanned, but the remaining vertices are unlabeled.

3. Choose any labeled but unscanned vertex v_i, whose label is $(\pm v_k, \delta(v_i))$.

    a. Attach the label $(+v_i, \delta(v_j))$ to each vertex $v_j \in A(v_i)$ that is unlabeled and for which $q_{ij} < c_{ij}$, where

    $$\delta(v_j) = \min[\delta(v_i), c_{ij} - q_{ij}].$$

    b. Attach the label $(-v_i, \delta(v_j))$ to each vertex $v_j \in A^{-1}(v_i)$ that is unlabeled and for which $q_{ji} > 0$, where

    $$\delta(v_j) = \min[\delta(v_i), q_{ji}].$$

    The vertex v_i is now labeled and scanned, and v_i should be marked in some way because its scanning is complete. The vertices v_j in substeps a and b are now labeled but unscanned.

4. Go to step 3 unless either t is labeled, in which case set $v_i \longleftarrow t$ and go to step 5, or t is unlabeled and no more labels can be placed, in which case go to step 7.

5. a. If the label on v_i is of the form $(+v_j, \delta(v_i))$, change the flow along the edge (v_j, v_i) from q_{ji} to $q_{ji} + \delta(t)$.

    b. If the label on v_i is of the form $(-v_j, \delta(v_i))$, change the flow along arc (v_i, v_j) from q_{ji} to $q_{ji} - \delta(t)$.

6. If $v_j = s$, erase all labels and go to step 2. If $v_j \neq s$, set $v_i \longleftarrow v_j$ and go to step 5.

7. Stop.

Note that if V_m is the set of labeled vertices and $\tilde{V}_m$ is the set of unlabeled ones, then the cut-set $V_m \longrightarrow \tilde{V}_m$ is the minimum cut-set. In each complete cycle of the algorithm following initialization for which a labeling of t results, steps 2 to 4 lead to the increment in flow that is possible from s to t through the flow-augmenting path set up, and steps 5 to 6 characterize the backtracking necessary to change the existing edge flows for realizing this increment. If the terminal vertex cannot be labeled at any cycle, then no more increments of flow from s to t are possible and the maximum flow has been realized.

The algorithm described is suitable for implementation in a digital computer. Variants of the algorithm may also be used to construct the flow-augmenting paths needed to assign the maximum flow from source to sink. Such variants often can be used with hand calculations to illustrate the principles expeditiously. The following example presents one variant in which, instead of labeling each vertex $v_j \in A(v_i)$ and each vertex $v_j \in A^{-1}(v_i)$ as in step 3, only one vertex is labeled and the process is continued with one of the newly labeled vertices.

Example 3.3. In Fig. 3.3, vertices v_2 and v_3 represent factories, which are capable of producing a commodity at rates of 25 and 15 units, respectively. Vertices v_4, v_5, and v_6 represent depots, which are capable of receiving the commodities at rates of 20, 10, and 5 units, respectively. The number associated with each edge in Fig. 3.3 denotes the edge capacity. The max-flow min-cut algorithm will be used to determine the rates at which v_2 and v_3 should produce and the routes over which the commodity should be shipped, so that the depots receive those at the maximum possible rate.

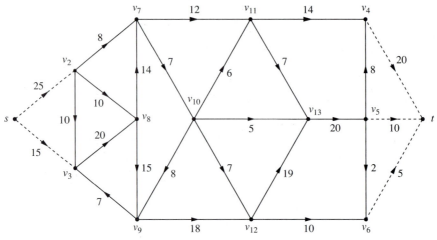

FIGURE 3.3
The directed graph representing the flow problem in Example 3.3. The dashed edges serve to convert the original problem into a one-source, one-sink problem.

After introducing source s and sink t with edges incident on v_2 and v_3 from s and edges incident on t from v_4, v_5, and v_6 as shown by the dotted lines in Fig. 3.3, the max-flow min-cut algorithm may be applied to the resulting one-source and one-sink network. Note that the capacities of the two edges from the source vertex to nodes v_2 and v_3, representing the factories, are the production rates of the commodities. Similarly, the capacities of the three edges from the depots to the sink node are the commodity consumption rates. So as to facilitate the understanding of how the algorithm is implemented, the edges of the graph are labeled as follows after the completion of each cycle. Each edge has two numbers associated with it, separated by a comma. The first number denotes the capacity and the second number denotes the actual flow through the edge before the start of the next cycle. Initially, all edge flows are taken to be zero, though suitable other initial values could also be assigned. The vertices are labeled as described in a variant of the algorithm. The state of the network after the first cycle is completed is shown in Fig. 3.4. To avoid clutter, we omit the plus and minus prefixes in the vertex labelings, since those are not really necessary in this problem; only those vertices that occur in the flow-augmenting path in each cycle are labeled. The label on t indicates that it is to receive an additional 10 units along a flow-augmenting path through v_5. By backtracking from t, it is clear that this flow-augmenting path consists of vertices $t, v_5, v_{13}, v_{12}, v_9, v_8, v_3, v_2$, and s. The labels on the edges in the flow-augmenting path are updated, thus completing the cycle.

The states of the network after the completion of the second, third, fourth, fifth, and final cycles of iteration are shown in Figs. 3.5, 3.6, 3.7, 3.8, and 3.9, respectively. In Fig. 3.5, 10 units of incremental flow are realized from s to t through the sequence of intermediate vertices v_2, v_8, v_7, v_{11}, and v_4. Thus, each of the first two flow-augmenting paths from s to t realizes 10 units of flow. The remaining flow-augmenting paths realize successively 5, 5, 2, and 2 units of flow, as shown in Figs. 3.6, 3.7, 3.8, and 3.9. Therefore, the maximum flow from s to t is 34 units. The cut-set (minimum cut-set) that realizes this maximum flow consists of edges (v_7, v_{11}), (v_7, v_{10}), (v_8, v_9), and (v_9, v_3). Removal of these edges separates the graph into two parts, namely G_m and $\tilde{G}_m$. G_m

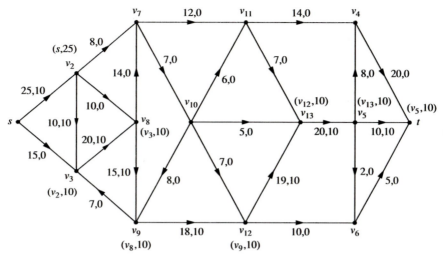

FIGURE 3.4
The state of the network after completion of the first cycle in the labeling algorithm for maximum flow. A complete cycle includes backtracking from sink t to source s for assigning the flow, which in this case is 10 units.

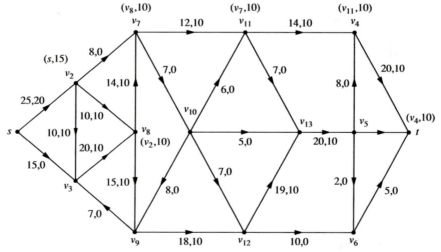

FIGURE 3.5
The state of the network after completion of the second cycle in the labeling algorithm for maximum flow. A complete cycle includes backtracking from sink t to source s for assigning the flow, which in this case is 10 units.

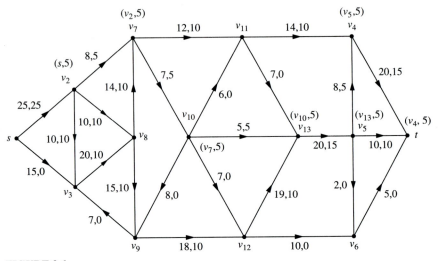

FIGURE 3.6
The state of the network after completion of the third cycle in the labeling algorithm for maximum flow. A complete cycle includes backtracking from sink t to source s for assigning the flow, which in this case is 5 units.

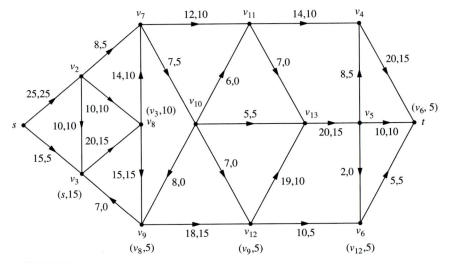

FIGURE 3.7
The state of the network after completion of the fourth cycle in the labeling algorithm for maximum flow. A complete cycle includes backtracking from sink t to source s for assigning the flow, which in this case is 5 units.

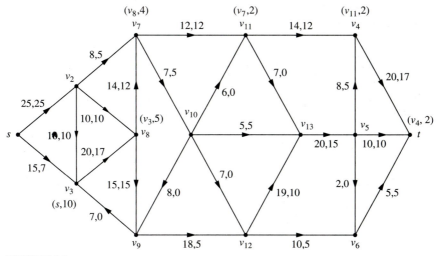

FIGURE 3.8
The state of the network after completion of the fifth cycle in the labeling algorithm for maximum flow. A complete cycle includes backtracking from sink t to source s for assigning the flow, which in this case is 2 units.

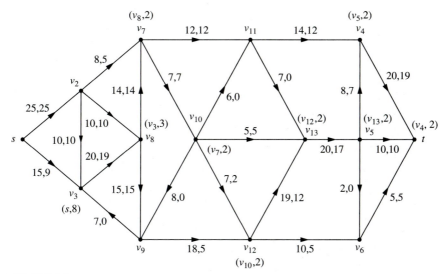

FIGURE 3.9
The state of the network after completion of the sixth cycle in the labeling algorithm for maximum flow. A complete cycle includes backtracking from sink t to source s for assigning the flow, which in this case is 2 units.

consists of vertices $\{s, v_2, v_3, v_8, v_7\}$ and edges (s, v_2), (s, v_3), (v_2, v_7), (v_2, v_3), (v_2, v_8), (v_3, v_8), and (v_8, v_7). $\tilde{G}_m$ consists of the remaining vertices and remaining edges of the original graph, excluding, of course, the edges present in the minimum cut-set. Note that the forward edges of the minimum cut-set, which are directed from G_m toward $\tilde{G}_m$ and constitute the minimum cut, are saturated, whereas the only backward edge (v_9, v_3) directed from $\tilde{G}_m$ to G_m carries zero units of flow. The final flow assignment for the original problem is shown in Fig. 3.10.

Example 3.4. A certain number of families denoted by $a_1, a_2, \ldots, a_m$ want to go for an outing in cars $b_1, b_2, \ldots, b_n$. Knowing the number s_i of people in the family a_i and the number d_j of seats in car b_j, we wish to arrange the seating so that no two members of the same family are in the same car.

A little thought shows that there are two constraints on the data that must be satisfied in order for a solution to exist. These are

$$(a) \quad n \geq \max_{1 \leq i \leq m} \{s_i\} \quad \text{and} \quad (b) \quad \sum_{j=1}^{n} d_j \geq \sum_{i=1}^{m} s_i.$$

Constraint (a) is necessary to ensure that there are at least as many cars as there are members of the largest family so that no two members of the same family will be in the same car. Constraint (b) is necessary to ensure that there will be at least one seat available per person. The problem may be solved by using the max-flow min-cut algorithm in the following manner. Assign a source s with each edge connecting s and vertex a_i, directed from s toward a_i, for $i = 1, 2, \ldots, m$. The assigned capacity of edge (s, a_i) is s_i. Assign a sink, t, with each edge connecting t and vertex b_j, directed from b_j toward t, with capacity d_j, for $j = 1, 2, \ldots, n$. Next, assign edges, each of unity

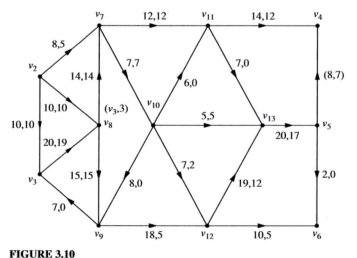

FIGURE 3.10
The final state of the network for the original two-source three-sink flow problem.

capacity and directed from vertex a_i, $i = 1, 2, \ldots, m$, to vertex b_j, $j = 1, 2, \ldots, n$. The edges directed from a_i to b_j with assigned flows of 1 correspond to a seating arrangement for the family a_i. The application of the max-flow min-cut labeling algorithm to the resulting directed graph comprising the $m + n + 2$ nodes and $m + n + mn$ edges leads to the solution of the problem. To facilitate understanding, the reader is urged to do the problem for specific values of m, n, s_1, s_2, \ldots, s_m and d_1, d_2, \ldots, d_n.

3.3 INTERCONNECTION AND ROUTING ALGORITHMS

An m-dimensional metric space is usually associated with any physical interconnection or routing problem. A vertex (node or point) v_i may be represented by the m-tuple $(v_{i1}, v_{i2}, \ldots, v_{im})$ where v_{ik} is the coordinate of v_i along the kth dimension. The distance metric or weight $d(v_i, v_j)$ associated with an edge joining vertices v_i and v_j is

$$d(v_i, v_j) = \left\{ \sum_{k=1}^{m} |v_{ik} - v_{jk}|^p \right\}^{1/p}, \tag{3.2}$$

where the notational dependence on integers m and p is not shown explicitly on the left-hand side of Eq. (3.2) for the sake of brevity. Since $d(v_i, v_j)$ is a measure associated with a metric space, it can be verified that (a) $d(v_i, v_j) = 0$ implies $i = j$; (b) $d(v_i, v_j) = d(v_j, v_i)$ for all i, j (symmetry property); and (c) $d(v_i, v_k) \le d(v_i, v_j) + d(v_j, v_k)$ for any triple (i, j, k) (triangle inequality). The distance measure in Eq. (3.2) is nonnegative. For points in a plane $m = 2$. The metric associated with the $p = 1$ case is called the *rectilinear* or *Manhattan metric,* whereas that associated with the $p = 2$ case is known as the *Euclidean metric.*

In the construction of digital computers requiring use of high-frequency circuitry, it is often necessary to minimize total wire lengths when connecting specified terminals to reduce capacitance and delay-line effects of long wire leads. This subject has a broader consequence, including applications outside the domains of electrical engineering proper. Consider, for example, the trend toward LSI and VLSI, where design and packaging costs often exceed the cost of components used because of high circuit density. To cut down the cost, minimizing the interconnection costs becomes desirable, even though other constraints, depending on the problem at hand, may also be of significance. Similar considerations have to be given in interconnection problems arising in thin-film and printed circuit technologies. Section 3.3.1 will consider an abstract formulation of the interconnection problem; each succeeding paragraph will be concerned with some of the special cases that are of interest in a layout design problem.

3.3.1 Problem Formulation

The generalized formulation, from which other known problems such as the minimal spanning tree problem (C_n), the traveling salesperson problem (T_n), the Fermat problem (F_n), and the Steiner problem (S_n) fall out as special cases, is credited to Melzak [255]. Let M be a metric space with a metric d having the following properties:

1. M is finitely compact.
2. There exists a geodesic in M joining every two points of M.
3. For all pairs of points $v_i, v_j \in M$, $d(v_i, v_j)$ is the length of a geodesic joining v_i and v_j.

3.3.1.1 GENERALIZED FORMULATION OF PROBLEM ($S_{n\alpha\beta\gamma}$). Given three nonnegative real numbers α, β, γ, and n distinct points $v_1, v_2, \ldots, v_n \in M$, find an integer k and the locations of k points, $q_1, q_2, \ldots, q_k \in M$, and then construct a tree, T, over the vertices $v_1, v_2, \ldots, v_n, q_1, q_2, \ldots, q_k$ so as to minimize the sum (cost function)

$$L(T) + \alpha \sum_{j=1}^{n} \delta(v_j) + \beta \sum_{j=1}^{k} \delta(q_k) + \gamma k, \tag{3.3}$$

where $\delta(v_j)$ is the degree of vertex v_j and $L(T)$ is a cost measure for constructing T.

It can be seen that the following problems fall out as special cases of the foregoing general formulation.

3.3.1.2 C_n PROBLEM (MST). Given a set $V = (v_1, v_2, \ldots, v_n)$ of distinct points with $n \geq 3$, find the shortest or *minimal spanning tree* (MST) whose vertices are these n points (i.e., no extra vertices can be introduced). It can be confirmed that in this problem $\alpha = 0$ and $\max(\beta, \gamma) \gg 1$ in the expression Eq. (3.3), since the MST vertices are not degree-constrained and the cost function is to be minimized without allowing extra points.

3.3.1.3 F_n PROBLEM (MFT). Given a convex polygon with the set of vertices $V = \{v_1, v_2, \ldots, v_n\}$, find the point $q = q_0$ that minimizes the sum $\sum_{j=1}^{n} w_j d(q, v_j)$, where $w_j > 0$, for all j. The case when $w_j = 1$ corresponds to the minimization of total interconnection length in this problem. It can be confirmed that here $\beta = 0$ and $\alpha > \gamma \gg 1$ in the expression Eq. (3.3). These restrictions on α, β, and γ imply that the priority is on keeping the degrees of most of the vertices in the tree T minimum and also on keeping the number of extra vertices to the smallest nonzero integer possible. For a suitable value of α, it then follows that the solution leading to the minimum cost function is obtained when $k = 1$, $\delta(q_1) = n$, $\delta(v_k) = 1$ for $k = 1, 2, \ldots, n$. The statement $\beta = 0$ implies that $\delta(q_k) = n$ for arbitrary n, and the constraints set on α, β, and γ lead to the F_n problem irrespective of the number n of specified vertices.

3.3.1.4 T_n PROBLEM (TS). Given a set $V = \{v_1, v_2, \ldots, v_n\}$ of distinct points with $n \geq 3$, find the shortest *unbranched* tree (a tree is unbranched if and only if the degree of each of its vertices is no greater than 2) with these n points as vertices. The T_n problem is obtained by setting $\max(\beta, \gamma) \gg \alpha \gg 1$ in the expression Eq. (3.3).

3.3.1.5 S_n PROBLEM (SMT). Given a set $V = \{v_1, v_2, \ldots, v_n\}$ of distinct points with $n \geq 3$, find the shortest tree whose vertices *contain* (i.e., an arbitrary number of extra points, called *Steiner points,* could be introduced) these *n*-points. The S_n problem is obtained by setting $\alpha = \beta = \gamma = 0$ in the expression Eq. (3.3).

3.3.1.6 ST_n PROBLEM. The ST_n problem can be viewed in some respects as a slight generalization of the S_n problem. The difference is that in the ST_n problem each element V_i of the vertex set $V = \{V_1, V_2, \ldots, V_n\}$ is a compact component that is not restricted to be just a point or vertex. Any such V is called an *n*-terminal set, and its n components are called *terminals.* The ST_n problem can be stated this way: Given a terminal set V, find the shortest net N (a net is understood to denote a finite set of connected plane-rectifiable arcs) such that the set union of V and N is a connected set.

3.3.2 Minimal Spanning Tree (MST) Algorithms

A set of n vertices is given. A weight or cost is associated with an edge between a pair of distinct vertices. When there is no edge between a pair of distinct vertices, an edge of weight infinity (or a suitably large finite number) may be inserted so that the resulting graph is complete. Therefore, the problem of interconnecting a set of n points by a router of minimum total weight is equivalent to the problem of finding an MST in a weighted complete graph. Of course, the task of extracting an MST from any simple graph can then also be completed as a special case of the MST construction in a complete graph. Mathematically, if $G = (V, E)$ is a connected undirected linear graph with $|V| = n$ vertices and $|E| = e$ edges, and if $d(v_i, v_j)$ is the edge weight of edge $(v_i, v_j) \in E$ connecting vertices $v_i, v_j \in V$, the objective is to find a spanning tree $T = (V, \hat{E}), \hat{E} \subseteq E$ such that $\sum_{(v_i, v_j) \in \hat{E}} d(v_i, v_j)$ is minimum. The first simple but useful algorithm for constructing an MST is due to Kruskal [207].

3.3.2.1 KRUSKAL'S PROCEDURE. First, the set of edges is ordered, based on their weights, in a nondecreasing manner. Following this sorting, an MST is constructed by iteratively applying this rule: "Among the edges of the graph G not yet chosen, choose an edge of least weight that does not form any loop with those edges already chosen." The set of edges eventually chosen must form a spanning tree, and the fact that this is an MST can be substantiated as follows. Let the edges chosen be called $e_1, e_2, \ldots, e_{n-1}$. Let T_i be a subtree consisting of edges $e_1, e_2, \ldots, e_{i-1}, e_i$. Hypothesize that T is an MST chosen so that it has at least one edge in common with T_{n-1} (this is always possible) and that T_{n-1} is not an MST. Let e_i be the first edge of T_{n-1} that is not in T (i.e., edges $e_1, e_2, \ldots, e_{i-2}, e_{i-1}$ are common to both T and T_{n-1}). Then the graph formed from e_i and the edges in T (for the sake of brevity, this graph may be denoted by the set union, $T \cup \{e_i\}$, of the edge set in T and e_i) has exactly one loop containing e_i, because T is a tree and e_i is an additional edge inserted. This loop must contain an edge, e_a, not in T_{n-1}. Then $T(-e_a) \cup \{e_i\}$ is a tree with $n - 1$ edges where $T(-e_a)$ denotes T with edge e_a removed. From the construction rule, it is evident that the weight of edge e_a is greater than or equal to the weight of edge e_i. If the inequality prevails, $T(-e_a) \cup \{e_i\}$ is of lesser total weight than T, contradicting the fact that T is an MST. If the weights of e_i and e_a are equal, the new tree $T_a \equiv T(-e_a) \cup \{e_i\}$ is again an MST with edges $e_1, e_2, \ldots, e_{i-1}, e_i$ in common with T_{n-1}. Repeat the argument on T_a as in T until either a tree identical to T_{n-1} results or the fact that T (or a tree derived from it and having the same total length) is an MST is contradicted.

Kruskal's algorithm belongs to the class of *greedy algorithms*. If all the edge weights in the graph are distinct, there is a unique MST, because then the algorithm leads to such a tree in a unique way. The initial phase of sorting by weight can be done in $O(e \log n)$ operations. After sorting, the tree can be grown in $O(eA(e, n))$ operations, where $A(e, n)$ is a functional inverse of Ackermann's function [3]. $A(e, n)$ is a very slow-growing function, and the worst-case time for the tree-growing phase is bounded by $O(e + n \log *n)$, where

$$\log *n = \min\{i \mid \log \log \cdots \log n \le 1\} \tag{3.4}$$

with log repeated i times on the right-hand side of Eq. (3.4). Even if the length of the branches is a computable function of time, the procedure demands that data for all branches be stored simultaneously. The method is applicable in any dimensions (m arbitrary) and any metric (p arbitrary). Try to justify whether the restriction of metric space is necessary for the algorithm to work and also whether negative edge weights can be tolerated. Another publication [235], which developed these ideas independently, appeared in 1957, but the procedures presented there were identical to Kruskal's.

3.3.2.2 PRIM-DIJKSTRA PROCEDURE. This method [97, 304] requires neither initial sorting of the edges nor testing for a circuit or loop at each stage, as in the previous procedure. The algorithm to be discussed is called the *nearest neighbor algorithm,* or the fragment-building algorithm. Select any vertex v_1 in the graph. Determine the edge, say (v_1, v_2), of least weight incident on v_1. The edge (v_1, v_2) belongs to the tree being grown. From all edges incident on v_1 and v_2, an edge of least weight is selected and included in the growing tree. This process is continued until n nodes and $(n - 1)$ edges are included in the tree, which then can be proved to be an MST. The proof follows from the fact that, given n nodes with k of these nodes connected in a subtree whose edges are also the edges of the MST over the n nodes, the shortest edge between any one of the k nodes and any of the remaining $(n - k)$ nodes must be an edge of the MST. If several edges of equal length qualify to be the shortest edge, then each of these is an edge of some MST containing the k-node subtree as a subgraph. Substantiation of this fact is possible by considering a k-node subtree whose edges belong to an MST over n nodes, where $n > k$. Let $(v_1, v_{k+1}), (v_2, v_{k+2}), \ldots, (v_r, v_{k+r})$ be the shortest edges of equal weight that can connect the k-node subtree to any of the remaining $r = (n - k)$ nodes. Next, assume that one of these shortest edges, say (v_1, v_{k+1}), is not an edge of any MST over the n nodes. In the MST, then, the path from v_1 to v_{k+1} must include exactly one branch, say (v_i, v_{k+i}), that connects the k-node subtree to its complement. If this branch belongs to the set of branches $(v_2, v_{k+2}), (v_3, v_{k+3}), \ldots, (v_r, v_{k+r})$, i.e., $2 \le i \le r$, replace edge (v_i, v_{k+i}) by edge (v_1, v_{k+1}) to get another MST. On the other hand, if the condition $2 \le i \le r$ is not satisfied, then replace (v_i, v_{k+i}) by (v_1, v_{k+1}) to obtain an n-node tree shorter than an MST, which leads to a contradiction. Therefore, substantiation of the statement made has been completed. The operations here are comparisons. If one selects the kth edge (for $k = 1, 2, \ldots, n - 1$), $[k(n - k) - 1]$ comparisons are sufficient in the worst case. Therefore, the number of operations sufficient to implement the algorithm is

$$\sum_{k=1}^{n-1} [k(n - k) - 1] = \frac{n^3}{6} - \frac{7n}{6} + 1. \tag{3.5}$$

Of course, much better running time can be achieved than is indicated by Eq. (3.5). Kerschenbaum and Van Slyke [186] demonstrated that the number of operations was $O(n^2)$. Suppose that for each vertex not yet in the growing tree, a record is kept of the vertex in the tree to which it is closest. Then the determination of the kth vertex to be added to the partially grown tree requires $n - k$ comparisons for $k = 2, 3, \ldots, n$ (because the first vertex in the tree is arbitrarily selected). After adding the kth vertex, the information about the closest vertices can be updated with another $(n - k)$ comparisons. Therefore, the total number of comparisons required to implement the Prim-Dijkstra algorithm via use of the artifice mentioned is

$$\sum_{k=2}^{n} 2(n - k) = n^2 - 3n + 2. \tag{3.6}$$

The data storage for the algorithm may be reduced from $O(n^2)$ to $O(n)$ by replacing the input array containing weights of edges between pairs of nodes with an edge length function that calculates required internode edge lengths as they are needed. This strategy is useful in extending the size of the problem to be solved on a machine with limited core storage. Again note that the present algorithm applies for arbitrary integers m and p in Eq. (3.2). A different implementation of the algorithm [407] runs in $O(e \log n)$ time.

3.3.2.3 SOLLIN'S PROCEDURE. When a graph has a large number of edges, a procedure attributed to Sollin [40] leads to efficient algorithms. This procedure is summarized next. First, for each vertex the minimum-weight edge incident on it is found, which can be done in $O(e)$ operations. The groups of vertices that are connected by these edges form connected components. Each of these connected components is shrunk into a new vertex. The process is repeated on each of these new vertices and continued until only a single vertex remains. The edges traced at different stages constitute an MST. The number of stages in the worst case is $O(\log n)$, so that the algorithm can be implemented in $O(e \log n)$ operations. Yao [423] used this algorithm after initializing his data structure by partitioning the set of edges incident on each node into k levels $E_1, E_2, \ldots, E_k$ so that edge $(v_r, v_s) \in E_i$, $(v_k, v_l) \in E_j$ for $i < j$ if $d(v_r, v_s) \le d(v_k, v_l)$. This can be done in $O(e \log k)$ time by repeatedly applying an algorithm called the *linear median-finding algorithm* [75], which may be quite complicated to implement. The MST algorithm due to Sollin can then be implemented in $O[(e/k) \log n]$ operations. Therefore, the overall time complexity in Yao's modification and use of the procedure under discussion here is $O[e \log k + (e/k) \log n]$ operations, which simplifies to $O(e \log \log n)$ operations by choosing $k = \log n$. Cheriton and Tarjan [75] have produced other MST algorithms, that can be implemented in $O(e \log \log n)$ operations.

3.3.3   Minimal Fermat Tree (MFT) Problem

The problem to be discussed here is attributed to Fermat. A general formulation of the problem for arbitrary m and p in Eq. (3.2) is given next.

> **Generalized Fermat Problem.** Let there be n specified points $v_k = (v_{k1}, v_{k2}, \ldots, v_{km})$, $k = 1, 2, \ldots, n$ in an m-dimensional metric space with a metric $d(v_i, v_j)$ shown in Eq. (3.2). Let there be n positive numbers w_k, $k = 1, 2, \ldots, n$, called weights. Find a point $q = (x_1, x_2, \ldots, x_m)$ such that the cost function,
>
> $$C(q) = \sum_{k=1}^{n} w_k d(q, v_k), \tag{3.7}$$
>
> is minimized.

Kuhn has discussed in detail the case when $p = 2$ and m is arbitrary [209]. If the points v_k, $1 \le k \le n$, are not collinear, then $C(q)$ is a strictly convex function of q. If the points are collinear, then $C(q)$ is piecewise linear and convex on the line through them and strictly convex elsewhere. In the following discussion, attention will be focused on the situation when $C(q)$ is a strictly convex function of q.

From elementary results in convexity theory, $C(q)$ in Eq. (3.7) has a unique minimum at $q = q_0$ in m-dimensional Euclidean space when the metric is Euclidean. The point $q = q_0$ can be located using an algorithm due to Weiszfeld [401], slightly modified by Kuhn, who also gave a convergence proof for the algorithm subject, of course, to this modification. Some of the results dealing with the solution to the Fermat problem are also available in ref. [281].

The algorithms for solution to the MST problem are metric-independent. However, when extra points are permissible for obtaining trees shorter than MSTs, the metric used must be taken into account. So far, the solution to the MFT problem in Euclidean metric ($p = 2$, m is an arbitrary positive integer) was discussed. The MFT problem over rectilinear metric ($p = 1$) in m-dimensional space is considered in ref. [115].

3.3.4   Traveling Salesperson (TS) Problem

This classical problem is concerned with the construction of a minimal spanning tree over n specified vertices subject to the constraint that the degree of each vertex in the constructed tree is not greater than 2; more specifically, except for the initial and terminal vertices, which are of degree 1, all remaining vertices in the tree are of degree 2, and the tree is called an unbranched tree. This degree-constrained MST is actually a path and is referred to as a *Hamiltonian path*. A modification of the basic problem requires the construction of a circuit or loop (where each vertex is of degree 2) of minimum total length containing, exclusively, the specified vertices. Such a loop is called a *Hamiltonian loop*. The imposition of the degree constraint on the vertices alters the computational complexity for the solution to the problem in a very great way. In fact, even to this day no computationally feasible exact method for problems with large n exists. Minimal spanning tree algorithms, however, provide useful lower bounds on the length of the unbranched tree in this problem [157]. A comprehensive survey of the traveling salesperson problem, including description of heuristic approaches, is available in ref. [39]. Theoretically, the problem can always be solved by enumerating all $(n - 1)!/2$ Hamiltonian paths and then picking the shortest one. Exact procedures based on dynamic programming [156] and the branch and bound technique [232] reduce the time for solution but still are of exponential order in the worse case.

3.3.5 Steiner Minimal Tree (SMT)

In this section, useful necessary conditions satisfied by a Steiner minimal tree (SMT) constructed in a plane ($m = 2$) will be stated and proved. The proof given will be analytic as opposed to those based on the use of mechanical [131, 372] and other [85] analogies.

> **Theorem 3.2.** Let S_n be an SMT in Euclidean metric over vertices $v_1, v_2, \ldots, v_n, q_1,$ $q_2, \ldots, q_k$, where the v_i's are the given vertices and the q_i's are the additional or Steiner vertices, all situated on a plane. If $\delta(q_i)$ is the degree of vertex q_i, then
>
> a. $\delta(q_i) = 3$, for $i = 1, 2, \ldots, k$ and, furthermore, any pair of edges incident at q_i subtends an angle of 120° at q_i.
> b. $\delta(v_i) \leq 3, i = 1, 2, \ldots, n$.
> c. $0 \leq k \leq n - 2$.
> d. T_n is non-self-intersecting.
>
> *Proof.*
>   (a) Consider any Steiner vertex q_i, $1 \leq i \leq k$. Then $\delta(q_i) \neq 1$, because otherwise the tree length would needlessly be increased. Let $d(\mathbf{a}, \mathbf{b})$ denote the distance between the vectors $\mathbf{a}, \mathbf{b}$ from the origin to the points a, b. Suppose $\delta(q_i) = 2$. Then two edges would connect q_i to two distinct tree-vertices, say a, b. However,
>
> $$d(\mathbf{a}, \mathbf{b}) \leq d(\mathbf{a}, \mathbf{q}_i) + d(\mathbf{b}, \mathbf{q}_i). \tag{3.8}$$
>
> Therefore, the tree length can be shortened by deleting q_i and connecting a with b directly, thereby contradicting the hypothesis that S_n is an SMT. Therefore, $\delta(q_i) \neq 2$. Assume, next, that $\delta(q_i) = 4$, as shown in Fig. 3.11. Split vertex q_i to yield two vertices q_{i1}, q_{i2}, as shown in Fig. 3.12. Then, the length l of the subtree in Fig. 3.12 that belongs to S_n is
>
> $$l(q_{i1}, q_{i2}) = d(\mathbf{q}_{i1}, \mathbf{v}_1) + d(\mathbf{q}_{i1}, \mathbf{v}_2) + d(\mathbf{q}_{i1}, \mathbf{q}_{i2}) + d(\mathbf{q}_{i2}, \mathbf{v}_3) + d(\mathbf{q}_{i2}, \mathbf{v}_4). \tag{3.9}$$

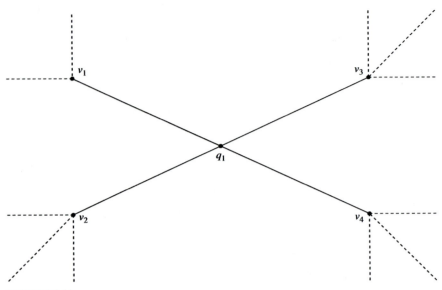

FIGURE 3.11
A vertex q_1 having degree 4 in a hypothetical tree.

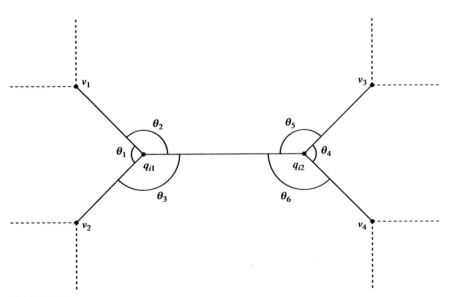

FIGURE 3.12
The graph obtained after splitting vertex q_i in Fig. 3.11 into vertices q_{i1} and q_{i2} with a connecting edge q_{i1}, q_{i2} inserted.

Denote the vector joining the origin to vertex v_i by $\mathbf{v}_i$. At a minimum, the gradients of the scalar function l must be zero. That is,

$$\frac{\partial l}{\partial \mathbf{q}_{i1}} = 0 = \frac{(\mathbf{q}_{i1} - \mathbf{v}_1)}{d(\mathbf{q}_{i1}, \mathbf{v}_1)} + \frac{(\mathbf{q}_{i1} - \mathbf{v}_2)}{d(\mathbf{q}_{i1}, \mathbf{v}_2)} + \frac{(\mathbf{q}_{i1} - \mathbf{q}_{i2})}{d(\mathbf{q}_{i1}, \mathbf{q}_{i2})} \qquad (3.10)$$

$$\frac{\partial l}{\partial \mathbf{q}_{i2}} = 0 = \frac{(\mathbf{q}_{i2} - \mathbf{v}_3)}{d(\mathbf{q}_{i2}, \mathbf{v}_3)} + \frac{(\mathbf{q}_{i2} - \mathbf{v}_4)}{d(\mathbf{q}_{i2}, \mathbf{v}_4)} + \frac{(\mathbf{q}_{i1} - \mathbf{q}_{i2})}{d(\mathbf{q}_{i1}, \mathbf{q}_{i2})} \qquad (3.11)$$

Note that the angle θ between two vectors $\mathbf{a}, \mathbf{b}$ in a real m-dimensional vector space is given by

$$\cos \theta = \frac{\mathbf{a}^\mathrm{T} \mathbf{b}}{\|\mathbf{a}\| \, \|\mathbf{b}\|} \qquad (3.12)$$

where the superscript "T" denotes "transpose" and $\|\mathbf{a}\|$ is the ordinary Euclidean norm of vector $\mathbf{a}$. Note that

$$\|\mathbf{q}_{ij} - \mathbf{v}_r\| = d(\mathbf{q}_{ij}, \mathbf{v}_r) \qquad (3.13)$$

for $j = 1, 2$, and $r = 1, 2, 3$. Premultiplying Eq. (3.10) successively by $(\mathbf{q}_{i1} - \mathbf{v}_1)^\mathrm{T}/d(\mathbf{q}_{i1}, \mathbf{v}_1)$, $(\mathbf{q}_{i1} - \mathbf{q}_{i2})^\mathrm{T}/d(\mathbf{q}_{i1}, \mathbf{q}_{i2})$, and $(\mathbf{q}_{i1} - \mathbf{v}_2)^\mathrm{T}/d(\mathbf{q}_{i1}, \mathbf{v}_2)$ and then using Eqs. (3.12) and (3.13), one gets

$$1 + \cos \theta_1 + \cos \theta_2 = 0$$
$$1 + \cos \theta_2 + \cos \theta_3 = 0 \qquad (3.14)$$
$$1 + \cos \theta_1 + \cos \theta_3 = 0$$

with $\theta_1, \theta_2, \theta_3$ defined in Fig. 3.12.

The solution relevant to Eq. (3.14) is

$$\theta_1 = \theta_2 = \theta_3 = 120°. \qquad (3.15)$$

Similarly, by operating on Eq. (3.11), it can be shown that

$$\theta_4 = \theta_5 = \theta_6 = 120°, \qquad (3.16)$$

where θ_4, θ_5, and θ_6 are also defined in Fig. 3.12. Therefore, given the tree in Fig. 3.12, which is a part of S_n, it is always possible to obtain a shorter S_n, which contradicts the hypothesis that T is an SMT. Therefore, $\delta(q_i) \neq 4$ in an SMT.

Next, assume that $\delta(q_i) > 4$. Consider, for example, $\delta(q_i) = 6$, as in Fig. 3.13. The argument to be given next can be adapted for any $\delta(q_i) > 4$. In Fig. 3.14,

$$d(\mathbf{q}_i, \mathbf{v}_5) = d(\mathbf{q}_{i3}, \mathbf{v}_5), \qquad d(\mathbf{q}_i, \mathbf{v}_6) = d(\mathbf{q}_{i3}, \mathbf{v}_6)$$

and

$$\sum_{j=1}^{4} d(\mathbf{q}_i, \mathbf{v}_j) \geq \sum_{j=1,3} d(\mathbf{q}_{i1}, \mathbf{v}_j) + \sum_{j=2,4} d(\mathbf{q}_{i2}, \mathbf{v}_j) + d(\mathbf{q}_i, \mathbf{q}_{i1}) + d(\mathbf{q}_i, \mathbf{q}_{i2}).$$

Thus, again a shorter tree than S_n can be obtained, contradicting the hypothesis that S_n is an SMT. Therefore, $\delta(q_i) \neq 6$ and, by adapting and combining the arguments just given, the only possible value for $\delta(q_i)$ is

$$\delta(q_i) = 3.$$

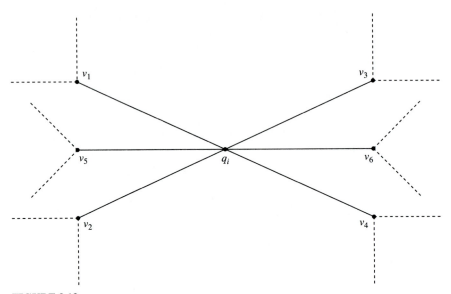

FIGURE 3.13
A vertex q_1 having degree 6 in a hypothetical tree.

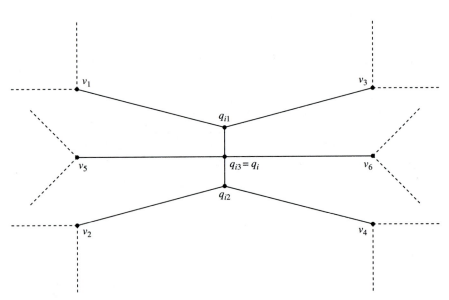

FIGURE 3.14
The graph obtained after splitting vertex q_1 in Fig. 3.13 to create a vertex q_{i3} of degree 4, and two vertices q_{i1} and q_{i2}, each of degree 3, with connecting edges inserted as shown.

Furthermore, from Eqs. (3.15) and (3.16), it is clear that any pair of edges incident at q_i subtends an angle of $120°$ at q_i.

(b) Consider any fixed vertex v_i, $1 \le i \le n$. The cases $\delta(v_i) = 1$, $\delta(v_i) = 2$ are certainly possible by trivial constructions. The argument advanced in the proof of (a) can be applied to prove that $\delta(v_i)$ cannot be greater than 3. Therefore, $\delta(v_i) \le 3$.

(c) A spanning tree over $(n + k)$ vertices has $(n + k - 1)$ edges. If the number of degree r vertices in the set, $\{v_1, v_2, \ldots, v_n\}$, is n_r, then from the results in (a) and (b), and from the fact that $n = n_1 + n_2 + n_3$, it follows from Theorem 2.1 that

$$3k + n_1 + 2n_2 + 3n_3 = 2(n + k - 1),$$

which leads to the equation

$$k = n_1 - 2 - n_3. \tag{3.17}$$

Therefore, $k \le n-2$, since $n_1 \le n$. From Eq. (3.17), it is clear that $k = n-2$, provided $n_2 = n_3 = 0$ or $n = n_1$. When $k = n - 2$, the Steiner minimal tree is said to be a *full* SMT.

(d) The impossibility for nontrivial intersection of any two edges in S_n can be confirmed by observing that no vertex in a Steiner tree can be of degree 4 or greater, as already proved in (a) and (b).

The proof of the theorem is now complete.

An important special case of the SMT problem is the $n = 3$ case, because the construction of an SMT over three given points is often used to obtain a suboptimum Steiner tree [114] for large n. Theorem (3.3), pertaining to the $n = 3$ case, is stated and proved next.

Theorem 3.3. Given three points v_1, v_2, v_3, if each angle of the triangle $v_1v_2v_3$ is less than $120°$, then the Steiner point q_1 is the point at which each of the three sides v_1v_2, v_2v_3, v_1v_3 subtends an angle of $120°$. If, however, an angle of triangle $v_1v_2v_3$, say the angle at vertex v_2, is equal to or larger than $120°$, then the point q_1 coincides with the vertex v_2.

Proof. An alternative proof, independent of Theorem 3.2, can be given. Suppose, first, that each angle of triangle $v_1v_2v_3$ is less than $120°$. Consider an arbitrary point q inside the triangle, as in Fig. 3.15. Join q to v_1, v_2, v_3 and rotate triangle v_1qv_2 through $60°$ about v_1 to obtain triangle $v_1q'v_3'$ as shown in Fig. 3.16. Note that triangles $v_1v_2v_3'$ and v_1qq' are equilateral triangles. Then

$$\sum_{k=1}^{3} d(\mathbf{v}_k, \mathbf{q}) = d(\mathbf{v}_3', \mathbf{q}') + d(\mathbf{q}', \mathbf{q}) + d(\mathbf{q}, \mathbf{v}_3). \tag{3.18}$$

Usually, the path $v_3'q'qv_3$ from v_3' to v_3 is a broken line with angles at q' and q. Such a path is shortest when it is straight. In that case,

$$\angle v_1qv_3 = 180° - 60° = 120° \qquad \angle v_1qv_2 = \angle v_1q'v_3' = 120°.$$

Thus, each of the sides v_1v_2, v_2v_3, and v_1v_3 subtends an angle of $120°$ at the Steiner point $q = q_1$ in an SMT.

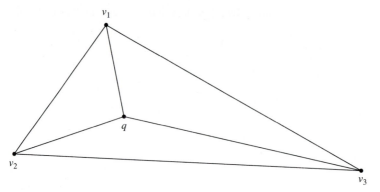

FIGURE 3.15
An arbitrary vertex q inside a triangle whose corners are the three specified vertices, v_1, v_2, and v_3.

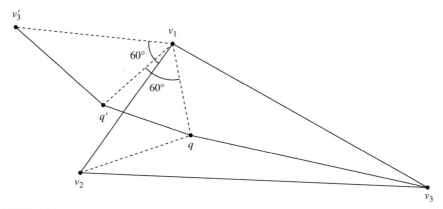

FIGURE 3.16
Construction of the Steiner tree over the three vertices v_1, v_2, and v_3.

The case when one angle, say $\angle v_1 v_2 v_3$, is 120° or greater can be handled by adding simple arguments to the fact that the Steiner point q_1 is in the convex hull of the vertices v_i, $i = 1, 2, \ldots, n$; and if q_1 does not coincide with a given vertex, then it is not on the boundary of the convex hull of the vertices v_i, $i = 1, 2, \ldots, n$.

The SMT, S_3, over three given vertices can be constructed in the following manner. Assume that each angle of the triangle $v_1 v_2 v_3$, where v_1, v_2, v_3 are prescribed vertices, is less than 120°, as the other case is trivial. Then, construct equilateral triangles on any two sides, say on $v_1 v_2$ and $v_2 v_3$. The Steiner point q_1 lies at the intersection of lines $v_3 v_3'$ and $v_1 v_1'$ as shown in Fig. 3.17. If the equilateral triangles $v_1 v_2 v_3'$, $v_2 v_3 v_1'$, and $v_1 v_3 v_2'$ are drawn outward on the sides of any triangle $v_1 v_2 v_3$, as shown in Fig 3.17, then the line segments $v_1 v_1'$, $v_2 v_2'$, $v_3 v_3'$ are equal. Furthermore, the length l of the SMT, S_3, is

$$l = \sum_{k=1}^{3} d(q_1, v_k) = d(v_1, v_1') = d(v_2, v_2') = d(v_3, v_3'). \qquad (3.19)$$

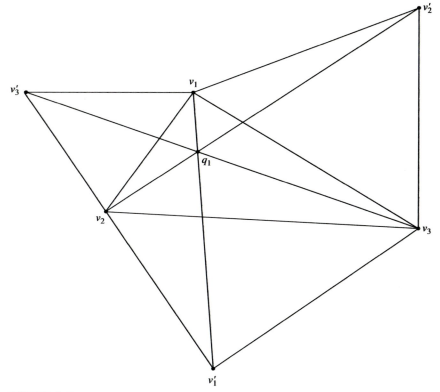

FIGURE 3.17
A straightforward method for locating the Steiner point in the case of three specified vertices.

Several additional comments pertaining to S_3 are relevant. First, the tree S_3 is the same as the F_3 tree obtained as a solution to the Fermat problem when $n = 3$ and $w_k = 1$ for all k in Eq. (3.5). Second, it is easily proved that any one of the three ellipses through the Steiner point q_1 with two of the vertices v_1, v_2, v_3 as foci is tangent at q_1 to the circle, through q_1, centered at the third vertex. Third, S_3 is full except in the trivial case when the triangle $v_1v_2v_3$ contains an angle greater than or equal to 120°.

Next, a set of necessary conditions satisfied by a Steiner minimal tree (SMT) over the rectilinear metric are discussed. These results were introduced in ref. [148] and apply in the case of a plane.

Theorem 3.4. Let S_n be an SMT in rectilinear metric over vertices $v_1, v_2, \ldots, v_n, q_1, q_2, \ldots, q_k$, where the v_i's are prescribed vertices and the q_i's are Steiner vertices on the plane. Then

(a) $\delta(q_i) = 3$ or 4, $i = 1, 2, \ldots, k$

(b) $\delta(v_i) \le 4$, $i = 1, 2, \ldots, n$

(c) $0 \le k \le n - 2$.

Proof. It is evident that in rectilinear metric, the degree of any vertex, fixed or Steiner, in a plane cannot exceed 4, as substantiated next.

(a) $\delta(q_i) \neq 1$, for otherwise the tree length would needlessly increase, and $\delta(q_i) \neq 2$ as implied by the triangle inequality. The possibilities for $\delta(q_i) = 3$ or 4 can be illustrated by simple constructions in Figs. 3.18 and 3.19.

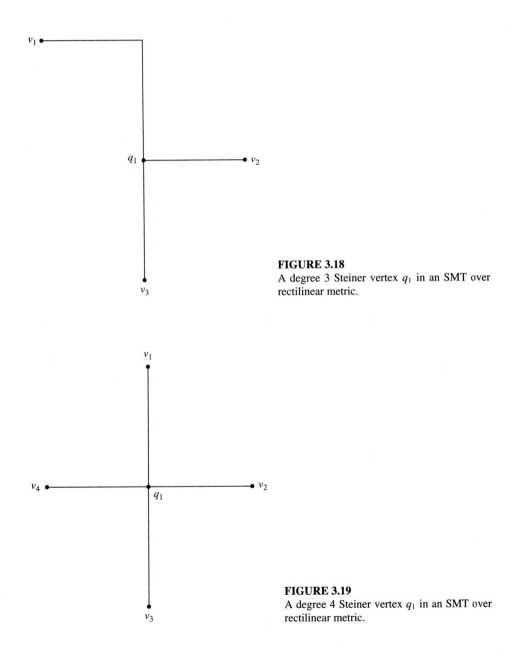

FIGURE 3.18
A degree 3 Steiner vertex q_1 in an SMT over rectilinear metric.

FIGURE 3.19
A degree 4 Steiner vertex q_1 in an SMT over rectilinear metric.

(b) The fact that $\delta(v_i)$ can be 1, 2, 3, or 4 is justified by simple constructions. Figure 3.18 illustrates the $\delta(v_i) = 1$ case. In Fig. 3.20, $\delta(v_2) = 2, \delta(v_5) = 3$, and in Fig. 3.21, $\delta(v_5) = 4$.

(c) If the number of degree r vertices in the set, $(v_1, v_2, \ldots, v_n)$, is n_r, and if there are k_3 and k_4 Steiner vertices of degrees 3 and 4, respectively, where $k_3 + k_4 = k$, then, by applying Theorem 2.1 to the SMT with $(n + k - 1)$ edges, one gets

$$3k_3 + 4k_4 + n_1 + 2n_2 + 3n_3 + 4n_4 = 2(n_1 + n_2 + n_3 + n_4) + 2k - 2$$

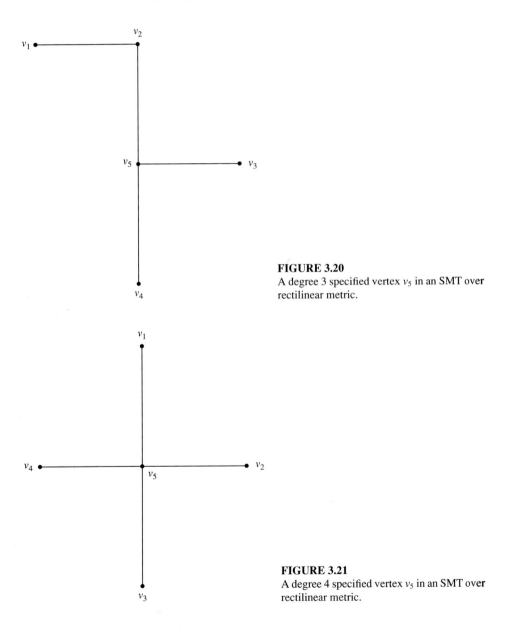

FIGURE 3.20
A degree 3 specified vertex v_5 in an SMT over rectilinear metric.

FIGURE 3.21
A degree 4 specified vertex v_5 in an SMT over rectilinear metric.

after substituting $n = n_1 + n_2 + n_3 + n_4$. Consequently,

$$k = n_1 - n_3 - 2n_4 - k_4 - 2 \leq n_1 - 2. \tag{3.20}$$

Therefore, $k \leq n - 2$, since $n_1 \leq n$.

From Eq. (3.20), it is clear that $k = n - 2$, provided $n_2 = n_3 = n_4 = k_4 = 0$, implying that $n = n_1$. In ref. [148] explicit schemes are given for construction of SMTs in a plane when $n \leq 5$. The result in the $n = 3$ case is summarized next. It holds even when $m > 2$.

Theorem 3.5. Let $(v_{k1}, v_{k2}, \ldots, v_{km})$ be the coordinates of v_k, $k = 1, 2, 3$. Denote by $(p_j(1), p_j(2), p_j(3))$ the permutation of integers $(1,2,3)$, for $j = 1, 2, \ldots, m$ so that

$$v_{p_j(1)j} \geq v_{p_j(2)j} \geq v_{p_j(3)j}, \qquad j = 1, 2, \ldots, m.$$

Then the Steiner point is located at $v_{p_1(2)1}, v_{p_2(2)2}, \ldots, v_{p_m(2)m}$.

Proof. In general, there will be no more than $3 - 2 = 1$ Steiner point when $n = 3$. The Steiner point will be obtained from a solution $(q_{11}, q_{12}, \ldots, q_{1m})$ that minimizes the following cost function:

$$C(q_{11}, q_{12}, \ldots, q_{1m}) = \sum_{j=1}^{m} \sum_{k=1}^{3} |q_{1j} - v_{kj}| \tag{3.21}$$

Observe the sum-separable nature of the cost function and use the fact that the minimum of

$$\sum_{k=1}^{3} |q_{1j} - v_{kj}|$$

occurs when $q_{1j} = v_{p_j(2)j}$, $j = 1, 2, \ldots, m$, to get the result.

3.4   PLACEMENT AND PARTITIONING

Although the problems of partitioning and assignment, placement, interconnection, and routing are intimately related, historically they have been treated separately because of the inherent computational complexity of the total problem. Placement is the process of positioning modules in a physical environment, such as on a backplane or a printed circuit board, whereas partitioning is the process of assigning logic elements to modules, so that in both cases certain constraints are satisfied. The three-level backplane was usual in integrated circuit design in the 1960s. On the lowest level, sets of logic elements form modules. Interconnected sets of modules define boards, and interconnected sets of boards define the backplane.

3.4.1   Placement

For convenience we consider the placement of modules on a board. Forming a board involves positioning a set of modules into various slots in the board. The various circuit elements on the modules lead to connection pins located on the sides of the modules. On the basis of the given logic design, various subsets of these pins, termed *signal sets,* must be interconnected to form *nets.* When some nets are more critical than others, the corresponding signal sets must be weighted.

Formally, the module placement problem consists of finding the optimum placement of modules on the board with respect to some norm defined on the interconnections, such as minimal weighted wire length. Practical constraints that usually enter into the placement problem are (*a*) wire buildup in the routing channels of the board; (*b*) signal cross talk, which must be avoided without use of expensive shielding techniques; (*c*) signal echo, which must be eliminated; (*d*) severe heat source concentrations, which cannot be permitted; (*e*) ease and neatness of wirability—a very desirable feature to reduce construction and maintenance costs. When all of these considerations cannot be simultaneously implemented, minimization of *total weighted wire length* is sought. Two mathematical problems are related to the placement problem. The *linear assignment problem* is a special case of the *quadratic assignment problem,* and the quadratic assignment problem is a special case of the placement problem. The linear assignment problem, described next, is a variant of the general linear programming problem.

3.4.1.1   THE LINEAR ASSIGNMENT PROBLEM.   A real ($n \times n$) matrix $[a_{ij}]$ is given, and one is required to find the nth order permutation p that minimizes $\sum_{i=1}^{n} a_{ip(i)}$, where $p(i) \triangleq j$ is assignment of i. For example, given n persons and n jobs and the cost a_{ij} of assigning person i to job j, the linear assignment problem requires finding an assignment involving one and only one person for each job so that the total cost is minimum. As there are $n!$ ways by which n persons can be assigned to n jobs in this problem, efficient solution algorithms were desired and obtained. The preliminaries given next are necessary for understanding one such algorithm, due to Kuhn [208].

> **Definition 3.2.** A set of elements of a matrix will be said to be *independent* if no two of them lie in the same line (the word *line* applies to both the rows and the columns of the matrix).

One needs to choose n independent elements of the matrix $[a_{ij}]$, such that the sum of these elements is minimum, in order to solve the problem under consideration. Kuhn's algorithm depends on Konig's theorem, quoted next.

> **Konig's theorem.** If m is the maximum number of independent zero elements of a matrix $\mathbf{A}$, then there are m lines that contain all the zero elements of $\mathbf{A}$.

Obviously, the solution to the linear assignment problem does not change if the matrix $\mathbf{A} = [a_{ij}]$ is replaced by the matrix $\mathbf{B} = [b_{ij}]$, obtained by subtracting an arbitrary constant from each element in $\mathbf{A}$.

Kuhn's algorithm (the Hungarian Method).

1. Subtract the smallest element in $\mathbf{A}$ from each element of $\mathbf{A}$, obtaining a matrix $\mathbf{A}_1$ with nonnegative elements and at least one zero element. Set $k = 1$.
2. Find a minimal set S_k of lines that contain all the zeros of $\mathbf{A}_k$. Let the cardinality of this set be $|S_k| \triangleq n_k$. If $n_k = n$, there is a set of n independent zeros, and the elements of $\mathbf{A}$ in these n positions constitute the required solution; go to step 4.
3. If $n_k < n$, let h_k denote the smallest element of $\mathbf{A}_k$ that is not in any line belonging to the set S_k. Then $h_k > 0$. For each line in S_k, add h_k to every element of that line; then subtract h_k from every element of $\mathbf{A}_k$. Call the new matrix $\mathbf{A}_{k+1}$. Go to step 2 and set $k \longleftarrow k + 1$.
4. Stop. The sum of the elements of the matrix is decreased by at least $n(n - n_k)h_k$ after each application of step 3. So the process must terminate after a finite number of steps.

This algorithm naturally applies even if negative elements occur in matrix $\mathbf{A} = [a_{ij}]$. Kuhn's algorithm will be illustrated by the following nontrivial example.

Example 3.5. The given cost assignment matrix is

$$[a_{ij}] = \mathbf{A} = \begin{bmatrix} 4 & 3 & 1 & 2 \\ -2 & -1 & 6 & 8 \\ 1 & 1 & 2 & 3 \\ -1 & -1 & 4 & 1 \end{bmatrix}.$$

Therefore, the minimum element in $\mathbf{A}$ is -2.

Step 1: $\quad \mathbf{A}_1 = \begin{bmatrix} 6 & 5 & 3 & 4 \\ 0 & 1 & 8 & 10 \\ 3 & 3 & 4 & 5 \\ 1 & 1 & 6 & 3 \end{bmatrix}$

Step 2: $\mathbf{A}_2$ is obtained after noting that a minimal set S_1 of lines that contain all zeros of $\mathbf{A}_1$ is just <u>column 1</u> (or <u>row 2</u>) of $\mathbf{A}_1$.

Step 3: $\quad \mathbf{A}_2 = \begin{bmatrix} 6 & 4 & 2 & 3 \\ 0 & 0 & 7 & 9 \\ 3 & 2 & 3 & 4 \\ 1 & 0 & 5 & 2 \end{bmatrix}$

Step 2: $\quad$ On $\mathbf{A}_2$, a minimal set consists of <u>rows 2 and 4</u>, for example.

Step 3: $\quad \mathbf{A}_3 = \begin{bmatrix} 4 & 2 & 0 & 1 \\ 0 & 0 & 7 & 9 \\ 1 & 0 & 1 & 2 \\ 1 & 0 & 5 & 2 \end{bmatrix}$

Step 2: $\quad$ On $\mathbf{A}_3$, a minimal set consists of, for example, <u>columns 1, 2, and 3</u>.

Step 3: $\quad \mathbf{A}_4 = \begin{bmatrix} 4 & 2 & 0 & 0 \\ 0 & 0 & 7 & 8 \\ 1 & 0 & 1 & 1 \\ 1 & 0 & 5 & 1 \end{bmatrix}$

Step 2: On $\mathbf{A}_4$, a minimal set consists of row 1, columns 1 and 2.

Step 3: $\quad \mathbf{A}_5 = \begin{bmatrix} 4 & 2 & 0 & 0 \\ 0 & 0 & 6 & 7 \\ 1 & 0 & 0 & 0 \\ 1 & 0 & 4 & 0 \end{bmatrix}$

A minimal set of lines that contain all zeros of $\mathbf{A}_5$ consists of four elements, which equals the order of $\mathbf{A}$. Therefore, the algorithm terminates. A solution is

$$[a_{21} + a_{42} + a_{13} + a_{34}] = [-2 + -1 + 1 + 3] = 1.$$

Note that the solution is not unique [in the sense that combination of different a_{ij}'s (independent) could have given the same sum]. An alternative solution is

$$[a_{21} + a_{32} + a_{13} + a_{44}] = [-2 + 1 + 1 + 1] = 1.$$

Of course, the *value* (in this case 1) of the solution is unique. Also, the sequence $\mathbf{A} \rightarrow \mathbf{A}_1 \rightarrow \mathbf{A}_2 \rightarrow \mathbf{A}_3 \rightarrow \mathbf{A}_4 \cdots$ is not unique. For example, if on $\mathbf{A}_2$ the minimal set is taken to consist of columns 1 and 2, then we proceed as follows. A superscript is used on the resulting matrices to distinguish from the previous case.

Step 3: $\quad \mathbf{A}_3^{(1)} = \begin{bmatrix} 6 & 4 & 0 & 1 \\ 0 & 0 & 5 & 7 \\ 3 & 2 & 1 & 2 \\ 1 & 0 & 3 & 0 \end{bmatrix} \neq \mathbf{A}_3$

Step 2: On $\mathbf{A}_3^{(1)}$, a minimal set consists of rows 2 and 4, and column 3.

Step 3: $\quad \mathbf{A}_4^{(1)} = \begin{bmatrix} 5 & 3 & 0 & 0 \\ 0 & 0 & 5 & 7 \\ 2 & 1 & 1 & 1 \\ 1 & 0 & 3 & 0 \end{bmatrix}$

Step 2: On $\mathbf{A}_4^{(1)}$, a minimal set consists of rows 1, 2, and 4.

Step 3: $\quad \mathbf{A}_4^{(1)} = \begin{bmatrix} 5 & 3 & 0 & 0 \\ 0 & 0 & 5 & 7 \\ 1 & 0 & 0 & 0 \\ 1 & 0 & 3 & 0 \end{bmatrix}$

So, again $\left(\sum a_{ip(i)} \right)_{\min} = 1$.

H.W. Kuhn's algorithm, described earlier, is not very efficient, though it is remarkably simple and straightforward. Munkres's algorithm [267], based on Kuhn's work, requires not more than $(11n^3 + 12n^2 + 31n)/6$ operations on a matrix $\mathbf{A}$ of order n, where the types of operations are "scan," "add," and "subtract."

3.4.1.2 THE QUADRATIC ASSIGNMENT PROBLEM. Here, in addition to an $(n \times n)$ cost matrix, $\mathbf{C} = [c_{ij}]$, there is also an $(n \times n)$ distance matrix, $\mathbf{D} = [d_{kl}]$, and the problem is to find the minimum of

$$\sum_i \sum_j c_{ij} d_{p(i)p(j)}$$

over all permutations p. If $\mathbf{C}$ and $\mathbf{D}$ are symmetric, then the quadratic assignment problem is formulated, where minimization of

$$\sum_{i<j} \sum c_{ij} d_{p(i)p(j)}$$

is required. Though there are $n!$ ways of assignment, there are no computationally feasible solution methods available for reasonably large n. To comprehend the problem better, the following analogy is helpful. Given are n people and a matrix $[c_{ij}]$, where c_{ij} is a measure of the amount of contact needed between two people i and j. Also given are n possible offices for these people and a matrix $[d_{kl}]$, where d_{kl} is the distance between offices k and l. If person i is assigned to office $p(i)$ and person j is assigned to office $p(j)$, then the cost of this assignment is taken to be $c_{ij} d_{p(i)p(j)}$. The quadratic assignment problem then requires that the total cost be minimized.

The quadratic assignment problem is a special case of the placement problem. In the general placement problem, one is concerned with sets of points, whereas in the quadratic assignment problem, one deals with only the simpler problem of pairs of points. Therefore, when each signal set of a placement problem involves no more than two modules, then the placement problem reduces to the quadratic assignment problem. Often, the placement problem is converted to an associated quadratic placement problem. This conversion is accomplished by taking as elements of the cost matrix, $\mathbf{C} = [c_{ij}]$, the sum of the weights of the signal sets common to modules i and j, $i \neq j$, and $c_{ii} = 0$, for all i. The distance matrix remains the same and is identical to the distance matrix in the original placement problem.

Note that, in general, the optimum solution of the associated quadratic assignment problem may not necessarily coincide with the optimum solution to the original placement problem. For direct approaches to tackling the placement problem, including those based on constructive initial placement, iterative placement improvement, pairwise interchange, and branch and bound, the reader may consult the references cited in [46] and [56].

3.4.2 Partitioning

Given a detailed description of the logic design of the entire system, the partitioning problem requires subdivision of the entire system into a hierarchy of subsystems so that constraints of space, external connection requirements of circuits, and other parameters important in packaging the particular technological product are incorporated. In a backplane using integrated circuit technology, for example, an acceptable partition requires the set of blocks (each block consists of one or more gates required for performing logic functions), which are interconnected by nets (each net is a physical connection of electrical conductors that make particular blocks electrically common), to be divided into modules of blocks so that some objectives are met. The objectives could be the minimization of the number of modules, the minimization of the total number of electrical connections between modules rather than the number of such modules, or even the minimization of the maximum delay through the circuit. When the cost of a module is considerably greater than the cost of a block (as, for example, when the modules are LSI chips and the blocks are gates), obviously a lower-cost solution would result from a reduction in the number of modules. Some other constraints, such as the occurrence of feedback loops in one partition or the need for access to certain signals for monitoring purposes, could sometimes outweigh economic considerations.

Consider the situation just alluded to in which the number of modules is more important in cost considerations than the number of blocks. It has been demonstrated that the use of redundant blocks could be helpful for reducing the number of modules in the partitioning phase of layout. When the modules are LSI chips, the pin capacity of the modules limits the number of blocks that can be used to less than the block capacity. If the modules are to be used efficiently, the objective should be to bury as many nets as possible within the modules so that they will not use pins. The algorithms advanced in refs. [327] and [328] to solve the partitioning problem are of a heuristic nature. Usually, the procedure involves several steps. In the first the blocks of the logic design are assigned to groups, and in the second the groups are allocated to modules. The groups are not random collections of blocks but are functional in the sense that the blocks they contain are interconnected and perform the logic function required to generate the outputs given the inputs. The procedure of determining the block members and input nets of a group, given its output nets, is called *group generation.* The output nets are called the *initiate nets.* More than one block may be allocated to a module if the block capacity or pin capacity of the module is not exceeded. However, each group is allocated to only one module. Detailed descriptions of partitioning techniques and references are available in [46] and [56].

3.5 PARALLEL COMPUTATION

There has been a trend in recent years toward using several processors operating in parallel to implement the computational chores in certain algorithms, as opposed to using one central processing unit operating in serial or sequential mode. This remark underscores the fact that many problems do not permit immediate parallelization. A rich body of theoretical results is available to single out problems that are easily parallelizable and those that are not. Just as P is the class of problems that are solvable by algorithms implementable in polynomial sequential time, *NC* denotes the class of problems that can be associated with well-parallelizable algorithms. More precisely, NC represents the class of problems that are solvable by a *polylogarithmic-time algorithm,* which takes $O(\log^k n)$ parallel time for some constant integer k where the problem size is n. Like the uncertainty concerning whether or not P = NP (Section 3.1), the major question in parallel computation involves the resolution of either the truth or falsity of the statement P = NC. It is believed [130] that NC constitutes a proper subclass of P. The boundary between well-parallelizable problems and those that do not appear to admit parallelization readily (such problems are called *hardly parallelizable*) lies somewhere between NC and the class of P-complete problems, defined next.

> **Definition 3.3** **[130].** A problem P_i belonging to the class P is P-complete if every other problem in P can be transformed to P_i in a polylogarithmic parallel time using a polynomial number of processors.

When an algorithm is implementable in polylogarithmic time using a polynomial number of processors, it is called an *efficient algorithm.* Efficient parallel algorithms constitute the subject-matter of a recent text [130], which the interested reader may consult for specific details. In Definition 3.3, P_i is in the subclass of hardest problems in P from the point of view of finding an efficient parallel implementation for its solution. The importance of P-completeness stems from the fact that any problem belonging to this class is hardly parallelizable. The max-flow min-cut problem, described in Section 3.1, is an example of a problem that has been proved [130] to be P-complete. On the other hand, the shortest-path problem, also described in Section 3.1, belongs to class NC. Thus, two different problems, both belonging to class P (and, therefore, solvable by a sequential algorithm implementable in polynomial time), might have different capabilities concerning parallelization. The notion of P-completeness suggests that certain algorithms may be inherently sequential whereas other algorithms for solving problems in the P class by serial computation are also well-parallelizable. Among parallel algorithms, a subclass may be defined to be optimal when the product of the parallel time and the number of processors is linear in the size of any problem belonging to the subclass. The parallel computation thesis suggests a time-complexity and space-complexity trade-off. The hypothesis can be stated in this manner: The class of problems solvable with unbounded parallelism in time complexity that is described by a function of the problem size is equivalent to the class of problems solvable by a sequential or serial computation whose space complexity is described by the same function of the problem size. Thus, sequential space is related to parallel time.

A model for the parallel computer is the P-RAM (parallel random access memory), which has several processors working synchronously and sharing a common random access memory as shown in Fig. 3.22. Each processor is a random access machine with a finite *control* part, which is simply a string from the set of all strings of finite length on the Boolean alphabet {0, 1}, such as a program for a Turing machine, and a list of finitely many *constants,* each of which may be representable with infinite precision. Therefore, both a parallel computer and a serial computer are essentially Turing machines. The differences in the two modes of computation stem from the standpoints of space and time complexities. The motivation behind parallel computer architecture originates from an attempt to mimic the operation of the brain, since different parts of the brain appear to carry out separate and independent sensory functions as described in Chapter 1. Also from that chapter, a neural network

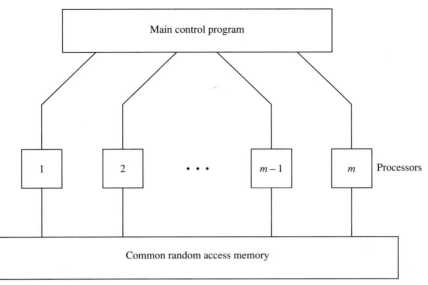

FIGURE 3.22
A model for parallel random access memory (P-RAM) showing several processors working synchronously and sharing a common random access memory.

may be viewed as an extreme case of fine-grain[1] parallel computing architecture with the added features of adaptivity of processor architectures and asynchronicity of processor operations. The processing elements in an artificial neural network operating with a high degree of parallelism are also suited for the implementation of associative memory, as described next.

3.6 ASSOCIATIVE MEMORY

Chapter 1 showed that the mechanism by which the brain stores information is very different from the one by which traditional computers store information, by location and in binary code. Therefore, if an artificial neural network (ANN) is to provide reliable information on the functioning of the brain, it must be capable of distributed storage of information over many units rather than centralized storage in any particular unit. Such storage should be based on the concept that long-term information storage in the brain is a consequence of adaptation in synaptic connections between neurons, whereas the activities of the neurons present the stored patterns. The recall of stored information in the brain relies primarily on associations with other stored data, and this phenomenon leads to the notion of associative memory in an ANN.

---

[1]The *grain size* is measured by the execution time, including both processing time and communication time, of a typical program. Fine grain leads to a much higher degree of parallelism, and also to higher communication overhead, than coarse-grain, medium-grain, and large-grain machines.

Definition 3.4 Associative memory. An associative memory is a system that provides a mapping from a space of inputs to a space of outputs in a way that requires the mapping to be fault-tolerant to either a degree of incompleteness or some acceptable level of noise in each of the input patterns belonging to the space of inputs.

Consider a set of discrete-valued vector pairs, $(\mathbf{x}_i, \mathbf{y}_i)$, $i = 1, 2, \ldots, L$, where $\mathbf{x}_i$ and $\mathbf{y}_i$ are, respectively, r- and p-dimensional vectors in the input and output spaces. The associative memory that stores $(\mathbf{x}_i, \mathbf{y}_i)$, $i = 1, 2, \ldots, L$, must ideally provide $\mathbf{y}_i$ as output not only when $\mathbf{x}_i$ is the input but also when either a noisy version of $\mathbf{x}_i$ or a partial (incomplete) version of $\mathbf{x}_i$ is available as input. When $\mathbf{x}_i = \mathbf{y}_i$, $i = 1, 2, \ldots, L$, the process is referred to as *autoassociative;* otherwise it is *heteroassociative.* Naturally, the desired properties in an associative memory can only be approximated.

3.6.1 The Linear Associator: Solution by Hebbian Rule

Consider the possibility of providing the input/output description of the associative memory through the linear transformation

$$\mathbf{y} = \mathbf{W}\mathbf{x} \tag{3.22}$$

where $\mathbf{y}$ and $\mathbf{x}$ are, respectively, representative vectors from the output and input spaces, whereas $\mathbf{W}$ is a $(p \times r)$ weight matrix that characterizes approximately the associative memory. A learning law due to Hebb [152], described here and in Section 1.3.3, gives the weight matrix under certain restrictions on the input vectors $\mathbf{x}_i$, $i = 1, 2, \ldots, L$. Hebb hypothesized that correlated neuron activities increase the strength of the synaptic link. Thus, the synaptic weight w_{ij} between neurons i and j increases when both neurons emit pulses and decreases in the complementary situation. Consequently, to store a prototype $(\mathbf{x}_i, \mathbf{y}_i)$, one must modify the weight matrix by

$$\Delta \mathbf{W} = \gamma \mathbf{y}_i \mathbf{x}_i^T, \tag{3.23}$$

where γ is a positive learning factor. Therefore, starting from a zero-valued weight matrix, Hebb's rule generates $\mathbf{W}$, which characterizes the associative memory storing $(\mathbf{x}_i, \mathbf{y}_i)$ for $i = 1, 2, \ldots, L$, by the relation

$$\mathbf{W} = \sum_{i=1}^{L} \mathbf{y}_i \mathbf{x}_i^T, \tag{3.24}$$

where the learning factor has been normalized to unity for convenience. When the vectors in the real-valued set $\{\mathbf{x}_1, \mathbf{x}_2, \ldots, \mathbf{x}_L\}$ are orthonormal, i.e.,

$$\mathbf{x}_i^T \mathbf{x}_j = \begin{cases} 1 & i = j, \\ 0 & \text{otherwise}, \end{cases} \tag{3.25}$$

then the prototypes stored in associative memory can be recalled exactly; using Eqs. (3.24) and (3.25), one may easily show that

$$\mathbf{W}\mathbf{x}_k = \mathbf{y}_k \qquad k = 1, 2, \ldots, L. \tag{3.26}$$

The requirement that the set of vectors in input space be orthonormal for exact recall to be possible is very stringent, because the number of vector pairs that can be stored in that case cannot exceed r, the dimension of the input space. Anderson [23] and Kohonen [197] investigated linear associative neural networks. Variants of the Hebbian rule have been proposed [182].

3.6.2 Linear Associator: Solution by Generalized Inverse

An alternative approach to the solution for $\mathbf{W}$ satisfying Eq. (3.26) is obtained by expressing Eq. (3.26) in the form

$$\mathbf{W}[\mathbf{x}_1 \ \mathbf{x}_2 \cdots \mathbf{x}_L] = [\mathbf{y}_1 \ \mathbf{y}_2 \cdots \mathbf{y}_L] \tag{3.27}$$

and then solving the foregoing system of linear equations by the method of generalized inverse. To solve for $\mathbf{W}$ in Eq. (3.27), we require a generalized inverse $\mathbf{G}$ of

$$\mathbf{X} \triangleq [\mathbf{x}_1 \ \mathbf{x}_2 \cdots \mathbf{x}_L]. \tag{3.28}$$

$\mathbf{G}$ is usually nonunique and satisfies the matrix equation

$$\mathbf{XGX} = \mathbf{X}. \tag{3.29}$$

The matrix $\mathbf{G}$ in Eq. (3.29) is sometimes referred to as a *pseudoinverse* to distinguish it from cases in which more constraints are imposed on a generalized inverse than the one conveyed through Eq. (3.29). In fact, a generalized inverse can be made unique by the imposition of certain additional constraints. This unique generalized inverse, called the *Moore-Penrose inverse,* is defined next.

> **Definition 3.5.** A pseudoinverse $\mathbf{G}$ of a complex-valued rectangular matrix $\mathbf{X}$ is called the Moore-Penrose inverse if (*a*) $\mathbf{XGX} = \mathbf{X}$, (*b*) $(\mathbf{XG})^H = \mathbf{XG}$, (*c*) $\mathbf{GXG} = \mathbf{G}$, and (*d*) $(\mathbf{GX})^H = \mathbf{GX}$, where the superscript H (for "Hermitian conjugate") denotes the operation of complex conjugate transpose. Notationally, the Moore-Penrose inverse of $\mathbf{X}$ is denoted by $\mathbf{X}^+$.

The Moore-Penrose inverse is unique, and it gives the minimum-norm least squares solution to any system of linear equations. That is, among all solutions to Eq. (3.27) for $\mathbf{W}$ that minimize the squared error,

$$E(\mathbf{W}) = \sum_{k=1}^{L} [\mathbf{y}_k - \mathbf{W}\mathbf{x}_k]^H [\mathbf{y}_k - \mathbf{W}\mathbf{x}_k],$$

the Moore-Penrose inverse $\mathbf{X}^+$ of $\mathbf{X}$ gives a weight matrix $\mathbf{W}_0 = \mathbf{Y}\mathbf{X}^+$ of minimum norm $\|\mathbf{W}_0\|$ where for $\mathbf{W} = [w_{ij}]$,

$$\|\mathbf{W}\|^2 = \sum_{i=1}^{p} \sum_{j=1}^{r} |w_{ij}|^2.$$

When the matrix $\mathbf{X}$ in Eq. (3.28) is of full rank, $\mathbf{XX}^H$ is nonsingular; and the solution for $\mathbf{W}$ in Eq. (3.27), obtained after computing a pseudoinverse or in this case the Moore-Penrose inverse,

$$\mathbf{X}^+ = \mathbf{X}^H(\mathbf{XX}^H)^{-1} \tag{3.30}$$

of $\mathbf{X}$, is

$$\mathbf{W} = \mathbf{YX}^+ = \mathbf{YX}^H(\mathbf{XX}^H)^{-1} \tag{3.31}$$

where

$$\mathbf{Y} \triangleq [\mathbf{y}_1 \ \mathbf{y}_2 \ \cdots \ \mathbf{y}_L]. \tag{3.32}$$

Note that for most applications of our concern the entries of matrices and vectors are real-valued, the superscript H may be replaced by the notation T for transpose, and Eq. (3.31) is then changed to Eq. (3.33),

$$\mathbf{W} = \mathbf{YX}^+ = \mathbf{YX}^T(\mathbf{XX}^T)^{-1}. \tag{3.33}$$

Note that the Moore-Penrose inverse $\mathbf{X}^+$ of a real-valued matrix $\mathbf{X}$ is expandable as a power series [308, p. 64],

$$\mathbf{X}^+ = \sum_{k=1}^{\infty} \mathbf{X}^T(\mathbf{I} + \mathbf{XX}^T)^{-k} = \lim_{\lambda \to 0^+} \mathbf{X}^T(\lambda\mathbf{I} + \mathbf{XX}^T)^{-1}. \tag{3.34}$$

By substituting Eq. (3.34) into Eq. (3.33), it follows that the solution for the weight matrix obtained from application of the Hebbian rule is derived from the solution using the Moore-Penrose inverse by keeping only the first term in the expansion given in Eq. (3.34).

3.6.3 Implementation of Associative Memory

Different implementations of an associative memory are possible. One popular implementation involves the learnmatrix [371] network shown in Fig. 3.23. The core is a resistive network built as a matrix with r rows and p columns. In addition, there are p thresholding devices from which the components of the p-dimensional output vector emerge. These threshold values are indicated in the figure by $\theta_1, \theta_2, \ldots, \theta_p$. Every resistive element is connected between each row-column junction of the matrix. Thus, there are altogether rp resistors in the learnmatrix network of Fig. 3.23. It is pedagogically useful to describe the topology of the core resistive network by a complete bipartite graph, $K_{r,p}$, as shown in Fig. 3.24, where the nodes in one part are the r row junctions associated with the r rows and the nodes in the other part are the p column junctions associated with the p columns. Each edge in $K_{r,p}$ represents a resistor. The learnmatrix network and its variants, which are characterized by a highly regular and modular architecture that is characteristic of ANN models, are suitable for fabrication using VLSI technology [307].

In the learnmatrix network, the input and output vectors are binary vectors, and the threshold values belong to the set of positive integers. The components of the r-dimensional input vector, $\mathbf{x} = [x_1 \ x_2 \cdots x_r]^T$, are introduced as a set of r

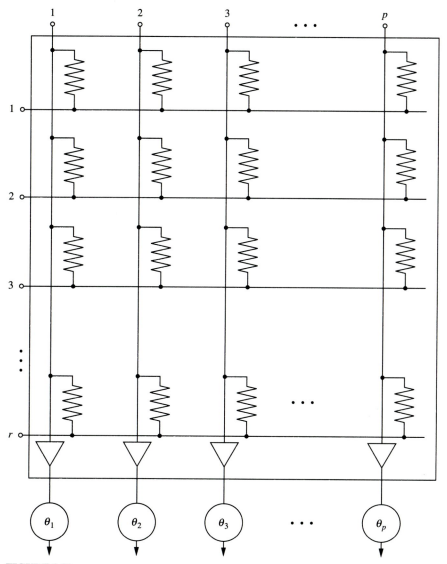

FIGURE 3.23
Implementation of a learnmatrix network.

voltages. The input to the ith threshold unit is given by $\sum_{j=1}^{r} w_{ij} x_j$, where w_{ij} is the conductance of the resistor connecting the ith row to the jth column and is also binary-valued. Note that this implementation realizes an equation that is generated after taking the transpose of both sides of Eq. (3.22). There is no conceptual difference between the presentations here and in Section 3.6.1. The weight matrix here is actually the transpose of the weight matrix in Section 3.6.1 although the same notation **W** is used for both. The output y_i from the ith threshold unit is binary-valued, i.e.,

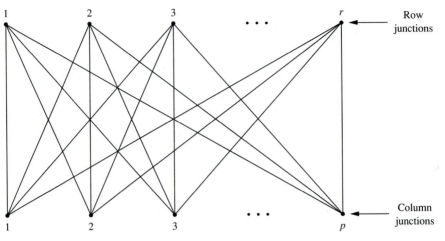

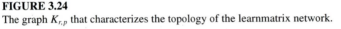

FIGURE 3.24
The graph $K_{r,p}$ that characterizes the topology of the learnmatrix network.

$$y_i = \begin{cases} 1 & \text{if } \sum_{j=1}^{r} w_{ij}x_j \geq \theta_i \\ 0 & \text{otherwise.} \end{cases} \tag{3.35}$$

The storing and recall are done in the following manner. It is required, say, to store the binary vector pairs $(\mathbf{x}_i, \mathbf{y}_i), i = 1, 2, \ldots, L$, whose elements are drawn from the set, $\{0, 1\}$. As before, $\mathbf{x}_i$ and $\mathbf{y}_i$ are, respectively, r-dimensional and p-dimensional vectors. It is assumed that the vector pairs, $(\mathbf{x}_i, \mathbf{y}_i)$, are presented sequentially, starting with $(\mathbf{x}_1, \mathbf{y}_1)$ and ending with $(\mathbf{x}_L, \mathbf{y}_L)$. Let $w_{ij}^{(k)}$ denote the weight connecting the ith row to the jth column after the presentation of $(\mathbf{x}_k, \mathbf{y}_k)$. The initial weights are

$$w_{ij}^{(0)} = 0, \qquad i = 1, 2, \ldots, r \qquad \text{and} \qquad j = 1, 2, \ldots, p. \tag{3.36}$$

The weight update rule is described by the Hebbian rule (see Section 1.3.3) but is implemented with Boolean arithmetic:

$$w_{ij}^{(k)} = w_{ij}^{(k-1)} + (x_{ki} \odot y_{kj}). \tag{3.37}$$

The x_{ki} and y_{kj} are, respectively, the ith component in the vector $\mathbf{x}_k$ and the jth component in the vector $\mathbf{y}_k$, whereas $+$ and $\odot$ denote, respectively, the Boolean sum and Boolean product operations. These are also referred to as the logical sum and logical product operations. Boolean arithmetic is built by deploying the operations on the elements of the set $\{0, 1\}$ according to the following rules:

$$0 + 0 = 0, \qquad 0 + 1 = 1 + 0 = 1, \qquad 1 + 1 = 1,$$

$$0 \odot 0 = 0, \qquad 0 \odot 1 = 1 \odot 0 = 0, \qquad 1 \odot 1 = 1.$$

The weight matrix $\mathbf{W}$ is obtained by repeated application of Eq. (3.37) starting with $k = 1$ and ending with $k = L$,

$$\mathbf{W} = [w_{ij}^{(L)}] \triangleq [w_{ij}]. \tag{3.38}$$

The weight matrix $\mathbf{W}$ here is an $r \times p$ matrix, which after updates with the exemplar pairs $(\mathbf{x}_i, \mathbf{y}_i)$ for $i = 1, 2, \ldots, L$ assumes the final form (applying Boolean arithmetic)

$$\mathbf{W} = \sum_{i=1}^{L} \mathbf{x}_i \mathbf{y}_i^{\mathrm{T}}. \tag{3.39}$$

The recall phase involves the application of an input row vector, say $\mathbf{x}_k = [x_{k1}\ x_{k2} \cdots x_{kr}]^{\mathrm{T}}$, which premultiplies the ith column of $\mathbf{W}$ to yield the ith component $\hat{y}_{ki}$ of a p-dimensional vector $\mathbf{y}_k$.

$$\hat{y}_{ki} = \sum_{j=1}^{r} w_{ji} x_{kj} \qquad i = 1, 2, \ldots, p. \tag{3.40}$$

Note that $\hat{y}_{ki}$ in Eq. (3.40) is computed using ordinary arithmetic instead of Boolean arithmetic. The binary output vector $\mathbf{y}_k$ whose ith component is y_{ki} is obtained by the thresholding rule in Eq. (3.35) for $i = 1, 2, \ldots, p$.

Example 3.6. It is specified that

$$\mathbf{x}_1 = [1\ 0\ 1\ 0\ 1]^{\mathrm{T}}$$
$$\mathbf{y}_1 = [1\ 0\ 0\ 1\ 0]^{\mathrm{T}}$$
$$\mathbf{x}_2 = [1\ 1\ 0\ 1\ 0]^{\mathrm{T}}$$
$$\mathbf{y}_2 = [0\ 1\ 0\ 0\ 1]^{\mathrm{T}}.$$

The associative memory matrix for storing $(\mathbf{x}_1, \mathbf{y}_1)$ and $(\mathbf{x}_2, \mathbf{y}_2)$ is obtained by applying Eqs. (3.36) and (3.37). The reader may verify that $\mathbf{W}^{(1)} \triangleq [w_{ij}^{(1)}]$ and $\mathbf{W}^{(2)} \triangleq [w_{ij}^{(2)}]$ are easily calculated to be

$$\mathbf{W}^{(1)} = \begin{bmatrix} 1 & 0 & 0 & 1 & 0 \\ 0 & 0 & 0 & 0 & 0 \\ 1 & 0 & 0 & 1 & 0 \\ 0 & 0 & 0 & 0 & 0 \\ 1 & 0 & 0 & 1 & 0 \end{bmatrix}$$

$$\mathbf{W}^{(2)} = \begin{bmatrix} 1 & 1 & 0 & 1 & 1 \\ 0 & 1 & 0 & 0 & 1 \\ 1 & 0 & 0 & 1 & 0 \\ 0 & 1 & 0 & 0 & 1 \\ 1 & 0 & 0 & 1 & 0 \end{bmatrix}$$

The preceding result agrees with that obtainable from Eq. (3.39). Note that $L = 2$, implying that the final weight matrix $\mathbf{W}$ is equal to $\mathbf{W}^{(2)}$. In the recall phase, multiply $\mathbf{x}_1^{\mathrm{T}}$ and each column of $\mathbf{W}^{(2)}$ according to Eq. (3.40) to yield

$$\hat{\mathbf{y}}_1 = [\,3\ 1\ 0\ 3\ 1\,]^{\mathrm{T}}.$$

Similarly, on applying $\mathbf{x}_2$, the corresponding elements of the output vector $\hat{\mathbf{y}}_2$ are calculated by Eq. (3.40) to yield

$$\hat{\mathbf{y}}_2 = [\,1\ 3\ 0\ 1\ 3\,]^{\mathrm{T}}.$$

On thresholding all the units at 2, i.e., by setting $\theta_1 = \theta_2 = \theta_3 = \theta_4 = \theta_5 = 2$, the output vectors $\mathbf{y}_1$ and $\mathbf{y}_2$ are obtained from $\hat{\mathbf{y}}_1$ and $\hat{\mathbf{y}}_2$, respectively, by applying Eq. (3.35),

$$\mathbf{y}_1 = [\,1\,0\,0\,1\,0\,]^T$$

$$\mathbf{y}_2 = [\,0\,1\,0\,0\,1\,]^T.$$

Next, suppose that a noisy version of either $\mathbf{x}_1$ or $\mathbf{x}_2$ were applied. Specifically, consider the vector $[\,1\,0\,0\,1\,0\,]^T$, whose Hamming distances from $\mathbf{x}_1$ and $\mathbf{x}_2$ are, respectively, 3 and 1 (the *Hamming distance* between two binary-valued vectors or code words is the number of positions at which they differ). The output vector associated with this input, on application of Eq. (3.40), is $[\,1\,2\,0\,1\,2\,]^T$, which, after thresholding, produces the output vector $[\,0\,1\,0\,0\,1\,]^T$. This happens to be $\mathbf{y}_2$ associated with the input vector $\mathbf{x}_2$, which is closer to the test exemplar according to the distance measure selected. Thus, the noisy version of an input may be associated with the correct output. Note that the choice of threshold may be as crucial as the interconnection weights in the extraction of satisfactory performance from a designed network.

Example 3.6 illustrates how, with the progress of recursion, the weight matrix becomes more and more filled, possibly leading to error in the reliable storage of patterns. The associative memory tends to exhibit "optimal" storage capacity for sparsely coded input/output patterns. The storage capacity is a function of r, p, L, and the number of 1s or active components in the input and output vectors. In the analysis of optimal storage capacity conducted by Palm [282], the number of active components or 1s varies logarithmically in the dimensions (r and p) of the input and output vectors, and the number of patterns L that can be stored is much larger than p.

3.7 CONCLUSIONS

The topics presented in this chapter are concerned with algorithms, their implementation on serial as well as parallel computers, and their classifications in terms of computational complexity of implementation on digital computers. These lead into the concept of associative or content-addressable memory, which provides a simple illustration of collective computation in an artificial neural network.

The popular model for evaluation of computational complexity is the Turing machine. The description of this machine, albeit brief, encompasses important fundamentals needed to cultivate an appreciation of any type of computing, including neurocomputing. In conjunction with the Turing machine, languages and deterministic as well as nondeterministic machines are discussed; algorithms executed by those machines are commonly referred to as deterministic and nondeterministic algorithms. The problem classes P, NP, and NP-complete are defined in terms of the nature of the time bound (polynomial or exponential) and type of machine (deterministic or nondeterministic) required to execute algorithms for solving problems on traditional computers. Problems solvable on deterministic (nondeterministic) machines whose running times are bounded by a polynomial function of the size of inputs belong to P (NP). Problems that are in NP and are at least as hard as every other problem in NP constitute the NP-complete class. The task of constructing an NP-completeness proof for a problem A is difficult in general. It consists of showing that A belongs to NP; selecting a problem B known to be NP-complete; and constructing a polynomial-time transformation from B to A. This will be illustrated in detail in Chapter 6. Although the answer to the question of whether a problem solvable in polynomial time by a nondeterministic algorithm is also solvable in polynomial time by a deterministic algorithm is not in sight, the classifications cited provide impetus for the construction of good suboptimal algorithms to solve problems belonging to the NP-complete class. For computational complexity analysis of algorithms that may be candidates for implementation on parallel computing machines with several processors, the classes NC and P-complete are needed in addition to class P. The outstanding theoretical question here is whether or not P = NC, which if true would imply that all polynomial-time solvable sequential algorithms could be massively parallelized.

Two popular problems, both belonging to class P, are described with illustrative examples. The shortest-path problem also belongs to class NC and, therefore, is well-parallelizable. The max-flow min-cut problem, though in P, also belongs to the P-complete class and is hardly parallelizable. The Achilles heel, with respect to parallel computation, of the algorithm for finding the maximum flow is that it works in stages.

Neural networks, the topic of focus in this text, provide an alternative approach to solving hard combinatorial optimization problems. A number of such hard problems are encountered in layout design of large-scale circuits involving printed circuit board (PCB), integrated circuit (IC), and very large scale integrated circuit (VLSI) technologies. The importance of fabricating neural networks on VLSI chips justifies presentation of some typical hard problems faced in the layout area. Many of these problems have been proved to belong to the NP-complete class and therefore provide alternative arenas for application of neural network structures and principles to achieve satisfactory suboptimum solutions. To wit, the rectilinear Steiner tree problem, which has been encountered in routing and interconnection, was proved to be a member of the NP-complete class [125] and a suboptimal algorithm for its solution was advanced in ref. [219]. The algorithm in the latter reference belongs to the class of greedy algorithms and therefore is not suitable for parallel implementation [130]. Heuristic-based fast suboptimal algorithms for the problem are also available [358, 359]. Several theoretical issues and practical applications of the Steiner problem are discussed in a recent special issue of the journal *Algorithmica* on this topic (vol. 7, no. 2/3, 1992). The readers of this text will find the neural network–based approach to the finding of the SMT to be of interest.[2]

Neurocomputing differs from traditional computing significantly. Address-oriented information storage, which requires precise knowledge of the memory

---

[2]Jayadeva and Basabi Bhaumik. A neural network for the Steiner minimal tree problem. *Biological Cybernetics*, 70:485–494, 1994.

address, is replaced by content-addressable (associative) memory, which permits information recall based on partial knowledge of content without knowing its storage location. The associative memory concept, illustrated by the learnmatrix neural network, and the algorithm for training the network, based on the Hebbian rule, introduce the reader to the possibilities of collective computation in preparation for an in-depth study of a variety of structures that can be trained to perform such computations.

PROBLEMS

3.1. Find the shortest distance from the node labeled v_1 to the node labeled v_n in Fig. P3.1 using the labeling algorithm of Dijkstra and the edge weights marked on the graph.

3.2. Consider the graph shown in Fig P3.2, where each nondirected edge is to be considered as equivalent to two directed edges of equal cost in opposite directions. The weight associated with each edge is marked directly on Fig P3.2. Apply Dijkstra's algorithm to find the length of the of the shortest path for each of the following:

    (*a*) From the node labeled v_1 to the node labeled v_3

    (*b*) From the node labeled v_1 to the node labeled v_4

3.3. Use Dijkstra's labeling algorithm to construct a shortest path from the node labeled v_1 to the node labeled v_2 in Fig. P3.3, where the weight associated with each edge is indicated. Show the permanent labels on the vertices required in the construction of the shortest path by Dijkstra's algorithm. Note that some of the edges in the network are non-oriented.

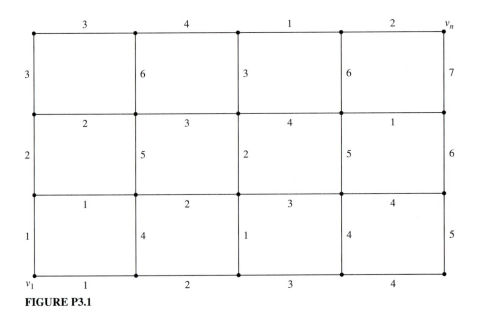

FIGURE P3.1

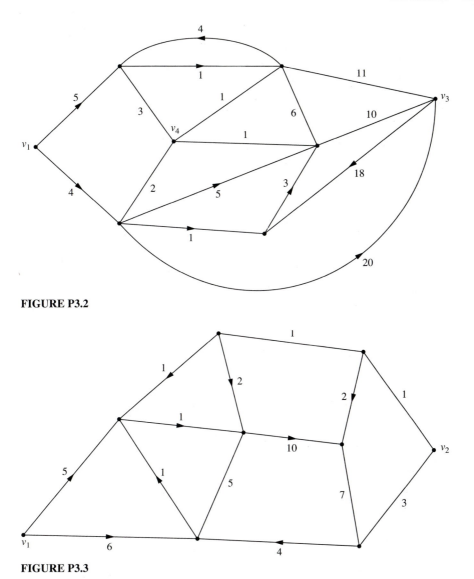

FIGURE P3.2

FIGURE P3.3

3.4. A company has branches in each of six cities, $C_1, C_2, \ldots, C_6$. The fare (in some unspecified unit of currency) for a direct flight from C_i to C_j is given by the (i, j)th entry in the following matrix (∞ indicates that there is no direct flight):

$$
\begin{array}{c@{\quad}cccccc}
 & C_1 & C_2 & C_3 & C_4 & C_5 & C_6 \\
C_1 & 0 & 10 & 30 & 40 & 15 & 20 \\
C_2 & 10 & 0 & \infty & 25 & 10 & \infty \\
C_3 & 30 & \infty & 0 & 15 & 20 & 25 \\
C_4 & 40 & 25 & 15 & 0 & \infty & 80 \\
C_5 & 15 & 10 & 20 & \infty & 0 & 9 \\
C_6 & 20 & \infty & 25 & 80 & 9 & 0
\end{array}
$$

The company is interested in computing a table of cheapest routes between pairs of cities. Prepare such a table.

3.5. Consider the directed communication net shown in Fig. P3.5, where the edge weights are indicated. Using the labeling algorithm for maximum flow assignment, obtain the maximum flow assignment from the source node s to sink node t. Also, identify the minimum cut.

3.6. Consider the directed graph for a transport network shown in Fig. P3.6. The capacity for each edge is marked. Determine the value of the maximum flow from source node s to sink node t.

3.7. Find a minimal spanning tree (MST) for the graph in Fig. P3.7. The edge weights are marked. Name the algorithm you used to obtain your MST and state if this MST is unique.

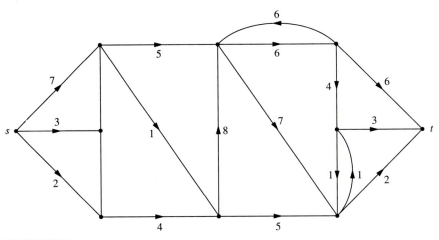

FIGURE P3.5

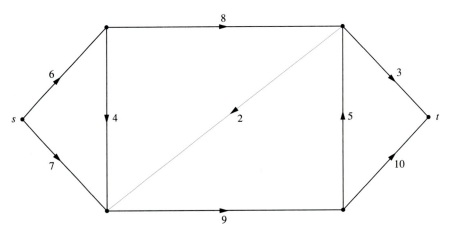

FIGURE P3.6

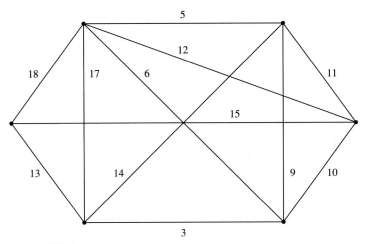

FIGURE P3.7

3.8. Consider Table P3.8 of airline distances in kilomiles between six of the largest cities in the world, namely, London (L), Mexico City (MC), New York (NY), New Delhi (ND), Beijing (Be), and Seoul (Se). After drawing an appropriate graph, determine the length of the route (traced by an edge-sequence) that an airline can follow so that each city may be visited at least once, subject to the constraint that the total number of miles traveled is minimum.

3.9. Three points in the plane constitute the vertices of an equilateral triangle, each of whose sides is of length 10 centimeters.

   (*a*) Calculate the length L_1 of wiring required to connect the three points using a Steiner minimal tree in Euclidean metric.

   (*b*) Calculate the length L_2 of wiring required to connect the three points using a minimal spanning tree in Euclidean metric.

   (*c*) Calculate the ratio L_1/L_2.

3.10. Four points in the plane constitute the vertices of a square, each of whose sides is of length 10 centimeters. The diagonals of this square are parallel to the horizontal and vertical axes.

   (*a*) Calculate the length l_1 of wiring required to connect the four points using a Steiner minimal tree in rectilinear metric.

TABLE P3.8
Airline distance in kilomiles between six cities

	L	MC	NY	ND	Be	Se
L	—	5.6	3.5	4.5	5.1	5.7
MC	5.6	—	2.1	8.9	7.8	7.6
NY	3.5	2.1	—	7.3	6.8	6.9
ND	4.5	8.9	7.3	—	2.5	3.1
Be	5.1	7.8	6.8	2.5	—	0.65
Se	5.7	7.6	6.9	3.1	0.65	—

(b) Calculate the length l_2 of wiring required to connect the four points using a minimal spanning tree in rectilinear metric.

(c) Calculate the ratio, l_1/l_2.

3.11. N.K. Bose and his student J.H. Lee conjectured that for any set of points in a plane the ratio of the lengths of the Steiner minimal tree and the minimal spanning tree in rectilinear metric is never less than the ratio obtained in part (c) of Problem 3.10. This conjecture appeared in Dr. Lee's Ph.D. dissertation, submitted in 1975 to The University of Pittsburgh.[3] The proof of the conjecture appeared in 1976 [172].

(a) Calculate the minimum value of the ratio when the number of points specified on the plane is three if these points be permitted to have arbitrary locations.

(b) Can the value of the ratio, when the number of points located arbitrarily on the plane is 5, equal the value you obtained in part (c) of Problem 3.10?

3.12. In the conjecture named after them, Gilbert and Polak [131] hypothesized in 1968 that for any set of points in a plane, the ratio of the lengths of the Steiner minimal tree and the minimal spanning tree constructed over those points in Euclidean metric is never less than the ratio obtained in part (c) of Problem 3.9. The solution was given 22 years later in ref. [100] and was announced in the *New York Times* on October 30, 1990; a more detailed and easily accessible documentation of the proof has recently appeared.[4] Knowing that the Steiner problem in Euclidean metric belongs to the class of NP-complete problems, give your opinion, with justifications whenever possible, on any impact the solution to the Gilbert-Polak conjecture might have on the design of routers, where interconnection length as well as time complexity in the implementation of algorithms may be of concern.

3.13. A variation of Steiner's problem occurs in printed and integrated circuit technology. Suppose that n electrical junctions are to be connected with the shortest possible length of wire. Moreover, the wires must run in the horizontal and vertical directions. Find the coordinates of the Steiner point or points (if those are necessary) in each of the following cases, where the coordinates of the specified points representing the electrical junctions are given. In each case determine the length of the resulting rectilinear Steiner tree.

(a) $n = 3$; coordinates of the specified points in the plane are $(0, 10)$, $(2, 1)$, and $(3, 4)$

(b) $n = 3$; coordinates of the specified points in the plane are $(0, 10)$, $(2, 10)$, and $(3, 5)$

(c) $n = 4$; coordinates of the specified points in the plane are $(0, 10)$, $(5, 10)$, $(0, 0)$, and $(5, 0)$

(d) $n = 4$; coordinates of the specified points in the plane are $(1, 4)$, $(2, 8)$, $(3, 2)$, and $(4, 12)$

(e) $n = 4$; coordinates of the specified points in the three-dimensional space are $(3, 4, 5)$, $(3, 2, 1)$, and $(-2, 6, 0)$

3.14. Consider the rectangular grid Fig. P3.14, where the grid points are all uniformly spaced and some of their coordinates are explicitly shown. As it is a uniform large grid, only

---

[3]J.H. Lee. Aspects of partitioning and routing of multinets in multilayers. Ph.D. dissertation, completed under the supervision of N.K. Bose, Department of Electrical Engineering, University of Pittsburgh, 1975.

[4]D.Z. Du and F.K. Hwang. A proof of the Gilbert-Polak conjecture on the Steiner problem. *Algorithmica*, 7(2/3): 121–135, 1992.

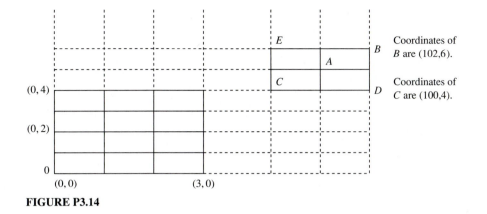

FIGURE P3.14

portions are shown. The grid may be traversed from one grid point to another by restricting movement to the horizontal and vertical directions, i.e., in rectilinear metric. Let the number of shortest paths between the origin 0 and point C be N_C. The coordinates of C are $(100, 4)$.

(a) Find N_C, i.e., write an expression for it, without necessarily evaluating it.

(b) Will the number of shortest paths from 0 to points D and E, respectively, be the same? If yes, justify your answer. If no, which number would be larger?

(c) Find the number of shortest paths between point 0 and point B that *do not* go via point C.

3.15. Answer whether each of the statements below is true or false.

(a) Kruskal's minimal spanning tree (MST) algorithm applies only if the specified edge weights are real and positive.

(b) The length of a Steiner minimal tree (SMT) is always shorter than the length of the corresponding MST no matter what the geometric distribution is of the fixed vertices.

(c) An SMT, when used to connect n fixed vertices in rectilinear metric, is always nonunique when $n \geq 4$.

(d) A full SMT is considered to have the degree of each of its fixed vertices exactly equal to one.

(e) In VLSI chips, pin capacity of the module usually limits the number of blocks that can be used to less than the block capacity.

(f) In VLSI chips, the cost of a module is comparable to the cost of a gate, and so minimization of the number of modules during partitioning is not important.

(g) In the routing of printed circuit boards, the minimum length constraint is always the dominating constraint.

(h) The set of NP-hard problems is a subset of the set of NP-complete problems.

(i) It is required to compute a shortest path between two specified vertices in a graph, each of whose edge weights is real and positive. This shortest path is unique if the edge weights are distinct.

(j) A square matrix whose entries are real and distinct is given. Kuhn's algorithm applied to this matrix yields a linear assignment that is unique.

(*k*) An MST is constructed over a graph of $(n + 1)$ nodes having real and positive edge weights. Suppose that the edge weights of the MST are $l_1, \ldots, l_n$. Then, among all lengths of possible spanning trees in the graph, the length $(l_1 + l_2 + \cdots + l_n)$ is a minimum. Suppose the sum of squares of the edge weights of a spanning tree has to be minimized over all spanning trees of the prescribed graph. This minimum is also attained in the MST, where it assumes the minimum value $l_1^2 + l_2^2 + \cdots + l_n^2$.

(*l*) The statement in part (*k*) also holds when the edge weights are real but allowed to assume negative values.

(*m*) The degree of any Steiner vertex cannot exceed 4 in any SMT using the rectilinear metric in any dimensions.

(*n*) There exists only one SMT in a plane over four specified points when using the Euclidean metric.

(*o*) There exists only one SMT in a plane over three specified points when using the Euclidean metric.

3.16. A cost assignment matrix in a linear assignment problem is specified to be

$$\mathbf{A} = \begin{bmatrix} 4 & 1 & 2 & 3 \\ 2 & 3 & 4 & 5 \\ 3 & 1 & 2 & 6 \\ 8 & 2 & 3 & 6 \end{bmatrix}$$

Apply Kuhn's algorithm to find a minimum cost assignment for this matrix. Is your answer unique?

3.17. The following vector pairs, $(\mathbf{x}_i, \mathbf{y}_i)$ are specified for $i = 1, 2, 3$:

$$\mathbf{x}_1 = [1\,0\,0\,1\,0]^T \qquad \mathbf{y}_1 = [1\,0\,0\,1\,0]^T$$
$$\mathbf{x}_2 = [1\,0\,1\,0\,1]^T \qquad \mathbf{y}_2 = [1\,0\,1\,0\,1]^T$$
$$\mathbf{x}_3 = [1\,1\,0\,0\,1]^T \qquad \mathbf{y}_3 = [1\,1\,0\,1\,0]^T$$

(*a*) With all weights and thresholds specified from the vector pairs provided, find a learnmatrix associative memory by applying the procedure described in the text. Test to see if perfect recall is achievable in this case.

(*b*) Suppose that $\mathbf{x}_1$ is replaced by vectors, each of which is at unity Hamming distance (i.e., the corresponding binary digits in two vectors are not similar at one position) from $\mathbf{x}_1$. Check if the associative memory you designed in part (*a*) is able to associate $\mathbf{y}_1$ with each of the noisy versions of $\mathbf{x}_1$.

(*c*) Change the weight matrix you obtained in part (*a*) so that perfect recall of the specified association is possible with properly selected thresholds. Test for generalizability using the test exemplars in part (*b*) and the weight matrix as well as thresholds for this part.

(*d*) Summarize your observations regarding the possible trade-off between good recall and good generalization.

PART

II

FEEDFORWARD NETWORKS

A feedforward network is characterizable by a directed acyclic graph G, which essentially describes the topological structure of the network. A directed edge of G represents a weighted connection with the signal flowing along the direction of the arrow. The nodes of G comprise source nodes (called *input nodes* because the external inputs are applied here), sink nodes (called *output nodes* because the outputs are processed as well as extracted here), and *hidden* nodes (not directly accessible at either the input or the output, and sometimes called *processing nodes* because computations of interest occur here). Some examples of feedforward networks are shown in Fig. 4.1. The inputs can be either continuous-valued, belonging to a subset of the n-dimensional real Euclidean space $\mathbb{R}^n$, or discrete-valued. One particular case of discrete-valued inputs is binary inputs, which belong to $\{a, b\}^n$, the n-fold Cartesian product of $\{a, b\}$, where a and b are 0 and 1, respectively, in the unipolar case and -1 and 1, respectively, in the bipolar case.

Among feedforward networks is a subclass characterizable by a layered graph, as shown in Figs. 4.1a and 4.1b. This type of feedforward network is also referred to as a layered feedforward network, and the connections are between immediate neighboring or adjacent layers only. The layer that connects to the input signal is called the input layer. The layer that provides the output signal is called the output layer. An intermediate layer does not have direct access to the outside world, i.e., its interaction with the outside world must be through the input or output layer. Therefore, such an intermediate layer is called a *hidden* layer. A layered feedforward network is said to be *fully connected* if its underlying graph is a complete layered graph.

There are two ways to count layers in feedforward networks. One way counts the input layer, whereas the other does not. A unit in the input layer is either a sensor that produces a signal on application of an external stimulus, or simply a "placeholder" that receives a signal and maintains it for a short period of time. In general, the input layer does not perform any significant computation, so it will not be counted as a layer in the convention adopted here; an n-layer network will have $n - 1$ hidden layers and one output layer. In an actual circuit implementation, there may be drivers or linear units that serve as relays. These units are used to realize the high density of connections and have no functional role. To avoid confusion, they are not counted as layers.

In feedforward networks that are not of the layered type, direct connections from the input to any of the intermediate and/or output layers may exist. These connections, illustrated in Fig. 4.1c, are called *shortcut connections*. They are introduced for faster convergence of learning, as will be discussed in Section 5.2.

PROBLEMS TO BE ADDRESSED.   The problems that need to be addressed in feedforward networks include the following:

1. *Scope of representation.* What can and cannot be computed using a feedforward network?
2. *Learnability.* A key motivation for studying neural networks is that they do not require explicit programming. A neural network should learn the desired transformation or extract the rules from preset examples, called *training exemplars*. The learnability problem has two aspects: (*a*) *loading and training* and (*b*) *generalization*. The question of loading has been posed as follows. Given a set of input-output training data and a neural network with a fixed structure, is there a choice of parameters (weights) so that the network will yield the correct input-output mapping for ideally all the training exemplars? If the answer is yes, the training problem seeks to find whether loading can be done in time that is a polynomial function of the dimension of input vectors. Another question is the capability for generalization of the learned solution. The most important measure of successful learning is the degree of correct prediction of outputs when the given inputs do not belong to the set of exemplars used in training. The test inputs are from the same problem and follow the same probability distribution as the exemplars used in training. The important question is summarized next: Assuming that a set of training exemplars is successfully loaded on a given network, with what level

of confidence can we expect valid generalizations, i.e., correct predictions with small probability of error?

3. *Network complexity and physical realizability.* Given a task, how many units and connections are required in a network to achieve the desired loading and generalization property? The size of the network in terms of the number of units and connections should be a polynomial function of the dimension of inputs and outputs. The most severe physical constraint of current VLSI technology is on the number of connections. Also, the range and resolution of the connection weights that can be realized in a network with many connections are limited.

4. *Network synthesis.* The preceding questions are analysis questions. An engineer needs also to face the synthesis question; i.e., given a task, how does one design a network to solve the problem, or how does one map a task to a network structure so as to ensure fast learning, valid generalization, and acceptable network complexity subject to the physical realizability constraints of current technology? What are the design principles? Is it possible to have an algorithm that constructs an optimal or acceptable suboptimal network for a class of tasks?

Most of these questions have been addressed at least in part. Few results are available on the problem of network synthesis.

Feedforward networks are in principle used for pattern classification and recognition and for function approximation. Pattern classification is important in concept learning or concept formation. Engineering applications will be discussed in the last chapter.

PARALLEL AND LOCAL COMPUTATION. An important motivation for studying neural networks is the need to construct fast approximate solutions to hard problems by a network of simple processors operating in parallel, with each providing local and partial solutions. This translates to limiting the connections of each unit to units within a certain neighborhood or to bounding the number of connections between units by a certain constant. Complete connections, where every unit is connected to every other unit, or full connections, where a unit is connected to every input unit and/or units in adjacent layers, should be avoided. This statement applies to all types of neural networks and is an important issue that Minsky and Papert [261] raised. It has practical implication in the realizability of neural networks using existing technology. Many researchers seemingly have overlooked this problem. Most of the results discussed in the literature use fully connected feedforward networks or completely connected recurrent networks. Exceptions to the last statement can be found in a recently published analysis [329] of ill-conditioning during training in fully connected and sparsely connected layered networks.

CHAPTER
4

PERCEPTRONS AND THE LMS ALGORITHM

The perceptron was among the first and simplest learning machines that are trainable. The mode of training is supervisory, because the steps in the algorithm involve the comparison of actual outputs with desired outputs associated with the set of training patterns. Supervisory training applies as well to the LMS (least mean square) algorithm, also discussed in this chapter. The LMS algorithm was developed for adaptive systems research geared toward diverse applications, including noise cancellation and adaptive equalization. Accompanying the structural simplicity of the perceptron is a powerful convergence theorem. Notwithstanding the importance, originality, and applicability of perceptrons, they have limitations; analysis in the setting of mathematical logic indicates that the causes of such limitations are linked to the architecture of the perceptron and the nature of the problems to be learned.

In general, a perceptron is *not* a single TLU, because it also has a layer of fixed processing units. A single TLU, sometimes called a one-unit single-layer perceptron, is just a special case of the perceptron when each of the fixed processing units is assigned the identity transfer characteristic. In this book, the term *perceptron* denotes the class of two-layer feedforward networks (*a*) whose first-layer units have fixed functions with fixed connection weights from the inputs and (*b*) whose connection weights linking this first layer to the second layer of outputs are learnable, together with the thresholds of the units in that output layer. We use the phrase *multilayer learning networks* to denote feedforward networks that have more than one layer of learnable parameters.

It is often said that a perceptron cannot compute the exclusive-OR (XOR) function. This is actually not the case. With the right processing layer, a perceptron can compute XOR or even its more general form, the parity function. However, the number of connections in the processing layer must satisfy the order condition to be discussed in Section 4.3. This order condition applies not only to perceptrons but also to multilayer learning networks (Chapter 5). The difference between a perceptron and a multilayer learning network is that the perceptron learning algorithm is incapable of searching for the right processing layer. But without the right connections required by the order of the function, a multilayer learning network cannot learn the XOR function either.

First, we introduce the reader to the perceptron and the learning rules associated with it in Section 4.1, where the perceptron convergence theorem is also proved for a class of training exemplars. Subsequently, the LMS algorithm is discussed in Section 4.2, where attention is directed to stringent conditions that must be satisfied for this algorithm to converge. In Section 4.3, some general properties of linear predicate families that apply to a perceptron, independent of the problem being tackled, are briefly presented. The important concept of order, introduced in Section 4.3, is useful not only to perceptrons *but also to multilayer trainable networks* discussed in Chapter 5. Illustrative examples in the text and the exercises at the end of the chapter will contribute to the readers' comprehension of the important concepts discussed.

4.1   ROSENBLATT'S PERCEPTRON

The perceptron, first introduced in the late 1950s [320, 321] by Frank Rosenblatt at Cornell University, is a two-layer feedforward network of threshold logic units (TLUs), as illustrated in Fig. 4.1*a*. The TLUs in the first layer have fixed connection weights and thresholds and are sparsely connected to inputs, which constitute the *retina*. The second layer consists of a single TLU with trainable connection weights from the first-layer units and threshold, where those parameters are adjustable using training exemplars. Rosenblatt's perceptron evolved as the merger of two concepts proposed during the 1940s. The first of these was due to McCulloch and Pitts [250], who proposed a threshold logic model for neurons as described in Chapter 1. However, the McCulloch-Pitts network used fixed weights and thresholds. The second concept was the proposal by Hebb [152] that learning is realized through changes in the synapses between neurons. As a student at Cornell the senior author of the present text was fortunate to know Dr. Rosenblatt, a truly remarkable pioneer, during the 1960s, when more criticism was being heaped on the perceptron for its limitations than it deserved. The pessimistic attitude that prevailed discouraged many from entering the field and generalizing the concept of the perceptron to multilayer feedforward networks. The latter was not done until after a gap of more than a decade; note, however, that unlike the algorithm for training the perceptron, the popular backpropagation algorithm, described later, for training multilayer feedforward networks, cannot be guaranteed to converge.

In the general case the perceptron is not just a single TLU connected directly to the inputs. Actually, it has two layers of computation units, although the functions computed by the first layer are not learnable but fixed. Only the weights

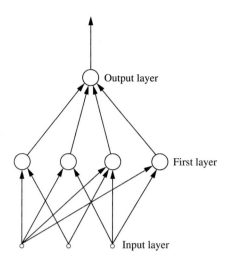

(*a*)

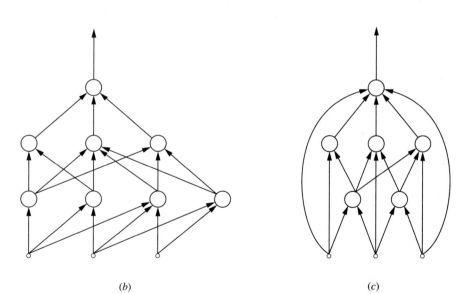

(*b*)   (*c*)

FIGURE 4.1
Examples of feedforward networks: (*a*) two-layer, (*b*) multilayer, (*c*) nonlayered with shortcut connections.

to the second-layer single TLU are learnable. In this sense, the first layer is not a hidden layer, because it has been exposed to the inputs by fixed connections. The first layer performs a fixed transform on the inputs. If the inputs are applied directly to the trainable TLU, it is a single-TLU perceptron. A single-TLU perceptron, which is a single-layer perceptron, is just a special case of the perceptron in which the first-layer units each have the transfer characteristic of identity. In this book, perceptrons are two-layer feedforward networks whose first-layer units have fixed functions and whose second-layer parameters alone are learnable. Multilayer feedforward networks are feedforward networks that have more than one layer of learnable weights.

Researchers initially hoped that the perceptron would be capable of computing any function using locally connected first-layer units and that the number of connections and units in the network would scale at most as a polynomial function of the size of the retina. The task of computing the function could then be decomposed into simpler tasks on portions of the inputs, allowing their execution in parallel. In that case, the function could be computed faster using resources that scale as a polynomial function of the retina size. In this chapter the reader will see that even functions that are not very complex cannot be so computed. This is not only true for perceptrons; it is also true for multilayer feedforward networks.

4.1.1   Definitions

Let $\mathbf{R} = \{x_1, x_2, \ldots, x_n\}$ be a set of n real variables x_i, $i = 1, 2, \ldots, n$, defined over an n-dimensional finite subspace in $\mathbb{R}^n$. The components of $\mathbf{R}$ are sometimes arranged as a two-dimensional array that is referred to as a *retina*.

A *predicate* or *decision function,* which has two possible values represented either by linguistic or numerical variables, is defined on $\mathbf{R}$. Thus, the representations could be TRUE and FALSE, HIGH and LOW, 1 and 0, 1 and -1, or any other set of two distinct real numbers or symbols.

Definition 4.1. Let $\mathbf{\Phi}$ be a family of M (partial) functions defined on the elements of $\mathbf{R}$. Then Ψ is a *linear threshold function* (LTF) with respect to $\mathbf{\Phi}$ if there exists a set of coefficients $\{w_i\}_{i=1}^{M+1}$ such that

$$\Psi(\mathbf{x}) = T_b\left(\sum_{i=1}^{M} w_i\phi_i(\mathbf{x}) + w_{M+1}\right) = T_b\left(\sum_{i=1}^{M} w_i y_i + w_{M+1}\right) \tag{4.1}$$

for $\mathbf{x} = \{x_i, \ldots, x_k\} \subseteq \mathbf{R}$ with $1 \le i \le k \le n$, $y_i = \phi_i(\mathbf{x}) \in \Phi$,

$$T_b(x) = \begin{cases} 1 & \text{if } x > 0 \\ \alpha & \text{if } x \le 0, \end{cases} \tag{4.2}$$

where α may be 0, -1, or a small positive number. The parameter $\theta = -w_{M+1}$ is called the *threshold,* which is the negative of the *bias,* w_{M+1}. Sometimes the expression

$$\Psi(\mathbf{x}) = T_b\left(\sum_{i=1}^{M+1} w_i\phi_i(\mathbf{x})\right)$$

is used, with the understanding that $\phi_{M+1}(\mathbf{x}) = 1$.

In Eq. (4.2) the inequality $>$ may be replaced by $<$, $\le$, or $\ge$, with associated changes, needed to realize a dichotomy, for the other inequality in the same equation.

To reinforce this flexibility and arbitrariness, the choice here is different from that used to define the characteristic of a TLU in Eq. (1.1) of Chapter 1.

Note that $\mathbf{x}$ need not contain every variable in $\mathbf{R}$; that is, $\mathbf{x}$ may be a proper subset of $\mathbf{R}$. The ϕ_i's are called *partial functions* because they involve only part of the computation required for Ψ and are usually simpler than Ψ. The partial functions may be any real, single-valued, and linearly independent set of functions. These functions may be predicate functions; they could also be *identity transforms*, i.e., $y_i = \phi_i(\mathbf{x}) = x_i$.

Sometimes we use the notation $\Psi(\mathbf{x}) = [statement]$ to denote a predicate function, where $[statement]$ denotes that the output is 1 when the statement is true and it is either 0 or -1 otherwise. If a predicate function assumes values from the set $\{0,1\}$, it is said to be *unipolar binary;* if from $\{-1,1\}$, it is said to be *bipolar binary.*

If each component of the set $\mathbf{R}$ is a unipolar binary variable, so that $\mathbf{x} \in \{0,1\}^n$, the logical operations involving $\{x_1, x_2, \ldots, x_n\}$ can be expressed in arithmetic form. The union, intersection, and exclusive-OR logical operations denoted by $\cup$, $\cap$, and $\oplus$, respectively, are expressed in the following arithmetic forms:

$$\bigcup_i x_i \quad \text{is expressed as } T_b\left(\sum_i x_i\right)$$

$$\bigcap_i x_i \quad \text{is expressed as } T_b\left(\prod_i x_i\right)$$

$$x_1 \oplus x_2 \quad \text{is expressed as } T_b[x_1(1 - x_2) + (1 - x_1)x_2].$$

Such arithmetic forms of binary logical functions will be used throughout this book.

The set of all LTFs with a given $\mathbf{\Phi}$ is denoted by $L(\mathbf{\Phi})$. It is easy to see that any $\Psi \in L(\mathbf{\Phi})$ can be computed by a TLU (McCulloch-Pitts neuron) with M inputs $\{y_i\}_{i=1}^M = \{\phi_i(\mathbf{x})\}_{i=1}^M$, properly chosen weights $\{w_i\}_{i=1}^M$, and threshold $-w_{M+1}$. Such a TLU is a special case of a perceptron, which is formally defined next.

Definition 4.2. A *perceptron* is a feedforward network that has one layer of fixed processing units and a trainable TLU and is capable of computing any $\Psi \in L(\mathbf{\Phi})$ for a given $\mathbf{\Phi}$ by adjusting the weights and threshold of its trainable TLU. The fixed processing units computing $\phi_i \in \mathbf{\Phi}$ may be realized by any fixed device.

Note that if the partial function ϕ_i is a predicate, it may be computed by TLUs as well. Such preprocessing TLUs, however, have *fixed* weights and thresholds. It is possible to include more than one TLU in the output layer of a perceptron. The important point in the definition of the perceptron architecture is that only the connections from the layer of fixed processing units to the unit (or units) in the output layer directly above it, and possibly the thresholds of the output unit (or units), are trainable. Again, note that the underlying graph characterizing a perceptron is not required to be layered in the foregoing definition, because fixed connection weights from the inputs to the output layer, as in Fig. 4.1c, could be permitted.

4.1.2   Linear Separability of Training Patterns

In this section it is assumed that every input $\mathbf{x}$ contains all the variables in $\mathbf{R}$. There-fore, an input $\mathbf{x}$ can be denoted as an n-dimensional vector $\mathbf{x} = (x_1 \, x_2 \cdots x_n)^T \in \mathbb{R}^n$. An input vector is called a *pattern,* an *exemplar,* or a *sample,* and the n-dimensional space $\mathbb{R}^n$ is called a *pattern space.* Suppose that there are M neurons in the first layer. The output from the jth neuron in this layer is denoted by

$$y_j = \phi_j(\mathbf{x}) \qquad \text{for } j = 1, 2, \ldots, M.$$

The vector $(y_1 \, y_2 \cdots y_M)^T = \mathbf{\Phi}(\mathbf{x}) = (\phi_1(\mathbf{x}) \, \phi_2(\mathbf{x}) \cdots \phi_M(\mathbf{x}))^T$, which is the input vector to the trainable TLU, is called a *first-layer image pattern.* It represents the image of the original pattern $\mathbf{x}$ in the space $\mathbb{R}^M$ with $\phi_1(\mathbf{x}), \phi_2(\mathbf{x}), \ldots, \phi_M(\mathbf{x})$ as the coordinate axes. The space to which the image patterns belong is called the *image pattern space,* or the first-layer *image space.* The mapping $\mathbf{\Phi}(\mathbf{x}) : \mathbb{R}^n \longrightarrow \mathbb{R}^M$ from the original pattern space (referred to as the *feature space*) to the image pattern space, as illustrated in Fig. 4.2, is nonlinear.

A surface that separates the patterns into different classes is called a *decision surface.* Patterns belonging to one class all lie on one side of the decision surface, and patterns belonging to the other class lie on the other side of the decision surface. In the case of a perceptron, the decision surface is the hyperplane defined in the image pattern space by

$$\sum_{i=1}^{M} w_i y_i + w_{M+1} = 0.$$

A perceptron categorizes a set of image patterns into two classes according to whether $\sum_{i=1}^{M} w_i y_i + w_{M+1} > 0$ or $\sum_{i=1}^{M} w_i y_i + w_{M+1} < 0$, and the hyperplane in

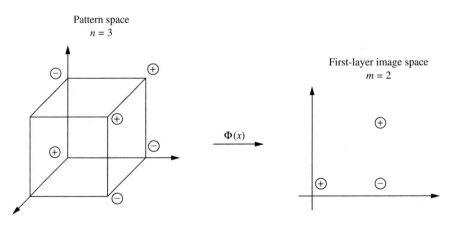

FIGURE 4.2
A nonlinear map transforms not linearly separable patterns in the original pattern (feature) space to linearly separable patterns in the image space.

that case is called a *linear dichotomy*. A linear threshold function then defines *linear separability* of the image patterns $\{(\phi_1(\mathbf{x})\,\phi_2(\mathbf{x})\cdots\phi_M(\mathbf{x}))^{\mathrm{T}} \mid \mathbf{x} \subseteq \mathbf{R}\}$ in the image pattern space.

Given the dimension of an image pattern space and a set of image patterns, what is the likelihood that the image patterns are linearly separable in the image pattern space? In other words, how effective is a perceptron as a pattern classifier? Given N binary image patterns in $\mathbb{R}^M$, there are a total of 2^N distinct classifications of these patterns into two categories (*dichotomies*). The reader can verify that the number of linear dichotomies of N image patterns achievable by a perceptron that has M processing units in the first layer (and an output TLU with M trainable connection weights and a trainable bias w_{M+1}) is

$$L(N, M) = \begin{cases} 2\sum_{i=0}^{M}\binom{N-1}{i} & \text{for } N > M + 1 \\ 2^N & \text{for } N \le M + 1 \end{cases} \tag{4.3}$$

if the image patterns are in *general positions*. When $N > M$, N points are in general positions in an M-dimensional space if and only if no $(M + 1)$ points lie on an $(M - 1)$-dimensional hyperplane. When $N \le M$, N points are in general positions if no $(M - 2)$-dimensional hyperplane contains all the points. Therefore, the probability $p_{N,M}$ that a dichotomy chosen at random will be computable by a perceptron with given $(\phi_1\,\phi_2\,\cdots\,\phi_M)^{\mathrm{T}}$ is

$$p_{N,M} = \frac{L(N, M)}{2^N} = \begin{cases} 2^{1-N}\sum_{i=0}^{M}\binom{N-1}{i} & \text{for } N > M + 1 \\ 1 & \text{for } N \le M + 1. \end{cases} \tag{4.4}$$

In Fig. 4.3, plots of this probability function versus the nonnegative real-valued parameter λ with $N = \lambda(M + 1)$ are shown. For any value of M and $\lambda = 2$,

$$p_{2(M+1),M} = \tfrac{1}{2}. \tag{4.5}$$

As M increases, the probability function tends to a threshold function with threshold at $\lambda = 2$. That is, for any small real positive number ϵ,

$$\lim_{M \to \infty} p_{(2+\epsilon)(M+1)} = 0 \tag{4.6}$$

$$\lim_{M \to \infty} p_{(2-\epsilon)(M+1)} = 1. \tag{4.7}$$

These limits mean that if $0 < N < 2(M + 1)$, a perceptron given in Eq. (4.1) will correctly classify the N image patterns with asymptotic probability 1, as $M \to \infty$. In other words, for large M, a perceptron with $M + 1$ parameters can almost certainly achieve any dichotomy of fewer than $2(M + 1)$ image patterns. On the other hand, it will almost certainly fail to achieve any dichotomy of more than $2(M + 1)$ image patterns. This statement leads us to define the *capacity C* of a perceptron with $M + 1$ parameters by

$$C = 2(M + 1). \tag{4.8}$$

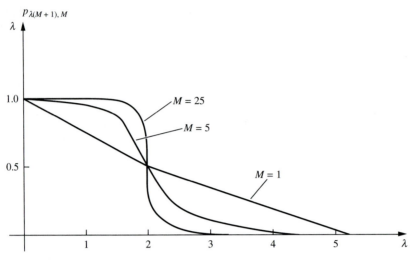

FIGURE 4.3
Plots of the probability function $p_{N,M}$ in Eq. (4.4) versus the parameter λ for three choices
of M, with $N = (\lambda)(M + 1)$.

Note that N is not the number of patterns in the original pattern (feature) space;
it is the number of patterns of the generic type $(y_1\ y_2 \cdots y_M)^T$ in the image space.
Let the number of patterns in the original pattern space be N_0. It is easy to see that
$N \le N_0$ (why?). Recall that the preceding discussion is given in the image pattern
space, where all image patterns are represented by the vertices of an M-dimen-
sional hypercube, because the first-layer TLUs have only binary-valued states.
Also, the preceding discussion applies to N image patterns in an M-dimensional
space provided that the representations of those patterns are in general positions
(implying that no subset of $M + 1$ vertices lies in the same $(M - 1)$-dimensional
face).

   If the patterns in the original pattern space are linearly separable, a single trainable TLU or, in other words, a perceptron with each first-layer unit having identity
transfer characteristic, $y_i = \phi_i(\mathbf{x}) = x_i$, $i = 1, 2, \ldots, n$, will be able to classify the
patterns. If they are not linearly separable, the first layer is needed to map the patterns into an image space where they may become linearly separable. The mapping
performed by the first-layer units must be nonlinear to achieve this (why?). The first
layer may use two mechanisms to achieve this mapping from not linearly separable
to linearly separable distributions. One way is by increasing the dimension of the
image space, and the other way is by reducing the number of patterns in the image space. The former is achieved by increasing M. The latter can be achieved by
mapping multiple patterns in the same class to one image pattern, i.e., by reducing
N. Both methods increase the probability that patterns in the image space will be
linearly separable.

Example 4.1. The predicate function XOR, $\Psi(x_1, x_2) = x_1 \oplus x_2$, cannot be computed with a single TLU. If x_1 and x_2 represent features, the XOR problem is equivalent to a pattern classification problem in the two-dimensional feature space that requires unipolar binary patterns $(0,1)$ and $(1,0)$ to belong to one class, and patterns $(0,0)$ and $(1,1)$ to belong to another class. This requirement cannot be achieved by a single straight line, as shown in Fig. 4.4a. Note that by Eq. (4.8) the capacity of a two-input single TLU is 6 and the number of patterns in this case is only 4. Although the number of patterns is less than the capacity of the perceptron, the patterns are still not linearly separable. (From the definition of capacity, a perceptron with three parameters can almost certainly achieve any dichotomy of fewer than six image patterns. This seems to be a contradiction. Justify this.)

In the single-TLU case the two partial functions are the identity functions, $\phi_1(x_1) = x_1$ and $\phi_2(x_2) = x_2$. If we expand $\mathbf{\Phi}$ to include $\phi_3(x_1, x_2) = T_b(x_1 x_2 - 0.5)$, the image space becomes three-dimensional. The patterns mapped into the image space are shown in Fig. 4.4b. It is obvious that they are linearly separable. The architecture of a network capable of realizing the predicate function using this set of partial functions is shown in Fig. 4.4c. You can set values for connection weights in this figure that will enable the network to synthesize the XOR function. Note that the thresholds of the units are zero, because fixed, unity inputs are allowed. The capacity of this perceptron is $2 \times (3 + 1) = 8$.

Another way is to change the partial functions to $\phi_1(x_1, x_2) = T_b(x_2 - x_1 x_2 - 0.5)$ and $\phi_2(x_1, x_2) = T_b(x_1 - x_1 x_2 - 0.5)$. The patterns mapped into the image space are shown in Fig. 4.4d. Patterns $(0,0)$ and $(1,1)$ in feature space are mapped to the same point, namely, the origin $(0,0)$ of the image space. The number of patterns is reduced to three, and they become linearly separable in this image space. A perceptron that realizes the predicate function using this set of partial functions is shown in Fig. 4.4e. Again, you can set values for connection weights in this figure that will enable the network to synthesize the XOR function. The capacity of this perceptron, like that of a two-input single TLU in the first case, is 6. However, the patterns are now linearly separable.

The mapping patterns in multilayer trainable TLU networks will be discussed in greater detail in Chapter 5.

Nonlinear analog preprocessing. The partial functions in Example 4.1 are realized using TLUs. Nonlinear analog units may also be used in the first layer. In the image pattern space, these lead to an increase in the dimension of the image space with a corresponding increase in the capacity of the machine. In the feature space, nonlinear analog units permit realization of a smooth nonlinear decision surface instead of piecewise linear decision surfaces in the case where only TLUs are used in the first layer. One class of useful nonlinear preprocessors is made up of the polynomial functions. That is, the partial function $\phi_i(\mathbf{x})$ is a monomial of the form

$$\phi_i(\mathbf{x}) = x_1^{k_1} x_2^{k_2} \cdots x_n^{k_n}, \tag{4.9}$$

where k_j for $j = 1, 2, \ldots, n$ could be any finite nonnegative integer. Shown in Fig. 4.5 is a network that can realize any quadratic decision surface, generated by a bivariate second-degree polynomial, in the original pattern space by using analog first-layer units.

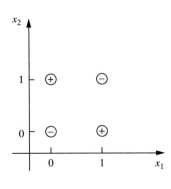

(a)

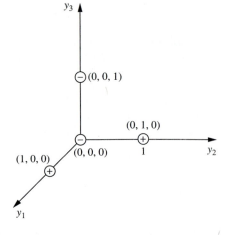

(b)

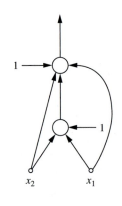

(c)

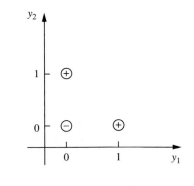

(d)

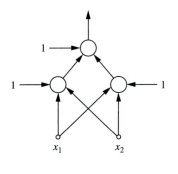

(e)

FIGURE 4.4

The various figures in Example 4.1. The axes in (*a*) and (*d*) are labeled in the manner indicated to avoid clutter. The labelings of the coordinates in (*b*) remove ambiguity and also promote notational brevity. Networks in (c) and (e) can realize the XOR function.

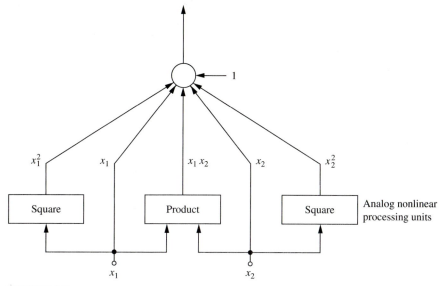

FIGURE 4.5
Analog network for realizing any quadratic decision surface in the two input variables, x_1 and x_2. The connection weights are not shown.

4.1.3   Perceptron Learning Algorithms

We have shown that a perceptron can implement various decision functions by adjusting the weights and threshold of its trainable TLU. The next question is how to determine the weights and threshold in a given problem. The neural network approach involves parameter learning from examples, rather than explicit programming. Prescribed are a set of input patterns whose classifications are known. This set, called the training sample set or training exemplar set, will be used to determine the parameters.

Let the training exemplar set be $\{\mathbf{x}(i)\}_{i=1}^{N}$ where i is the index associated with the ith training pattern. For simplicity, suppose that these exemplars are members of either of two known classes, C_+ and C_-. Let the value of the real-valued variable d_i determine the class to which $\mathbf{x}(i)$ belongs. If $\mathbf{x}(i) \in C_+$, then $d_i > 0$, and if $\mathbf{x}(i) \in C_-$, then $d_i < 0$.

The inputs to the trainable TLU are elements of the column vectors $\mathbf{y}(i) = (\phi_1(\mathbf{x}(i))\ \phi_2(\mathbf{x}(i))\ \cdots\ \phi_M(\mathbf{x}(i))\ 1)^{\mathrm{T}}$, obtained by appending 1 to the end of each image pattern vector so as to enable the threshold to be learned in the same way as a weight. An image pattern vector with 1 appended is sometimes referred to as the *augmented image pattern vector* that belongs to the augmented image pattern space. In the network the appended 1 is realizable, as was shown earlier, by an additional weighted connection from a constant unity-valued input. The threshold of the TLU is then set to zero. The equivalent threshold is the negative of the weight, w_{M+1}, of this additional connection, i.e., $\theta = -w_{M+1}$. If the inputs $\{x_i\}_{i=1}^{n}$ are connected directly to the trainable TLU without the first layer, then the generic $\mathbf{y}(i)$ is definable directly in terms of the inputs as $\mathbf{y}(i) = (x_1 \ x_2 \ \cdots \ x_n \ 1)$ (the index i is eliminated in the right-hand side to avoid notational clutter), so that $M = n$.

The parameter estimation or training problem involves finding a solution weight vector $\mathbf{w}^\mathsf{T} = (w_1 \ w_2 \ \cdots \ w_M \ w_{M+1})$, either exactly (if a solution exists) or approximately (subject to an error criterion), such that

$$\mathbf{Sw} = \mathbf{d},$$

where

$$
\mathbf{S} = \begin{bmatrix}
\phi_1(\mathbf{x}(1)) & \cdots & \phi_M(\mathbf{x}(1)) & 1 \\
\phi_1(\mathbf{x}(2)) & \cdots & \phi_M(\mathbf{x}(2)) & 1 \\
\vdots & \ddots & \vdots & \vdots \\
\phi_1(\mathbf{x}(N)) & \cdots & \phi_M(\mathbf{x}(N)) & 1
\end{bmatrix}, \quad
\mathbf{w} = \begin{bmatrix} w_1 \\ \vdots \\ w_M \\ w_{M+1} \end{bmatrix}, \quad
\mathbf{d} = \begin{bmatrix} d_1 \\ d_2 \\ \vdots \\ d_N \end{bmatrix}. \quad (4.10)
$$

Equation (4.10) can be solved using the pseudoinverse of $\mathbf{S}$. When $N > M + 1$ and the matrix $\mathbf{S}$ is of full rank, it is easy to verify that

$$\mathbf{w} = (\mathbf{S}^\mathsf{T}\mathbf{S})^{-1}\mathbf{S}^\mathsf{T}\mathbf{d} = \mathbf{S}^+\mathbf{d}, \tag{4.11}$$

where $\mathbf{S}^+$ denotes the Moore-Penrose inverse, which was defined in Section 3.6.2 as the minimum-norm least squares generalized inverse. When $\mathbf{S}$ is not of full rank, this pseudoinverse can always be obtained in the limit [308, p. 64] as

$$\mathbf{S}^+ = \lim_{\epsilon \to 0^+} \left(\mathbf{S}^\mathsf{T}\mathbf{S} + \epsilon\mathbf{I}\right)^{-1}\mathbf{S}^\mathsf{T}. \tag{4.12}$$

The foregoing solution minimizes the mean square error in Eq. (4.13) and is unique by virtue of the fact that among all such least mean squares (LMS) solutions of the inconsistent system of equations in Eq. (4.10) it yields one having minimum norm. The mean squared error is

$$e^2 = \frac{1}{N}\|\mathbf{d} - \mathbf{Sw}\|^2 = \frac{1}{N}(\mathbf{d} - \mathbf{Sw})^\mathsf{T}(\mathbf{d} - \mathbf{Sw}). \tag{4.13}$$

The computation of the pseudoinverse matrix can cause problems if the determinant of $\mathbf{S}^\mathsf{T}\mathbf{S}$ is vanishingly small, i.e., if $\mathbf{S}^\mathsf{T}\mathbf{S}$ is ill-conditioned. Also, the network must have simultaneous access to all the training patterns in order for it to be able to compute the pseudoinverse.

Since the first-layer units in a perceptron are fixed, we shall discuss the perceptron learning algorithm for a single trainable TLU to simplify the presentation. For the general case, one only needs to consider the first-layer image patterns as the training patterns. Before introducing the perceptron learning algorithm, we introduce a *dual space* of the augmented (first-layer image) pattern space containing the augmented pattern vector $\mathbf{y}(i)$. This dual space, called the *weight space,* is an $(M + 1)$-dimensional space, each of whose coordinates represents a weight. A particular choice of the weights is represented by a point in this weight space. The weights can also be represented by a vector $\mathbf{w}$ from the origin of the weight space to the point. For a pattern vector $\mathbf{y}$ there is a hyperplane in the weight space defined by

$$\mathbf{w} \cdot \mathbf{y} = 0, \tag{4.14}$$

whose left-hand side is described by the inner product, $\mathbf{w}^T\mathbf{y}$, of the real-valued vectors $\mathbf{w}$ and $\mathbf{y}$. This hyperplane is called the *pattern hyperplane*. Each pattern hyperplane divides the weight space into two half-spaces, referred to as the positive and negative half-spaces. Weight points representing weight vectors in the positive half-space produce a TLU output of $+1$, whereas those in the negative half-space produce a TLU response of either 0 or -1. If the training patterns are linearly separable, there exists at least one weight vector $\mathbf{w}$ such that

$$\begin{aligned} \mathbf{w} \bullet \mathbf{y} > 0 \qquad &\text{for each } \mathbf{y} \in C_+ \\ \mathbf{w} \bullet \mathbf{y} < 0 \qquad &\text{for each } \mathbf{y} \in C_-. \end{aligned} \qquad (4.15)$$

For each training pattern, there is a corresponding pattern hyperplane in the weight space, and all the points on one side of the hyperplane will produce the desired TLU output for the given training pattern. Call this half-space the *solution region* for the given pattern. If the intersection of the solution regions for all the training patterns is nonempty, then there is a solution to the classification problem. This region of intersection is called the problem solution region, and any weight point in this region will satisfy the inequalities in Eq. (4.15). It is easy to show that the solution region, if it exists, is a convex polyhedral cone with its vertex at the origin. These concepts are illustrated in Fig. 4.6.

The perceptron learning (training) algorithm is an iterative procedure that updates its weights using one training exemplar at a time. In a network with

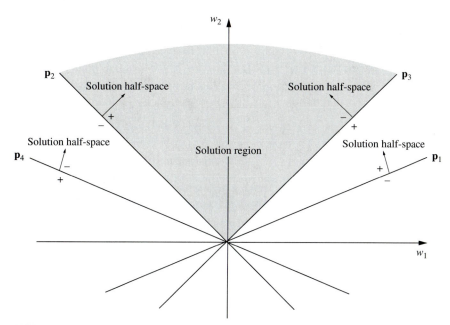

FIGURE 4.6
The solution region corresponding to the region of intersection of the half-spaces in weight space. The $+$ and $-$ signs next to each line indicate the positive and negative half-spaces set up by the line. Pattern vectors $\mathbf{p}_1$ and $\mathbf{p}_2$ are in C_+, and pattern vectors $\mathbf{p}_3$ and $\mathbf{p}_4$ are in C_-.

substantially fewer parameters than are required to memorize all training patterns, convergence to a solution may not be reached when each training pattern is presented only once. The input training patterns in $\{\mathbf{x}(i)\}_{i=1}^{N}$ need to be presented repeatedly either sequentially or randomly. Each presentation in this sequence is denoted as $\mathbf{x}(k)$. The weight vector at the kth presentation is denoted by $\mathbf{w}(k)$, and the corresponding augmented image space pattern is denoted by $\mathbf{y}(k)$. If a pattern is misclassified (i.e., the weight point characterizing the weight vector in the weight space lies on the wrong side of the pattern hyperplane), an obvious correction strategy is to move the weight point along the direction normal to the given pattern hyperplane toward the correct side. Suppose that for a training pattern, $\mathbf{y}(k) \in C_+$ and $\mathbf{w}(k) \cdot \mathbf{y}(k) < 0$. In that case, the weight point $\mathbf{w}(k)$ should be moved toward the positive side of the pattern hyperplane. Since the vector $\mathbf{y}(k)$ is on the normal to the hyperplane in weight space for pattern $\mathbf{y}(k)$ and since it points to the positive side of the hyperplane, the weight vector should be updated according to

$$\mathbf{w}(k + 1) = \mathbf{w}(k) + c\mathbf{y}(k), \tag{4.16}$$

where the positive number c is called a *correction increment*. Similarly, for a pattern $\mathbf{y}(k) \in C_-$, if $\mathbf{w}(k) \cdot \mathbf{y}(k) > 0$, then the updated weight vector should be

$$\mathbf{w}(k + 1) = \mathbf{w}(k) - c\mathbf{y}(k). \tag{4.17}$$

For a sufficiently large c, the weight point will be moved to the correct side of the hyperplane for this pattern.

The perceptron learning algorithm is based on the foregoing simple idea. There are several versions of the algorithm based on the choice of c.

4.1.3.1 FIXED-INCREMENT RULE. In this rule c is any number greater than zero, and the weight vector is updated according to the following equation (the $\mathbf{w}(k) \cdot \mathbf{y}(k) = 0$ case may be handled in ways different from that selected here):

$$\mathbf{w}(k + 1) = \begin{cases} \mathbf{w}(k) + c\mathbf{y}(k) & \text{if } \mathbf{w}(k) \cdot \mathbf{y}(k) \leq 0 \text{ and } \mathbf{y}(k) \in C_+ \\ \mathbf{w}(k) - c\mathbf{y}(k) & \text{if } \mathbf{w}(k) \cdot \mathbf{y}(k) > 0 \text{ and } \mathbf{y}(k) \in C_- \\ \mathbf{w}(k) & \text{if } \mathbf{y}(k) \text{ is correctly classified.} \end{cases} \tag{4.18}$$

To simplify the presentation, replace $\mathbf{y}(i)$ with $-\mathbf{y}(i)$ for all training patterns $\mathbf{y}(i)$ belonging to C_-. Remember that $\mathbf{y}(i)$ is an augmented pattern vector:

$$\mathbf{y}(i) \rightarrow -\mathbf{y}(i) \qquad \text{for all } \mathbf{y}(i) \in C_-. \tag{4.19}$$

This convention will be adopted in all discussions on perceptron learning. Form an *adjusted augmented training set* by taking the union of patterns in C_+ and the new set of patterns in Eq. (4.19). To avoid notational cluttering, we denote a generic element of this adjusted augmented training set by $\mathbf{y}(k)$. Then, the fixed-increment rule becomes

$$\mathbf{w}(k + 1) = \begin{cases} \mathbf{w}(k) + c\mathbf{y}(k) & \text{if } \mathbf{w}(k) \cdot \mathbf{y}(k) \leq 0 \\ \mathbf{w}(k) & \text{if } \mathbf{w}(k) \cdot \mathbf{y}(k) > 0. \end{cases} \tag{4.20}$$

4.1.3.2 ABSOLUTE CORRECTION RULE.

The correction increment c is chosen so that after each update, it will correctly classify the current pattern. That is, if $\mathbf{w}(k) \cdot \mathbf{y}(k) \leq 0$, then

$$\mathbf{w}(k + 1) \cdot \mathbf{y}(k) = \mathbf{w}(k) \cdot \mathbf{y}(k) + c\mathbf{y}(k) \cdot \mathbf{y}(k) > 0. \qquad (4.21)$$

Therefore, c must be greater than $|\mathbf{w}(k) \cdot \mathbf{y}(k)|/\|\mathbf{y}(k)\|^2$. Usually, c is chosen to be the smallest integer greater than $|\mathbf{w}(k) \cdot \mathbf{y}(k)|/\|\mathbf{y}(k)\|^2$. The end effect of applying the absolute correction rule can also be realized using the fixed-increment rule if each pattern is presented repeatedly until it is correctly classified.

4.1.3.3 FRACTIONAL CORRECTION RULE.

The correction increment c is chosen such that the magnitude of the difference of the distances from the pattern hyperplane in weight space between the new weight vector $\mathbf{w}(k + 1)$ and the old weight vector $\mathbf{w}(k)$ is proportional to the shortest distance from the old weight vector to the pattern hyperplane in the weight space. The dot product $\mathbf{w}(k) \cdot \mathbf{y}(k)$ is proportional to the (signed) normal distance from the weight point $\mathbf{w}(k)$ to the pattern hyperplane of $\mathbf{y}(k)$. The quantity $|\mathbf{w}(k + 1) \cdot \mathbf{y}(k) - \mathbf{w}(k) \cdot \mathbf{y}(k)|$ is proportional to the magnitude of the difference of the distances referred to above. Therefore, the fractional correction rule requires that

$$|\mathbf{w}(k + 1) \cdot \mathbf{y}(k) - \mathbf{w}(k) \cdot \mathbf{y}(k)| = \lambda|\mathbf{w}(k) \cdot \mathbf{y}(k)|. \qquad (4.22)$$

Substituting $\mathbf{w}(k + 1) = \mathbf{w}(k) + c\mathbf{y}(k)$ into Eq. (4.22), one gets

$$c = \lambda \frac{|\mathbf{w}(k) \cdot \mathbf{y}(k)|}{\|\mathbf{y}(k)\|^2}. \qquad (4.23)$$

If $\lambda > 1$, this rule becomes the same as the absolute correction rule. It can be shown that the algorithm based on the rule converges for $0 < \lambda < 2$.

Note that a pattern correctly classified at one iteration may become misclassified in a later iteration. The algorithm is considered to have produced convergence when all patterns have been cycled once and there is no correction required to any of the weights. Note that the perceptron rules apply to both binary and analog patterns. To illustrate Rosenblatt's perceptron algorithm, we take the pattern and image spaces to be the same in Example 4.2.

Example 4.2. Here, the fixed-increment rule is applied to a classification problem in a 2-D pattern space using a single TLU. The patterns in the pattern space are shown in Fig. 4.7. The training patterns, whose elements belong to the *ternary set* $\{0, 1, -1\}$, are as follows:

$$C_+ = \{(1, 1), (1, -1), (0, -1)\}$$
$$C_- = \{(-1, -1), (-1, 1), (0, 1)\}.$$

The augmented training set is

$$\{(1, 1, 1), (1, -1, 1), (0, -1, 1), (-1, -1, 1), (-1, 1, 1), (0, 1, 1)\}.$$

The adjusted augmented training set is

$$\{(1, \; 1, \; 1), \; (1, \; -1, \; 1), \; (0, \; -1, \; 1), \; (1, \; 1, \; -1), \; (1, \; -1, \; -1), \; (0, \; -1, \; -1)\}.$$

After inspection of Fig. 4.7 it can be concluded that the patterns in C_+ and C_- are linearly separable. Therefore, we can expect the perceptron learning algorithm to be able to provide a solution weight vector. We apply the fixed-increment rule with $c = 1$ and an initial weight vector $\mathbf{w}(0) = (1 \; 0 \; 0)^\mathsf{T}$; the initial weight vector was randomly selected. The training exemplars are presented sequentially in each iteration. The result is shown in Table 4.1.

The weight vector $(3 \; -2 \; 0)^\mathsf{T}$ yields the decision surface $3y_1 - 2y_2 = 0$, which is plotted in Fig. 4.7. By inspecting the training sequence, one may notice that a pattern correctly classified at one step (Table 4.1) may become misclassified later. Compare, for example, the first line in iteration 1 with the first line in iteration 2. In this example, the training patterns were always presented in the same order, and every pattern was presented once in each iteration. However, the convergence is still guaranteed if the patterns are picked at random. Nevertheless, the number of steps required to converge may vary with different orderings of the presented patterns.

4.1.4 Derivation of the Perceptron Algorithm as Gradient Descent

Readers familiar with optimization theory should realize that the perceptron algorithm is an implementation of the gradient descent method. According to this, the mean squared error $E(\mathbf{w})$ has associated with it a gradient, ∇E. The vector $-\nabla E$ points in the direction in which $E(\mathbf{w})$ will decrease at the fastest possible rate, and therefore the weight update equation is

$$\mathbf{w}(k + 1) = \mathbf{w}(k) - c\nabla E, \tag{4.24}$$

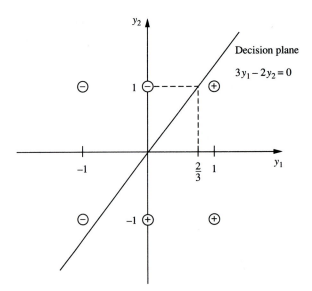

FIGURE 4.7
Training patterns in the feature space and the decision surface learned to classify the two categories of patterns in Example 4.2.

TABLE 4.1
Table for Example 4.2

Adjusted pattern	Weight applied	$\mathbf{w} \cdot \mathbf{y}$ $\triangleq \mathbf{w}^T\mathbf{y}$	Update?	New weight
		Iteration 1		
$(1, 1, 1)$	$(1, 0, 0)$	1	No	$(1, 0, 0)$
$(1, -1, 1)$	$(1, 0, 0)$	1	No	$(1, 0, 0)$
$(0, -1, 1)$	$(1, 0, 0)$	0	Yes	$(1, -1, 1)$
$(1, 1, -1)$	$(1, -1, 1)$	-1	Yes	$(2, 0, 0)$
$(1, -1, -1)$	$(2, 0, 0)$	2	No	$(2, 0, 0)$
$(0, -1, -1)$	$(2, 0, 0)$	0	Yes	$(2, -1, -1)$
		Iteration 2		
$(1, 1, 1)$	$(2, -1, -1)$	0	Yes	$(3, 0, 0)$
$(1, -1, 1)$	$(3, 0, 0)$	3	No	$(3, 0, 0)$
$(0, -1, 1)$	$(3, 0, 0)$	0	Yes	$(3, -1, 1)$
$(1, 1, -1)$	$(3, -1, 1)$	1	No	$(3, -1, 1)$
$(1, -1, -1)$	$(3, -1, 1)$	3	No	$(3, -1, 1)$
$(0, -1, -1)$	$(3, -1, 1)$	0	Yes	$(3, -2, 0)$
		Iteration 3		
$(1, 1, 1)$	$(3, -2, 0)$	1	No	$(3, -2, 0)$
$(1, -1, 1)$	$(3, -2, 0)$	5	No	$(3, -2, 0)$
$(0, -1, 1)$	$(3, -2, 0)$	2	No	$(3, -2, 0)$
$(1, 1, -1)$	$(3, -2, 0)$	1	No	$(3, -2, 0)$
$(1, -1, -1)$	$(3, -2, 0)$	5	No	$(3, -2, 0)$
$(0, -1, -1)$	$(3, -2, 0)$	2	No	$(3, -2, 0)$

where c is a suitable constant. If we define an error function at an iteration as

$$e_k(\mathbf{w}(k), \mathbf{y}(k)) = \tfrac{1}{2}(|\mathbf{w}(k) \cdot \mathbf{y}(k)| - \mathbf{w}(k) \cdot \mathbf{y}(k)), \tag{4.25}$$

then

$$\frac{\partial e_k(\mathbf{w}(k), \mathbf{y}(k))}{\partial \mathbf{w}(k)} = \tfrac{1}{2}(\mathbf{y}(k) \, T_b(\mathbf{w}(k) \cdot \mathbf{y}(k)) - \mathbf{y}(k)), \tag{4.26}$$

where

$$T_b(\mathbf{w}(k) \cdot \mathbf{y}(k)) = \begin{cases} 1 & \text{if } \mathbf{w}(k) \cdot \mathbf{y}(k) > 0 \\ -1 & \text{if } \mathbf{w}(k) \cdot \mathbf{y}(k) \le 0. \end{cases} \tag{4.27}$$

Substitution of Eq. (4.26) into (4.24) yields the fixed-increment rule,

$$\mathbf{w}(k + 1) = \mathbf{w}(k) + \frac{c}{2}(\mathbf{y}(k) - \mathbf{y}(k) \, T_b(\mathbf{w}(k) \cdot \mathbf{y}(k))). \tag{4.28}$$

The error function in Eq. (4.25) is minimum when $\mathbf{w}(k) \cdot \mathbf{y}(k) > 0$. Note that this procedure differs from the standard gradient descent algorithm in that the error function is different for each training pattern. The foregoing error function can be considered as an estimate of the true error function,

$$E(\mathbf{w}) = \frac{1}{N} \sum_{\mathbf{y} \in \mathbf{Y}} e_k(\mathbf{w}, \mathbf{y}(k)), \qquad (4.29)$$

that should be minimized, where $\mathbf{Y}$ is the set of all training patterns. It can be shown that all solutions must lie in a single open convex polyhedral cone with its vertex at the origin. That is, the error function $E(\mathbf{w})$ in the weight space has a unique valley with flat bottom. Therefore, convergence is guaranteed with gradient descent when the step size is appropriately chosen. This statement is no longer true when the gradient descent method is applied to networks with multilayer trainable units, in which the error functions have complicated topography with many local minima.

The gradient descent method for optimization is very simple and general. Only local information, for estimating a gradient, is needed for finding the minimum of the error function. However, there is an implicit assumption that is equivalent to requiring global information. The assumption is that the error function topography has only one extremum where the gradient vector is zero. Just because of its simplicity and generality, the gradient descent method can easily get stuck at any local minimum, oscillate, or diverge when the error function becomes more complicated, as is the case of networks with multilayer trainable units, to be described later.

4.1.5   The Perceptron Convergence Theorem

It will be shown in this section that the perceptron learning algorithm, using any one of the correction rules, converges. We will only prove the result for the fixed-increment rule with $c = 1$. Actually, the value of c is unimportant as long as it is positive, since for any fixed c one can scale the pattern by c (i.e., let $\mathbf{y}'(i) = (1/c)\mathbf{y}(i)$) without changing the separability of the patterns. The proof can be modified for the absolute correction rule. This follows from the observation that the absolute error correction rule is equivalent to the fixed-increment rule if each pattern is presented repeatedly until it is correctly classified. Similarly, convergence with the fractional correction rule can also be proved if $0 < \lambda < 2$.

Recall that to simplify the presentation, we let

$$\mathbf{y}(i) \rightarrow -\mathbf{y}(i) \qquad \text{for all } \mathbf{y}(i) \in C_-. \qquad (4.30)$$

Theorem 4.1   Perceptron convergence theorem [261, 273, 320]. If the training set is linearly separable, i.e., if there exists a $\mathbf{w}$ such that $\mathbf{w} \cdot \mathbf{y} > 0$ for all adjusted augmented training patterns, then perceptron learning using the fixed-increment rule will find a solution $\mathbf{w}^*$ in finite time such that $\mathbf{w}^* \cdot \mathbf{y} > 0$ for all training patterns. In other words, there exists a k_0 such that $\mathbf{w}(k_0) = \mathbf{w}(k_0 + 1) = \mathbf{w}(k_0 + 2) = \cdots$ and $\mathbf{w}^* = \mathbf{w}(k_0)$.

Proof. Let $\mathbf{Y}$ be the set of all training patterns. Although $\mathbf{Y}$ is a finite set, the training patterns are presented repeatedly in learning. For notational convenience, we feel free to denote $\mathbf{y}(i)$ by $\mathbf{y}_i$ and $\mathbf{w}(k)$ by $\mathbf{w}_k$. Relabel the training patterns in successive steps of the algorithm as $\mathbf{y}_1, \mathbf{y}_2, \ldots, \mathbf{y}_k, \ldots$ Let the corresponding weight vectors be $\mathbf{w}_1, \mathbf{w}_2, \ldots, \mathbf{w}_k, \ldots$ Assume that the patterns and weight vectors at those steps where there is no change to the previous weight vector, i.e., $\mathbf{w}_{k+1} = \mathbf{w}_k$, are removed from the sequences.

Since in each step where correction is needed, $\mathbf{w}_j \cdot \mathbf{y}_j \leq 0$ and the weight vector is updated using the fixed-increment rule with $c = 1$, we have

$$\mathbf{w}_{k+1} = \mathbf{w}_1 + \mathbf{y}_1 + \mathbf{y}_2 + \cdots + \mathbf{y}_k. \tag{4.31}$$

Because the patterns are linearly separable, there exists a solution region $\mathbf{W}$ such that for any $\mathbf{w} \in \mathbf{W}$, $\mathbf{w} \cdot \mathbf{y} > 0$ for all the training patterns. Pick a $\mathbf{w}^* \in \mathbf{W}$, and let

$$\min_{\mathbf{y} \in \mathbf{Y}} \mathbf{y} \cdot \mathbf{w}^* = \alpha \qquad \text{and} \qquad \beta = \mathbf{w}_1 \cdot \mathbf{w}^* \tag{4.32}$$

where $\alpha > 0$. Taking the inner product with $\mathbf{w}^*$ of both sides of Eq. (4.31), we have

$$\mathbf{w}_{k+1} \cdot \mathbf{w}^* = \mathbf{w}_1 \cdot \mathbf{w}^* + \mathbf{y}_1 \cdot \mathbf{w}^* + \mathbf{y}_2 \cdot \mathbf{w}^* + \cdots + \mathbf{y}_k \cdot \mathbf{w}^*. \tag{4.33}$$

From Eq. (4.32), noting that all the $\mathbf{y}_i \cdot \mathbf{w}^*$ terms in Eq. (4.33) are positive, we have

$$\mathbf{w}_{k+1} \cdot \mathbf{w}^* \geq k\alpha + \beta. \tag{4.34}$$

Since

$$(\mathbf{w}_{k+1} \cdot \mathbf{w}^*)^2 \leq |\mathbf{w}_{k+1}|^2 |\mathbf{w}^*|^2, \tag{4.35}$$

therefore

$$|\mathbf{w}_{k+1}|^2 \geq \frac{(\mathbf{w}_{k+1} \cdot \mathbf{w}^*)^2}{|\mathbf{w}^*|^2} \geq \frac{(k\alpha + \beta)^2}{|\mathbf{w}^*|^2}. \tag{4.36}$$

Thus, the squared magnitude of the weight vector grows at least quadratically with the number of correction steps. Next, we obtain an upper bound for the squared magnitude of the weight vector growth from another line of reasoning. Since $\mathbf{w}_{j+1} = \mathbf{w}_j + \mathbf{y}_j$ for all j, we have

$$|\mathbf{w}_{j+1}|^2 = |\mathbf{w}_j|^2 + 2\mathbf{w}_j \cdot \mathbf{y}_j + |\mathbf{y}_j|^2 \tag{4.37}$$

Since $\mathbf{w}_j \cdot \mathbf{y}_j \leq 0$ (why?),

$$|\mathbf{w}_{j+1}|^2 - |\mathbf{w}_j|^2 \leq |\mathbf{y}_j|^2 \qquad \text{for all } j. \tag{4.38}$$

The preceding inequality is summed over $j = 1, 2, \ldots, k$ and simplified to yield

$$|\mathbf{w}_{k+1}|^2 \leq \sum_{j=1}^{k} |\mathbf{y}_j|^2 + |\mathbf{w}_1|^2 \leq kA + |\mathbf{w}_1|^2 \tag{4.39}$$

where $A = \max_{\mathbf{y} \in \mathbf{Y}} |\mathbf{y}|^2$. This inequality shows that the squared length of the weight vector cannot grow faster than linearly with the number of correction steps. For sufficiently large k, Eqs. (4.36) and (4.39) become contradictory. Therefore, k cannot be larger than k_m which is the solution to the equation:

$$k_m A + |\mathbf{w}_1|^2 = \frac{(k_m \alpha + \beta)^2}{|\mathbf{w}^*|^2}. \tag{4.40}$$

Therefore, the number of correction steps must be less than k_m if the patterns are linearly separable. The training patterns are repeated until a solution vector is found.

The first proof of Theorem 4.1 is due to Rosenblatt [320]. This theorem has been proved in many different ways. For a geometric proof of the theorem, see ref. [273].

The bound k_m is almost useless for estimating the number of steps required for finding a solution, since it depends on a known solution vector. This leads to a problem. If corrections to the weights stop, we know a solution is found. However, we will not be able to know whether the updates should cease if there is no a priori knowledge of the linear separability of the patterns. In practice, we must set a maximum number of steps for which we allow the algorithm to run. Then, if we stop the algorithm after 10^6 steps, the solution may be just one step away at the $(10^6 + 1)$st step.

Convergence speed. Theorem 4.1 shows that the perceptron algorithm converges in a finite number of steps if a solution exists. However, it has been shown that the algorithm may not have polynomial-time convergence [261]. Baum showed that the perceptron algorithm is polynomial in the dimension of the input and the inverse of an accuracy parameter for "nonmalicious distributions" [34]. The result is obtained in a modified framework of Valiant's distribution-free learning [382], which will be discussed later in Chapter 6.

Following are some practical considerations to speed up the convergence when implementing the perceptron learning algorithm. If the vectors $\mathbf{y}(i)$ are binary, with elements drawn from the set $\{\alpha, 1\}$, then α is -1 in the bipolar case, but it is chosen to be a small nonzero number, like 0.1, in the unipolar case. This will lead to faster convergence in almost all cases. The reason is that if $\alpha = 0$, the updates of a weight connected to an input variable will be zero when the corresponding variable is zero in the training pattern. Making α nonzero ensures that a weight will be updated whenever required.

Another way to accelerate the convergence of the perceptron algorithms is to use adaptive bias, i.e., either estimate the threshold during learning by modifying the learning algorithm or set the thresholds initially to manually estimated values. To illustrate the problem, we give the following example. The detailed verification is left as an exercise.

> **Example 4.3.** Given are the following two classes of augmented patterns with only one pattern in each class: $C_+ = \{(57.595722, -99.759033, 1)\}$, and $C_- = \{(41.887859, -72.551994, 1)\}$. Surprisingly, it may take many thousands of iterations for any of the perceptron error correction rules to converge to a solution. By properly estimating the threshold, the number of iterations for convergence can be reduced to well below 50. See Problem 4.12.

4.2   THE WIDROW-HOFF LMS ALGORITHM

The Widrow-Hoff or Least Mean Square (LMS) algorithm [408, 409] uses a linear rule for training a perceptron. Widrow called a trainable TLU, allowing both analog and real input values, an *Adaline* (adaptive linear element). Let $d(k)$ be the desired real-valued output for the augmented pattern $\mathbf{y}(k)$, and suppose that the corresponding weight vector is $\mathbf{w}(k)$. The error at the kth iteration is

$$e_k = d(k) - \mathbf{w}(k) \cdot \mathbf{y}(k).$$

The LMS algorithm is also a gradient descent algorithm requiring the squared error function,

$$e_k^2 = (d(k) - \mathbf{w}(k) \cdot \mathbf{y}(k))^2 = (d(k) - \mathbf{w}^T(k)\mathbf{y}(k))^2, \tag{4.41}$$

to be minimized at the kth iteration. In general, $\mathbf{y}(k)$ and $\mathbf{w}(k)$ are random vectors, so that e_k^2 is a random variable. Note that e_k^2 is not the ensemble mean squared error, $E(e_k^2)$, where $E(\bullet)$ denotes the expectation operator. See Problem 4.15 for review and further details on what follows.

The difference between the LMS algorithm and the perceptron algorithm is that the error minimized by the LMS algorithm is a continuous quantity. Both can be applied to the same neural network architecture, whose topology is described by the generic graph described in Section 4.1. Remember that e_k^2 is the squared error from one pattern. Then

$$\hat{\nabla}_k = \frac{\partial e_k^2}{\partial \mathbf{w}} = -2e_k\mathbf{y}(k), \tag{4.42}$$

where $\hat{\nabla}_k$ is an approximation of the true gradient ∇_k of the ensemble mean square error. If we restrict, for the time being, the parameter vector $\mathbf{w}(k)$ to be deterministic, it is routine to verify that

$$\nabla_k = \frac{\partial E(e_k^2)}{\partial \mathbf{w}(k)} = 2(\mathbf{Q}\mathbf{w}(k) - \mathbf{P}), \tag{4.43}$$

where $\mathbf{Q} = E(\mathbf{y}(k)\mathbf{y}^T(k))$ is the $N \times N$ autocorrelation matrix of all the N training patterns $\{\mathbf{y}(k)\}_{i=1}^N$, and $\mathbf{P} = E(d(k)\mathbf{y}(k))$ (recall that $\mathbf{y}(k)$ is a column vector) is a vector of crosscorrelations. Applying the gradient descent rule (Section 4.1.4), we find that using $\hat{\nabla}_k$ yields

$$\mathbf{w}(k + 1) = \mathbf{w}(k) + 2\alpha e_k\mathbf{y}(k), \tag{4.44}$$

where α is a suitable learning parameter that influences stability and convergence rate. Since, as mentioned before, the gradient in Eq. (4.42) is only an approximation to the true gradient of the ensemble mean squared error, the algorithm discussed falls under the general theory of stochastic approximation.

We will show next that the estimate $\hat{\nabla}_k$ in Eq. (4.42) is an unbiased estimate of the gradient of the ensemble mean squared error when the weight parameter vector is treated to be deterministic. The expectation operator E is applied to both sides of Eq. (4.42) to yield

$$E(\hat{\nabla}_k) = -2E(e_k\mathbf{y}(k)) = -2E((d(k) - \mathbf{w}^T(k)\mathbf{y}(k))\mathbf{y}(k)), \tag{4.45}$$

which, using Eq. (4.43), simplifies to

$$E(\hat{\nabla}_k) = 2E(\mathbf{y}(k)\mathbf{y}^T(k)\mathbf{w}(k) - d(k)\mathbf{y}(k)) = \nabla_k. \tag{4.46}$$

Because the mean value of $\hat{\nabla}_k$ equals the true gradient ∇_k, it is by definition an *unbiased estimate*. Because the gradient estimate is unbiased, the LMS algorithm could be made a true gradient descent algorithm in the limiting sense, by estimating ∇_k at each step but not updating the weights until many estimates have been accumulated. In this way, the updating rule in Eq. (4.44) may be made to approach the updating using the true gradient. However, up to this point the rule in Eq. (4.44) that updates the weights in each iteration has been of interest. We examine next the convergence in the mean of this updating rule, by treating the weight vector as a random vector.

The optimal solution $\mathbf{w}^*$ that minimizes the mean squared error is obtained by setting $\nabla_k = 0$ in Eq. (4.43). Provided $\mathbf{Q}$ is not singular (the autocorrelation matrix $\mathbf{Q}$ is then positive-definite), this solution is

$$\mathbf{w}^* = \mathbf{Q}^{-1}\mathbf{P}. \qquad (4.47)$$

The optimal solution in Eq. (4.47) (referred to as the *Wiener solution*) requires a priori knowledge of the signal statistics conveyed through the matrices $\mathbf{Q}$ and $\mathbf{P}$. Usually, that information is not completely available. The LMS algorithm enables one to obtain an accurate estimate of the true solution without computing $\mathbf{Q}^{-1}$ and $\mathbf{P}$. Assume that all the training pattern vectors are linearly independent. Then apply the expectation operator to both sides of Eq. (4.44) to get

$$E(\mathbf{w}(k+1)) = E(\mathbf{w}(k)) + 2\alpha E(e_k \mathbf{y}(k)), \qquad (4.48)$$

which, after substituting the value of e_k from Eq. (4.41), expands to

$$E(\mathbf{w}(k+1)) = E(\mathbf{w}(k)) + 2\alpha E(d(k)\mathbf{y}(k)) - 2\alpha E(\mathbf{y}(k)\mathbf{y}^{\mathrm{T}}(k)\mathbf{w}(k)). \quad (4.49)$$

From Eq. (4.44) we see that $\mathbf{w}(k)$ depends only on $\mathbf{y}(i)$, $i = 1, 2, \ldots, k-1$. A random vector, which is a collection of random variables, is said to be independent if it has independent components. If we assume that the pattern vectors are independent over time, then $\mathbf{w}(k)$ is independent of $\mathbf{y}(k)$. After inserting $\mathbf{Q}$ and $\mathbf{P}$, Eq. (4.49) becomes

$$E(\mathbf{w}(k+1)) = E(\mathbf{w}(k)) + 2\alpha\mathbf{P} - 2\alpha\mathbf{Q}E(\mathbf{w}(k)). \qquad (4.50)$$

The relation $\mathbf{P} = \mathbf{Q}\mathbf{w}^*$ is then substituted into Eq. (4.50) to yield

$$E(\mathbf{w}(k+1)) = (\mathbf{I} - 2\alpha\mathbf{Q})E(\mathbf{w}(k)) + 2\alpha\mathbf{Q}\mathbf{w}^*. \qquad (4.51)$$

The preceding equation was derived from the assumption of statistical independence that was made on the relevant random vectors. Actually, the weaker assumption, that they are uncorrelated, suffices.

Next apply the *affine transformation*,

$$\mathbf{w}(k) = \mathbf{B}\mathbf{v}(k) + \mathbf{w}^*, \qquad (4.52)$$

where $\mathbf{B}$ is an orthonormal matrix (i.e., $\mathbf{B}^{\mathrm{T}}\mathbf{B} = \mathbf{I}$) that diagonalizes the real symmetric autocorrelation matrix $\mathbf{Q}$. Then the matrices $\mathbf{\Lambda}$ and $\mathbf{Q}$ are said to be related by a *similarity transformation*,

$$\mathbf{\Lambda} = \mathbf{B}^{-1}\mathbf{Q}\mathbf{B},$$

where $\mathbf{\Lambda}$ is a diagonal matrix whose diagonal elements are the eigenvalues of $\mathbf{Q}$.[1] Substitute Eq. (4.52) into Eq. (4.51) and iterate to get

$$E(\mathbf{v}(k)) = (\mathbf{I} - 2\alpha\mathbf{\Lambda})^k\mathbf{v}(0). \tag{4.53}$$

The solution $E(\mathbf{v}(k))$ in the new coordinate system approaches zero asymptotically, provided the right-hand side of Eq. (4.53) goes to zero as $k \to \infty$. This result is guaranteed if

$$-1 < 1 - 2\alpha\lambda_{\max} < 1 \tag{4.54}$$

where $\lambda_{\max}$ is the largest eigenvalue of the nonnegative definite matrix $\mathbf{Q}$. Since $\lambda_{\max} > 0$ (excluding the trivial case of a null matrix), a sufficient condition for asymptotic convergence of $E(\mathbf{w}(k))$ to the optimal solution $\mathbf{w}^*$ via application of the learning rule in Eq. (4.44) is

$$\frac{1}{\lambda_{\max}} > \alpha > 0. \tag{4.55}$$

The foregoing result is arrived at under the severe restriction that the pattern vectors are linearly independent over time. Since there can be only n linearly independent vectors in an n-dimensional pattern space, this assumption can only be true for $\mathbf{w}(k)$ when $k < n$. Since convergence requires large k, we must require n to be large to guarantee small error after a finite number of steps. Proof of convergence of the LMS algorithm under more relaxed conditions becomes much more complex. Interested readers are referred to refs. [108] and [410].

The updating rule in Eq. (4.44) may be normalized to produce

$$\mathbf{w}(k + 1) = \mathbf{w}(k) + \frac{\alpha}{|\mathbf{y}(k)|^2}e_k\mathbf{y}(k). \tag{4.56}$$

The change of the error e_k corresponding to a weight change using the normalized updating rule in Eq. (4.56) is then

$$\Delta e_k = d(k) - \mathbf{w}(k + 1) \bullet \mathbf{y}(k) - d(k) + \mathbf{w}(k) \bullet \mathbf{y}(k),$$

which, after substituting from Eq. (4.56), becomes

$$\Delta e_k = -\alpha\frac{e_k\mathbf{y}(k) \bullet \mathbf{y}(k)}{|\mathbf{y}(k)|^2} = -\alpha e_k. \tag{4.57}$$

Therefore, the error for the kth training pattern is reduced by a factor of α as the weight vector is adjusted. The value of α, usually chosen to be between 0 and 1, controls the stability and convergence speed [411]. Total error correction, corresponding to the absolute correction rule, is achieved with $\alpha = 1$.

---

[1]In the case of complex-valued matrices the counterpart of an orthonormal matrix is a *unitary* matrix ($\mathbf{B}$ is unitary if $\mathbf{B}^H\mathbf{B} = \mathbf{I}$, where the superscript H denotes the complex conjugate transpose or Hermitian operator), which allows a *Hermitian* matrix $\mathbf{Q}$ (for which $\mathbf{Q} = \mathbf{Q}^H$) to be related to a diagonal matrix $\mathbf{\Lambda}$ of its eigenvalues (all of which are real) by the similarity transformation described above.

The LMS algorithm behaves better than the perceptron algorithms when the patterns are nonseparable, since it converges under certain conditions to a solution that minimizes the mean squared error even if the patterns are not linearly separable. However, the LMS algorithm may converge to a solution that does not separate linearly separable training patterns.

4.3 ORDER OF A PREDICATE AND A PERCEPTRON

The concept of *order of a predicate* for a perceptron, introduced by Minsky and Papert [261], provides a measure of the number of connections from the input variables to units at the first hidden layer that is required to compute a predicate function. Order was defined in [261] for perceptrons whose first-layer functions are fixed. However, the definition of order and the related results apply as well to networks where the connection weights to the hidden units are learned.

In this section, all the input vectors are assumed to be binary with $\{0, 1\}$ values. Before defining order, the support of a partial predicate function is first defined.

Definition 4.3. The *support*, $\mathbf{S}(\phi)$, of a partial predicate function $\phi \in \mathbf{\Phi}$ is the smallest subset $\mathbf{S} \subseteq \mathbf{R}$ such that for every $\mathbf{x} \subseteq \mathbf{R}$,

$$\phi(\mathbf{x}) = \phi(\mathbf{x} \cap \mathbf{S}). \tag{4.58}$$

In other words, the support is the subset of $\mathbf{R}$ on which ϕ really depends. For example, let $\mathbf{R}$ be arranged as a one-dimensional binary array $\{x_n, x_{n-1}, \ldots, x_1, x_0\}$ and let $\phi(\mathbf{x}) = T_b(x_1 x_0)$; then the support of ϕ is $\{x_0, x_1\}$. The number of elements in $\mathbf{S}(\phi)$, or the size of the support $\mathbf{S}(\phi)$, is denoted by $|\mathbf{S}(\phi)|$. In this case, $|\mathbf{S}(\phi)| = 2$. Recall that for a given $\mathbf{\Phi}$ we use $L(\mathbf{\Phi})$ to denote the set of all predicates whose elements are the linear threshold functions with respect to $\mathbf{\Phi}$.

Definition 4.4. The order of a predicate function Ψ is the smallest number k for which a set of predicates $\mathbf{\Phi}$ can be found such that

$$|\mathbf{S}(\phi)| \leq k \quad \text{for all } \phi \in \mathbf{\Phi}, \quad \text{and} \quad \Psi \in L(\mathbf{\Phi}). \tag{4.59}$$

Note that the order of Ψ is a property of Ψ alone and does not depend on the choice of $\mathbf{\Phi}$. Thus, the concept of order is an absolute concept. The next example gives a particular predicate whose order is 1, and the succeeding example explains in detail why the order of the predicate representing the identity function (complementary exclusive-OR or CXOR) is not 1 but 2, as is also the case with the XOR function.

Example 4.4. Let $\mathbf{R}$ be arranged as a one-dimensional binary array $\{x_n \, x_{n-1} \cdots x_1 \, x_0\}$. The order of $\Psi(\mathbf{x}) = [x_n \, x_{n-1} \cdots x_1 \, x_0$ is a binary representation of an even number] is 1. Since only one partial predicate $\phi = x_0$ is needed to compute the function, $\Psi(\mathbf{x}) = T_b(1 - \phi)$.

Example 4.5. In this example, the representations of exclusive-OR (XOR) and identity functions in terms of the Boolean variables are given, and then the order of the simplest perceptron needed for computing the identity function is obtained.

Let the Boolean variables be x_1 and x_2. Denote the complements of x_1 and x_2 by $\bar{x}_1$ and $\bar{x}_2$, respectively. The XOR logic function is representable by

$$T_b(x_1\bar{x}_2 + \bar{x}_1 x_2)$$

or, equivalently,

$$T_b(x_1(1 - x_2) + (1 - x_1)x_2).$$

Then, $T_b((\bullet)) = 1$, provided that

$$x_1 + x_2 - 2x_1 x_2 > 0 \qquad \text{or} \qquad 2x_1 x_2 - x_1 - x_2 < 0.$$

The identity function, $x_1 \equiv x_2$, is representable by

$$T_b(x_1 x_2 + \bar{x}_1 \bar{x}_2)$$

or, equivalently,

$$T_b(2x_1 x_2 - x_1 - x_2 + 1).$$

The perceptron $\Psi(x_1, x_2) = P_B[x_1 \equiv x_2]$ is not of order 1, as is also the case for the XOR problem. Hypothesize the order to be 1 so that

$$\Psi(x_1, x_2) = P_B[\alpha x_1 + \beta x_2 - \theta].$$

Then

$$
\begin{array}{lll}
\Psi(1, 0) = 0 & \text{implies} & \alpha \le \theta \\
\Psi(0, 1) = 0 & \text{implies} & \beta \le \theta \\
\Psi(1, 1) = 1 & \text{implies} & \alpha + \beta > \theta \\
\Psi(0, 0) = 1 & \text{implies} & 0 > \theta.
\end{array}
$$

Therefore, from the first two conditions in this example,

$$\alpha + \beta \le 2\theta;$$

and this inequality, with the third, implies that

$$\theta < 2\theta,$$

which would make θ positive, contradicting the fourth condition. So, the order must be 2 (by additional elementary arguments on support of partial predicates).

It must be understood that a conjunction $x_1 \cap x_2$ of two unipolar binary variables, x_1 and x_2, that realizes the AND gate can be computed by the thresholding of a linear form. To wit, the predicates $T_b(x_1 + x_2 - 1.5)$ and $T_b(x_1 x_2)$ involving, respectively, a linear and a quadratic form, both realize the AND gate; but the order of both predicates is 1 and not 2. Note, however, that the product term $x_1 x_2$ in the representation $T_b(2x_1 x_2 - x_1 - x_2 + 1)$ for the CXOR cannot be replaced by a linear form, consistent with the obtained order for the identity type of predicate function. The next two examples illustrate further the computation of the important characterizing function of order for different predicate functions.

Example 4.6. Let **R** be arranged as a binary two-dimensional array, and consider the predicate $\Psi_{\text{convex}} = [\mathbf{x}$, as a 2-D discrete figure in **R**, is convex]. Convexity of **x** requires that for any two points x_p and x_q in **R** that belong to **x**, any point x_r on the line joining x_p and x_q also belongs to **x**. The order of Ψ_{convex} is 3, because it can be computed with partial predicates that look at any three points on a line and cannot be computed by partial predicates of smaller support. (Note that in actual implementation the selection of $\mathbf{\Phi}$ depends on how a "line" is defined in a discrete space.)

Example 4.7. Let the elements in **R** be unipolar binary. The counting predicate $\Psi_M = [|\mathbf{x}| = M$, or there are M elements in **x** that are 1] is of order 2. This statement can be shown by observing that $-(|\mathbf{x}| - M)^2 + \epsilon > 0$, where $0 < \epsilon < 1$, is true only when $|\mathbf{x}| = M$. Hence,

$$\Psi_M = T_b(-(|\mathbf{x}| - M)^2 + \epsilon). \tag{4.60}$$

To find the order, we need to express the foregoing as a linear summation:

$$\begin{aligned}
\Psi_M &= T_b(-(|\mathbf{x}| - M)^2 + \epsilon) \\
&= T_b(-|\mathbf{x}|(|\mathbf{x}| - 1) + (2M - 1)|\mathbf{x}| - M^2 + \epsilon) \\
&= T_b\left(-\left(\sum_i x_i\right)\left(\sum_j x_j\right) + 2M \sum_i x_i - M^2 + \epsilon\right) \tag{4.61} \\
&= T_b\left(-2\sum_{i>j} x_i x_j + (2M - 1)\sum_i x_i - M^2 + \epsilon\right)
\end{aligned}$$

Since the predicate cannot be computed by a perceptron of order 1, the order of the predicate is 2.

Before we can prove the order of more complicated predicates, we need to investigate a special class of simple predicates and their properties.

Definition 4.5. The *mask* of a set A with respect to **x** is defined as

$$\phi_A(\mathbf{x}) = [\text{all members of } A \text{ are in } \mathbf{x}] = [A \subset \mathbf{x}]. \tag{4.62}$$

In the Boolean function notation, a mask is given as the conjunction of all the elements in A. If $A = \{x_1, \ldots, x_n\}$, then $\phi_A(\mathbf{x}) = \cap_{i=1}^n x_i$ or, alternatively, $\phi_A(\mathbf{x}) = T_b(x_1 x_2 \cdots x_n)$. Since $\phi_A(\mathbf{x})$ may also be expressed as (generalized discussion following Example 4.5)

$$\phi_A(\mathbf{x}) = T_b(x_1 + x_2 + \cdots + x_n - (n - 0.5)),$$

all masks are therefore of order 1. We first state and prove a simple but useful theorem.

Theorem 4.2. Every predicate Ψ is a linear threshold function with respect to all the masks, i.e., $\Psi \in L$ (all masks).

Proof. It is known that any Boolean function $\Psi(x_1, x_2, \ldots, x_n)$ can be written in the disjunctive normal form $\cup_i C_i(\mathbf{x})$ where each $C_i(\mathbf{x})$ is a conjunction of the n binary variables $\cap_{i=1}^{n} z_i$, where each z_i is either x_i or $\bar{x}_i$. For any value assignment of the n binary input variables, at most one of the $C_i(\mathbf{x})$ can be true; therefore,

$$\Psi(\mathbf{x}) = T_b\left(\sum_i C_i(\mathbf{x})\right), \tag{4.63}$$

where each conjunction term is written as a product of n binary variables. Then replace each $\bar{x}_i$ with $1 - x_i$ and multiply out as follows:

$$A\bar{x}_i B = A(1 - x_i)B = AB - Ax_iB \tag{4.64}$$

where A and B are arbitrary products of binary variables. After combining terms, $\Psi(\mathbf{x})$ in Eq. (4.63) is rewritten as

$$\Psi(\mathbf{x}) = T_b\left(\sum_i w_i\phi_i(\mathbf{x})\right)$$

where each ϕ_i is a mask and each w_i is an integer.

The number of variables in a product term in Eq. (4.64) is less than or equal to n. Equation (4.64) is referred to as the *positive normal form*. With it, we can show that the order of a function can be determined by examining its representation as a linear threshold function with respect to the set of masks.

Theorem 4.3. A predicate function is of order k if and only if k is the smallest number for which there exists a set $\mathbf{\Phi}$ of masks satisfying

$$|S(\phi)| \le k \qquad \text{for all } \phi \in \mathbf{\Phi} \text{ and } \Psi \in L(\mathbf{\Phi}). \tag{4.65}$$

Proof. As in the proof of Theorem 4.2, each ϕ_i in $\Psi = T_b\left(\sum_i w_i\phi_i\right)$ can be replaced by its positive normal form. Subsequent to that operation, the size of the support of ϕ_i remains invariant, and hence the order is also invariant.

The following theorem can be proved by using Theorem 4.3.

Theorem 4.4. The predicate $\Psi_{\text{parity}}(\mathbf{x}) = [|\mathbf{x}| \text{ is an odd number}]$ is of order $|\mathbf{R}|$.

Proof. Consider computing Ψ_{parity} using masks, i.e.,

$$\Psi_{\text{parity}} = T_b\left(\sum_i w_i\phi_i\right), \tag{4.66}$$

where all ϕ_i's are masks. Because $\Psi_{\text{parity}}(\mathbf{x}) = 1$ for any $\mathbf{x}$ whose size $|\mathbf{x}| = 1$, all the singleton masks x_i must be present with positive coefficients in Eq. (4.66). These coefficients may be arbitrarily chosen as long as they are positive, so they may be (but are not necessarily) assigned equal positive values. If, say, $x_i = 1$ and $x_j = 1$ such that $|x| = 2$, and $\Psi_{\text{parity}}(\mathbf{x}) = 0$, then the masks $x_ix_j, i > j$ must be present. The coefficient of an x_ix_j mask must be negative and large enough to cancel the positive contributions of the two singleton masks x_i and x_j. To prove by induction, assume that all masks with $|\mathbf{R}| - 1$ or fewer variables are present, and, without loss of generality, assume that $\Psi_{\text{parity}}(\mathbf{x}) = 0$ for any $\mathbf{x}$ such that $|\mathbf{x}| = |\mathbf{R}| - 1$. Then to make $\Psi_{\text{parity}}(\mathbf{x}) = 1$ for any $\mathbf{x}$

such that $|x| = |\mathbf{R}|$, the mask with $|\mathbf{R}|$ variables must not only be present but must also have a coefficient large enough to cancel the negative contributions of all the masks with $|\mathbf{R}| - 1$ variables. Therefore, all the masks must be present to compute Ψ_{parity}. As a consequence, based on Theorem 4.3, the order of Ψ_{parity} is $|\mathbf{R}|$.

Minsky and Papert [261] proved Theorem 4.4 by applying a *group invariance theorem*. The coefficients for masks ϕ_i whose support sizes $|\mathbf{S}(\phi_i)|$ are the same can be made equal. To make the computation reliable, assume that we require $\sum_i w_i \phi_i \geq 1$ for odd parity and $\sum_i w_i \phi_i \leq 0$ for even parity. In that case, assuming that unit value is assigned to the coefficients for all the singleton masks, it is easy to prove the following corollary:

Corollary. To realize the function Ψ_{parity} as an LTF over the set of all masks, the coefficients grow at least as fast as $2^{|\mathbf{S}(\phi_i)|-1}$. Therefore, the ratio of the magnitudes of the largest and the smallest coefficients is at least $2^{|\mathbf{R}|-1}$.

This corollary poses a serious problem in hardware implementation if the parity function is to be realized for large $|\mathbf{R}|$ using only masks, because it is impossible to realize such a large range of coefficients in a single circuit. The problem may be avoided if we do not limit ourselves to masks only in the first layer, as is the case with multilayer trainable networks, discussed later in Chapter 5. The foregoing theorem shows that to compute the seemingly not so complicated function Ψ_{parity}, at least one unit in the first layer must be connected to all the input variables. The function may still be said to be computable in parallel by the first-layer units; however, the computation is no longer local in any sense. The requirement that at least one unit (before connecting to the output unit) have connections to all input variables holds for both perceptrons and multilayer networks.

Minsky and Papert [261] proved that the order of another important geometric predicate $\Psi_{connected}(\mathbf{x}) = [\mathbf{x}$ as a figure in a 2-D $\mathbf{R}$ is connected] is at least $C|\mathbf{R}|^{1/2}$ where C is a constant. The connectivity predicate is an important function in image processing and analysis. We shall not go into the different proofs and many details related to $\Psi_{connected}$ since the results on Ψ_{parity} already illustrate the main problems. Interested readers are referred to the classic book by Minsky and Papert [261].

The significance of the concept of order is that for a perceptron order limits the predicates that are computable. A perceptron with a given order O_1 cannot be trained to compute any predicate whose order is greater than O_1. This conclusion is the most important one in ref. [261]. Therefore, if we want to increase the likelihood for a given network to be able to learn an arbitrary set of examples, or if we know that the network needs to compute high-order functions, the number of connections must be high. The connection complexity will be further discussed in Chapter 6. Multilayer trainable networks also cannot escape the requirement of order. For such networks, there must be at least one unit below the output node for which the number of connections, direct or indirect, to input units equals the order of the function being computed. However, so many connections need not be made to one unit. Several layers of units can be used as relays. If the order is N, and M layers of trainable TLUs with the same number of connections are used, the maximum number of connections to a unit will be $N^{1/M}$. This reduction can be achieved at the expense of $(N-1)$ TLUs. However, the actual number of units required may be much more than this in order to achieve the same functional capability of one TLU with N connections, because of the analog factor, to be discussed in Chapter 6.

4.4 CONCLUSIONS AND SUGGESTIONS

The perceptron was introduced as a tool for learning about thirty-five years ago. At about the same time, the LMS algorithm was developed with a similar objective of classifying patterns in feature space. Many other ramifications of these early techniques also appeared, as summarized in ref. [409], to which the reader is referred for additional references and chronological descriptions of events leading up to and including the backpropagation rule, to be described in detail in the following chapter.

The graph-based characterization of a two-layer feedforward neural network, and the issues in analysis and design to be addressed by such networks, are introduced. The perceptron, a generalization of the TLU introduced in Chapter 1, is defined in Section 4.1. For the reader to understand the computing capabilities of a perceptron, a linear threshold function is defined with respect to a family of predicates on an arbitrary set of variables. The restriction is explained that patterns must be linearly separable in feature space for the perceptron rule to be successfully applied. The perceptron convergence theorem is enunciated and proved; in spite of the limitations in scope for applying the perceptron rule, this convergence theorem was of groundbreaking significance, not only in theoretical considerations but also from the implementational standpoint. For the sake of brevity, the presentation is restricted to the two-class perceptron training algorithm. This can quite conveniently be generalized to the multicategory case [428].

Section 4.2 is devoted to the LMS algorithm, developed for training adaptive elements and applied subsequently to diverse problems in adaptive signal processing and adaptive control. The LMS algorithm, however, may converge to a solution that does not separate linearly separable training patterns, which the perceptron is guaranteed to handle. If some error in classification can be tolerated, however, the LMS algorithm is likely to yield better results than the perceptron rule when the patterns are not linearly separable. It is worth emphasizing that, unlike the perceptron rule, which guarantees convergence, the sufficient conditions available for convergence in the case of the LMS algorithm are usually too stringent and therefore have to be considerably relaxed when applied in practice.

In Section 4.3, the important concept of order of a predicate is introduced. Roughly, whenever a given problem is of low order, the perceptron performs well, whereas when the order is unbounded, serious problems of size, scaling, and density of units and connections are encountered. Thus, order is important in crucial issues concerning feasibility and cost of a neural network to compute various functions with retinas of increasing size.

PROBLEMS

4.1. Write down all the linear threshold functions $L(\Phi)$ and the corresponding Boolean functions for the following case, where Φ is the family of predicates defined on the two-variable space $\mathbf{R}$ (*Hint:* There are 16 Boolean functions of two variables):

$$\mathbf{R} = \{x, y\}, \qquad \Phi = \{\phi_1 = x, \ \phi_2 = y\}.$$

Does $L(\Phi)$ include all the Boolean functions of x and y? If not, what functions are not included?

4.2. (*a*) Consider a rectangular grid. The coordinates of the grid points, ordered lexicographically, by a row-by-row scan from left to right and bottom to top are $(0,0)$, $(0,1), \dots, (0,M), (1,0), (1,1), \dots, (1,M), \dots, (N,0), (N,1), \dots, (N,M)$. The edges of the grid are traversed either horizontally or vertically. Let $T(N,M)$ denote the number of shortest paths from $(0,0)$ to (N,M). Then justify that $T(N,M)$ is the solution to the two-dimensional difference equation,

$$T(N,M) = T(N, M-1) + T(N-1, M),$$

with boundary conditions

$$T(0,M) = 1 \qquad \text{and} \qquad T(N,0) = 1.$$

Subsequently, show that the solution for $T(N,M)$ is

$$T(N,M) = \binom{N+M}{M} = \binom{N+M}{N}.$$

(*b*) The two-dimensional difference equation,

$$L(N,M) = L(N-1, M) + L(N-1, M-1),$$

with boundary conditions

$$L(1,M) = 2 \qquad \text{and} \qquad L(N,1) = 2N,$$

occurs in the solution of $L(N,M)$ given in Eq. (4.3). Verify the solution by any method you know.

4.3. Given is a perceptron with analog nonlinear preprocessing units as shown in Fig. 4.5. What types of decision surfaces can be realized? What is the capacity of the machine?

4.4. Design a perceptron with one layer of analog preprocessing units to realize any circular decision surfaces. What is the capacity of the machine?

4.5. Before applying the perceptron learning algorithm, a pattern vector of the form $(y_1 \ y_2 \ \cdots \ y_M)^T$ is extended by appending a 1 so that the augmented vector is $(y_1 \ y_2 \ \cdots \ y_M \ 1)^T$. Why is this done? Can a different constant be used instead of 1, for example, 0, 5, -10? In case a nonzero constant different from 1 is used, then after convergence, what is the equivalent threshold of the TLU without the connection to the input set at this constant value? Can different constants be used for different patterns?

4.6. Apply the perceptron learning algorithm to classify the following three-dimensional unipolar binary patterns before augmentation:

$$\text{Class A: } \{x\} = \{(0,0,0), \ (1,1,1)\}$$
$$\text{Class B: } \{x\} = \{(0,0,1), \ (0,1,1)\}$$

Draw a figure of the perceptron obtained, with its connections, weights, threshold, and transfer characteristic specified.

4.7. Apply the absolute correction rule to the following unaugmented unipolar binary patterns. After augmentation and adjustment, a ternary set results.

$$C_+: \{(0,0), (0,1)\}, \qquad C_-: \{(1,0), (1,1)\}.$$

4.8. Apply the fixed-increment rule with $c = 1$ to the following three-dimensional unipolar binary patterns before augmentation:

$$C_+: \{(0,0,0), \quad (1,0,0), \quad (1,0,1), \quad (1,1,0)\}$$
$$C_-: \{(0,0,1), \quad (0,1,1), \quad (0,1,0), \quad (1,1,1)\}$$

Let $\mathbf{w}_0 = (-1 \ -2 \ -2 \ 0)^T$ denote the initial weight vector.

4.9. Show that the pseudoinverse solution $\mathbf{w}^* = S^+\mathbf{d}$ minimizes the mean squared error

$$e^2 = \frac{1}{N}\|\mathbf{d} - S\mathbf{w}\|^2 = \frac{1}{N}(\mathbf{d} - S\mathbf{w})^T(\mathbf{d} - S\mathbf{w})$$

in the case when all entries are real-valued.

4.10. (*a*) Use the general gradient descent update equation

$$\mathbf{w}(k + 1) = \mathbf{w}(k) - c\left\{\frac{\partial E(\mathbf{w}, \mathbf{x})}{\partial \mathbf{w}}\right\}_{\mathbf{w} = \mathbf{w}(k)}$$

and the error function

$$E(\mathbf{w}, \mathbf{y}, T) = \frac{1}{8\|\mathbf{y}\|^2}\left[(\mathbf{w}^T\mathbf{y} - T) - |\mathbf{w}^T\mathbf{y} - T|\right]^2,$$

where $T > 0$, to derive a perceptron error correction algorithm.

(*b*) Let $c = T = 1$. Apply the algorithm obtained in (*a*) to the patterns in Problem 4.7.

(*c*) Discuss the effects of increasing T on the convergence of the algorithm for linearly separable patterns.

4.11. Consider an augmented pattern vector $\mathbf{y}(k) = (y_1(k) \cdots y_n(k) \ 1)^T$ and a weight vector $\mathbf{w} = (w_1 \cdots w_n \ w_{n+1})^T$. Assume that the augmented pattern vectors belonging to class C_- have been multiplied by -1. Call the totality of patterns after this modification the resulting set or the adjusted augmented pattern set.

(*a*) Show that if the patterns are linearly separable, then a solution $\hat{\mathbf{w}}$ exists such that $\hat{\mathbf{w}}^T\mathbf{y} > T$ for each pattern vector $\mathbf{y}$ in the resulting set where T is a nonnegative real number. What is the geometric interpretation in the weight space?

(*b*) The normal distance from an extended pattern vector $\mathbf{y}(k)$ to a decision hyperplane defined by $\mathbf{w}^T\mathbf{y}(k) = 0$ is

$$d = \frac{|\mathbf{w}^T\mathbf{y}(k)|}{\|\mathbf{w}\|}$$

Let

$$\alpha = \max_{\mathbf{w}} \ \min_{\{\mathbf{y}(k)\}_{k=1}^N} \ \frac{|\mathbf{w}^T\mathbf{y}(k)|}{\|\mathbf{w}\|}$$

where N is the number of patterns. Then the condition

$$\frac{|\mathbf{w}^T\mathbf{y}(k)|}{\|\mathbf{w}\|} \geq \alpha$$

gives the optimal decision hyperplane in the sense that the minimum distance from all the extended training patterns to it is the largest possible.

Find the minimum distance from all training patterns to the decision hyperplane obtained after convergence of the following modified fixed-increment rule:

$$\mathbf{w}(k+1) = \begin{cases} \mathbf{w}(k) + \mathbf{y}(k) & \text{if } \mathbf{w}^T\mathbf{y}(k) \leq T \\ \mathbf{w}(k) & \text{if } \mathbf{w}^T\mathbf{y}(k) > T. \end{cases}$$

4.12. You are given the following two classes of patterns, before augmentation, with only one pattern in each class: $C_+ = \{(57.595722, -99.759033)\}$ and $C_- = \{(41.887859, -72.551994)\}$. Surprisingly, it may take many thousands of iterations for any of the perceptron error correction rules to converge to a solution. Augment the patterns in the standard way to $C_+^a = \{(57.595722, -99.759033, 1)\}$, and $C_-^a = \{(41.887859, -72.551994, 1)\}$.

(a) Write a computer program implementing any of the perceptron error correction rules to verify this.

(b) Provide an explanation as to why it takes so long to solve such a simple problem, and suggest a general method to speed up the convergence of the perceptron algorithms that will reduce the iterations required for convergence to well below 50 in this case.

(c) Repeat (a) and (b) using the Widrow-Hoff LMS algorithm.

(d) Generalize your method obtained in (b) to patterns of higher dimensions.

4.13. In many applications, some components of the training vectors are not specified, either because they are not available or because of too much noise in the measurement. These components are called *uncertain* components. In different patterns, the uncertain components may be different. Generalize the perceptron algorithms to patterns with uncertain components.

4.14. Derive Eq. (4.43) in text.

4.15. Consider the adaptive linear element (combiner) shown in Fig. P4.15. The kth augmented pattern vector and the weight vector are, respectively,

$$\mathbf{y}(k) = [y_1 \; y_2 \; \cdots \; y_n \; 1]^T \quad \text{and} \quad \mathbf{w}(k) = [w_1 \; w_2 \cdots w_n \; w_{n+1}]^T.$$

The desired response to $\mathbf{y}(k)$ is $d(k)$, and the present error of the linear combiner is

$$e_k = d(k) - \mathbf{y}(k) \bullet \mathbf{w}(k).$$

(a) In the μ-LMS algorithm, an instantaneous gradient $\hat{\nabla}_k$ is calculated to be

$$\hat{\nabla}_k = \frac{\partial e_k^2}{\partial \mathbf{w}(k)}.$$

The weight update based on this estimate instead of the true gradient is

$$\mathbf{w}(k+1) = \mathbf{w}(k) - \mu \hat{\nabla}_k, \quad \mu > 0.$$

Show that the weight update simplifies to

$$\mathbf{w}(k+1) = \mathbf{w}(k) + 2\mu e_k \mathbf{y}(k).$$

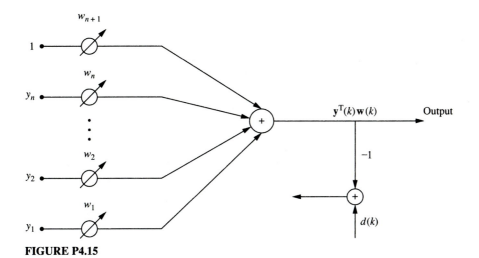

$y^T(k)w(k)$

Output

-1

$d(k)$

FIGURE P4.15

(b) Comment on the use of the instantaneous gradient, the size of μ, and the step size corresponding to the period during which a small finite number of exemplars may be presented without appreciable change in the weight vector.

4.16. In a certain training scheme, the weights $w_1, w_2, \ldots, w_n$ were ordered as follows:

$$w_1 > w_2 > w_3 > \cdots > w_{n-1} > w_n > 0.$$

The elements $x_1, x_2, \ldots, x_n$ of a training pattern vector were also ordered as follows:

$$0 < x_1 < x_2 < x_3 < \cdots < x_{n-1} < x_n.$$

The weight w_i need not be associated with x_i. A neural network designer remembers only that it is possible to obtain the correct association from a particular one-to-one correspondence between the weight w_i and the signal $x_{p(i)}$ for $i = 1, 2, \ldots, n$, which maximizes the value of the expression

$$E_p = \sum_{i=1}^{n} w_i x_{p(i)}$$

over all possible permutations p of the integer index set $\{1 \ 2 \ \cdots \ n\}$. Help the neural network designer by identifying the expression that produces that maximum.

4.17. Consider two vectors:

$$\mathbf{v} = (v_1 \ v_2 \ \cdots \ v_m)$$
$$\mathbf{w} = (w_1 \ w_2 \ \cdots \ w_m).$$

It is specified that

$$v_1 > v_2 > \cdots > v_m > 0$$
$$0 > w_1 > w_2 > \cdots > w_m.$$

It is required to find a permutation p for $1, 2, \ldots, m$ corresponding to each of the following cases. Identify each permutation by writing the expression for the optimization desired.

(a) $S_1 = \sum v_i w_{p(i)}$ has to be a minimum.

(b) $S_2 = \sum v_i^2 w_{p(i)}^2$ has to be a maximum.

4.18. Suppose there are eight binary inputs $\mathbf{x} = (x_7 x_6 \cdots x_0)$, where $x_7 x_6 \cdots x_0$ can be considered as a binary number $\mathbf{x}$. Let $B(\mathbf{x})$ be the decimal representation of the binary number. For example, 35 is the decimal (radix 10) representation of the binary (radix 2) number 00100011. Design the simplest perceptron to compute the predicate function,

$$\Psi_1 = \begin{cases} 1 & B(\mathbf{x}) \geq 8 \\ 0 & \text{otherwise.} \end{cases}$$

What is the support of Ψ_1?

Let Ψ be a linear threshold function with respect to the family of predicates $\mathbf{\Phi}$ defined on the retina $\mathbf{R} = (x_7, x_6, \ldots, x_0)$. Then Ψ has the representation

$$\Psi(\mathbf{x}) = P_B \left[\sum_{\phi_i \in \Phi} \alpha_i \phi_i(\mathbf{x}) - \theta \right],$$

where $\mathbf{x}$ is a subset of $\mathbf{R}$, θ is a real number denoting threshold, Φ_i is a predicate that belongs to the family $\mathbf{\Phi}$, and

$$P_B[y] = \begin{cases} 1 & \text{if } y \geq 0 \\ 0 & \text{if } y < 0. \end{cases}$$

What are the supports of the partial predicates ϕ_i? What is the order of the perceptron you have designed?

4.19. Repeat Problem 4.18 with Ψ_1 replaced by the predicate function,

$$\Psi_2 = \begin{cases} 1 & B(\mathbf{x}) \geq 8 \quad \text{and} \quad B(\mathbf{x}) \text{ is odd} \\ 0 & \text{otherwise.} \end{cases}$$

4.20. Consider the predicate function,

$$\Psi(\mathbf{x}) = P_B \left[a \sum_{x_i \in \mathbf{R}} x_i + b \sum_{x_i} \sum_{\substack{x_j \\ i<j}} x_i x_j - c \right],$$

where a, b, and c are real constants. What is the order of $\Psi(\mathbf{x})$? If $\Psi(\mathbf{x})$ is expressed in the form,

$$\Psi(\mathbf{x}) = P_B \left[\alpha_i \phi_i(\mathbf{x}) - \theta \right],$$

write α_i, $\phi_i(\mathbf{x})$, and θ in terms of a, b, c, and the x_i's. If a perceptron is to implement $\Psi(\mathbf{x})$, how many connections to the output threshold logic unit exist, given that the cardinality of the retina is $|\mathbf{R}|$?

4.21. What is the order of the predicate $\varphi(|\mathbf{x}|) = [|\mathbf{x}| = M_1 \vee |\mathbf{x}| = M_2)]$, where $M_1 < M_2$ and M_1, M_2 are arbitrary positive integers?

4.22. In a *diameter-limited* perceptron, for each $\phi_i(\mathbf{x}) \in \mathbf{\Phi}$, the set of points (defined by specializations of the set of variables $\{x_1, x_2, \ldots, x_n\}$ in $\mathbf{x}$) on which $\phi_i(\mathbf{x})$ depends is restricted so as not to exceed a certain *fixed diameter* (measured, say, according to the Euclidean metric) in the Euclidean space. Can a diameter-limited perceptron compute Ψ_{convex}? Why?

4.23. Answer whether each of the following statements is true or false.

(a) A diameter-limited perceptron can compute Ψ_{convex}.

(b) The order of the predicate $\Psi(|X| < M)$ is 1, where M is an arbitrary but fixed positive integer and $|X|$ denotes the number of points in the finite set X.

(c) The predicate $\Psi_{\text{connected}}$ cannot have an order greater than 3.

(d) The predicate Ψ_{convex} is of order 3.

(e) All Boolean functions of two variables have order 1.

(f) The conjunction

$$y_1 \wedge y_2 \wedge \cdots \wedge y_n \triangleq y_1 \, y_2 \, \cdots \, y_n$$

of the Boolean variables $y_1, y_2, \ldots, y_n$ (each either assumes the value 1 or 0) is of order 1.

(g) The disjunction

$$y_1 \vee y_2 \vee \cdots \vee y_n \triangleq y_1 + y_2 + \cdots + y_n$$

of the Boolean variables $y_1, y_2, \ldots, y_n$ (each assumes either the value 1 or 0) is of order 1.

(h) The counting predicate that recognizes that a finite set X has M points is of order 4.

4.24. Each accompanying part has one correct answer. Identify this correct answer by circling the appropriate letter (capital A, B, C, etc.).

(a) The Widrow-Hoff learning law is obtained after calculating the gradient $\nabla F(\mathbf{w})$ of the expression

$$F(\mathbf{w}) = p - 2\mathbf{w}^T\mathbf{q} + \mathbf{w}^T\mathbf{R}\mathbf{w},$$

where p is a scalar, $\mathbf{w}$ and $\mathbf{q}$ are vectors, $\mathbf{R}$ is a matrix, and the superscript T denotes transpose operation. The gradient $\nabla F(\mathbf{w})$ is

A. $-2\mathbf{q} + \mathbf{R}\mathbf{w}$.
B. $-2\mathbf{q} + 2\mathbf{R}\mathbf{w}$.
C. $-\mathbf{q} + \mathbf{R}\mathbf{w}$.
D. $-\mathbf{q} + 2\mathbf{R}\mathbf{w}$.
E. none of the above.

(b) The order of the predicate $\Psi(|X| = M_1 \vee |X| = M_2 \vee |X| = M_3)$, where $0 < M_1 < M_2 < M_3$ and M_1, M_2, M_3 are integers, is

A. 2.
B. 4.
C. 6.
D. 8.
E. none of the above.

(c) The orders of the predicates $\Psi_1 = T_b(x_7 + x_6 + x_5 + x_4 + x_3 + 5x_0 - 6)$ and $\Psi_2 = T_b(\sum_{i=3}^{7}(x_0 x_i - 1))$, where x_k for $k = 0, 3, \ldots, 7$ are unipolar binary variables, are

A. both equal to 2.
B. both equal to 1.
C. different from each other.
D. none of the above.

(d) When a real symmetric matrix (complex Hermitian matrix) is transformed to a diagonal matrix by a similarity transformation using an orthonormal (unitary) linear transformation, the original matrix and the resulting diagonal matrix have
A. their traces and determinants invariant.
B. their traces same and determinants different.
C. their determinants same and traces different.
D. none of the above.

CHAPTER
5

MULTILAYER
NETWORKS

Multilayer feedforward network structures are characterized by directed layered graphs. In Chapter 4, we saw that to realize a nonlinear map for transforming a not linearly separable problem in the input feature space to a linearly separable problem in the first-layer image pattern space, a perceptron designer must find answers to questions such as how many TLUs or nonlinear analog preprocessors should be in the first layer, how those should be connected to the inputs, and what the values of the connection weights should be so that the desired linear separability property is achieved, before the perceptron convergence theorem becomes applicable. For perceptrons the designer's options are limited to either empirical or random choices. If a choice is improper, the problem posed cannot be tackled. For example, in the case of the perceptron shown in Fig. 4.4e, choice of the mapping functions $\phi_1(X) = T_b(10x_1 + 2x_2 - 1)$ and $\phi_2(X) = T_b(x_1 + 10x_2 - 5)$, where $X = (x_1, x_2) \in \mathbb{R}^2$, does not lead to the computation of the XOR function no matter how the connection weights to the trainable TLU are adjusted. The reason is that the improper choice of weights to the first-layer units leads to the mapping of two patterns, characterized by $(1,1)$ and $(0,1)$, belonging to different classes in the feature space, to the same point $(1,1)$ in the first-layer image pattern space. Therefore, the desired linear separability cannot be achieved by any means with such a perceptron structure. Generally this type of problem can be remedied only by allowing the structure, connection weights, and thresholds at all levels to be obtained from learning rather than by being predetermined. When the first-layer units in a perceptron are replaced by trainable TLUs, the resulting structure becomes a special case of a trainable multilayer network. Actually, Minsky and Papert [261] called this special structure with one trainable hidden layer a Gamba perceptron.

For arbitrary patterns, binary or nonbinary, a Gamba perceptron may not suffice. From network complexity, performance, and implementation considerations, a larger number of hidden layers, with corresponding increase in the number of hidden units and connections, may be required, necessitating the study of trainable multilayer networks. The capabilities of a three-layer feedforward structure can be appreciated from the implications of a remarkable mathematical result, due to Kolmogorov, on the existence of exact representations, which is described in Section 5.1. This section also contains some recent results on approximate representations using multilayer feedforward networks. The training of interconnection weights and thresholds in a fixed multilayer feedforward network by the popular method of backpropagation is discussed in Section 5.2. The name *backpropagation* derives from the fact that computations are passed forward from the input to the output layer, following which calculated errors are propagated back in the other direction to change the weights to obtain a better performance. The possibilities of training for the structure as well as for connection weights and thresholds are investigated in Section 5.3. The methods of training discussed so far are based on supervisory learning done on the basis of direct comparison of actual outputs with desired values. When the learning goal is not defined in terms of a specific set of exemplars, the network may be expected to use available information in the form of correlation data on the input signals to produce output signals that can be associated with each input category. Section 5.4 is devoted to the topic of unsupervised learning in feedforward networks for the principal component analysis approach as well as for self-organization. In Section 5.5, another multilayer feedforward structure called the *probabilistic neural network*, which has a network structure similar to backpropagation but has (usually) a Gaussian-shaped characteristic rather than a sigmoid activation function, is described along with a variant. The training mechanism is quite different from the iterative approach in backpropagation. Conclusions are drawn in Section 5.6, especially pertaining to properties of multilayer networks.

5.1 EXACT AND APPROXIMATE REPRESENTATION USING FEEDFORWARD NETWORKS

Multilayer feedforward networks offer immense scope for exact representation of a broad class of input/output maps, as suggested by Kolmogorov's theorem (described next). However, practical design considerations, which include the actual construction of the neural network, demand an appreciation of the possibilities of approximation for meeting a desired error criterion. After all, the learning of an input/output mapping from a set of exemplars that a neural network is designed to realize and to generalize as well when presented with new inputs, may be described in terms of approximation theory.

5.1.1 Exact Representation: Kolmogorov's Theorem and Its Consequences

In 1900, Professor David Hilbert, the eminent mathematician from the University of Goettingen, delivered a lecture before the International Congress of Mathematicians at Paris, where he presented 23 problems[1] from the discussion of which "advancement of science may be expected." Some of these deep and difficult problems have been related to applications, where useful insights into the *existence,* but not the *construction,* of solutions to problems have been deduced. For instance, Artin's solution of Hilbert's seventeenth problem had an impact on the realizability theory of passive electrical networks [47].

Another of the great mathematician's problems is having some impact in the area of neural networks. The thirteenth problem of Hilbert extended an invitation to settle his conjecture about the impossibility of the solution of the general equation of the seventh degree by compositions of continuous functions of two variables. He showed that if his conjecture were true, it would be necessary to prove that the seventh-degree polynomial equation

$$x^7 + a_3 x^3 + a_2 x^2 + a_1 x + 1 = 0$$

is not solvable for its roots (which are continuous functions of the three independent parameters a_1, a_2, a_3) with the help of any continuous functions of only two of the parameters. The problem just stated is then reformulated as, "Are there continuous functions of three variables that are not representable by superposition of a composition of functions in a lesser number of variables?"

V. I. Arnold demonstrated the falsity of Hilbert's conjecture by proving that every continuous function $f(x_1, x_2, x_3)$ in the real variables x_1, x_2, x_3 whose domains belong to the closed unipolar cube

$$I_3 = [0, 1]^3 \triangleq \{(x_1, x_2, x_3) \in \mathbb{R}^3 \mid 0 \le x_i \le 1, \ i = 1, 2, 3\}$$

can be represented in the form

$$f(x_1, x_2, x_3) = \sum_{k=1}^{9} h_k(g_k(x_1, x_2), x_3),$$

where h_k and g_k are real, continuous functions.

Kolmogorov improved Arnold's result by demonstrating the feasibility of an alternate representation,

$$f(x_1, x_2, x_3) = \sum_{k=1}^{7} h_k(g_{k1}(x_1) + g_{k2}(x_2) + g_{k3}(x_3)),$$

where h_k and g_{kj}, for $j = 1, 2, 3$, are real continuous functions. Furthermore, the g_{kj}'s can be chosen once and for all independently of f. Kolmogorov generalized his results by proving the following theorem [201] over an n-dimensional cube,

$$I_n = [0, 1]^n \triangleq \{(x_1, \ldots, x_n) \in \mathbb{R}^n \mid 0 \le x_i \le 1, \ i = 1, 2, \ldots, n\}. \qquad (5.1)$$

---

[1] S. Iyanaga and Y. Kawada, eds. *Encyclopedic Dictionary of Mathematics.* MIT Press paperback edition, Cambridge, MA, 1980, pp. 632–633.

Theorem 5.1   (Kolmogorov's theorem). Any continuous function $f(x_1, x_2, \ldots, x_n)$ of n variables $x_1, x_2, \ldots, x_n$ on I_n ($n \geq 2$) can be represented in the form

$$f(x_1, x_2, \ldots, x_n) = \sum_{j=1}^{2n+1} h_j \left(\sum_{i=1}^{n} g_{ij}(x_i) \right), \tag{5.2}$$

where h_j and the g_{ij}'s are continuous functions of one variable; furthermore, the g_{ij}'s are fixed, monotone increasing functions that are not dependent on $f(x_1, x_2, \ldots, x_n)$.

In Kolmogorov's *exact* representation shown in Eq. (5.2), a *univariate* monotone increasing function $g_{ij}(x)$ over a domain I of x satisfies the property

$$[g_{ij}(x_1) - g_{ij}(x_2)](x_1 - x_2) > 0$$

for any distinct values x_1, x_2 of x in I. The representation in Eq. (5.2) is also valid if I_n is replaced by any closed and bounded domain. Several authors have improved in several ways the representation in Eq. (5.2). Lorentz [239] showed that one can replace the h_j's by one single-variable function h. Sprecher [367] replaced functions g_{ij} by $\lambda_i g_j$, where the λ_i's are constants, to obtain another exact representation equation,

$$f(x_1, x_2, \ldots, x_n) = \sum_{j=1}^{2n+1} h \left(\sum_{i=1}^{n} \lambda_i g_j(x_i) \right), \tag{5.3}$$

which is a considerably improved version of Eq. (5.2). A neural network realization of the mapping of the input variables x_1, x_2 to the output $f(x_1, x_2)$ in the special case when $n = 2$ in Eq. (5.3) is shown in Fig. 5.1 [133]. This type of realization, in the case of n input variables for the n-input one-output case, requires $2n + 1$ units in the layer directly below the output layer and $n(2n + 1)$ units in the layer two levels below the output layer. The total number of connections, which is $2n^2 + 3n + 1$, excluding any connections from inputs or output, equals the total number of units in the two hidden layers. Therefore, the underlying graph characterizing the structure is layered but not a complete layered graph. Sprecher obtained another refinement that led to the following exact representation.

Sprecher's representation. For each preassigned number $\delta > 0$ there is a rational number ϵ, $0 < \epsilon < \delta$, such that every continuous function $f(x_1, x_2, \ldots, x_n)$ of n variables, defined on I_n, can be represented as

$$f(x_1, x_2, \ldots, x_n) = \sum_{j=1}^{2n+1} h \left(\sum_{i=1}^{n} \lambda^i g[x_i + \epsilon(j-1)] + j - 1 \right), \tag{5.4}$$

where the function h is real and continuous; g is real, monotone increasing, continuous, and dependent on n; and λ is a constant independent of $f(x_1, x_2, \ldots, x_n)$.

Sprecher's representation leads directly to a neural network realization of the vector map

$$\mathbf{f} : [0, 1]^n \longrightarrow \mathbb{R}^m,$$

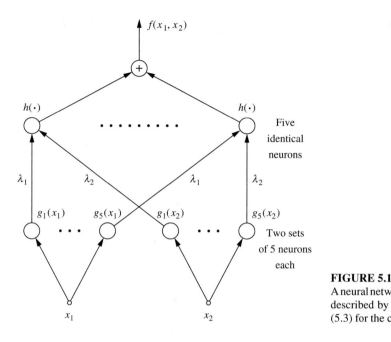

FIGURE 5.1
A neural network for the mapping described by the function in Eq. (5.3) for the case when $n = 2$.

where

$$\mathbf{f} = [f_1(x_1, \ldots, x_n) \cdots f_m(x_1, \ldots, x_n)]^{\mathrm{T}} \in \mathbb{R}^m.$$

In the limiting case when $\epsilon = 0$, this network realization is shown in Fig. 5.2, where, again, there are two hidden layers and an output layer, whereas the inputs are the independent real variables $x_1, x_2, \ldots, x_n$. The three-layered network is formed from the node-coalesced cascade or concatenation of the complete bipartite graphs $K_{n,2n+1}$ and $K_{2n+1,m}$. When $m = 1$, the numbers of nodes in the two hidden and one output layers and of edges (excluding those from the input nodes and the output node) in the complete layered graph are, respectively, $3n + 2$ and $2n^2 + 3n + 1$. In comparison to the n-input generalization of the structure in Fig. 5.1, the corresponding structure of Fig. 5.2 has a lesser number of nodes but the same order of connections. The numbers inside the nodes of the hidden layer just below the output layer are the negatives of the thresholds. The threshold of each unit in the other hidden layer is zero when $\epsilon = 0$.

5.1.2 Approximate Representations

A pessimistic note on the utilitarian value of Kolmogorov's theorem was conveyed by Lorentz [239]:

> I do not know of any applications of Kolmogorov's theorem, except perhaps that the multivariable case of the Weierstrass approximation theorem follows from its single-variable case. Perhaps Kolmogorov's theorem is of the nature of pathological examples, whose main purpose is to disprove hopes that are too optimistic.

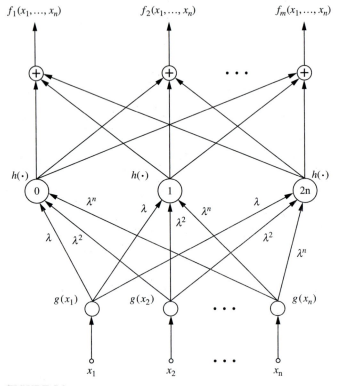

FIGURE 5.2
The neural network for the vector-valued mapping **f** from the n-dimensional cube to $\mathbb{R}^m$ in the limiting case of Sprecher's representation. The numbers inside the units in one of the hidden layers are the biases.

Consider the mapping H from I_n to $\mathbb{R}^{2n+1}$ given by

$$z_j = \sum_{i=1}^{n} \lambda_i g_j(x_i), \qquad j = 1, \ldots, 2n + 1.$$

By Kolmogorov's theorem, there exists a homeomorphic (one-to-one from one metric space onto another so that the mapping and its inverse are both continuous) embedding H of I_n into $\mathbb{R}^{2n+1}$ so that on the image $H(I_n)$ each continuous function f takes the special form

$$f = \sum_{j=1}^{2n+1} h(z_j).$$

Unfortunately, the functions g_j and h could be very nonsmooth even for a differentiable function f. Furthermore, Kolmogorov's theorem is only an existence result. In fact, for an arbitrarily specified $f(x_1, \ldots, x_n)$ there is no constructive procedure that leads to the representation in Eq. (5.2), even though the existence of the representation is guaranteed.

In view of the difficulties just mentioned, investigations have been initiated for approximate representations, subject to the neuron transfer characteristic nonlinearities commonly encountered in multilayer feedforward training, using the popular backpropagation algorithm. Under these constraints the exact representation of Kolmogorov fails to provide not only the number of layers but also the number of neurons necessary in each hidden layer. Irie and Miyake [174] obtained an integral formula that suggests the realization of functions of several variables by three-layer networks, by analogy with the principle of computerized tomography. However, in this integral formula the neuron transfer characteristic must satisfy the condition of absolute integrability; so it cannot be a sigmoid function. Moreover, the function to be realized is given by an integral representation, and the formula does not give the realization theorem of functions by networks with a finite number of neurons.

The results of research activities steered toward meeting the need for approximate realization procedures are found in refs. [87, 122, 133, 166, 174, 336]. Giroso and Poggio [133] showed that any continuous vector-valued mapping whose components are square-integrable on compact subsets of $\mathbb{R}^n$ can be approximately represented in the sense of L^2 norm (i.e., the integral of the square of the magnitude of the error of approximation can be made to approach zero in the limit) by a three-layer feedforward network with sigmoidal nonlinearities (discussed in Section 1.3.2) in the transfer characteristics of the units. Although the sigmoid type of nonlinearity is assumed, the results obtained belong to the class of existence results for approximate realizations with wide-ranging types of activation functions, so long as these functions satisfy an explicit set of assumptions that vary from one result to another. Subsequent research revealed that only two layers in a feedforward network are sufficient for such approximations. Cybenko [87] considered approximating a specified absolutely integrable function $f(x_1, x_2, \ldots, x_n)$ in the real variables $x_1, x_2, \ldots, x_n$ by finite linear combinations of the form,

$$\sum_{j=1}^{N} \alpha_j \sigma(\mathbf{w}_j^T \mathbf{x} - \theta_j), \tag{5.5}$$

where α_j and θ_j are fixed real numbers and $\mathbf{w}_j, \mathbf{x}$ are, respectively, $(n \times 1)$ weight and input vectors. The main result of Cybenko is a demonstration of the fact that sums of the form in Eq. (5.5) are dense on the unit cube with respect to the supremum (uniform) norm if σ is any continuous sigmoidal function and N is allowed to be arbitrarily large. In other words, given $\epsilon > 0$ and an absolutely integrable function $f(x_1, x_2, \ldots, x_n)$ over the n-dimensional cube I_n, there exists a sum $h(x_1, x_2, \ldots, x_n)$ of the form in Eq. (5.5) for which

$$|h(\mathbf{x}) - f(\mathbf{x})| < \epsilon, \qquad \text{for all } \mathbf{x} = [x_1 \cdots x_n]^T \in I^n.$$

Thus, any absolutely integrable function can be uniformly approximated by a neural network having only one hidden layer employing continuous sigmoidal nonlinearities. The drawback is that the approximating properties focus only on existence, and for a specified value of error ϵ the number N of terms in the summation Eq. (5.5) could be impractically large. Attention has been directed toward improving upon these problems.

5.2 FIXED MULTILAYER FEEDFORWARD NETWORK TRAINING BY BACKPROPAGATION

Here we assume that the neural network is structurally fixed in the sense that the nodes and edges of the underlying layered graph have been preset. Like the perceptron, whose algorithm can be viewed as an application of the gradient descent method encountered in optimization theory, a multilayer network that involves the minimization of an error function in the least mean square sense is also trained by applying this gradient descent method. The *backpropagation algorithm* (BPA), also called the *generalized delta rule,* provides a way to calculate the gradient of the error function efficiently using the chain rule of differentiation. The error after initial computation in the forward pass is propagated backward from the output units, layer by layer, justifying the name "backpropagation." This algorithm has been rediscovered several times with minor variations [62, 214, 287, 324, 325, 402]. We follow the presentation by Rumelhart, Hinton, and Williams [324, 325]. The Ph.D. thesis of Werbos [402], along with tutorials on other developments on backpropagation, is contained in a recent monograph [404].

The BPA can be applied not only to a multilayer feedforward network whose structure is characterized by a layered graph but also to a similar network whose structure is not so constrained; i.e., in addition to layered connections, units at a given layer may be connected to units at layers not immediately above it, as shown in Fig. 4.1c. However, to make the algorithm easier to understand, we restrict the subsequent presentation to layered feedforward networks. Once this is understood, generalization to the training of structures characterized by multipartite graphs is straightforward, as will be illustrated by a nontrivial example.

Let the training set be $\{\mathbf{x}(k), \mathbf{d}(k)\}_{k=1}^{N}$, where $\mathbf{x}(k)$ is the input pattern vector to the network and $\mathbf{d}(k)$ is the desired output vector for the input pattern $\mathbf{x}(k)$. The output of the jth output unit is denoted by y_j. Connection weights from the ith unit, in one layer, to the jth unit, in the layer above, are denoted by w_{ij}. To avoid ambiguity, the superscript l in $w_{ij}^{(l)}$ will be used to denote the fact that the layer containing the jth unit is l layers below the output layer. When $l = 0$, the output layer is defined, and the superscript may be omitted. Refer to Fig. 5.3 for an illustration of notations.

Let m be the number of output units. Suppose that $d_j(k)$ is the desired output from the jth output unit whose actual output in response to the kth input exemplar $\mathbf{x}(k)$ is y_j, for $j = 1, 2, \ldots, m$. Define the sum of squares of the error over all output units for this kth exemplar by

$$E(k) = \frac{1}{2} \sum_{j=1}^{m} [y_j(k) - d_j(k)]^2 \tag{5.6}$$

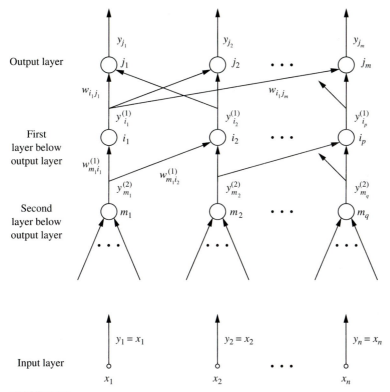

FIGURE 5.3
A typical multilayer feedforward network structure.

and the total classification error over the set of N exemplars by

$$E_T = \sum_{k=1}^{N} E(k). \tag{5.7}$$

In Eq. (5.6), the constant multiplier of value $\frac{1}{2}$ does not influence the minimization but has been inserted for convenience in representation following the gradient calculation. The process of computing the error $E(k)$ in Eq. (5.6) is called a *forward pass*.

After presentation of a training pattern $\mathbf{x}(k)$, the classification error can be computed. The objective is to determine how the error is reducible by the adjustment of network parameters. How the error $E(k)$ is affected by the output from unit j at the output layer is determined easily from Eq. (5.6) by computing

$$\frac{\partial E(k)}{\partial y_j} = y_j - d_j. \tag{5.8}$$

Recall that the net input to unit j in the output layer is of the form

$$s_j = \sum_i y_i^{(1)} w_{ij} - \theta_j, \tag{5.9}$$

where $y_i^{(1)}$ is the output from the ith unit in the first layer below the output layer, w_{ij} is the connection weight multiplying $y_i^{(1)}$, and θ_j is the threshold of unit j. Remember that the negative of the threshold is defined to be the bias. This choice of notation should provide a good balance between avoidance of clutter and reduction of ambiguity.

The transfer characteristic of output unit j, described by the input/output relationship $y_j = f_j(s_j)$, should be such that $\partial f_j / \partial s_j$ exists and is finite. A popular choice for f_j is the sigmoidal function, which, after using Eq. (5.9), provides the mapping described in the following equation, where the positive real parameter λ determines the slope of the function at a point and is called the *activation gain:*

$$y_j = \frac{1}{1 + \exp(-\lambda s_j)} = \frac{1}{1 + \exp\left[-\lambda\left(\sum_{i=1}^{n} w_{ij} y_i^{(1)} - \theta_j\right)\right]}. \qquad (5.10)$$

Recall from Chapter 1 that the sigmoidal function is differentiable and therefore continuous everywhere. It is also a bounded and a monotonically nondecreasing function. Its derivative is positive and approaches zero as the magnitude of the argument s_j approaches infinity. Variants of the sigmoidal function in Eq. (5.10) exist; they are specifically referred to as *logsigmoid without bias* in the MATLAB® *Neural Network Toolbox*. How the error $E(k)$ in Eq. (5.6) is affected by the input s_j in Eq. (5.9) to the jth unit of the output layer can be computed from

$$\frac{\partial E(k)}{\partial s_j} = \frac{\partial E(k)}{\partial y_j} \frac{dy_j}{ds_j}, \qquad (5.11)$$

where, assuming $\lambda = 1$ in Eq. (5.10),

$$\frac{dy_j}{ds_j} = \frac{d}{ds_j}\left(\frac{1}{1 + \exp(-s_j)}\right) = y_j(1 - y_j). \qquad (5.12)$$

Therefore, substituting Eqs. (5.8) and (5.12) in Eq. (5.11), we have

$$\frac{\partial E(k)}{\partial s_j} = (y_j - d_j)y_j(1 - y_j). \qquad (5.13)$$

Since unit i in the layer just below the output layer is connected to unit j of the output layer by interconnection weight w_{ij}, we need to calculate

$$\frac{\partial E(k)}{\partial w_{ij}} = \frac{\partial E(k)}{\partial s_j} \frac{\partial s_j}{\partial w_{ij}} = \frac{\partial E(k)}{\partial s_j} y_i^{(1)}. \qquad (5.14)$$

Since $\partial E(k)/\partial s_j$ was computed in Eq. (5.13), therefore Eq. (5.14) permits the computation of $\partial E(k)/\partial w_{ij}$ for the connection weights to each unit in the output layer from the units in the layer directly below it. It can now be said that the error has been propagated down one layer.

Next, let us determine how the error $E(k)$ is affected by connection weights from units that are located in layers that are two or more levels below the output layer. Recall that $w_{mi}^{(l)}$ denotes the connection weight to the ith unit in the layer that is l levels below the output layer from the mth unit in the layer that is $(l + 1)$ levels below the output layer. The output from the ith unit in the layer that is l levels below the output layer is denoted by $y_i^{(l)}$, and the net input to it is $s_i^{(l)}$. This net input is related to the corresponding output by the map

$$y_i^{(l)} = f_i^{(l)}\left(s_i^{(l)}\right).\tag{5.15}$$

Furthermore, $s_i^{(l)}$ may be expressed as a weighted sum of the outputs $y_m^{(l+1)}$ from the units in the layer directly below by

$$s_i^{(l)} = \sum_m y_m^{(l+1)} w_{mi}^{(l)} - \theta_i^{(l)},\tag{5.16}$$

where $w_{mi}^{(l)}$ are the connection weights and $\theta_i^{(l)}$ is the threshold of unit i in level l below the output layer. The reader is reminded that $l = 0$ corresponds to the output layer, and in this case the superscript in the variables was omitted for the sake of brevity without causing any confusion. By applying the chain rule, the following derivative is computed for each unit corresponding to the case, $l = 1$:

$$\frac{\partial E(k)}{\partial w_{mi}^{(1)}} = \frac{\partial E(k)}{\partial y_i^{(1)}}\frac{\partial y_i^{(1)}}{\partial s_i^{(1)}}\frac{\partial s_i^{(1)}}{\partial w_{mi}^{(1)}}.\tag{5.17}$$

Calculations similar to that in Eq. (5.12) and use of Eq. (5.16) allow Eq. (5.17) to be expressed by

$$\frac{\partial E(k)}{\partial w_{mi}^{(1)}} = \frac{\partial E(k)}{\partial y_i^{(1)}}y_i^{(1)}\left(1 - y_i^{(1)}\right)y_m^{(2)}.\tag{5.18}$$

The output from unit i may be connected to more than one unit at the layer above as in Fig. 5.3. Summing over all connections emanating from unit i to the layer above, we have

$$\frac{\partial E(k)}{\partial y_i^{(1)}} = \sum_j \frac{\partial E(k)}{\partial s_j}w_{ij},\tag{5.19}$$

since from Eq. (5.9)

$$\frac{\partial s_j}{\partial y_i^{(1)}} = w_{ij}.\tag{5.20}$$

Since $\partial E(k)/\partial s_j$ was already computed in Eq. (5.13), therefore Eq. (5.19) may be calculated from Eqs. (5.13) and (5.20). Substitution of Eq. (5.19) in Eq. (5.18) then permits the computation of $\partial E(k)/\partial w_{mi}^{(1)}$. The procedure summarized in Eqs. (5.18) and (5.19) for the $l = 1$ case is repeated until $\partial E(k)/\partial w_{mi}^{(l)}$ is computed for all connections. At each layer, the partial derivatives $\partial E(k)/\partial s_j^{(l)}$ are saved for computations at the next layer. These partial derivatives will, however, not be needed after the computations for the layer immediately below are completed. For the layered topology, only the communication between units in adjacent layers is required for computations. The process of computing the partial derivatives $\partial E(k)/\partial w_{ij}^{(l)}$ from the output layer all the way down to connections linking the input variables to units at the first layer is called the *backward pass*.

There are two approaches for applying the gradient descent method to the training of a multilayer feedforward neural network. The first is based on *periodic updating* and the second on *continuous updating*. In either case, the exemplars are repeatedly presented, either sequentially or at random, until (it is hoped) the algorithm converges, although there is no guarantee for that to happen. When the exemplars from the training set are presented to the network sequentially, an entire pass through all the elements of the training set constitutes an *epoch*. When such an entire pass occurs without error, training will be considered to be complete.

In the periodic updating approach the gradient,

$$\frac{\partial E_T}{\partial \mathbf{w}} = \sum_{k=1}^{N} \frac{\partial E(k)}{\partial \mathbf{w}}, \tag{5.21}$$

is computed over all N exemplars, one by one, where $\mathbf{w}$ has all the weights arranged as a vector, so that

$$\frac{\partial E(k)}{\partial \mathbf{w}} = \left[\frac{\partial E(k)}{\partial w_1} \; \frac{\partial E(k)}{\partial w_2} \; \cdots \; \frac{\partial E(k)}{\partial w_M} \right]^{\mathrm{T}}, \tag{5.22}$$

with M denoting the total number of weights in the network. The weights are updated only once a cycle, after all the training patterns are presented, according to the *generalized delta update rule*,

$$\mathbf{w}^{\text{new}} = \mathbf{w}^{\text{old}} - \eta \frac{\partial E_T}{\partial \mathbf{w}}, \tag{5.23}$$

where η is a small constant greater than zero, referred to as the *learning rate*. In Eq. (5.23), $\mathbf{w}^{\text{new}}$ and $\mathbf{w}^{\text{old}}$ may be viewed as weight vectors at time indices $k+1$ and k, respectively, and therefore may also be denoted by $\mathbf{w}(k+1)$ and $\mathbf{w}(k)$.

The continuous updating approach requires that the weights be updated after each training pattern is presented. That is, after all the partial derivatives $\partial E(k)/\partial w_{ij}^{(l)}$ are computed for all connections in the network, the weights are updated according to

$$\mathbf{w}^{\text{new}} = \mathbf{w}^{\text{old}} - \eta \frac{\partial E(k)}{\partial \mathbf{w}}. \tag{5.24}$$

The preceding update equation is equivalent to considering $\partial E(k)/\partial \mathbf{w}$ as an approximation to $\partial E_T/\partial \mathbf{w}$.

In both cases, the step size η is called the learning rate. The two approaches are essentially the same. It has been argued in the second approach that when η is large, one particular pattern may force the weights into a local minimum of the cost function. However, it is also likely that one pattern may push the weights into a region closer to the desired solution, resulting in a quicker convergence. There is no guarantee of convergence to the desired solution in either approach. The second approach has the advantage of not requiring storage for all $\partial E(k)/\partial w_{ij}^{(l)}$. No general definite conclusions on the speed of convergence in the two approaches currently exist. Larger values of η in the gradient descent formulation may lead to faster convergence. However, they may also lead to oscillation. One attempt at increasing the speed of convergence while minimizing the possibility of oscillation involves adding a momentum term to the basic gradient descent formulation. In this case, the weight vector at time index $(k + 1)$ is related to the weight vectors at time indices k and $(k - 1)$ by

$$\mathbf{w}(k + 1) = \mathbf{w}(k) - \left[\eta\frac{\partial E}{\partial \mathbf{w}} + \beta\Delta\mathbf{w}(k - 1)\right], \tag{5.25}$$

where β is a constant that determines the effect of past weight changes on the current weight change. It can be shown that Eq. (5.25) is equivalent to a low-pass filtering of weight changes. For stability of this filter, β should be within a certain range (see Problem 5.14), and it is often chosen to be around 0.9. This low-pass filter attenuates the noise when computing the partial derivatives. It also smoothes out the high-frequency variations of the error surface in the weight space. This effect is useful when the error surface contains long ravines that are characterized by sharp curvatures across the ravine and a gently sloping floor. The sharp curvatures tend to cause divergent oscillations across the ravine.

Though this presentation has been given for layered topology, the reader is reminded that the procedure is easily adaptable when the characterizing graph for the neural network is multipartite. To justify the preceding comment and to enhance the reader's comprehension of the material presented, the following example illustrates how backpropagation applies to a nonlayered structure. To accommodate the nonlayered situation, a minor and obvious change of notation is appropriate, whereby the units are numbered sequentially and not by layers.

Example 5.1. Consider the network shown in Fig. 5.4. In order to learn the threshold, all the units are connected to a constant input, and each sigmoidal transfer characteristic is given a threshold $\theta = 0$. The two input variables, x_1 and x_2, occur at units 1 and 2 and are identified only for convenience. All the bias connection weights are assumed to be linked to a single constant input source of value a, denoted as unit 3, which is not explicitly shown. The processing units are numbered from 4 to 8. The output units are numbered 7 and 8. Note that the underlying topology of the network is not a layered graph. Let $x_1(k)$ and $x_2(k)$ form one set of input patterns in a forward pass. Let y_j, $j = 4, 5, 6, 7, 8$, denote the outputs from units 4 through 8 due to the pattern vector, $(x_1(k)\ x_2(k))^T$, applied as input. The error $E(k)$ is computed as in Eq. (5.6). By realizing that s_7 and s_8 are the respective inputs to the output units 7 and 8, Eqs. (5.13) and (5.14) directly lead to the following equations:

$$\frac{\partial E(k)}{\partial s_7} = (y_7 - d_7)y_7(1 - y_7) \tag{5.26}$$

$$\frac{\partial E(k)}{\partial s_8} = (y_8 - d_8)y_8(1 - y_8) \tag{5.27}$$

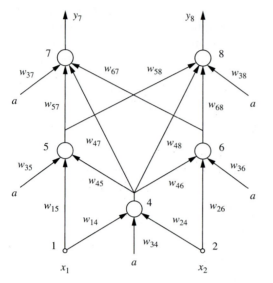

FIGURE 5.4
The multilayer feedforward neural network structure in Example 5.1.

$$\frac{\partial E(k)}{\partial w_{i7}} = \frac{\partial E(k)}{\partial s_7} \frac{\partial s_7}{\partial w_{i7}} = \frac{\partial E(k)}{\partial s_7} y_i \qquad \text{for } i = 4, 5, 6 \qquad (5.28)$$

$$\frac{\partial E(k)}{\partial w_{37}} = \frac{\partial E(k)}{\partial s_7} \frac{\partial s_7}{\partial w_{37}} = \frac{\partial E(k)}{\partial s_7} a. \qquad (5.29)$$

Then the y_i values obtained from the forward pass and the current connection weights are substituted into the preceding equations to obtain the values of these partial derivatives. Similarly, the partial derivatives for unit 8 can be obtained. It can be said that the error now has been propagated to the output of units 5 and 6. Partial derivatives for connections to units 5 and 6 can therefore be computed using Eqs. (5.18) and (5.19), after incorporating the notational modification. Note that partial derivatives for connections to unit 4 cannot be carried out yet since its output is connected not only to units 7 and 8 but also to units 5 and 6. Computations for connections to units 5 and 6 must be carried out first before those to unit 4 can be done. We should first determine how the error is affected by the output of units 5 and 6. Let us consider unit 5. We see y_5 is connected to units 7 and 8. Therefore, changes in y_5 will affect the error through its connections to units 7 and 8. We may consider its effect on the error through the connection $5 \to 7$ first:

$$\left[\frac{\partial E(k)}{\partial y_5} \right]_{5 \to 7} = \frac{\partial E(k)}{\partial s_7} \frac{\partial s_7}{\partial y_5} = \frac{\partial E(k)}{\partial s_7} w_{57}. \qquad (5.30)$$

To find the total effect of y_5 on the error, i.e., $\partial E(k)/\partial y_5$, Eq. (5.30) should be summed over all connections emanating from unit 5, or

$$\frac{\partial E(k)}{\partial y_5} = \left[\frac{\partial E(k)}{\partial y_5} \right]_{5 \to 7} + \left[\frac{\partial E(k)}{\partial y_5} \right]_{5 \to 8} = \frac{\partial E(k)}{\partial s_7} w_{57} + \frac{\partial E(k)}{\partial s_8} w_{58}. \qquad (5.31)$$

Note that $\partial E(k)/\partial s_7$ and $\partial E(k)/\partial s_8$ have been computed previously from Eqs. (5.26) and (5.27). Then the effect on the error caused by changes in the weights to unit 5, i.e., $\partial E(k)/\partial w_{m5}$, can be computed:

$$\frac{\partial E(k)}{\partial s_5} = \frac{\partial E(k)}{\partial y_5}\frac{dy_5}{ds_5} = \frac{\partial E(k)}{\partial y_5}y_5(1-y_5) \qquad (5.32)$$

$$\frac{\partial E(k)}{\partial w_{m5}} = \frac{\partial E(k)}{\partial s_5}\frac{\partial s_5}{\partial w_{m5}} = \frac{\partial E(k)}{\partial y_5}y_5(1-y_5)y_m \qquad \text{for } m = 1,3,4. \qquad (5.33)$$

The partial derivatives $\partial E(k)/\partial s_6$ and $\partial E(k)/\partial w_{m6}$ can be computed similarly. Next, computation for unit 4 can be carried out:

$$\frac{\partial E(k)}{\partial y_4} = \left[\frac{\partial E(k)}{\partial y_4}\right]_{4\to5} + \left[\frac{\partial E(k)}{\partial y_4}\right]_{4\to6} + \left[\frac{\partial E(k)}{\partial y_4}\right]_{4\to7} + \left[\frac{\partial E(k)}{\partial y_4}\right]_{4\to8}$$

$$= \frac{\partial E(k)}{\partial s_5}w_{45} + \frac{\partial E(k)}{\partial s_6}w_{46} + \frac{\partial E(k)}{\partial s_7}w_{47} + \frac{\partial E(k)}{\partial s_8}w_{48}. \qquad (5.34)$$

Note that $\partial E(k)/\partial s_i$, $i = 5,6,7,8$, have all been computed previously. Then

$$\frac{\partial E(k)}{\partial w_{m4}} = \frac{\partial E(k)}{\partial y_4}\frac{dy_4}{ds_4}\frac{\partial s_4}{\partial w_{m4}} = \frac{\partial E(k)}{\partial y_4}y_4(1-y_4)y_m \qquad \text{for } m = 1,2,3. \qquad (5.35)$$

Note that $y_3 = a$. This step completes the computation of the partial derivatives of the error with respect to all the connection weights.

The next example illustrates how the Neural Network Toolbox of MATLAB solves a training and classification problem by applying backpropagation.

Example 5.2. A neural network will be trained by using the capital letters T and L and their rotated versions. To simplify the presentation by reducing the size of the problem, we draw each letter on a figure with nine squares, arranged in three rows and three columns to form a larger square. Each of the smaller squares is either filled or unfilled as needed to represent the letter. Each letter is also rotated clockwise through 90°, 180°, and 270°. Thus, the letters and their rotated versions constitute a set of eight exemplars as shown in Fig. 5.5. The problem is to design a feedforward neural network with one hidden layer so that the network is trained to produce an output value 1 when the input pattern is either T

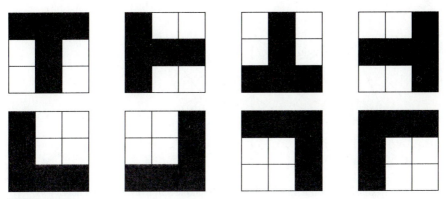

FIGURE 5.5
The letters T and L and their rotated versions in Example 5.2.

or any of its rotated versions, and 0 in the complementary situation. There are altogether nine inputs at the input layer. These inputs are associated with the nine small squares used to represent the letters. The input is 1 when a square is filled and 0 otherwise. The hidden layer is assumed to have three units, and the output layer has only one unit. Thus, the topology of the network to be trained is described by the graph in Fig. 5.6, where to avoid clutter the arrows associated with the edges from the input nodes at the bottom to the output nodes at the top are not shown. Each unit in the hidden layer of the ANN being designed is assigned a tansigmoid-with-bias transfer characteristic, as sketched in Fig. 5.7; the net input to a tansigmoid unit is mapped to a value in the interval $(-1, 1)$. Because the output values of the ANN are between 0 and 1, the output unit is assigned a logsigmoid-with-bias transfer characteristic as sketched in Fig. 5.8; the net input to a logsigmoid unit is mapped to an output value in the interval $(0, 1)$.

The eight exemplars constituting an epoch were sequentially presented repeatedly until the network was trained with acceptable error. The initial weight matrix and the biases are created with random elements between -1 and $+1$.

Results. On application of the backpropagation algorithm with the set of initial weights and biases, a satisfactory result for this problem was obtained after 5938 epochs with a learning rate of 0.001. The final network values yielded a sum of squared error of 0.124976. As a word of caution, since the number of training exemplars is very small in comparison with the number of network parameters in this example, the capability for valid generalization is therefore severely curtailed. Reasons for this will be found in Chapter 6. The connection weight matrix for the edges connecting the nine inputs impinging on the input layer to the three units in the hidden layer is as

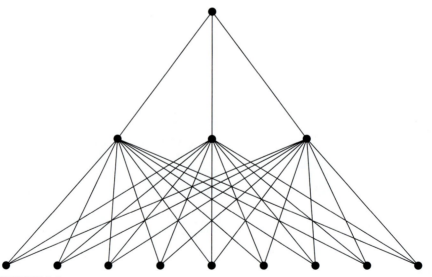

FIGURE 5.6
The graph for the feedforward neural network trained in Example 5.2. To avoid clutter the arrows associated with the edges are not shown.

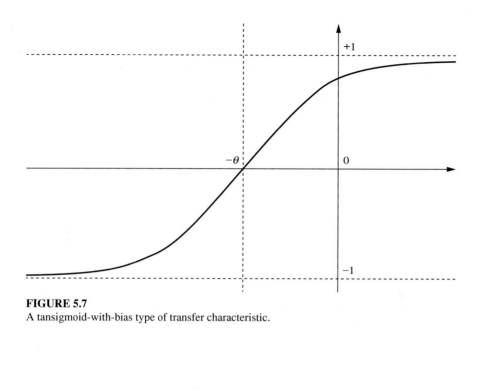

FIGURE 5.7
A tansigmoid-with-bias type of transfer characteristic.

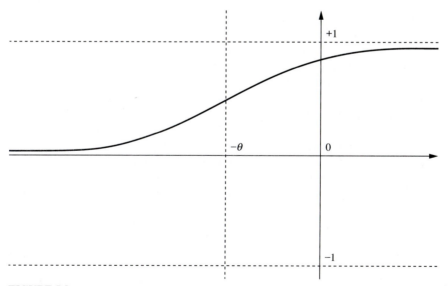

FIGURE 5.8
A logsigmoid-with-bias type of transfer characteristic.

follows, after rounding to three decimal places so that the matrix may be conveniently written (when space is not a constraint, the values will be given to four decimal places):

$$\begin{bmatrix} -0.943 & -0.948 & 0.538 & -0.607 & 0.254 & 0.929 & -0.596 & 0.774 & 0.140 \\ 0.742 & -0.430 & 0.716 & 0.310 & -1.288 & -0.135 & 0.431 & -0.143 & 0.535 \\ 0.530 & -0.437 & -0.338 & -0.404 & 1.598 & 0.134 & -0.625 & 0.399 & -0.127 \end{bmatrix}.$$

The bias vector yielding the threshold values for the three units in the hidden layer is

$$[\, 1.0021 \quad -0.3599 \quad -0.3504 \,]^{\mathrm{T}}.$$

The weight vector for the three edges connecting the units in the hidden layer to the output layer and the bias for the output unit are, respectively,

$$[\, 0.2615 \quad -1.4469 \quad 1.3431 \,]^{\mathrm{T}} \qquad \text{and} \qquad -0.0564.$$

The trained network was able to recall satisfactorily when the exemplar patterns were supplied as inputs even when some noise was permitted.

Since the transfer characteristics of the units are described by continuous functions to implement the binary decision rule, the following selection was made. Values of an output greater than 0.85 were assigned the value 1, whereas values of output less than 0.15 were assigned the value 0. After training for 5938 epochs, using 8,843,153 floating-point operations, the following outputs were obtained in the recall phase, after the patterns in Fig. 5.5 were presented sequentially as inputs.

$$0.8759 \qquad 0.8690 \qquad 0.8615 \qquad 0.9018$$
$$0.1486 \qquad 0.0765 \qquad 0.1361 \qquad 0.1310.$$

Selection of random weights and biases during initialization may slow training. If we take the other extreme, when all weights, say to an output unit, are identical, it is possible to gravitate toward the situation when weight updates in accordance with the generalized delta update rule will not break the state of equality of the weights, necessitating the need for *symmetry breaking*. Also, if not enough neurons are used in the hidden layer, it is possible that no set of weights and biases may exist that will produce outputs reasonably close to the targets. The criterion used for stopping also does not have to be unique. Depending on the nature of the error surface, it may be necessary to consider the magnitude of the change in error instead of the magnitude of error. For instance, in the case of a locally flat error surface, a small magnitude of change of error might motivate the use of a larger step size to speed up the process. These and other implementational concerns will be summarized in Section 5.2.1.

The next two examples illustrate the use of the Neural Network Toolbox of MATLAB in function approximation, where the backpropagation rule may be applied. It is important to bear in mind that the degree of success in approximation is function-dependent. That is, for some functions it works well, but for others it does not.

Example 5.3. It is desired to train a neural network to approximate the plot of the function $f(x) = \sin 2\pi x$ over the interval $0 \le x \le 1$.

The ANN chosen for the job is characterized by a directed graph with one node in the input layer, three nodes in the hidden layer, and one node in the output layer, as shown in Fig. 5.9. Each unit in the hidden layer of the ANN being designed is assigned

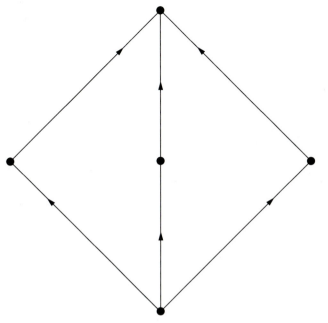

FIGURE 5.9
The graph of the feedforward neural network structure in Example
5.3. The arrows associated with the edges are shown.

a *tansigmoid-with-bias* transfer characteristic, similar to the one sketched in Fig. 5.7.
The output unit is assigned a linear-with-bias (i.e., affine) transfer characteristic, as
sketched in Fig. 5.10. Ten exemplars, represented by 10 input values for x in $0 \leq
x \leq 1$, associated with their respective correct output values computed according to
$f(x) = \sin 2\pi x$, were used in one epoch of the training phase. These exemplars were
repeatedly presented until the sum-of-squared-error goal was reached.

Results. The initial values for the weight vector for connections linking the input node
to the three hidden layer nodes and the bias vector for the units in the hidden layer were,
respectively,

$$[-0.9271 \quad 0.6668 \quad 0.7952]^{\mathrm{T}} \quad \text{and} \quad [-0.9572 \quad -0.4353 \quad -0.4374]^{\mathrm{T}}.$$

The weight vector for connections linking the hidden layer nodes and the output layer
node and the bias for the output unit were, respectively,

$$[0.5498 \quad 0.7362 \quad -0.2600]^{\mathrm{T}} \quad \text{and} \quad -0.6033.$$

The corresponding final values were

$$[-2.3298 \quad 1.4824 \quad 4.0922]^{\mathrm{T}} \quad \text{and} \quad [-0.2696 \quad -1.3397 \quad -2.0824]^{\mathrm{T}}$$

and

$$[-2.3032 \quad 4.1309 \quad -3.0782]^{\mathrm{T}} \quad \text{and} \quad 0.0517.$$

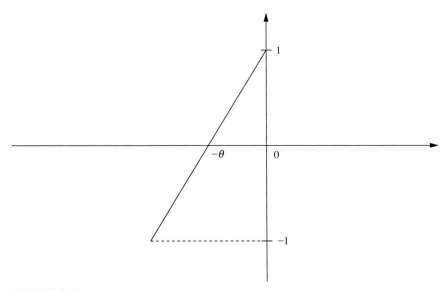

FIGURE 5.10
The linear-with-bias type of transfer characteristic, also referred to as the affine characteristic.

The final values were reached after training for 17,214 epochs with a learning rate of 0.01. The final sum-of-squared-error goal was 0.02, whereas the actual value of this error was 0.0199995.

Example 5.4. It is desired to train a neural network so that it is capable of approximating the plot of the function $f(x_1, x_2) = x_1^2 + x_2^2$ over the intervals $0 \leq x_1 \leq 1$ and $0 \leq x_2 \leq 1$.

The ANN chosen for this job is characterized by a complete layered directed graph with 2 nodes in the input layer, 10 nodes in the hidden layer, and 1 node in the output layer. The reader may verify that the underlying undirected graph that characterizes this ANN topology is formed from the node coalescence of $K_{2,10}$ and $K_{10,1}$.

To train the structure, 441 exemplars on a (21×21) uniformly spaced grid in the (x_1, x_2)-plane were selected in an epoch. Each unit in the hidden layer was assigned a logsigmoid-with-bias transfer characteristic, similar to the one sketched in Fig. 5.8. The output unit of the ANN was assigned an affine (linear-with-bias) transfer characteristic. The Neural Network Toolbox of MATLAB was used to train the ANN. This toolbox permits the deployment of an adaptive learning rate, where the parameter η in Eq. (5.23) is adjusted according to an algorithm during training to minimize training time.

Results. With an initial learning rate of 0.0005 and training for 68,718 epochs, use of the adaptive feature mentioned before resulted in a final sum-of-squared-error value of 0.0199984, which was considered adequate. The final connection weight matrices of the $K_{2,10}$ and $K_{10,1}$ subgraphs and the final values for the biases of the units were also obtained. Fig. 5.11 is the plot of the function $f(x_1, x_2)$, generated in the recall phase. The correct values at the points of sampling are identified by circles.

The sum of squared error as a function of the number of epochs is plotted in Fig. 5.12. This plot is not typical but is intended to serve as one measure for performance

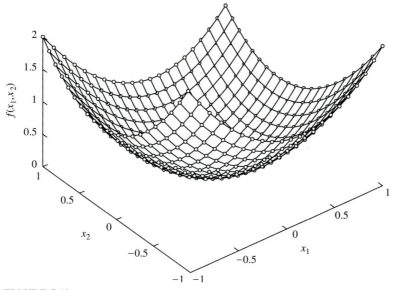

FIGURE 5.11
The plot of the function $f(x_1, x_2) = x_1^2 + x_2^2$, generated in the recall phase in Example 5.4, after training with a square array of 441 training samples equally spaced every 0.1 unit in the interval $[-1, 1]$ along each axis and on lines of same length parallel to these axis segments. The circles represent true values of exemplars.

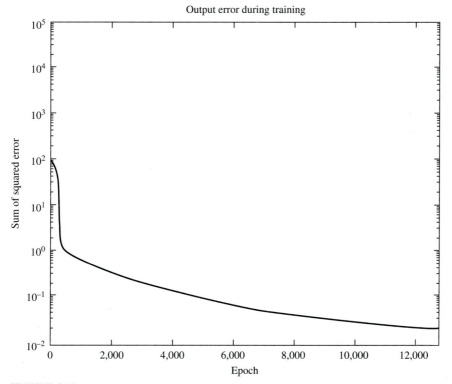

FIGURE 5.12
The sum of squared error as a function of the number of epochs in Example 5.4.

Absolute error

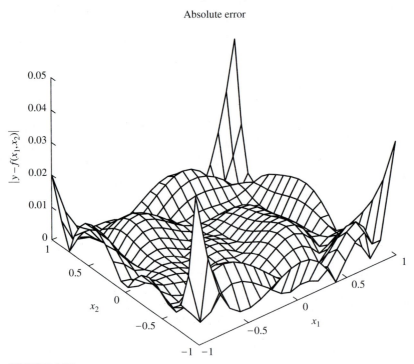

FIGURE 5.13
The sum-of-squared-error plot in Example 5.4 during the recall phase.

evaluation for this example. The sum of squared error can be plotted either as a function of input-target pairs (associated with exemplars used in training, where the input-target pairs are sequenced according to a row-by-row scan of the (21×21) grid points in the (x_1, x_2) plane used to generate the target values in the exemplars) or as a function of the independent variables. The plot in Fig. 5.13 is the latter plot.

Additional information pertaining to the test phase can also be generated. The plots in Figs. 5.11 and 5.13 are consistent from the standpoint of greater errors being observed at the corners of the bowl-shaped curve plotted during the recall phase in Fig. 5.11.

5.2.1 Implementation Considerations for Backpropagation

As we have seen, the activation function must be differentiable for backpropagation to be feasible. We tabulate next several implications of this requirement, especially in comparison to the perceptron algorithm studied in Chapter 4.

1. In the case of perceptrons, the output is either 1 or 0. However, when the activation function is sigmoidal, an output of 1 or 0 requires some weights to be infinity for a finite-sized network (why?). Therefore, the desired output is required to be from the set $\{\epsilon_1, 1 - \epsilon_2\}$ instead of $\{0, 1\}$, where the ϵ_i's are small positive real numbers.

The larger the ϵ_i's are, the smaller the range of weights required, which facilitates physical realizability. However, the larger the ϵ_i's are, the smaller is the tolerance of the network to noise in the input patterns. The difference $1 - \epsilon_1 - \epsilon_2$ determines the capability for noise tolerance of a unit.

2. Unlike the perceptrons, the error function may not reach zero either, because it may be stuck at a local minimum and because the weights may oscillate in the neighborhood of the global minimum. Therefore, the stopping criterion should not be $E = 0$. Instead, the algorithm should stop when either $E < \epsilon$ or $|\Delta E| < \delta$, where ϵ and δ are small positive real numbers. In addition, the maximum number of iterations allowed should be specified a priori, because the algorithm may not converge.

3. If all of the weights are initially chosen the same, the change of weights may also be the same. Then the weights will remain the same after updating. This problem is solved by starting with small, random weights. This approach is called *symmetry breaking* in the literature.

4. As with a perceptron, if the input patterns are binary, then $\{\alpha, 1\}$ should be used instead of $\{0, 1\}$, where α may either be -1 or a small positive number, e.g., 0.1. This choice will lead to faster convergence in almost all cases. The reason is that if $\alpha = 0$, the updates of a weight connected to an input variable will be zero when the corresponding variable is zero in the training pattern. Making α nonzero ensures that a weight will be updated whenever it is required.

5. The BPA generally slows down by an order of magnitude every time a layer is added to the network, because the error signal is attenuated each time it goes through a layer. Therefore, the convergence speed is limited by the slow adaptation of the connections in layers close to the input units. To overcome this problem, shortcut connections from lower layers directly to the output units may be made. These connections allow the error signal to be directly passed to lower layers close to the input units [211]. Note, however, that the structure then is not layered.

The BPA is simple, general, and widely used for training multilayer feedforward networks. However, there is no guarantee of convergence to the right solution, unlike the perceptron algorithm (although for a special class of patterns), where the error function has only one minimum and all gradients in its neighborhood point away from it. When infinitesimal step size is required to guarantee convergence, it takes forever to converge. The BPA may fail to converge as a result of inappropriate choice of step size, which may lead to oscillation. In cases where convergence is feasible, results on the rate of convergence of the algorithm may not be available. Besides the momentum coefficient β, the adaptive bias method, introduced for perceptron algorithms, may also be used to improve the rate of convergence of the BPA.

5.2.2 Variants of BPA

Many variants of the foregoing BPA are possible. Since the BPA is a gradient descent algorithm, all techniques available for improving upon the gradient descent procedure apply to BPA. Those include making the learning rate η and the coefficient for the momentum term either gradually decay or adaptive [175, 390]. Also, any second derivative–based nonlinear optimization method, such as the Newton-Raphson method or the conjugate gradient method, may be adapted for the training of feedforward networks [36, 288]. However, these variants also share problems present in the standard BPA and may converge faster in some cases and slower in others. Comparison of the speeds of convergence of different schemes for implementing backpropagation is not clear-cut, though Fahlman presents a detailed discussion on the benchmarking of backpropagation-type algorithms [107]. In a recent paper [178], the parity problem was chosen as the benchmark test for comparing the methods of conjugate gradient backpropagation and conventional backpropagation. In all test cases involving the use of 3-, 4-, and 5-bit parity problems on neural network architectures with one or two hidden layers, the conjugate gradient–based method performed better.

Fahlman introduced a variant of the BPA, called *quick-prop* [107], which seems to give faster convergence in many cases. It is a second-order–based method combined with heuristics. The quick-prop algorithm is based on two assumptions that may not hold in general: (1) The error vs. weight curve for each weight can be approximated by a parabola that opens upward, and (2) the change in the slope of the error curve, as seen by each weight, is not affected by all the other weights that are changing at the same time. Everything else proceeds as in the standard BPA, except that the update for each weight is computed according to

$$w(k + 1) = w(k) + \eta[\Delta w(k)] = w(k) + \eta \left[\frac{S(k)}{S(k-1) - S(k)} \Delta w(k-1) \right],$$

where $S(k)$ and $S(k-1)$ are the current and previous values of $\partial E / \partial w$. Note that each connection weight must be stored in addition to the memory required in the standard BPA. Only the periodic updating approach can be used for the quick-prop algorithm in its present form.

Another algorithm for training multilayer networks is the Madaline III algorithm (multiple-Adaline) by Andes et al. [26]. Widrow and Lehr [409] point out that the Madaline III algorithm has advantages over the backpropagation algorithm in analog hardware implementation, whereas the backpropagation algorithm is more efficient in digital computer simulation and digital hardware implementation.

No matter which variant of the gradient descent method is used for training multilayer networks, the inescapable problem is that all of these optimization methods are based on the assumption of a single minimum of the function. Therefore, variants of the BPA may work better in some cases and worse in others. No analysis or comprehensive experimental studies exist to indicate when a particular variant or the standard BPA works better. Therefore, the neural network training problem encounters all of the drawbacks inherent in nonlinear optimization. Unless a priori global information is available, no existing method guarantees convergence to the global minimum in finite time. One way is to transform the problem so that there is only one minimum, sacrificing space complexity to reduce time complexity. Another way is to add noise randomly to the weights in order to escape from a local minimum, as in the Boltzmann machine, to be discussed in Chapter 8.

Different approaches exist that avoid use of any gradient information. In a *genetic algorithm* [265, 406], instead of one network, a group (called a *population*) of networks is considered. The complete set of weights for each of the networks is coded as a binary string. Each weight string has a different evolution path. An error function, called the *fitness function,* is used to evaluate the fitness of each weight string. The weight string giving less classification error is considered as fitter. Successive strings are constructed by performing genetic operations, such as mutation and crossover, on old strings, based on the principle of *survival of the fittest.* The genetic operations basically involve exchanges of bits within and between strings. Fitter strings are more likely to survive and affect the new strings constructed. How the weights are encoded and the type of genetic operations selected are both crucial in the performance of the search. Genetic algorithms have the ability to adapt to the problem being solved and are suggested by the evolutionary process of natural selection. Since no differentiation is required, neither the fitness function nor the transfer characteristics of the units need be differentiable. Therefore, TLUs can be used instead of sigmoidal function units. Another approach that is not gradient-based, offers several advantages, and holds future promise is described in Section 5.3.

5.2.3   Temporal Signal Recognition and Prediction

So far, we have only considered input patterns that are spatial in nature, i.e., input patterns that can be arranged along one or more spatial axes such as a vector or an array. In many tasks, the input pattern comprises one or more temporal signals, as in speech recognition, time series prediction, and signal filtering. A simple, commonly used method converts the temporal signal at the input into a spatial pattern by using a *tapped delay line,* which provides the signal values at different time instants. This conversion is illustrated in Fig. 5.14.

A neural network using the tapped delay lines is sometimes called a *time-delay network.* The input to a unit connected to the taps on a delay line is

$$h_i(t) = \sum_{i=0}^{n} w_i x(t - i). \tag{5.36}$$

Equation (5.36) shows a convolution, and the weights form the unit impulse response sequence of a finite-impulse-response (FIR) filter. A further generalization is obtained by also replacing the internal connection weights in the network by tapped delay lines [29, 396]. The resulting network is sometimes called a *spatiotemporal* or *internal delay line network.*

There are two difficulties with this scheme of temporal signal processing. The first is the problem of determining the beginning and end of a temporal pattern. For example, to recognize a word in speech processing, it is usually necessary to isolate the word from the rest of the speech signal. This task is a difficult open problem and is one of the bottlenecks in developing large-vocabulary continuous speech recognizers. The other difficulty is *time warping* [155]. A time warp transforms a temporal

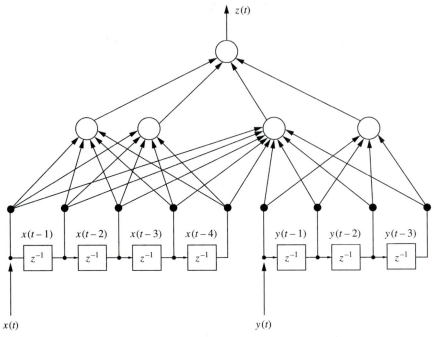

FIGURE 5.14
A time-delay neural network converts a temporal signal to a spatial pattern at the input using tapped delay lines.

signal $x(t)$ to $x(\theta(t))$, where $\theta(t)$ is a strictly monotonically increasing smooth function of time t. Time warping has the effects of speeding up or slowing down the signal and translating it backward or forward in time. In general, the recognition of a temporal signal must be insensitive to a class of time-warping transformations. For example, in speech recognition, pronouncing a word slower or faster should not affect its recognition. The tapped delay line approach becomes insufficient when warping is involved, because a warped signal would be considered to be a different spatial pattern from the original one.

A more general approach should apply a set C of warping transformations to a temporal signal and find the nearest match, where C is the class of warping transformations to which the recognition should be insensitive. The idea of converting a temporal signal to a spatial pattern still applies here. However, all the warped versions of the spatial patterns should be matched (see Problem 5.18), which can be achieved by performing the warping transformation either in the spatial domain or in the time domain. In the spatial domain, a time-warped signal will be represented as a different spatial pattern but with the same categorization. In the time domain, the temporal signal will be transformed by a sequence of time warps and compared to the prototype. This time domain approach is the basic idea in the nearest-matched-filter spatiotemporal network proposed by Hecht-Nielsen [155].

An alternative to the tapped delay lines is to convolve the input temporal signal with smoothing filters having different window sizes and peak locations [374]. For example, the filter may be of the following form:

$$f(t, \tau_i) = \left(\frac{t}{\tau_i}\right)^\sigma \exp\left[\sigma\left(1 - \frac{t}{\tau_i}\right)\right]. \qquad (5.37)$$

The filter response achieves the peak magnitude of 1 at $t = \tau_i$. The width of the filter response is controlled by the spread σ. Instead of passing the temporal signal through many z^{-1} unit delay units, the signal is passed through several filters with increasing τ_i. This step effectively provides a smoothed as well as a delayed version of the signal.

5.3 STRUCTURAL TRAINING OF MULTILAYER FEEDFORWARD NETWORKS

The procedure proposed in refs. [51, 52] for designing neural networks by using the feedforward topology requires the construction of a Voronoi diagram (VoD), described in Chapter 2, over a finite set of points in multidimensional feature space. Recent results in computational geometry have shown that such diagrams can be constructed, in expected (average) time linear in the number of points, for an arbitrary but fixed dimension of the space. A substantial portion of the September 1992 "Special Issue on Computational Geometry" published by *Proceedings of the IEEE* [377] was devoted to the development of numerically stable, efficient algorithms for constructing Voronoi diagrams. It is anticipated that in the near future such algorithms, which work well even when the number of points in the plane exceeds 1 million, will be generalized to higher dimensions, motivated especially by the encouraging results in ref. [104]. Progress toward that goal is being achieved. However, it is important to attend to the simultaneous curse of high dimensions and high cardinality of the point set characterizing exemplars by developing fundamental techniques rather than to depend solely on advances in coding. It is also conceivable that advances in parallel computational geometry will further facilitate the construction of Voronoi diagrams, especially in higher-dimensional space.

Lack of any convergence criterion, mentioned earlier, is a severe drawback for error backpropagation structures, especially when different classes of patterns are close to each other in multidimensional feature space. The procedure in [52] has excellent discriminating capabilities in such situations and is also able to perform better in noisy cases where a test input pattern deviates from an exemplar, such as in handwritten characters targeted for recognition. For vision and image-processing applications, it is important to recognize patterns independently of certain transformations such as translation, rotation, or scaling; different approaches have been suggested to solve this problem of invariant pattern recognition [41, 83, 98, 206, 269, 351]. It is possible to show that if a given set of points whose Voronoi diagram has been constructed undergoes translation, rotation, or scaling, or a combination of these operations, then the VoD of the transformed points can be found by subjecting the VoD of the original set of points to an identical transformation. However, since the invariance in image processing and vision applies to rotation and scaling of the original images and not the feature points that occur in VoDs, the direct utilization of this property of VoDs in such applications may not be forthcoming. Therefore, research into what modifications or adaptations are needed for such a possibility to materialize may be rewarding. Last but not least, the procedure in ref. [52] provides the starting point for the development of a mathematical realizability theory for neural networks by allowing the derivation of alternative structures that provide various exact representations of a given input/output description. The basis for improvement over existing techniques is the utilization of the geometric structure inherent in a given problem, a feature missing from most design and training algorithms that are in use presently.

In Chapter 4, we saw that a single-TLU perceptron (devoid of any hidden layer) can solve only a linearly separable problem; i.e., the two classes of patterns can be separated by a hyperplane. Problems that are not linearly separable can be solved, as has been seen earlier in this chapter, by using multilayer neural networks with neurons having nonlinear transfer characteristics. A single-TLU perceptron can implement the equation of a hyperplane. A layer (we do not count the input layer, because it is just a fan-out layer and does not change from one design to another) of n neurons can be used to implement the equations of n distinct hyperplanes. Therefore, any region that can be expressed as the intersection of a finite number of closed half-spaces, whose boundaries are defined by the hyperplanes, can be implemented by a two-layer neural network having one neuron in the upper layer. Several such distinct, possibly overlapping, regions can be implemented by a two-layer network having a corresponding number of neurons in the upper layer. The number of neurons in this upper layer, then, equals the number of such regions. Finally, the union of a finite number of such distinct regions, which classify a particular pattern in feature space, can be implemented by introducing a third layer to combine the corresponding outputs from the second layer. The number of neurons in the third layer is equal to the number of classes of patterns. This statement agrees with the consequences of Kolmogorov's theorem, which, applied to multilayer feedforward neural networks, implies the sufficiency of three layers for realizing a broad class of input/output mappings.

Suppose that the data D constitute a set of points, each represented by a vector $\mathbf{x}$ in the multidimensional feature space that is a subspace of the d-dimensional real Euclidean space $\mathbb{R}^d$. Each $\mathbf{x}$ is associated with a class from a finite set C of possible classes. A nonlinear map $f(\mathbf{x})$ of $\mathbf{x}$ from the set D to the set C may be assumed to be a single-valued function; i.e., for each arbitrary but fixed $\mathbf{x}$ the value of $f(\mathbf{x})$ is unique. A subset S of D constitutes the training set, and the objective after training is to generalize so that a point outside the training set is properly classified. It will be seen in Chapter 6 that in worst-case computational complexity studies for valid generalization, the training exemplars and test exemplars are drawn according to an unknown and arbitrary probability distribution. Fixed and known probability distributions have also been considered. The hyperplanes used for splitting the training set are not unique and can be obtained in many ways. The Voronoi diagram provides a partition of the points belonging to the training set S in $\mathbb{R}^d$ by convex regions, called Voronoi cells, each of which defines the *region of influence* of an exemplar. Each Voronoi cell of the VoD contains those points of the space that are closest to the given point among the totality of such points whose VoD has been constructed. This feature makes such a partitioning of the space especially useful for training neural networks. The local update feature of a VoD also facilitates incorporation of new exemplars to the training set, which in turn leads to the training of the structure in addition to traditional training of connection weights and thresholds.

5.3.1   Algorithm for Design Based on VoD

Given a set of patterns belonging to k distinct classes in the multidimensional feature space, it is desired to synthesize a neural network to obtain the classification for each input pattern. The following design procedure leads to such a neural network. For convenience, the transfer characteristic of each neuron is a unipolar hard-limiter with bias, so that the output is either 1 or 0, though this restriction can easily be lifted. Consult Definition 5.2 in Section 5.3.2 for the formal definitions of hyperplanes and half-spaces before reading the material below.

1. For the ith ($i = 1, 2, \ldots, k$) class of patterns, described by specified points in feature space, obtain a convex hull C_i using a standard procedure.
2. a. When $k = 2$ and the interiors of the two convex hulls do not intersect (implying that a hyperplane can be situated in the region between the two hulls), the two classes are linearly separable. One neuron can handle this situation; proceed to step 5. When $k = 2$, and the interiors of the two convex hulls have a nonempty intersection, proceed to step 4.
   b. When $k > 2$, for each class i ($i = 1, 2, \ldots, k$) form a convex hull C_i' over the specified points *not* belonging to the ith class by merging the remaining convex hulls. If there is a class j for which the interiors of C_j and C_j' have a nonempty intersection, the classes are not linearly separable; proceed to Step 3. If the interiors of each pair of convex hulls C_i and C_i' do not intersect, then the classes are linearly separable, and there exists a hyperplane H_i for the ith class that can separate the points of this class from the remaining points. There will be k such hyperplanes, and consequently k neurons in a single layer will be necessary as well as sufficient; proceed to step 5.
3. Suppose that the classes are not linearly separable but that the interiors of the convex hulls of every pair of classes do not intersect; i.e., each class can be separated from another class by a hyperplane. In this case, the classes are *pairwise linearly separable* [273] and two layers of neurons are necessary. The number of neurons in the first layer equals the number of required hyperplanes and is at least $(k + 1)$ and at most $k(k - 1)/2$. The number of neurons in the second layer equals the number of classes. Proceed to step 5. If the convex hulls of at least one pair of classes have a nonempty intersection, then the classes are not pairwise linearly separable, and three layers of neurons are required; proceed to step 4.

4. Obtain a Voronoi diagram over all the specified points using any suitable algorithm for the purpose. Form a cluster or clusters (in case of edge-disjoint Voronoi cells) of Voronoi cells for each class of patterns. Each cluster is described by a finite number of hyperplanes.

   a. If a cluster is convex, then it can be described by an intersection of half-spaces delimited by a finite number of hyperplanes. Consider a hyperplane $H: \sum_{i=1}^{d} w_i x_i - \theta = 0$, where a point in d-dimensional space has coordinates $(x_1, x_2, \ldots, x_d)$, and $w_1, w_2, \ldots, w_d$ and θ are constants. The half-spaces described by $\sum_{i=1}^{d} w_i x_i - \theta > 0$ and $\sum_{i=1}^{d} w_i x_i - \theta < 0$ are denoted by H^+ (the positive half-space) and H^- (the negative half-space), respectively. Each neuron in the first layer has a transfer characteristic that enables it to transform an input pattern into a Boolean variable by assigning the value 1 if the input pattern lies in H^+ and the value 0 if the pattern lies in H^-; other choices besides unipolar hard-limiters are also possible. The w_i's yield the connection weights of the edges connecting the corresponding input components (x_i's) to the neuron, and θ represents the threshold of the neuron ($-\theta$ is the bias). Thus, each convex cluster (polytopic region) can be implemented using two layers. The number of neurons in the first layer equals the number of hyperplanes supporting the cluster (region). Only one neuron is required in the second layer to perform the AND operation.

   b. If a cluster is not convex, it cannot be implemented with two layers using only AND gates in the second layer. However, it can be described as a union of a finite number of convex regions, each of which is expressible as an intersection of a finite number of closed half-spaces. Every such convex region (bounded or unbounded) requires one neuron in the second layer. For each class of patterns formed by one or more clusters, only one neuron is required in the third layer, to perform the OR operation to combine the relevant outputs from the second layer. If a class has more than one cluster, the OR neuron corresponding to this class in the third layer combines the outputs of the neurons in the second layer for the convex regions covering the clusters of this class. The number of neurons in the third layer equals the number k of distinct classes.

5. The equation of each hyperplane mentioned in the previous steps determines the connection weights and the bias of the neurons in the first layer. If the classes are linearly separable, proceed to step 7.

6. a. Implement each convex region obtained in step 4 using the AND prototype shown in Fig. 5.15. The inputs to the AND neuron come from the neurons in the first layer, which are used to describe the supporting hyperplanes H_i, $i = 1, 2, \ldots, n$, of the convex region. If this region lies in H_i^+, the connection weight from the corresponding neuron in the first layer is 1, as shown with a solid line in Fig. 5.15; if it is in H_i^-, the connection weight is -1, as shown with a dashed line in Fig. 5.15; if the hyperplane does not support the convex region, then the corresponding connection weight is 0 and is omitted. The bias for an AND neuron is $m - n + 0.5$ when the convex region is supported by n hyperplanes and belongs to H_i^-, for $i = 1, 2, \ldots, m$ (implying a negative superscript for each of those m hyperplanes in the Boolean expression for this region). If the classes are pairwise linearly separable, proceed to step 7.

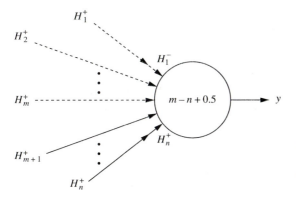

FIGURE 5.15
The AND prototype implementing $y = H_1^- \cap H_2^- \cap \cdots \cap H_m^- \cap H_{m+1}^+ \cap \cdots \cap H_n^+$.
The value of bias is inside the circle.

   b. An AND neuron in step 6a implements the membership of an input pattern in a convex region R^+; the output from the neuron is 1 when an input pattern is in the region and 0 if the pattern is outside. The complement of R^+ is denoted by R^-. For each class in R^+, $i = 1, 2, \ldots, n$, use the outputs of the appropriate AND neurons from the second layer (corresponding to the convex regions covering the various clusters of this class) as inputs to an OR neuron prototype shown in Fig. 5.16. Sometimes a region can be expressed more simply by using the regions outside some of the convex regions available (denoted by R^-). When the region for a class is expressible as $R_1^- \cup R_2^- \cup \cdots \cup R_m^- \cup R_{m+1}^+ \cup \cdots \cup R_n^+$, the bias for the OR neuron for this class is $m - 0.5$ (m is the number of inputs that are complemented, implying that the connection weight multiplying each such input is -1); see Fig. 5.16.
7. Stop.

   In this algorithm the values of the biases for the AND as well as the OR neurons are summarized. The unipolar binary logic function AND of n inputs, m of which are complemented, can be realized with connection weights of $+1$ for the uncomplemented inputs, connection weights of -1 for the complemented inputs, and a bias of $(m - n + 0.5)$. For the unipolar OR function, the bias is $(m - 0.5)$, independent

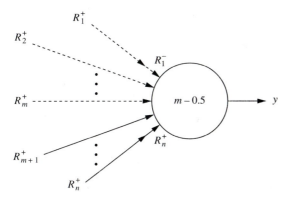

FIGURE 5.16
The OR prototype implementing $y = R_1^- \cup R_2^- \cup \cdots \cup R_m^- \cup R_{m+1}^+ \cup \cdots \cup R_n^+$.
The bias value is inside the circle.

of n. If the inputs are bipolar, then the AND and OR neurons have biases $-(n-1)$ and $(n-1)$, respectively. The last statement is left for verification by the reader.

Example 5.5. Two classes of patterns are represented by crosses and circles in two-dimensional feature space in Fig. 5.17. Each class consists of five patterns. The coordinates of the points and the class to which each belongs are given in the accompanying table. These points are numbered sequentially from top to bottom starting from the left and extending to the right.

Point number	Coordinates	Class
1	(1.25, 4.4)	1
2	(2.4, 1.1)	1
3	(3.0, 3.25)	2
4	(4.75, 8.1)	1
5	(4.75, 5.45)	2
6	(6.0, 4.3)	2
7	(7.1, 2.2)	1
8	(8.3, 7.5)	2
9	(9.5, 3.75)	2
10	(11.8, 6.5)	2

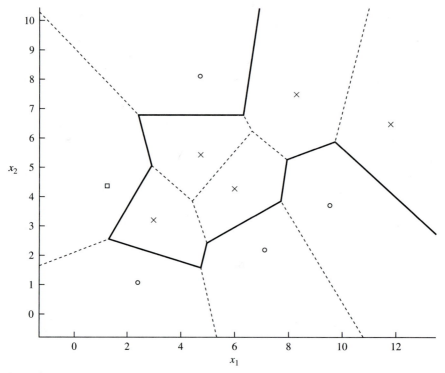

FIGURE 5.17
Two classes, each containing five patterns, represented in two-dimensional feature space. Also shown is the Voronoi diagram over those 10 points. See the detailed description in Example 5.6.

A neural network will be designed using the 10 patterns as training exemplars. For the sake of brevity, only highlights illustrating the usage of the algorithm are given in this section, and the reader is invited to fill in the gaps to ensure comprehension. The reader also may derive additional benefit by going through some of the simpler examples in ref. [52] beforehand.

Starting with the algorithm, one is quickly led to step 4, which requires the construction of a VoD over the set of 10 points using one of several programs that are available for the purpose. To conserve space, this VoD is also shown in Fig. 5.17. Both the solid and the dotted lines in Fig. 5.17 are used for showing this VoD, because the solid lines may also be used to describe the boundary or decision surface that separates the two classes of patterns. This decision surface has 10 edges, each of which is a portion of a particular hyperplane. If $\mathbf{x} = [x_1 \ x_2]^T$ denotes the two-dimensional feature vector, the equations of these hyperplanes H_i for $i = 1, 2, \ldots, 10$, which give the weights of the connections from the input layer to the first hidden layer of neurons and the bias of each neuron, may be easily obtained (as stated in step 5) and are given here:

$$3.55x_1 - 0.60x_2 - 18.48 = 0$$

$$-2.65x_2 + 17.95 = 0$$

$$3.50x_1 + 1.05x_2 - 15.67 = 0$$

$$1.75x_1 - 1.15x_2 + 0.68 = 0$$

$$0.60x_1 + 2.15x_2 - 6.30 = 0$$

$$4.10x_1 - 1.05x_2 - 17.84 = 0$$

$$1.10x_1 - 2.10x_2 - 0.38 = 0$$

$$3.50x_1 - 0.55x_2 - 24.91 = 0$$

$$1.20x_1 - 3.75x_2 + 10.41 = 0$$

$$2.30x_1 + 2.75x_2 - 38.59 = 0.$$

The regions containing the patterns belonging to a particular class may be expressed in several ways in terms of the intersections of the half-spaces set up by the hyperplanes. The bias of each neuron in the second hidden layer is calculated from the formula given in step 6a. Finally, the connections to the output layer of neurons are obtained (also nonuniquely as described in step 6b), and the bias of each neuron in the output layer is calculated by the formula given in step 6b. One particular realization is shown in Fig. 5.18. It is important to remember that synthesis is always nonunique, and alternate structures that realize the same input-output description may be obtained.

Example 5.5 illustrates the main steps in the derivation of a multilayer neural network following the tessellation of the space by a VoD. Such a design may also be obtained from the Delaunay tessellation, which, in the two-dimensional space, is derived by taking the geometric dual of a VoD and is called a Delaunay triangulation. For another procedure that also leads to a multilayer feedforward network through partitioning of space by hyperplanes using an entropy-based optimization

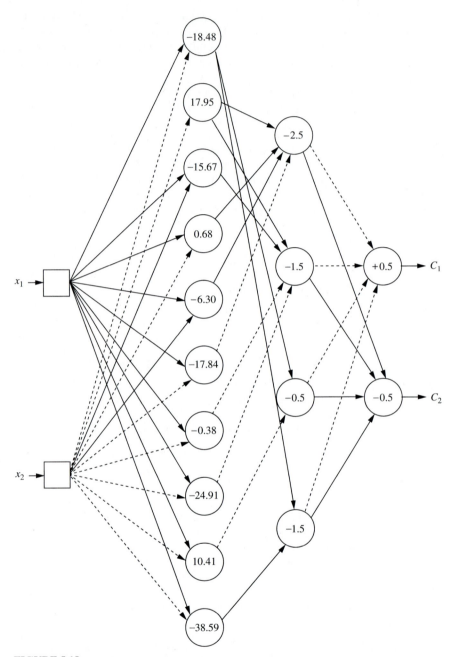

FIGURE 5.18
One neural network realization of the solution to the problem posed in Example 5.6. The numbers inside the circles are biases, or the negatives of the neuron thresholds. The output layer has an AND neuron (to reduce the number of neurons in the preceding layer) and an OR neuron below it. To avoid notational clutter, connection weights are not shown.

criterion, refer to ref. [55]. The tessellation of the space could also be done from VoDs constructed in other metrics. Of particular interest has been the rectilinear metric, where preliminary results are very promising [290]. In that case *all* the weights in the resulting neural network belong to the ternary set $\{0, +1, -1\}$. Although the number of units required is higher than in the case detailed here, the easy direct readout of the connection weights from the VoD and the suitability for hardware implementation justify the need for further investigations.

5.3.2 Robustness and Size Issues

The VoD-based approach has been analyzed [127] with respect to the *n*-bit parity problem to obtain an understanding of the trade-off between the size complexity of the network and the important property of *robust generalization,* which demands satisfactory performance in cases where an uncertain input pattern deviates from a training exemplar. The parity problem has been chosen because the computation of its order requires at least one partial predicate whose support is the whole base space of input points [261], which makes it a difficult problem to tackle and where backpropagation does not yield very good results.

   Let $R = \{x_1, x_2, \ldots, x_n\}$ be a set of n real variables x_i, $i = 1, 2, \ldots, n$, defined over an n-dimensional finite subspace of the n-dimensional Euclidean space $\mathbb{R}^n$. Let x_i, $i = 1, 2, \ldots, N$, denote the exemplars in the n-dimensional feature space $\mathbb{F}^n$, which is a subspace of $\mathbb{R}^n$. The VoD over the set of N points in $\mathbb{F}^n$ is first constructed. To define the parity function, the variables x_i, $i = 1, 2, \ldots, n$, are restricted to the binary set, $\{0, 1\}$. Let $|X|$ denote the number of 1s in X. The parity function $\psi_{\text{parity}}(X)$, seen in Section 4.3, is defined next, for convenience.

   Definition 5.1. The simple predicate function,

$$\psi_{\text{parity}}(X) = [\, |X| \text{ is an odd number}\,],$$

is called the *parity function,* where, notationally, $\psi_{\text{parity}}(X)$ is 1 (TRUE) when the expression within the [ ]'s is TRUE and is 0 otherwise. When X is defined over a certain subspace of $\mathbb{R}^n$, $\psi_{\text{parity}}(X)$ is said to be associated with the n-bit parity problem.

The notion of a hyperplane, encountered in Sections 4.1.2 and 5.3.1, is central to the construction of Voronoi cells. It is formally defined next to facilitate reading and easy identification.

   Definition 5.2. A *hyperplane* in $\mathbb{F}^n$ is the set of points $x \in \mathbb{F}^n$ that satisfy the equation $H : \sum_{i=1}^{n} \alpha_i x_i + \delta = 0$, where x has coordinates $(x_1, x_2, \ldots, x_n)$, and $\alpha_1, \alpha_2, \ldots, \alpha_n$ and δ are constants. The half-spaces described by $\sum_{i=1}^{n} \alpha_i x_i + \delta > 0$ and $\sum_{i=1}^{n} \alpha_i x_i + \delta < 0$ are denoted by H^+ (the positive half-space) and H^- (the negative half-space), respectively.

   Let H_k, $k = 1, 2, \ldots, L$, denote the hyperplanes in the VoD constructed. The Euclidean distance of x_i from the hyperplane H_k is denoted by $d(x_i, H_k)$. A measure of robustness is obtained from the minimization of $d(x_i, H_k)$ over all relevant indices k and i.

Definition 5.3. The scalar

$$r = \min_i \{ \min_k d(x_i, H_k) \}$$

provides a measure of robustness for a neural network designed by using the VoD.

The trade-off between robustness and complexity of realization is studied for the parity function by considering, first, the 2-bit parity case, which is the exclusive-OR (XOR) problem. The VoD for this case is easily obtainable from a horizontal and a vertical line that partition the plane into four quadrants. A reduced VoD is generated by using the following rule. Obtain the midpoint in $\mathbb{F}^2$ of each pair of exemplars that belong to different classes; obviously, there are four such points. One line passes through any two of these midpoints of least proximity to an exemplar of one class, and the other line passes through the remaining two midpoints. The VoD and the reduced VoD so obtained are shown in Fig. 5.19. The neural networks derived from the VoD and the reduced VoD are shown, respectively, in Fig. 5.20 and Fig. 5.21. The measure of robustness of the neural network

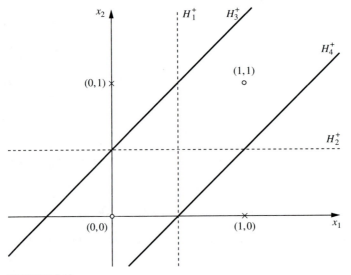

FIGURE 5.19
VoD and reduced VoD for the 2-bit parity (XOR) problem. Dashed lines show the VoD ($r = 0.5$), and solid lines show the reduced VoD ($r = 0.35$).

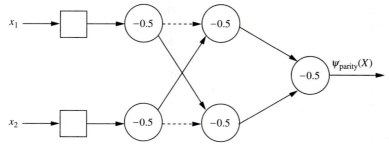

FIGURE 5.20
A neural network (VONNET) based on the VoD for the 2-bit parity problem. The solid
and dashed lines are associated, respectively, with weights $+1$ and -1. The values
inside the circles are the biases.

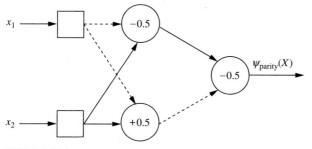

FIGURE 5.21
The reduced VONNET for the 2-bit parity problem. The solid and dashed lines are associated,
respectively, with weights $+1$ and -1. The values inside the circles are the biases.

(VONNET) obtained from the VoD is $\frac{1}{2}$. The corresponding measure in the neural
network of lower complexity (reduced VONNET), obtained from the modification of
the VoD, is only $1/(2\sqrt{2})$. Therefore, the ratio of the robustness measures for the
reduced VoD- and VoD-based networks is $1/\sqrt{2}$ in the 2-bit parity problem. Fig.
5.22 shows the neural network for the 8-bit parity case derived from the reduced
VoD, obtained via generalization of the rule just enunciated for the 2-bit parity case,
where the ratio of measures of robustness for the VoDs associated with the reduced
VONNET and the full VONNET is $1/\sqrt{8}$. A dramatic reduction in the size of the
reduced VONNET is realized: the full VONNET in the 8-bit case required 137 neurons and 1160 connection weights, but the reduced VONNET requires only 9 neurons and 72 connection weights. For the n-bit parity case, the full VONNET requires
$(2^{n-1}+n+1)$ neurons and $(2^{n-1}(n+1)+n)$ connection weights, whereas the reduced
VONNET requires $(n + 1)$ neurons and $n(n + 1)$ connection weights.

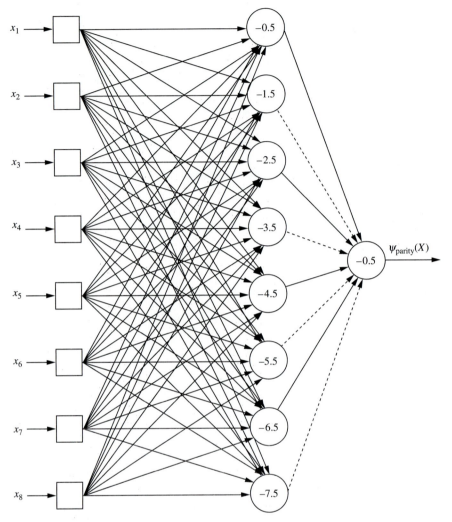

FIGURE 5.22
A reduced VONNET for the 8-bit parity problem. The values inside the circles are the biases.

5.4   UNSUPERVISED AND REINFORCEMENT LEARNING

In both the perceptron algorithm and the backpropagation procedure, the correct output for the current input is required for learning. This type of learning is called *supervised learning*. Two other types of learning are essential in the evolution of biological intelligence: *unsupervised learning* and *reinforcement learning*. In unsupervised learning a system is only presented with a set of exemplars as inputs. The system is not given any external indication as to what the correct responses should be nor whether the generated responses are right or wrong. Statistical clustering methods [117], without knowledge of the number of clusters, are examples of unsupervised learning. Reinforcement learning is somewhere between supervised learning, in which the system is provided with the desired output, and unsupervised learning, in which the system gets no feedback at all on how it is doing. In reinforcement learning the system receives a feedback that tells the system whether its output response is right or wrong, but no information on what the right output should be is provided.

Basically, unsupervised learning aims at finding a certain kind of regularity in the data represented by the exemplars. Roughly speaking, regularity means that much less data are actually required to approximately describe or classify the exemplars than the amount of data in the exemplars. To find meaningful regularity, there must be some redundancy in the input data. Examples exploiting data regularity include vector quantization for data compression and Karhunen-Loeve expansion, often referred to as principal component analysis, for dimension reduction.

In reinforcement learning, because no information on what the right output should be is provided, the system must employ some random search strategy so that the space of plausible and rational choices is searched until a correct answer is found. Reinforcement learning is usually involved in exploring a new environment when some knowledge (or subjective feeling) about the right response to environmental inputs is available. The system receives an input from the environment and produces an output as response. Subsequently, it receives a reward or a penalty from the environment. The system learns from a sequence of such interactions.

5.4.1 Principal Component Analysis Networks

We first describe an unsupervised learning algorithm performing principal component analysis. A principal component analysis identifies M orthogonal directions representing, in descending order, the largest variance in the data, where M is less than or equal to the dimension of the data. Mathematically, principal component analysis requires finding the eigenvectors of the covariance matrix $\mathbf{C} = E[(\mathbf{x} - \bar{\mathbf{x}})(\mathbf{x} - \bar{\mathbf{x}})^\mathrm{T}]$ of the real (no restriction) data vector $\mathbf{x}$. (Note that in this section the uppercase letter E denotes the expectation operator.) The eigenvalues of $\mathbf{C}$, a real symmetric nonnegative definite matrix, are real and nonnegative and may be ordered starting with the largest. In this section, we restrict the discussion to zero-mean data, i.e., $\bar{\mathbf{x}} = 0$. Note that for convenience some vectors are defined to be row vectors in this section. All other vectors not specifically noted are column vectors. Principal component analysis seeks to describe data optimally in higher dimensions using data in lower dimensions. In other words, the objective is to reconstruct the N-dimensional input $\mathbf{x}$ optimally from the M-dimensional output $\mathbf{y}$, when $N > M$. The input and the output are related by a linear transformation $\mathbf{y} = \mathbf{W}\mathbf{x}$, where $\mathbf{W}$ is a matrix having M rows and N columns. The optimality is based on minimization of the mean square error (definable by the trace, denoted by Tr, of a matrix),

$$e_M^2 \triangleq E[(\mathbf{x} - \hat{\mathbf{x}})^\mathrm{T}(\mathbf{x} - \hat{\mathbf{x}})] = \mathrm{Tr}\{E[(\mathbf{x} - \hat{\mathbf{x}})(\mathbf{x} - \hat{\mathbf{x}})^\mathrm{T}]\}, \qquad (5.38)$$

in the case when $\hat{\mathbf{x}}$ is a linear estimate of $\mathbf{x}$, i.e., $\hat{\mathbf{x}} = \hat{\mathbf{Q}}\mathbf{y}$, where $\hat{\mathbf{Q}}$ is an $N \times M$ matrix. In the following theorem, the eigenvalues λ_i of $\mathbf{C}$ are assumed to be ordered as

$$\lambda_1 \geq \lambda_2 \geq \cdots \geq \lambda_N \geq 0,$$

and λ_i is referred to as the ith largest eigenvalue.

Theorem 5.2. The mean squared error e_M^2 in Eq. (5.38) is minimized by an $(M \times N)$ matrix $\hat{\mathbf{W}}$ whose ith row is the eigenvector of the covariance matrix corresponding to the ith largest eigenvalue. The optimal linear estimate is given by

$$\hat{\mathbf{x}} = \hat{W}^{\mathsf{T}}\mathbf{y}. \tag{5.39}$$

Proof. Let $\mathbf{P}$ and $\mathbf{Q}$ be two $N \times N$ matrices. Let an $N \times N$ matrix $\mathbf{W}_1$ be obtained by setting the elements of the last $(N - M)$ rows of $\mathbf{P}$ to 0s. This is expressed as

$$\mathbf{W}_1 = \mathbf{I}_M\mathbf{P}, \tag{5.40}$$

where $\mathbf{I}_M$ is an $N \times N$ matrix in which the first M diagonal elements are 1 and all other elements are 0. Also, expand the $\mathbf{y}$ vector to an $N \times 1$ vector $\mathbf{y}_1$ by appending $(N - M)$ 0s. Then this new output vector and the original input vector are related by a linear transformation, $\mathbf{y}_1 = \mathbf{W}_1\mathbf{x}$. An estimate of $\mathbf{x}$ from $\mathbf{y}$ can be expressed as $\hat{\mathbf{x}} = \mathbf{Q}\mathbf{y}_1$. Then, Eq. (5.38) can be written as

$$e_M^2 = \mathrm{Tr}\{E[(\mathbf{x} - \mathbf{Q}\mathbf{I}_M\mathbf{P}\mathbf{x})(\mathbf{x} - \mathbf{Q}\mathbf{I}_M\mathbf{P}\mathbf{x})^{\mathsf{T}}]\} = \mathrm{Tr}[(\mathbf{I} - \mathbf{Q}\mathbf{I}_M\mathbf{P})\mathbf{C}(\mathbf{I} - \mathbf{Q}\mathbf{I}_M\mathbf{P})^{\mathsf{T}}], \tag{5.41}$$

where $\mathbf{I}$ is an identity matrix of appropriate order. Differentiating Eq. (5.41) with respect to $\mathbf{P}$ and setting the result to zero yields

$$\mathbf{I}_M\mathbf{Q}^{\mathsf{T}}(\mathbf{I} - \mathbf{Q}\mathbf{I}_M\mathbf{P})\mathbf{C} = 0. \tag{5.42}$$

The minimum value of e_M^2 then becomes

$$e_M^2 = \mathrm{Tr}[(\mathbf{I} - \mathbf{Q}\mathbf{I}_M\mathbf{P})\mathbf{C}]. \tag{5.43}$$

When $M = N$, i.e., if the dimensions of $\mathbf{y}$ and $\mathbf{x}$ are equal, the condition for optimality is $\mathbf{I} - \mathbf{Q}\mathbf{P} = 0$, which requires $\mathbf{Q} = \mathbf{P}^{-1}$, as expected. From this relation and Eq. (5.42), we have

$$\mathbf{I}_M\mathbf{Q}^{\mathsf{T}}\mathbf{Q} = \mathbf{I}_M\mathbf{Q}^{\mathsf{T}}\mathbf{Q}\mathbf{I}_M \qquad 1 \leq M \leq N. \tag{5.44}$$

For Eq. (5.44) to hold for every M, $\mathbf{Q}^{\mathsf{T}}\mathbf{Q}$ must be diagonal. Suppose that $\mathbf{Q}^{\mathsf{T}}\mathbf{Q} = \mathbf{D}$, where $\mathbf{D}$ is a diagonal matrix. Then $\mathbf{Q}$ can be expressed as $\mathbf{Q} = \hat{\mathbf{Q}}\sqrt{\mathbf{D}}$ where $\sqrt{\mathbf{D}}$ is a diagonal matrix whose diagonal elements are square roots of those of $\mathbf{D}$. Obviously, $\hat{\mathbf{Q}}^{\mathsf{T}}\hat{\mathbf{Q}} = \mathbf{I}$, implying that $\hat{\mathbf{Q}}$ is an orthonormal matrix.

From Eq. (5.44), we have

$$\mathbf{I}_M\mathbf{Q}^1 = \mathbf{I}_M\mathbf{Q}^1\mathbf{Q}\mathbf{I}_M\mathbf{P}. \tag{5.45}$$

Postmultiplying both sides of Eq. (5.45) by $\mathbf{P}^{\mathsf{T}}$ gives

$$\mathbf{I}_M = \mathbf{I}_M(\mathbf{P}^{\mathsf{T}})^{-1}\mathbf{P}^{\mathsf{T}} = \mathbf{I}_M\mathbf{Q}^{\mathsf{T}}\mathbf{P}^{\mathsf{T}} = \mathbf{I}_M\mathbf{Q}^{\mathsf{T}}\mathbf{Q}\mathbf{I}_M\mathbf{P}\mathbf{P}^{\mathsf{T}} = \mathbf{D}_M\mathbf{P}\mathbf{P}^{\mathsf{T}}, \tag{5.46}$$

where $\mathbf{D}_M$ is the matrix obtained from $\mathbf{D}$ by keeping only the first M diagonal elements nonzero. For Eq. (5.46) to hold for all M, $\mathbf{P}\mathbf{P}^{\mathsf{T}}$ must also be diagonal. Actually, when $M = N$ we have $\mathbf{P}\mathbf{P}^{\mathsf{T}} = \mathbf{D}^{-1}$, which is a diagonal matrix whose diagonal elements are the reciprocals of those of $\mathbf{D}$.

Express $\mathbf{P}$ as $\mathbf{P} = \sqrt{\mathbf{D}^{-1}}\hat{\mathbf{P}}$, implying that $\hat{\mathbf{P}}$, like $\hat{\mathbf{Q}}$, is an orthonormal matrix. Then it is easy to see that $\hat{\mathbf{Q}} = \hat{\mathbf{P}}^{-1} = \hat{\mathbf{P}}^{\mathrm{T}}$, implying that $\hat{\mathbf{P}}$ is an orthonormal matrix. The error e_M^2 can now be expressed as

$$e_M^2 = \mathrm{Tr}\left[\mathbf{C} - \hat{\mathbf{Q}}\sqrt{\mathbf{D}}\mathbf{I}_M\sqrt{\mathbf{D}^{-1}}\hat{\mathbf{P}}\mathbf{C}\right] = \mathrm{Tr}\left[\mathbf{C} - \hat{\mathbf{P}}^{\mathrm{T}}\mathbf{I}_M\hat{\mathbf{P}}\mathbf{C}\right] = \mathrm{Tr}\left[\mathbf{C} - \mathbf{I}_M\hat{\mathbf{P}}\mathbf{C}\hat{\mathbf{P}}^{\mathrm{T}}\right]. \tag{5.47}$$

Since $\mathbf{C}$ is fixed, the error will be minimized if the quantity $\hat{e}_M^2$ given next is maximized:

$$\hat{e}_M^2 = \mathrm{Tr}[\mathbf{I}_M\hat{\mathbf{P}}\mathbf{C}\hat{\mathbf{P}}^{\mathrm{T}}] = \sum_{i=1}^{M}\hat{\mathbf{p}}_i\mathbf{C}\hat{\mathbf{p}}_i^{\mathrm{T}}, \tag{5.48}$$

where $\hat{\mathbf{p}}_i$ is the ith row vector of $\hat{\mathbf{P}}$. Since $\hat{\mathbf{P}}\hat{\mathbf{P}}^{\mathrm{T}} = \mathbf{I}$, we have $\hat{\mathbf{p}}_i\hat{\mathbf{p}}_i^{\mathrm{T}} = 1$. We can use the Lagrangian method to find the maximum of $\hat{e}_M^2$ subject to the constraint of $\hat{\mathbf{p}}_i\hat{\mathbf{p}}_i^{\mathrm{T}} = 1$. Define

$$L_\lambda = \sum_{i=1}^{M}\hat{\mathbf{p}}_i\mathbf{C}\hat{\mathbf{p}}_i^{\mathrm{T}} + \sum_{i=1}^{M}\lambda_i\left(1 - \hat{\mathbf{p}}_i\hat{\mathbf{p}}_i^{\mathrm{T}}\right), \tag{5.49}$$

where the λ_i's are the Lagrange multipliers. Differentiating L_λ with respect to $\hat{\mathbf{p}}_j$ gives us the necessary condition

$$\mathbf{C}\hat{\mathbf{p}}_j^{\mathrm{T}} = \lambda_j\hat{\mathbf{p}}_j^{\mathrm{T}}. \tag{5.50}$$

This expression shows that $\hat{\mathbf{p}}_j^{\mathrm{T}}$'s are the normalized eigenvectors of $\mathbf{C}$. Therefore,

$$\hat{e}_M^2 = \sum_{i=1}^{M}\lambda_i. \tag{5.51}$$

Equation (5.51) will be maximized if the eigenvectors $\{\hat{\mathbf{p}}_j^{\mathrm{T}}\}_{j=1}^{M}$ correspond to the largest eigenvalues of $\mathbf{C}$, because it is a symmetric nonnegative definite matrix and therefore has nonnegative eigenvalues. Since $\mathbf{W} = \mathbf{I}_M\mathbf{P}$, we conclude that the error $\hat{e}_M^2$ is minimized by a $\hat{\mathbf{W}}$ whose ith row is the eigenvector of $\mathbf{C}$ corresponding to the ith largest eigenvalue, and the optimal linear estimate is given by $\hat{\mathbf{x}} = \hat{\mathbf{W}}^{\mathrm{T}}\mathbf{y}$.

We will show next that principal component analysis can be realized in a network setting through unsupervised learning. We use a one-layer network with M linear units and N dimensional inputs. The network computes $\mathbf{y} = \mathbf{W}\mathbf{x}$, where the ith row of $\mathbf{W}$ is the weight vector for the ith unit. Such a network is shown in Fig. 5.23. All the units are linear, i.e.,

$$y_i = \sum_{j=1}^{N}w_{ij}x_j = \mathbf{w}_i\mathbf{x}, \tag{5.52}$$

where $\mathbf{w}_i$ is the ith row vector of the $\mathbf{W}$ matrix and $\mathbf{x}$ is the input (column) vector. The objective is to make the weight vectors converge to the eigenvectors of the covariance matrix of $\mathbf{x}$. Although the network used here is a one-layer network, it is discussed in this section together with unsupervised learning in multilayer networks only for the sake of simplicity.

Sanger showed that the following learning rule will enable the row vectors of $\mathbf{W}$ to converge to the first M eigenvectors of the covariance matrix $\mathbf{C}$ [337]:

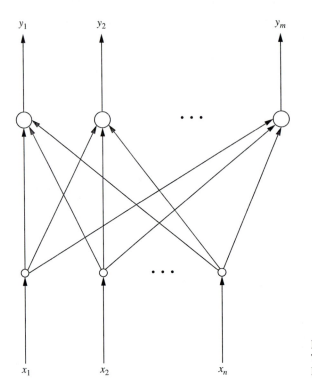

FIGURE 5.23
The neural network computing
Eq. (5.52) for $i = 1, 2, \ldots, M$.

$$\mathbf{W}(k + 1) = \mathbf{W}(k) + \eta \left(\mathbf{y}(k)\mathbf{x}^T(k) - \text{LT}[\mathbf{y}(k)\mathbf{y}^T(k)]\mathbf{W}(k) \right), \qquad (5.53)$$

where η is a positive real number that decays as k increases, and $\text{LT}[\cdot]$ is an operator that makes its matrix argument lower triangular by setting all entries above the diagonal to zero. The scalar expression of this learning rule shows more clearly the effect of the LT operator:

$$w_{ij}(k + 1) = w_{ij}(k) + \eta \left(y_i(k)x_j(k) - y_i(k)\sum_{q=1}^{i} y_q(k)w_{qj}(k) \right). \qquad (5.54)$$

Notice that the upper index of summation only extends to i.

It can be shown that the foregoing learning rule converges, and after convergence the ith row vector of $\mathbf{W}$ will equal the eigenvector (up to a $\pm$ sign) of $\mathbf{C}$ associated with the ith largest eigenvalue. The proof is left as an exercise.

The learning rule in Eq. (5.54) is not local, because computation of the updates of weights at the ith unit requires the outputs and weights at all the preceding $i - 1$ units. Sanger designed a semilocal implementation of the learning rule by reformulating Eq. (5.54) as

$$w_{ij}(k + 1) = w_{ij}(k) + \eta y_i(k)\left(\left[x_j(k) - \sum_{q=1}^{i-1} y_q(k)w_{qj}(k) \right] - y_i(k)w_{ij}(k) \right). \qquad (5.55)$$

The first term inside the square brackets can be propagated from the preceding units. Such an implementation is illustrated in Fig. 5.24.

Other works on principal component analysis networks include refs. [276] and [323]. In the latter, lateral connections among the output units are used. Sanger [338] proposed an extension to networks where the units are nonlinear, characterized, say, by a hard-limiter or a sigmoidal function. However, convergence in the nonlinear case has not been proved.

5.4.2   Self-Organization in a Perceptual Network

Another type of unsupervised learning takes place in a system acquiring specially tuned functional capabilities without supervision. This is represented by the work of Linsker [228, 229]. Linsker's network is a multilayer network as shown in Fig. 5.25. All of the units in the network are linear. The units are organized into 2-D layers A, B, C, etc., with feedforward connections to each unit from units in an overlying neighborhood in the previous layer, called a *perceptive field*. Layer A is the input layer, simulating the retina in a visual system. The focus is on the case where there is no input, but instead only random activity of the units in layer A, with no correlation among the units. The emphasis on random inputs is motivated by the observation that certain feature-analyzing cells emerge in the retina even before birth in certain primates, and therefore prior to the onset of structured visual stimuli. These feature-analyzing neurons detect light-dark contrast and orientation of an edge or bar [170]. Therefore, to simulate this phenomenon, only random signals should be fed to the input layer of the network.

The structure of Linsker's network is also motivated by the organizational principles in mammalian visual systems. A multilayer network is used because both the retina and the cortex in a biological visual system are organized in layers of neurons with interconnections between and within layers. Each unit in a layer receives input only from neurons in a diameter-limited region of the previous layer. This is analogous to the visual system, where the neurons within an anatomical layer (at least

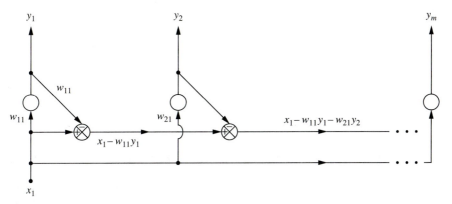

FIGURE 5.24
Sanger's implementation of the learning rule in Eq. (5.53) for one input.

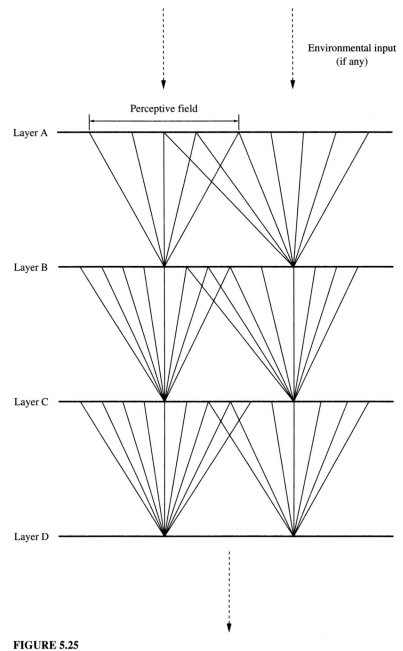

FIGURE 5.25
Linsker's multilayer network.

during the early stages of development) perform approximately the same processing function on its inputs, and each neuron receives input from a diameter-limited receptive field.

The model is based on two major simplifications.

1. All of the units are linear. Nonlinear units would more closely approximate the properties of biological neurons, but a linear network is much easier to analyze. If a linear network can develop feature-analyzing functions, insights gained from understanding linear networks may be extended to nonlinear networks. Mathematically, a multilayer neural network with linear transfer characteristics for the neurons is equivalent to a single-layer linear network. The objective in Linsker's work is not to implement a particular transformation, but rather to study what transformations can be developed by a network without supervision. In various types of feature analysis an invariant response to certain variations in the features is sought. This invariance is hard to realize in a single step. Decomposing this task into multiple stages will make the learning easier. This strategy can be implemented in a multilayer network.

2. No feedback connections are used. In a biological visual system, there are feedback connections from later stages to earlier stages. There are lateral connections within a layer as well. Linsker first chooses to understand the development properties of networks without feedback, just as one must understand a feedback control system's open-loop transfer function first before investigating closed-loop properties.

The response y_k at unit k is given by

$$y_k = \alpha_1 + \sum_i w_i x_i, \tag{5.56}$$

where x_i's are the inputs to unit k, the w_i's are the corresponding connection weights, and α_1 is a threshold. A modified Hebbian rule is used for learning the weights:

$$\Delta w_i = \alpha_2 x_i y_k + \alpha_3 x_i + \alpha_4 y_k + \alpha_5, \tag{5.57}$$

where α_j's are arbitrary constants with $\alpha_2 > 0$. These parameters may be adjusted to produce different behaviors. The weights are *clipped* to prevent them from growing indefinitely. Linsker tested two types of clipping [228]. In one type, the weights are clipped to belong to the range $w^- \leq w_i \leq w^+$. Alternatively, two types of connections are used: excitatory and inhibitory. The excitatory weights are clipped to the range $0 \leq w_i \leq w^+$. The inhibitory weights are clipped to the range $w^- \leq w_i \leq 0$. Both ways of clipping lead to the same results.

Take an average of the rule in Eq. (5.57) over an ensemble of many presentations. After some algebraic manipulations, it is possible to show that

$$\overline{\Delta w_i} \triangleq E[\Delta w_i] = \eta \left[\sum_j c_{ij} w_j + \left(k_1 + \frac{k_2}{N} \sum_j w_j \right) \right], \tag{5.58}$$

where k_1 and k_2 are combinations of the constants $\{\alpha_i\}_{i=1}^5$ and the c_{ij}'s are the elements of the covariance matrix $\mathbf{C}$. The weights are actually updated using this rule instead of the one in Eq. (5.57).

It can be shown that the rule in Eq. (5.57) is equivalent to the average of the gradient descent learning rule $\Delta w_i = -\eta \partial E / \partial w_i$, where the error function is of the form

$$ E = -\frac{1}{2}\mathbf{w}^{\mathrm{T}}\mathbf{C}\mathbf{w} + c\left(d - \sum_j w_j\right)^2. \tag{5.59} $$

For further in-depth analysis of Linsker's network, see refs. [228, 242, 425].

Simulation results. In the simulation, Linsker adopted a layer-by-layer strategy in learning the weights. All weights are set to random values within the range. The weights from layer A to layer B are learned first. After the weights of interconnections from A to B are stabilized and combined with the covariance matrix $\mathbf{C}_A$ of inputs to layer A, the covariance matrix $\mathbf{C}_B$ of inputs to layer B can be computed as a linear transformation of $\mathbf{C}_A$ using the weights from layer A to layer B. This process allows the connection weights from layer B to layer C to be learned. This process is repeated for all the remaining layers in sequence.

A few parameters for each layer determine the stabilized weights for the connections to that layer. These parameters include k_1, k_2, and the size of the perceptive field. The first type of feature-analyzing units emerges in layer B. There is a parameter regime in which each weight reaches its excitatory limit w^+ and then stabilizes. Thereafter, each unit in layer B computes the local average of the activity in its perceptive field in layer A.

Once layer B is stabilized, nearby units are positively correlated. As a result of this correlation, a new type of feature-analyzing units, called *center-surround units*, emerges in layer C. This type of unit acts as a contrast-sensitive filter. It responds maximally to a bright circular spot centered on the unit's receptive field against a dark background. A reverse type of center-surround unit also emerges. This type of unit responds maximally to a dark spot on a bright background.

The correlation between the center-surround units in layer C determines the feature-analyzing units that may emerge in layer D. The behaviors of the units in the succeeding layers emerge in a similar fashion. Actually, progressively sharper center-surround units are observed in layers C through F.

For layer G Linsker used a larger receptive field. This produced a new type of feature-analyzing units called *orientation-selective units*. A unit of this type responds maximally to a bright edge or bar against a dark background, or its complement, when the edge or bar has a particular orientation. The emergence of orientation-selective units in a system with symmetric architecture and parameters describes a broken-symmetry phenomenon. Each orientation-selective unit will develop to favor an arbitrary orientation in a feedforward-only network. Linsker [228] showed that if lateral connections between nearby units in the orientation-selective layer are included, the orientation preferences of the units in the layer can become organized into certain arrangements. Units with similar orientation preferences develop to occupy irregular band-shaped regions. This development is strikingly similar to the orientation columns found in biological visual systems.

Based on these results, Linsker proposed a principle for unsupervised learning networks: Network connections should develop in a way that maximizes the amount of information that is preserved when signals are transformed at each processing stage, subject to certain constraints. This principle is in concert with the principal component analysis network discussed earlier. In principal component analysis the objective is to best reconstruct a higher-dimension input from a lower-dimension output. In other words, principal component analysis aims to preserve the maximum amount of information in dimension reduction.

Center-surround and orientation-selective cells are found in mammalian visual systems. It is notable that a simplified linear model without feedback can develop similar functions using only random stimuli. Of course, this similarity does not prove that the feature-analyzing cells in the mammalian visual system develop in the same way as in this network.

5.4.3 Reinforcement Learning

The difficulty with reinforcement learning stems not only from the possibility that precise information about the error is unavailable but also from the likelihood that reward or penalty may be implemented only after many action steps. An example is a chess game. The only knowledge available is that the game is either lost or won. A loss may be due to errors at several of the earlier moves. In order to learn where and when errors are made, strategies should be identified to reward the right moves and punish the wrong ones.

A random search component is necessary for reinforcement learning. One way to implement the random search is by use of stochastic output units. A *stochastic unit* is a unit whose output depends on a probability distribution function. For example, the output z_i of a stochastic TLU may assume either the $+1$ or -1 state according to the probabilities,

$$P(z_i = +1) = \frac{1}{1 + \exp[-2(\sum_j w_{ij} y_j - \theta_i)/T]} \qquad (5.60)$$

$$P(z_i = -1) = \frac{1}{1 + \exp[2(\sum_j w_{ij} y_j - \theta_i)/T]}, \qquad (5.61)$$

where the y_j's are the outputs of units connected to the stochastic output unit i, and T is a parameter determining the probability for the two transitions and is referred to as the *temperature*. Its meaning will become clearer when we discuss simulated annealing and Boltzmann machines in Chapter 8. The meanings of the other parameters are self-evident. Similarly, a unit may assume an output value within a continuous range according to a probability distribution function. Another alternative is simply to add a random noise to the output value of a unit.

Barto and Anandan [30] proposed the associative reward-and-penalty algorithm for learning the weights of these stochastic units using the reinforcement signal. Assume that the reward signal from the environment is $r = +1$ and the penalty signal is $r = -1$. The basic idea is to encourage the unit to do what it has just done if the action receives a reward, and to do the opposite if a penalty is received. Therefore, for the kth input pattern, we may construct the desired output as follows:

$$\hat{d}_i(k) = \begin{cases} y_i(k) & \text{if } r(k) = +1 \\ -y_i(k) & \text{if } r(k) = -1. \end{cases} \tag{5.62}$$

Once a desired output has been constructed, the learning problem can be turned into a supervised one. The Widrow-Hoff LMS algorithm may be applied. In Chapter 4 the Widrow-Hoff LMS learning rule was written as

$$\mathbf{w}(k + 1) = \mathbf{w}(k) + 2\alpha e_i(k)\mathbf{y}(k), \tag{4.44}$$

where $e_i(k)$ is the difference between the desired output $d_i(k)$ and the actual output $z_i(k)$ for the kth input pattern vector $\mathbf{y}(k)$, i.e., $e_i(k) = d_i(k) - z_i(k)$. Although we constructed an estimate of the real desired output $d_i(k)$, our actual output here is a random variable rather than a deterministic one as in the Widrow-Hoff LMS algorithm. Reward or penalty for a stochastic unit should depend on its average behavior. Therefore, we modify the error definition into

$$e_i(k) = \hat{d}_i(k) - E[z_i(k)] \tag{5.63}$$

where $E[z_i(k)]$ is either approximated by the short-time average of the output of the stochastic unit (by averaging the output value $z_i(k)$ over a short time period) or is found by computing the average from the probability function of z_i if this is known, as in Eqs. (5.60) and (5.61). Then the learning rule becomes

$$\mathbf{w}(k + 1) = \begin{cases} \mathbf{w}(k) + \alpha(+1)(z_i(k) - E[z_i(k)])\mathbf{y}(k) & \text{if } r(k) = +1 \\ \mathbf{w}(k) + \alpha(-1)(-z_i(k) - E[z_i(k)])\mathbf{y}(k) & \text{if } r(k) = -1, \end{cases} \tag{5.64}$$

where the learning rate is made to depend on the reinforcement signal $r(k)$. It has been observed that it is desirable to make $\alpha(+1)$ much larger than $\alpha(-1)$.

The preceding discussion, which deals with learning weights to output units, can be generalized to multilayer feedforward networks by propagating the error $e_i(k)$ in Eq. (4.44) as in the backpropagation algorithm in Section 5.2. Reinforcement learning converges much more slowly than its supervised learning counterpart. This outcome is expected, because the network is asked to learn the same task with much less information. However, it has been shown to work faster than a blind trial-and-error approach if the learning already done can be generalized [5].

A more sophisticated approach is to construct a model of the environment. The model is just an auxiliary learning network that uses the input from the environment, the output from the main learning network, and a reinforcement signal to generate estimates of the desired outputs for the main learning network [31, 414]. The architecture of such a learning scheme is illustrated in Fig. 5.26. There are two ways to use the auxiliary network. In one approach, the auxiliary network is trained to provide a continuous estimate of the reinforcement signal. This approach is useful in problems where the environmental reinforcement signal is only provided after long time intervals. For example, Barto, Sutton, and Anderson [31] used a single-unit learning network, called the *associative search element,* and an auxiliary single-unit network, called the *adaptive critic element,* to learn to balance an inverted pendulum on a cart. The pendulum was linked to the cart but free to fall under gravity in a plane perpendicular to the ground. It could be kept from falling by moving the cart back and forth, similar to balancing a broom on the hand. The auxiliary network learned to provide a continuous estimate of the reinforcement signal, called the *critic signal,* as shown by the dashed line in Fig. 5.26.

In another approach, the auxiliary network is first trained to minimize the square of the difference between the real environmental reinforcement signal r and the estimated reinforcement signal $\hat{r}$. This is a supervised learning problem, and the backpropagation algorithm can be applied. If the auxiliary network is a good model of the environment, the real reward r will be maximum when the estimated reward $\hat{r}$ is maximum. Therefore, at the second stage, the two networks are trained

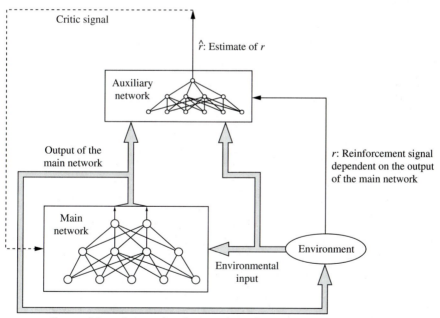

FIGURE 5.26
A reinforcement learning network that uses an auxiliary network.

together to maximize the total reward over all the input patterns. This again becomes a supervised learning problem and can be solved using the backpropagation algorithm. However, the connection weights in the auxiliary network are not changed. The auxiliary network simply backpropagates the error signal down to the main network. The connection weights in the main network are changed according to gradient descent to maximize the output $\hat{r}$ of the auxiliary network.

Although the discussion in this section is limited to reinforcement learning in feedforward networks, the idea can be generalized to recurrent networks, i.e., to networks with graphs that contain loops.

5.5   THE PROBABILISTIC NEURAL NETWORK

Another multilayer feedforward network is the *probabilistic neural network* (PNN). In addition to the input layer, the PNN has two hidden layers and an output layer. The major difference from a feedforward network trained by backpropagation is that it can be constructed after only a single pass of the training exemplars in its original form and two passes in a modified version. The activation function of a neuron in the case of the PNN is statistically derived from estimates of probability density functions (PDFs) based on training patterns.

Suppose that members of a set of exemplar patterns belong to k classes, $S_1, S_2, \ldots, S_k$. Assume that the observable pattern is $\mathbf{x} \in \mathbb{R}^m$, whose a posteriori probability, $p_r(S_i \mid \mathbf{x})$, that it is from class S_i is, by Bayes' rule,

$$p_r(S_i \mid \mathbf{x}) = \frac{p(\mathbf{x} \mid S_i)p_r(S_i)}{p(\mathbf{x})}, \tag{5.65}$$

where $p(\mathbf{x} \mid S_i)$, $i = 1, 2, \ldots, k$, is the a priori PDF of the pattern in classes to be separated; $p_r(S_i)$, $i = 1, 2, \ldots, k$, are the a priori probabilities of the classes (may be assumed to be equally likely); and $p(\mathbf{x})$ is assumed to be constant. The decision rule is to select class S_i for which $p_r(S_i \mid \mathbf{x})$ is maximum. This will happen if, for all $j \neq i$,

$$p(\mathbf{x} \mid S_i)p_r(S_i) > p(\mathbf{x} \mid S_j)p_r(S_j). \tag{5.66}$$

If we assume that the a priori probabilities $p_r(S_i)$ of the classes are known and the a priori PDF, $p(\mathbf{x} \mid S_i)$, is Gaussian, then the estimator for the a priori PDF is

$$\hat{p}(\mathbf{x} \mid S_i) = \frac{1}{(2\pi)^{m/2}\sigma_i^m |S_i|} \sum_{j=1}^{n_i} \exp\left[\frac{-(\mathbf{x} - \mathbf{x}_j^{(i)})^{\mathrm{T}}(\mathbf{x} - \mathbf{x}_j^{(i)})}{2\sigma_i^2}\right], \tag{5.67}$$

where $\mathbf{x}_j^{(i)}$ is the jth exemplar pattern or training pattern from class S_i, $|S_i| = n_i$ denotes the cardinality of the set of patterns in class S_i, and σ_i is a smoothing parameter.

The layers constituting the topology in the PNN are organized as follows. The input layer has m units, to which the m-dimensional input vector $\mathbf{x} \in \mathbb{R}^m$ is applied. The first layer has one pattern unit for each pattern exemplar. Therefore, each such pattern unit may be associated with a generic term depicted in the summation of

Eq. (5.67) for the ith class. The second hidden layer contains one summation unit for each class. Each summation unit is used to realize a sum of the type in Eq. (5.67) from the outputs in the previous layer. The output layer is the decision layer used for implementing the decision rule by selecting the maximum a posteriori probability, $p_r(S_i \mid \mathbf{x})$, from the outputs of the preceding summation layer for each i. The decision layer can be implemented by a winner-take-all competitive network, described in Chapter 9. The topology for the PNN is shown in Fig. 5.27. The network is constructed by setting the weight vector to one of the pattern units equal to each distinct pattern vector in the training set from a certain class and then connecting the outputs of the pattern units to the appropriate summation unit for that class. Note that each new exemplar causes a new unit in the first hidden layer to be assigned to it, with the pattern vector equaling the input weight vector. To see how the computation proceeds from the data applied to the input layer, let us rewrite the negative of the argument of the exponential in the generic term for the summation of Eq. (5.67) as

$$\frac{\|\mathbf{x} - \mathbf{x}_j^{(i)}\|^2}{2\sigma_i^2} = \frac{1}{\sigma_i^2}\left[\mathbf{x}^T\mathbf{x}_j^{(i)} - \frac{1}{2}\left(\|\mathbf{x}\|^2 + \|\mathbf{x}_j^{(i)}\|^2\right)\right], \tag{5.68}$$

where the norm of the real-valued vector $\mathbf{x}$ is

$$\|\mathbf{x}\| = \sqrt{\mathbf{x}^T\mathbf{x}}. \tag{5.69}$$

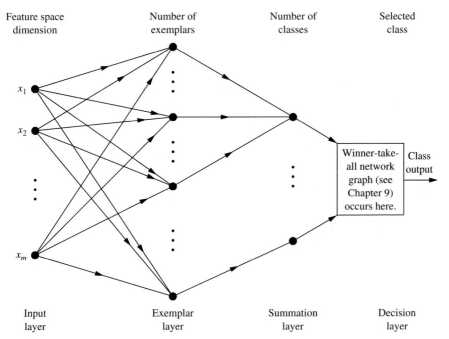

FIGURE 5.27

Graph of the PNN showing the input layer nodes, exemplar layer nodes (each with Gaussian activation function), summation layer nodes, and the decision layer.

Therefore, the generic term within the summation in Eq. (5.67) may be realized by the structure in Fig. 5.28. The summing element implements the computation of the inner product of the vectors $\mathbf{x}$ and $\mathbf{x}_j^{(i)}$ and adds it to the bias term, $-\frac{1}{2}(\|\mathbf{x}\|^2 + \|\mathbf{x}_j^{(i)}\|^2)$, following which there is a multiplication by $-1/\sigma_i^2$ and exponentiation. Each unit in the second hidden layer sums the relevant outputs from the first hidden layer. Following multiplication of the sum by the term

$$\frac{p_r(S_i)}{(2\pi)^{m/2}\sigma_i^m|S_i|},$$

one obtains the estimate $\hat{p}(\mathbf{x} \mid S_i)$ in Eq. (5.67). This estimate is used in place of $p(\mathbf{x} \mid S_i)$ to compute $p_r(S_i \mid \mathbf{x})$ in Eq. (5.65) for each i, which then provides the inputs for the output layer to make its decision based upon the rule in Eq. (5.66). This decision involves selection of the maximum element from its set of inputs so that the appropriate class number is generated at the output. The original PNN used the same smoothing parameter σ_i for all classes and used a single pass to construct the network [365]. A modified approach [66] used a distinct smoothing parameter for each class and a second pass of the training pattern to calculate the smoothing parameter by multiplying a constant times the average minimum distance between training samples within the same category. Let $d_j^{(i)}$ denote the distance between the jth exemplar pattern and the nearest exemplar pattern in class S_i. Then the average minimum distance between exemplars in class S_i is

$$d_{\mathrm{avg}}(i) = \frac{1}{|S_i|}\sum_{j=1}^{n_i} d_j^{(i)},$$

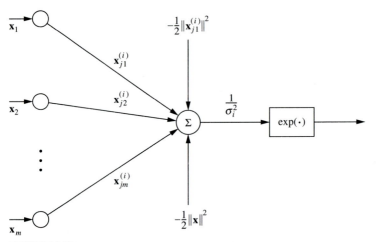

FIGURE 5.28
Structure realizing the generic Gaussian function in the estimator for the a priori PDF in a PNN.

where $|S_i| = n_i$. The smoothing parameter σ_i for class S_i is assigned as

$$\sigma_i = gd_{\text{avg}}(i),$$

where g is a constant that has been found experimentally to be between 1.1 and 1.4 for satisfactory performance.

The construction time for the PNN is very small in comparison to the backpropagation-trained feedforward network. However, as the cardinality of the training set increases, the PNN storage requirements for the weights may become appreciable, since all exemplars must be stored. In its simplest form, the PNN is a rote memorization scheme, which may have a severely limited capability for valid generalization; the network's performance may be very poor on the test exemplars. This may be resolved by clustering the training set. Therefore, the PNN is suited in classification problems for which fast learning is more important than generalization. Critical to the versatility and performance of the network is the choice of the smoothing parameters, and more research is recommended on better guidelines for their selection. The PNN classifier has sometimes been accepted as belonging to the class of radial basis function (RBF) classifiers. We prefer, however, to associate RBF classifiers topologically with a feedforward network having only one hidden layer.

Example 5.6. This example illustrates the calculation of the smoothing parameters and the evaluation phase. Consider three classes of data in two-dimensional feature space. The feature vectors are as follows:

Class S_1 : $\quad \mathbf{x}_1^{(1)} = [1\ 1]^{\text{T}} \qquad \mathbf{x}_2^{(1)} = [0\ 1]^{\text{T}} \qquad \mathbf{x}_3^{(1)} = [1\ 3]^{\text{T}}$

Class S_2 : $\quad \mathbf{x}_1^{(2)} = [3\ 4]^{\text{T}} \qquad \mathbf{x}_2^{(2)} = [4\ 3]^{\text{T}} \qquad \mathbf{x}_3^{(2)} = [5\ 3]^{\text{T}}$

Class S_3 : $\quad \mathbf{x}_1^{(3)} = [-3\ -3]^{\text{T}} \qquad \mathbf{x}_2^{(3)} = [-4\ -4]^{\text{T}} \qquad \mathbf{x}_3^{(3)} = [-2\ -3]^{\text{T}}.$

Since the training exemplars are clustered into classes, the connection weights of the neural network are already determined. The input layer has two units (the dimension of feature space), the first hidden layer has nine units (the total number of exemplars), the second hidden layer has three units (the number of classes), and the output layer is just a decision layer that selects the maximum from its inputs and outputs the corresponding class number. In this problem the graph characterizing the connections between the input layer and the first hidden layer of nodes is $K_{2,9}$; the weights associated with the edges, directly obtained from the feature vectors, are shown in Fig. 5.29, which is the sketch of the network for this example. Note that if the training data were not available in clustered form, an algorithm to do the clustering would be needed prior to the first pass. This requirement is a drawback of the method.

The smoothing parameters will be calculated next. The Euclidean distances between the points representing the training patterns in feature space for each class are first calculated. For example, if $d_{ij}^{(k)}$ denotes the Euclidean distance between feature vector $\mathbf{x}_i^{(k)}$ and $\mathbf{x}_j^{(k)}$ in class k, then

$$d_1^{(1)} = \min\left(d_{12}^{(1)}, d_{13}^{(1)}\right) = \min(1, 2) = 1$$

$$d_2^{(1)} = \min\left(d_{21}^{(1)}, d_{23}^{(1)}\right) = \min\left(1, \sqrt{5}\right) = 1$$

$$d_3^{(1)} = \min\left(d_{31}^{(1)}, d_{32}^{(1)}\right) = \min\left(2, \sqrt{5}\right) = 2.$$

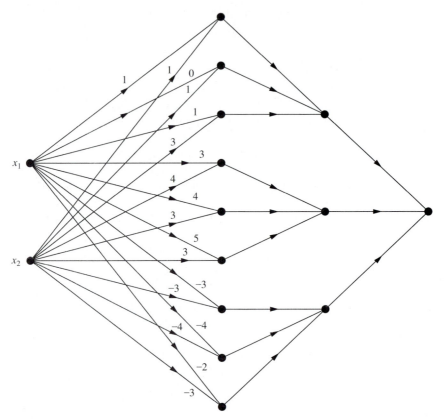

FIGURE 5.29
Graph for the PNN structure needed in Example 5.7 including the weights for the graph $K_{2,9}$ over the input layer nodes and the exemplar layer nodes.

In this example, we selected the value of the constant g as 1.2. Then the smoothing parameter σ_1 is

$$\sigma_1 = (1.2)\frac{1 + 1 + 2}{3} = 1.6.$$

The reader can easily verify that

$$d_1^{(2)} = \sqrt{2}, \qquad d_2^{(2)} = 1, \qquad d_3^{(2)} = 1, \qquad \sigma_2 = 1.36568$$

$$d_1^{(3)} = 1, \qquad d_2^{(3)} = \sqrt{2}, \qquad d_3^{(3)} = 1, \qquad \sigma_3 = 1.36568.$$

The calculations in the testing phase will be illustrated next by treating the exemplar vector $\mathbf{x}_1^{(1)}$ as a test vector $\mathbf{x}$. First we assume that

$$p_r(S_1) = p_r(S_2) = p_r(S_3) = \tfrac{1}{3}.$$

For this example $m = 2$ and $|S_1| = |S_2| = |S_3| = 3$. Then for category S_1,

$$\|\mathbf{x}_1^{(1)}\|^2 = 2, \qquad \mathbf{x}^T\mathbf{x}_1^{(1)} = 2$$

$$\|\mathbf{x}_2^{(1)}\|^2 = 1, \qquad \mathbf{x}^T\mathbf{x}_2^{(1)} = 1$$

$$\|\mathbf{x}_3^{(1)}\|^2 = 10, \qquad \mathbf{x}^T\mathbf{x}_3^{(1)} = 4$$

$$p_r(S_1 \mid \mathbf{x}) = \frac{p_r(S_1)}{(2\pi)\sigma_1^2(3)} \sum_{j=1}^{3} \exp\left[\frac{1}{\sigma_1^2}\left\{\mathbf{x}^T\mathbf{x}_j^{(1)} - \frac{1}{2}\left(\|\mathbf{x}\|^2 + \|\mathbf{x}_j^{(1)}\|^2\right)\right\}\right]$$

$$= 15.7525 \times 10^{-3}.$$

A similar set of calculations for categories S_2 and S_3 should yield (the reader is invited to verify these)

$$p_r(S_2 \mid \mathbf{x}) = 625.7411 \times 10^{-6}$$

$$p_r(S_3 \mid \mathbf{x}) = 13.44437 \times 10^{-6}.$$

The a posteriori probabilities just calculated are entered as inputs to the decision layer, whose output should be class 1 because

$$\max_i \{ p_r(S_i \mid \mathbf{x}) \} = p_r(S_1 \mid \mathbf{x}),$$

which is consistent with the fact that $\mathbf{x} = \mathbf{x}_1^{(1)}$ belongs to class S_1.

In an M.S. thesis in electrical engineering, completed in August 1994 at The Pennsylvania State University, Horst Max William Prehl documented Example 5.6 and made a detailed comparison of the performance in the training and testing phases of various multilayer feedforward neural network training algorithms, including the PNN and backpropagation, using Holstein sire data, Fisher's iris data, and image feature vector data. His conclusions were that the results for each neural network depend on the type of training and evaluation data.

5.6 CONCLUSIONS AND SUGGESTIONS

Problems that are not linearly separable can be solved with multilayer feedforward neural networks, possessing one or more hidden layers in which the neurons have nonlinear transfer characteristics. It has been shown that a feedforward network with one hidden layer of sigmoidal units and a linear output unit may approximate any absolutely integrable function arbitrarily closely, provided that the number of hidden units is allowed to be unbounded. For pattern classification problems, a more insightful solution may be provided by three-layer networks, each with two hidden layers and one output layer (the input layer is not counted since it is just a fan-out layer). They are capable of realizing arbitrarily complex decision regions based on the following rationale:

1. A neuron with a bipolar or unipolar hard-limiter type of transfer characteristic can implement the equation of a hyperplane, which splits the space into two disjoint

open half-spaces. A layer of m neurons can be used to implement the equations of m distinct hyperplanes.

2. Since any convex region can be expressed as the intersection of a finite number of closed half-spaces whose boundaries are hyperplanes, the interior of a convex region can be implemented by a two-layer neural network having one neuron in the upper layer. Several such distinct, possibly overlapping, regions can be implemented by a two-layer network where the number of neurons in the upper layer is equal to the number of such regions.

3. Finally, the union of a finite number of distinct regions can be implemented by introducing a third layer to combine the appropriate outputs from the second layer. The number of neurons in the third layer is equal to the number of classes to be identified.

Thus, for a set of patterns (exemplars) belonging to several classes, it is conceivable that a tessellation of the space can yield the number of layers (one, two, or three), the number of neurons in each layer (or a good estimate of this number), and their connection weights for a neural network whose topology is characterizable by a layered graph. Though this possibility is consistent with the implications of Kolmogorov's existence result for exact representation, which was proved in a more general setting, exact representations of arbitrary continuous functions require neuron characteristics that are impossible to realize in practice. Thus, an underlying approximation is inevitable in the actual design of any multilayer neural network. For example, in training a network, a set of inputs that are associated with a function is presented to the network, and the parameters are adjusted to make the output of the network close to the known function value.

Backpropagation, though a very popular training procedure, not only is slow and lacks guaranteed convergence but also requires a priori choices for the number of units in the hidden layers as well as for the number of layers; the pursuit of the optimal values may be error-prone and involve many trials. Recent research has also revealed that the training algorithms using backpropagation may be slow to converge because the training problem using gradient descent–based methods is usually ill-conditioned and may not be solved more efficiently by higher-order optimization methods [329]. As in the perceptron-trained network, learning in a backpropagation-trained ANN is not local; that is, if new training exemplars are added after initial learning, the whole network has to relearn. Also, how learning will be generalized in a network trained using backpropagation is hard to predict and control. Nevertheless, backpropagation has been widely used in pattern classification applications, occurring in speech recognition and image coding, because it can fit multidimensional data of high complexity on the basis of simple training data. A variant of backpropagation has been applied for learning complex-valued patterns by a multilayer feedforward network in which weights, thresholds, input signals, and output signals may be complex-valued [274]. Since frequency response samples are complex-valued, the foregoing variant could be used in filter design. This observation is also valid on transforms used for preprocessing digitized image data, which may be required to train a neural network in robust recognition tasks.

A method of designing multilayer feedforward neural nets other than through backpropagation has also been described here. This approach facilitates the derivation of equivalent structures (consistent with nonuniqueness of design) capable of realizing a specified input-output description. Other methods for designing neural networks, based on Voronoi diagrams [269] or decision trees [351], either lead to very large designs or are ad hoc in nature, and their complexity is not addressed. Training of such networks has only been marginally addressed, and the issue of equivalent designs has not been discussed in any of the approaches including that in [55], where partitioning of space has been based on an optimality criterion using a concept akin to entropy. The method presented in Section 5.3, based on Voronoi diagrams as proposed in [51] and [52], also addresses the problem of exact representation, and though the number of representative points is not fixed, it is finite, implying that connection weights are trained simultaneously with the network structure. (The need for training of structures in addition to interconnection weights is discussed in more detail in Chapter 7 and in [221].) This approach does not have difficulty in separating patterns that are very similar but belong to different classes. To exploit the advantages fully, it is important to extract the graph-theoretic properties of the VoD that are relevant to neural network design. This is especially true because, though a neural network with only one hidden layer can indeed interpolate a given data set satisfactorily, estimates are not given for the number of neurons in the hidden layer (or layers). Indeed, that number could be prohibitively large if only one hidden layer is chosen. The VoD provides useful information about the number of neurons in each layer. The neural network may also be constructed from the abstract dual of a VoD, namely the Delaunay tessellation, and fast methods for constructing the latter in higher dimensional Euclidean space are being developed [126]. The important role of computational geometry and parallel computational geometry in such efforts is stated.

The training problem in multilayer feedforward neural networks is primarily *overdetermined;* i.e., the number of training data points is greater than or equal to the number of training parameters. In applications of neural networks in areas such as continuous speech recognition, the amount of training data available may *far* exceed the number of parameters chosen for training (exceptions to this may occur; large multilayer networks with a single hidden layer containing over 4000 hidden units have been successfully trained, using online backpropagation and a speech corpus with over 6 million training samples, when there were more than a million free parameters [264] in the network). Some redundancy in the training data is also necessary for deployment of unsupervised learning. Remarkable feature extraction properties have been demonstrated by unsupervised learning in multilayer feedforward networks. The technique, based on principal component analysis, is analyzed in sufficient generality and detail. A model of self-organization that uses a layered topology is also described.

The principal advantage of the PNN is fast construction that does not require an iterative procedure as the backpropagation algorithm does. It can be effective in situations where there is sparse data in a real-time environment. When the size of the training exemplar set is large, various clustering techniques can be applied to generate a smaller set of representative exemplars. The main disadvantage is the amount of computation required after training when a new output is to be calculated. A learning algorithm similar to the PNN has been presented for estimation of continuous variables in [366]. The Cerebellar Model Arithmetic Computer (CMAC) has a similar structure and provides another alternative to backpropagation [259]. The hybrid learning schemes employed in training a class of multilayer feedforward networks will be considered in Chapter 9.

A different approach to the organization of search in parameter space so that there is a high likelihood of locating either an optimal or near-optimal solution is provided by the genetic algorithms. Unlike the usual backpropagation, where the gradient descent methods and their variants iteratively refine a trial solution until no further improvements result, the genetic search, inspired by biological evolution, cross-breeds trial solutions by selective reproduction, recombination, and mutation, permitting only the fittest solutions to survive after several generations. We alert the reader to the simple and supportive exposition given by P. J. Denning.[2] Documentation of claims on a higher chance of locating a global optimum by genetic search is, however, only empirical.

PROBLEMS

5.1. To compute predicates other than linear threshold functions using a multilayer feedforward network, the output-input transfer characteristic of a neuron must be differentiable. Otherwise, learning cannot be achieved, because backpropagation using the generalized delta rule cannot be applied. Is this statement correct? Why? You should feel free to interpret the statement from various standpoints while writing your answer.

5.2. Let the index of summation k satisfy $1 \leq k \leq |X|(|X| - 1)/2$ in

$$\phi(X) = T_b\left(\sum_{x_i,x_j \in X, i<j} \alpha_k x_i x_j - \theta \right),$$

where α_k and θ are unknown real-valued parameters. An example is given in Fig. P5.2 for $|X| = 4$. Given are training sets Y_1 and Y_2, and $\phi(X) = 1$ if $X \in Y_1$ and $\phi(X) = 0$ otherwise. What learning algorithm should you use to train this network to compute $\phi(X)$? Why?

5.3. Write a computer program to implement the backpropagation algorithm to train the two-layer network in Fig. P5.3 to compute the exclusive-OR function $x_1 \oplus x_2$. Test the program and give the transfer characteristics of neurons used, the weights and thresholds obtained, the total number of iterations, the total number of weight corrections, and the total number of calculations (multiplications, additions, and divisions) required for

---

[2]P.J. Denning. Genetic algorithms. *Scientific American*, 80:12–14. January–February 1992.

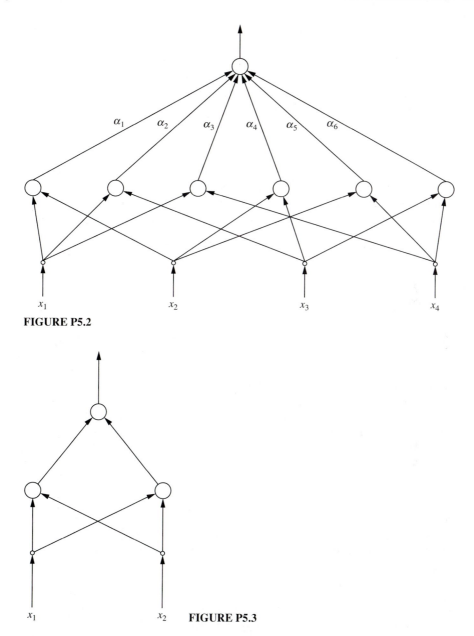

FIGURE P5.2

FIGURE P5.3

convergence (provided convergence does occur). Start the program with different random initial weights and thresholds, and determine how often it converges to a solution. What you have done is achievable for a broader class of problems by use of the Neural Network Toolbox in MATLAB.

5.4. Repeat Problem 5.3 for the network in Fig. P5.4.

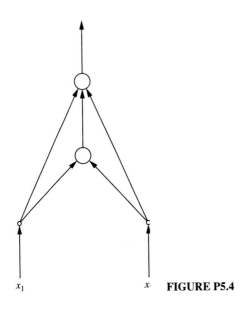

x_1 x **FIGURE P5.4**

5.5. Write a general program that can apply the backpropagation algorithm to any multilayer feedforward network. You may choose to write the program in C language if you are familiar with the basics of C; such a program listing is available in ref. [283].

5.6. Design a feedforward network to compute the parity function. The dimension of the input patterns should be no less than 10. Write programs to apply the BPA and the quick-prop to train the network. Test the program and give the transfer functions used, the weights and thresholds obtained, the total number of iterations, the total number of weight corrections, and the total number of calculations (multiplications, additions, and divisions) required for convergence (provided convergence does occur). Start the program with different random initial weights and thresholds, and determine how often it converges to a solution. Again, use of the MATLAB Neural Network Toolbox is encouraged.

5.7. The exclusive-OR (XOR) function acting on two inputs, x_1 and x_2, provides one of the simplest examples of a not linearly separable function (it is, however, *nonlinearly* separable). Nonlinear functions of x_1, x_2 are known to yield nonlinear decision boundaries. Consider the function

$$y(x_1, x_2) = w_0 + (w_1 x_1 + w_2 x_2) + (w_{11} x_1^2 + w_{12} x_1 x_2 + w_{22} x_2^2),$$

which includes the superposition of a constant, a linear form, and a quadratic form. Justify whether the above function, with proper choice of weights $w_0, w_1, w_2, w_{11}, w_{12}$, and w_{22}, can be used to realize the XOR logic function that maps the bipolar binary variables (x_1, x_2) according to the following rule:

$$(1, 1) \longrightarrow -1, \qquad (1, -1) \longrightarrow +1$$
$$(-1, -1) \longrightarrow -1, \qquad (-1, 1) \longrightarrow +1$$

5.8. Investigate the case when the function in the preceding problem is replaced by

$$y(x_1, x_2, \ldots, x_n) = w_0 + \sum_{i=1}^{n} w_i x_i + \sum_{i=1}^{n} \sum_{i=1}^{n} w_{ij} x_i x_j,$$

which is formed from the superposition of a constant, a linear form in n variables, and a quadratic form in the same variables. To do this problem, first generalize the mapping of the XOR function from the case involving two bipolar binary variables to the case of $n > 2$ bipolar binary variables. You are asked to achieve this generalization by starting with the XOR of x_1 and x_2. The XOR mapping is then repeated on the resulting variable and x_3. The process is continued until all the n variables are used up. Such a generalization of XOR leads to the *parity function* of n variables. Determine whether this parity function can be computed by suitably thresholding $y(x_1, x_2, \ldots, x_n)$ for selected values of n like $n = 3$ and $n = 4$.

5.9. Investigate the case when $y(x_1, x_2)$ in Problem 5.7 is replaced by

$$y(x_1, x_2) = \sum_{i=0}^{3} \sum_{j=0}^{3} w_{ij} x_1^i x_2^j,$$

which is a polynomial of partial degree 3 in each variable, subject to the constraint, $w_{11} = w_{20} = w_{02} = 0$.

5.10. The synaptic weight vector whose transpose multiplies the input feature vector $\mathbf{x}$ is denoted by $\mathbf{w}$. Both $\mathbf{x}$ and $\mathbf{w}$ are real-valued input vectors, each having n components. The inner product, $\mathbf{w}^T\mathbf{x}$, of $\mathbf{w}$ and $\mathbf{x}$ is applied as input to a unit having a linear transfer characteristic with zero bias.

(*a*) The input-output mapping of this unit is described therefore by

$$f(\mathbf{x}, \mathbf{w}) = \mathbf{w}^T\mathbf{x}.$$

Calculate the first-order gradient vector $\nabla_{\mathbf{w}} f(\mathbf{x}, \mathbf{w})$ with respect to the weight vector $\mathbf{w}$.

(*b*) Suppose that the scalar $\mathbf{w}^T\mathbf{x}$ is applied as input to a unit characterized by the sigmoid transfer characteristic,

$$f(u) = \frac{1}{1 + e^{-u}},$$

so that the output from the unit is $f(\mathbf{w}^T\mathbf{x})$. Calculate the gradient vector $\nabla_{\mathbf{w}} f(\mathbf{w}^T\mathbf{x})$ in this case.

5.11. The input to a unit may not necessarily be a bilinear function of the weight and input vectors. You will study about nonlinear synaptic contacts in Section 7.2. Suppose that the inputs x_1 and x_2 are raised to their second powers and then combined so that the resulting expression, $w_1 x_1^2 + w_2 x_2^2 + w_3$ (where w_1, w_2, w_3 are weights), serves as the input to a unit whose transfer characteristic is described by the hard-limiter,

$$f(u) = \begin{cases} 1 & u > 0 \\ 0 & u \le 0. \end{cases}$$

Starting with an initial choice of the weight vector $[w_1 \ w_2 \ w_3]^T$, investigate the possibility of implementing a learning rule capable of generating a decision surface that leads to the solution of the XOR problem.

5.12. The feedforward neural network can be used for data compression. The structure involves an input layer, one hidden layer, and an output layer. The input exemplar applied to the input layer is mapped to itself at the output layer, and the signal encoded as the output from the hidden layer represents the compressed data. Therefore, the number of units at the output layer equals the dimension of the input vector, whereas the hidden layer units are less in number if compression is to take place. For instance, to achieve 2:1 compression, the number of hidden layer units must be half the number of output units. Represent each of the letters E, H, F, L, M, and N as an (8 × 5) binary image composed of 40 squares (8 rows of 5 squares). Denote a filled square by 1 and an unfilled square by 0. Represent each letter as a binary sequence of length 40 generated from a row-by-row scan of the corresponding image. The set of binary sequences constitutes an epoch to be used for training. Let the number of hidden layer units be 20, each of which is characterized by a logsigmoid-with-bias type of transfer characteristic. Let the number of output units be 40, each of which is characterized by another suitable nonlinearity, which you are asked to choose.

(a) Train the structure using the backpropagation algorithm. For this purpose, use the MATLAB Neural Network Toolbox, if you have access to that software.

(b) Test the performance of your trained network by determining whether the characters you used for training can be recalled.

(c) Test the capability of your neural network for generalization by using as inputs the representations of characters other than those used for training.

(d) Test the performance of your trained network when the input is noisy by reversing one or two pixel values in the digitized image of the characters used for training.

(e) State how you will modify your feedforward structure so that the compressed data after transmission through a communication channel may be reconstructed at the receiving end to yield the original data.

5.13. Design a suitable multilayer feedforward network capable of plotting the bivariate function

$$f(x_1, x_2) = \cos(2\pi x_1) \cos(2\pi x_2), \qquad 0 \le x_i \le 0.5, \qquad i = 1, 2,$$

by using as exemplars the values of the function evaluated over, say, 441 sample points in the (x_1, x_2)-plane. You may select one or two hidden layers, each having between 5 and 10 units. Remember that the network should have the potential for interpolating between the sample points so that a continuous map from the space of inputs to the output is well approximated. Comment on the success or lack of it in reaching your goals.

5.14. To improve the performance of the BPA, a momentum term is introduced as shown in the following equation:

$$\mathbf{w}(k + 1) = \mathbf{w}(k) - \Delta\mathbf{w}(k) = \mathbf{w}(k) - \left[\eta \frac{\partial E(k)}{\partial \mathbf{w}} + \beta \Delta\mathbf{w}(k - 1) \right].$$

It is mentioned in the text that this is equivalent to a low-pass filtering of weight changes with $\Delta\mathbf{w}(k)$ as the output and $\partial E(k)/\partial\mathbf{w}$ as the input to the filter. Find out the transfer function of this filter and show that it is indeed a low-pass filter. For this filter to be stable, what is the range of β?

5.15. A critical goal during training is to make the hidden layer (in a network with, say, one such layer) small enough to improve the generalization performance and large enough to permit learning. Justify this statement and analyze how an optimal number of hidden nodes may be arrived at (in the sense that both larger and smaller numbers of hidden nodes produce larger mean-squared errors). The reader will find other details in the next chapter.

5.16. Show that the learning rule in Eq. (5.54) will converge to a $\mathbf{W}$ matrix whose ith row vector $\mathbf{w}_i$ equals the eigenvector (up to to a $\pm$ sign) of $\mathbf{C}$ with the ith largest eigenvalue. *Hint:* Equation (5.54) can be written in the following form:

$$E[\Delta w_{ij}(k)] = E[w_{ij}(k+1) - w_{ij}(k)]$$

$$= \eta E[y_i(k)x_j(k)] - \eta E\left[y_i(k)\sum_{q=1}^{i} y_q(k)w_{qj}(k)\right]$$

$$= \eta E\left[\sum_{q=1}^{N} w_{iq}(k)x_q(k)x_j(k)\right] -$$

$$\eta E\left[\sum_{r=1}^{N} w_{ir}(k)x_r(k)\sum_{q=1}^{i}\sum_{s=1}^{N} w_{qs}(k)x_s(k)w_{qj}(k)\right]$$

$$= \eta\left[\sum_{q=1}^{N} w_{iq}(k)c_{qj} - \sum_{q=1}^{i}\left(\sum_{r=1}^{N}\sum_{s=1}^{N} w_{ir}(k)c_{rs}w_{qs}(k)\right)w_{qj}(k)\right] \quad (5.70)$$

In matrix-vector form, the result becomes the following:

$$\frac{E[\Delta\mathbf{w}_i(k)]}{\eta} = \mathbf{w}_i(k)\mathbf{C} - \sum_{q=1}^{i-1}\left(\mathbf{w}_i(k)\mathbf{C}\mathbf{w}_q^T(k)\right)\mathbf{w}_q(k) - \mathbf{w}_i(k)\mathbf{C}\mathbf{w}_i^T\mathbf{w}_i(k) \quad (5.71)$$

Note that the first two terms in Eq. (5.71) can be interpreted as the projection of the row vector $\mathbf{w}_i(k)\mathbf{C}$ into the subspace orthogonal to the space spanned by the row vectors $\{\mathbf{w}_q(k)\}_{q=1}^{i-1}$.

5.17. Show that the learning rule in Eq. (5.58) is equivalent to the average of the gradient descent learning rule $\Delta w_i = -\eta \partial E/\partial w_i$ where the error function is defined in Eq. (5.59). Determine the parameters c and d in terms of $\{\alpha_i\}_{i=1}^{5}$.

5.18 Design a neural network for temporal signal recognition that is insensitive to a class of time warping transformations, using both the spatial domain and the time domain approaches as discussed in Section 5.2.3. Discuss the advantages and disadvantages in each approach.

5.19. Consider five exemplars representing two classes:

$$S_1 = \{(0,0),(0,4),(4,0)\}, \qquad S_2 = \{(2,2),(4,4)\}.$$

Use the method given in Section 5.3 to obtain a feedforward neural network that can separate these exemplars. It is claimed that the given exemplars may be separated with a feedforward neural network with a single hidden layer consisting of two neurons. Justify or refute this claim.

5.20. A benchmark problem for neural networks is the *two-spirals problem*. It is desired to distinguish between the points belonging to two intertwined spirals. Generate the exemplars using the following equations:

$$\text{Spiral 1: } x = \frac{\theta}{4}\cos\theta, \qquad\qquad y = \frac{\theta}{4}\sin\theta, \qquad\qquad \theta \geq 0$$

$$\text{Spiral 2: } x = \left(\frac{\theta}{4} + 0.8\right)\cos\theta, \qquad y = \left(\frac{\theta}{4} + 0.8\right)\sin\theta, \qquad \theta \geq 0,$$

where θ takes 51 equally spaced values between 0 and 20 radians. Use the method given in Section 5.3 to construct a feedforward neural network that performs the desired classification. Also, use the method of backpropagation of errors to solve this problem.

To compare the decision regions formed by the networks, generate a uniform grid of 100×100 test samples in the square $[-5,5]^2$. Now plot the points classified as belonging to the first spiral by the two networks. Comment on the differences between the two decision regions.

CHAPTER
6

COMPLEXITY OF LEARNING USING FEEDFORWARD NETWORKS

The question of the scope of functions that are computable by perceptrons and multi-layer feedforward networks was considered in Sections 4.1 and 5.1. The answer was very encouraging. However, just knowing that a neural network exists for computing a function is not sufficient. We must also consider the complexity issues in using a neural network to learn the function. The issue of the existence of a network solution to compute a function becomes meaningless if an unrealistic amount of time, an excessively large number of training exemplars, or an impracticably large network is required to meet the desired goal of learning the function. In this chapter we consider these complexity questions. This material is for the more advanced student. However, the conclusions arrived at are of interest to all designers and users of neural networks. The exposure to graph theory in Chapter 2 and to computational complexity fundamentals in Chapter 3 would be useful for digesting the topics presented here.

6.1 LEARNABILITY IN ANN

Valiant proposed a formal framework for learning from examples [382]. The framework for the neural network setting is described in this section. Examples for learning a concept are drawn from an *environment* (input space) X according to an unknown and arbitrary probability distribution p. A *concept* is defined as a function,

$$f^*: X \longrightarrow \{0, 1\},$$

describing a mapping from X to a Boolean alphabet. A *concept class* is a collection of concepts over the environment. The probability distribution specifies how likely an example from X is drawn for learning. For example, the environment may be a set of visual images of moving objects, and the concept could be "a life-threatening situation." For a boy who is growing up in the jungle, the situation of "an approaching tiger" will be encountered more often than "an approaching car." In the former setting, the function f^* should yield a 1 if the approaching tiger causes a life-threatening situation and 0 otherwise. Given that ϵ and δ are two tolerance parameters whose values lie between 0 and 1, the goal of a learning algorithm for a neural network is to produce, with a probability of at least $(1 - \delta)$, a feedforward network, using exemplars $(x, f^*(x))$, $x \in X$ drawn according to any distribution p, that will correctly predict the outcome of f^* for at least a fraction $1 - \epsilon$ of future (test) exemplars. Such a correct prediction based on learning from exemplars is referred to as a *valid generalization*. The function realized by the network is called a *hypothesis, $f : X \longrightarrow \{0, 1\}$,* that approximates f^*.

A function is *efficiently learnable* if and only if there exists a learning algorithm satisfying the following properties:

1. The algorithm runs in polynomial time in $\delta^{-1}, \epsilon^{-1}$, parameters that quantify function complexity, and the dimension n of input.
2. For every probability distribution p of sampling exemplars in X, the algorithm produces, in polynomial time, with a probability of at least $(1 - \delta)$, a feedforward network that will correctly predict the outcome of f^* for at least a fraction $1 - \epsilon$ of future exemplars. The *confidence parameter δ* accounts for the small, but nonzero, chance that some exemplars happen to be very atypical, and the *error parameter ϵ* incorporates the possibility of error even when the randomly drawn exemplars are representative of the concepts being learned.

The first condition accounts for the efficiency in learning. The second condition is referred to as *distribution-free learning;* that is, the learning algorithm works well for any probability distribution. It seems to be a strong requirement. However, all future exemplars are assumed to be drawn from the same probability distribution that was used during the learning process. In practice, the performance of learning does depend on the distribution of the training exemplars and on the nature of the function to be learned. First, there is the question whether the function can be sufficiently specified by N input-output pairs, where N is a polynomial in the dimension of the input space. If an exponential number of training exemplars are required, there is no hope that the network can learn the function in polynomial time in n with valid generalization, because just one scan of the training exemplars requires exponential time. Intuitively, such functions are not interesting, because there is little regularity to be discovered (i.e., little knowledge is conveyed). Second, there is the question of the distribution of the training exemplars. The manner in which the N exemplars are sampled from the entire sample space affects the generalization to future exemplars. For example, in a classification problem, exemplars close to the decision surface, referred to as *boundary exemplars,* carry more information for training the network. Actually, the boundary exemplars tell us about the shape of the decision surface to be learned. This not only cuts down the learning time, since the number of exemplars can be small, but also in general should yield a good generalization after the boundary exemplars are successfully learned. Of course, these desired properties are achieved because of the a priori knowledge that the exemplars are at the boundary. A priori knowledge, however, on the distribution of the training exemplars may not be available. Therefore, the distribution-free condition comes into play. The learnability problem in its most general form involves two questions: (1) the time it takes to find the network to learn a function and (2) the performance of the learned network on future exemplars. In this section, we address the first question. The second question will be discussed in Section 6.2.

In general, the problem of finding the network involves finding the graph as well as the connection weights of the network. This is a difficult problem and remains open. In the following, it is assumed that the graph of the network is given, and only the weights are to be learned. On the assumption that the function can be specified sufficiently accurately by a number N of training exemplars from a given distribution, where N is polynomial in n, can a given network find a set of weights and thresholds such that the network will produce the correct output for the N exemplars in polynomial time in the dimension of the input? This problem is discussed next.

6.1.1 The Problem of Loading

Judd [179] defined the loading problem as follows. For a feedforward network with a given graph and a given set of exemplars, does there exist a set of edge weights for the graph so that the network produces the correct output for all the exemplars? The reader should bear in mind that loading and training (or learning) a network are different concepts. The problem of loading as defined by Judd [179] and by Blum and Rivest [43] is a binary decision problem. The search problem of finding the weights, i.e., the training problem, is at least as hard. For example, as a binary decision problem, the loading problem for a single trainable TLU is polynomial if all training exemplars are available at the same time, because the loading problem in this case can be formulated as a linear programming problem. Polynomial-time algorithms exist for linear programming problems [134, 184, 187]. However, finding the weights for a single-TLU perceptron using the incremental perceptron algorithm is not polynomial-time in the worst case [261]. Loading in this section is considered as batch-style; i.e., all exemplars are available at once. The problem is at least as hard with incremental algorithms such as backpropagation, where the exemplars are available only one at a time.

Judd made an important contribution by showing that the problem of loading is NP-complete for several classes of networks. Judd also showed that the problem remains NP-complete even if the networks are required to produce the correct output for only two-thirds of the loading exemplars. This implies that even the task of loading a neural network approximately is intrinsically difficult in the worst case.

It is proven that for a class of networks and loading exemplars, any algorithm will perform poorly on some network and exemplars in that class.

Blum and Rivest showed that the problem of training a very simple three-node network is NP-complete [43]. More specifically, they showed that for a network with three TLUs, if P ≠ NP, then any polynomial-time algorithm in the dimension of the input (the number n of input Boolean variables) will fail to load some sets of exemplars. This result occurs even though there exists a choice of weights with which the network correctly classifies the set of exemplars (in which case we say that the set of exemplars is *consistent* with the network). However, this result should not prevent us from loading the exemplars on a larger network. Actually, Blum and Rivest [43] showed that a given set of exemplars that is NP-complete to load on one network may be polynomial for another network. Their main results [43] are presented next.

Consider a network with one hidden layer of two TLUs and an output TLU as shown in Fig. 6.1. Each unit in the hidden layer is connected to all input nodes. The unit in the output layer has exactly two inputs, which are the outputs from the units in the layer below. The three units are referred to as U_1, U_2, and U_3. This network will be referred to as the three-node network. Assume that a loading algorithm for this network is presented with a set of N binary exemplars. Each is either a *positive exemplar* (defined to be an input for which the desired network output is $+1$) or a *negative exemplar* (defined to be an an input for which the desired output is -1). The loading problem for the three-node network differs greatly in a computational sense from the loading problem for the single-TLU perceptron, which is implementable in polynomial time using linear programming. The loading problem for the three-node network belongs to the class of NP-complete problems. This problem

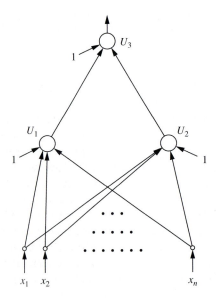

FIGURE 6.1
A three-node network.

belongs to the NP class because the maximum number of bits needed for each weight and threshold is the same as that needed for the weights of a perceptron. Raghavan [306] showed that the number of bits needed is at most $O(n \log n)$ per weight (and threshold). Therefore, one can certainly write down all the weights and thresholds, or equivalently pick those nondeterministically, and then verify whether the network so produced classifies all exemplars correctly in polynomial time in the dimension n of the input space.

To see why loading such a simple network might be hard, assume that the output node computes the logical AND function of its inputs, i.e., outputs $+1$ when it receives inputs $(+1, +1)$ from nodes U_1 and U_2, and outputs -1 for all the other pairs of binary inputs. When the network is presented with a positive exemplar, we know that both hidden nodes U_1 and U_2 must output $+1$. Therefore, we know how the weights of the connections to these nodes should be modified in this case. When the network is presented with a negative exemplar, however, we only know that either U_1 or U_2 (or both) should output -1. Both nodes can be made to output -1 if the positive and negative exemplars are linearly separable. If that is the case, the loading problem can be solved using a single-TLU perceptron. Assume the exemplars are not linearly separable. Then for some negative exemplars, a choice must be made to have either U_1 output -1 or U_2 output -1. It may be necessary that the correct combination of choices over all or at least a large number of the negative exemplars be made in order to train the network correctly. The number of such combinations increases exponentially. We may not be able to do much better than just to try all combinations blindly and see if one happens to work. This obviously would take exponential time. What makes the loading problem hard is this combinatorially large number of possible states that the hidden units may take in order to reach the desired output state. To prove that the problem of loading the three-node network is NP-complete, we transform the known NP-complete problem of set-splitting to the network loading problem. In order to understand the transformation more clearly, the network loading problem is given a geometrical interpretation.

6.1.1.1 THE GEOMETRIC POINT OF VIEW. A binary exemplar pattern is represented as a vertex of the binary cube $\{0, 1\}^n$ in the n-dimensional Boolean pattern space. The vertex associated with each loading exemplar is colored white (w) or blue (b) depending on whether the exemplar is positive or negative. Each of the linear threshold functions computed by U_1 and U_2 generates an $(n-1)$-dimensional hyperplane in the pattern space. The two hyperplanes divide the space into four cones (sometimes referred to as *quadrants*) associated with the four possible pairs of outputs for nodes U_1 and U_2. If the hyperplanes are parallel, then either one or two of these cones are degenerate (nonexistent). The outputs of the hidden units U_1 and U_2 become the image patterns that serve as inputs to TLU U_3. The output unit, again, can classify only linearly separable patterns in this image pattern space. Therefore, the two hidden units must transform the patterns in the original pattern space into a linearly separable distribution in the first-layer image space.

The three-node network loading problem is equivalent to the following problem. Given a collection of points represented as a subset of the vertices in $\{0, 1\}^n$, where each point is colored white or blue, does either of the following exist?

1. A single hyperplane that separates the white points from the blue points
2. Two hyperplanes that partition the points so that one cone contains either all the white points and no blue points or all the blue points and no white points

In the first case, since all points of one color are mapped to two cones on the same side of one hyperplane, the output TLU U_3 can also separate the patterns in the image space. This outcome corresponds to linear separability of the training set. In the second case, the two hidden units transform a not linearly separable training set in the original pattern space to a linearly separable one in the image pattern space. If the answers to both cases are negative, then the two hidden units can only map all points of one color to two diagonal quadrants in the image pattern space. This result is not linearly separable for U_3. Therefore, the answer to the loading problem will also be negative.

Consider now a restricted version of the second case.

> Given $O(n)$ points in $\{0, 1\}^n$, each point colored white or blue, do two hyperplanes exist that partition the points so that one cone contains all the white points and no blue points?

Blum and Rivest called this problem the *quadrant* (or *cone*) *of positive Boolean examples* problem (white points are assumed to be positive exemplars). The quadrant of positive Boolean exemplars problem corresponds to having an AND function at the output node of the three-node network. Once it is shown that this is NP-complete, the proof can be extended to the full problem.

> **Lemma 6.1**   **[43].** The quadrant (cone) of positive Boolean examples problem is NP-complete.

> **Proof.** The proof is through transformation (refer to Chapter 3) of an instance of a known NP-complete problem—set-splitting—into the quadrant of positive Boolean examples problem, such that the constructed instance has a solution if and only if the set-splitting instance has a solution. Lovász[1] proved that the following set-splitting problem is NP-complete [124]:

> Given a finite set S and a collection C of subsets $c_i \subseteq S$, do there exist disjoint sets S_1, S_2 such that $S_1 \cup S_2 = S$ and for all $i, c_i \not\subseteq S_1$ and $c_i \not\subseteq S_2$?

[1]L. Lovász. Covering and coloring of hypergraphs. *Proc. 4th Southeastern Conference on Combinatorics, Graph Theory, and Computing*, Utilitas Mathematica Publishing, Winnipeg, Manitoba, Canada, 1973, pp. 3–12.

The set-splitting problem is also known as the *2-nonmonotone colorability* or *hypergraph 2-colorability* problem. For a given instance of the set-splitting problem,

$$S = \{s_i\}, \quad C = \{c_j\}, \quad c_j \subseteq S, \quad |S| = n,$$

the following quadrant of positive Boolean examples problem is constructed.

- Let the origin 0^n be colored white.
- For each s_i, insert a blue point at the origin's neighbor whose ith coordinate is 1, i.e., the blue point is at $(0,0,\ldots 0,1,0,\ldots 0)$ where only the ith component is nonzero and 1. Call this point p_i.
- For each $c_j = \{s_{j1}, \ldots, s_{jk_j}\}$, insert a white point at the location obtained by summing the coordinates of $p_{j1}, p_{j2}, \ldots, p_{jk_j}$, i.e., at $\sum_{i=1}^{k_j} p_{ji}$.

For example, let $S = \{s_1, s_2, s_3\}$, $C = \{c_1, c_2\}$, $c_1 = \{s_1, s_2\}, c_2 = \{s_2, s_3\}$. The solution to this set-splitting problem is given by $S_1 = \{s_1, s_3\}$ and $S_2 = \{s_2\}$. Therefore, application of the rules just enumerated yields blue points at coordinate positions $(1,0,0), (0,1,0)$, and $(0,0,1)$ and white points at positions $(0,0,0), (1,1,0)$, and $(0,1,1)$, as shown in Fig. 6.2. Next, it is shown that the given instance of the set-splitting problem has a solution if and only if the constructed instance of the quadrant of positive Boolean examples problem has a solution.

Sufficiency. Given that S_1 and S_2 constitute a solution to the set-splitting instance, let P_1 be the hyperplane $\sum_{i=1}^{n} a_i x_i + \frac{1}{2} = 0$, where $a_i = -1$ if $s_i \in S_1$ and $a_i = n$ if $s_i \notin S_1$. Similarly, let P_2 be the hyperplane $\sum_{i=1}^{n} b_i x_i + \frac{1}{2} = 0$, where $b_i = -1$ if $s_i \in S_2$ and $b_i = n$ if $s_i \notin S_2$. Let $\mathbf{a} = (a_1 \ldots a_n)^T$ and $\mathbf{b} = (b_1 \ldots b_n)^T$.

For each $s_i \in S_1$, which corresponds to a blue point $\mathbf{p}_{bi}$, we have $\mathbf{a} \cdot \mathbf{p}_{bi} + \frac{1}{2} = -\frac{1}{2} < 0$. A white point $\mathbf{p}_{wi}$ either has at least one bit, say bit j, equal to 1 and $s_j \notin S_1$, or is the origin. This condition occurs because S_1, S_2 form a solution to the set-splitting

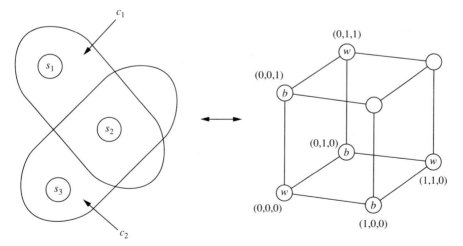

FIGURE 6.2
An example of converting a set-splitting problem into a quadrant of positive Boolean examples problem; after Blum and Rivest [43].

problem and, therefore, each $c_i \subset S$ must contain at least one s_j from S_2 and at least one s_k from S_1, where $j \neq k$. Thus, for any white point $\mathbf{p}_{wi}$, the inequality $\mathbf{a} \cdot \mathbf{p}_{wi} + \frac{1}{2} > 0$ must hold. That is, all white points are on the positive side of P_1, and all blue points corresponding to $s_i \in S_1$ are on the negative side of P_1. Similarly, all white points are on the positive side of P_2, and all blue points corresponding to $s_i \in S_2$ are on the negative side of P_2. Therefore, the cone described by $\mathbf{a} \cdot \mathbf{p} + \frac{1}{2} > 0$ and $\mathbf{b} \cdot \mathbf{p} + \frac{1}{2} > 0$ contains all the white points and no blue points. This is a solution to the quadrant of positive Boolean examples problem.

Necessity. Assume that P_1 and P_2 comprise a solution to the quadrant of positive Boolean examples problem. Let S_1 be the set of blue points separated from the origin by P_1, and S_2 be those blue points separated by P_2. Place any blue point separated by both planes in either S_1 or S_2 arbitrarily. It is obvious that $S_1 \cap S_2 = \varnothing$. Also, $S_1 \cup S_2 = S$, because all blue points are separated from the origin by at least one of the planes, and each blue point corresponds to an $s_i \in S$. Consider some $c_j = \{s_{j1}, \ldots, s_{jk_j}\}$ and the corresponding blue points $\mathbf{p}_{j1}, \ldots, \mathbf{p}_{jk_j}$. If $c_j \subset S_1$, then P_1 must separate all the $\mathbf{p}_{ji}$ from the origin. Let P_1 be described by the equation $\mathbf{a} \cdot \mathbf{p}_i + c = 0$. This means that $\mathbf{a} \cdot \mathbf{p}_{ji} + c$ have the same sign for all $\mathbf{p}_{ji}$. Therefore, $\mathbf{a} \cdot (\mathbf{p}_{j1} + \cdots + \mathbf{p}_{jk_j}) + c$ also has the same sign. However, the point $(\mathbf{p}_{j1} + \cdots + \mathbf{p}_{jk_j})$ is a white point. This means that some white points are in the same quadrant with blue points. This contradicts the assumption that P_1 and P_2 form a solution to the quadrant of positive Boolean examples problem. Therefore, no c_i can be contained in S_1. The same statement holds for S_2, and the lemma is proved.

The foregoing lemma shows that the problem of loading is NP-complete if the output TLU only computes an AND function of the outputs of the two hidden units. To extend the result to an output TLU with other functions, Blum and Rivest used a "gadget" consisting of six new points in three additional dimensions, as shown in Fig. 6.3. The "gadget" enables us to show that the only way for two hyperplanes to separate the white and blue points would be to map all the white points into one cone in the (U_1, U_2) image space. Now we are ready to prove the main theorem of this section.

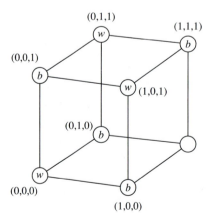

FIGURE 6.3
The gadget; after Blum and Rivest [43].

Theorem 6.1. The problem of training the three-node network is NP-complete.

Proof. Convert an instance of a set-splitting problem in the same way as in Lemma 6.1, but add three additional dimensions, represented by $x_{n+1}, x_{n+2}, x_{n+3}$. The three new dimensions are introduced to make the problem of loading the three-node network equivalent to a quadrant of positive Boolean examples problem. This step is necessary to take care of the case where a single plane can separate the white points from the blue points. The basic idea is to show that there exists a training set that corresponds to the quadrant of positive Boolean examples problem such that no single plane can separate all white points from all blue points, and no two planes can bound all blue points in one quadrant. Therefore, any solution for loading the network must map all white points in one quadrant in the image pattern space. Therefore, as shown in Lemma 6.1, it is equivalent to a solution to the set-splitting instance. The case where all blue points are mapped to one quadrant can be treated identically. This proves that the problem of loading the three-node network is NP-complete.

The incorporation of the three additional dimensions is illustrated in Fig. 6.3. For obvious reasons, only the coordinates of placed points in the three added dimensions are shown. Place white points at the origin and at

$$(0,0,\ldots 0,1,0,1), (0,0,\ldots 0,0,1,1)$$

and blue points at

$$(0,0,\ldots 0,1,0,0), (0,0,\ldots 0,0,1,0), (0,0,\ldots 0,0,0,1), (0,0,\ldots 0,1,1,1).$$

Let the two planes,

$$P'_1 : \sum_{i=1}^{n} a_i x_i + \frac{1}{2} = 0$$

$$P'_2 : \sum_{i=1}^{n} b_i x_i + \frac{1}{2} = 0,$$

(6.1)

constitute a solution to a quadrant of positive Boolean examples instance in n dimensions. The white points on the cube in the additional dimensions can be separated from the blue points by appropriately expanding the weights of planes P'_1 and P'_2 to the three new dimensions:

$$P_1 : \sum_{i=1}^{n} a_i x_i + x_{n+1} + x_{n+2} - x_{n+3} + \frac{1}{2} = 0$$

$$P_2 : \sum_{i=1}^{n} b_i x_i - x_{n+1} - x_{n+2} + x_{n+3} + \frac{1}{2} = 0.$$

(6.2)

P_1 separates the blue point at $(0,0,\ldots 0,0,0,1)$ from the white points, and P_2 separates the other three blue points from the white points.

6.1.1.2 OTHER HARD NETWORKS. Blum and Rivest showed that the problem of loading simpler networks, obtained by restricting the number of independent parameters in the three-node network, is also NP-complete. One such simpler network is obtained by assigning equal weights to the connections to the two hidden units U_1 and U_2. Only their thresholds are allowed to be different. The resulting network is still NP-complete for loading. Note that if the thresholds are also made the same, the three-node network equivalently reduces to a simple one-layer perceptron, and the loading problem becomes of polynomial time. Thus, adding the single extra free parameter of threshold at an additional unit results in intractability. Another simplified network is obtained by limiting the weights to be either $+1$ or -1. The loading problem for this network is also NP-complete.

How about networks that have more hidden units? Consider a family of two-layer, n-input, single-output networks with $k > 2$ TLUs in the hidden layer. Each hidden unit is connected to all n inputs, and the output unit computes the AND function. That is, the response at the output node is $+1$ if and only if all of its inputs are $+1$. Denote this family of networks by Λ. This class is a straightforward generalization of the three-node network to networks with more than two hidden nodes with a restriction. The restriction is that the output node computes the AND logic function of its inputs. There is the following theorem for this class of networks.

> **Theorem 6.2   [43].** For any network of the family Λ such that the number of hidden units, k, is bounded by some fixed polynomial in the dimension n of the inputs, the loading problem is NP-complete.

The preceding theorem can be proved by converting it to the three-node network. Then the proof of Theorem 6.1 can be applied. This is left as an exercise.

6.1.2   Using an Appropriate Network to Get Around Intractability

We have seen several classes of networks for which any loading algorithm will encounter hard problems. However, in practice we are not limited to a given fixed network to learn from some exemplars. Rather, given the exemplars, we are free to choose the network, subject to realizability and generalizability requirements. Therefore, we ask the following question: Is it possible that a set of exemplars that is hard to load on one network might be easier to load on another network? A case where the answer to the preceding question is in the affirmative is described first.

Two networks are given next such that the loading problem is NP-complete for the first but is polynomial-time for the second [43]. The second network also has a larger function representation capacity than the first in that it can be trained correctly on any set of exemplars the first can correctly classify.

The first network is a modification of the three-node network in which the output unit computes the XOR function of the outputs of the two hidden units. Obviously, this output unit cannot be a TLU, because a TLU cannot compute the XOR function. A product unit [101] or a product synaptic contact [227] can be used, because XOR can be computed as a threshold function of the product of the outputs of the two hidden units, assuming that the hidden unit outputs are bipolar binary (see Problem 5.7). This network is called the 3NX network [43]. Blum and Rivest showed that if the inputs to the network are three-valued inputs from the discrete n-dimensional ternary cube $\{-1, 0, +1\}^n$ (which is the natural generalization of the n-dimensional bipolar binary cube), then the loading problem of the 3NX network is NP-complete.

The second network is a one-layer perceptron with an expanded input representation. This perceptron has $2n + n(n-1)/2$ inputs, consisting of the original n inputs, their squares, and all $n(n-1)/2$ distinct products of pairs of the original n inputs. This network is referred to as P^2. Note that this is the bivariate polynomial network shown in Fig. 4.5 and is an example of the high-order networks using sigma-pi units [132, 325]. The number of weights in P^2 is of order $O(n^2)$, compared with $O(n)$ for 3NX. However, the loading problem for P^2 takes polynomial time, because it is just a perceptron with $O(n^2)$ inputs. Recall that the actual training of the network (i.e., finding the weights), using the perceptron algorithm, may not be polynomial-time.

Theorem 6.3. Any set of training exemplars that 3NX can correctly classify can also be correctly classified by P^2.

This theorem can be proved by observing that the XOR function can be computed by realizing the product of the two hyperplanes whose equations are set up at the two hidden units. The proof is left as an exercise.

Theorem 6.3 shows that, by increasing the representation capacity of a network, it is possible to remove as well as to introduce computational intractability. In terms of the network representational capacities, we have

$$P \subseteq 3\text{NX} \subseteq P^2,$$

where P is a single-TLU perceptron, whose loading problem takes polynomial time. Loading of 3NX is NP-complete, but loading of P^2 again takes polynomial time.

The reason that network P^2 can be both more powerful than 3NX and easier to load is that predefined nonlinear transformations are done for the network and the exemplars are mapped to a higher-dimensional space. By using P^2 instead of 3NX, improved time complexity, in a worst-case computational sense, is achieved. But this gain is not without a price. First, space complexity is higher because the order of the number of weights increases from $O(n)$ to $O(n^2)$. Second, the increase in the number of weights implies that the number of loading exemplars needed must also increase to constrain those weights so that valid generalization on new exemplars can be expected (see Section 6.2). Theorem 6.3 can be extended in the obvious way to networks like 3NX with $k > 2$ hidden units.

The preceding arguments show that increasing the representation capacity of a network may in some cases increase and in other cases decrease the complexity of the loading problem. If a given set of exemplars is hard to load on a particular network, one may try to increase the capacity of the network in order to make loading easier. However, there is no guarantee that this will be the case. For the family Λ of two-layer networks discussed earlier, one way to increase the function representation capacity is by adding more units in the hidden layer. Blum and Rivest showed that for the class of Λ networks, if one adds only relatively few nodes to the hidden layer, then there will be loading sets that are hard for both the original and the enlarged network, so this approach is not likely to be of help in the worst case.

The implications of Theorem 6.3 are examined for a wider class of networks. Given two networks N and N', define an N'/N-loading algorithm as one that will correctly load N' using any set of exemplars that N can correctly classify. For example, we have just seen a $P^2/3NX$-loading algorithm. Next, the graph k-vertex coloring problem is used to show that the number of hidden units may have to be increased substantially to avoid NP-completeness. The graph *k-vertex coloring problem* requires the coloring of a graph consisting of, say, n vertices connected by a specified number of edges using k allowed colors. A solution is an assignment of one of the k colors to each vertex so that no edge has both endpoints of the same color. For example, any subgraph of a graph that is a spanning tree is always vertex colorable with two colors. Any bipartite graph is also 2-vertex colorable. Because the chromatic number of a graph is the minimum value of k for which the graph is k-vertex colorable, the chromatic number of any complete bipartite graph is therefore 2 (see Problem 2.18). The graph k-vertex coloring problem is known to be NP-complete for $k \geq 3$. The following theorem is given without proof:

> **Theorem 6.4   [43].** Given network $N \in \Lambda$ with k hidden units and $N' \in \Lambda$ with k' hidden nodes ($k' > k$), then N'/N-loading is as hard as coloring a k-colorable graph with k' colors.

Since the problem of coloring a k-vertex colorable graph with $2k - \epsilon$ colors for a general k is NP-hard, the foregoing theorem implies that to avoid NP-completeness one must in general at least double the number of hidden units. A more recent coloring approximation algorithm suggests that one might wish to add n^ϵ ($0 < \epsilon < 1$) hidden units [240], where ϵ depends on the number k of hidden units and n is the number of input variables to the network. Of course, there is no guarantee that adding these hidden units will actually help, in the sense of worst-case computational complexity analysis.

Note that neither is it necessary to use all the nonlinear polynomial terms of a given degree to gain the reduction in learning time complexity as in the $P^2/3NX$ case, nor is it sufficient just to add a few hidden units at random as shown in Theorem 6.4. In practice, if a priori knowledge of the particular task at hand is available, nonlinear polynomial terms can be chosen to fit the particular problem, as in the case of the high-order networks [132]. The networks with product units [101] and quasi-polynomial synapses and product synaptic contacts [227] are further generalizations. Liang and Jamali showed that the type and number of nonlinear terms that are required may be learned instead of being prespecified [227].

Instead of varying the network until fast loading can be achieved, the VoD method in Section 5.3, as well as the growth algorithms and networks with nonlinear synapses and nonlinear synaptic contacts to be discussed in Chapter 7, could be attractive alternatives. However, the growth networks may suffer from poor generalization because too many parameters may be grown. This topic will be further discussed in Section 6.2.

Blum and Rivest used TLUs as network nodes. Their proofs break down when the differentiable sigmoidal transfer characteristics are used instead. Judd [179] showed that, for some classes of networks, loading is NP-complete for a wide variety of unit transfer characteristics, including the differentiable sigmoidal functions.

Another question to ask is this: If we require a network to load only a majority of the exemplars and not all of them (even if there is a choice of weights and thresholds that will correctly classify all the exemplars), will the loading problem be easier? The answer to this question is still negative. Judd [179] showed that there exist network and exemplar set pairs for which the problem of loading correctly more than two-thirds of the exemplars is NP-hard.

The worst-case analysis results in this section are useful for giving us a better theoretical understanding of the loading problem. However, we caution the reader that such analysis does not imply that the loading problem is always hard for any training set and networks on average. Most probable average behavior analysis will be more useful in practice than the traditional worst-case analysis, which assigns a blanket categorization of a problem to the NP-complete class.

6.2 GENERALIZABILITY OF LEARNING

After a network has successfully learned a set of N training exemplars, the usefulness of the learned network depends on the accuracy of the network's predictions of the output for future exemplars drawn according to the same probability distribution as the training exemplars. That is, can the learned network provide valid generalization to unseen exemplars? The number of training exemplars used in learning is an important factor in the generalization capability of the learned network. How well a given network learns a function using N exemplars depends on two issues: the number of learnable parameters in the network and the number of parameters necessary to describe the function. These two issues are like two sides of the same sword.

First, a sufficient number of training exemplars are required to describe the function. Obviously, there is no way a network can learn the variations in the function that are not reflected in the training exemplars. This is why future exemplars should be from the same probability distribution. Second, if the number of training exemplars used is not sufficient to pin down the free parameters in the network to capture the regularity in the data, the best the network can do is assign some random components to some parameters.

In this section, we only consider the number of training exemplars necessary to pin down the parameters in a network. Generalization in this sense should be measured using test exemplars similar to the training exemplars. It is meaningless to evaluate capability for generalization using exemplars that reflect variations not captured in the training exemplars. Test exemplars are picked from the same probability distribution that underlies the training exemplars, as given in the definition for learnability at the beginning of Section 6.1.

Under the assumption that future test exemplars are picked from the same probability distribution as the training exemplars, good generalization means that the performance observed during training will persist with a high probability for exemplars not used in training. Good generalization is not equivalent to good approximation of the function to be learned. For example, assume that the function learned matches the desired one for 80 percent of the training exemplars. If the generalization capability is good, one can expect with high probability that the network would correctly predict the value of the desired function for 80 percent of the test exemplars. As commented at the beginning of Section 6.1, the distribution of the training exemplars also affects the generalization capability of the learned network. In a classification problem, exemplars close to the decision surface carry more information on the shape of the decision surface to be learned. If boundary exemplars can be successfully learned, one can usually expect a good generalization. This requires a priori knowledge that the exemplars are at the boundary.

In this section, we consider distribution-free learning as described at the beginning of Section 6.1. We require a sufficiently high confidence level for valid generalization with any distribution of the training exemplars, as long as future test exemplars are drawn from the same distribution. The problem of generalization considered here is measured in a probabilistic sense and is described as follows. Assume that, after training using a set of exemplars of a function sampled according to an arbitrary probability distribution p, a network finds a set of weights such that it produces the correct input-output mapping for $1 - \gamma$ percent of the training exemplars. The question is, will it correctly predict the outcome of the function for at least a fraction $1 - \epsilon$ of future test exemplars? The parameters γ and ϵ are small positive real numbers. The future test exemplars are assumed again to be picked by following the same probability distribution as the training exemplars. Of course, if a set of weights cannot be found (in polynomial time) to classify (most of) the training exemplars correctly, the question of generalization becomes meaningless. We know that for a given network and exemplar set, a choice of weights to satisfy all (or most) of the training exemplars may not be possible. If this is the case, an algorithm may run forever and will not be able to load the exemplars. For example, a single TLU can never learn the XOR function. More generally, a perceptron with an order lower than the predicate to be learned can never learn the function. To concentrate on the generalization problem, we assume that the exemplars can be learned by the network in question.

6.2.1 VC Dimension and Generalization

Consider the following question: Given a network with a set of parameters that can be adjusted during learning, how many training exemplars are required so that valid generalization can be expected? Simply put, what is the number N of training exemplars required to pin down all the free parameters in the network sufficiently?

The treatment of the problem of valid generalization presented here is quite general. The results hold for arbitrary learning algorithms, not just for the back-propagation algorithm. The results are based on the notion of capacity introduced by Cover [86] and developed by Vapnik and Chervonenkis [386, 385]. The particular measures of capacity used are the maximum number of dichotomies that can be induced on a set of N points, and the Vapnik-Chervonenkis (VC) dimension, defined shortly. The analysis assumes that the units are TLUs.

Let the environment X be a subset of an n-dimensional space $\mathbb{R}^n$. For example, if the environment X consists of a set of speech signals, a speech signal can be represented by its samples at n points. Each sample is a real number equal to the amplitude of the signal. If the environment is a digital image, the brightness of all n pixels may be represented as a point in $\mathbb{R}^n$. If the environment is a set of animals, each coordinate in $\mathbb{R}^n$ can represent a feature of an animal that belongs to that set.

Let $f^* : \mathbb{R}^n \longrightarrow \{0, 1\}$ define a function, also called *concept*, in the environment. We are given a set $\mathbf{X}$ of training exemplars drawn at random according to some distribution p on $\mathbb{R}^n \times \{0, 1\}$. A training exemplar is an input-output pair $(\mathbf{x}, f^*(\mathbf{x}))$, $\mathbf{x} \in \mathbb{R}^n$. The goal is to use the set of training exemplars to produce a hypothesis $f : \mathbb{R}^n \longrightarrow \{0, 1\}$ that approximates f^* such that with a probability of at least $(1 - \delta)$, $f(\mathbf{x}) = f^*(\mathbf{x})$ for at least a fraction $(1 - \epsilon)$ of future exemplars drawn at random according to the same distribution p. The error probability $e(f)$ of f with respect to p is defined as the probability that $f(\mathbf{x}) \neq f^*(\mathbf{x})$ for a random exemplar from the distribution p. The generalizability probability $G(f)$ of f is defined as $G(f) = 1 - e(f) = \text{Prob}(f(x) = f^*(x))$ for $\mathbf{x}$ randomly drawn from $\mathbf{X}$ according to the distribution p.

Consider a feedforward network whose weights can be adjusted to approximate a function. Let F be the set of functions that can be obtained by changing the weights of the given network. In learning, the weights are changed so that a function $f \in F$ with small error $e(f)$ can be found. For every $f \in F$, define an *agreement set*

$$A_f = \{\mathbf{x} \in \mathbf{X} \mid f(\mathbf{x}) = f^*(\mathbf{x})\}$$

for $\mathbf{x}$ drawn from $\mathbf{X}$ according to p. The agreement sets for different functions f are different. $G(f)$ is the probability that an exemplar is in A_f, i.e., the probability that $f(\mathbf{x}) = f^*(\mathbf{x})$ for an exemplar randomly drawn from $\mathbf{X}$ according to p.

Consider a sample sequence of independent and identically distributed random variables. Let a particular value of a random variable in the process be the assignment (say, bipolar binary or unipolar binary values) of the outcome of two mutually exclusive events (like "heads" and "tails" in a coin-tossing experiment). If one event occurs with a probability p, then the other event occurs with probability $(1 - p)$. Then the random variables are called Bernoulli random variables, and the corresponding random process generated with the preceding probabilistic description of the random variables is a *Bernoulli process*. In fact, provided p does not equal either 0 or 1, any sequence of either the unipolar or bipolar binary values belongs to a Bernoulli process. We can consider each exemplar to belong to a Bernoulli process such that $f(\mathbf{x}) = f^*(\mathbf{x})$ with a probability $G(f)$, and $f(\mathbf{x}) \neq f^*(\mathbf{x})$ with a probability $1 - G(f)$. With N exemplars, we have N independent, identically distributed Bernoulli trials. Let n_f be the number of exemplars in A_f for the N exemplars. Then, by Bernoulli's theorem, when N is sufficiently large, the frequency of agreement $g_N(f) = n_f/N$ can be made arbitrarily close to the probability $G(f)$. In learning, we adjust the weights to maximize $g_N(f)$ and to achieve $g_N(f) = 1$ if possible. The question now is this: Will maximizing $g_N(f)$ also maximize $G(f)$?

Note the difference between $G(f)$ and $g_N(f)$. Whereas $g_N(f)$ measures how well f approximates f^* only on the N given exemplars, $G(f)$ measures how well f approximates f^* on all possible exemplars drawn from $\mathbf{X}$ according to p. That is, $g_N(f)$ is biased on the specific training exemplars given. If we maximize only $g_N(f)$, we may arrive at a choice of weights in the network that implements a function f that has no error on the training set, i.e., $g_N(f) = 1$, but is erroneous on most other exemplars, therefore yielding $G(f) \approx 0$. Recall that the other exemplars are also from the same distribution as the training exemplars.

We want to be assured that the probability that there is some $f \in F$ such that the probability that $g_N(f)$ of the specific function learned by the network differs significantly from $G(f)$ is very small. This probability of difference should be very small even in the worst case. Mathematically, this requires that $g_N(f)$ converge uniformly in probability to $G(f)$ for any $f \in F$. This is formally expressed as

$$\text{Prob}[\sup_{f \in F} |g_N(f) - G(f)| > \epsilon] \leq \delta, \tag{6.3}$$

where "sup" denotes the supremum. Conversely, $1 - \delta$ is our confidence that

$$\sup_{f \in F} |g_N(f) - G(f)| \leq \epsilon.$$

In summary, to have a good estimation of f^* it is desirable that $g_N(f)$ be maximized during learning and also that $g_N(f)$ converge uniformly to $G(f)$ as in Eq. (6.3) for any $f \in F$.

Vapnik and Chervonenkis [385, 386] found the following bound on the probability of uniform convergence.

Theorem 6.5   [385]. The probability that there exists at least one $f \in F$ such that the frequency $g_N(f)$ obtained from a set of N exemplars will deviate from the corresponding probability $G(f)$ by more than the amount ϵ is bounded by the inequality

$$\text{Prob}[\sup_{f \in F} |g_N(f) - G(f)| > \epsilon] < 6\Delta_F(2N)\exp(-\epsilon^2 N/4), \tag{6.4}$$

where $\Delta_F(2N)$ measures the size of the set F, i.e., the function representation capacity of the network.

Since the term $\exp(-\epsilon^2 N/4)$ decays exponentially as N grows, the right-hand side can be made small by increasing N, therefore guaranteeing uniform convergence if the function $\Delta_F(2N)$ does not grow too fast.

The *growth function* $\Delta_F(N)$ is the maximum number of partitions of a set of N arbitrary exemplars into two classes that can be implemented by a given neural network. We say a set S of N exemplars is *shattered* by a neural network if all two-class partitions on S can be implemented by the network. If S is shattered by a network, then $\Delta_F(|S|) = 2^N$, where $|S|$ denotes the number of exemplars in S. For example, a single TLU (a linear threshold function) with two input features (and therefore two connection weights) and a threshold shatter a set of three arbitrary points in feature space, because any two-class partition of three points in a two-dimensional space can be done with a straight line. However, a single TLU with two inputs and a bias cannot shatter a set of four arbitrary points, because a partitioning of four points to realize the XOR type of function in a two-dimensional space cannot be done with one straight line (see Fig. 4.4). If $\Delta_F(2N)$ in Eq. (6.4) grows exponentially for all N (as 2^{2N}), there is no hope of generalization, because the right-hand side of Eq. (6.4) cannot be made small by increasing N. However, a given network may not be able to implement all 2^{2N} binary functions on $2N$ points by varying its weights. In that case, $\Delta_F(2N)$ may grow as a polynomial in $2N$, and the right-hand side of Eq. (6.4) can be made arbitrarily small by increasing N.

Vapnik and Chervonenkis [385, 386] discovered that the function $\Delta_F(N)$ grows as 2^N as N increases from zero up to a certain point. After that the growth slows, as illustrated in Fig. 6.4. The point where the growth of $\Delta_F(N)$ starts to be slower than exponential gives what is called the *Vapnik-Chervonenkis dimension* (VC dimension) of F. This is denoted by d_{VC}. In other words, d_{VC} is the cardinality of the largest $S \subset \mathbb{R}^n$ that is shattered by F, i.e., the largest N such that $\Delta_F(N) = 2^N$. If arbitrarily large finite sets can be shattered by F, then the VC dimension of F is infinite.

Example 6.1. Consider a one-layer perceptron (i.e., a single TLU) with M inputs and a nonzero threshold. Recall the definition of $L(N, M)$ in Section 4.1.2. Replacing the number of inputs M by a variable n (in Section 4.1.2, M was the number of TLUs producing the image space; here, the image space may be replaced by the original

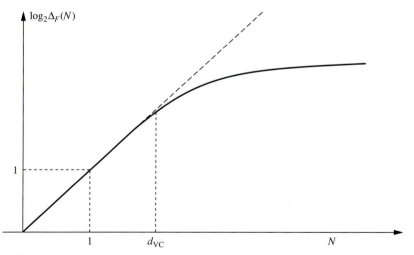

FIGURE 6.4
The function $\Delta_F(N)$ grows proportionally to 2^N as N increases from zero up to d_{VC}. After that, growth slows.

pattern space and there are n input patterns), we note that the capacity $L(N, n)$ is exactly $\Delta_F(N)$ for the perceptron, i.e.,

$$\Delta_F(N) = L(N, n) = 2 \sum_{i=0}^{n} \binom{N-1}{i}. \tag{6.5}$$

From Section 4.1.2, we know that $L(N, n) = 2^N$ for $N \le n + 1$, and $L(N, n) < 2^N$ for $N > n + 1$. Therefore, the VC dimension d_{VC} of the linear threshold function

$$T_b(w_0 + w_1 x_1 + w_2 x_2 + \cdots + w_n x_n + w_{n+1})$$

that has $n + 1$ weight parameters (the w_i's) is $d_{VC} = n + 1$. If the bias $w_{n+1} = 0$, then it is not difficult to show that $d_{VC} = n$.

The calculation of the VC dimension is usually not easy. In such cases, computing its lower and upper bounds may be expedient as well as useful. Proving upper bounds on the VC dimension is usually more difficult, because it is easier to find some shattered set of a certain size rather than show that no set of a certain size can be shattered. When d_{VC} is infinite, $\Delta_F(N) = 2^N$ for all N. Then, the right-hand side of Eq. (6.4) cannot be made smaller by increasing the number of training exemplars. However, if d_{VC} is finite, it can be shown [385, 386] that

$$\Delta_F(N) \le N^{d_{VC}} + 1. \tag{6.6}$$

Therefore, if d_{VC} is finite, we can increase the number of training exemplars to make the generalization error small. The reason is that when N is large, the growth of $\Delta_F(2N)$ is only polynomial in N whereas $\exp(-\epsilon^2 N/4)$ decays exponentially.

Theorem 6.5 gives a bound on the probability that $g_N(f)$ will be different from $G(f)$ by ϵ. It is not related to how well the exemplars are learned by a network. A more useful bound is the probability of error $e(f) = 1 - G(f)$ when most of the exemplars are successfully learned by the network. Such a bound is given in the following theorem.

Theorem 6.6   [44, 385]. Let F be a class of functions on $\mathbb{R}^n$ with suitable measurability conditions [44]. Assume $N \ge 1$, $0 < \epsilon, \gamma \le 1$. If N exemplars $(\mathbf{x}, f^*(\mathbf{x}))$, $\mathbf{x} \in \mathbb{R}^n$ are randomly chosen according to the distribution p, then the probability that there exists a function $f \in F$ such that $e(f) > \epsilon$ but f disagrees with only a fraction $(1 - \gamma)\epsilon$ of the training exemplars is bounded by the inequality

$$\text{Prob}[e(f) > \epsilon \mid e_N(f) \le (1 - \gamma)\epsilon] < 8\Delta_F(2N)\exp(-\gamma^2 \epsilon N/4), \tag{6.7}$$

where $e_N(f) = 1 - g_N(f)$.

The probability in Eq. (6.7) is a conditional probability that, if most of the exemplars are correctly learned by a network, tells us how confident we can be about the performance of the network on future exemplars drawn according to the same distribution. This inequality is similar to the one in Eq. (6.4). Both inequalities tell us that if valid generalization is expected, the function representation capacity $\Delta_F(N)$ cannot grow faster than the exponential term.

In summary, the training of a neural network with a set of exemplars is a process of selecting an $f \in F$ by adjusting the network's weights so that $g_N(f)$ is maximized. Whether the level of performance of the network on the training exemplars will continue on future exemplars depends on the function representation capacity of the network, i.e., the size of the set F. The VC dimension can be viewed as a measure of the capacity of the neural network. It tells us about the largest set of points that may be shattered by the network or machine. If the function representation capacity $\Delta_F(N)$ of the network has a finite d_{VC}, valid generalization can be expected. The larger the function representation capacity $\Delta_F(N)$ of the network, the larger the VC dimension, and the greater the number of training exemplars needed to achieve the required generalization.

6.2.2 Sufficient Conditions for Valid Generalization in Feedforward Networks

Sufficient conditions on the number of training exemplars required for valid generalization can be obtained using Eq. (6.7). To apply Eq. (6.7), one must estimate $\Delta_F(N)$, or the VC dimension of a given network. This problem can be difficult for complicated networks. Three examples are considered here.

Example 6.2. Consider a feedforward network with discrete weights; i.e., each weight can take only one of a finite number of values. This example is practical, for in digital implementation of neural networks the weights are discrete. Assume that each weight can only assume k different values, and the total number of weights is W. Then there are only k^W possible combinations of weight values. The number of binary functions implementable by this network thus must be equal to or less than k^W. Therefore, $\Delta_F(2N) \leq k^W$. Note that in this case $\Delta_F(2N)$ does not depend on the number of training exemplars. Using this bound of the VC dimension, we let the right-hand side of Eq. (6.7) be smaller than δ. Then, letting $\gamma = \frac{1}{2}$, we have

$$8\Delta_F(2N)\exp(-\epsilon N/16) \leq 8(k^W)\exp(-\epsilon N/16) < \delta. \tag{6.8}$$

For valid generalization, the number of training exemplars N must satisfy

$$N > \frac{16}{\epsilon}\left(W \ln k - \ln\left(\frac{\delta}{8}\right)\right). \tag{6.9}$$

Example 6.3. From Example 6.1 we know that for a one-layer perceptron (i.e., a single TLU) with a nonzero threshold and n inputs the VC dimension $d_{VC} = n + 1$. In Eq. (6.6), set $d_{VC} = n + 1$ and assume $\gamma = \frac{1}{2}$. Eq. (6.7) in Theorem 6.6 now becomes

$$\text{Prob}[e(f) > \epsilon \,|\, e_N(f) \leq (1 - \gamma)\epsilon] < 8[(2N)^{n+1} + 1]\exp(-\epsilon N/16) \tag{6.10}$$

$$\approx 8(2N)^{n+1}\exp(-\epsilon N/16) = 8\exp[(n + 1)\ln(2N) - \epsilon N/16].$$

Let

$$8\exp[(n + 1)\ln(2N) - \epsilon N/16] < \delta. \tag{6.11}$$

For Eq. (6.11) to hold for small δ, the exponent in the square bracket must be negative as N becomes bigger. Therefore, we must have $N > N_m$, where N_m is the solution to the following equation:

$$(n + 1)\ln(2N_m) = \epsilon N_m/16. \tag{6.12}$$

A smaller ϵ may substantially increase N_m and, consequently, the number of exemplars needed if good generalization is desired. For example, let $\epsilon = 0.1$ and $n = 4$. According to Eq. (6.12), we should have $N > N_m \approx 6,012$! This perceptron has only four weights and one threshold to be determined. This awfully large number of exemplars required shows that such a worst-case analysis may not be very meaningful in practice.

Example 6.4. Baum and Haussler [35] found an upper bound on the VC dimension d_{VC} for a general feedforward network with E edges and K TLUs ($K \geq 2$) to be

$$d_{VC} \leq 2W \log_2(eK) \quad \text{and} \quad \Delta_F(N) < (eNK/W)^W \quad \text{for all } N \geq W, \tag{6.13}$$

where $W = E + K$ is the number of weights (include one weight for each edge in the graph and one threshold for each TLU), and e is the base of the natural logarithm. Using this estimate and Theorem 6.6, Baum and Haussler [35] proved the following theorem:

Theorem 6.7   [35]. Assume that a feedforward network with a fixed graph G and $W = E + K$ weights (E edges and K TLUs, $K \geq 2$) is trained using N random training exemplars drawn according to a distribution p. Assume that $0 < \epsilon \leq \frac{1}{2}$. If a choice of weights can be found such that at least a fraction $1 - \epsilon/2$ of the N training exemplars are correctly classified, where

$$N \geq \frac{32W}{\epsilon} \ln \frac{32K}{\epsilon}, \tag{6.14}$$

then one has a confidence of at least $1 - 8\exp(-1.5W)$ that the network will correctly classify all but a fraction ϵ of future exemplars drawn according to the same distribution.

Proof. The proof is straightforward using Theorem 6.6 with $\gamma = \frac{1}{2}$ and the bound $\Delta_F(N) < (eNK/W)^W$ given in Example 6.4. It is left as an exercise.

As illustration of Theorem 6.7, consider a two-layer fully connected feedforward network with 10 hidden units and one output unit. Let the input vector be from $\mathbb{R}^{10}$ and $\epsilon = 0.1$. Then $W = E + K = 110 + 11 = 121$. Using Eq. (6.14), we have $N \geq 316, 196$! Similar to what was observed in Example 6.3, this number is impractically large and the bound may be too loose.

6.2.3   Necessary Conditions for Valid Generalization in Feedforward Networks

The results just given are sufficient conditions for valid generalization in each case. The bounds all appear to be too loose, leading to impractical results.

For feedforward networks with one hidden layer of K fully connected TLUs taking input from $\mathbb{R}^n$, Baum and Haussler [35] found a more practical necessary condition on the number of training exemplars required for valid generalization. This is obtained based on the following lower bound of the VC dimension,

$$d_{VC} \geq 2 \left\lfloor \frac{K}{2} \right\rfloor n, \tag{6.15}$$

for such networks, where $\lfloor \frac{K}{2} \rfloor$ denotes the largest integer not greater than $K/2$. For large K and n, $2 \lfloor \frac{K}{2} \rfloor n$ is approximately the number of weights in the network. Using this result, Baum and Haussler proved the following theorem.

> **Theorem 6.8 [35].** Consider any learning algorithm used in the training of a feedforward network with one hidden layer of K fully connected TLUs, and let $0 < \epsilon \leq \frac{1}{8}$. If the algorithm uses N exemplars, where
>
> $$N < \frac{2 \left\lfloor \dfrac{K}{2} \right\rfloor n - 1}{32\epsilon}, \tag{6.16}$$
>
> to learn a functional mapping from $\mathbb{R}^n$ to $\{0, 1\}$, then there exists a distribution p for which
>
> (a) a choice of weights exists such that the network exactly classifies random exemplars from these distributions, but
> (b) the learning algorithm will have a probability of at least 0.01 of finding a choice of weights having an error greater than ϵ, i.e., $\text{Prob}(e(f) > \epsilon) \geq 0.01$.

Applying Theorem 6.8 to the example following Theorem 6.7 with $\epsilon = 0.1$, we have a necessary condition for valid generalization, namely, N cannot be less than 31. Notice the big gap between the sufficient condition and necessary condition. Since there are 121 free parameters in the network, this lower bound is obviously too small to pin down all weights. This bound is also very loose.

In summary, provided

$$N \geq O\left(\frac{W}{\epsilon} \ln \frac{K}{\epsilon}\right), \qquad \left(0 < \epsilon \leq \frac{1}{2}\right),$$

random training exemplars can be learned on a general feedforward network with K TLUs and W weights so that at least $100(1 - \epsilon/2)$ percent of the exemplars are correctly classified, then one has confidence approaching certainty that the network will correctly classify a fraction $(1 - \epsilon)$ of future test exemplars drawn according to the same distribution. Conversely, for a fully connected feedforward network with one hidden layer, any learning algorithm using fewer than $O(W/\epsilon)$ random training exemplars may fail, for at least a fixed fraction of the time, to find a choice of weights that will correctly classify more than $100(1 - \epsilon)$ percent of the future exemplars. In such cases, the learned network is particularly deceiving, because it may find a choice of weights such that the network will correctly classify all the training exemplars.

Based on the $O(W/\epsilon)$ condition, a more practical and appropriate number of training exemplars may be the number of weights times the inverse of the accuracy parameter ϵ. For example, if an accuracy level of 90 percent, corresponding to $\epsilon = 0.1$, is required, about 10 times as many training exemplars as the number of weights in the network are needed. This is in fact the rule of thumb suggested by Widrow [408]. In our example of a network with 121 weights, 1,210 training exemplars will be required. This seems to be more reasonable. Note that the above bounds are obtained under the distribution-free condition with randomly picked training exemplars. If a priori knowledge is available about the distribution of the exemplars, a substantially lesser number of exemplars may be necessary for valid generalization. One example is when the training exemplars along the boundaries between pattern classes are used.

6.2.4   Discussions and Ways to Improve Generalization

There is a big gap between the sufficient condition $O[(W/\epsilon)\ln(K/\epsilon)]$ and the necessary condition $O(W/\epsilon)$ on the training set size for networks with one hidden layer of TLUs. Both conditions appear to be too loose. The closing of this gap remains an interesting open problem. Also, apart from a sufficient condition, the case of multiple hidden layers is largely open.

The foregoing results provide bounds on the probability of poor generalization in the worst case. Results on the average generalizability of learning and on distribution-dependent learning also exist [343, 387]. Schwartz et al. [343] studied the average generalizability in terms of the "volume" in the weight space, briefly introduced here.

Consider all the possible weights of a given feedforward network with a fixed graph in the weight space. Every vector $\mathbf{w}$ in the weight space represents a set of weights with which the network implements a function $f_\mathbf{w}(\mathbf{x})$. The volume in the weight space occupied by all the possible weights may be found by

$$V_a = \int p(\mathbf{w})\,d\mathbf{w}, \tag{6.17}$$

where $p(\mathbf{w})$ is a density distribution of the possible weights. Since the weight point may move within a neighborhood and still implement the same function, the weight space is partitioned into regions, each of which corresponds to a function $f_\mathbf{w}(\mathbf{x})$ that can be implemented by the network. These regions are mutually disjoint because different functions cannot have the same weight point. The volume of the weight space that implements a specific function f is given as

$$V_a(f) = \int p(\mathbf{w})\chi_f(\mathbf{w})\,d\mathbf{w}, \tag{6.18}$$

where $\chi_f(\mathbf{w})$ is the *characteristic function*,

$$\chi_f(\mathbf{w}) = \begin{cases} 1 & \text{if } f_\mathbf{w}(\mathbf{x}) = f(\mathbf{x}) \text{ for all input vector } \mathbf{x} \\ 0 & \text{otherwise.} \end{cases} \tag{6.19}$$

The ratio of the preceding two quantities, $R_a(f) = V_a(f)/V_a$, gives us the fraction of the weight space that implements the function f. The function representation capacity of the network then can be defined as

$$C_a = -\sum_f R_a(f) \log_2 R_a(f). \tag{6.20}$$

Each time an input-output training pair $\{x_i, f(x_i)\}$ is learned by the network, it constrains the region of possible weights for the network. This condition can be expressed as follows. Let the characteristic function in the weight space for a function $f_w(x_i)$ that correctly computes $f(x_i)$ be

$$\chi(f_w, x_i) = \begin{cases} 1 & \text{if } f_w(x_i) = f(x_i) \\ 0 & \text{otherwise.} \end{cases} \tag{6.21}$$

Then the volume of the region of possible weights after successfully learning N exemplars is

$$V_N = \int p(\mathbf{w}) \prod_{i=1}^{N} \chi(f_w, x_i) \, d\mathbf{w}. \tag{6.22}$$

The volume of the weight space that is consistent with both f and the N training exemplars is

$$V_N(f) = \int p(\mathbf{w}) \chi_f(\mathbf{w}) \prod_{i=1}^{N} \chi(f_w, x_i) \, d\mathbf{w} = V_a(f) \prod_{i=1}^{N} \chi(f, x_i). \tag{6.23}$$

The last step was obtained because $\chi_f(\mathbf{w}) \prod_{i=1}^{N} \chi(f_w, x_i) = \prod_{i=1}^{N} \chi(f, x_i)$; i.e., the product is nonzero only when $f_w = f$. Therefore, the term $\prod_{i=1}^{N} \chi(f, x_i)$ can be factored outside the integral. A generalizability measure can then be obtained after averaging $V_N(f)$ over all possible training sequences. Intuitively speaking, the volume of the set $(\prod_{i=1}^{N} \chi(f_w, x_i)) \backslash (\chi_f(\mathbf{w}) \prod_{i=1}^{N} \chi(f_w, x_i))$ provides a measure of the generalizability of learning. The smaller this volume, the higher the probability of valid generalization. The foregoing formulations can be applied to TLUs as well as units with differentiable transfer characteristics. The obtained generalizability measure is an average over all possible network weight choices consistent with the training exemplars. It may not be representative for a specific case in question. Interested readers are referred to refs. [90] and [343] and the references cited therein for more details.

The intuition on generalization is consistent with our knowledge of function approximation. We know that if a function $y = f(x)$ with too many free parameters, e.g., a high-order polynomial, is used to fit a given set of data points (x_i, y_i), then it may "overfit" the data. The fitted function may pass through all the specified data points (x_i, y_i) without interpolating error. However, the interpolating function could be highly oscillatory, leading to large errors at points not included in the original data set. Such an overly fitted function does not detect the regularity. It simply memorizes the right output values for the training data points. This case is illustrated in Fig. 6.5.

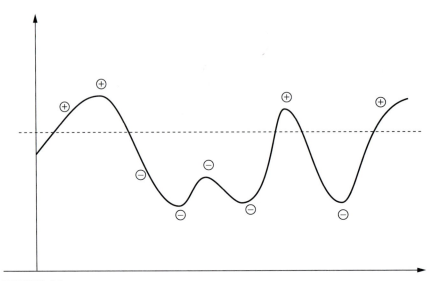

FIGURE 6.5
An illustration of overfitting in function approximation. Assume that the desired classification is
done by the dotted straight line. The overfitted oscillating curve will not generalize well.

Assume that the desired classification in the figure is the dashed straight line. The
overfitted oscillating curve will not generalize well. The analogy to the requirements
of good filter design is worth citing. A filter whose frequency response interpolates
well over a set of frequency points over, say, a passband may be less desirable than
one whose characteristic optimizes the performance over the whole band by minimizing, say, the maximum ripple, as in the Chebyshev type of filter design [48].
This analogy explains the phenomenon of *overtraining* in applying a backpropagation algorithm to feedforward networks. Overtraining is the phenomenon by which
after a certain number of training epochs, more training epochs will further reduce
the learning error (only slightly in many cases) on the training set but will produce
greater and greater errors (usually by a very appreciable amount) on test exemplars.
The reason is similar to that of overfitting as illustrated in Fig. 6.5. This is usually
an indication that either the network used is too large or the training set is too small.
　　A learning strategy that seeks a compromise between learning time and generalization is to use an oversized network and to stop the training early to avoid
overtraining. An oversized network may allow quick learning. At the beginning of
learning, the weights in the network are randomly initialized. As training progresses,
more and more weights are adjusted and put to use. This phenomenon is referred
to as the *increase of the number of effective parameters* in training [398]. If the
training is stopped at the right time, the number of parameters effectively used to
approximate the training data may be appropriate. The problem is how to determine
a good stopping criterion. One simple approach is to keep a subset, say 10 percent,
of the training set as the *validation set*. The validation set is not used in training.

The network's performance is evaluated on both the training set and the validation set. The training should stop either before the error on the validation set starts to increase or when it no longer decreases. This is a heuristic approach and assumes that the validation set is representative of any future test set. Another requirement is that the number of exemplars in the training set should be large enough such that removal of a subset of data from the training set is affordable and evaluation using the validation set is meaningful. This will not be the case when the training set is small.

Weigend and Rumelhart [398] proposed a measure for the number of effective parameters in a feedforward network with a single hidden layer. Their analysis is based on the eigenvalue spectra of the covariance matrix C of hidden unit activations. The entry c_{ij} in the ith row and jth column of the covariance matrix gives the correlation between the output values y_i and y_j, computed over the training set at two hidden units. Specifically,

$$c_{ij} = E[(y_1 - \bar{y}_i)(y_j - \bar{y}_j)],$$

where $\bar{y}_i = E[y_i]$ is the mean of y_i over the training set. The eigenvalues correspond to the variances captured by the corresponding eigenvectors. The number of significantly sized eigenvalues is a measure of the number of effective hidden units, referred to as the *effective dimension* of the space of hidden unit outputs, i.e., the image pattern space. This dimension can be viewed as the effective rank of the covariance matrix.

Weigend and Rumelhart [398] observed in experiments that a backpropagation type of gradient descent algorithm extracts one significant eigenvector after another during training. The dimension of the hidden unit output space is essentially zero before the training starts, and then increases. When training stops, the number of significantly sized eigenvalues gives the effective dimension of the hidden unit output space. Eigenvalue analysis may also be applied to the matrix W of weights between inputs and hidden units, whose numbers of rows and columns are equal to the dimension of the input space and the number of hidden units, respectively. The weight matrix can be decomposed into two orthogonal matrices and one diagonal matrix by *singular value decomposition* (SVD) [308]. As with the eigenvalues of the covariance matrix C already mentioned, the number of significantly sized singular values obtained from the diagonal matrix in the SVD of the weight matrix is also essentially zero at the beginning of training and increases as training proceeds. These observations support the strategy of using an oversized network for learning with an appropriate stopping criterion. The key difficulty is the determination of an appropriate stopping criterion.

There is also a converse problem. If a function with too few parameters, i.e., too small a network, is used to fit a set of training exemplars, both fitting error and interpolation error may be large. Then the size of the network needs to be increased. Because it is difficult to predetermine the right size of network for a problem, efficient learning algorithms that learn not only the weights but also the network graph may be a useful research direction. Efforts along that direction have already been made as pointed out in Chapter 5. However, analysis for valid generalization in networks that adapt their graphs, the number of learnable parameters, or the transfer characteristics of the units or synapses is a difficult open problem. The representation capacity Δ_F of this type of network needs to be investigated before its generalization capability can be well understood.

In general, a smaller network generalizes better than a larger one. Therefore, algorithms that either penalize the complexity of the network during backpropagation learning [275, 399] or prune the network after learning [216, 398] have been proposed. The basic idea in refs. [275, 399] is to add an extra term to the error function that will penalize size complexity of the network. Simple versions of this approach penalize either the sum of the squares of the weights or the number of nonzero weights. Nowlan and Hinton proposed the soft weight-sharing scheme [275]; it uses a more complicated penalty term in which the distribution of weight values is modeled as a mixture of multiple Gaussians. Weights with very similar values are clustered into subsets.

Another approach to improve generalization involves pruning the network after the training set has been learned. A network pruning method called *optimal brain damage* was proposed by Le Cun et al. [216]. The method uses information-theoretic measures to select an optimal set of weights for removal. Following this, the network needs to be retrained. The basic idea in their procedure is to remove the connections that have the least effect on the training error to be minimized. A simple implementation is to delete connections whose weights have small magnitude. After the deletion, the network should be retrained. Then the procedure for removal of small-magnitude weights may be repeated. This simple implementation, however, significantly slows down the learning process. Furthermore, it is not always true that the training error is less sensitive to small-magnitude weights. Removal of some small-magnitude weights may significantly increase the error. The sensitivity of a weight on the training error can be measured by the change in the error if a weight is made zero. However, a direct implementation of this would require a prohibitively large amount of computations. The method proposed in [216] provides an approximate measure of the sensitivity of weights using the Taylor expansion of the backpropagation training error function E. Consider the training error E as a function of all the weights, i.e., $E = E(w_1, w_2, \ldots, w_n)$. Then the change ΔE in the error function due to a perturbation of weights is given by the Taylor expansion:

$$\Delta E = \sum_i \frac{\partial E}{\partial w_i} \Delta w_i + \frac{1}{2} \sum_i \frac{\partial^2 E}{\partial w_i^2} (\Delta w_i)^2 + \frac{1}{2} \sum_{i \neq j} \frac{\partial^2 E}{\partial w_i \partial w_j} \Delta w_i \Delta w_j$$

$$+ O(\|\Delta \mathbf{w}\|^3). \tag{6.24}$$

The goal is to find a set of weights whose deletion will increase E the least. Three simplifications are made to reduce the amount of computations to a practical level. First, since the deletion of weights is performed after the learning has converged to a minimum of the error function, $\partial E / \partial w_i \approx 0$. Therefore, the first term on the right-hand side of Eq. (6.24) can be neglected. Second, the error function is assumed to be approximately quadratic, so the last term on the right-hand side of Eq. (6.24) can also be neglected. Lastly, the third term on the right-hand side of Eq. (6.24) is assumed to be much smaller than the second term and can be removed. Then, Eq. (6.24) reduces to

$$\Delta E \approx \frac{1}{2} \sum_i \frac{\partial^2 E}{\partial w_i^2} (\Delta w_i)^2. \tag{6.25}$$

The second-order derivatives $(\partial^2 E/\partial w_i^2)$ can be computed by backpropagation in much the same way as the standard backpropagation algorithm is used for computing first-order derivatives. The derivation of the computation procedure for the second-order derivatives is left as an exercise.

The "optimal brain damage" procedure for improving generalization is summarized as follows:

1. Choose a network structure that could learn the training data in a reasonable amount of time. This normally implies that a (slightly) oversized network be chosen.
2. Train the network until the training error is sufficiently small.
3. Compute the second-order derivatives $(\partial^2 E/\partial w_i^2)$ for each weight.
4. Compute the sensitivity for each weight

$$s_i = \frac{1}{2} \frac{\partial^2 E}{\partial w_i^2} (\Delta w_i)^2.$$

5. Sort the weights by the sensitivity and delete some weights with low sensitivity. Go to step 2.

Deleting a weight means removing the connection, or setting the weight to zero and freezing it there. The procedure should stop either when the network is considered to be sufficiently small for the training set (e.g., when the number of weights is about 10 percent of the number of exemplars in the training set) or when the network is unable to learn the training set in an acceptable amount of time. In the latter case, the network should revert to the version before the last removal of weights.

A challenge to postlearning analysis and pruning methods is to minimize relearning after pruning. It may be that after pruning, the network requires an impractically long time to learn the training set, whereas the previous larger network is able to learn quickly, as illustrated by the $P \subseteq 3 \, NX \subseteq P^2$ example in Section 6.1.2.

6.3 SPACE COMPLEXITY OF FEEDFORWARD NETWORKS

There are two aspects of computational complexity: *time complexity* and *space complexity*. The problems of loading and generalization address the time complexity of network learning algorithms. In this section, we discuss the space complexity of neural networks. Space complexity of a network includes three parameters as functions of the input dimension and the concepts to be learned, namely, the number of units, the number of connections (maximum number of connections to a unit as well as total number of connections in the network), and the numerical range (and resolution) of the weights. For example, in the case of a perceptron those three parameters depend on the order of the predicate to be learned and on the dimension of the input.

The numerical range and resolution of the weights are related to the space complexity of the network, because a large numerical range and fine resolution of the weights require complicated circuitry to realize. As shown in Chapter 4, the range of weights could be exponential in the size $|\mathbf{R}|$ of the input array or retina $\mathbf{R}$ for perceptrons. More specifically, it was shown that for the parity function ψ_{parity} when only masks are used at the first layer, the weights grow at least as order $2^{|\mathbf{R}|-1}$ with a resolution of 1. An appropriate choice of the network may avoid this problem. However, the price paid may be in the form of more complicated units, a larger number of units, and/or more connections. From a VLSI layout viewpoint, the preceding three effects all translate into an increase in the area required on a chip to implement the network. The scaling property of the maximum number of connections to a unit (that is, how the maximum number of connections to a unit increases as the network is scaled up) is more important from a physical realizability point of view, for it is difficult to lay out many connections to a single unit in VLSI technology. Even if many connections can be made to a single unit, there will be a reliability problem, because noise associated with the many connections may accumulate beyond the tolerance level. Worth noting are techniques for implementing large numbers of connections in analog VLSI, for example, the resistive network-sharing connections by Mead [253] and the complementary metal-oxide-semiconductor (CMOS) chip by Salam et al. [333, 334].

A simple way to reduce the maximum number of connections to a unit is to use several layers of linear or nonlinear units, producing analog output with low fan-in, as relays. A *linear relay* produces as its output the sum of all its inputs. The linear unit relay scheme will reduce the maximum number of connections to a unit. More precisely, to realize W connections using M layers of identical linear units as relays, the maximum number T of connections to a unit will be $T = W^{1/(M+1)}$. However, this reduction is achieved at the expense of $[(W - T)/(T - 1)]$ linear units. If threshold logic units are used as such relays, more units will be required to implement an equivalent network owing to the analog nature of the computation [1] (see Section 6.3.2).

Although high connectivity is difficult to realize, it is essential for the functioning of neural networks. What is important is not the absolute number of connections, but how the space complexity of a network scales up as a function of the dimension of the input space. We explain next, using the order of a perceptron and the analog nature of neural computation, why high connectivity is required for the functioning of neural networks.

6.3.1 Order of a Function and the Complexity of a Network

A key motivation for artificial neural networks is the hope that fast, approximate solutions to hard problems can be found by a network of simple processors providing local and partial solutions in parallel. The connections should be local in some sense. In this spirit, attempts should be made to avoid fully connected feedforward networks. This important problem, raised by Minsky and Papert [261], has practical implications in hardware implementations of artificial neural networks.

Order-limited or *diameter-limited* networks (see Problem 4.22) as defined in ref. [261] are examples of locally connected networks. The two concepts are defined only for perceptrons in ref. [261]. A perceptron is order-limited if the maximum number of connections from the input space to any first-layer unit is a fixed number, independent of the dimension of the input space, i.e., the number of input variables. A perceptron is diameter-limited if the input units connected to any first-layer unit are within a fixed diameter in the input space, independent of the number of input units, where the input units are arranged in a two-dimensional array. Examples of order-limited perceptrons are the perceptron for computing $\psi_{\text{convexity}}$ and ψ_M as defined in Section 4.3. Note that these two examples are not diameter-limited. The human visual system at the early processing stage is believed to be diameter-limited.

The two concepts can be generalized to multilayer feedforward networks and even recurrent networks. A network is *order-limited* if, independent of the size of the network, a unit is connected only to a fixed number of units. A network is *diameter-limited* if a unit is only connected to units so that the maximum distance is a fixed number independent of the size of the network. The units may be arranged in a two-dimensional or three-dimensional space. The distance may be the actual Euclidean distance, or it may be defined by the delays incurred in the transmission of signals. The key in both concepts is that the number of connections is fixed even when the network size, i.e., the number of units, grows.

Some results have appeared on the number of hidden units required in a two-layer network for it to be able to implement any function on N training exemplars [169]. These results give the number of hidden units required to implement any two-class dichotomy of N training exemplars. From results on generalization of learning in the previous section, we know that generally a network capable of implementing any function on N training exemplars does not yield good generalization in the worst case.

A more relevant question that needs to be answered is the size of a network required to implement a specific function or class of functions. Especially important is how the size increases as the network is scaled up, for learning the same function or the same class of functions. As in most computational processes, there is a trade-off between time complexity and space complexity. We saw in Section 6.1 that loading a small network is NP-complete, but loading a larger network may be possible in polynomial time.

The order of a function (Section 4.3) provides a measure of the space complexity a perceptron must have for it to compute the function. The order of a perceptron limits the predicates that it can compute. A perceptron with a given order O_1 cannot be trained to compute predicates whose order is greater than O_1, as seen in Chapter 4. This conclusion is the most important one in ref. [261]. Therefore, if we want to increase the likelihood for a given perceptron to be able to load an arbitrary set of exemplars, or if we know that the network needs to compute higher-order functions, the number of connections to the first-layer units must be high.

The order of a perceptron not only dictates the number of connections to the first-layer units but also provides an estimate of the number of units at the first layer. Equivalently, the number of units at the first layer is the number of connections to the output unit (assume there is only one output unit). Under the condition that the units in the first layer compute only mask functions, an estimate of how many units are required in the first layer, as a function of the size of the retina (i.e., input space), can be derived from the order of the predicate the perceptron is to compute. Actually, for a predicate of bounded order, we can prove the following theorem:

> **Theorem 6.9.** For a perceptron to compute a predicate of bounded order r, the number of first-layer units grows polynomially in the size of the retina $|\mathbf{R}|$ provided that the units in the first layer compute only mask functions. More specifically, it grows slower than, or at most at the same rate as, $O(|\mathbf{R}|^r)$.

The proof is left as an exercise. An open problem is how the order is related to the scaling of the number of first-layer units when the units are not limited to masks.

A multilayer feedforward network cannot escape the curse of the order of a predicate. The number of connections from the input space to units at the first layer may be less than the order, but more units (and more layers) are required. Somewhere before the final output unit, the effective connections, i.e., direct connections from the input plus indirect connections from inputs through intermediate units, must be equal to or more than the order. Otherwise, the network will not be able to learn the function. Use of a multilayer network allows the number of connections to be more evenly distributed to many units. The price paid is more units and, in general, a higher number of total connections.

6.3.2 High Connectivity in Analog Neural Computations

Another reason neurons have high connectivity is the analog nature of the computations carried out by biological neurons. In this section, we show that the analog mode of computation makes the computational power of an individual neuron proportional to the square of the number of inputs n, whereas the order of the unit's size is only linear in n. The size of a unit is assumed to be dominated by the size of the connection tree merging to it. This result contrasts with traditional logic gates, such as AND gates, in which both the computational power and the size are linear in n.

Let us consider an n-input AND gate. The AND gate can be replaced by a tree of two-input AND gates as shown in Fig. 6.6. The size of the n-input gate is approximately proportional to n. It may vary from one physical implementation to

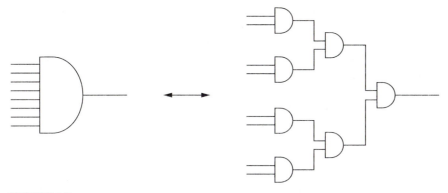

FIGURE 6.6
An AND gate can be equivalently replaced by a tree structure of two-input AND gates. The two
circuits compute the same function.

another. The size of the tree is proportional to the number of two-input gates in the
tree, which is approximately n. Hence, there is no essential gain or loss in the overall
network size if only two-input gates are used.

The situation with a neural network is drastically different. A unit makes a decision based on the values of its inputs. The computation involves analog parameters
and, in some cases, even analog signals. To show that there is an inherent advantage
in using units with a large number of inputs for such analog processing, consider a
TLU with n inputs. Suppose that we replace this single n-input TLU with a network
of two-input units. The network of two-input units is required to be able to implement
any threshold function of n variables that the single n-input TLU can.

The size of the n-input TLU is approximately proportional to n. Let us consider
the size of the network of two-input TLUs in order for it to be able to implement any
threshold function of n variables. Suppose we have a network with M two-input
TLUs that can implement any threshold function of n inputs. We know that a two-
input TLU can compute 14 out of the $2^{2^2} = 16$ switching functions of two variables;
the remaining cases are not linearly separable. Hence, the network can compute at
most 14^M different threshold functions. On the other hand, the number of linear
threshold functions computable by an n-input TLU is more than $2^{[n(n+1)/2]+8}$ for $n \geq$
8 [268]. Therefore, for the network with M two-input TLUs to be able to compute
the same set of n-input threshold functions, we must have

$$14^M \geq 2^{[n(n+1)/2]+8}. \tag{6.26}$$

Thus, the number M of two-input TLUs should at least be of order n^2.

There is no guarantee that there is a network with n^2 two-input units that can
replace the n-input unit. This equation shows only that there is no smaller network
that will do it. The situation becomes even worse when logic more sophisticated than
threshold logic is involved. In general, the fancier the logic, the more it pays to have
plenty of inputs to a unit.

The difference between an AND gate and a TLU is due to the analog nature of computation carried out by a TLU to make a global decision using threshold logic. With a network of two-input TLUs, the intermediate discrete decisions waste most of the information carried by the intermediate analog signals. A bigger network makes up for this lost analog information by providing an abundance of intermediate discrete decisions. For example, the intermediate analog signals may be soft decisions (analog values between 0 and 1, instead of just 0 or 1) carrying not only the decision (0 or 1, depending on which is closer) but also information about how reliable the decision is (i.e., how close). We need several bits to encode an approximate value for this measure of reliability if we use discrete signals.

From the foregoing analysis, two conclusions useful for engineering design of neural networks can be drawn. First, a network using units that accept analog inputs and yield analog outputs, e.g., units with sigmoidal transfer characteristic, may require fewer units to realize the same function compared with networks that use units with discrete input or output signals. Second, if TLUs are used and the maximum number of connections exceeds the physical realizability constraint on the connections of TLUs, linear or nonlinear units producing analog outputs should be used as relays in a tree structure, in the fashion shown in Fig. 6.6. This will produce a smaller circuit than that obtainable by using TLUs as relays. Note that the total number of learnable weights in two circuits will be the same, because all the intermediate relay connections are fixed with a gain of 1; i.e., they are simple wires.

6.4   SUMMARY AND DISCUSSION

This chapter considers the various complexity issues in feedforward networks. The problems of loading and valid generalization are treated in the distribution-free learnability framework. These results provide bounds on the probability of poor generalization. Results on the average generalizability of learning and on distribution-dependent learning also exist. Interested readers are referred to [90, 343, 387] and the references cited therein. The problem of learning a decision rule for two-class pattern classification with respect to a family of probability measures has recently been considered and more results can be expected in the future about learnability with respect to other families of probability measures.[2]

The loading problem is shown to be NP-complete for many simple two-layer networks with a wide variety of node functions, including threshold logic and differentiable sigmoidal functions [43, 179]. This result occurs even for approximate loading. This type of worst-case analysis result is useful for giving us a better theoretical understanding of the problem. However, that should not be taken to imply that the loading problem is always hard for any training set and networks on

---

[2] S.R. Kulkarni and M. Vidyasagar, "Learning decision rules for pattern classification under a family of probability measures." *IEEE Trans. Information Theory,* to appear.

average. Most probable average behavior analysis will be more useful in practice than the traditional worst-case analysis, which assigns a blanket categorization of NP-completeness to a problem.

Note that the loading problem is different from the learning problem. The former is only concerned with whether there exists a choice of weights that will correctly classify the training exemplars. The latter requires that such a choice be actually found if it exists. Obviously, learning is at least as hard as loading, and definitely harder when learning is incremental.

Two networks are given in Section 6.1.2 where the loading problem for the second is of polynomial time complexity on any set of loading exemplars that the first can correctly classify, even though the loading problem for the first is NP-complete. This observation brings out two points. First, a larger network does not necessarily imply a higher computational complexity in time. Increasing the representation capacity of a network may increase or decrease the complexity of the loading problem. Second, it provides theoretical support for the idea that (1) varying the size of a network to find an appropriate network and (2) finding an appropriate input encoding for one's loading problem are important parts of the learning process. Variable-structure networks provide an alternative to the trial-and-error approach of varying the representation capacity of a network until fast (approximate) learning is achieved. There is a trade-off between increasing the size of the network to ease the loading problem and maintaining valid generalization. The larger a network is, the more training exemplars will be required for valid generalization. In some applications, there could be a dearth of such exemplars.

The problem of how many training exemplars are required so that valid generalization from a trained network can be expected is examined in Section 6.2. This is necessary to settle in applications where such exemplars are abundant. The problem is then formulated in terms of uniform convergence of the frequency of correct learning over the training set to the corresponding true probability over the entire distribution of exemplars. Conditions for valid generalization for several networks are given in Section 6.2.2. The important property of generalization is the subject of computational learning theory [27], which has been developed only during the last few years to a state of acceptable, but far from complete, maturity. An intuitive interpretation of the generalization problem uses the phenomenon of overfitting in function approximation and filter design. This interpretation explains the overtraining problem in feedforward networks using backpropagation. Some researchers have even suggested different error functions to improve generalization in such networks [180].

In general, a smaller network generalizes better than a larger one. Therefore, algorithms that penalize the complexity of the network during learning [275, 399] or prune the network after learning [216, 398] are promising. A challenge to postlearning analysis and pruning methods is to minimize relearning after pruning. After pruning, the network may require an impractically long time to learn the training set, whereas the previous larger network is able to learn quickly. This result occurs because reducing the size of a network may increase the complexity of the loading problem. Derivation of conditions for valid generalization in networks that adapt their graphs, the number of learnable parameters, or the transfer characteristics of the units or synapses constitutes a difficult open problem. The representation capacity of this type of network, which itself is a difficult problem to settle, needs to be solved before its generalization capability can be well understood.

In Section 6.3, the problem of space complexity is considered. The space complexity of a network is determined by the type of function it is required to learn and the dimension of the input space (or size of the input array). High-order functions require networks with high space complexity. In other words, hard problems require large networks. This conclusion tells us that at least in the worst case, the intrinsic computational complexity of a problem cannot be avoided by simply using an analog system. A multilayer feedforward network also cannot escape the curse of the order of a function. The most important physical realizability constraint is the scaling property of the maximum number of connections to a unit when the network is scaled up. It is shown in Section 6.3.2 that, owing to the analog nature of computations in biological neural networks, use of units with many inputs offers space complexity savings over use of many units with a small number of inputs. Therefore, a compromise is necessary to accommodate the conflicting requirements of physical realizability and space complexity. Worth noting are techniques for sharing connections in analog VLSI implementations of neural networks.

PROBLEMS

6.1. Prove Theorem 6.2 by converting it to the three-node network.

6.2. Prove Theorem 6.3.

6.3. Prove Theorem 6.7. *Hint:* Use Theorem 6.6 with $\gamma = \frac{1}{2}$ and the bound $\Delta_F(N) < (eNK/W)^W$.

6.4. Prove Theorem 6.9.

6.5. Suppose that the domain of interest is the natural numbers. Let S denote the set $\{0,1,4\}$ and let F denote the class of sets $\{0,2,4\}$, $\{0,2\}$, $\{2\}$, $\{4\}$, $\{0,1,2\}$, $\{0,4\}$, $\{0,1,4\}$, $\{1,2\}$, $\{1,4\}$. F *shatters* S provided $\{f \cap S \mid f \in F\}$ is the power set of S, which is defined to be the set of all subsets of S [272]. Determine whether F shatters S.

6.6. Consider the input space to be a subspace of the n-dimensional real Euclidean space and the output space to be Boolean (unipolar or bipolar). Suppose that the computational structure is a McCulloch-Pitts neuron. Consider a set of m points in the input space, which, in particular, are represented by m vertices of an n-cube, $\{-1, 1\}^n$. Let $D(n,m)$ denote the number of linear dichotomies of the set of m points. It is known [387] that $D(n,m)$ satisfies the difference equation

$$D(n, m) = D(n - 1, m - 1) + D(n, m - 1)$$

with boundary conditions

$$D(n, 1) = 2 \quad \text{and} \quad D(2, m) = 2m.$$

Note that $D(n, m)$ is equal to *twice* the number of ways in which a set of m points in the n-dimensional space can be partitioned by an $(n-1)$-dimensional hyperplane generated by a McCulloch-Pitts neuron. This is because for each distinct partition there are two distinct classifications [273].

(a) Show that the solution for $D(n,m)$ when $m > n$ is given by

$$D(n, m) = 2 \sum_{j=0}^{n-1} \binom{m-1}{j}.$$

State what happens when $m \leq n$.

(b) Calculate the VC dimension of the function counting theorem exemplified by the solution in part (a).

6.7. Derive an efficient method for computing the second-order derivatives $(\partial^2 E/\partial w_i^2)$ needed for the "optimal brain damage" procedure. (*Hint:* A procedure very similar to the backpropagation algorithm for computing first-order derivatives can be found.)

CHAPTER
7

ADAPTIVE-STRUCTURE NETWORKS

In Chapter 6 we saw that the complexity of loading a set of exemplars on a network depends on the choice of the network graph. For a fixed graph, if the choice is improper, the loading problem may be NP-complete. The problem of actually finding out the weights is at least as hard as the loading problem. For example, we saw in Chapter 5 that the backpropagation algorithm (BPA) is not guaranteed to converge, it does not scale up very well, and in those situations when it converges it may not converge to the right solution and also may be extremely slow. The graph that characterizes the topology of the network must be decided before the algorithm can be applied. A major difficulty in doing so is the choice of the number of nodes in each layer of the graph, the number of layers, and the number of edges between the layers as well when the graph is not a fully connected multipartite graph. It was mentioned in the beginning of Section 6.1 that the complete learning problem using multilayer feedforward networks requires learning both the graph of the network and the connection weights. That feature was incorporated in the method of design based on the use of Voronoi diagrams, as described in Section 5.2. In this chapter we expand on the VoD-based design procedure to include additional learning algorithms, which grow or adapt the graph that characterizes a multilayer feedforward network so as to classify any linearly nonseparable clusters of patterns.

In Section 7.1, the so-called *growth algorithms* are introduced. The reader will be able to draw some analogies between these algorithms and VoD-based design in that they both have the feature of training for structure as well as connection weights. However, the methods adopted to reach the goal are quite different. The algorithms in this chapter are based on the principle of decomposition and subgoaling, whereas the VoD construction depends on the resources in computational geometry. Both approaches, though, dispense with the drawbacks of fixed structures and incorporate the learning of graphs that characterize growing (or shrinking) structures. In a complete adaptive neural system that is not just an abstraction from neurobiology in the model-theoretic sense, the restrictions of synaptic characteristics with regard to linearity need to be removed. Section 7.2 is devoted to the results of recent research on the outcome of employing synapses with nonlinear transfer characteristics (sometimes referred to as nonlinear synapses). Section 7.3 summarizes the topics covered and also gives the pros and cons.

The lack of adequate attention to the need for structural training may account for some of the problems encountered in designing artificial neural systems to mimic the performance of biological neural systems in the areas of cognition, thought, and language. The problems largely follow from the belief that the capabilities of a biological neural network can be captured by a relatively simple structure as long as a large number of learned connection weights are permitted in the ANN. Winograd and Flores refute that belief and underscore the importance of structure in modeling sensory functions:

> Work over the years in neuroanatomy and neurophysiology has demonstrated that living organisms do not fit this image. Even an organism as small as a worm with a few hundred neurons is highly structured, and much of its behavior is the result of built-in structure, not learning. [420]

A living system has an evolving structure that is shaped by interactions. Structural coupling is the basis for changes in an individual during its lifetime through learning and also through reproduction or evolution. The structural change of a living or autopoietic system takes place through continuous production and destruction of its components (cells, synaptic connections, etc.). When this process is interrupted, the system disintegrates or dies. The contents of this chapter are motivated by this biological process of change. Both growth and shrinkage of structures are part of structural adaptation.

7.1   GROWTH ALGORITHMS

There is a class of learning algorithms that grow a multilayer feedforward network to classify any linearly nonseparable clusters of patterns [116, 225, 226, 244, 257, 424]. These algorithms are used to learn the graph and the connection weights of the network simultaneously. Convergence to the correct classification is guaranteed in a finite number of steps. In fact, the algorithms are able to grow a network of layered TLUs with specified nodes, connections, and weights to solve any linearly separable or not linearly separable classification problem. The algorithms are fast and overcome the problems of nonconvergence (or slow convergence) and local minima that may be associated with the backpropagation type of algorithms. A key difficulty with growth algorithms, however, is that an overly large network may be grown, leading to poor generalization. In the worst case, a single neuron may be added for a single exemplar, though most growth algorithms make some attempts to prevent this from happening.

Growth algorithms are consistent with and can be considered as implementations of a proposal by Valiant [382]. In this seminal work on a theory of the learnable, Valiant concluded that because the class of learnable concepts is severely limited, the only way of teaching more complicated concepts is to build them up from simple, learnable ones. This conclusion suggests a decomposition of the learning process and supports the principle of problem decomposition and subgoaling for neural networks, proposed by Liang [225]. On the basis of Valiant's work [382] and of results on the complexity of the problem of loading, Baum [33] proposed the development of algorithms with the freedom to recruit new units into the network as it evolves to classify training exemplars correctly.

The principle of problem decomposition and subgoaling has played a key role in the success of the symbolic artificial intelligence paradigm. This general principle is applicable to the design of neural networks and learning algorithms. Based on this principle, a problem should be decomposed into subgoals so that each subgoal can be learned quickly using a subnetwork with a known graph. The overall network is built up from these simpler subnetworks, and it achieves the global goal by putting together all the subgoals learnable by the subnetworks. Three types of decompositions are identified [225]: serial subgoal decomposition, parallel subgoal decomposition, and diameter-limited subgoal decomposition. The strategy of dividing into smaller networks is also consistent with Hebb's idea of using many small *cell assemblies* to realize intelligence [152]. Within each cell assembly, the units should be tightly coupled or highly connected. Units in different assemblies are only loosely coupled or sparsely connected.

The basic strategy applied to all growth algorithms is one of *divide and conquer.* One starts with a single TLU. If the training set, no matter whether it is linearly separable or not, cannot be learned in a given time (e.g., in a time that is a polynomial function in the dimension of the input) by the TLU, divide the original training set into two smaller subsets and test to see whether each subset may be learned separately with an additional TLU. If a subset still cannot be learned within a specified time, divide it up again. Eventually, in the worst case, a subset contains only two exemplars, each belonging to a different class. A TLU can always separate two exemplars.

Note that if the training patterns are binary, then a single hyperplane can always separate any particular pattern from all the remaining patterns. The reason is that each binary pattern is representable as a vertex of a hypercube, and any one vertex of a hypercube is separable from the remaining vertices by a hyperplane. The connection weights from the input layer to a single TLU, together with its threshold, may be trained by applying a perceptron learning algorithm. However, complications may arise in the case of analog patterns. For example, a pattern belonging to one class cannot be separated by a single hyperplane from the other class if it is enclosed by patterns belonging to the other class. For digital patterns, pathological cases (for instance, a pattern that occurs in two different classes because of poorly collected or stored data) will not permit separation, either linearly by hyperplanes or nonlinearly by more complicated decision surfaces.

Almost all growth algorithms discussed in this chapter use either the *pocket algorithm* [123], which is a simple extension of the perceptron algorithm, or its variant. When the exemplars are not linearly separable, the standard perceptron algorithm seems to wander through the weight space. The weight vector may fall in the region in weight space that yields the fewest errors most of the time, although it may repeatedly jump back and forth between other weight vectors. The pocket algorithm stores ("puts in the pocket") the weight vector that yields the fewest errors when it cycles through the training set once. The algorithm stops after cycling through the training set a given number of times. After the algorithm stops, the weight vector stored is the one that gives the fewest errors up to that time. When the exemplars are picked randomly rather than cycled, the pocket algorithm stores the weight vector that has survived the longest without modification. In either case, the stored weight vector will be the one that gives the minimum possible number of errors, with a probability approaching unity as the training time increases. Unfortunately, as in the analysis of convergence of the perceptron algorithm, no bound is available on the training time required to find such a weight vector, which is not necessarily the one that minimizes the mean squared error.

The pocket algorithm may improve the generalization capability of the network grown or, equivalently, reduce the size of the network. Any perceptron correction rule may be used without affecting the convergence of the growth algorithms. Four growth algorithms are discussed in this section. The upstart algorithm [116] and the divide-and-conquer algorithm [225, 226] are presented in detail because they not only are simple but also best illustrate the basic idea.

7.1.1 The Upstart Algorithm

Denote the ith TLU by u_i and the response of u_i to an input exemplar j by y_i^j. For the sake of convenience, let the index $i = 0$ be associated with the initial TLU. Denote the desired or target response of u_i to input exemplar j by t_i^j. The unipolar TLU output is either 0 or 1. These are referred to as the OFF and ON states, respectively. The use of a unipolar TLU is crucial for the algorithm to work, as will become obvious in the discussion of the algorithm.

The algorithm starts with a single TLU, u_0. After training for a given amount of time using a perceptron-type algorithm (e.g., the pocket algorithm applied to the entire training set), u_0 may be linked to two kinds of errors:

$$\text{wrongly ON} \qquad y_0^j = 1, \qquad \text{but } t_0^j = 0$$

$$\text{wrongly OFF} \qquad y_0^j = 0, \qquad \text{but } t_0^j = 1.$$

Another TLU, which is ON only for exemplars that wrongly turn u_0 ON, can be used to correct the wrongly ON errors. This TLU is labeled u_{1n}. The connection strength from u_{1n} to u_0 is assigned a large negative value. Then u_{1n} will send a large inhibitory or negative signal to u_0 so that it will be OFF. The TLU u_{1n} should not be ON when u_0 is correctly ON. Otherwise, the large negative signal may turn u_0 wrongly OFF. Nor should u_{1n} be ON when u_0 is wrongly OFF, because the negative signal will further inhibit u_0. Exemplars that correctly turn u_0 OFF should be removed from the training set for u_{1n}, because neither the absence of signal (u_{1n} OFF) nor a large negative signal (u_{1n} ON) from u_{1n} will change the state of u_0 in this case. Similarly, to correct the wrongly OFF errors, a TLU can be used that is ON only for exemplars that wrongly turn u_0 OFF. Call this TLU u_{1p}. The connection strength from u_{1p} to u_0 is assigned a large positive value; then u_{1p} will send a large positive signal to u_0 so that it will be ON. Obviously, u_{1p} should output zero for all other exemplars. As in the u_{1n} case, exemplars that correctly turn u_0 ON could be removed from the training set for u_{1p}. The TLUs u_{1n} and u_{1p} are called the *daughter* units for the *parent* unit u_0. The graph of a network grown by the algorithm is illustrated in Fig. 7.1. Each daughter unit is then trained to respond as just described. If u_{1p} and u_{1n} cannot achieve this within a given time, they act as new parent units and enlist new daughter units to correct their errors. The graph of the network constructed by the upstart algorithm is a binary tree with shortcuts; i.e., all units are directly

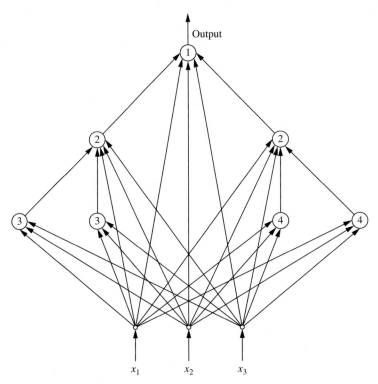

FIGURE 7.1
A network grown by the upstart algorithm; the integers in the TLUs indicate the order in which growth takes place.

connected to the inputs. Each time, a daughter unit is trained to be in the ON state for a smaller subset of exemplars. Eventually, in the worst case, a daughter unit is trained to be ON for only one exemplar. A TLU can always be trained to respond to any single binary exemplar. Consequently, the algorithm always converges.

Frean [116] uses a modified perceptron algorithm instead of the pocket algorithm to train the TLUs. The algorithm is derived by changing the parameter c in the perceptron fixed-increment rule to

$$\frac{T}{T_0} \exp\left(\frac{-|\eta^i|}{T}\right). \tag{7.1}$$

This factor decreases with $|\eta^i|$, which measures how serious the error is for exemplar i. The rationale is that an error whose $|\eta^i|$ is large is difficult to correct without causing other errors. Therefore, that error should be weighted less significantly than those with small $|\eta^i|$. The *temperature* parameter T controls how strongly this weighting is biased toward small $|\eta^i|$. During training T is reduced linearly from T_0 to close to zero. At high T, the fixed-increment rule is recovered, but as T decreases, the weights are *frozen*. In ref. [116], T_0 was set to 1, and 1000 passes were made through the training set. The algorithm was tested on the parity function and the random mapping function. The parity functions for input dimension $n = 3$ to $n = 10$ were tried. In all cases, a network with n total TLUs was produced. Results for higher dimensions were not reported.

7.1.2 Learning by Divide and Conquer

We demonstrate in this section the development of a growth algorithm based on the simple idea of divide and conquer [225, 226]. The network grown is a layered network having either one or two hidden layers expanding widthwise only. In this algorithm, weights of connections to the first and second hidden layers and to the output unit are simultaneously learned using a perceptron-type algorithm. Weights of connections to the second hidden layer and to the output unit are either 1 or -1. The partition of the pattern space learned by this algorithm has a simple geometric interpretation—each unit at the second hidden layer represents a hyperregion, with units at the first layers specifying the hyperplane boundaries of the region.

Given two arbitrary, linearly nonseparable classes of training exemplars X and Y, the global goal is to classify input patterns correctly as belonging to one of the classes. Because the two classes are not linearly separable, no single straight line or hyperplane can separate them. However, a straight line or hyperplane can divide the training patterns into two subsets although each subset may contain exemplars from both classes. If a correct classification cannot be found in N steps, we consider it unlearnable using a single TLU, where N is a positive integer that is polynomial in the dimension of the input pattern vectors. Then the single TLU is required only to separate the training patterns into two subsets (note that how a set is divided into subsets may affect the size of the network built and its generalization capability). The next task becomes that of using a TLU to classify each of the two subsets created.

This process continues until all the subsets become linearly separable. This goal can always be achieved eventually, because when a subset has only two patterns, each belonging to a different class, it is linearly separable. In practical applications linear separability usually occurs earlier, with more than two patterns in a subset. This suggests a decomposition of the learning task. Learning the global goal of classifying all the training exemplars can be decomposed into tasks of learning simpler and learnable subgoals. These subgoals are the results of division of the training set into subsets. Once all subsets become linearly separable, the learning of the classifications of the subsets is easily completed. Each time, a TLU is used to divide a set or a subset into two subsets. These TLUs form the first hidden layer of the network. TLUs at the second hidden layer pick out those subsets that belong to X. A single TLU is used at the output layer. It outputs 1 when any one of the TLUs in the second layer outputs 1. An output of 1 from the overall network therefore indicates that the pattern belongs to X. This is the standard divide-and-conquer strategy that has proven itself time and again in science, engineering, everyday life, politics, war, and so on.

Depending on the perceptron algorithm used, the divide-and-conquer strategy may excessively subdivide the pattern space, leading to poor generalization. It may be possible to introduce a merging stage afterward that will group adjacent regions to reduce redundancy. Thus, the algorithm consists of two stages: splitting and merging. The first is splitting, which decomposes the task so that the smaller tasks become learnable in an acceptable amount of time. The second step, merging, removes redundancy in order to reduce the size of the network and, one hopes, to realize a better generalization. To be useful, the merging stage should be achievable in polynomial time in the dimension of the input. This goal may not always be possible. How the merging stage can be efficiently implemented is likely to be based on heuristics and is an open problem; a possible direction is suggested later in this section. The multilayer networks created by the splitting stage has a structure as shown in Fig. 7.2. Following is the pseudocode of the splitting stage of the algorithm.

THE DIVIDE-AND-CONQUER ALGORITHM.

1. Let L be the list of sets to be classified, $\mathbf{W}^{(1)}$ be the list of first-layer weight vectors, and $\mathbf{W}^{(2)}$ be the list of second-layer weight vectors associated with the sets in L. Initially, let $L = ((X \cup Y))$, $\mathbf{W}^{(1)} = ()$ = a list that is initially empty, and $\mathbf{W}^{(2)} = (())$, a list containing one empty list. Associate the empty list, which may be viewed as a zero-dimensional null vector, in $\mathbf{W}^{(2)}$ with the set $(X \cup Y)$ in L.
2. Go to step 4 if L is empty; otherwise, go to step 3.
3. Let A_i = first element of list L; call $DIVIDE(A_i, L, \mathbf{W}^{(1)}, \mathbf{W}^{(2)})$; go to step 2.
4. Growth of the network is represented by the growth of $\mathbf{W}^{(1)}$ and $\mathbf{W}^{(2)}$. $\mathbf{W}^{(1)}$ and $\mathbf{W}^{(2)}$ grow from empty lists to lists of connections and weights specifying a three-layer network correctly classifying the two linearly nonseparable classes.
   a. *First hidden layer.* Each weight vector $\mathbf{w}_k$ in $\mathbf{W}^{(1)}$ specifies the connection weights and threshold of a single TLU at the first layer. The inputs to the TLU are the training exemplars. The weights of the connections are simply the first

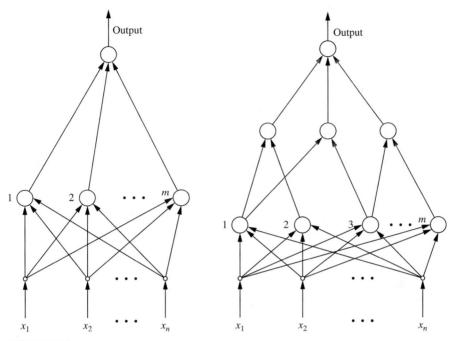

FIGURE 7.2
Two types of networks constructed by the divide-and-conquer algorithm.

n components of $\mathbf{w}_k$. The threshold of the TLU is the negative of the $(n + 1)$st component of $\mathbf{w}_k$. The output of the kth TLU at the first layer is 1 when $\mathbf{w}_k^T \mathbf{x} \triangleq \mathbf{w}_k \cdot \mathbf{x} \geq 0$, and -1 otherwise.

b. *Second hidden layer.* Each weight vector $\mathbf{w}_i^{(2)}$ in $\mathbf{W}^{(2)}$ specifies the connection weights and threshold of a single TLU at the second layer. The inputs to the TLU are the outputs of the first-layer TLUs specified by the pointers associated with each component of $\mathbf{w}_i^{(2)}$. The weights of the connections are simply the corresponding components of $\mathbf{w}_i^{(2)}$. The threshold of the ith TLU is $\|\mathbf{w}_i^{(2)}\|^2$. The output of the ith TLU at the second layer is 1 when $\mathbf{w}_i^{(2)} \cdot \mathbf{x} \geq \|\mathbf{w}_i^{(2)}\|^2$, and 0 otherwise.

c. *Output layer.* The single TLU at the third layer takes as its inputs all the outputs of the second-layer TLUs. The weights are all equal to 1. The threshold of the third-layer TLU is also 1. If $\mathbf{x} \in X$, the final output is 1; otherwise, it is 0 or -1 depending on the choice of the transfer characteristic of the third-layer TLU.

Procedure *DIVIDE*$(A_i, \; L, \; \mathbf{W}^{(1)}, \; \mathbf{W}^{(2)})$.

1. Add a TLU U_k with an arbitrary initial weight vector $\mathbf{w}_{k0}$.
   a. Apply the pocket algorithm for N iterations, using A_i as the training set, where N is a positive number that is polynomial in the dimension of the training

patterns. If a solution is found such that $\mathbf{w}_k^T\mathbf{x} \geq 0 \; \forall\mathbf{x}(\mathbf{x} \in A_i \wedge \mathbf{x} \in X)$ and $\mathbf{w}_k^T\mathbf{x} < 0 \; \forall\mathbf{x}(\mathbf{x} \in A_i \wedge \mathbf{x} \in Y)$ before or on the Nth iteration, then append $\mathbf{w}_k$ to the list of first-layer weight vectors $\mathbf{W}^{(1)}$, call $CONQUER(A_i, \mathbf{w}_i^{(2)}, \mathbf{w}_k)$, and go to step 2.

  b. Otherwise, after N iterations,

    i. If the hyperplane $\mathbf{w}_k^T\mathbf{x} = 0$ divides A_i into two subsets regardless of membership, append $\mathbf{w}_k$ to the list of first-layer weight vectors $\mathbf{W}^{(1)}$, and go to step 2.

    ii. Otherwise, apply the pocket algorithm. When the hyperplane $\mathbf{w}_k^T\mathbf{x} = 0$ divides A_i into two subsets, append $\mathbf{w}_k$ to the list of first-layer weight vectors $\mathbf{W}^{(1)}$, and go to step 2.

2. For each set A_m in the list of sets L, do the following:

  a. If $\mathbf{w}_k^T\mathbf{x} \geq 0$ or $\mathbf{w}_k^T\mathbf{x} < 0$ for all $\mathbf{x} \in A_m$, keep A_m in L unchanged.

  b. If A_m is divided into two subsets A_{m1} and A_{m2} by the hyperplane $\mathbf{w}_k^T\mathbf{x} = 0$, then append the new subsets A_{mj} to the list L of sets to be classified and do

    i. If a subset A_{mj} of A_m contains only patterns of one class, then

      A. If $\mathbf{x} \in Y$ for all $\mathbf{x} \in A_{mj}$, then remove A_{mj}.

      B. If $\mathbf{x} \in X$ for all $\mathbf{x} \in A_{mj}$, then append $\mathbf{w}_{mj}^{(2)} = \mathbf{w}_m^{(2)}$ to the list $\mathbf{W}^{(2)}$, where $\mathbf{w}_m^{(2)}$ is the second-layer weight vector associated with A_m, and call $CONQUER(A_{mj}, \mathbf{w}_{mj}^{(2)}, \mathbf{w}_k)$. Recall that the list $\mathbf{W}^{(2)}$ is initially a list containing a zero-dimensional null vector.

    ii. If the subset A_{mj} contains patterns from both X and Y, then do

      A. Associate with A_{mj} a new weight vector $\mathbf{w}_{mj}^{(2)} = (\mathbf{w}_m^{(2)} \; a_j)$, where $a_j = 1$ if all the patterns in A_{mj} lie on the positive side of the hyperplane (i.e., $\mathbf{w}_k^T\mathbf{x} \geq 0$ for any one $\mathbf{x} \in A_{mj}$); otherwise, $a_j = -1$. Note that the sign of a_j can be determined by testing the sign of $\mathbf{w}_k^T\mathbf{x}$ using any single pattern from A_{mj}.

      B. Associate with a_j a pointer pointing to the weight vector $\mathbf{w}_k$ of the first-layer TLU U_k.

      C. Append the new weight vector $\mathbf{w}_{mj}^{(2)}$ to the list $\mathbf{W}^{(2)}$.

    iii. Remove $\mathbf{w}_m^{(2)}$ from the list $\mathbf{W}^{(2)}$ after A_{m1} and A_{m2} have *both* been processed and also remove A_m from L.

3. Return.

Procedure $CONQUER(A_i, \mathbf{w}_i^{(2)}, \mathbf{w}_k)$.

1. Remove A_i from the list of sets L.
2. Append a_i to the end of $\mathbf{w}_i^{(2)}$; that is, let $\mathbf{w}_i^{(2)} = (\mathbf{w}_i^{(2)} \; a_i)$, where $a_i = 1$ if $\mathbf{w}_k^T\mathbf{x} \geq 0$ for all $\mathbf{x}(\mathbf{x} \in A_i \wedge \mathbf{x} \in X)$, otherwise $a_i = -1$.
3. Associate with a_i a pointer that points to the weight vector $\mathbf{w}_k$ in the first-layer TLU U_k.
4. Return.

The graph of the network constructed is generally a layered graph with two hidden layers. The algorithm may stop at the first hidden layer if all the members of one class of exemplars are contained in a single hyperregion bounded by the hyper-planes represented by the first-layer TLUs. The graphs of the two types of networks constructed by the algorithm are shown in Fig. 7.2. An example of the partitioned hyperregions generated by the algorithm is shown in Fig. 7.3.

In Step 1*a* of *DIVIDE,* the Widrow-Hoff LMS algorithm or a perceptron er-ror correction rule may be used as well. The pocket algorithm may give a parti-tion that requires a smaller number of units in the final network, but this result is not guaranteed. From the description of the algorithm, it may appear that a record has to be kept of which exemplar belongs to which subset. This is not necessary because it can be decided from the first-layer TLUs already built in $\mathbf{W}^{(1)}$. When-ever training using exemplars belonging to one subset is needed, a procedure can be called to decide if a pattern belongs to the current subset. The decision is made simply from the outputs of TLUs already in $\mathbf{W}^{(1)}$. It is easy to prove the following theorem.

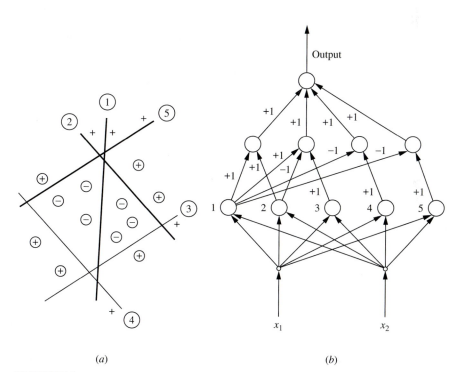

(a)   (b)

FIGURE 7.3
An example of the hyperregions partitioned by the divide-and-conquer algorithm: (*a*) The nu-merical labels for the hyperplane indicate the order in which the hyperplanes are generated. The + sign near the numerical labels indicates the positive half-space for that hyperplane; (*b*) the network implementing the partition in (*a*). The TLUs are assigned the same labels as the hyperplanes. The network output is 1 for an input exemplar labeled with a ⊕.

Theorem 7.1. Given any two classes of training exemplars, X and Y, that are finite and either linearly separable or nonlinearly separable, the foregoing divide-and-conquer algorithm always converges in a finite number of steps to the correct classification of the training patterns.

The network just described yields the correct classification, but it may have redundant hidden units at both layers and redundant connections from the first hidden layer to the second one. This redundancy partitions the pattern space into small hyperregions, which produce an overly large layered network, and usually leads to poor generalization. This problem may be overcome by a merging step that should merge adjacent small hyperregions belonging to the same class into a single region. Thus, the number of units at the second hidden layer may be reduced. Redundant connections from the first hidden layer to remaining units at the second hidden layer should be removed. Units at the first hidden layer that do not connect to any units at the second hidden layer could be removed. If, after merging, there is only one unit left at the second hidden layer, that unit becomes the output unit and the resulting network has only one hidden layer instead of two. The result of merging the partitions given in Fig. 7.3 and the corresponding simplified network are shown in Fig. 7.4. A possible way of merging is to treat all the connection weight vectors from the first hidden layer to the second hidden layer as conjunction terms in a Boolean function. This Boolean function should then be minimized under certain constraints and using

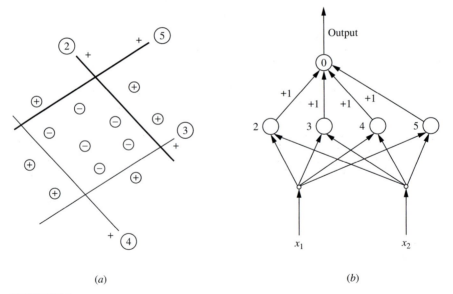

(a)   (b)

FIGURE 7.4
(a) The result of merging the hyperregions in Fig. 7.3; (b) the network for the merged partitions shown in (a).

some heuristics. This merging step may be possible as a result of the following two features:

1. The weights of connections from the first hidden layer to the second hidden layer are binary-valued. These values are either $+1$ or -1.
2. Each one of these weight vectors corresponds to a hyperregion bounded by the hyperplanes. A $+1$ indicates that the hyperregion lies on the positive side of the corresponding hyperplane, and a -1 indicates that the hyperregion lies on the negative side of the corresponding hyperplane. Because of this simple geometric interpretation, the first hidden layer may be called the *hyperplane layer*, and the second hidden layer may be called the *hyperregion layer*. For example, the two weight vectors $(+1, -1, +1)$ and $(-1, -1, +1)$ indicate that the hyperregion is really only bounded by the second and third hyperplanes. The first hyperplane should be removed.

As commented earlier, the development of an effective and efficient merging algorithm is an open problem. Algorithms that penalize the complexity of the network during learning [275, 399] or prune the network after learning [216, 398], as discussed in Chapter 6, may provide useful ideas for development of the merging algorithm. This possibility will be considered further at the conclusion of this chapter.

7.1.3   Other Growth Algorithms

The two algorithms just presented well illustrate the common idea behind growth algorithms. Based on this idea, many variants of the growth algorithms can be designed. Two other growth algorithms are described next.

The *tiling algorithm* [257] grows a multilayered network as shown in Fig. 7.5. The algorithm starts with a single TLU, called the *master unit*. This master unit is trained using the pocket algorithm. After that, if there are exemplars incorrectly classified by the master unit, a TLU is introduced for each of the two subsets that contain exemplars from both classes. Such a TLU, called an *ancillary unit,* is trained using the pocket algorithm to separate a subset containing exemplars from both classes into subsets each having members from only one class. If an ancillary unit is unable to separate exemplars correctly into subsets of only single-class exemplars, these smaller subsets are again used to train additional ancillary units. This process is continued until at this layer each image pattern of the patterns in the layer below is associated with a unique target output; i.e., no two input patterns belonging to distinct classes will give rise to the same image pattern at this layer. This feature is called a *faithful representation.* Then a TLU is introduced at the next layer that takes for its input the image patterns in the current layer of TLUs. This unit becomes the master unit for the new layer. This process is then repeated in the new layer. Ultimately, the process will converge, because the number of units (master plus ancillary) decreases after each layer, as shown in Fig. 7.5. Eventually, the master unit at a new layer produces the correct output for each input pattern. Each layer has a bias unit

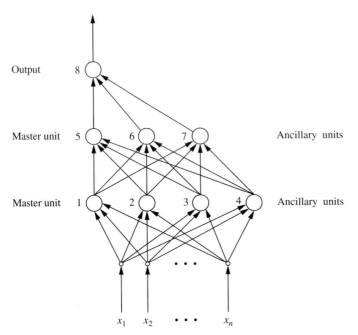

Output 8

Master unit 5   6   7   Ancillary units

Master unit 1   2   3   4   Ancillary units

x_1 x_2 $\cdots$ x_n

FIGURE 7.5
A network constructed by the tiling algorithm. The numbers in the units
indicate the ordering associated with the units being added. The network
starts with the unit labeled 1. The smallest number in each layer is associated
with the master unit for that layer, whose remaining units are the ancillary
units.

that is clamped to the $+1$ state. Denote the state of this bias unit at layer L (where
L denotes the number of layers above the layer of inputs) by y_{L0}. The output of the
master unit at layer L is denoted by y_{L1}. Outputs of the ancillary units are y_{Lk}, where
$k = 2, 3, \ldots, N_L$. An image pattern vector at layer L consisting of these components
is then denoted as $\mathbf{y}_L$. To prove that the number of units decreases after each layer,
it is sufficient to show that connection weights exist from layer L to the master unit
at layer $L + 1$ that enable it to correctly classify at least one more pattern than the
master unit at layer L. Let $\mathbf{y}_L^i = [y_{L1}^i \ y_{L2}^i \cdots y_{LN_L}^i]$ be the image patterns at layer L.
Each $\mathbf{y}_L^i$ is the image pattern of a certain number P_i of input patterns that have the
same desired output. Denote the desired bipolar binary output of $\mathbf{y}_L^i$ as d^i. The master
unit at layer $L + 1$ is connected to all the $N_L + 1$ units at layer L by a weight vector

$$\mathbf{w} = (w_{L0} \ w_{L1} \cdots w_{LN_L})^{\text{T}}.$$

Obviously, the weight vector with

$$w_{L1} = 1 \quad \text{and} \quad w_{Lj} = 0 \quad \text{for } j \neq 1$$

would produce a master unit at layer $L + 1$ that functions exactly the same as the
master unit at layer L. Assume that we want to correctly classify all the patterns the

master unit at layer L does plus an additional pattern whose image at layer L is $\mathbf{y}_L^{io}$. Since the pattern is wrongly classified at layer L, we have

$$y_{L1}^{io} = -d^{io}.$$

The existence of this solution can be shown with the following weight assignments:

$$w_{Lj} = \begin{cases} 1 & \text{if } j = 1 \\ \alpha d^{io} y_{Lj}^{io} & \text{otherwise}, \end{cases} \tag{7.2}$$

where

$$\frac{1}{N_L} < \alpha < \frac{1}{N_L - 2}. \tag{7.3}$$

Assume that the output of the TLU used in the network is from the set $\{-1, +1\}$. For the additional pattern to be correctly classified, the output of the master unit at layer $L + 1$ with the preceding weights is

$$y_{(L+1)1} = \text{sgn}\left(-d^{io} + \alpha d^{io} \sum_{j \neq 1} (y_{Lj}^{io})^2\right) = \text{sgn}(-d^{io} + \alpha d^{io} N_L) = d^{io}, \tag{7.4}$$

where "sgn" denotes the signum (sign) function. The $T_b(\cdot)$ function introduced in Eq. (4.2) could have also been used here instead of the signum function. The last step is because $\alpha N_L > 1$ from Eq. (7.3). This result shows that the additional pattern is now correctly classified by the master unit at layer $L + 1$.

We also need to make sure that patterns already correctly classified by the master unit at layer L are not upset. For a pattern already correctly classified at layer L, we have

$$y_{(L+1)1} = \text{sgn}\left(d^i + \alpha d^{io} \sum_{j \neq 1} y_{Lj}^{io} y_{Lj}^i\right) = \text{sgn}\left(d^i\left(1 + \alpha d^{io} d^i \sum_{j \neq 1} y_{Lj}^{io} y_{Lj}^i\right)\right). \tag{7.5}$$

We would like to have

$$y_{(L+1)1} = \text{sgn}(d^i).$$

This need is satisfied by

$$\left(1 + \alpha d^{io} d^i \sum_{j \neq 1} y_{Lj}^{io} y_{Lj}^i\right) > 0.$$

In the worst case,

$$D = d^{io} d^i \sum_{j \neq 1} y_{Lj}^{io} y_{Lj}^i$$

may be $-N_L$. For this to happen, there are two possibilities. One of these is for the case

$$d^i = -d^{io} \quad \text{and} \quad y_{Lj}^i = y_{Lj}^{io} \quad \text{for } j \neq 1.$$

Since

$$y^i_{L1} = d^i \quad \text{and} \quad y^{io}_{L1} = -d^{io},$$

therefore

$$y^{io}_{L1} = y^i_{L1}.$$

In that case,

$$y^{io}_{Lj} = y^i_{Lj}$$

for all j. This equation means that the two patterns with different desired output have the same image pattern. That cannot happen, because the image patterns at layer L have a faithful representation. The other possibility is for the case

$$d^i = d^{io} \quad \text{and} \quad y^i_{Lj} = -y^{io}_{Lj} \quad \text{for } j \neq 1.$$

That cannot happen either, because for the bias unit it leads to the contradiction,

$$1 = y^i_{L0} = -y^{io}_{L0} = -1.$$

The least positive value that can be attained by D is actually $N_L - 2$. This can be seen by considering the two cases separately. For example, when $d^i = -d^{io}$, at least for one ancillary unit,

$$y^i_{Lj} = -y^{io}_{Lj}.$$

Therefore, there are at most $N_L - 1$ positive terms and at least one negative term in the summation, and $(N_L - 1) - 1 = N_L - 2$. Therefore, by choosing α according to Eq. (7.3), it is guaranteed that patterns already correctly classified by the master unit at layer L are also correctly classified by the master unit at layer $L + 1$ using the foregoing weight choice.

In summary, the master unit at layer $L + 1$ correctly classifies at least one more pattern than the master unit at layer L. Thus, the tiling algorithm converges. Note that the actual weights found by the pocket algorithm may not be those in Eq. (7.2). The tiling algorithm increases both the width and the depth (number of layers) of a network in the growth. Both the tiling algorithm and the upstart algorithm may grow a multilayer network with more than three layers. A multilayer network can always be translated into a three-layer network [351].

Marchand et al. [244] proposed an algorithm that grows a two-layer network, as shown in Fig. 7.6. The strategy of divide and conquer using one TLU in the hidden layer to separate a set of patterns belonging to one class is applied again. These authors showed that the image patterns are guaranteed to be linearly separable. Therefore, one TLU at the output will be able to learn the correct classification. Based on the growth algorithms discussed, variations were proposed that construct a neural network decision tree. Interested readers are referred to refs. [135, 351, 355].

Another neural network that determines its own size and topology is the cascade correlation (CC) network [147]. Training starts only with connections between the input and output layers of nodes. Then, as is necessary, hidden nodes are added,

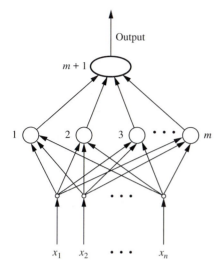

FIGURE 7.6
A network constructed by the growth algorithm of Marchand et al. [244]. The numbers indicate the ordering during the process of growth.

one at a time. The number of such nodes depends on the error bound set in the network, which employs supervised learning. The first hidden unit is connected only to the layer of inputs and trained using a type of gradient descent. After training for the input connections to this unit with its output deactivated, the interconnection weights are frozen, and then this node, along with all the input nodes, is connected to the output layer. The output weights are then trained, and the process is continued until the performance is satisfactory. Each new hidden node receives the network inputs plus the outputs from all previous hidden nodes. This process produces a cascade of hidden nodes between the input layer and the output layer. The graph of a CC network having four input nodes, two hidden nodes, and one output node is shown in Fig. 7.7. Note that the graph is not a layered graph. The size of the neural network, in terms of the total number of neurons and also the number of connections, is grown, and the training time is claimed to be fast. To offset the disadvantages of unbounded fan-in of the hidden and output units as more hidden units are added, irregularity of connections, and the propagation delay caused by the longest path through the network, some modifications in the original CC network have been suggested.[1] But the overall performance is expected to be inferior to other variable-structure networks such as the one based on VoD or Delaunay tessellations (DT). The latter is becoming especially attractive because of the emergence of fast neural network–based procedures for constructing Delaunay tessellations [126]. Algorithms for constructing the DT and the VoD in rectilinear metric by adding one planar site at a time have recently

---

[1]D.S. Phatak and I. Koren. Connectivity and performance tradeoffs in the cascade correlation learning architecture. *IEEE Trans. Neural Networks*, 5: 930–935, 1994.

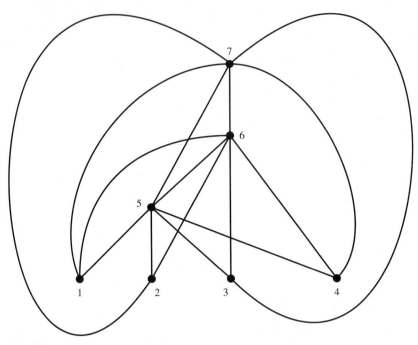

FIGURE 7.7
Graph showing connections in cascade correlation network having four input nodes, two hidden nodes, and one output node. Nodes 1, 2, 3, and 4 are the input nodes, and node 7 is the output node.

been reported [290]. Advantages of working with rectilinear metric include the connection weight values, which are either $+1$, 0 (no connection), or -1. The disadvantage is that three times the number of neurons required when using the Euclidean metric may be needed in the worst case, because the bisector of two arbitrary points in the plane can have up to three segments in the rectilinear metric.

7.2 NETWORKS WITH NONLINEAR SYNAPSES AND NONLINEAR SYNAPTIC CONTACTS

Growth algorithms may lead to an overly large network that may achieve poor generalization. In this section, an alternative to the growth algorithms is presented. Instead of growing more units and connections, the proposed new model grows more nonlinearities at the synapses. The new model has some flexibility in function representation, as in the growth algorithms, but at the same time it offers some control on the generalization capability of the network.

The focus of this section is on learning desired nonlinear transfer characteristics of synapses and on computational models of nonlinear synapses. Actually, in analog implementations it is often quite a chore to make the synapses linear, because of the inherent nonlinearity in the circuit elements. For example, Salam [332] used the nonlinear current-voltage characteristics between the drain-source current I_{ds} and the gate, drain, and source voltages V_g, V_d, V_s, respectively, of a single MOSFET (metal-oxide-semiconductor field-effect transistor) to implement a nonlinear synapse. The substrate of the MOSFET is connected to ground. The current I_{ds} is approximately a quadratic function of the gate voltage V_g in saturation mode and is reduced to a linear function of V_g in the so-called triode mode. The floating-gate nonvolatile memory technology for MOSFET has been a popular way for realizing adjustable weights in analog implementations of neural networks [103, 161, 217]. Construction of a neural chip with a complexity of 100K synapses has been demonstrated using one-megabit static-RAM fabrication technologies [217]. However, the nonlinearity of the synapses in analog implementations is often viewed as an imperfection. Examples of purposeful use of the inherent nonlinearity in analog implementation of synapses include the work on an analog multilayer feedforward network with nonlinear synapses [238] and the nonlinear-synapse Hopfield network [332].

With the foregoing exceptions of nonlinear analog synapses, many models currently used in neural network studies and electronic implementations make some or all of the following three simplifying assumptions.

1. The interaction of all postsynaptic signals is a simple summation in a latent period.
2. A synapse only *linearly* amplifies or attenuates the presynaptic signal. This feature is modeled by a connection weight that multiplies the presynaptic signal to produce the postsynaptic signal.
3. There is only one synaptic contact between two neurons.

These models are results of further simplifications of the McCulloch-Pitts model [250], which was introduced in Section 1.3. Because of these simplifications, all the nonlinearity necessary to achieve a desired transformation is restricted to the thresholds or activation functions of the neurons. Neurophysiological data show that the assumptions just listed are not true in a biological neural network; e.g., see Chapter 1 and refs. [63, 352]. In such networks the interaction between postsynaptic signals is more complicated than a simple summation. Several synapses may come into contact before acting on a neuron, as with the presynaptic inhibitive synapses. The transformation between the presynaptic and postsynaptic signals is not linear in a biological synapse. It is known that the transfer characteristic of a biological synapse may be better modeled by a nonlinear transformation than by a simple multiplication. A neuron may also have more than one synaptic contact with another neuron. However, because of the first two assumptions, such multiple synaptic connections are assumed to be modeled by a single connection weight. These disagreements between linear-synapse neural network models and biological neural networks prompted us to investigate nonlinear synaptic contacts and the effects of multiple synaptic connections between two neurons.

Several models that remove some of the foregoing simplifying assumptions have been reported. The *sigma-pi units* [324] and the *product units* [101] allow multiplication of synaptic signals. The product units require both the coefficients and the exponents of a product term to be learned. The product term is in the form of a polynomial, except that the exponents may be not only integers but also other real numbers. This type of term is referred to as a *quasi-polynomial term*. A special case of the sigma-pi units, called high-order neural networks, is investigated in ref. [132]. The high-order networks use sigma-pi units only at the input layer. Encouraging results are reported for these models. These models can be further generalized along the following lines.

1. The synaptic transfer characteristic in these models still provides only a linear amplification.
2. The nonlinear terms in the high-order, sigma-pi, and product unit networks must be *handcrafted* in the network using a priori knowledge before learning. Although this step is not necessarily a disadvantage, because embedding a priori knowledge may alleviate the load of the learning algorithm, it is still desirable to have a network that is able to learn nonlinear synaptic transformations and to determine by learning the number and type of nonlinear terms when there is no a priori knowledge available.
3. The number of learnable parameters is fixed in the sigma-pi units, product units, and most other high-order network models (except the growth networks discussed earlier). Again, this feature is not a disadvantage if a priori knowledge is available to choose the right number of learnable parameters. The number of learnable parameters should be kept minimal to ensure good generalization [35], which was also discussed in Chapter 6. However, when there is no a priori knowledge available, it is desirable to have a network that will gradually increase its total number of learnable parameters, subject to hardware constraint, if the training examples cannot be successfully loaded with a given number of learnable parameters.

One criticism to the introduction of a greater number of nonlinearities in a network is that the network complexity increases, making analysis and synthesis tasks more difficult. In general, one can always improve a fit to data by making a model more complex, and this may not be worth the price of throwing away elegance [101]. Durbin and Rumelhart defended their product units model [101] as being a natural extension of the simpler models. Nonlinear synapses and nonlinear synaptic contacts, in addition to being natural extensions toward more realistic models, may offer advantages both in improved learning behavior and in hardware implementation. A network with nonlinear synapses and nonlinear synaptic contacts is an alternative to linear-synapse networks with many neurons and connections for realizing highly nonlinear functions. This feature occurs because higher levels of nonlinearities can be realized using more complicated synapses and contacts. The advantage may be fewer connections if suitable hardware can be designed to realize the nonlinear synapses and contacts.

7.2.1   Quasi-Polynomial Synapses and Product Synaptic Contacts

From a computational point of view, when the synapses are restricted to being linear and the nonlinearities are confined to the units, the freedom to introduce and change independent nonlinear terms of the inputs is lost. Functions that involve nonlinear terms of individual inputs and cross product terms will not be readily learned. This characteristic limits the functions that can be realized by a given network. Recall that although a two-layer network can approximate arbitrarily closely any absolutely integrable function in a finite interval, it requires an increasing number of hidden units to do so. In a collection of networks with a fixed characterizing graph, the capabilities for good approximation might be very different.

Liang and Jamali [227] proposed to introduce at each synapse a transformation that may be either linear or nonlinear. The actual transformation should be learned. Both linear and nonlinear transformations may be learned by parameter adjustment. Moreover, the form of the transformation should be amenable to analysis and derivation of the learning algorithm. Liang and Jamali extended the work of Durbin and Rumelhart on product units [101] by proposing that quasi-polynomials be used to model the nonlinearity of synapses.

Thus, the postsynaptic signal becomes a quasi-polynomial function of the presynaptic signal. Observe that a quasi-polynomial synapse is now a computational unit, similar to a neuron, but with only one input. A postsynaptic signal then may have a product contact with other postsynaptic signals or a summation contact at a neuron. At a product contact, all the postsynaptic signals involved are multiplied together before being summed with other signals. At a summation contact, the signal is simply summed with other signals. The symbols for nonlinear synapses and nonlinear contacts are shown in Fig. 7.8. The number of terms, exponents, and coefficients of the quasi-polynomials modeling the synaptic function evolve in the direction of least error by a learning mechanism that is derived using the gradient descent method [324] as in backpropagation, discussed in Chapter 5. What such a network implements is a quasi-polynomial classifier. Another possibility is to use polynomial models of synaptic characteristics by allowing exponents to be updated by integer amounts only. The only difference between the learning algorithm formulations is that of forcing the increments to the exponents to be integers. This may cause discontinuities in the improvements of the network performance. The effect of such an algorithm is yet to be investigated. We believe that there will be no fundamental difference in the performance of trained networks with quasi-polynomial synapses and with polynomial synapses. Properties of polynomial classifiers were investigated by Schürmann [341, 342].

The quasi-polynomial synapse model is described next. The transformation at a synapse from unit i to unit j (units at the lowest level perform a sigmoidal transformation to scale all inputs to within $(0,1)$) is of the following form:

$$f_{ij}(y_i) = w'_{ij} y_i^{p_{ij}} + \sum_{a=1}^{m_{ij}} w_{aij} y_i^a, \tag{7.6}$$

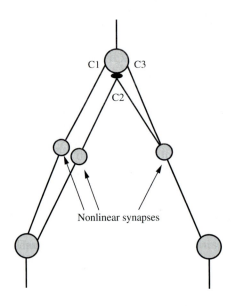

Nonlinear synapses

FIGURE 7.8
Illustration for a network with nonlinear synapses and with summation and product synaptic contacts. C1 and C3 are summation contacts, and C2 is a product contact.

where y_i is the output of unit i and m_{ij} is a positive integer that is updated during learning. The only exponent that is updated in each iteration during learning is p_{ij}. At any time, terms involving each of the integer exponents up to m_{ij} in addition to $y_i^{p_{ij}}$ are present. In the beginning,

$$m_{ij} = 0 \quad \text{and} \quad p_{ij} = 1.$$

During learning, the coefficients w'_{ij} and w_{aij} and the exponent p_{ij} are adjusted. When p_{ij} exceeds 2 for the first time, m_{ij} is set to 1 and a linear term is permanently added. Later on, whenever an integer value larger than $m_{ij} + 2$ is surpassed, a new term with an exponent of $m_{ij} + 1$ is introduced. The coefficient of the new term is set to zero when it is first introduced. Because the gradient descent updating rule may decrement as well as increment p_{ij}, when p_{ij} is reduced below m_{ij}, terms with exponents higher than p_{ij} can be removed.

Let

$$F_j(f_{1j}, f_{2j}, \ldots, f_{n_j j}) = \sum_{i=1}^{n_j} \prod_{k=1}^{k_i} f_{kj} + c_j, \tag{7.7}$$

where n_j is the total number of synaptic contacts at neuron j, and k_i is the number of postsynaptic signals involved in the ith synaptic contact. Note that if $k_i = 1$ for a given i, the corresponding product term in the equation becomes a simple summation term. Note additionally that some of the postsynaptic signals in the summation term and the product term may come from the same neuron. Also, some of the postsynaptic signals may have both a summation contact and one or more product contacts with a neuron, thus appearing in both the summation and product terms. From a computational point of view, allowing both summation and product contacts gives a network the freedom to add independent cross product terms in the quasi-polynomial F_j. Then the output of unit j is given as

$$y_j = \frac{1}{1 + e^{-\lambda F_j}}, \qquad \lambda > 0. \tag{7.8}$$

For every unit j, the learnable parameters from Eqs. (7.6), (7.7), and (7.8) are w_{aij}, w'_{ij}, p_{ij}, and c_j. The gradient descent formulation and associated computational arrangements for networks with quasi-polynomial synapses and product contacts can be easily derived [227]. The procedure is similar to that in the standard backpropagation algorithm [325] described in Chapter 5.

Features of this new model are summarized below:

1. Nonlinearity is introduced at each synapse. Each synapse is characterized by a quasi-polynomial type of transfer characteristic. Higher-order functions of a presynaptic signal can be added by learning. The postsynaptic signal may produce several quasi-polynomial terms that are functions of the presynaptic signal instead of just one linear or polynomial term.

2. The product terms in the new model are produced as the products of two or more postsynaptic signals following passage through the quasi-polynomial synapses. Because a postsynaptic signal may have several quasi-polynomial terms that are functions of an individual presynaptic signal and because these terms are learned, multiplication of two or more postsynaptic signals has two consequences. First, one product contact may produce many cross product terms of different degrees; second, the type and number of cross product terms that are present are not totally predetermined, but learned. Although what presynaptic signals can be involved in the quasi-polynomial cross product terms is determined from where the product contacts are handcrafted, the type and number of cross product terms that are actually there is *not predetermined*. This is in contrast with a product unit that produces only one quasi-polynomial term, whose coefficient and exponents are learned [101].

3. Since the number of learnable parameters needed is determined by learning, the new model is much like those in growth algorithms, which in general give poor generalization. There are several mechanisms in the new model that contribute to a possibly better generalization performance.

4. Unlike Durbin and Rumelhart [101], who treat a product as a unit (neuron), a product of postsynaptic signals is treated as a synaptic contact, i.e., a location where several synapses come into contact before acting on a neuron. The difference is that the neuron transfer characteristic acts uniformly on the product terms and summation terms in the new model. In a product unit [101], each product term is transformed by a neuron activation function before being summed with other signals.

An alternative to adding nonlinearity to the synapses and synaptic contacts is to allow adaptation of the transfer characteristics or, in other words, to allow the transfer characteristics of the units to be learned so as to approximate more functions better using fewer units and fewer connections. The backpropagation algorithm adjusts only the connection weights to approximate a target function. A more general approach is to adjust both the weights and the form of the neuron transfer characteristics to produce a better approximation using fewer units and connections. In such a scheme, variational calculus may be applied in a backpropagation scheme instead of simple partial derivatives.

7.2.2 Generalization of Learning and Hardware Considerations

Three cases are discussed below.

Case I. More parameters can be made available to the network (in hardware implementation or in simulation) as long as the algorithm calls for more parameters.[2] In this case, the new model is effectively another way of "growing" a network for a given task. From the discussion on learnability in Chapter 6 we know that a network with a fixed number of parameters may not be able to learn some functions or may require an exponential amount of time to do so. A network that learns not only the values of the parameters but also the number of parameters and their positions in the network may be able to overcome this, provided that some mechanism exists to prevent the network from having a function representation capacity that is too large, leading to poor generalization.

Case II. The total number of parameters available to the network is fixed, but the distribution of the parameters for each synapse can be determined during learning. The network learns what quasi-polynomial terms and, to some extent, how many terms should be present at each synapse, subject to the limit on the total number of parameters available. Synapses requiring more learnable parameters will get more. Overhead in the managing of the distribution of parameters to synapses is required.

Case III. The number of parameters available at each synapse is fixed. However, as in Case II, the type of quasi-polynomial terms and, to some extent, the number of terms (subject to the limit of parameters available at each synapse) that are present at each synapse are still determined by learning, although with less flexibility than Cases I and II. In order to apply Cases II and III, efficient algorithms capable of dynamic parameter release and assignment during learning need to be developed.

In all three cases, the model adaptively learns the distribution of the parameters (in a limited way in Case III). These schemes effectively correspond to adapting the

---

[2]In practice this growth is limited by the maximum resources available. Here it is assumed that the network is part of a larger system and will not use up all the parameters the larger system can supply.

structure of a network, although the network appears to have a fixed graph associated with it. Also, terms with small coefficients can be deleted during learning to allow the introduction of higher-degree quasi-polynomial terms without using a larger number of parameters.

Mechanisms should be designed to prevent the use of too many parameters, which leads to poor generalization. Even with these mechanisms, the generalization capability may still suffer since more parameters than necessary are used. To avoid this possibility, one can limit the number of parameters to suit a given task as in Cases II and III. The generalization capability of a network can be controlled by limiting the total number of parameters allowed. In Cases II and III there is still flexibility in learning what quasi-polynomial terms should be included in the synapses. Both Cases II and III offer some control on the generalizability of learning and flexibility in functional representation and may provide a compromise between the complexity of loading and generalizability of learning. However, fixing the number of parameters will not totally decide the representational capacity in Cases II and III because the flexibility of the distribution of the parameters to the synapses allows the networks to implement many more functions than do fixed parameters at fixed places. It is the flexibility, or capacity, in function representation of a network, not the number of parameters, that is crucial in the assessment of the generalization capability of a network. Determining the function representation capacity of the new networks, or their VC dimensions, could be a difficult problem, and its solution is necessary for a complete understanding of the generalization capability of this new model. Nevertheless, the number of parameters is one of the determining factors of the generalization capacity. Fixing the number of parameters does offer some control on the generalization capability of the network.

Hardware that recursively computes the quasi-polynomial at a synapse can be designed. Using such designs to implement the quasi-polynomial synapses provides an alternative way to realize highly nonlinear transfer characteristics with fewer connections but more complex synapses.

From the viewpoint of increasing the function representation capacity, increasing the number of terms of the quasi-polynomials at the synapses of a nonlinear synapse network is equivalent to increasing the size of a linear synapse network as in the growth networks. Increasing the nonlinearity of synapses should yield a better generalization than adding neurons and connections. This result can be attributed to the following reasons:

1. Most growth algorithms use hard-limiter threshold units. The networks in this section use sigmoidal activation functions for neurons. Information is not lost as a result of early, immature binary decisions from layer to layer, as in the growth algorithms [351]. Therefore, fewer parameters may be required than in networks using hard-limiter units, as discussed in Section 6.3. Of course, growth algorithms using units with sigmoidal activation functions could be developed as well.

2. In the quasi-polynomial synapse network, the inputs are scaled to belong to the interval $(0,1)$ at the first layer. As a result, higher-order terms have less influence,

because all signals have magnitudes less than 1. This effectively prevents the exponents of the quasi-polynomials from incrementing to impractically high values. Hence, the total number of parameters in the network is prevented from growing too large. This limiting capability is inherent and is not of a hard-limiter type (i.e., it does not prespecify a fixed degree for the synapse quasi-polynomials).

3. Growth algorithms may end up adding one neuron (and the corresponding connections) for one training sample. In general, growth algorithms only use training exemplars that cannot be loaded by existing units to train newly added units and connections. This feature is *localized* learning. Localized learning normally yields faster learning but at the price of poor generalization. However, as in the new model, the number of quasi-polynomial terms and all the added parameters of the quasi-polynomial of a synapse are affected by all training samples. The exponents may go up or down depending on the direction of the gradient. This is *global* learning versus the localized learning in the growth algorithms.

4. Terms with small coefficients in the quasi-polynomials can be deleted during learning to reduce the number of parameters. Elimination of units or connections during learning may be difficult in the localized-learning type of growth algorithms.

Even with the foregoing mechanisms, the generalization capability may still suffer, because more parameters than necessary are used. To avoid this drawback, the number of parameters can be limited to suit a given task in an implementation as in Cases II and III.

7.3   CONCLUSIONS AND SUGGESTIONS

The backpropagation-type algorithms try to find a solution by searching the entire weight space at the same time without knowing the mapping realized by the hidden layers. The growth algorithms discussed in Section 7.1 search the weight space of each hidden layer to implement a certain mapping. The goal of both approaches is the same: to make the image patterns linearly separable at the layer immediately below the output layer. The backpropagation-type algorithms are not constrained to any particular intermediate mappings or subgoals at the hidden layers. The growth algorithms choose a particular set of mappings at the hidden layers that lead to linear separability of the image patterns at the layer immediately below the output unit.

The foregoing analysis makes it clear that a backpropagation algorithm *may* find a better solution than the growth algorithms, in the sense that a smaller network with fewer connections may suffice. The reason is that, for a given network, no constraint is placed on the search space, and any possible intermediate mapping at the hidden layers may be explored. A growth algorithm may require a larger network than necessary, because the subgoals chosen may not be the optimal path of transformations leading to linear separability. However, the backpropagation-type algorithms may suffer from slow convergence because the entire weight space may be searched; they may also be stuck at local minima because no guidance is provided for circumventing the bottleneck. On the other hand, the growth algorithms converge fast and always find the right solution, because the subgoals decompose the problem into easier ones and provide guidance leading to linear separability. A desired solution would be a compromise between these two extremes.

In all the growth algorithms discussed, the basic principle of divide and conquer is ubiquitous. There are many different ways to divide the training set, corresponding to different algorithms. One important point to note is that the proofs of convergence for all the growth algorithms rely on one statement: One TLU can always separate at least one pattern from the rest of the patterns (except in certain pathological cases mentioned earlier). Therefore, in the worst case, a growth algorithm may add one neuron for each pattern and become a straightforward memorization. Although it may be argued that this may not happen in general, there is no guarantee it would not.

Another problem that needs to be considered is the connection complexity of the networks constructed by the growth algorithms. The networks grown by the two algorithms in Section 7.1.3 are either partially connected layered or partially connected multipartite networks. All units in the networks built by the upstart algorithm are fully connected to the input units and, therefore, their graphs are multipartite. Only the first layer of the network constructed by the divide-and-conquer algorithm is fully connected. Algorithms that construct networks with local connections should be investigated.

The worst-case learning time of a growth algorithm is of the order $O(M(N+2))$, where $M = \min(M_X, M_Y)$, and M_X and M_Y are the numbers of training exemplars in the two classes X and Y, respectively. N is the number of steps the pocket algorithm or other perceptron algorithms is allowed to run for each subset. N can be chosen to be a positive number that is a polynomial in the dimension of the inputs. This statement is equivalent to saying that if a perceptron learning algorithm does not converge to a solution in polynomial time, the problem will be considered unlearnable by the algorithm. A new TLU is then added. The worst case occurs when the training sets must be divided into subsets containing only two patterns with each belonging to a different class. The smaller the number N, the shorter the worst-case learning time. However, N may affect the size of the final network. The smaller N is, the larger (more TLUs) the final network usually is. This result agrees with the usual trade-off between time complexity and space complexity. The growth algorithms are therefore fast, and they overcome the problems of nonconvergence or slow convergence and local minima that may be associated with the backpropagation-type algorithms.

In summary, the main features of the growth algorithms are these:

1. Convergence in a finite number of steps to the correct classification is guaranteed for any set of nonlinearly separable patterns, no matter how high the degree of nonlinearity is.
2. The graph of the network and the connection weights required to classify the patterns are simultaneously learned. For any classification problem, the algorithms

grow a network from a single TLU with specified connections and weights to solve the given problem.

3. Fast learning can be achieved. There is a trade-off between the learning time and the size of the learned network.

4. The range of the weights of the learned network is easily controlled using the parameter N. Therefore, the problem of a large ratio between the largest and smallest weights can be overcome.

5. The networks constructed in general are fully connected, at least from the input layer.

6. It is possible that an overly large network may be grown, leading to poor generalization. One of the reasons for poor generalization is localized learning. That is, a newly added TLU is trained using only a subset of exemplars instead of the entire training set. This reason is the same one that justifies fast learning.

For good generalization, the pattern space should be partitioned into a minimum number of hyperregions, with each such hyperregion being as large as possible. Far from what is desired, a growth algorithm often yields redundant partitions. A possible way to reduce the size of the network constructed is to avoid or remove redundant partitions. A growth algorithm needs a perceptron-type algorithm that leads to an optimal or a near-optimal partitioning of the pattern space in the sense of network size and generalization capability. Algorithms that attempt to minimize the network size during backpropagation learning [275, 399], introduced in Section 6.2.4, may provide useful ideas. Another approach to improve generalization is to prune the network after the training set has been learned, as in the *optimal brain damage* [216] and eigenvalue spectrum analysis methods [398], also introduced in Section 6.2.4. The challenge here is to avoid or minimize relearning after pruning, as was illustrated in the merging step for removing redundant partitions in Section 7.1.2. A growth algorithm may be used to produce a network that quickly learns the training set in the posttraining eigenvalue spectrum analysis method. However, the pruned network may need to be retrained using backpropagation.

To replace a model that grows more units and connections, a network model that grows nonlinearity at synapses with nonlinear synaptic contacts is introduced in Section 7.2. This model seems to combine the desirable properties of the backpropagation learning and growth algorithms. However, further investigation and understanding of the model are required, especially in its generalization measure and its hardware implementation.

Analog implementations of synapses often are nonlinear in nature owing to the inherent nonlinearity in the circuit elements [103, 161, 217, 238, 332]. The difficulty is in learning the desired form of nonlinearity at the synapses. In addition to being natural extensions toward more realistic models, nonlinear synapses and nonlinear synaptic contacts whose nonlinearity can be learned may offer advantages both in improved learning behavior and in hardware implementation. A network with nonlinear synapses and nonlinear synaptic contacts is an alternative to using linear-synapse networks with many neurons and connections to realize highly nonlinear functions, because higher levels of nonlinearity can be achieved in the synapses and contacts. The advantage may be in fewer numbers of connections if suitable hardware is designed to realize the learnable nonlinear synapses and contacts.

Finally, we point out that the algorithms discussed in this chapter are connected with the structural training method using the Voronoi diagram, described in Chapter 5 and in ref. [290]. They share the common idea of determining the structure of the network based on the training data set. However, the methods used to arrive at that goal are totally different, though the divide-and-conquer principle can also be applied in VoD construction. In that case, however, all the points representing locations of sites must be known in advance; no incremental update is possible such as is required in real-time pattern classification. Local update, by adding one point in feature space at a time, leaves most of the VoD that has been already calculated unaffected, as seen for the L_2 metric in Chapter 5 and for the L_1 metric in ref. [290]. Pruning for better generalization is also feasible by merging appropriate regions in the VoD. This also leads systematically to alternative structures.

PROBLEMS

7.1. Write a computer program to implement the upstart algorithm. Test the algorithm on the 5-bit and 10-bit parity functions. In each case, use 70 percent of the binary patterns as training exemplars and the remaining as test exemplars.

7.2. Write a computer program to implement the divide-and-conquer algorithm. Test the algorithm on the following two-dimensional classification problem where the training exemplars are generated as follows:

> **Class 1.** 10 randomly sampled points inside the circle $x^2 + y^2 = 1$ and 20 randomly sampled points in the ring $\{x^2 + y^2 > 2\} \cap \{x^2 + y^2 < 4\}$.
> **Class 2.** 15 randomly sampled points in the ring $\{x^2 + y^2 > 1\} \cap \{x^2 + y^2 < 2\}$.

The network is to output a 1 for exemplars belonging to class 1. After the network has learned, examine the partition implemented by the network; manually identify and remove redundant partitions. Simplify the network corresponding to the new partition with redundancies removed. Compare the performance of the two networks on 40 test exemplars. The test exemplars are to be randomly sampled in the same regions where the training exemplars are generated. The same distribution should be used in sampling the test exemplars as used in sampling the training exemplars. However, attention should be given to programming using the random number generator so that most of the test exemplars are different from the training exemplars.

7.3. Derive the backpropagation learning algorithm for the network with quasi-polynomial synapses and product contacts.

7.4. It has been claimed that a standard multilayer feedforward network with a locally bounded piecewise continuous activation function (transfer characteristic of unit) can approximate any continuous function to any degree of accuracy if and only if the activation function is not a polynomial [222]. Though this type of result (other activities are reported in [405]) imposes minimal restrictions on the activation function of a unit, the number of units required in the hidden layer of the generic structure studied (consisting of an input layer, one hidden layer, and an output layer) can be impractically large. Investigate the scope of overcoming the drawback cited by using conveniently chosen nonlinearities for the activation function, the connection strengths of synapses, and synaptic contacts. Study the problem by starting with very small networks with nonlinearities as mentioned above.

PART
III

RECURRENT
NETWORKS

Feedforward networks, considered in Part II, implement mappings from the input pattern space to the output space. Once the weights are fixed, the states of the units are totally determined by inputs independent of the initial and past states of the units. Hence, the mapping is fixed. There are no dynamics involved. For more complicated information processing, dependence on the initial and past states and serial processing capabilities are required. These can be made possible by introducing cyclic connections described by directed loops in the network graph.

Once cyclic connections are included, a neural network, often called a *recurrent neural network,* becomes a nonlinear dynamic system. Such a system has very rich temporal and spatial behaviors, such as stable and unstable fixed points and limit cycles, and chaotic behaviors. These behaviors can be utilized to model certain cognitive functions, such as associative memory, unsupervised learning, self-organizing maps, and temporal reasoning.

Networks with cyclic connections are much harder to analyze and describe than feedforward networks, reflecting the difficulties of limited mathematical tools for nonlinear dynamic systems. The problems that need to be addressed in the study of recurrent networks include the following:

1. *Network synthesis and learning algorithm.* The network synthesis problem for recurrent networks is more complicated than for feedforward networks because the possibilities of the variations in the network graphs are much wider. We need to associate a task with the appropriate behaviors of a dynamic system. Then we need to design a network graph and the mechanism to determine its weights and state transition rules so as to implement the dynamic system. We also need algorithms that learn the desired behavior over time either with or without supervision or with only reinforcement signal. For a neural network to accomplish complex cognitive tasks, the following three ingredients seem necessary: It must be able to perform serial logic computation and processing; several subnetworks must work together; and there should be more than one type of functional unit and more types of connections than excitatory and inhibitory.

2. *Convergence and learnability.* After the network graph, its weights, and state transition rules are determined, we must investigate the dynamics of the system to see if it is what we want. Questions that need to be answered include the stability of the attractors such as point, limit cycle, and chaotic; the convergence rate; and whether the system will converge to local or global minimum of some predefined energy or error functions, etc. Similar to feedforward networks, the learning algorithms for recurrent neural networks also face the learnability problem. However, this problem is much harder to analyze than in the feedforward case and is a totally open problem.

3. *Size of the network.* Similar to feedforward networks, for a recurrent network to be useful in practice, the network size required is normally large. However, when the size of a network (number of connections and units) increases, its synthesis becomes more difficult and its dynamics become harder to manipulate. One way to reduce the space complexity is by limiting the connections to local neighborhoods only. This step dramatically slows down the state evolution and therefore convergence of the network. A good compromise needs to be struck. Methods for implementing large networks to realize complicated functions, possibly using a hierarchy of smaller subnetworks, are needed. The connections between the subnetworks may be sparse while the connections within the subnetworks are dense.

4. *Complexity of analog computation.* A fundamental question is this: Can biological or analog dynamic systems solve problems that are NP-hard for a Turing machine? This very difficult question touches on problems in both mathematics and physics. Treatment of this topic is beyond the scope of this book. We only briefly present the following conclusion: It has been shown that with $P \neq NP$, no analog computer or dynamic system can solve NP-hard problems with less than exponential resources (at least in the worst case) in the dimension of the input space and the problem size [258, 302, 388]. What nonlinear dynamic systems, such as neural networks, can solve are approximations to the NP-hard problems that can be encoded as limit sets of the network.

This part is organized into two chapters. Chapter 8 considers symmetric and asymmetric recurrent networks. Chapter 9 discusses unsupervised learning and self-organizing networks.

In Chapter 8, recurrent networks with symmetric connections, widely known as Hopfield networks, are first considered. Convergence to point attractors, memory capacity and spurious memory, and synchronous and asynchronous dynamics are discussed. Bidirectional associative memory is also discussed. Because a Hopfield network often gets stuck at a local minimum of the energy function, the simulated annealing algorithm is introduced to help alleviate the problem. The stochastic approach in simulated annealing leads us to the Boltzmann machine learning algorithm. Because symmetric networks cannot capture temporal patterns, asymmetric networks are then investigated. The dynamic behavior of asymmetric networks includes limit cycles and chaos, and these networks are capable of storing or generating temporal sequences of spatial patterns. The temporal sequence of patterns in an asymmetric network may play an important role in many cognitive functions. Then we consider learning in asymmetric networks. A generalization of the backpropagation algorithm to recurrent networks is presented.

Unsupervised learning and self-organization in recurrent networks are examined in Chapter 9. Unsupervised competitive learning and its applications are discussed. The hybrid learning algorithms with both an unsupervised and a supervised phase, typically present in the counterpropagation and radial basis function networks, are also discussed here. The counterpropagation network applies winner-take-all unsupervised competitive learning at the unsupervised phase. The second part of this chapter considers the adaptive resonant network, feature maps, and unsupervised learning in multilayer networks. Simple analysis that provides insight into the dynamic process of self-organizing maps is presented.

CHAPTER
8

SYMMETRIC AND ASYMMETRIC RECURRENT NETWORKS

A recurrent network has feedback paths, which make it a sequential rather than a combinational network, permitting it to exhibit temporal behavior. All possible connections between neurons are allowed. A major component of an intelligent system is its ability to recognize and associate similar patterns. From perusal of Section 3.6, the reader learned that a memory system that can recall a pattern from memory based on the contents of an input is an associative or content-addressable memory. If a pattern is recalled from memory when a sufficiently similar pattern is presented, the memory is *autoassociative*. The other type of associative memory, in which the input and output vectors may have entirely different connotations, is a *heteroassociative* memory. In a heteroassociative memory, patterns are given in pairs. When a pattern sufficiently similar to one of the patterns in a pair is presented, the other pattern is recalled. In a biological associative memory, perfect recall is possible even with incomplete or noisy excitation, which serves as a *key*. A biological memory is also highly *distributed,* a feature that endows the biological system with remarkable fault tolerance properties. Compared with the digital computer, biological memory is realized with very slow and inexact components. It is the *collective computational capability* of the biological memory that is responsible for performing cognitive tasks beyond the reach of electronic computers.

Much effort has been devoted to using a neural network as an associative memory model since the 1950s [22, 197, 233, 417]. Some of these earlier results were brought to the reader's attention in Section 3.6. The linear associative memories described there exhibit certain drawbacks. Because the mapping is linear, inputs that are close in the domain space map to points in the range space that are also close. Thus, similar exemplars that need to be mapped to dissimilar outputs cannot be accommodated. Not only can contextual information be lost; linear associative memories have very low capacities, especially when good generalization is required. Various *nonlinear associative memories* exist to remedy the problem, at least partially. Some such memories, based on feedforward networks, have already been encountered in Chapters 4 and 5. For example, the perceptron is a nonlinear heteroassociative memory that was seen to be somewhat limited in scope. In 1982, Hopfield formulated an associative memory as stable attractors in a dynamic system and used an energy function for analysis [162].

In Section 8.1 the Hopfield model is introduced. The Hopfield network is an example of autoassociative memory with feedback. The basic model consists of a set of processing elements that compute the weighted sums of the inputs and threshold the outputs to binary values. Naturally, thresholding is a nonlinear operation. It will be shown that an *energy function,* partly akin to the *Lyapunov function* occurring in stability investigations of nonlinear dynamic systems, exists for this model and that the processing elements with binary-valued outputs converge to a stable local energy minimum. The state at such a minimum is referred to as an *equilibrium point,* which is responsible for memory. Although the iterative process of state updates does converge, spurious memories exist and the memory capacity is low. As with the proof for the perceptron convergence theorem encountered in Chapter 4, the reader is introduced to the proof of convergence for the discrete Hopfield network. In addition to the standard proof, a graph theory–motivated proof is also provided. Continuous (analog) Hopfield networks, using resistor-capacitor combinations and sigmoid transfer characteristics, are also studied, and it will be shown that the properties of this type of network mimic the discrete counterpart. The bidirectional associative memory (BAM), which is heteroassociative and a variation of the Hopfield network, is described. The analog counterparts of these results are developed in Section 8.2, where the relation to the more recent *cellular neural network* (CNN) is also pointed out.

In Section 8.3 the simulated annealing method of optimization, which leads to the Boltzmann machine (BM) in Section 8.4, is introduced. The distinguishing feature is that the learning rule for such a machine is not deterministic but stochastic. The BM, being a generalization of the Hopfield network, can serve also as a heteroassociative memory in addition to an autoassociative memory. Since the Boltzmann machine operates stochastically, it does not converge to the same solution at every try if the solution to the problem is not unique. Like the Hopfield network, the BM has an associated energy function. It has the capability for gravitating to an improved solution over time as iterations are continued on the data. The difficulty is that the BM is slow, and variants such as the *Cauchy machine* have been introduced to speed up convergence. In Section 8.5, the restriction of symmetry, underlying the presentations in Sections 8.1, 8.2, and 8.4, is eliminated; this increases the versatility of the network considerably. Characteristically, a summary and a discussion are provided in the final section, followed by a set of representative problems that readers should find useful for facilitating their comprehension of the important concepts presented in this chapter.

The topology of the structures considered in this chapter can be conveniently characterized by particular types of undirected graphs. The graph characterizing a Hopfield network, for example, is a complete graph, whereas that characterizing a BAM is a bipartite graph. The graph for a BM is a complete graph in general, but because of the presence of hidden units that are not accessible to the outside world, the connections are usually structured, implying that the graph that characterizes the topology of the BM is actually a proper subgraph of the complete graph. The actual graph in both cases is directed, and distinction is needed between signal flows from node i to node j and from node j to node i. We will concentrate mostly on symmetric networks in the following sections, but a more concise description of the scope as well as the prospects of asymmetric networks is also provided at the later parts of this chapter.

8.1   SYMMETRIC HOPFIELD NETWORKS AND ASSOCIATIVE MEMORY

Physical systems made up of a large number of simple elements can exhibit collective *emergent phenomena* (implying that a collective property cannot be inferred from an individual element) through (local) interaction between elements. Examples include stable magnetic orientations, flow patterns, clouds, and snowflakes. Hopfield asked whether analogous collective emergent phenomena in a network of simple interacting neurons have useful computational correlates [162]. (A word of caution regarding the analogy of physical systems with biological nervous systems is appropriate. No analogy is perfect. Unlike physical systems, a nervous system has a very complicated nonuniform structure, composed of a large collection of simple but inhomogeneous neurons that interact in complicated ways.)

Consider a network in which every unit is connected to every other unit and the connections are symmetric. The connections are *symmetric* if the connection weights from unit i to unit j and from unit j to unit i are identical for all i and j. Such a network is called a Hopfield network (Fig. 8.1) in its original form, after the author of an influential paper [162]. Hopfield further presented the idea that a physical system whose dynamics in state space are dominated by a number of locally stable states (called *attractors*) can be regarded as an associative memory. A *point attractor* may be viewed as a special state (in the state space associated with a dynamic nonlinear feedback system) to which the state equations characterizing the dynamic system bring the system, from a rich class of initial states, after a sufficiently long temporal evolution. Let the state vectors $\{\mathbf{y}^s\}_{s=1}^n$ corresponding to the point attractors of the system represent the information, in the form of patterns, to be stored. Examples of such patterns include the coding pattern of a sentence and the pattern of a cascade of scan lines from an image. The set of initial states from which the system evolves to the same attractor state constitutes the *basin of attraction* for that attractor. The initial state of the system may be set at a partial or distorted pattern, represented as

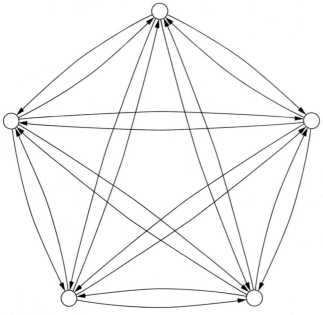

FIGURE 8.1
The structure of a Hopfield network.

$\mathbf{y}^s + \Delta\mathbf{y}$, and as long as it is still within the basin of attraction of an attractor $\mathbf{y}^s$, the system will evolve in time until its output reaches an equilibrium point (steady state of autonomous systems) $\mathbf{y} \approx \mathbf{y}^s$. This process is, effectively, the recall of the stored information from partial or distorted information. Therefore, if a neural network can be organized such that patterns are made to correspond to its attractors, it can function as an associative memory. A Hopfield network is such a network, and the graph characterizing its topology, in its most commonly used form, is K_N, the complete graph over N nodes.

A Hopfield network may be constructed using TLUs for nonlinear components. The outputs of the TLUs are assumed, without loss of generality, to be bipolar binary here. That is, the threshold function is now given as

$$T_b(x) = \begin{cases} 1, & x \geq 0 \\ -1, & x < 0. \end{cases} \tag{8.1}$$

An equilibrium state may be either stable or unstable. Instead of precise definitions of the various types of stabilities available in textbooks on nonlinear system theory, an intuitive interpretation is adequate for our purpose here. An equilibrium state may be considered stable if, whenever the system is perturbed from that state of equilibrium, it eventually returns to the original point in the state space of trajectories; otherwise, the equilibrium state is unstable. Each pattern or information to be stored is coded as a binary vector, called a *pattern vector*. Units in the network are appropriately ordered so that unit i corresponds to bit i in the pattern vectors. A pattern vector is *stored* in the network if at a stable equilibrium the states of the TLUs are identical (or almost identical) with the pattern vector.

An intuitive way to store a set of n binary pattern vectors in a Hopfield network is to set each weight w_{ij} to the accumulated correlations of the the ith and jth components, y_i^s and y_j^s, of all the n binary pattern vectors $\mathbf{y}^s$ (for $s = 1, 2, \ldots, n$), each containing N bits of information, as shown below. The integer N also represents the number of units in the network, because each unit can then be associated with one bit of stored information.

$$w_{ij} = \frac{1}{N} \sum_{s=1}^{n} y_i^s y_j^s, \qquad i \neq j. \tag{8.2}$$

The value of w_{ii} is either 0 or positive for each i. When the value of w_{ii} is nonzero, corresponding to the case of a nonzero-diagonal connection weight matrix, the graph is not a *simple* graph, because self-loops are added to the basic complete graph. The thresholds of the units are usually set to zero, though this may not always be the case [266]. For example, in the spin representation of the Hopfield network, the threshold θ_i for the ith unit is set at

$$\theta_i = -\sum_{j \neq i} w_{ij}.$$

The memory capacity is improved substantially by such a choice [266, p. 103], which incorporates the biological fact that neurons spend most of their time in the resting state and have a low level of activity. A modification of Eq. (8.2) may also be applied to compute each bias weight that links the unity-valued external input to a unit, whose threshold is then set to the negative of this bias. Equation (8.2), like the Hebbian type of rule, models Hebb's hypothesis [152] that the synaptic strength change in the brain is proportional to the correlation between the presynaptic and postsynaptic neuron states. However, Eq. (8.2) is also more general than a standard Hebbian rule, because the connection weight w_{ij} between neurons i and j is increased not only when they are both activated but also when they are both inactive for a given pattern. The weight is decreased when the units i and j are in different states (that is, one is active and the other is inactive) for a given pattern. This correlation is summed and averaged over all patterns to be stored.

The weights in Eq. (8.2) can be either precomputed or learned. The weights may be learned by repeatedly setting the units to the patterns to be stored, either sequentially or at random. In that case the weights are updated by

$$w_{ij}^{\text{new}} = \alpha w_{ij}^{\text{old}} + (1 - \alpha) y_i^s y_j^s, \tag{8.3}$$

where $0 < \alpha < 1$ should be appropriately chosen. After the weights are determined, the state transition at each unit is governed by

$$y_i(k + 1) = T_b(h_i(k)) = T_b\left(\sum_j w_{ij} y_j(k) - \theta_i\right), \tag{8.4}$$

where

$$h_i(k) = \sum_j w_{ij} y_j(k) - \theta_i.$$

In an associative recall, the states of the units in a Hopfield network are initialized to values representing partial and distorted versions of the stored patterns. The network then evolves according to the state transition (or updating) rule in Eq. (8.4). The updating could be implemented either synchronously or asynchronously. In the former case all units are updated simultaneously at each time index. This is also called the parallel mode of operation. In the latter case the units are selected at random for updating. If the updating is performed at a single node at a time index in sequence, then it is called a serial mode of operation. In the biologically motivated mode of asynchronous updating, the network is considered to have reached an *attractor* when all the units have ceased to change their states. It is expected that the network states associated with an attractor will correspond to the stored pattern that is closest to the initial pattern according to the Hamming distance measure.

The state update in Eq. (8.4) may generate three types of trajectories in state space for a nonlinear dynamic feedback system such as a recurrent neural network. These types of trajectories lead, respectively, to *fixed points, limit cycles,* and *chaos.* A fixed point (point attractor) in state space repeats itself under the update dynamics of Eq. (8.4) (see Section 8.5.3). A limit cycle is a cycle of states of an arbitrary but fixed finite length. Trajectories that evolve in state space in an uncorrelated and irregular fashion lead to chaotic dynamics (see Section 8.5.1). Fixed points are least sensitive to the update rule and initial conditions, and the chaotic phenomenon is most sensitive. Limit cycles are usually somewhat sensitive to the update rule. An attractor could be either a fixed point (unique point attractor), a limit cycle (periodic orbit), or chaotic (aperiodic strange attractor). In the area of artificial neural networks, so far the fixed-point attractors have found the greatest relevance. However, chaotic attractors are known to provide interpretations of phenomena such as the occurrence of epileptic seizures in biological neural networks. An impressive body of current literature exists in the area of chaotic dynamical systems. Here it suffices to say that very simple nonlinear difference or differential equations with appropriate initial conditions are capable of modeling very complex trajectories in state space.

Several questions need to be answered. First, with the weights determined by Eq. (8.2), can the pattern vectors become the point attractors of the network? If yes, then starting from a partial and distorted version of one of the patterns stored, can the network dynamics evolve to the state of a pattern vector stored? Starting from an arbitrary initial state of the network, where will the network dynamics stabilize? How many patterns can be stored with small recall error? Answers to these and other questions are provided in the remaining parts of this section.

8.1.1   Convergence Proofs

First, we want to find out whether the updating process for the weights described in Eq. (8.4) converges. Note that *updating,* in the current context, requires the transition rule to be applied to a unit and the state of the unit to be either changed or kept the same depending on the outcome of the evaluation of the transition rule.

The states of the units may, as mentioned before, be updated either *synchronously* (i.e., fully parallel) or *asynchronously*. In synchronous updating, the transition rule is applied to all the units simultaneously. The Little-Shaw model is based on synchronous updating [233, 234]. Asynchronous updating is of either the *simple* or the *general* type. In simple asynchronous updating, only one unit is randomly selected for evaluation and updating at each time step; the Hopfield model is based on simple asynchronous updating [162]. In general asynchronous updating, each unit makes the decision to update itself independently and randomly by following a probability distribution over time. As a result, a subset of units may be randomly selected at each time step for evaluation and updating. Both the number of units and the membership in the subsets are random. Usually, the probability that a unit will update itself is a constant per unit time, although different units may have different such constants.

The simple and general asynchronous modes of updating may be considered to be approximately equivalent, because if each unit runs independently, the probability that two or more units choose to update at exactly the same time instant is very small. The simple asynchronous mode is normally used in computer simulation. The synchronous and general asynchronous modes are appropriate for hardware implementation. In a digital computer (software) implementation of a Hopfield network, the simple asynchronous type of update is usually implemented in a serial mode. A network running in a serial mode evaluates the transition rule at all the units one by one. The order of evaluation is unimportant and may be different in each iteration. However, each unit must be evaluated once before the start of the next iteration. When the number of units in a network is large, the serial mode is statistically equivalent to a simple asynchronous mode, because each unit is assigned equal probability for updating.

We first show a proof of convergence for the simple asynchronous updating case using an energy function [162]. Let $\mathbf{W} = \{w_{ij}\}$ be the weight matrix and $\boldsymbol{\theta} = [\theta_1\ \theta_2\ \cdots\ \theta_N]^T$ be the threshold vector.

Theorem 8.1   [162]. If a Hopfield network evolves by simple asynchronous updating, it will converge to a stable state.

Proof. Let $\mathbf{y}(k)$ be the state vector at time index k. Define an energy function

$$E(k) = -\tfrac{1}{2}\mathbf{y}^T(k)\mathbf{W}\mathbf{y}(k) + \mathbf{y}^T(k)\boldsymbol{\theta}. \tag{8.5}$$

For simple asynchronous updating, one unit i is changed at a time by $\Delta y_i(k)$, where

$$\Delta y_i(k) = \begin{cases} 0, & \text{if } y_i(k) = T_b(h_i(k)) \\ 2, & \text{if } y_i(k) = -1 \text{ and } h_i(k) \geq 0 \\ -2, & \text{if } y_i(k) = +1 \text{ and } h_i(k) < 0. \end{cases} \tag{8.6}$$

The change $\Delta E(k)$ of the energy function due only to $\Delta y_i(k)$, the change in $y_i(k)$, is given by

$$\Delta E(k) = -\Delta y_i(k)\left(\sum_j w_{ij}y_j(k) - \theta_i\right) - \frac{w_{ii}}{2}(\Delta y_i(k))^2$$

$$= -(\Delta y_i(k))h_i(k) - \frac{w_{ii}}{2}(\Delta y_i(k))^2.$$

(8.7)

Since $(\Delta y_i(k))h_i(k) \geq 0$ (from Eq. (8.6)), and $w_{ii} \geq 0$, we have $\Delta E(k) \leq 0$. Because $E(k)$ is bounded from below, the energy must converge, so $\Delta E(k) = 0$ for all $k > T_0$, where T_0 is some positive integer. When $\Delta E(k) = 0$, then either $\Delta y_i(k) = 0$ (i.e., $y_i(k) = T_b(h_i(k))$) or $\Delta y_i(k) = 2$ and both $h_i(k) = 0$ and $w_{ii} = 0$. In the latter case, $y_i(k + 1) = 1 = T_b(h_i(k + 1))$. Therefore, the network must reach a stable state if the value of energy has converged to a constant. This proves that with the weights determined by Eq. (8.2) a Hopfield network with simple asynchronous updating must converge to a stable state.

Bruck [59] proved the convergence properties of the Hopfield network without using an energy function. He showed that the problem of finding the global minimum of the energy function associated with the network running in a simple asynchronous mode is equivalent to that of finding the minimum cut in the undirected graph associated with the network. Based on this relation, an elementary proof for convergence in the simple asynchronous mode can be obtained without involving the concept of an energy function. Using this elementary proof, convergence properties in the synchronous mode can be inferred by realizing that mode to be a special case of the simple asynchronous mode.

8.1.2 Computation in a Network and Minimum Cuts in a Graph

We now show the relation between the computation performed by a Hopfield network and the problem of finding a minimum cut (MC) in an undirected graph. A Hopfield network in the simple asynchronous mode actually performs a local search for a minimum of the energy function $E(k)$ in Eq. (8.5). Consider a network H with N units operating in the simple asynchronous mode. Let L_H denote the local search algorithm, described as follows, performed by the network H.

Algorithm L_H for searching $\min(E(\mathbf{y}))$.

1. Start with an initial assignment $\mathbf{y} \in \{-1, +1\}^N$.
2. Choose a unit $i \in \{1, \ldots, N\}$ at random.
3. Perform the *energy-reducing transition*

$$y_i = T_b\left(\sum_j w_{ij}y_j - \theta_i\right).$$

4. Go to step 2.

For this algorithm to stop, the stopping criterion must be global in the sense that not one of the units changes state. Modification for software implementation is straight-forward. Hardware implementation causes no problem either, once it is realized that the states will not change after the algorithm has converged.

Next, we show that the problem of finding an MC in a graph is equivalent to an optimization problem with a quadratic cost function [146, 284, 296]. Recall the definition for a cut-set given in Definition 3.1. Though the notion of a minimum cut was encountered in the discussion of the maximum-flow minimum-cut problem in Chapter 3, it is defined here for convenience in the context of the notation to be used. In particular, we do not require the graph to be directed. Therefore, here a cut-set is also a cut.

Definition 8.1. Let $G = (V, E)$ be a weighted and undirected graph, with $\mathbf{W}$ being an $N \times N$ symmetric matrix of weights for the edges of G. Let V_1 be a subset of V and let $V_{-1} = V \backslash V_1$, where $\backslash$ is the notation for set-difference. The set of edges each of which has a vertex in V_1 and another in V_{-1} is called a *cut-set* of the graph G. A *minimum cut* in a graph is a cut-set for which the sum of the corresponding edge weights is minimal over all V_1.

The following theorem holds [146, 296].

Theorem 8.2. Let $G = (V, E)$ be a weighted, undirected graph, and let $\mathbf{W}$ be the matrix of its edge weights. Then the MC problem in G is equivalent to the problem of minimizing $Q_G(\mathbf{y})$, where $\mathbf{y} \in \{-1, +1\}^N$ and

$$Q_G(\mathbf{y}) = -\frac{1}{2} \sum_{i=1}^{N} \sum_{j=1}^{N} w_{ij} y_i y_j. \tag{8.8}$$

Proof. Assign a bipolar binary-valued variable y_i to every node $i \in V$. Let V_1 and V_{-1} be the sets of nodes in G that are associated with the values 1 and -1, respectively, of y_i. Let W^{++} denote the sum of the weights of the edges in G that have both endpoints in the set V_1. Let W^{--} and W^{+-} denote, respectively, the sum of the edges with both endpoints in V_{-1} and the sum of the edges with one endpoint in V_1 and the other in V_{-1}. Thus,

$$Q_G = -(W^{++} + W^{--} - W^{+-}). \tag{8.9}$$

This can also be written as

$$Q_G = -(W^{++} + W^{--} + W^{+-}) + 2W^{+-} = -\frac{1}{2} \sum_{i=1}^{N} \sum_{j=1}^{N} w_{ij} + 2W^{+-}. \tag{8.10}$$

The first term in Eq. (8.10) is a constant equal to the negative of the sum of weights of edges in G. Hence, minimization of Q_G is equivalent to minimization of W^{+-}, which is actually the sum of edge weights of a cut in G.

Based on Theorem 8.2, it is easy to prove the following [59]. A neural network of order N will be defined by $H = (\mathbf{W}, \boldsymbol{\theta})$, where $\mathbf{W}$ is an $N \times N$ real symmetric matrix and $\boldsymbol{\theta}$ is an $N \times 1$ vector. The element w_{ij} in the ith row and jth column of $\mathbf{W}$

equals the weight of the edge connecting neuron i to neuron j, and the ith element of θ is the threshold of neuron i.

Theorem 8.3. Let $H = (\mathbf{W}, \theta)$ define a network, where $\mathbf{W}$ is an $N \times N$ real symmetric zero-diagonal matrix. Let G be a weighted graph with $(N + 1)$ nodes and weight matrix

$$\mathbf{W}_G = \begin{pmatrix} \mathbf{W} & \theta \\ \theta^\mathsf{T} & 0 \end{pmatrix}.$$

The problem of finding a state $\mathbf{y}$ in H for which the configuration energy E is a global minimum is equivalent to the MC problem in the corresponding graph G.

Proof. Note that the graph G is built out of H by adding one node to H. This additional node is connected to all the other N nodes. The weight of the edge joining the additional node to node i is $-\theta_i$. Now, if the state of the additional node is constrained to the value 1, then for all $\mathbf{y} \in \{-1, 1\}^N$,

$$Q_G\left([\mathbf{y}^\mathsf{T}\ 1]^\mathsf{T}\right) = E(\mathbf{y}), \tag{8.11}$$

where $E(\mathbf{y})$ is the energy function E defined in Eq. (8.5). For the reader's convenience, a step-by-step proof of the equality in Eq. (8.11) is given next, since it is the key to the verification of the theorem.

$$Q_G\left[(\mathbf{y}^\mathsf{T}\ 1)^\mathsf{T}\right] = -\frac{1}{2}\sum_i^{N+1}\sum_j^{N+1} w_{ij} y_i y_j$$

$$= -\frac{1}{2}\sum_i^{N}\sum_j^{N+1} w_{ij} y_i y_j - \frac{1}{2}\sum_j^{N+1} w_{(N+1)j} y_{N+1} y_j$$

$$= -\frac{1}{2}\sum_i^{N}\left[\sum_j^{N} w_{ij} y_i y_j + w_{i(N+1)} y_i y_{(N+1)}\right]$$

$$\quad -\frac{1}{2}\sum_j^{N} w_{(N+1)j} y_{N+1} y_j - \frac{1}{2} w_{(N+1)(N+1)} y_{N+1} y_{N+1}$$

Since $w_{(N+1)(N+1)} = 0$, $w_{i(N+1)} = -\theta_i$, $i = 1, 2, \ldots, N$, and $y_{N+1} = 1$, the preceding equation becomes

$$Q_G\left[(\mathbf{y}^\mathsf{T}\ 1)^\mathsf{T}\right] = -\frac{1}{2}\sum_{i=1}^{N}\left[\sum_{j=1}^{N} w_{ij} y_i y_j - \theta_i y_i\right] - \frac{1}{2}\sum_j^{N}(-\theta_j) y_j$$

$$= -\frac{1}{2}\sum_{i=1}^{N}\sum_{j=1}^{N} w_{ij} y_i y_j + \sum_i^{N} \theta_i y_i$$

$$= -\frac{1}{2}\mathbf{y}^\mathsf{T}\mathbf{W}\mathbf{y} + \theta^\mathsf{T}\mathbf{y}$$

$$= E(\mathbf{y})$$

Note that $[\mathbf{y}^\mathsf{T}\ 1]^\mathsf{T}$ is the same as the augmented vector in Chapter 4. The equivalence then follows from Theorem 8.2.

The relation between a Hopfield network and the MC problem leads to the following interpretation of the algorithm L_H.

Algorithm L_H for searching the MC in G.

1. Start with a random cut.
2. Choose a node k at random.
3. Compare the sum of weights of the edges that belong to the cut and are incident at node k with the sum of weights of the other edges incident at node k. Move node k to the side of the cut that will result in a *decrease* in the weight of the cut. Ties (the case of equality) are broken by placing node k in V_1.
4. Go to step 2.

The implementation of the stopping criterion in this algorithm is in accordance with the comments following the algorithm L_H for searching $\min(E(\mathbf{y}))$. This enables us to obtain an elementary convergence proof for the Hopfield network [59].

> **Theorem 8.4.** Let $H = (\mathbf{W}, \boldsymbol{\theta})$ define a network with a real symmetric zero-diagonal matrix $\mathbf{W}$. If H is running in a simple asynchronous mode, it will always converge to a stable state.

> **Proof.** Based on the foregoing discussions, the network H is running algorithm L_H to obtain the minimum cut in G. In each iteration the value of the cut is nonincreasing (ties are broken, as already described); thus, the algorithm will always stop at a cut whose sum of weights corresponds to a local minimum.

This proof is for the special case of a zero-diagonal matrix. It will now be shown that other general cases can be reduced to this case.

> **Lemma 8.1   [60].** Let $H = (\mathbf{W}, \boldsymbol{\theta})$ define a network where $\mathbf{W}$ is a real symmetric matrix with nonnegative diagonal elements. Let $\hat{H} = (\hat{\mathbf{W}}, \hat{\boldsymbol{\theta}})$ be obtained from H as follows. The topology of the network $\hat{H}$ is characterized by a bipartite graph, with a connection weight matrix
> $$\hat{W} = \begin{pmatrix} \mathbf{0} & \mathbf{W} \\ \mathbf{W} & \mathbf{0} \end{pmatrix},$$
> and the neurons in the network are associated with a vector of thresholds
> $$\hat{\boldsymbol{\theta}} = \begin{pmatrix} \boldsymbol{\theta}^{\mathrm{T}} & \boldsymbol{\theta}^{\mathrm{T}} \end{pmatrix}^{\mathrm{T}}.$$
> *(a)* For a simple asynchronous mode of operation in H there exists an equivalent simple asynchronous mode of operation in $\hat{H}$, provided $\mathbf{W}$ has a nonnegative diagonal.
> *(b)* There exists a simple asynchronous mode of operation in $\hat{H}$ that is equivalent to a synchronous mode of operation in H.

> **Proof.** The topology of the new network $\hat{H}$ is characterized by a bipartite graph having $2N$ nodes. Therefore the nodes of $\hat{H}$ can be naturally divided into two sets. Let P_1 denote the first set of N nodes and P_2 denote the second set of N nodes. It can be seen

from the definition of a bipartite graph describing $\hat{\mathbf{W}}$ that no two nodes of P_1 (or of P_2) are connected by an edge, as illustrated in Fig. 8.2. P_1 and P_2 are, from that standpoint, independent sets of nodes in $\hat{H}$. Observe also that P_1 and P_2 are symmetric in the sense that a node $i \in P_1$ has an edge set similar to that of a node $(i + N) \in P_2$.

Proof of (a). Let $\mathbf{v}_0$ be an initial state of H; therefore, the *states of the units represented by nodes* (referred to henceforth, for brevity, as *states of nodes*) in both P_1 and P_2 are $\mathbf{v}_0$. Let $(i_1, i_2, \ldots)$ be the order by which the states of the nodes are evaluated in a simple asynchronous mode of operation in H. It can be shown that starting from the initial state $(\mathbf{v}_0, \mathbf{v}_0)$ in $\hat{H}$ and using the order $(i_1, (i_1 + N), i_2, (i_2 + N), \ldots)$ for updating will result in the following.

(i) The state of the nodes in P_1 will be equal to the state of the nodes in P_2 in $\hat{H}$ after an arbitrary even number of evaluations.

(ii) The state of H at time index k is equal to the state of nodes in P_1 at time index $2k$, for an arbitrary k.

Part (i) can be proven by induction. Given that at some arbitrary time k the state of P_1 is equal to the state of P_2, it can be shown that after updating node i and then node $(N + i)$ the states of P_1 and P_2 remain equal. There are two cases, described next:

- If the state of node i does not change as a result of the evaluation, then by the symmetry of $\hat{H}$ there will be no change in the state of node $(N + i)$.
- If there is a change in the state of node i, then, because $\hat{w}_{i(N+i)}$ is nonnegative, it is straightforward to show that there will be a change in the state of node $(N + i)$.

The proof of (ii) follows from (i), as explained next. From (i), the state of P_1 is equal to the state of P_2 right before a node in P_1 is updated. Assume that the current

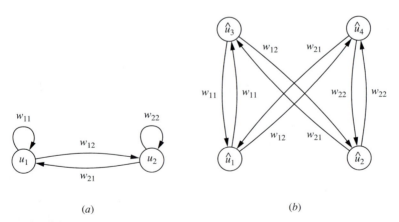

(a)   (b)

FIGURE 8.2
A bipartite graph in (b) is obtained from a Hopfield network graph with self-loops in (a) for $N = 2$.

state of H is the same as the state of P_1 in $\hat{H}$. Then updating node $i \in P_1$ will have the same result as updating $i \in H$. By induction, (ii) holds.

Proof of (b). Assume as in part *(a)* that $\hat{H}$ has the initial state $(\mathbf{v}_0, \mathbf{v}_0)$. Alternate updating of all nodes in P_1 synchronously and then all nodes in P_2 synchronously is equivalent to a synchronous mode of operation in H. The equivalence is in the sense that the state of H is equal to the state of the subset of nodes, either P_1 or P_2 of $\hat{H}$, at the time index at which the last updating was performed. Moreover, when the nodes in P_1 are updated in parallel, P_2 remains at the previous state of the network H. As long as P_2 keeps to the previous state of the network H, whether the nodes in P_1 are updated in parallel or one by one, the result will be the same after all units in P_1 are updated once. This is because the process of updating nodes in P_1 does not depend on the state of P_1. Therefore, there is a simple asynchronous mode of operation in $\hat{H}$ that is equivalent to the synchronous mode of operation in H.

Based on the foregoing, we have the following theorem [59].

Theorem 8.5. Let $H = (\mathbf{W}, \boldsymbol{\theta})$ define a neural network.

(a) If H is operating in a simple asynchronous mode and $\mathbf{W}$ is a symmetric matrix with nonnegative elements on the diagonal, the network will always converge to a stable state.

(b) If N is operating in a synchronous mode, then for an arbitrary symmetric matrix $\mathbf{W}$, the network will always converge to either a stable state or a cycle of length 2; i.e., the cycles in the state space are of length ≤ 2.

Proof.

Proof of (a). By part *(a)* of Lemma 8.1, every network H with nonnegative diagonal symmetric matrix $\mathbf{W}$ running in a simple asynchronous mode can be transformed to an equivalent network $\hat{H}$. $\hat{H}$ also runs in a simple asynchronous mode. $\hat{\mathbf{W}}$ is a symmetric, zero-diagonal matrix. By Theorem 8.4, $\hat{H}$ will converge to a stable state; hence, H will also converge to a stable state, which is equal to the state of nodes in P_1.

Proof of (b). By part *(b)* of Lemma 8.1, every network H operating in a synchronous mode can be transformed to an equivalent network $\hat{H}$ running in a simple asynchronous mode. The connection matrix $\hat{\mathbf{W}}$ is a symmetric, zero-diagonal matrix. By Theorem 8.4, $\hat{H}$ will converge to a stable state. When $\hat{H}$ reaches a stable state, there are two cases.

1. The state of nodes in P_1 is equal to the state of nodes in P_2; in this case H will converge to a stable state, which is equal to the state of nodes in P_1.

2. The states of nodes in P_1 and P_2 are distinct; in this case H will oscillate between the two states defined by the states of nodes in P_1 and P_2; i.e., H will converge to a cycle of length 2.

Bruck also showed that a network H running in a synchronous mode with an antisymmetric matrix $\mathbf{W}$ and zero diagonal and zero thresholds $(\boldsymbol{\theta} = \mathbf{0})$ will always converge to a cycle of length 4.

8.1.3   Capacity and Spurious Memory

It has just been shown that the Hopfield network will converge to stable states. Next, we answer the question regarding what these stable states are. In other words, we need to determine whether the pattern vectors to be stored are indeed the attractors of the network. The property of stability of an attractor enables the network to drive a small amount of perturbation in the state back to the attractor. In neural networks the point attractors are very commonly used for storing patterns. It is also possible to store time-varying patterns as limit cycles in feedback networks.

A fixed point in state space (phase space) will be called *robust stable* if small perturbations neither change nor eliminate it. The stability condition for a pattern vector indexed by p, associated with a point attractor $\mathbf{y}^p = (y_1^p \, y_2^p \cdots y_N^p)^\mathrm{T}$, is

$$y_i^p = T_b\left(\sum_j w_{ij} y_j^p - \theta_i\right), \qquad i = 1, 2, \ldots, N, \tag{8.12}$$

where $w_{ii} = 0$. Substituting Eq. (8.2) for the weights yields

$$y_i^p = T_b\left(\frac{1}{N} \sum_{j\neq i} \sum_s y_i^s y_j^s y_j^p - \theta_i\right)$$

$$= T_b\left(\frac{1}{N} y_i^p \sum_{j\neq i} (y_j^p)^2 + \frac{1}{N} \sum_{j\neq i} \sum_{s\neq p} y_i^s y_j^s y_j^p - \theta_i\right)$$

$$= T_b\left(\frac{N-1}{N} y_i^p + \delta_i^p\right), \tag{8.13}$$

where

$$\delta_i^p = \frac{1}{N} \sum_{j\neq i} \sum_{s\neq p} y_i^s y_j^s y_j^p - \theta_i \tag{8.14}$$

is called the *crosstalk term* because it contains the contributions of the remaining pattern vectors $\mathbf{y}^s$, $s \neq p$. Note that in the last step, use was made of the fact that the elements of the pattern vector are either $+1$ or -1, which implies that

$$\frac{1}{N} \sum_{j\neq i} (y_j^p)^2 \equiv \frac{N-1}{N}.$$

Assuming N is large, we replace $(N-1)/N$ by its approximant, 1. Therefore, if for all i, either $y_i^p \delta_i^p \geq 0$ or $y_i^p \delta_i^p < 0$, and $|\delta_i^p| < 1$, then

$$T_b(y_i^p + \delta_i^p) = T_b(y_i^p) = y_i^p. \tag{8.15}$$

Therefore, $\mathbf{y}^p$ is an attractor, and the pattern is stored.

Next, we analyze the crosstalk term and find out when its magnitude will be less than 1 for all the patterns to be stored. To simplify the analysis, assume that the patterns to be stored are totally random. Each pattern is independent of other patterns, and each bit of a pattern can be either $+1$ or -1 with equal probability independent of other bits in the same pattern. Thus, different stored patterns are assumed to be uncorrelated, and each pattern is assumed to be unbiased in the sense that in any stored state the numbers of active and quiescent neurons are (about) equal. Under this assumption, each $y_i^s y_j^s y_j^p$ term in the crosstalk δ_i^p, Eq. (8.14), is also a random variable with equal probability of being either -1 or $+1$ independently of the other terms. Without loss of generality, it is assumed that each of these components is of zero mean and unit variance. Thus, δ_i^p is the summation of $(N-1)(n-1) \approx Nn$ independent random variables when both N and n are sufficiently large. Each of the $(N-1)(n-1)$ randomly signed contributions (either $+1/N$ or $-1/N$) associated with the summation in the crosstalk term of Eq. (8.14) has zero mean and variance $1/N^2$. In that case, it follows from the *central-limit theorem*[1] that the probability distribution $P(\delta_i^p)$ of the crosstalk term δ_i^p is approximately a Gaussian distribution with a mean $m = -E(\theta_i)$ and a variance $\sigma^2 = n/N$,

$$P(\delta_i^p) = \frac{1}{\sigma \sqrt{2\pi}} \exp\left(-\frac{(\delta_i^p + E(\theta_i))^2}{2\sigma^2}\right). \tag{8.16}$$

We assume that the mean of the threshold, considered to be a random variable, is zero; i.e.,

$$E(\theta_i) = 0.$$

From the distribution it can then be seen that the probabilities for δ_i^p to be positive and negative are each equal to $1/2$; hence, the probability that δ_i^p has a different sign from y_i^p is also $1/2$. Therefore, the probability P_e for the crosstalk term to cause an error in bit i of the pattern ($\delta_i^p y_i^p < 0$ and $|\delta_i^p| > 1$) equals half of the sum of the areas under the distribution in Eq. (8.16) over the disjoint intervals extending from 1 to $+\infty$ and from -1 to $-\infty$. Since these two areas are equal,

$$P_e = \frac{1}{\sigma \sqrt{2\pi}} \int_1^\infty \exp\left(-\frac{x^2}{2\sigma^2}\right) dx, \tag{8.17}$$

which simplifies to

$$P_e = \frac{1}{\sigma \sqrt{2\pi}} \int_1^\infty \exp\left(-\frac{x^2}{2\sigma^2}\right) dx = \frac{1}{2}\left(1 - \text{erf}\left(\sqrt{N/2n}\right)\right) \tag{8.18}$$

---

[1]This theorem states that the sum of a large number M of independent and identically distributed random variables approaches a Gaussian probability distribution function centered at M times the component mean value, with a variance that is M times the variance of the original underlying probability distribution function.

where erf(x) is the *error function* given by

$$\text{erf}(x) = \frac{2}{\sqrt{\pi}} \int_0^x \exp(-\tau^2)d\tau. \tag{8.19}$$

The values of erf(x) can be found from a mathematical handbook. For example, when $n = 0.185N$, we have $P_e = 0.01$; i.e., each bit has 0.01 probability of being erroneous, or, equivalently, 1% of the bits in a pattern may be erroneous.

An important point to note is that Eq. (8.18) gives the probability of the number of bits that may be different from the stored pattern. We need to know whether this error will trigger the network to move farther away from the stored pattern. A more sophisticated mean field analysis of the problem yields the conclusion that for $n > 0.138N$ the error will trigger an avalanche-like increase in divergence from the stored patterns. It has been shown that at $n = \alpha N$, where $\alpha = 0.138$, there is a *phase transition:* the average number of error bits jumps from about 1.5% to about 100% [19, 20]. Therefore, for $n > 0.138N$, the memory becomes useless. Actually, Amit et al. [19, 20] obtained the phase diagram shown in Fig. 8.3 for the Hopfield network. The network is a useful memory only in areas A and B. Along the boundaries of the different regions the probability of error has jump discontinuities. Interested readers are referred to refs. [19, 20, 129, 158]. P_e gives the probability of error in a single bit of the pattern. A stricter requirement on the error is that all bits in a pattern must

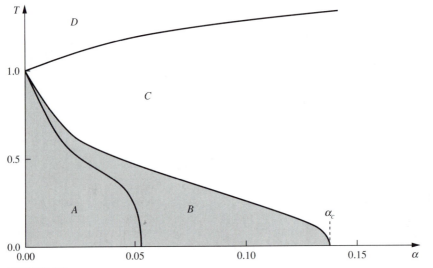

FIGURE 8.3
The phase diagram of the Hopfield network. Patterns to be stored are attractors only in areas A and B. The vertical axis is the "temperature" reflecting the randomness of state transitions at neurons, to be discussed in Section 8.3. (*Source:* Reprinted with permission from D. Amit, H. Gutfreund, and K. Sompolinsky, "Storing Infinite Numbers of Patterns in a Spin-Glass Model of Neural Networks," *Physical Review Letters* 55(14): 1532 (1985). Copyright © 1985 The American Physical Society.)

be recalled with very small probability of error. For example, one may require that $(1 - P_e)^N > 0.99$; i.e., the probability that all bits of a pattern are correctly recalled must be larger than 0.99. An even more stringent requirement is that all bits in *all* stored patterns must be recalled with very small probability of error; that is, requiring $(1 - P_e)^{nN} > 0.99$. In both cases, it is shown that the capacity of the memory is proportional to $N/\ln N$ [251, 400]. Why this is so is left as an exercise problem. To tackle the problem of memory limitations on the number of stored patterns, a small nonzero fraction of misaligned bits is allowed, and equilibrium is considered to have been reached if a sufficiently small number of units change state.

With the weights determined by Eq. (8.2), it has been shown that there are other attractors in the network in addition to the patterns to be stored. Amit et al. [18] showed that thresholded linear combinations of an odd number of the stored patterns may also be attractors of the network. These are referred to as the *mixed states*. As an example, consider a state that is formed from three random patterns by the *majority* rule:

$$y_i^{\text{mix}} = T_b(y_i^{p_1} + y_i^{p_2} + y_i^{p_3}). \tag{8.20}$$

Substituting y_j^{mix} in place of y_j^p into the right-hand side of Eq. (8.12) and using Eq. (8.2) yield

$$y_i^p = T_b\left(\frac{1}{N}\sum_j\sum_s y_i^s y_j^s y_j^{\text{mix}} - \theta_i\right)$$

$$= T_b\left(\frac{1}{N}y_i^{p_1}\sum_j y_j^{p_1} y_j^{\text{mix}} + \frac{1}{N}y_i^{p_2}\sum_j y_j^{p_2} y_j^{\text{mix}}\right.$$

$$\left. + \frac{1}{N}y_i^{p_3}\sum_j y_j^{p_3} y_j^{\text{mix}} + \frac{1}{N}\sum_j\sum_{s\neq p\in\{p_1,p_2,p_3\}} y_i^s y_j^s y_j^{\text{mix}} - \theta_i\right). \tag{8.21}$$

If the patterns are random, then $\sum_j y_j^{p_k} y_j^{\text{mix}} = N/2$ on average. To justify this, we adopt the argument advanced by Amit in [17]. Each bit in each of the three patterns has a probability of $\frac{3}{4}$ of being in the majority among the three bipolar bits that vote in the corresponding bit of $\mathbf{y}^{\text{mix}}$. To be in the minority, the two remaining bits must be of opposite sign. Thus, in $\mathbf{y}^{\text{mix}}$, three-fourths of the bits are of the same sign as in any of the three patterns y^{p_i}, $i = 1, 2, 3$, and one-fourth are of opposite sign. Hence,

$$y_i^p = T_b\left(\tfrac{1}{2}(y_i^{p_1} + y_i^{p_2} + y_i^{p_3}) + \text{crosstalk terms}\right). \tag{8.22}$$

Similar to the stored-pattern case, if the crosstalk term either has the same sign as y_i^{mix} or is less in magnitude than $|\tfrac{1}{2}(y_i^{p_1} + y_i^{p_2} + y_i^{p_3})|$, the mixed state is an attractor of the network. Other linear combinations of odd numbers of stored patterns may also become attractors of the network as well. Sums of even numbers of stored patterns are not mixed states of the network, because the sum may be zero on some units and the states of a unit can only be ± 1. (As an exercise, consider what happens if the TLUs used are unipolar binary with states of either 0 or 1).

We have shown that additional minima of the energy function may occur in addition to those that correspond to the stored patterns in the network. These additional minima or attractors that are unintentionally introduced are called the *spurious states*. The mixed states constitute only one type of spurious states that are possible in a Hopfield network. Another set of spurious states contains members that are not correlated to any of the stored patterns. This type of spurious state may occur when the number of stored patterns is large; it is called the *spin glass state* [19]. The signs and magnitudes of the weights, in this case, are distributed randomly, and interactions may take place between units that are widely separated. Some of the important contributions discussed in this section are linked to the *Ising model* in spin glass physics [17].

It has been shown that in some cases the number of spurious states in a Hopfield network can be an exponential function of the number of patterns to be stored. It may be so even when these pattern vectors form an orthogonal set [61]. A surprising result is that the spurious states can be exponential in the number n of the patterns to be stored even when n is small compared to the number N of units in the network. The following theorem is from ref. [61].

> **Theorem 8.6.** Let $N = 2^m$. For every k in $0 \leq k < m$ there exists a set of 2^k orthogonal pattern vectors $\{\mathbf{y}_1, \mathbf{y}_2, \ldots, \mathbf{y}_{2k}\}$, where $\mathbf{y}_i \in \{-1, 1\}^N$, such that when the element w_{ij} in the ith row and jth column of the interconnection weight matrix $\mathbf{W}$ is computed according to
>
> $$ w_{ij} = \begin{cases} \sum_{i=1}^{2^k} y_i y_j & i \neq j, \\ 0 & \text{otherwise,} \end{cases} \tag{8.23} $$
>
> the network specified by $(\mathbf{W}, \mathbf{0})$ has 2^{2^k} stable states, where $\mathbf{0}$ is the all zero or null threshold vector.

The proof is based on polynomial representations of Boolean functions. For the proof and other related results, see ref. [61]. We caution the reader that this is a worst-case scenario. The average behavior of a network is more useful in practice than a theoretical worst-case analysis.

Another class of attractors in the network are the "negatives" of the stored patterns if the thresholds are zero. This is because when the thresholds are all zero, the state transition equation, Eq. (8.4), is symmetric with respect to y_i and $-y_i$. This can also be seen from the symmetry in y_i and $-y_i$ exhibited in the energy equation.

8.1.4   Correlated Patterns

If the stored patterns are not totally random and independent, both bitwise and patternwise, the crosstalk term in general will be more significant. One way for offsetting this is by recoding the patterns before storage, i.e., before the calculation of the weights. This will make the patterns more like independent random patterns. Another approach to overcome the problem of correlated patterns is via the *projection method*, which is also called the *pseudoinverse* method [183, 200, 292]. If the number n of patterns to be stored is less than the number N of units, the weight matrix $\mathbf{W}$ can be determined by solving the following system of N equations:

$$\mathbf{W}\mathbf{y}^s = \mathbf{y}^s \text{ for } s = 1, 2, \ldots, n \tag{8.24}$$

$$\mathbf{W}\mathbf{y}^s = \mathbf{0} \text{ for } s = n + 1, \ldots, N, \tag{8.25}$$

where $\mathbf{y}^s$, $s = 1, \ldots, n$, are the patterns to be stored. If the patterns to be stored are linearly independent, and the vectors $\mathbf{y}^s$, $s = n + 1, \ldots, N$, are also chosen to be linearly independent, a unique $\mathbf{W}$ can be found. With the $\mathbf{W}$ so determined, the pattern vectors to be stored become stable states of the network.

An interpretation of the $\mathbf{W}$ matrix is that the N column vectors of $\mathbf{W}$ are the basis vectors. They are not necessarily orthogonal. The projections of a pattern to be stored onto these basis vectors equal the pattern vector, implying that $\mathbf{W}$ is an idempotent matrix. A pattern to be stored is expressed as a linear combination of the column vectors in $\mathbf{W}$. The maximum number of patterns that can be stored is $N - 1$, because for N linearly independent patterns $\mathbf{W}$ reduces to an identity matrix. Then *any* pattern becomes a stable state of the network, and it is no longer a useful associative memory, as is easily substantiated next. If $\mathbf{y}^s$, $s = 1, 2, \ldots, N$, are linearly independent, define the *pattern matrix* $\mathbf{Y}_N = [\mathbf{y}^1 \ \mathbf{y}^2 \ \cdots \ \mathbf{y}^N]$ for the set of N pattern vectors. Since all the patterns are linearly independent, $\mathbf{Y}_N^{-1}$ exists, and Eq. (8.25) does not exist, so that

$$\mathbf{W}\mathbf{Y}_N = \mathbf{Y}_N \rightarrow \mathbf{W} = \mathbf{Y}_N \mathbf{Y}_N^{-1} = \mathbf{I}. \tag{8.26}$$

If some of the patterns to be stored are linearly dependent, $\mathbf{W}$ is not unique. This problem can be tackled by considering only a maximal subset, containing the patterns that are linearly independent. $\mathbf{W}$ is determined by increasing the dimension of the *null space*—the linear vector space generated from vectors $\mathbf{y}^z$ such that $\mathbf{W}\mathbf{y}^z = \mathbf{0}$. These vectors are stored in the network as spurious memory states. With the weight matrix so determined, the determination of the possible spurious memories is left as an exercise.

Assume that there are n linearly independent pattern vectors in all the patterns to be stored. A direct method to determine the weight matrix from these n linearly independent pattern vectors follows. The weight matrix obtained from this method will guarantee that all the n linearly independent patterns become the stable states of the network. Define an $n \times n$ *overlap matrix* $\mathbf{P}$ as

$$\mathbf{P} = \frac{1}{N}\mathbf{Y}_n^T\mathbf{Y}_n, \tag{8.27}$$

where $\mathbf{Y}_n = [\mathbf{y}^1 \ \mathbf{y}^2 \ \cdots \ \mathbf{y}^n]$ is the $N \times n$ *pattern matrix* for the set of n pattern vectors. The n pattern vectors are linearly independent, so the inverse $\mathbf{P}^{-1}$ exists. If we postmultiply the pattern matrix by $\mathbf{P}^{-1}$, we have

$$\mathbf{X} = \mathbf{Y}_n\mathbf{P}^{-1}, \tag{8.28}$$

where $\mathbf{X}$ is an $N \times n$ matrix. Since $\mathbf{P}$ is a symmetric matrix, therefore,

$$\mathbf{X}^T\mathbf{Y}_n = N\mathbf{P}^{-1}\mathbf{P} = N\mathbf{I}, \tag{8.29}$$

where $\mathbf{I}$ is the $n \times n$ identity matrix. This shows that $\mathbf{X}^T/N$ is the left pseudoinverse matrix of $\mathbf{Y}_n$; hence, the method is referred to as the pseudoinverse method. If we choose the $N \times N$ weight matrix $\mathbf{W}$ as

$$\mathbf{W} = \frac{1}{N}\mathbf{Y}_n\mathbf{X}^T, \tag{8.30}$$

then (post-multiply both sides of Eq. (8.30) by $\mathbf{Y}_n$ and use Eq. (8.29))

$$\mathbf{W}\mathbf{y}^s = \mathbf{y}^s \quad \text{for all } s = 1, 2, \ldots, n. \tag{8.31}$$

Therefore, if the weights are chosen according to Eqs. (8.27) through (8.30), all the linearly independent pattern vectors $\mathbf{y}^s$, $s = 1, 2, \ldots, n$, are guaranteed to be the stable states of the network. Note that components of these pattern vectors can be only either $+1$ or -1. Otherwise, satisfaction of Eq. (8.31) does not mean stable states, because the unit outputs can only be ± 1. The weight matrix is the unique one that transforms any vector orthogonal to the pattern vectors to a zero vector. That is,

$$\mathbf{W}\mathbf{y} = \mathbf{0} \tag{8.32}$$

for any $\mathbf{y}$ orthogonal to all the pattern vectors.

Unlike Eq. (8.2), Eq. (8.30) for determining the weights is not local. To compute a weight in Eq. (8.2), only the states of the units connected by the edge associated with that weight are required. In neurological terms, only the states of the presynaptic and postsynaptic neurons are required. Such a situation is in the spirit of the Hebbian rule. In Eq. (8.30), however, the states of all units in the network are required to compute a weight. An iterative algorithm using only local information has been proposed [96], which converges to the same result given in Eq. (8.30).

8.1.5   Hopfield Networks with Variations in the Connection Weights

In this part, we consider the behavior of a Hopfield network whose connections are not exactly determined by Eq. (8.2). In a digital hardware implementation the weights can assume only a finite number of discrete values. In an analog hardware implementation the weights can assume values only within a given range. In both cases the convergence is not affected as long as the symmetry of the connection weights is maintained. However, these constraints on the weights have some effect on how close the attractors are to the actual patterns to be stored. Several attractors, representing different stored patterns, may merge into one attractor that may not be associated with any of the patterns to be stored. In other words, discretization, which limits the range of the weights, reduces the capacity of the network as an associative memory.

An interesting extreme case arises when the weights are limited to be binary. It has been shown that for binary weights the phase transition of the bit error occurs at $\alpha = 0.1$ instead of at $\alpha = 0.138$, where $\alpha = n/N$ is the ratio of the number of patterns stored over the number of units in the network [384]. This is a rather surprising result because it shows that the gain in memory capacity by changing from binary weights to arbitrary weights is only 38 percent, whereas the circuit complexity increases at least logarithmically with the number of weight values allowed (it is assumed that the network is to be used as an associative memory for arbitrary binary patterns).

In a hardware implementation the weights may also vary slightly from their specified values because of noise or inaccuracy in the components. Such small random variations are also known to affect the memory capacity of the network [360].

Another type of variation on weights is called *dilution*. The basic idea here is to cut off some connections (i.e., make some weights zero) randomly according to a given probability distribution in order to reduce the connection complexity. A *weak dilution* is said to occur if the probability of setting a weight to zero is low and the majority of the nonzero connections are maintained. A *strong dilution* occurs if the majority of the connections are cut and only an infinitesimal fraction of the connections are maintained as $N \rightarrow \infty$. In the case of weak dilution, when the symmetry of the connections is maintained, the network behaves in essentially the same way but with reduced memory capacity [67, 158, 360]. For the strong dilution case, it has been shown that if the average number K of connections from each unit does not exceed a number proportional to $\log N$ as $N \rightarrow \infty$, and the dilution is performed independently on w_{ij} and w_{ji}, then $n \leq 2K/\pi$ patterns may be stored in the network [91, 158].

8.1.6   Bidirectional Associative Memory

Kosko [203] extended the Hopfield network to a Bidirectional Associative Memory (BAM) for pairwise association of patterns. The BAM is a resonance model, in the sense that information is passed back and forth between two layers of units until an overall stable state is reached. The graph of a bidirectional associative memory is bipartite and is shown in Fig. 8.4, where for the sake of simplicity the feedforward and feedback edges between a unit in one part and a unit in another part are shown through arrows on a common edge. Each unit is a TLU, as in the discrete Hopfield network. Information passes from layer A, with N units, to layer B, with M units, through the $M \times N$ connection matrix $\mathbf{W}$. Information passes backward from B to A through the transposed $N \times M$ matrix $\mathbf{W}^{\mathrm{T}}$. As a result, though $\mathbf{W}$ may not be a symmetric matrix, a BAM is a symmetric network, because the overall interconnection weight matrix

$$\begin{pmatrix} \mathbf{0} & \mathbf{W} \\ \mathbf{W}^{\mathrm{T}} & \mathbf{0} \end{pmatrix}$$

is symmetric. The Hopfield network is said to be autoassociative, because it uses a partial and noisy pattern to recall the best match of itself. The BAM is heteroassociative, because the association is between pairs of patterns $\{(\mathbf{x}^i, \mathbf{y}^i)\}_{i=1}^n$, where $\mathbf{x}^i \in \{-1, 1\}^N$ is an $N \times 1$ vector and $\mathbf{y}^i \in \{-1, 1\}^M$ is an $M \times 1$ vector.

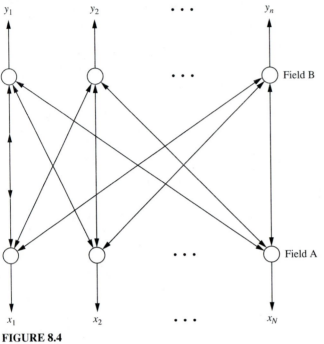

FIGURE 8.4
A bidirectional associative memory.

In a BAM a pattern vector $\mathbf{x}$ presented to layer A will be fed through $\mathbf{W}$ to layer B, producing a pattern vector $\mathbf{y}$ in layer B. Assume that the stable states in the BAM are $\{\mathbf{x}^i, \mathbf{y}^i\}$, $i = 1, 2, \ldots, n$. If $\mathbf{x}$ is closer to $\mathbf{x}^j$ than to any other stored vectors $\mathbf{x}^i$, $i \neq j$, the image $\mathbf{y}$ of $\mathbf{x}$ should be closer to $\mathbf{y}^j$. Then $\mathbf{y}^j$ is fed back to A through $\mathbf{W}^{\mathrm{T}}$. The sequence of the recall continues as follows:

$$\mathbf{x} \rightarrow \mathbf{W} \rightarrow \mathbf{y}$$
$$\mathbf{x}' \leftarrow \mathbf{W}^{\mathrm{T}} \leftarrow \mathbf{y}$$
$$\mathbf{x}' \rightarrow \mathbf{W} \rightarrow \mathbf{y}'$$
$$\mathbf{x}'' \leftarrow \mathbf{W}^{\mathrm{T}} \leftarrow \mathbf{y}'$$
$$\vdots$$
$$\mathbf{x}^j \rightarrow \mathbf{W} \rightarrow \mathbf{y}^j$$
$$\mathbf{x}^j \leftarrow \mathbf{W}^{\mathrm{T}} \leftarrow \mathbf{y}^j$$
$$\vdots$$

Finally, the network reaches the stable state, $(\mathbf{x}^j, \mathbf{y}^j)$.

The connection weights are determined from the principle of superposition of the correlations between pairs of bits of all patterns, as in the Hopfield network. The difference is that only the correlations between the two layers are used; i.e., the connection weight from the ith unit in A to the jth unit in B is given by

$$w_{ij} = \sum_s x_j^s y_i^s, \quad \text{or in matrix form} \quad \mathbf{W} = \sum_s \mathbf{y}^s (\mathbf{x}^s)^{\mathrm{T}}. \quad (8.33)$$

The connection weight from the jth unit in A to the ith unit in B is symmetric in the sense that it equals the above value. The connection weights can be either computed before the network is used or learned using the Hebbian rule [202, 204]. The proof of convergence for the Hopfield network can be easily extended to show that the BAM will converge to a stable state. We present the following theorem for BAM stability [203, 204]. Remember that for any matrix $\mathbf{W}$, symmetric or asymmetric, a BAM is always a symmetric network. Therefore, the stability can be expected for an arbitrary real matrix $\mathbf{W}$.

Theorem 8.7. The BAM is stable for every interconnection weight matrix $\mathbf{W}$ and for simple asynchronous, general asynchronous, and synchronous state updates.

Proof. General asynchronous and synchronous updatings are limited in the sense that they are subject to the condition that field A and field B must update alternately. Without loss of generality, assume that all the TLUs in the network have zero threshold. Define an energy function

$$E(\mathbf{x}, \mathbf{y}) = -\tfrac{1}{2}\mathbf{x}^{\mathrm{T}}\mathbf{W}^{\mathrm{T}}\mathbf{y} - \tfrac{1}{2}\mathbf{y}^{\mathrm{T}}\mathbf{W}\mathbf{x}. \quad (8.34)$$

Observe that

$$\mathbf{x}^{\mathrm{T}}\mathbf{W}^{\mathrm{T}}\mathbf{y} = (\mathbf{x}^{\mathrm{T}}\mathbf{W}^{\mathrm{T}}\mathbf{y})^{\mathrm{T}} = \mathbf{y}^{\mathrm{T}}\mathbf{W}\mathbf{x}.$$

Therefore, the energy function can be simplified to

$$E(\mathbf{x}, \mathbf{y}) = -\mathbf{y}^{\mathrm{T}}\mathbf{W}\mathbf{x}. \quad (8.35)$$

Denote the state changes in layers A and B by $\Delta\mathbf{x}$ and $\Delta\mathbf{y}$, respectively. With $\Delta\mathbf{x} = (\Delta x_1 \ \Delta x_2 \ \cdots \ \Delta x_N)^{\mathrm{T}}$, it is easy to show that

$$\Delta E = E(\mathbf{x} + \Delta\mathbf{x}, \mathbf{y}) - E(\mathbf{x}, \mathbf{y}) = -\sum_i \left(\Delta x_i \left(\sum_j w_{ij} y_j \right) \right). \quad (8.36)$$

Each of the terms $(\Delta x_i(\sum_j w_{ij} y_j))$ inside the first summation is always positive or zero, as in the Hopfield network. Therefore, $\Delta E \le 0$. The equality holds when there is no state change. Similarly, it can be shown that $\Delta E \le 0$ for state changes $\Delta\mathbf{y}$. Since the energy E is bounded from below, the state changes in a BAM with any $\mathbf{W}$ converge for simple asynchronous state changes (only one unit in A or B is updated at a time by Δx_i or Δy_j). Similar conclusions can be drawn for general asynchronous state changes (any number of units in A or B are updated at a time) and for synchronous state changes (all units in A or B are updated at the same time).

An interesting question to ask is whether this proof of convergence for general asynchronous state changes and synchronous state changes holds for the Hopfield network. The answer is no. The proof holds for the BAM because there are no lateral connections among units in the same layer. It is left as an exercise to show that if there are (symmetric) lateral connections, the proof just given would not hold for general asynchronous state changes and synchronous state changes.

8.2   SYMMETRIC NETWORKS WITH ANALOG UNITS

The Hopfield networks discussed in the preceding section use TLUs and are referred to as discrete Hopfield networks. Real neurons are not simple binary devices; they are capable of graded response in which the strengths of the output signals are coded by the short-term average frequency of the action potentials. Another simplification of the Hopfield networks discussed in the preceding section is the sudden change of states of the units; real neurons have integrative time delays. Furthermore, the state transition in real networks is continuous; it should be described by differential equations. Similarly, analog electronic circuits that implement neural network models have the same characteristics: graded response, integrative time delay, and continuous state transition.

8.2.1   Analog Hopfield Networks

Hopfield networks can be extended to networks with units having graded response [163]. These are referred to as *continuous* or *analog* Hopfield networks. The neuron model with continuous transfer characteristics, as described in Section 1.3.2, is used. The differential equations describing a network with graded response units are given as

$$C_i \frac{du_i}{dt} = \sum_j w_{ij} y_j - \frac{u_i}{R_i} + I_i, \tag{8.37}$$

where for unit i, C_i is the membrane capacitance, R_i is the transmembrane resistance, I_i is the external input current, y_i is the output potential of a unit, u_i is the instantaneous transmembrane potential, and w_{ij} represents the connection weight conductance from each of the other units. Let the activation function $y_i = g(u_i)$ of a neuron (and of an amplifier) be a nonlinear and monotone increasing function of the form shown in Fig 8.5. The fast-rising part of the curve can be approximated by a linear amplifier. The gain of the amplifier is given by the slope of the curve. Like any physical device, it must either saturate or cut off. Hence, the curve levels off, approaching asymptotes at both ends, as the magnitude of the input increases. The inverse function exists and is also monotonically increasing. The values approached by the asymptotes are unimportant and are assumed to be ± 1 here.

An electrical circuit implementing a network consisting of these graded response units is shown in Fig. 8.6. The inverters are used to realize inhibitive connections (i.e., negative weights). The equation describing the dynamics of the circuit in Fig. 8.6 is

$$C_i \frac{du_i}{dt} + \frac{u_i}{\rho_i} = \sum_j \frac{1}{R_{ij}}(y_j - u_i) + I_i. \tag{8.38}$$

Let

$$\frac{1}{R_i} = \frac{1}{\rho_i} + \sum_j \frac{1}{R_{ij}} \quad \text{and} \quad w_{ij} = \frac{R_i}{R_{ij}}. \tag{8.39}$$

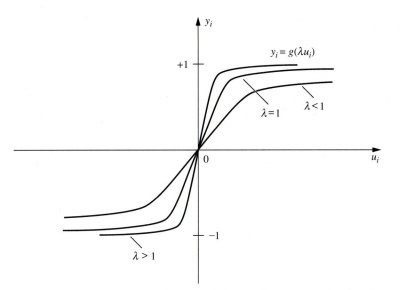

FIGURE 8.5
Sigmoidal nonlinear activation functions of a neuron (or an amplifier). The parameter λ scales the gain.

Then we have

$$\tau_i \frac{du_i}{dt} = -u_i + \sum_j w_{ij} y_j + I_i R_i, \qquad (8.40)$$

where $\tau_i = R_i C_i$. The form is similar to the one in Eq. (8.37) after multiplying both sides of Eq. (8.37) by R_i.

To implement the circuit, the R_{ij} values need to be determined to satisfy the relation in Eq. (8.39). In order to choose each R_{ij} independently, we may choose ρ_i to be small so that $R_i \approx \rho_i$. Then the weights can be determined independently by

$$w_{ij} \approx \frac{\rho_i}{R_{ij}}, \qquad (8.41)$$

where ρ_i is the input resistance of the amplifier. A small ρ_i, however, implies a large power consumption.

Denker [89] proposed a circuit to determine the weights independently without making ρ_i small. That circuit is shown in Fig. 8.7a. Assuming that node P in the circuit is a virtual ground, the node equation becomes

$$\sum_j \frac{y_j}{R_{ij}} + I_i = \frac{y_i}{\rho_i} + C_i \frac{dy_i}{dt}. \qquad (8.42)$$

Letting $\tau_i = \rho_i C_i$, $w_{ij} = \rho_i / R_{ij}$ and $\theta_i = -\rho_i I_i$, we have

$$\tau_i \frac{dy_i}{dt} = -y_i + \sum_j w_{ij} y_j - \theta_i. \qquad (8.43)$$

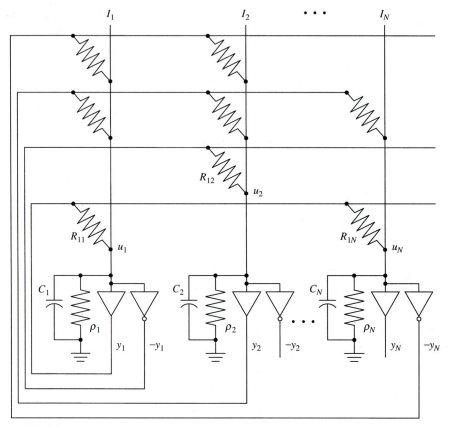

FIGURE 8.6
Analog circuit for a Hopfield network with continuous response.

Note that Eq. (8.43) is an ordinary linear differential equation. The circuit must be modified to make the equation nonlinear. One way is to add to Fig. 8.7a a subcircuit that realizes the nonlinear transfer characteristic of a neuron whose input is at virtual ground. The result is given in the circuit of Fig. 8.7b. The equation describing the system realized by a network of units shown in Fig. 8.7b now has the form

$$\tau_i \frac{dy_i}{dt} = -y_i + f_i\left(\sum_j w_{ij} y_j - \theta_i\right), \tag{8.44}$$

where $f_i(\cdot)$ describes the transfer characteristic of the unit scaled by ρ_i. This model of a neural network is frequently used in the literature, because it involves only the state variables y_i of the network, unlike Eq. (8.40), which contains both y_i and u_i. Similar to the continuous Hopfield network, the above results can be extended to a continuous BAM where the units have continuous monotonically increasing transfer characteristics [203, 204].

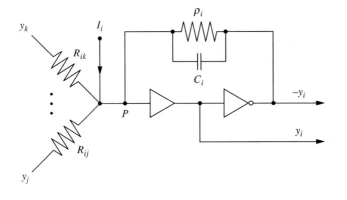

(a)

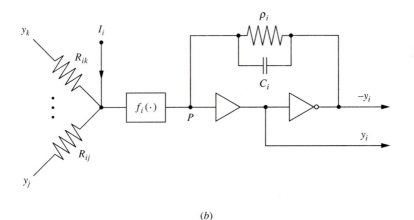

(b)

FIGURE 8.7
(a) A circuit to enable independent choice of the weights without requiring small
input resistance. (b) Modification of (a) to add a nonlinear transfer characteristic.

Many hardware implementations of the analog Hopfield network have been
reported [13, 137, 165, 253, 332, 334, 356]. The difficulties in VLSI implementation of the Hopfield networks include the large number of connections, of order
$O(n^2)$, and making them learnable and symmetric. The convergence of the Hopfield
network depends on the symmetry of connections, $w_{ij} = w_{ji}$. This condition may
be met in a digital implementation, but it is practically impossible in an analog implementation. If the connection weight matrix is far from being symmetric, the state
transitions of the network may become oscillatory or chaotic. When the connection
weights are random with a zero mean and a variance of σ^2, there is a transition from
stable to chaotic behavior as σ^2 is increased [361]. Salam [332] solved this problem
by using the same connection weight for both w_{ij} and w_{ji}. The connection weight
may be realized as a simple conductance for a linear synapse or as a metal-oxide-

semiconductor field-effect transistor (MOSFET) for a nonlinear synapse. Another advantage of sharing the two connection weights is that the maximum number of connections is cut in half. Since floating-gate nonvolatile memory technology for MOSFETs is often used to realize adjustable weights in analog implementations of Hopfield networks [103, 161, 217], the synapses realized are often nonlinear. Convergence of the network with such nonlinear synapses to stable states can be shown, similar to the proof in the following subsection, by defining an energy function [332].

The Hopfield network has also been implemented using optical technology (e.g., [2, 21, 167, 294, 393]), since it is easy to make many connections there. However, it is rather difficult to make many units in optical technology because of the inherent linearity of most optical media. Early efforts in optical implementation were in hybrid optoelectronic or photonic systems taking advantage of both technologies [109, 110]. The price paid is the cost of conversion between optical and electrical signals. Efforts towards developing fully optical neural networks using nonlinear optical devices have been reported [110].

8.2.2 Convergence Proof

Applying the same technique used in the discrete Hopfield network, let the energy function E for the network defined in Eq. (8.37) be

$$E = -\frac{1}{2}\sum_i \sum_j w_{ij} y_i y_j - \sum_i I_i y_i + \sum_i \frac{1}{R_i} \int_0^{y_i} g_i^{-1}(y)\, dy, \qquad (8.45)$$

where the inverse function, g_i^{-1}, is related to g_i in $y_i = g(u_i)$ through the constraint equation $g_i^{-1}[g_i(\cdot)] = g_i[g_i^{-1}(\cdot)] = 1$. The function g_i is assumed to be a monotonically increasing differentiable function. This assumption guarantees the existence of the inverse function, which is also monotonically increasing. Therefore, g_i^{-1} has a positive slope everywhere. Assuming the connections are symmetric, we have

$$\frac{dE}{dt} = -\sum_i \frac{dy_i}{dt}\left(\sum_j w_{ij} y_j - \frac{u_i}{R_i} + I_i\right). \qquad (8.46)$$

The expression inside the parentheses in Eq. (8.46) is the right-hand side of Eq. (8.37). Therefore,

$$\frac{dE}{dt} = -\sum_i C_i \frac{dy_i}{dt}\frac{du_i}{dt} = -\sum_i C_i (g_i^{-1}(y_i))'\left(\frac{dy_i}{dt}\right)^2. \qquad (8.47)$$

Since $g_i^{-1}(y_i)$ is a monotonically increasing function, its derivative $(g_i^{-1}(y_i))' > 0$. Also, C_i is positive. Therefore,

$$\frac{dE}{dt} \le 0, \quad \text{and} \quad \frac{dE}{dt} = 0 \rightarrow \frac{dy_i}{dt} = 0 \quad \text{for all } i. \qquad (8.48)$$

Using the boundedness property of E, it can be concluded that the time evolution of the network seeks out the minima of E in the state space and stops at such points.

Actually, E is a Lyapunov-like function of the system described in Eq. (8.37). More detailed analysis of the dynamic behavior of the Hopfield network may be found in ref. [335].

For convergence to energy minima, we assumed that the connection weight matrix is symmetric. In practice, an approximation to symmetry can sometimes be sufficient, similar to the discrete case. It can be shown by a linear approximation near an attractor that the energy approaches that of an attractor asymptotically [17]. In practice, the energy is considered to have reached the minimum after finite time. Zak showed that Eq. (8.37) can be modified so that the energy does reach the value assumed at an attractor in a finite number of steps [426].

8.2.3 Relation between Stable States of Discrete and Analog Hopfield Networks

For a given symmetric connection weight matrix, the stable states of the analog Hopfield network have a simple correspondence with the stable states of the discrete network. To make the relation clearer, we assume that $g_i(0) = 0$ and the external inputs $I_i = 0$. For the discrete network, assume the thresholds are zero. The energy function for the analog network now becomes

$$E = -\frac{1}{2}\sum_i \sum_j w_{ij} y_i y_j + \sum_i \frac{1}{R_i} \int_0^{y_i} g_i^{-1}(y)\, dy. \tag{8.49}$$

In the usual case the maxima and minima of the first term in the N-dimensional hypercube $[-1, 1]^N$ lie at corners of the hypercube (why?). If the interconnection weight matrix $\mathbf{W}$ is either positive-definite or negative-definite, there may also be an extremum in the interior of the hypercube (why?). The connection weight matrix determined by the Hebbian rule often is neither nonnegative-definite nor nonpositive-definite but indefinite.

The discrete network searches for the energy minima at the corners of the hypercube. The extrema of

$$E = -\frac{1}{2}\sum_i \sum_j w_{ij} y_i y_j \tag{8.50}$$

for the discrete network are exactly at the same corners as the extrema of the first term in Eq. (8.49) for the analog case.

The second term in Eq. (8.49) alters the overall picture somewhat. To understand the effect of the second term better, we use a scaled notion of the neuron activation function. Replace

$$y_i = g(u_i) \qquad \text{by} \qquad y_i = g(\lambda u_i) \tag{8.51}$$

and

$$u_i = g^{-1}(y_i) \qquad \text{by} \qquad u_i = (1/\lambda)g_i^{-1}(y_i). \tag{8.52}$$

The scaling factor λ changes the gain of the sigmoid curve without altering the output asymptotes, as shown in Fig. (8.5). The second term in Eq. (8.49) now becomes

$$+\frac{1}{\lambda}\sum_i \frac{1}{R_i}\int_0^{y_i} g_i^{-1}(y)\,dy. \qquad (8.53)$$

The integral is zero for $y_i = 0$ and positive otherwise. In the high-gain limit, when $\lambda \to \infty$, this second term becomes negligible, and the energy expression becomes the same as that of the discrete network with zero thresholds. The stable points of a very high-gain analog Hopfield network therefore correspond to the stable points of the discrete network.

For finite λ, the contribution of the second term in Eq. (8.49) to the total energy is not negligible. The integral in Eq. (8.53) increases monotonically as $y_i \to \pm 1$. Its contribution may be very large near all surfaces, edges, and corners of the hypercube if the activation function $g(u_i)$ approaches the asymptotes very slowly. This leads to an energy function that still has its maxima at corners, but the minima become displaced slightly toward the interior of the hypercube. As λ decreases, each minimum moves further inward and eventually disappears when it coalesces with a saddle point of the energy function. Ultimately, for very small λ, the second term dominates, and the only minimum is at $y_i = 0$ for all i. In Fig. 8.8, the upper right and lower left corners are the stable minima for infinite gain. Unstable extrema are at the other two corners. The minima are moved inward in the finite-gain case. When the gain is large enough, each minimum can be associated with a well-defined minimum for the discrete case. As the gain is increased in an analog network, each minimum moves towards a corner of the hypercube.

8.2.4   Cellular Neural Networks

The Hopfield networks, in general, are completely connected. The number of connections, therefore, scales as the square of the number of units. This presents a serious problem in the VLSI implementation of large networks.

Chua and his colleagues introduced the Cellular Neural Network (CNN) [77, 78, 79, 80]. A CNN is an analog Hopfield network in which the connections are limited to units in local neighborhoods of individual units with bidirectional signal paths. It is a strongly diluted Hopfield network and has a structure similar to a cellular automaton. Units in a CNN are arranged in a d-dimensional array. Typically, $d = 2$, because this provides a good match to computations in image processing applications. An example of a two-dimensional CNN is shown in Fig. 8.9.

Assume that a two-dimensional cellular neural network has M rows and N columns. Denote the unit at the ith row and jth column by $u(i, j)$. A *neighborhood* is defined as

$$N_r(i, j) = \{u(p,q) \mid \max(|p - i|, |q - j|) \le r,\ 1 \le p \le M;\ 1 \le q \le N\}, \quad (8.54)$$

where r controls the size of the neighborhood. For the example in Fig. 8.9, $r = 1$.

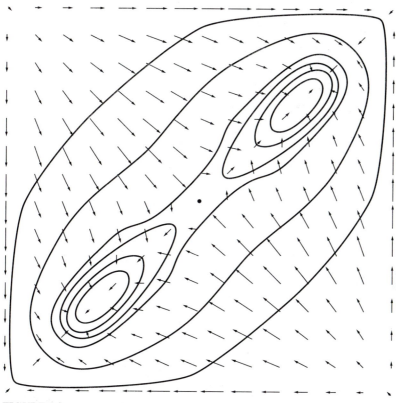

FIGURE 8.8

Energy-descending directions in a two-neuron, two-attractor network. The ordinate and abscissa are the outputs of the neurons. The dot at the center is a saddle point of the energy function. (*Source:* Reprinted with permission from J.J. Hopfield, "Neurons with Graded Response Have Collective Computational Properties like Those of Two-State Neurons," *Proceedings of the National Academy of Sciences,* 81:3088–3092 (1984). Copyright ©1984 J.J. Hopfield (published by National Academy Press).)

The unit at the center of an N_r-neighborhood is connected to all the other units within the neighborhood, but not to any unit outside that neighborhood. All connections are symmetric; thus, a CNN is a symmetric recurrent network. Therefore, by using an appropriately defined energy function, its stability can be proved in the same way as an analog Hopfield network. An initial condition at each node starts the response dynamics, and the system ultimately evolves to a stable state. Actually, a CNN can also be used as an associative memory. In computing the weights of connections from a unit in a CNN for an associative memory by Eq. (8.2), only units within the N_r-neighborhood are used to compute the correlation. This may cause problems in associative recall from a pattern that is partially missing, especially if the missing part is located outside the N_r-neighborhood. Units that are not connected to any units corresponding to the nonmissing part of the input pattern will not be able

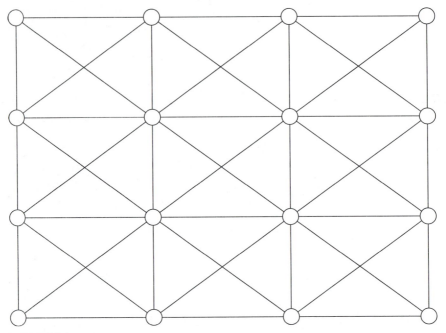

FIGURE 8.9
A two-dimensional cellular neural network structure.

to respond in any way until the association is propagated to units in its neighborhood. The speed of associative recall will be much slower than in the completely connected network. Since a CNN is a strongly diluted Hopfield network, its memory capacity is severely limited.

The biggest advantage of the CNN is that its interconnections are local, making it well suited for VLSI implementation of large networks. A two-dimensional CNN can be viewed as a parallel nonlinear two-dimensional filter, which is highly suited for image processing applications. Therefore, the most popular application for cellular neural networks has been in image processing, essentially because of their analog features and sparse connections, which are conducive to real-time processing. Cellular neural networks for noise removal, shape extraction, edge detection, and Chinese character recognition have also been demonstrated [80].

Although only symmetric cellular neural networks have been investigated, asymmetric CNNs may also be possible for applications involving temporal variations of spatial patterns. Analysis of the dynamic behavior would become more difficult in that case (see Section 8.5).

8.3   SEEKING THE GLOBAL MINIMUM: SIMULATED ANNEALING

In the Hopfield network, many local minima are used to store information. Its ability to function as an associative memory depends on reliable recall of the local minima.

However, in many cases, the network is required to reach the global minimum, such as in optimization tasks. A Hopfield network follows a gradient descent rule. Once it reaches a local minimum, it is stuck there. To find the global minimum of a function using only local information, some randomness must be added to the gradient descent rule to increase the chance of hitting the global minimum. Next, we introduce the simulated annealing method for optimization.

8.3.1 Simulated Annealing in Optimization

Many problems in science and engineering can be formulated as optimization problems. There are two basic strategies for heuristic search for a minimum of a function: divide-and-conquer and iterative improvement. The first strategy is problem-specific, because an effective decomposition of the problem depends on the nature of the problem itself. Iterative improvement, commonly known as gradient descent, is a general method. Its difficulty is that it often gets stuck at a local minimum. *Simulated annealing* (SA) [189] is a method that introduces randomness to allow the system to jump out of a local minimum. The method draws an analogy between optimization of a cost function in a large number of variables with minimization of an energy function in statistical mechanics.

Statistical mechanics is the central discipline of condensed-matter physics. It offers a body of methods for analyzing aggregate properties of physical systems with a very large number of particles. For a given physical system with a set of possible states or configurations $\{\alpha_i\}$, define an energy function E. The total energy of the system at configuration α_i is denoted as E_{α_i}. If the system is at a temperature T greater than absolute zero (zero Kelvin, i.e., -273 degrees Celsius), there will be *thermal fluctuations,* which are state transitions that cause the configuration energy to either increase or decrease slightly. When the system only fluctuates around constant average values without drifting far away, it is said to have reached *thermal equilibrium.*

A fundamental result from statistical mechanics shows that in thermal equilibrium the probability P_{α_i} of finding the system at a configuration α_i is given by the *Boltzmann-Gibbs distribution*

$$P_{\alpha_i} = \frac{1}{Z} \exp\left\{ \frac{-E_{\alpha_i}}{k_B T} \right\}, \tag{8.55}$$

where T is the temperature in Kelvin and k_B is the *Boltzmann constant.* Since the "temperature" in simulated annealing and neural networks is not related to the physical temperature at all, we will normalize the Boltzmann constant to 1 in this book. The denominator Z in the preceding equation is called the *partition function* and is given as

$$Z = \sum_i \exp\left\{ \frac{-E_{\alpha_i}}{T} \right\}. \tag{8.56}$$

The Boltzmann-Gibbs distribution holds for systems with a very large number of particles, unless the system is constrained so that it cannot explore all its possible states.

Suppose there are two configurations α_i and α_j. Then the ratio of the probabilities of the two configurations is given by

$$\frac{P_{\alpha_i}}{P_{\alpha_j}} = \exp\left\{ -\frac{(E_{\alpha_i} - E_{\alpha_j})}{T} \right\}. \tag{8.57}$$

If the temperature is very high, the probabilities of finding the system at high and low energy levels are roughly the same, because the large denominator T makes the difference in probabilities between different configurations small. That is, due to thermal agitation, the system is almost equally likely to transit to states that increase its energy as to states that decrease the energy. When the temperature is reduced, the probability of finding the system at a high energy state decreases. The system is more likely to assume a configuration with low energy. When the temperature is very low, the probability of the system assuming a configuration with an energy higher than the lowest level becomes negligibly small, and the system is said to be *frozen* at the configuration with the lowest energy. However, the system should not be set at a low temperature for finding the minimum energy configuration. Experiments that seek the low-temperature state of a material are done by careful *annealing*. In annealing, the substance is first melted at high temperature. The temperature is then lowered slowly. The substance is kept for a long time at temperatures in the vicinity of the freezing point. An example is the growing of a single crystal from a melt. If the temperature drops very rapidly, the resulting crystal will have many defects, or the substance may form a *glass,* which has only metastable, locally optimal structures and no crystalline order.

Iterative optimization is much like the microscopic transitions of particles in statistical mechanics, which seeks out the system configuration with the minimum energy. The cost function plays the role of the energy function. The many variables play the roles of the particles. Accepting only transitions that lower the cost function is much like extremely rapid quenching from high temperature to $T = 0$. It is not surprising that the resulting solutions are often local minima.

The SA method introduces a stochastic ingredient into the gradient descent rule using the parameter T and an annealing procedure. The resulting algorithm allows both downhill and uphill state transitions. The probability of an uphill motion is controlled by T. This procedure was first introduced by Metropolis et al. [256] in 1953 for computer simulation of a collection of atoms in equilibrium at a given temperature. The stochastic state transitions can be described by a set of probabilities $P(\alpha_i \to \alpha_j)$. However, such a set of transition probabilities may not lead to thermal equilibrium. Instead, it may lead to a limit cycle or chaotic behavior. We are mainly interested in thermal equilibrium, because analysis is much simplified at equilibrium. A sufficient condition on $P(\alpha_i \to \alpha_j)$ that guarantees equilibrium is that the probability of transitions from α_i to α_j equals that from α_j to α_i on average; i.e.,

$$P_{\alpha_i} P(\alpha_i \to \alpha_j) = P_{\alpha_j} P(\alpha_j \to \alpha_i). \tag{8.58}$$

If this condition is satisfied, the system will reach equilibrium according to the Boltzmann-Gibbs distribution, and

$$\frac{P(\alpha_i \to \alpha_j)}{P(\alpha_j \to \alpha_i)} = \frac{P_{\alpha_j}}{P_{\alpha_i}} = \exp\left(-\frac{E_{\alpha_j} - E_{\alpha_i}}{T}\right) = \exp\left(-\frac{\Delta E}{T}\right), \qquad (8.59)$$

where $\Delta E = E_{\alpha_j} - E_{\alpha_i}$.

The Metropolis algorithm adopted in ref. [189] satisfies the condition in Eq. (8.58). It uses the following transition probability:

$$P(\alpha_i \to \alpha_j) = \begin{cases} 1 & \text{if } \Delta E < 0; \\ \exp\left(-\Delta E/T\right) & \text{otherwise.} \end{cases} \qquad (8.60)$$

At each step a variable is given a small random displacement; in other words, the state is changed from α_i to α_j. The resulting change in energy ΔE is computed. If the energy is reduced (i.e., $\Delta E < 0$), the transition is accepted, and the new configuration is used as the starting point of the next step. If $\Delta E \geq 0$, the transition from a lower to a higher energy state is accepted with a probability $P(\Delta E) \triangleq \exp(-\Delta E/T)$. This can be realized by generating a random number uniformly distributed in the interval $(0, 1)$. If the random number is less than $P(\Delta E)$, the transition is accepted; otherwise, the original state is used as the starting point for the next step. Repeating the procedure many times simulates the thermal motion of atoms in thermal contact with a heat bath at temperature T, leading to a Boltzmann-Gibbs distribution. Note that the Metropolis simulation can be carried out in parallel; i.e., many transitions can occur simultaneously.

In summary, the SA process consists of the following four components:

1. A concise description of the configurations (the states) of the system.
2. A random number generator, based on which random state transitions are selected.
3. A quantitative cost function, capturing the criteria and constraints of the optimization problem.
4. An annealing schedule, which consists of a sequence of temperatures and the number of steps at each temperature. An annealing procedure normally consists of melting the system at high temperature and then lowering the temperature by slow stages to the freezing temperature. At each temperature the Metropolis simulation must proceed long enough for the system to reach a steady state (i.e., thermal equilibrium). There is no fixed annealing schedule that will work for any problem. A trial-and-error process is required to identify a satisfactory annealing procedure.

The basic principle of SA is to assign any state a nonzero probability at nonzero temperature. Arrival at the global minimum is not guaranteed in *finite time*. Simulated annealing actually employs an adaptive divide-and-conquer strategy. At high temperatures the energy differences among the states are reduced. The fine details of the energy differences among the states start to have an effect on the state transitions only at low temperature. This corresponds to a coarse search at high temperatures in the global topography and a fine search at low temperatures in the local terrain around the state into which the system finally settles. An important point made by Kirkpatrick et al. [189] is that an average-behavior analysis is more useful in assessing the value of a heuristic for optimization than is the traditional worst-case analysis. A worst-case analysis simply assigns a blanket categorization of NP-completeness to many optimization problems. It appears that in a large number of difficult problems that arise in engineering, the most probable behavior of the solution to an optimization problem is more useful than the worst-case performance evaluation.

Statistical mechanics provides methods for computing macroscopic properties from microscopic averages. An ensemble average can be obtained using the partition function Z. The average thermal energy $\langle x \rangle$ of a variable x is given by

$$\langle x \rangle = \sum_i x_{\alpha_i} P_{\alpha_i}, \tag{8.61}$$

where P_{α_i} is the probability of finding x at x_{α_i}. For example, the *average thermal energy* of a system is defined as

$$\langle E(T) \rangle = \sum_i E_{\alpha_i} P_{\alpha_i}. \tag{8.62}$$

Define the *free energy* of a system as

$$F(T) = -T \ln Z. \tag{8.63}$$

It can be easily shown that

$$F(T) = \langle E(T) \rangle - TS, \tag{8.64}$$

where S is the *entropy*, defined as

$$S = -\frac{\partial F}{\partial T} = -\sum_i P_{\alpha_i} \ln P_{\alpha_i}. \tag{8.65}$$

Then the *average energy* can be expressed as

$$\langle E(T) \rangle = \frac{\partial (F(T)/T)}{\partial (1/T)}. \tag{8.66}$$

The rate of change of the average energy with respect to the temperature is given by

$$C(T) = \frac{d\langle E(T) \rangle}{dT} = \frac{[\langle E^2(T) \rangle - \langle E(T) \rangle^2]}{T^2}. \tag{8.67}$$

In statistical mechanics $C(T)$ is called the *specific heat*. A large value of C signals a change in the state of the order in a system. It can be used in the simulated annealing process to indicate that freezing has begun, implying that very slow cooling is required.

The analogy between the processes of cooling a fluid and optimization may fail in one important respect. In ideal fluids all the atoms are similar and the ground state is a regular crystal. An optimization problem may contain many distinct, noninterchangeable elements, and optimization is subject to many conflicting constraints. Research in condensed-matter physics on systems with quenched-in randomness (i.e., not all atoms are alike) may lend some insight. A feature of such systems, termed *frustration,* is that interactions favoring different and incompatible kinds of ordering may be simultaneously present. The magnetic alloys known as *spin glasses* are among the best-understood examples of the frustration phenomenon [353, 369]. The physical properties of spin glasses at low temperatures may provide some guide to the understanding of optimization problems subject to conflicting constraints [189].

8.3.2 Stochastic Networks: Applying Simulated Annealing to Hopfield Networks

The idea of simulated annealing in searching for the global minimum is generally applicable. It can be applied to search for the global minimum in a discrete Hopfield network. To apply simulated annealing, the transition rule of the units, Eq. (8.4), is made stochastic according to a probability distribution. The transition probability should be a function of the energy change ΔE and the "temperature" parameter T.

Any transition probability that satisfies the condition in Eq. (8.58) can be applied; it will lead to a Boltzmann-Gibbs distribution of the states at thermal equilibrium. A network of TLUs whose state transition rule is probabilistic, leading to Boltzmann-Gibbs distribution at equilibrium, is sometimes called a Boltzmann machine (BM) [4]. However, the term *Boltzmann machine* is more often used to denote a class of learning networks to be discussed in the next section.

To allow parallel computation of the stochastic transition rules, ΔE should be computable locally. It should be computed using only states of the presynaptic and postsynaptic units. Because the connection weight matrix is symmetric, the energy function in Eq. (8.5) for the discrete Hopfield network can be used. When y_i changes from -1 to $+1$ and $w_{ii} = 0$ in Eq. (8.7), the energy change is

$$\Delta E_i = E(y_i = +1) - E(y_i = -1) = -2\left(\sum_j w_{ij}y_j - \theta_i\right).$$

This quantity can be computed locally. The following transition probabilities may be used.

$$P(y_i = +1) = \frac{1}{1 + \exp(\Delta E_i/T)} = \frac{1}{1 + \exp[-2(\sum_j w_{ij}y_j - \theta_i)/T]} \quad (8.68)$$

and

$$P(y_i = -1) = 1 - \frac{1}{1 + \exp(\Delta E_i/T)}. \quad (8.69)$$

It can be verified that this choice of the transition probabilities satisfies the condition in Eq. (8.59). Therefore, the global state will follow the Boltzmann-Gibbs distribution at thermal equilibrium. An effective annealing schedule is usually determined empirically.

8.4   A LEARNING ALGORITHM
FOR THE BOLTZMANN MACHINE

Another possible extension of the Hopfield network can be obtained by introducing hidden units. The state of these hidden units can acquire an internal representation of the input patterns. The response of the network then depends not only on the current input and the connection weights but also on the current internal representation. This will certainly provide a network with a much richer set of possible responses to stimuli.

However, once hidden units are added, the "credit-assignment" problem of determining how the weights should be modified to reduce the error arises, as it does in the feedforward networks. The problem is more complicated here, because there are cyclic connections in the network. Ackley et al. [4] developed a learning algorithm based on the Boltzmann-Gibbs distribution at thermal equilibrium for networks with hidden units and symmetric connections. Symmetry is required because convergence to stable states is guaranteed. Such a learning network is called a *Boltzmann machine* or *Boltzmann learning machine*. Note that the structure of a BM is more general than that of a Hopfield network because of the possibility of hidden units.

8.4.1   Learning the Underlying Structure
of an Environment

The units of a BM are partitioned into two functional groups: a nonempty set of v visible units and a set, which may be empty, of h hidden units. As in the feedforward networks, the visible units are either connected to the external stimuli or provide the outputs of the network. The role of hidden units in a BM is similar to that in a feedforward network. These hidden units make the BM more versatile than a Hopfield network. For example, the BM is capable of realizing a parity function, which cannot be done by a Hopfield network. The graph characterizing the completely connected BM structure over v visible units and h hidden units is $K_{(v+h)}$. The total number of feedback and feedforward connections is $(v+h)(v+h-1)$, and the maximum number of distinct interconnection weights in this symmetric network is half the total number of connections. A state vector for the visible units is a v-bit binary vector, which may also be called an *environmental vector* or an exemplar from the environment. There are 2^v possible states of the visible units. The structure of the environment is defined by the probability distribution of the states of the visible units over all the 2^v possible states.

Learning in the BM involves the finding of the connection weights of the network so that at thermal equilibrium the network achieves the same probability distribution over the 2^v states of the visible units as observed in the environment. The network then is said to be a perfect model of the environment [4]. This should be achieved without any environmental input.

With no environmental input the network is started with totally randomized initial states of all the $v + h$ units. The visible units are free to assume any state determined by the transition rule. A total randomization of the network corresponds to infinitely high temperature. It can be achieved by setting each unit with equal probability of transition between its two states. To learn the weights, the network runs in two modes. One mode is called the *clamped mode,* in which the visible units are set to an environmental vector and then the network is allowed to run until it reaches thermal equilibrium. The other mode is the *free run mode,* in which the visible units are unclamped; all the units are free to assume any state determined by the probability transition rule.

Unless the number of hidden units is exponentially large compared to the number of the visible units, it will be impossible to achieve a perfect model of the environment. This is because even if the network is completely connected, the $(v + h - 1)(v + h)/2$ distinct weights and the $v + h$ thresholds of the network will be insufficient to model the probability distribution of all the 2^v states of the visible units. However, if there are regularities in the examples, it may be possible to use the hidden units to capture these regularities to achieve a good match with the environment.

The difference between the network's model and the environment is based on the difference between the two probabilities: the probability $P(\mathbf{v}_\alpha)$ of the α state of the visible units when their states are determined by the environment (i.e., the probability of the α state of the visible units appearing in the exemplars) and the probability $\hat{P}(\mathbf{v}_\alpha)$ of the α state of the visible units appearing when the whole network is running freely. An information-theoretic metric G of this difference, called the *asymmetric divergence* or *information gain* [210, 312], is given by

$$G = \sum_\alpha P(\mathbf{v}_\alpha) \ln \frac{P(\mathbf{v}_\alpha)}{\hat{P}(\mathbf{v}_\alpha)} \geq 0. \tag{8.70}$$

Eq. (8.70) follows from the arguments advanced next. The logarithm function of a real variable x satisfies the condition $\log x \leq x - 1$. For any two sets of probabilities $\{p_i\}$ and $\{q_i\}$, $p_i \geq 0$, $q_i \geq 0$ for each i, and $\sum_i p_i = \sum_i q_i = 1$. Therefore,

$$\sum_i p_i \log\left(\frac{q_i}{p_i}\right) \leq \sum_i p_i \left(\frac{q_i}{p_i} - 1\right)$$

$$\leq \sum_i q_i - \sum_i p_i$$

$$\leq 0.$$

Since $\sum_i p_i \log(p_i/q_i) = -\sum_i p_i \log(q_i/p_i)$, it easily follows that

$$\sum_i p_i \log\left(\frac{p_i}{q_i}\right) \geq 0.$$

Replace $\{p_i\}$ and $\{q_i\}$ in the above expression by the sets of probabilities $\{P(\mathbf{v}_\alpha)\}$ and $\{\hat{P}(\mathbf{v}_\alpha)\}$ under consideration here, and Eq. (8.70) follows.

In Eq. (8.70), G is zero if and only if the two probability distributions are identical. The term $\hat{P}(\mathbf{v}_\alpha)$ depends on the weights; therefore, G can be changed by adjusting the weights of the network. To perform gradient descent, we need to know the partial derivatives of G with respect to each weight. Finding these partial derivatives in a nonlinear network with feedback loops can be very difficult. The derivation is straightforward for the Boltzmann machine, because we are concerned only with the relations at the thermal equilibrium, where the state of the network follows the Boltzmann-Gibbs distribution. When a network is free-running at equilibrium, the probability distribution over the visible units is given by

$$\hat{P}(\mathbf{v}_\alpha) = \sum_\beta \hat{P}(\mathbf{v}_\alpha \wedge \mathbf{h}_\beta) = \frac{\sum_\beta \exp(-E_{\alpha\beta}/T)}{\sum_\lambda \sum_\mu \exp(-E_{\lambda\mu}/T)}, \tag{8.71}$$

where $\mathbf{v}_\alpha$ is a state vector of the visible units, $\mathbf{h}_\beta$ is a state vector of the hidden units, and $E_{\alpha\beta}$, defined next, is the configuration energy of the system in state $\mathbf{v}_\alpha \wedge \mathbf{h}_\beta$:

$$E_{\alpha\beta} = -\frac{1}{2} \sum_i \sum_j w_{ij} y_i^{\alpha\beta} y_j^{\alpha\beta} + \sum_i \theta_i y_i^{\alpha\beta}. \tag{8.72}$$

The second term in Eq. (8.72), involving the thresholds, can be combined with the first term by adding a unit p that is always at 1 state. Then the second term is equivalent to $-\sum_i (w_{ip} + w_{pi}) y_p^{\alpha\beta} y_i^{\alpha\beta}$, where $w_{ip} = w_{pi} = -\frac{1}{2}\theta_i$, $w_{pp} = 0$, and $y_p^{\alpha\beta} = 1$ always. Therefore, the energy expression is simplified into the form

$$E_{\alpha\beta} = -\frac{1}{2} \sum_i \sum_j w_{ij} y_i^{\alpha\beta} y_j^{\alpha\beta}. \tag{8.73}$$

Differentiating Eq. (8.71) and using Eq. (8.73) yield

$$\frac{\partial \hat{P}(\mathbf{v}_\alpha)}{\partial w_{ij}} = \frac{\sum_\beta y_i^{\alpha\beta} y_j^{\alpha\beta} \exp(-E_{\alpha\beta}/T)}{T \sum_\lambda \sum_\mu \exp(-E_{\lambda\mu}/T)} -$$

$$\frac{\sum_\beta \exp(-E_{\alpha\beta}/T) \sum_\lambda \sum_\mu \exp(-E_{\lambda\mu}/T) y_i^{\lambda\mu} y_j^{\lambda\mu}}{T \left(\sum_\lambda \sum_\mu \exp(-E_{\lambda\mu}/T) \right)^2}$$

$$= \frac{1}{T} \left(\sum_\beta \hat{P}(\mathbf{v}_\alpha \wedge \mathbf{h}_\beta) y_i^{\alpha\beta} y_j^{\alpha\beta} - \hat{P}(\mathbf{v}_\alpha) \sum_\lambda \sum_\mu \hat{P}(\mathbf{v}_\lambda \wedge \mathbf{h}_\mu) y_i^{\lambda\mu} y_j^{\lambda\mu} \right). \tag{8.74}$$

From this derivative the gradient of G can be obtained next. Note that $P(\mathbf{v}_\alpha)$ is the probability of the states of the visible units in the clamped mode and is independent of w_{ij}. Therefore, after differentiating G in Eq. (8.70) and substituting Eq. (8.74),

$$\frac{\partial G}{\partial w_{ij}} = -\sum_\alpha \frac{P(\mathbf{v}_\alpha)}{\hat{P}(\mathbf{v}_\alpha)} \frac{\partial \hat{P}(\mathbf{v}_\alpha)}{\partial w_{ij}}$$

$$= -\frac{1}{T} \sum_\alpha \left[\frac{P(\mathbf{v}_\alpha)}{\hat{P}(\mathbf{v}_\alpha)} \left(\sum_\beta \hat{P}(\mathbf{v}_\alpha \wedge \mathbf{h}_\beta) y_i^{\alpha\beta} y_j^{\alpha\beta} - \right. \right.$$

$$\left. \left. \hat{P}(\mathbf{v}_\alpha) \sum_\lambda \sum_\mu \hat{P}(\mathbf{v}_\lambda \wedge \mathbf{h}_\mu) y_i^{\lambda\mu} y_j^{\lambda\mu} \right) \right]. \tag{8.75}$$

Using conditional probability, we have

$$P(\mathbf{v}_\alpha \wedge \mathbf{h}_\beta) = P(\mathbf{h}_\beta \mid \mathbf{v}_\alpha)P(\mathbf{v}_\alpha), \tag{8.76}$$

$$\hat{P}(\mathbf{v}_\alpha \wedge \mathbf{h}_\beta) = \hat{P}(\mathbf{h}_\beta \mid \mathbf{v}_\alpha)\hat{P}(\mathbf{v}_\alpha). \tag{8.77}$$

Both $P(\mathbf{h}_\beta \mid \mathbf{v}_\alpha)$ and $\hat{P}(\mathbf{h}_\beta \mid \mathbf{v}_\alpha)$ correspond to the probabilities of finding the hidden units in state $\mathbf{h}_\beta$ at equilibrium given the visible units are at state $\mathbf{v}_\alpha$ in the clamped and free modes. Therefore, they must be the same no matter whether the state $\mathbf{v}_\alpha$ is reached by clamping or by free-running. That is,

$$P(\mathbf{h}_\beta \mid \mathbf{v}_\alpha) = \hat{P}(\mathbf{h}_\beta \mid \mathbf{v}_\alpha). \tag{8.78}$$

Therefore, from Eq. (8.76) through Eq. (8.78) we have

$$\hat{P}(\mathbf{v}_\alpha \wedge \mathbf{h}_\beta)\frac{P(\mathbf{v}_\alpha)}{\hat{P}(\mathbf{v}_\alpha)} = P(\mathbf{v}_\alpha \wedge \mathbf{h}_\beta). \tag{8.79}$$

Also, note that since $\sum_\alpha P(\mathbf{v}_\alpha) = 1$, we have

$$\frac{\partial G}{\partial w_{ij}} = -\frac{1}{T}(p_{ij} - \hat{p}_{ij}), \tag{8.80}$$

where

$$p_{ij} \triangleq \sum_\alpha \sum_\beta P(\mathbf{v}_\alpha \wedge \mathbf{h}_\beta)y_i^{\alpha\beta} y_j^{\alpha\beta} \tag{8.81}$$

and

$$\hat{p}_{ij} \triangleq \sum_\lambda \sum_\mu \hat{P}(\mathbf{v}_\lambda \wedge \mathbf{h}_\mu)y_i^{\lambda\mu} y_j^{\lambda\mu}. \tag{8.82}$$

The value of p_{ij} is the average probability for the two units i and j to be both in the ON state when the visible units are clamped to environmental vectors, whereas $\hat{p}_{ij}$ is the average probability that the two units i and j are both in the ON state when the network is running freely. It is worth emphasizing again that both probabilities must be calculated at thermal equilibrium for the relation to be valid. Based on Eq. (8.80), if p_{ij} and $\hat{p}_{ij}$ at thermal equilibrium are known, the metric G can be minimized by

$$\Delta w_{ij} = \epsilon(p_{ij} - \hat{p}_{ij}), \tag{8.83}$$

where ϵ is step size.

A feature that makes this rule useful in parallel computation is that it uses only local information. The change of a weight depends only on the two units it connects, even though the change attempts to optimize a global measure. If there are no hidden units, it can be shown that the G space is concave, and the simple gradient descent rule will be able to find the global minimum. If there are hidden units, local minima may exist. The local minima corresponds to the different ways of using the hidden units to represent the higher-order constraints that are implicit in the probability distribution of the environmental vectors. This is similar to the case of perceptrons and multilayer feedforward networks.

Learning input-output mapping. The BM learning algorithm can also be formulated as an input-output model. The vector of the visible units is divided into two parts: the input vector $\mathbf{i}$ and the output vector $\mathbf{o}$. An environment specifies a set of conditional probabilities $P(\mathbf{o}_\beta \mid \mathbf{i}_\alpha)$. To estimate p_{ij}, the environment clamps the units associated with the input and also the output vector. To estimate $\hat{p}_{ij}$, the environment clamps only the input units, while the output and hidden units are allowed to run freely. The appropriate G measure in this case is

$$G = \sum_\alpha \sum_\beta P(\mathbf{i}_\alpha \wedge \mathbf{o}_\beta) \ln \frac{P(\mathbf{o}_\beta \mid \mathbf{i}_\alpha)}{\hat{P}(\mathbf{o}_\beta \mid \mathbf{i}_\alpha)}. \qquad (8.84)$$

The gradient $\partial G/\partial w_{ij}$ is of the same form as before.

8.4.2   The Learning Procedure

Monte Carlo simulation is used to implement the BM learning algorithm on a digital computer. Units are selected at random for updating according to the probabilities in Eq. (8.68) and (8.69). To obtain the statistics of p_{ij} and $\hat{p}_{ij}$ at a wide range of possible configurations, the statistics should be taken with the network at thermal equilibrium at fairly low temperatures, because at high temperatures thermal equilibrium is possible only at configurations corresponding to isolated, narrow, and very deep minima of the energy surface. However, if the network is started at a low temperature, it may get stuck quickly at local minima. For the Boltzmann-Gibbs distribution to hold, it may take a long time at low temperatures. The simulated annealing procedure for seeking global minimum can be applied to resolve this problem. The state transition probabilities given in Eq. (8.68) and (8.69) are followed. One should note, however, that the SA procedure is not used here for seeking the global minimum as in optimization. Instead, it is to ensure that the network reaches thermal equilibrium quickly following the Boltzmann-Gibbs distribution.

The function G is a measure of how well the two probability distributions match. If the environment specifies that only a small subset of all the possible patterns of the visible units occur, and the remaining patterns have a probability of zero, the learning algorithm will lead to infinitely large weights. This is because the only way to guarantee that certain patterns do not occur at nonzero temperatures in a BM is by giving them infinitely high energy. This requires infinite weights. A way to avoid this problem is to add a small amount of noise to the environmental vectors each time the visible units are clamped to estimate p_{ij}. The noise is added by randomly reversing each bit with a small probability. If the noise is small, the correct vectors will dominate the statistics, but every vector will have some chance of occurring. This technique was shown to work quite well [4]. However, when the probability distribution of the environment is concentrated on a very small subset of the patterns, it may not be sufficient to avoid very large weights.

Other parameters, such as the step size ϵ and the length of time over which p_{ij} and $\hat{p}_{ij}$ are estimated, all have significant effects on the learning. These parameters are normally selected on the basis of empirical observation. Following is the learning cycle of the algorithm with an annealing procedure [4].

1. *Estimation of p_{ij}:* Each environmental vector in turn is clamped over the visible units. For each environmental vector, the network is allowed to reach equilibrium twice, following an annealing schedule. For each environmental vector, after thermal equilibrium is reached, the probability $P(\mathbf{v}_\alpha \wedge \mathbf{h}_\beta)$ is estimated by the frequency with which state $\mathbf{v}_\alpha \wedge \mathbf{h}_\beta$ appears over a period D of time. Once the estimation of $P(\mathbf{v}_\alpha \wedge \mathbf{h}_\beta)$ is available, p_{ij} can be computed. To prevent the weights from growing too large, a small amount of noise may be introduced every time an environmental vector is clamped over the visible units. For example, each ON bit of a clamped vector may be set to OFF with a probability of 0.1, and each OFF bit may be set to ON with a probability of 0.05.
2. *Estimation of $\hat{p}_{ij}$:* The network runs freely without clamping and is allowed to reach thermal equilibrium the same number of times as in the clamped case for estimating p_{ij}: twice the number of environmental vectors used for clamping. The same annealing schedule is followed. Each time, after thermal equilibrium is reached, the probability $\hat{P}(\mathbf{v}_\alpha \wedge \mathbf{h}_\beta)$ is estimated by the frequency with which the state $\mathbf{v}_\alpha \wedge \mathbf{h}_\beta$ appears over the same period D of time. Once the estimation of $\hat{P}(\mathbf{v}_\alpha \wedge \mathbf{h}_\beta)$ is available, $\hat{p}_{ij}$ can be computed.
3. *Updating the weights:* All the weights are updated according to the gradient descent rule. In some applications, to simplify the computation, the weights may be incremented or decremented by a fixed step size, with the sign determined by $p_{ij} - \hat{p}_{ij}$.
4. *Test:* Exit either when the magnitude of the gradient is small enough or the number of updates exceeds a given limit. Otherwise, go to step 1.

Annealing schedule for equilibrium. When settling to equilibrium is required, all unclamped units are randomized with equal probability of ON or OFF. The network is allowed to run following an annealing schedule: m_1 iterations at temperature T_1, m_2 iterations at temperature $T_2, \ldots, m_i$ iterations at temperature T_i, where $T_1 > T_2 > \cdots > T_i$, and $m_1 \leq m_2 \leq \cdots \leq m_i$. The value of m_i is usually large because it takes longer for the network to evolve through states at lower temperatures. An iteration is defined as the time required for each unit to have a chance to change its state. If there are N_u unclamped units, an iteration here means that the units be randomly picked N_u times for updating.

An example of an annealing schedule is $T_1 = 20$, $m_1 = 4$, $T_2 = 15$, $m_2 = 8$, $T_3 = 12$, $m_3 = 10$, $T_4 = 10$, $m_4 = 20$. After this annealing schedule, it is assumed that the network has reached equilibrium.

During learning, each environmental vector is clamped over the visible units for the same number of times. One may ask how the probability distribution of the environmental vectors can be learned. This is achieved by estimating the probability distributions $P(\mathbf{v}_\alpha)$ and $\hat{P}(\mathbf{v}_\alpha)$ using the frequency of occurrence of states in the time domain instead of ensemble frequency. After the learning converges, the network is said to be a model of the environment if in a sufficiently large number of free runs with completely random initializations, $\hat{P}(\mathbf{v}_\alpha) \approx P(\mathbf{v}_\alpha)$ for all α, where the probabilities are understood to be the estimations by frequency of occurrences of states $\mathbf{v}_\alpha$.

When the BM trained by this learning algorithm is used for pattern completion or association, the visible units are clamped to the partial pattern. The remaining units are left unclamped. In such applications, the partial pattern may contain errors. If these errors are forced on the visible units, there may be a problem. A possible solution may be *soft clamping*, in which the visible units are not totally clamped to the partial pattern. They are allowed to change away from it with a small probability.

The learning algorithm for the BM has been applied to such problems as the encoder problem [4], learning 2D symmetries [346], speech recognition [231], and combinatorial optimization [143]. A major disadvantage of the algorithm is that it can be extremely slow, because thermal equilibrium is required. Efforts in speeding up the algorithm using electronic and optoelectronic hardware implementations have been reported [12, 109, 375]. Another way to speed up the learning is by modifying the algorithm. One modification, leading to a deterministic BM, is discussed next.

8.4.3   Mean Field Theory and the Deterministic Boltzmann Machine

In a neural network with many units it is impossible to solve exactly the dynamics of each unit. The *mean field approximation* from statistical mechanics is proven to be useful. In a mean field approximation, the fluctuating $h_i(t)$ is represented by its mean

$$\langle h_i(t)\rangle = \sum_j w_{ij}\langle y_j(t)\rangle - \theta_i. \tag{8.85}$$

From Eq. (8.68) and (8.69), we can compute

$$\langle y_i\rangle = P(y_i = 1)\times(+1) + P(y_i = -1)\times(-1)$$

$$= \frac{1}{1 + \exp[-2\langle h_i(t)\rangle/T]} - \frac{\exp[-2\langle h_i(t)\rangle/T]}{1 + \exp[-2\langle h_i(t)\rangle/T]} = \tanh(\langle h_i(t)\rangle/T). \tag{8.86}$$

Then, we have

$$\langle y_i\rangle = \tanh\left[\frac{1}{T}\left(\sum_j w_{ij}\langle y_j(t)\rangle - \theta_i\right)\right], \qquad i = 1, 2, \ldots, N. \tag{8.87}$$

The stochastic variables are removed in the above equation. However, the problem of solving N nonlinear equations with N unknowns remains.

Using the mean field approximation, Peterson and Anderson [293] proposed a method to speed up the Boltzmann machine learning algorithm. Instead of computing p_{ij} with Monte Carlo simulation and simulated annealing, they proposed to approximate p_{ij} with $m_i m_j = \langle y_i\rangle\langle y_j\rangle$, where

$$\langle y_i\rangle = \sum_\alpha\sum_\beta P(\mathbf{v}_\alpha \wedge \mathbf{h}_\beta)y_i^{\alpha\beta} = \tanh\left[\frac{1}{T}\left(\sum_j w_{ij}\langle y_j(t)\rangle - \theta_i\right)\right]. \tag{8.88}$$

There is one equation for each unit in the network. For a clamped unit, $m_i = \pm 1$. Similarly, $\hat{p}_{ij}$ can also be computed using mean field approximation. Solution of the N unknowns from N nonlinear equations can be obtained by numerical iterative methods, combined with a gradual lowering of T, known as *mean field annealing* [42]. This approach is found to be 10 to 30 times faster than the Monte Carlo approach on some problems [295].

8.5 ASYMMETRIC RECURRENT NETWORKS

Symmetric networks always converge to stable point attractors. As such, a symmetric network cannot generate, learn, or store a temporal sequence of patterns. This leads us to the study of asymmetric networks. The dynamics of an asymmetric network include limit cycles and chaos. With appropriate choice of weights, temporal sequences of spatial patterns can be generated and stored. Temporal sequences of spatial patterns may play an important role in applications such as symbolic reasoning and task planning. These functions are necessary for high-level intelligence. In the remaining part of this chapter, the dynamics of asymmetric networks and learning algorithms for asymmetric networks are discussed.

8.5.1 Phase Transition from Stationary to Chaotic

Chaos in a recurrent neural network is characterized by a time evolution that progresses through a set of distorted patterns in a notably irregular manner. In a *stationary state*, on the other hand, the state from one time index to the next does not change. When the recurrent network cycles through a predetermined sequence of patterns, a *limit cycle* is said to occur. It has been shown that an asymmetric network with a large number of units may undergo a transition from stationary states to chaos through an intermediate stage of limit cycles with increasing complexity. This phase transition occurs as the nonlinearities in the transfer characteristics of the units increase [361].

The network used in ref. [361] has N completely connected units with asymmetric random connection weights. Each weight follows a Gaussian distribution with zero mean and a variance V. Units in the network are assumed to have the following type of sigmoidal transfer characteristic:

$$f(h_i) = \tanh(\alpha h_i), \tag{8.89}$$

where $h_i = \sum_j w_{ij} y_j$, and $w_{ii} = 0$. The nonlinearity of a unit is defined as the product of the scaling factor α and the variance of the weights V (i.e., αV). For example, it was shown that for $N \geq 100$, in almost all cases a rapid convergence to a zero fixed point is observed for $\alpha V > 1$, whereas for $\alpha V > 2$ the behavior is chaotic [361]. As αV increases above unity, nonzero stationary states and limit cycles are observed. The limit cycles become increasingly more complex as αV increases, and finally the motion becomes chaotic. As $N \to \infty$, it is shown using the mean-field theory that there is a sharp transition from a stationary phase to a chaotic phase occurring at a critical value of αV [361]. Point attractors can be used in associative memories for storing stationary patterns, as shown in the case of Hopfield networks. Along the same line, limit cycle attractors can be used for associative memories of temporal sequences of patterns and also as pattern sequence generators. However, the role of chaos in a neural network or a biological neural system is controversial and less well understood.

Skarda and Freeman [357] studied the olfactory bulb of animals by analyzing the recording of the EEG (electroencephalograph) gross potentials in the range 10 to 160 Hz from an array of 64 electrodes covering a large fraction of the olfactory bulb. Based on the analysis, they hypothesized that the neural dynamics responsible for odor recognition and discrimination are chaotic. It was suggested that sensory information is registered in the olfactory bulb in the form of a spatial-temporal pattern of chaotic activity covering the entire olfactory bulb. All the neurons in the olfactory bulb are equally involved in the process. The signal manifests as a carrier wave or wave packet for a few tens of milliseconds.

Chaotic behavior is not predictable but is not random either, although the statistics associated with it portray it to be like noise. It has been shown that chaotic motion in a nonlinear system with many degrees of freedom is often controlled by only a small number of parameters, which are combinations of the original variables [280]. Although the chaotic motion of the system occurs in a very high-dimensional space, it is actually confined to a subspace of low dimensionality. This subspace, often referred to as the *strange attractor*, may have a noninteger dimension [243]. Skarda and Freeman showed in their simulation that a few parameters can control the behavior of their model to change progressively from resting to chaotic limit cycle oscillation to "epileptic seizures." The simulated system qualitatively resembles the different modes in the real olfactory system. In the research of *complex systems* [370, 176] and *artificial life* [212, 213], it has also been proposed that a dynamic system at the edge of transition from point attractors to chaos may function as a universal computing machine [212, 353].

8.5.2 Spatial and Temporal Patterns

In general, to store or generate a temporal sequence of spatial patterns, the connections of a recurrent network need to be made asymmetric. Suppose we want an associative memory network with N units to recall a sequence of N patterns, $\{\mathbf{y}^s\}_{s=1}^n$, in order. The sequence is *cyclic*, meaning that $\mathbf{y}^{an+k} = \mathbf{y}^k$, where a is a positive integer.

Hopfield suggested [162] the following form of asymmetric connections to store sequences of patterns.

$$w_{ij} = \frac{1}{N} \sum_s y_i^s y_j^s + \frac{\lambda}{N} \sum_s y_i^{s+1} y_j^s, \tag{8.90}$$

where λ is a positive constant determining the strength of the asymmetric components in the connections relative to the symmetric components. If such a network reaches the kth pattern, then the input to unit i is

$$h_i^k = \sum_j w_{ij} y_j^k = \frac{1}{N} \sum_j \sum_s y_i^s y_j^s y_j^k + \frac{\lambda}{N} \sum_j \sum_s y_i^{s+1} y_j^s y_j^k$$

$$= \frac{1}{N} \sum_j y_i^k \left(y_j^k\right)^2 + \frac{\lambda}{N} \sum_j y_i^{k+1} \left(y_j^k\right)^2 + \frac{1}{N} \sum_j \sum_{s \neq k} y_i^s y_j^s y_j^k + \frac{\lambda}{N} \sum_j \sum_{s \neq k} y_i^{s+1} y_j^s y_j^k$$

$$= y_i^k + \lambda y_i^{k+1} + \text{crosstalk terms.} \tag{8.91}$$

If the number of patterns in the sequence is small and the patterns are uncorrelated, the crosstalk terms are small. For $\lambda > 1$, the second term dominates the sign of input to unit i. The network will change to the next pattern in the sequence.

The analysis just given requires that the network reach one of the patterns. A problem with this network is that it may never reach any of the patterns in the sequence if it starts at a state that is not identical to any one of the patterns in the sequence. Another problem is that there is no control on how long the network will stay at a particular pattern if it is reached. Modification to this network is necessary for it to produce stable pattern sequences [64].

An effective way of generating a sequence of patterns is to introduce time-varying weights including short-term connections, which are symmetric and responsible for reaching and maintaining a stable state, and long-term connections, which are responsible for transition to the next pattern. The asymmetric long-term connections gradually increase their strengths when the network stays at a stable state long enough [191, 362]. More precisely, the short-term connections are given by

$$w_{ij}^{\text{short}} = \frac{1}{N} \sum_s y_i^s y_j^s, \tag{8.92}$$

and the long-term connections are given by

$$w_{ij}^{\text{long}} = \frac{\lambda}{N} \sum_s y_i^{s+1} y_j^s. \tag{8.93}$$

The input to unit i is given by

$$h_i(t) = h^{\text{short}}(t) + h^{\text{long}}(t) = \sum_j w_{ij}^{\text{short}} y_j(t) + \sum_j w_{ij}^{\text{long}} \overline{y}_j(t), \tag{8.94}$$

where $\overline{y}_j(t)$ is the convolution of $y_j(t)$ and the causal weighting function $g(t)$ (i.e., $g(t) = 0$ for $t < 0$):

$$\overline{y}_j(t) = \int_{-\infty}^t g(t - v) y_j(v) \, dv. \tag{8.95}$$

The function $g(t)$ is nonnegative and is normalized so that $\int_0^\infty g(t) \, dt = 1$. In a digital implementation, the integral in Eq. (8.95) is replaced by a summation

$$\overline{y}_j(k) = \sum_{i=-\infty}^k g(k - i) y_j(i), \tag{8.96}$$

where $\sum_{i=0}^\infty g(i) = 1$.

Examples of $g(t)$ include the delayed step function $g(t) = (1/\tau) u(\tau - t)$, the exponential decay function $g(t) = (1/\tau) \exp(-t/\tau)$, and the delayed unit impulse function $g(t) = \delta(t - \tau)$, where τ is a positive real number. The function $g(t)$ represents a dynamic memory with either a time constant τ or a time delay τ. A time unit here is the time required to give each unit a chance to update once. In a simple asynchronous mode, a time unit means N random selections of single units for updating. $h^{\text{long}}(t)$ is the average of the state of unit j weighted by $g(t)$ over the time period τ. If the states of all units are time-persistent on the scale of τ, $h^{\text{long}}(t)$ will increase. For appropriate values of λ, the asymmetric part $h^{\text{long}}(t)$ will induce a transition to pattern $s + 1$ only after the network has stayed in state s for a time period T_0 which is of order τ.

Sompolinsky and Kanter [362] showed that $\tau > 4$ is sufficient to generate sequences. Note that for simple asynchronous updating, the time constant τ must be measured in the average number of updatings per unit. The choices of λ for three types of $g(t)$ were also given in ref. [362]. For the delayed step function, we should choose $\lambda > 1$. For the exponential decay function, $1 < \lambda < 2$ should be chosen. For the delayed unit impulse function, $\lambda > 1$ is required. In general, this method works well and is robust for appropriately chosen λ and τ. It has been shown that for large values of λ and the exponential decay function mentioned above, chaos could be produced instead of the desired sequence [313]. Kleinfeld and Sompolinsky [192] applied the above model of temporal sequence pattern generation to a class of biological systems known as central pattern generators. *Central pattern generators* (CPGs) control the muscles involved in executing well-defined rhythmic behaviors, such as breathing, chewing, walking, or swimming. CPGs consist of groups of neurons, typically in the spinal cord, that collectively produce a cyclic sequence with neither feedback from the controlled system nor continuous control from the brain. There is no single pacemaker neuron. In some cases, multiple pattern sequences can be generated from the same set of neurons. Kleinfeld and Sompolinsky modeled the CPG for swimming in the mollusk *Tritonia*. The signs of the connection strengths (weights) computed matched the signs of the actual synapses that were measured experimentally. As mentioned above, some CPG may generate multiple pattern sequences from the same set of neurons. This cannot be achieved with the method just presented. Storage or generation of multiple nonoverlapping sequences in the same network is an interesting topic.

Exponentially long sequences. An asymmetric network may produce exponentially long sequences of patterns. When the Hopfield network was discussed, we considered the convergence properties of symmetric networks running in a simple asynchronous mode based not only on the classical energy function approach but also the more recent graph-theoretic approach [59]. Bruck used the same approach to investigate the convergence properties of recurrent networks with a special type of asymmetric **W** running in a simple asynchronous mode and also in a synchronous mode. It is shown that a network with antisymmetric connection weight matrix can have exponentially (in the number of units) long cycles in their state space. We present the following two theorems and sketch the proof for the second one. The interested reader is referred to ref. [59].

Theorem 8.8. Let $N \geq 2$ be an even integer. There exists a network $H = (\mathbf{W}, \theta)$ of order N, denoted by $O(N)$, with an antisymmetric interconnection weight matrix $\mathbf{W}$, that, when operating in a simple asynchronous mode, has a cycle of length 2^N.

Theorem 8.9. Let N be a positive integer. There exists a network $H = (\mathbf{W}, \theta)$ of order $3N$, denoted by $O(3N)$, with an antisymmetric $\mathbf{W}$, that, when running in a synchronous mode, has a cycle of length 2^N.

Proof. The idea in the proof is to construct a linear shift register [59, 136] using N TLUs. In a shift register [48] the input to a unit is the output from the previous unit. The input to the first unit is a *mod 2* sum of the output from a certain subset of the units. There is a way to select the subset of units that sum up to be the input to the first unit in such a way that the shift register will go through all the possible states (2 to the power of the number of units) [48, 136] and generate a maximum-length sequence at the output. This maximum-length sequence, having a period $2^N - 1$, is also called a *pseudorandom sequence*. It has many interesting properties. To construct a linear shift register using linear threshold elements, two basic operations need to be implemented:

1. Identity with unit delay, to implement the function of a single cell in a shift register
2. XOR, to implement the *mod 2* operation

Both functions can be implemented using TLUs. The parity function of N variables, which is a generalization of the XOR logic function, requires a two-layer network with $O(N)$ units. Since the XOR function is realizable with two layers, a delay unit is required between any two units in the shift register with a total of another $O(N)$ units. In all, a linear shift register device with N cells can be implemented using $O(3N)$ TLUs. Hence, for every N, there is a network of TLUs of $O(3N)$ units that, when running in a synchronous mode, goes through a cycle of length 2^N.

Since an antisymmetric matrix is a special example of an asymmetric network, the above theorem shows that an asymmetric network can have an exponentially long cycle. We caution the reader that this is a worst-case analysis. The average behavior of a network is more meaningful in practice than a theoretical worst-case analysis is.

8.5.3 Learning in Asymmetric Networks: Recurrent Backpropagation

As mentioned at the beginning of this section, the dynamics of asymmetric recurrent networks include stable states, limit cycles, and chaos. One useful application of asymmetric recurrent networks with stable states is as an extension of the feedforward networks for pattern classification. The addition of recurrent connections to a feedforward network will increase the computational capability, because the network now becomes a dynamical system that has a temporal evolution of states. One may view this as adding serial processing capability to a feedforward network. After recurrent connections are added to a feedforward network, it is natural to investigate the extension of the backpropagation algorithm. Such an extension is needed to train recurrent networks as pattern classifiers and associative networks.

One way to extend the standard backpropagation algorithm to recurrent networks is based on the following observation. For every recurrent network, there exists a feedforward network that is equivalent to the recurrent network over a finite period of time [261, 325]. This is called *backpropagation through time* or *unfolding of time*. An example of the equivalent feedforward network for a recurrent network that is unfolded in time is shown in Fig. 8.10. The cost of this strategy is the manifold duplication of the units and connections of the recurrent network. It has not been used widely. Pineda [297, 298, 299], Almeida [10, 11], Rohwer and Forrest [319] independently provided an extension of the backpropagation algorithm to recurrent networks, known as *recurrent backpropagation* (RBP). RBP is a nonrule-based continuous-time formalism that emphasizes the dynamics of the network for computation. Recurrent backpropagation can be put into an algorithmic form for implementation on digital computers. Nevertheless, the intent of the formalism is to stay as close to the collective dynamics as possible.

The class of neural networks that can be trained by recurrent backpropagation is very general. As an example, consider the system described by Eq. (8.44), repeated below.

$$\tau_i \frac{dy_i}{dt} = f_i \left(\sum_j w_{ij} y_j - \theta_i \right) - y_i. \tag{8.97}$$

The fixed points $\mathbf{y}^\infty$ of the network are at the states where $dy_i/dt = 0$ for all i, i.e., the solutions of the nonlinear algebraic equations

$$y_i^\infty = f_i \left(\sum_j w_{ij} y_j^\infty - \theta_i \right). \tag{8.98}$$

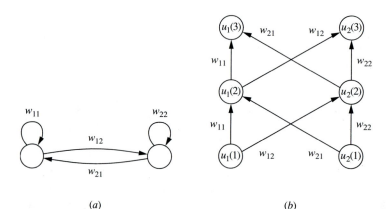

(a)   (b)

FIGURE 8.10
(a) A two-unit recurrent network. (b) Feedforward network equivalent to the recurrent network in (a), for three time steps, by unfolding of time.

They are implicit functions of the weight matrix $\mathbf{W}$ and the initial state $\mathbf{y}^0$. Assume that at least one fixed point in Eq. (8.98) exists and is an attractor. If the weight matrix $\mathbf{W}$ is lower (or upper) triangular, the network has connections in only one direction (i.e., it is a feedforward network). Then Eq. (8.98) can be solved recursively by computing $y_1^\infty, y_2^\infty, y_3^\infty, \ldots$ sequentially. Thus, when the units are properly labeled, this is just the forward propagation in the backpropagation algorithm for the feedforward network. In fact, the backpropagation algorithm for the feedforward network can be considered to be a direct method for calculating the fixed points when $\mathbf{W}$ is lower (or upper) triangular. As in the feedforward case, define the error function as

$$E = \frac{1}{2}\sum_k e_k^2 = \frac{1}{2}\sum_k (d_k - y_k^\infty)^2, \tag{8.99}$$

where the summation is over all the output units and d_k is the desired output at output unit numbered k. The gradient descent rule requires the update of weight w_{st} to be

$$\Delta w_{st} = -\eta \frac{\partial E}{\partial w_{st}} = \eta \sum_k e_k \frac{\partial y_k^\infty}{\partial w_{st}}. \tag{8.100}$$

To find the partial derivatives, differentiate both sides of Eq. (8.98) and assume all f_i's to be the same to get

$$\frac{\partial y_i^\infty}{\partial w_{st}} = f'(h_i)\left(\delta_{is}y_t^\infty + \sum_j w_{ij}\frac{\partial y_j^\infty}{\partial w_{st}}\right), \tag{8.101}$$

where $h_i = \sum_j w_{ij}y_j^\infty - \theta_i$ is the total input to unit i. Collecting all the partial derivatives to one side, we have

$$\sum_j p_{ij}\frac{\partial y_j^\infty}{\partial w_{st}} = \delta_{is}f'(h_i)y_t^\infty, \tag{8.102}$$

where p_{ij} are the entries of a matrix $\mathbf{P}$ with

$$p_{ij} = \delta_{ij} - f'(h_i)w_{ij}. \tag{8.103}$$

The partial derivatives can be found by multiplying both sides of the matrix equation generated from Eq. (8.102) by the inverse matrix $\mathbf{Q} = \mathbf{P}^{-1}$ (assuming $\mathbf{P}^{-1}$ exists), to get

$$\frac{\partial y_k^\infty}{\partial w_{st}} = q_{ks}f'(h_s)y_t^\infty. \tag{8.104}$$

Then from Eqs. (8.100) and (8.104), the gradient descent updating rule becomes

$$\Delta w_{st} = \eta\left(\sum_k e_k q_{ks}\right)f'(h_s)y_t^\infty = \eta\Delta_s y_t^\infty, \tag{8.105}$$

where $\Delta_s = \left(\sum_k e_k q_{ks}\right)f'(h_s)$.

From the foregoing, it is seen that a matrix inversion is required to compute the gradient descent updating rule. Pineda [297] and Almeida [10] found the following more efficient way of computing the partial derivatives. Let

$$\Delta_s = f'(h_s)z_s, \qquad (8.106)$$

where

$$z_s = \sum_k e_k q_{ks} \quad \text{or} \quad \mathbf{z} = \mathbf{Q}^T\mathbf{e}. \qquad (8.107)$$

Now multiplying both sides of the Eq. (8.107) with matrix $\mathbf{P}^T = (\mathbf{Q}^T)^{-1}$ and using the expression of p_{ij} in Eq. (8.103), we have

$$z_k - \sum_s f'(h_s)w_{sk}z_s = e_k. \qquad (8.108)$$

Rewrite Eq. (8.108) in the form

$$z_k = g\left(\sum_s f'(h_s)w_{sk}z_s + e_k\right), \qquad (8.109)$$

where $g(x) = x$ is the identity transfer characteristic. This is in exactly the same form as Eq. (8.98) for the fixed points of the network. Therefore, it can be found by constructing a network whose fixed points are given by Eq. (8.109) and then letting the network dynamics evolve to its fixed point. The differential equation for this network is given by

$$\tau\frac{dz_i}{dt} = -z_i + \sum_j f'(h_j)w_{ji}z_j + e_i. \qquad (8.110)$$

The network implementing Eq. (8.110) has the same graph as the original network. The connection weights in the new network from unit i to unit j is given by $f'(h_i)w_{ij}$. Each unit in the new network has an identity transfer characteristic and an external input e_i. We will call the new network the *transposed network*. This approach enables the gradient to be computed using entirely local information. An example of an original network and its transposed network is given in Fig. 8.11. The complete procedure for the RBP is the following.

1. Relax the original network to a fixed point.
2. Compute the error function using the state of the network found in step 1 and the desired output; if this error e_i is small enough, go to step 6.
3. Relax the transposed network to a fixed point using the error e_i found in step 2 as external input.
4. Update the weights according to Eqs. (8.105) and (8.106), where z_i is the fixed point found in step 3.
5. Go to step 1.
6. Stop.

Trainable recurrent networks definitely have a wider range of functionality than feedforward networks and symmetric recurrent networks. This is due to its ca-

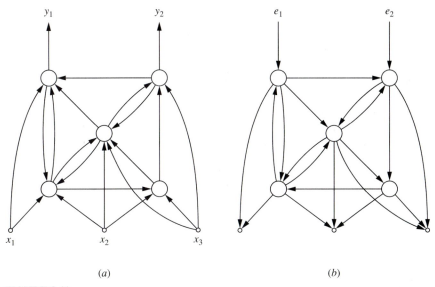

(a) $\qquad\qquad\qquad\qquad\qquad\qquad$ (b)

FIGURE 8.11
(a) The original recurrent network. (b) Its transposed network used in the recurrent backpropagation computation.

pability of having internal dynamic evolution of states. In other words, this is due to its serial processing capability. For example, the RBP can be used to train networks for pattern completion as an associative memory where the standard backpropagation with feedforward network is unsuitable. However, there is a risk associated with the RBP due to the asymmetry of the connections. We know that for asymmetric recurrent networks, the network may oscillate, or even fall into exponentially long cycles. Even when fixed points are reached, a critical problem is that the fixed point may not be stable. Therefore, the network could backpropagate incorrect error signals and fail to learn properly, as shown in ref. [354].

It is shown in ref. [354] that if the parameter η is chosen sufficiently small and if the network is small, RBP performs well, but standard backpropagation is shown to be more robust to a high learning rate than RBP. Simard et al. [354] also showed (using small networks) that application of simulated annealing to RBP increases the network's ability to learn. In summary, more in-depth understanding of the dynamic behavior of the RBP algorithm, with respect to issues of convergence, stability, learnability, etc. is necessary for it to be applied with a degree of confidence.

The problem of analyzing the asymptotic stability of asymmetric networks is a difficult one. Several fundamentally similar sufficient conditions for stability are given in refs. [28, 142, 159, 185, 247]. The basic idea is to require a certain form of matrix norm of the matrix $\mathbf{WW}^{\mathrm{T}}$ to be less than 1. There is a close resemblance between the stability of asymmetric networks and iterative numerical methods.

Finally, it is worth pointing out that one contribution of the RBP is the demonstration of the idea of two networks cooperatively running together with the objective of reducing the overall computational complexity (timewise). The readers are referred to refs. [289, 317, 318, 403, 415, 416] for other schemes of training recurrent networks through backpropagation.

8.6   SUMMARY AND DISCUSSION

This chapter discusses recurrent networks whose directed graphs contain cycles. We start with recurrent networks that are associated with symmetric connection weight matrices, giving rise to symmetric recurrent networks. One of the major capabilities of a symmetric recurrent network is associative memory. Although much effort has been devoted to using neural networks as associative memories since the 1950s, Hopfield's influential 1982 paper [162] motivated a new wave of extensive theoretical and experimental research in neural network associative memories, and neural networks in general for that matter. Hopfield made the simple but powerful analogy between a collective physical system seeking minimum energy states and associative memory. The discrete Hopfield network model is introduced in Section 8.1. Applications of the model in the tackling of hard problems are provided in Chapter 10, to which the reader is referred for implementational issues of the algorithm using recently developed software such as the MATLAB Neural Network Toolbox.

The main questions in the use of a Hopfield network as an associative memory include those concerning synchronous and asynchronous dynamics, the convergence to point attractors, and memory capacity and spurious memory. These are considered in Sections 8.1.1, 8.1.2, and 8.1.3. The pseudoinverse method for storing correlated patterns is considered in Section 8.1.4. Variations in the connection weights of the Hopfield network are discussed in Section 8.1.5. The Hopfield network is autoassociative. A heteroassociative memory model, the bidirectional associative memory, is presented in Section 8.1.6.

Neural networks built with analog circuits have continuous dynamics. Circuits and differential equations describing Hopfield networks using analog units are given in Section 8.2.1. The convergence of such analog networks and the relation with discrete networks are discussed in Sections 8.2.2 and 8.2.3.

A special class of symmetric analog networks, the cellular neural network (CNN), is discussed in Section 8.2.4. The CNN is basically a strongly diluted Hopfield network. It avoids the high connection complexity of a Hopfield network by limiting the connections to small neighborhoods of any unit. As a result, it is well matched with the current VLSI technology for large network hardware implementation. A CNN suits some applications very well, such as image processing.

In using a Hopfield network for associative memory, convergence to local minima (except spurious states) is sought, because the information is stored as states associated with local minima. However, in some applications the global minimum is desired. The Hopfield network runs a gradient descent algorithm and is inherently handicapped in the search for global minimum. The simulated annealing algorithm is introduced in Section 8.3 to alleviate the problem.

The stochastic approach in simulated annealing leads us to the Boltzmann machine learning algorithm in Section 8.4. The BM algorithm permits learning in a symmetric recurrent network with hidden units, which may capture an internal representation of a task. That capability will certainly provide a network with a much richer set of possible responses to stimuli. A Boltzmann machine is more general than a Hopfield network because of the possibility of hidden units. A major difficulty of the Boltzmann learning algorithm is its slow speed, because thermal equilibrium must be reached many times at different temperatures. A deterministic Boltzmann machine based on the mean field theory is briefly presented in Section 8.4.3.

Since symmetric networks cannot capture temporal patterns, asymmetric networks are investigated in Section 8.5. The dynamic behavior of asymmetric networks may include limit cycles and chaos and is capable of storing or generating a temporal sequence of spatial patterns. Temporal sequences of patterns may play an important role in many cognitive functions.

Finally, we consider learning in asymmetric networks. The recurrent backpropagation (RBP) learning algorithm is presented in Section 8.5.3. Although an elegant idea, RBP faces many unanswered questions. In general, understanding of recurrent networks with asymmetric connections is limited. This is a reflection on the limited mathematical tools available for analyzing the dynamics of general nonlinear systems.

PROBLEMS

8.1. Using the energy function approach, prove the convergence of a Hopfield network with unipolar binary units.

8.2. Let the number of stored patterns be n, and let N denote the number of units. Consider two definitions of recall error when using a Hopfield network as an associative memory. The first is defined by the probability that all bits in a pattern are recalled correctly and is given by $(1 - P_e)^N$, when P_e is the probability of error in one unit. Another definition is based on the probability that all bits in *all* stored patterns are recalled correctly (i.e., $(1 - P_e)^{nN}$). In both cases, show that the capacity of the memory is proportional to $N/\ln N$ [251, 400].

8.3. Implement a Hopfield net with binary responses. The input patterns to the net should be on a 2D array whose size is not less than 10×10. Design a set of n patterns to be stored in the net. Input patterns are to be obtained by randomly reversing each bit of a stored pattern with probability p. Test the network with different values of n and p ($4 < n \leq 15$, $0.05 \leq p \leq 0.2$) and different sets of patterns with different Hamming distances between patterns in a set. Analyze your results by discussing the factors that limit or otherwise affect the performance of the network and the relations between these factors.

8.4. It is shown in the text that linear combinations of odd numbers of stored patterns may become attractors of the network. Sums of even numbers of stored patterns are not mixed states of the network, because bipolar TLUs are used. Consider what happens if unipolar TLUs are used.

8.5. Show that the weight matrix determined in Eq. (8.30) is the unique one that transforms any vector orthogonal to the patterns to a zero vector. That is,

$$\mathbf{W}\mathbf{y} = 0$$

for any $\mathbf{y}$ orthogonal to all the linearly independent pattern vectors, $\mathbf{y}^s$, $s = 1, 2, \ldots, n$.

8.6. Propose an algorithm that will use only local information to compute the weight matrix in Eq. (8.30).

8.7. Show that if there are (symmetric) lateral connections, the stability proof for the BAM will not hold for subset asynchronous state changes and synchronous state changes.

8.8. Prove that in Eq. (8.70) the function G is always nonnegative using a procedure different from that given in the text. You may assume that all probabilities are nonzero in the problem.

8.9. In a successful annealing strategy for the Boltzmann machine, the network is run at a sequence of temperatures $T_1 > T_2 > \cdots > T_n$. The transition probabilities are given in Eqs. (8.68) and (8.69).

(a) Explain how the network behaves when the temperature T approaches absolute zero.

(b) At a nonzero temperature $T > 0$, when should the network be considered as converged, or more precisely, as having reached thermal equilibrium?

(c) In the above annealing process to minimize the energy, as T is lowered, on average, will $|\Delta E_i|$ increase or decrease? Why?

(d) At thermal equilibrium, what can you say about the number of units turning on and off? Why?

(e) In practice, will the Boltzmann machine always converge to the global minimum?

(f) Justify the above annealing strategy and explain why it could lead to lower energy states than the Hopfield algorithm.

8.10. Implement an associative memory of a temporal sequence of patterns using the scheme of short-term and long-term connections described in Section 8.5.2. This implementation may be obtained by expanding your programs in Prob. 8.3. The patterns should be on a 2D array of size not less than 10×10. Design a sequence of $n \geq 10$ patterns to be stored in the network. Test the different time average functions τ and λ. Analyze your computer simulation results. Explain the effects of different time average functions τ and λ.

8.11. In the proof of the convergence of the Hopfield net, the configuration energy is defined as

$$E = -\frac{1}{2} \sum_{i \neq j} w_{ij} y_i y_j + \sum_i y_i \theta_i.$$

Will the proof of the convergence be affected if the energy is defined by $\overline{E} = -E$? Justify your answer.

8.12. Let the number of stored patterns be n, and let N denote the number of neurons. When N is large the probability of an error in a single bit of a stored pattern in a binary response Hopfield net is

$$P = \frac{1}{\sqrt{2\pi\sigma^2}} \int_{N/2}^{\infty} \exp(-x^2/2\sigma^2) \, dx.$$

Given that the standard deviation $\sigma = \sqrt{(n-1)N/2}$, compute the probability that a stored pattern has

(a) No error in all its N bits

(b) Errors in 10 bits

for the cases when $n = 100$, $N = 1000$; $n = 200$, $N = 1000$.

CHAPTER
9

COMPETITIVE LEARNING AND SELF-ORGANIZING NETWORKS

In this chapter we investigate unsupervised competitive learning in neural networks through mutual near-range excitation and long-range inhibition between the units. Such *center-on surround-off* interaction patterns are widely observed in biological neural networks. Some motivations for competitive learning arise from the need in some pattern classification problems to select one input with the maximum value from a set of inputs and from the need in other instances to form appropriate clusters from the input data without supervision. A common subnetwork in competitive learning networks is a layer of units that selects a single (or a neighborhood of) *winner unit*(s), often referred to as the *winner-take-all* layer. The MAXNET, discussed in Section 9.1, is an example of such a layer. The graph that characterizes the topology of a MAXNET is a complete graph with self-loops added at each node. Competitive learning consists of two phases. In the first phase a winner unit is picked; in the second phase the connection weights to the winner unit from the inputs are updated. In Section 9.1 it is also shown that a competitive learning network can be used to implement an associative memory more efficiently than the Hopfield network can. Such a network is called a *Hamming net,* whose associated graph is a node-coalesced cascade of a complete directed bipartite graph and the graph for MAXNET just cited.

To overcome the so-called stability and plasticity dilemma in simple competitive learning networks, Grossberg and his group at Boston University developed the Adaptive Resonance Theory (ART), which is the topic of Section 9.2. ART1, which was designed to cluster binary-valued vectors, is the focus of discussion; a later development, ART2, is also introduced. Essentially, in both cases an input layer of

343

neurons is fully connected along both directions to an output layer of neurons. A third group of neurons is required to control the degree of match between patterns placed in the same cluster. The output layer is a winner-take-all layer. Basically, an ART network is a managed competition network allowing serial processing. The graph for the complete structure is essentially a node-coalesced cascade of a complete bipartite graph and a complete graph with self-loops added to each node of this complete graph.

One type of self-organizing feature map (SOFM), conceptualized and developed by Kohonen at the Helsinki University of Technology, is introduced in Section 9.3. The architecture for a SOFM has the special property of being able to create effectively topographically organized maps of the different features of exemplar patterns. The key to the SOFM's spatial organization capability is the ability to select a winning neighborhood instead of a single winner. Connections to the winning neighborhood are updated in a similar fashion. This spatial organization provides classification accuracy of noisy inputs, and that accuracy may be further enhanced by fine-tuning with supervised learning. This latter method, employing supervised learning principles, called learning vector quantization (LVQ), and also introduced by Kohonen, are discussed and shown to be useful for clustering abstract pattern vectors in data compression. Two other types of SOFMs are also discussed in Section 9.3: the topographic map from a presynaptic two-dimensional array to a post-synaptic two-dimensional array, by Willshaw, von der Malsburg, and Amari, and a multilayered self-organizing feature map, by Fukushima. The learning mechanism in a SOFM and ART is both competitive and unsupervised, or *self-organizing*.

Another competitive network, the counterpropagation network (CPN), where learning is integrated into a hierarchical system, is studied in Section 9.4. This network uses both supervised and unsupervised competitive learning (hybrid learning). The graph for the *full* CPN is a node-coalesced cascade of a complete bipartite graph, a complete graph with self-loops added, and another complete bipartite graph. The connection weights associated with the edges of one bipartite graph are obtained from unsupervised learning. Also discussed in Section 9.4 are radial basis function (RBF) neural networks, which are characterized by a node-coalesced cascade of two complete directed bipartite graphs and the deployment of a hybrid learning mechanism. Section 9.5 contains a brief summary and discussion. The reader should find the problems supplied at the end to be also of value.

9.1   UNSUPERVISED COMPETITIVE LEARNING

At the end of Chapter 5 we discussed unsupervised learning based on the Hebbian learning rule applied to feedforward networks. In this section we consider competitive learning. As implied by the name, in competitive learning only one unit (or a small number of units), which is called the winner (winners), is *on* or *activated* after the network stabilizes. Such networks are used to categorize or to find clusters in the input data in an unsupervised manner.

In a competitive learning network (CLN) an input vector belonging to a cluster may be represented by the ON state of a single unit (the winner), or each of a small number of units that either are spatially close together or have some other relations. When a single unit represents one cluster, the network is called a winner-take-all network. Sometimes, the output or readout units in a winner-take-all network are called *grandmother* units. The name is used because one unit must be present for every single category such as "a grandmother." A grandmother cell would be activated by a small class of inputs that constitute the patterns that belong to a class.

In this section, we focus the discussion on winner-take-all type of competitive networks unless otherwise stated. However, we believe that a more distributed version of competitive learning, where a group of units represents a cluster, may be more advantageous. In a winner-take-all network, N output units can represent only N categories. However, N units with binary outputs have the capacity to represent 2^N categories. A CLN with a more distributed representation is less well understood and is an interesting topic for research.

A winner-take-all CLN consists of an input layer and a competition, or output, layer. Units in the output layer are completely connected with the addition of self-connections. Therefore, the topology is characterized by a complete graph plus self-loops. Each unit has a self-excitatory connection, and inhibitory as well as excitatory connections to all the other units may exist. The input layer is connected fully to the output layer with feedforward connections only. An example is shown in Fig. 9.1.

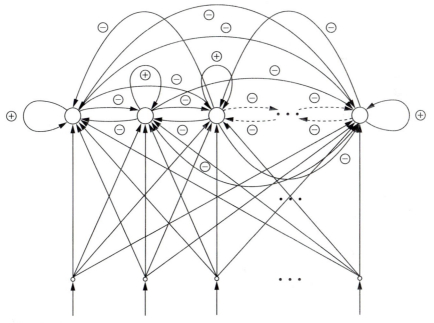

FIGURE 9.1
An example of a winner-take-all competitive learning network. Connections in output layer are excitatory if labeled with + and inhibitory if labeled with −.

9.1.1 Two Phases of Competitive Learning

Competitive learning involves two phases [198, 200]. The first phase is the *competition phase,* in which a winner is selected. The second phase is the *reward phase,* in which the winner is rewarded with an update of its weights. In Fig. 9.1, selection of the winner occurs at the output layer. Updating of the weights occurs on the connections from the input layer to the output layer.

Denote the connection weights from the input units to unit j at the output layer by a vector $\mathbf{m}_j$, and denote the input vector by $\mathbf{x}^i$, where the superscript i denotes the ith presentation of input data. Let I_j^i denote the scalar product of the two vectors $\mathbf{m}_j$ and $\mathbf{x}^i$:

$$I_j^i = \mathbf{m}_j \bullet \mathbf{x}^i = \sum_r m_{rj} x_r^i. \tag{9.1}$$

Then I_j^i is the input to output unit j. In Eq. (9.1) the first subscript in m_{rj} is associated with the connection weight from input unit r (i.e., the rth component of the input vector), and the second subscript is associated with unit j at the output layer. In the first phase I_j^i is evaluated over each output unit j, and the unit that gives the maximum value is declared to be the winner.

When the weight vectors $\mathbf{m}_j$ are unit-magnitude vectors, then selecting the maximum I_j^i over all possible values of j is equivalent to identifying the unit j at the output layer that satisfies

$$\| \mathbf{m}_j - \mathbf{x}^i \| \leq \| \mathbf{m}_k - \mathbf{x}^i \| \qquad \text{for all } k. \tag{9.2}$$

Therefore, the first phase implements a pattern classifier based on the minimum norm of the distances from the input vector to the representatives of each cluster, as shown in Eq. (9.2). For a type of optimal classification, the cluster representatives $\mathbf{m}_j$ should be at the center of the clusters. How the connection weight vectors $\mathbf{m}_j$ can be moved to the center of the clusters, starting from random initial settings, is tackled in the second phase, to be discussed later.

The picking out of a single winner from the evaluation of the inner products I_j^i over all values of j can be achieved by using lateral inhibition and a self-excitatory connection. One implementation is to use the following lateral connection weights in the competition layer having M output units:

$$w_{hk} = \begin{cases} 1, & h = k \\ -\delta, & h \neq k, \ \delta < 1/M \end{cases} \qquad 1 \leq h, \ k \leq M. \tag{9.3}$$

A winner-take-all network with lateral connections according to Eq. (9.3) is called a MAXNET [230]. Figure 9.2 plots the lateral connection weights w_{hk} in a MAXNET with the output units arranged linearly on the horizontal axis. First, the inner products I_j^i are computed. The input to unit j at the output layer is set to the computed value I_j^i, initially, for each j. Let the output of unit j at time index k be denoted by $y_j(k)$. Denote the initial time index by $k = 0$. Afterwards, the input vector is removed, and it no longer affects the state transitions in the output layer. Each unit in the output layer

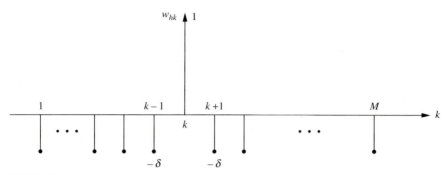

FIGURE 9.2
The connection weights of the MAXNET. The M output units are arranged on the horizontal axis.

has a sigmoidal activation function with zero threshold. It evolves according to the following equation:

$$y_j(k + 1) = T_f\left(y_j(k) - \delta \sum_{r \neq j} y_r(k)\right), \qquad y_j(0) = T_f(I_j^i), \qquad (9.4)$$

where $0 \leq T_f(x) \leq 1$, for all real values of the argument x. The function $T_f(x)$ is a sigmoidal function. It is assumed that the initial input I_j^i will not cause any of the output units to saturate.

The convergence of this network is guaranteed, because it is a symmetric network with positive self-connection weights. It can be shown that at steady state only the unit whose initial input value is the maximum has a nonzero output. Actually, by experiment, it has been shown that the network converges to such a state typically in less than 10 iterations [230]. For other types of winner-take-all networks, see [68, 112, 138, 139].

Once a winner has been picked, in the second phase of competitive learning the connection weights from the input units to the winner are updated so that the winning unit is more likely to win the next time the same or similar input vectors are presented. This update has the effect of moving the connection vector $\mathbf{m}_j$ toward the center of the cluster to which this input vector belongs. It can be achieved in several ways with the same basic idea. The basic idea in the second phase is to rotate the weight vector $\mathbf{m}_j$ toward the input vector $\mathbf{x}^i$ if unit j emerges as the winner with $\mathbf{x}^i$ as input. Rotation of the weight vector $\mathbf{m}_j$ toward the input vector $\mathbf{x}^i$ reduces the angle between the two vectors, which leads to an increase in the value of their inner product. As pointed out before, a maximum inner product corresponds to the smallest difference between two vectors, provided the weight vectors are normalized.

The two schemes shown in Fig. 9.3 correspond to two ways of updating the weight vectors. In Fig. 9.3a the new weight vector for the winner is given by

$$\mathbf{m}_j(k + 1) = \beta[\mathbf{m}_j(k) + \alpha(k)(\mathbf{x}^i - \mathbf{m}_j(k))], \qquad 0 \leq \alpha(k) \leq 1, \qquad (9.5)$$

where $\alpha(k)$ is the learning rate (which should decay with time) at time index k, and β is the normalization factor, given by

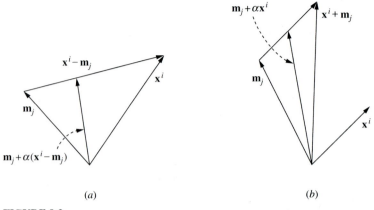

(a)   (b)

FIGURE 9.3
Two ways to rotate the winner weight vector $\mathbf{m}_j$ closer to an input vector $\mathbf{x}_i$.

$$\beta = \| \mathbf{m}_j(k) + \alpha(k)(\mathbf{x}^i - \mathbf{m}_j(k)) \|^{-1} . \qquad (9.6)$$

Other normalization schemes are also possible. The new weight vector for the winner in the case of Fig. 9.3b is given by

$$\mathbf{m}_j(k+1) = \beta[\mathbf{m}_j(k) + \alpha(k)\mathbf{x}^i], \qquad (9.7)$$

where the normalization factor β is given by

$$\beta = \| \mathbf{m}_j(k) + \alpha(k)\mathbf{x}^i \|^{-1} . \qquad (9.8)$$

Note again that only the connection weight vector for the winner is updated.

It is emphasized that the effect of updating the connection weight vector for the winner unit is to rotate it closer to the input vector. If the input vectors form a number of clusters, then, assuming that all the input vectors are presented to the network equally often, the connection strength vectors $\mathbf{m}_j$ will eventually reach equilibrium close to the centers of gravity of the clusters. Of course, there will be small fluctuations in the values of the weights of the connection vectors. To achieve stable clustering, it is desirable to use a decaying learning rate $\alpha(k)$. A larger value of α may be chosen initially to allow fast learning; then the value should be gradually reduced to allow refinement so that a stable clustering may result.

It has been shown that if the connection strength (weight) vector is updated according to Eq. (9.5), then the competitive learning algorithm is approximately a procedure for minimizing the error function [316]

$$E = \frac{1}{2}\sum_{j}\sum_{i} P(i, j) \| \mathbf{x}^i - \mathbf{m}_j \|^2, \qquad (9.9)$$

where the output unit j is the winner for input vector $\mathbf{x}^i$, and $P(i, j)$ is the *cluster membership function,* given by

$$P(i, j) = \begin{cases} 1, & \text{if unit } j \text{ is the winner for } \mathbf{x}^i; \\ 0 & \text{otherwise.} \end{cases} \qquad (9.10)$$

Note that $P(i, j)$ will change during learning, because changes in the weights may make a different unit the winner for an input.

Minimization of E by gradient descent yields, at time index k, the change in the connection strength (weight) vector to be

$$\Delta \mathbf{m}_j = -\alpha \frac{\partial E}{\partial \mathbf{m}_j} = \alpha \sum_i P(i, j)(\mathbf{x}^i - \mathbf{m}_j(k)). \tag{9.11}$$

The update to the weight in Eq. (9.11) is the summation of the updates in Eq. (9.5) over all input vectors for which unit j is the winner. Equation (9.5) is an approximation of the learning rule in Eq. (9.11) for minimizing the error E. The gradient vector $\partial E / \partial \mathbf{m}_j$ is approximated by the gradient of E for a single input vector. The stability and convergence for this incremental style of updating in Eq. (9.5) have been proved only for sparsely distributed input vectors [140]. Since competitive learning is a form of gradient descent, as just shown, we immediately conclude that there is the usual local minima problem, which is pervasive in all gradient descent–based algorithms. Local minima in this case correspond to different clusterings of the input vectors.

Competitive learning has been used for data compression during storage and transmission of signals and images. After the signal or image is organized into vectors, the basic idea is to find the clusters in the vectors. A vector is then represented by the representative or prototype vector of the cluster in which it falls. From the foregoing discussion, we know that this can be implemented by a competitive learning algorithm. For details, see [7, 200, 220] and the discussion in Chapter 10.

Competitive learning may also be extended to multiple-layer networks. One motivation for multilayer competitive learning is to capture the hierarchical categorization of data. Two objects may belong to one class but have different characteristics. For example, both apples and pears belong to the cluster "fruit," but each may form its own cluster. Multiple-layer competitive learning may be realized by having inhibitory connections from a neuron only to certain neighborhoods (which may overlap) instead of having complete connections to all the competition units. This will yield several units with nonzero outputs after competition at the first layer. These results are then used as inputs to the next competition layer and so on, until at the last layer only one unit fires for a given input, to represent the class to which this input belongs. An example of this is the Neocognitron network by Fukushima [118, 121]. Similarly, the competition units at a lower layer may be divided into groups, and within each group the inhibitory connections are complete. Therefore, each group produces one winner. The results of competition from all the groups are used as the input vector for the next competition layer. An example is the network in ref. [326] for feature extraction.

9.1.2 Using a Competitive Learning Network for Associative Memory

One application for the CLN is in associative recall. In this application, instead of learning the connection weight vectors $\mathbf{m}_k$, the Hamming distances (HDs) between the connection weight vectors and the input vector $\mathbf{x}$ are computed. The connection weight vector associated with the smallest HD to the input vector determines the recall result. A CLN used for this purpose is called a *Hamming network* (HN) [230]. The graph of a Hamming network is similar to that shown in Fig. 9.1. Assume that n is the dimension of the input pattern vector and M is the number of patterns to be stored. Each of the units at the competition layer has a zero threshold. However, the capability for simulating different thresholds is achieved by bias weights from an $(n + 1)$th input unit, added with its state set to 1 for every input vector. Therefore, there should be altogether $n + 1$ input units, whereas the number of output units at the competition layer is M. These output units are completely connected and a self-loop is allowed at each node to function as a winner-take-all subsystem. The number of feedforward connections from the input layer to the output layer is $(n + 1)M$, and M^2 directed graph connections are needed to connect the units in the output layer completely (because the weight matrix of order M at the output layer has all nonzero entries). Thus, the Hamming net requires M processing units (this excludes the input units) and a total number of $(n + 1)M + M^2$ connections to store M patterns, each of which has n components. The number of connections is consistent with the fact that the underlying graph for the network is a node-coalesced cascade of a complete bipartite graph $K_{n+1,M}$ and a multigraph, derived from the complete graph K_M by replacing each of its edges with two parallel edges, and to which self-loops are also added at each node. The lower part of the network, whose underlying graph is $K_{n+1,M}$, is of the feedforward type, so that the actual associated graph is directed. The upper part of the network, whose underlying graph is associated with the multigraph derived from K_M plus the self-loops at each node, is recurrent. Thus, the total number of directed edges in the associated directed graph must be $(n + 1)M + M^2$. It is assumed that the pattern vectors x^j to be stored and the input vectors x are bipolar binary, whose elements are drawn from the set $\{-1, +1\}^n$. The storage of the patterns is achieved by setting the weights of the connections from the input layer to the competitive layer according to the rule

$$m_{hj} = \frac{x_h^j}{2}, \qquad m_{(n+1)j} = \frac{n}{2}, \qquad h = 1, 2, \ldots, n, \qquad j = 1, 2, \ldots, M, \quad (9.12)$$

where x_h^j is the hth component of the jth pattern to be stored. The edge weights of the upper part having M nodes are assigned in accordance with the rule for MAXNET discussed earlier; that is, these weights are set to 1 for the connections from each node to itself (self-loops in the graph) and to the value $-\delta$ for each of the remaining edges with δ less than $1/M$. Then, after the thresholds of the units (which have non-saturating discrete binary activation functions) are set to zero, an augmented input vector from the set of exemplars is presented at the bottom of the network. The presentation is continued until the output values of the MAXNET are initialized. The input is then removed, and the MAXNET continues to operate until the output of one unit is positive. This unit gives the class to which the input belongs.

The input to unit j at the competition layer is

$$I_j = \sum_h m_{hj} x_h + \frac{n}{2}, \tag{9.13}$$

where x_h is the hth component of the generic input vector $\mathbf{x}$. It is easy to see that $2\sum_h m_{hj}x_h$ equals the number of bits at which $\mathbf{x}$ and $\mathbf{x}^j$ are the same minus the number of bits at which the two vectors are different. Therefore,

$$I_j = n - \text{HD}(\mathbf{x}, \mathbf{x}^j), \qquad (9.14)$$

where $\text{HD}(\mathbf{x}, \mathbf{x}^j)$ is the Hamming distance between the two vectors shown in parentheses. Therefore, the input to the jth unit at the competition layer will be maximum if the input pattern is closest to the jth stored pattern in accordance with the Hamming distance measure. The measure of closeness I_j sets the initial value of the units at the competition layer. The competition layer then picks out only the unit that received the maximum initial value. In this way, an incomplete and noisy input pattern is associated with a stored pattern that is closest to it.

The Hamming network implements the optimal minimum-error classifier (in Hamming distance) when bit errors are random and independent. The Hopfield network association results must be either worse than or equivalent to the Hamming network. The important difference is that as the number of bits n in the patterns increases, the number of connections increases only linearly in a Hamming network, whereas it increases quadratically in n in a Hopfield network. Another advantage of the Hamming network is that there is no spurious memory. Every recall is guaranteed to be one of the stored patterns, because this network decomposes the problem of finding the most similar pattern to two subproblems: computing the distances and picking the closest. The stored pattern can be obtained from the connection weights to the winning unit.

The foregoing procedure is summarized next, and a simple example is given. Here we find it convenient to denote $\mathbf{x}^i$ by $\mathbf{x}_i$ without abuse of notations.

- There are M n-dimensional bipolar exemplars $\mathbf{x}_i = (x_i^1 \ x_i^2 \ \cdots \ x_i^n)^{\mathrm{T}}$.
- Let $\text{HD}(\mathbf{x}_i, \mathbf{x}_j)$ denote the Hamming distance between the bipolar binary vectors $\mathbf{x}_i$ and $\mathbf{x}_j$. Then, $\text{HD}(\mathbf{x}_i, \mathbf{x}_j) = (n - \mathbf{x}_j^{\mathrm{T}}\mathbf{x}_i)/2$.
- The test pattern vector $\mathbf{y}_j$ is in the same cluster as $\mathbf{x}_i$ if $\text{HD}(\mathbf{x}_i, \mathbf{y}_j) = \min_k \text{HD}(\mathbf{x}_k, \mathbf{y}_j)$ or $\mathbf{y}_j^{\mathrm{T}}\mathbf{x}_i = \max_k \mathbf{y}_j^{\mathrm{T}}\mathbf{x}_k$.
- Let the weight matrix from the input to the neurons be $\mathbf{W} = (\mathbf{x}_1 \ \mathbf{x}_2 \ \cdots \ \mathbf{x}_M)$. For a test pattern $\mathbf{y}_j$, unit i in the competition layer is initialized to $\mathbf{y}_j^{\mathrm{T}}\mathbf{x}_i$.

Example 9.1. Suppose that there are three prototype patterns: $\mathbf{x}_1 = (1 -1 -1 -1)^{\mathrm{T}}$, $\mathbf{x}_2 = (-1 \ -1 \ -1 \ 1)^{\mathrm{T}}$, and $\mathbf{x}_3 = (-1 \ 1 \ 1 \ -1)^{\mathrm{T}}$. Then, the weight matrix is $\mathbf{W} = (\mathbf{x}_1 \ \mathbf{x}_2 \ \mathbf{x}_3)$. Now, suppose that four test patterns presented to this Hamming net are

$$\mathbf{y}_1 = (1 \ 1 \ -1 \ -1)^{\mathrm{T}},$$
$$\mathbf{y}_2 = (1 \ -1 \ -1 \ -1)^{\mathrm{T}},$$
$$\mathbf{y}_3 = (-1 \ -1 \ -1 \ 1)^{\mathrm{T}},$$
$$\mathbf{y}_4 = (-1 \ -1 \ 1 \ 1)^{\mathrm{T}}.$$

Then it can easily be verified that the Hamming net with these prototypes will associate $\mathbf{y}_1$ and $\mathbf{y}_2$ with $\mathbf{x}_1$ and will associate $\mathbf{y}_3$ and $\mathbf{y}_4$ with $\mathbf{x}_2$.

9.2   ADAPTIVE RESONANT NETWORKS

The stability of the clusters formed by a competitive learning network is not guaranteed. The winning unit may continue to change even when the same set of input vectors is continuously presented. This may be prevented from happening by gradually reducing the learning rate α to zero. However, the network will not then be able to learn new clusters. Grossberg calls this phenomenon the *stability and plasticity dilemma*. This dilemma questions:

> How can an organism's adaptive mechanisms be *stable* enough to resist environmental fluctuations (or irrelevant events) which do not alter its behavioral success, but *plastic* enough to rapidly change in response to environmental demands (or relevant events) that do alter its behavioral success?   [69]

The networks designed by this approach are better suited to adapt to unexpected changes as biological neural networks are geared to do. Carpenter and Grossberg contend that *adaptive resonance,* defined to be a state of collective activity of the behavioral system as a whole, arises when feedforward and feedback computations are consonant. Accordingly, they proposed the ART1 and ART2 networks to deal with the stability and plasticity dilemma [69, 70, 71]. ART is the acronym for *Adaptive Resonance Theory*. In this section the ART1 network and algorithm are first presented in detail. Although the ART1 network is implemented in [69, 71] using continuous-time units that are described by differential equations, it uses certain simplifying assumptions that allow its behavior to be described as a discrete-time pattern-clustering algorithm [263]. The discussion here uses the exposition in ref. [263] because it captures the essence of the network using terminologies more familiar to readers in engineering and computer science. Note that the ART1 algorithm is based on the hypothesis that all variables and vectors are unipolar binary, whose values are drawn from the set {0, 1}.

9.2.1   The ART1 Clustering Algorithm

The basic idea in ART1 is that the input vector is compared to the prototype vectors in order of decreasing similarity (using one criterion) until a prototype vector close enough to the input vector (by a second criterion) is found. Prototype vectors are stored in the network as connection weight vectors. Connection (prototype) weight vectors that have not been used for any cluster at a certain stage are all set to **1**, the vector of all ones. A weight vector of **1** indicates, therefore, that the associated output unit has not been used for any cluster so far. These unused prototype vectors participate in the competition in the same way as other prototype vectors, which represent stored patterns.

We first discuss the clustering algorithm implemented by the ART1 network before describing the network itself. Assume that there are a finite number of output units. The ON state of each output unit, indexed by j, indicates that the current input vector $\mathbf{x}$ belongs to the cluster represented by unit j. The prototype vector associated with unit j is denoted as $\mathbf{w}_j$. Initially, all prototype vectors are set to $\mathbf{1}$; i.e., $\mathbf{w}_j = \mathbf{1}$ for all j. The setting of all prototype vectors to $\mathbf{1}$ makes it possible for unused units to participate in the competition in the same way as the learned units. It ensures that an unused output unit will be employed to represent a new cluster only if the current input is not sufficiently similar to any of the already learned prototype vectors.

The ART1 clustering algorithm.

1. Set each prototype vector to $\mathbf{1}$, and enable all output units.
2. Among all the enabled output units, find the prototype vector $\mathbf{w}_j$ closest to the current input vector $\mathbf{x}$, where *closest* is defined in terms of the largest value of the similarity measure

$$s_1(\mathbf{w}_j, \mathbf{x}) = \frac{\mathbf{w}_j \bullet \mathbf{x}}{\beta + \| \mathbf{w}_j \|_1}, \qquad (9.15)$$

where $\| \mathbf{w}_j \|_1$ denotes simply the number of 1s in $\mathbf{w}_j$ and β is a small positive number.

For small β, $s_1(\mathbf{w}_j, \mathbf{x})$ is, approximately, the ratio of the number of 1s overlapping in $\mathbf{x}$ and $\mathbf{w}_j$ to the number of 1s in $\mathbf{w}_j$. In other words, it is the fraction of the 1s in $\mathbf{w}_j$ that are also in $\mathbf{x}$. Note that for two clusters whose prototype vectors have the same number of overlapping 1s in the input $\mathbf{x}$, the one with fewer 1s in its prototype vector will be selected as the winner. Since the prototype vector for an unused output unit is set to an all-1 vector, it follows that any output unit with a prototype vector that is not all 1 will be selected to be the winner over an unused unit. That is, an input will be compared to all existing clusters first in order of decreasing similarity. A new cluster is not formed unless all the existing clusters are sufficiently dissimilar according to the criterion, given next.
3. For the winning unit j selected in step 2, test whether the prototype vector is sufficiently similar to the input using the second similarity measure,

$$s_2(\mathbf{w}_j, \mathbf{x}) = \frac{\mathbf{w}_j \bullet \mathbf{x}}{\| \mathbf{x} \|_1}, \qquad (9.16)$$

which gives the fraction of 1s in $\mathbf{x}$ that are also in $\mathbf{w}_j$. It is easy to see that both similarity measures are needed to ensure that the two vectors are approximately the same. A threshold ρ, called the *vigilance parameter*, where $0 < \rho \leq 1$, is used to determine whether the two vectors are sufficiently similar. If $s_2(\mathbf{w}_j, \mathbf{x}) \geq \rho$, then $\mathbf{w}_j$ and $\mathbf{x}$ are considered to be sufficiently similar; go to step 4. Otherwise, reject the cluster represented by unit j, disable unit j, and go back to step 2.

The disabling of a winning unit ensures that all existing clusters are tested for similarity using s_2 before a new output unit is used to establish a new cluster.
4. Update the winning vector $\mathbf{w}_j$ to move it closer to $\mathbf{x}$. Output the index j of the winning unit as the category of $\mathbf{x}$. Then go to step 1 to accept the next input vector, if one is left; otherwise, go to step 5.

The operation of "move closer" is interpreted as making the updated proto-type vector to be the logical AND of $\mathbf{w}_j$ and $\mathbf{x}$. Thus, any 1 bit in $\mathbf{w}_j$ that is not in $\mathbf{x}$ is removed from $\mathbf{w}_j$.

5. Stop.

One reason that two similarity criteria are necessary in ART1 is that the vectors are unipolar binary. Both criteria are needed to ensure that the two vectors have 0s and 1s in the same places for most of the bits. Observe that if all the variables and vectors in ART1 are bipolar binary, with elements drawn from the set $\{-1, +1\}$, then it may not be necessary to have two criteria for similarity testing. An alternative is to compute the Hamming distance between a connection weight vector and an input vector, as in the Hamming network.

Key properties of the ART1 clustering algorithm follow [69, 263]. These are easy to prove and left to the reader for verification.

1. $\mathbf{w}_j = \cap \{\mathbf{x} \mid \mathbf{x} \in \mathbf{X}$ and $\mathbf{w}_j$ is updated using $\mathbf{x}\}$, where $\mathbf{X}$ is the training set. More-over, $\mathbf{w}_j \subseteq \mathbf{x}$ for all $\mathbf{x}$ used to update $\mathbf{w}_j$ in step 4 of the algorithm, where $\subseteq$ implies that all 1 bits in $\mathbf{w}_j$ also appear in $\mathbf{x}$.

2. Increasing the value of the vigilance factor ρ increases the number of clusters learned and decreases the size of each cluster, where *size* is defined as the number of input vectors in that cluster. This is called the *self-scaling property*.

3. Different orders of presentation of input vectors during learning can result in dif-ferent clusters. This property is true for any unsupervised clustering algorithm that is based on one-by-one presentation of the inputs.

4. No two clusters will have the same prototype vector; i.e., $\mathbf{w}_k \neq \mathbf{w}_h$, $h \neq k$.

5. The maximum number of clusters that can be learned is 2^n, no matter whether the set of input vectors is finite or infinite, where n is the dimension of the space to which the input vectors belong. This is because the input vectors are binary.

6. After a finite number of presentations of the training set, no new clusters will form, and the prototype vectors of the already learned cluster will not change. At this point, learning is said to have *stabilized*.

   An important point is that ART1 resolves the stability and plasticity dilemma by allowing the cluster prototype vectors to move along only one di-rection: shrinking by taking intersections. The stability property 6 is the simple direct result of the way the connection vectors are updated. They can be updated only by reducing the number of 1s in the vector.

7. After learning has stabilized, each input vector in the training set will access its cluster directly. Direct access means that a vector picked by maximum s_1 will also satisfy $s_2 \geq \rho$.

8. For any $\mathbf{x} \in \mathbf{X}$, if there exist $\mathbf{w}_j$ and $\mathbf{w}_h$, $h \neq j$ such that $\mathbf{w}_j \subseteq \mathbf{x}$ and $\mathbf{w}_h \subseteq \mathbf{x}$ and $\| \mathbf{w}_j \|_1 < \| \mathbf{w}_h \|_1$, then $\mathbf{x}$ belongs to cluster h. That is, an input vector $\mathbf{x}$ belongs to the cluster whose prototype vector is the largest subset of $\mathbf{x}$.

9.2.2   The ART1 Network

Figure 9.4 shows the general architecture of ART1. There is a layer of processing units, called the *feature* representation field (F_1), and a layer of output units, called the *category* representation field (F_2). The F_1 layer receives and holds the input exemplar for comparison with a pattern returned from the F_2 layer. The F_1 and F_2 layers are fully connected to each other in both directions. The output units are also connected among themselves in both directions so that the winner-take-all subsystem is realized. The graph is a complete bipartite graph that is node-coalesced at the top with a complete graph and self-loops. The main difference between this and the Hamming network studied in Section 9.1 is that the associated directed graph that characterizes the connections between the F_1 layer units and the F_2 layer units has both feedforward and feedback edges because the presence of feedback is quintessential to ART.

To understand how this network implements the ART1 algorithm, it is important to understand the function of the gain control unit G and the reset unit R. The G unit serves to provide a control signal for the F_1 layer and is characterized at any instant by a unipolar binary value. $G = 1$ if no unit at the output layer is ON, and $G = 0$ otherwise. G can be computed by using a TLU according to the following equation:

$$G = T_b\left(\sum_h x_h - n\sum_j y_j - 0.5\right), \tag{9.17}$$

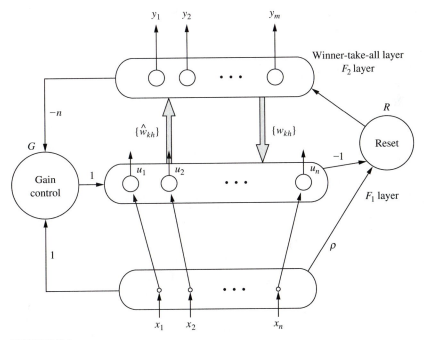

FIGURE 9.4
The architecture of the ART1 network.

where x_h is element h in the input vector, y_j is element j in the output vector, and n is the dimension of the input vector. Ignoring any all-zero input vectors, $1 \le \sum_h x_h \le n$, so if an output unit is ON, the sum inside the parentheses will be less than zero, and if no output unit is ON, the sum will be positive. The state of the unit u_h in the F_1 layer is then determined as follows:

$$u_h = \begin{cases} x_h, & \text{if } G = 1 \\ x_h \wedge w_{jh}, & \text{if } G = 0 \text{ and unit } j \text{ is the winner at the output layer,} \end{cases} \quad (9.18)$$

where the wedge denotes logical AND. This assignment can be realized by using TLUs with $\{0, 1\}$ binary outputs after receiving input signals from three sources and a threshold of 1.5:

$$u_h = T_b\left(x_h + \sum_j w_{jh} y_j + G - 1.5\right). \quad (9.19)$$

Note that if $G = 1$, we necessarily have $\sum_j w_{jh} y_j = 0$. When $G = 0$, since only one unit at the output layer can be ON, $\sum_j w_{jh} y_j = w_{kh}$, where unit k is the winning unit at the output layer, with $y_k = 1$. Thus, at least two out of the three summation terms must be present for $u_h = 1$. This is called the 2/3 rule in ref. [69].

The output layer, labeled F_2, is a winner-take-all competitive layer. When an input vector is first presented to the network, all the output units in F_2 are OFF, and $G = 1$. Therefore, the F_1 layer copies the input vector exactly: i.e., $u_h = x_h$. The connection strength $\hat{w}_{hj}$ from unit h at the F_1 layer to unit j at the F_2 layer is given by

$$\hat{w}_{hj} = \frac{w_{jh}}{\beta + \sum_h w_{jh}}, \quad (9.20)$$

where the feedback connection vector $\mathbf{w}_j$, whose hth component w_{jh} is the connection strength from unit j at the F_2 layer to unit h at the F_1 layer, are the prototype vectors mentioned in the ART1 algorithm.

Thus, the F_1 layer and the connection strengths $\hat{w}_{hj}$ compute the first similarity measure s_1 in Eq. (9.15). The F_2 layer selects a single winning unit. Once a winning unit is selected, $G = 0$. Then each unit in the F_1 layer computes $u_h = x_h \wedge w_{jh}$ using the feedback connections w_{jh}, where j is the winning unit at the F_2 layer and the wedge denotes logical multiplication (AND). The sum, $\sum_h u_h = \mathbf{w}_j \cdot \mathbf{x}$, of the outputs u_h of the F_1 layer units is exactly the numerator of the second similarity measure s_2 in Eq. (9.16).

Step 3 in the ART1 algorithm calls for the comparison of s_2 with the vigilance parameter ρ. This is achieved in the network by the reset unit R. The reset unit is a TLU with $\{0, 1\}$ output computing the following:

$$R = T_b\left(\rho \sum_h x_h - \sum_h u_h\right). \quad (9.21)$$

Thus, $R = 0$ if $s_2 \geq \rho$, and $R = 1$ if $s_2 < \rho$.

When $R = 0$, a *resonance* is said to occur, and the connection weights w_{jh} are updated as in the competitive learning networks, (Eqs. (9.5) or (9.7)):

$$\Delta w_{jh}(k + 1) = \alpha(k)y_j(k)(u_h(k) - w_{jh}(k)), \qquad 0 \leq \alpha(k) \leq 1, \quad (9.22)$$

where y_j is the output of the jth unit at the F_2 layer. Multiplication by y_j ensures that only the prototype weight vector associated with the winning unit j is updated. When $\alpha_k = 1$, this learning rule changes the prototype vector $\mathbf{w}_j$ to the logical AND of $\mathbf{w}_j$ and the current input vector $\mathbf{x}$ in one step.

When $R = 1$, all output units are reset to OFF, and the current winning unit (for the duration of learning the current input vector) is disabled. Once the winning unit is reset, $G = 1$, and another winning unit will be selected.

The foregoing process is repeated. If none of the patterns in the learned cluster is sufficiently similar to the input, they will all be disabled one by one, and an unused unit will be selected as the winning unit. Once an unused unit is selected, it will always pass the second similarity test, because the prototype vector for an unused unit is all 1s, and $s_2 = 1$ for an all-1 vector.

The similarity measures are based on the one-dimensional relation of overlapping. Therefore, ART networks are not capable of translation-, scaling- and rotation-invariant 2D binary pattern classification. In practice, the ART1 network may be very sensitive to noise in the input vectors and is difficult to adjust. The ART1 network is also inefficient in its storage requirements. Carpenter and Grossberg [70] proposed ART2 to improve on some of these problems. The principal difference between ART1 and ART2 is that the feature representation field layer F_1 of ART2 itself includes several processing layers and gain control signals. Input patterns and feedback signals from the F_2 layer are sent to different locations in F_1. Both ART1 and ART2 have been considered for practical applications by several research groups. However, the general finding seems to be that it is difficult to get ART2 to work as a whole system [24].

The ART network runs autonomously without external control signal. It searches all learned clusters in order of decreasing similarity, creates new clusters only when necessary, and accesses directly learned clusters. After all the units in the output layer are used, it will no longer respond to new classes of input vectors.

We believe that the most important contribution of the ART architecture is in its use of several subnetworks that work collectively by executing a *serial-nature algorithm*. This is the only realistic way for neural networks to accomplish any complicated task. This is consistent with the biological phenomenon about how limitations concerning the types of information available to individual units can be overcome when the units act together in suitably designed feedback configurations.

Example 9.2. Consider an ART1 network that accepts as input 5×5 binary patterns. The two-dimensional pattern can be transformed into a 25×1 vector via a row-by-row scan as illustrated in Fig. 9.5a. Therefore, the F_1 layer has 25 units. Assume that the F_2 layer has 5 units, the vigilance factor is chosen to be $\rho = 0.7$, and the constant

1	2	3	4	5
6	7	8	9	10
11	12	13	14	15
16	17	18	19	20
21	22	23	24	25

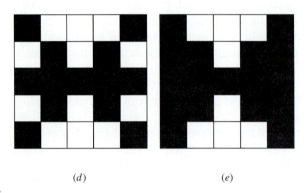

(a)   (b)   (c)

(d)   (e)

FIGURE 9.5
An example of ART1 clustering. (a) Conversion of the two-dimensional input pattern into a one-dimensional pattern. (b)–(e) Four input patterns to be clustered. Darkened pixels are set to 1, and blank pixels are set to zero.

$\beta = 0.5$. Initially, all prototype vectors are set to $\mathbf{1}$ vectors. Therefore, the feedback connection weight from the jth unit in F_2 to the hth unit in F_1 is given initially as

$$w_{jh}(0) = 1 \qquad j = 1, 2, 3, 4, 5 \qquad h = 1, 2, \ldots, 25.$$

The connection weight from the hth unit in F_1 to the jth unit in F_2 is given from Eq. (9.20) by

$$\hat{w}_{hj}(0) = \frac{w_{jh}(0)}{\beta + \sum_h w_{jh}(0)} = \frac{1}{25.5}.$$

Suppose that Fig. 9.5b is the first input pattern. Pixels 1, 7, 13, 19, and 25 are set to 1, and all other pixels are set to 0, as an outcome of a row-by-row scan starting from the topmost pixel on the left side. Since no prototype pattern has been learned, the first unit (i.e., $j = 1$) in F_2 becomes the winner. The connection weight from the first unit in F_2 to F_1 is updated by Eq. (9.22) as

$$\Delta w_{1h}(1) = y_1(x_h - w_{1h}(0)),$$

using $y_1 = 1$ and after assigning $\alpha = 1$. Thus, a new cluster is formed. This new cluster is represented by the first unit in F_2. The prototype for cluster 1 is given by the following connection weights:

$$w_{1h}(1) = \begin{cases} 1, & h = 1, 7, 13, 19, 25, \\ 0, & \text{otherwise,} \end{cases}$$

and, again from Eq. (9.20),

$$\hat{w}_{h1}(1) = \begin{cases} \frac{2}{11}, & h = 1, 7, 13, 19, 25, \\ 0, & \text{otherwise.} \end{cases}$$

Let Fig. 9.5c be the second input pattern, with nine nonzero pixels. The first unit becomes the winner in the F_2 layer. The second similarity measure as computed by the feedback connections is $\frac{5}{9} = 0.56 < \rho = 0.7$. Then unit 1 is disabled, the second unit in F_2 wins the competition, and a second new cluster is formed represented by the second unit in F_2. The prototype for cluster 2 is given by the following connection weights.

$$w_{2h}(2) = \begin{cases} 1, & h = 1, 5, 7, 9, 13, 17, 19, 21, 25, \\ 0, & \text{otherwise,} \end{cases}$$

and from Eq. (9.20),

$$\hat{w}_{h2}(2) = \begin{cases} \frac{2}{19}, & h = 1, 5, 7, 9, 13, 17, 19, 21, 25, \\ 0, & \text{otherwise.} \end{cases}$$

The third input pattern is as shown in Fig. 9.5d, with 13 nonzero pixels. The feedforward connections compute the inputs to the first two units in F_2. They are

$$\sum_h \hat{w}_{h1} x_h = 5 \times \tfrac{2}{11} = 0.91,$$

and

$$\sum_h \hat{w}_{h2} x_h = 9 \times \tfrac{2}{19} = 0.95,$$

respectively. Therefore, the second unit becomes the winner in the F_2 layer, as is obvious because Fig. 9.5d shares more pixels with Fig. 9.5c than with Fig. 9.5b. The second similarity measure is then computed by the feedback connections, which is $\frac{9}{13} = 0.69 < \rho = 0.7$. Therefore, unit 2 is disabled, and the input is compared with the first prototype. The similarity measure again falls below 0.7. Therefore, the first two units are disabled, and a third new cluster is formed, represented by the third unit in F_2. The prototype for cluster 3 can be similarly determined as previously.

Next, Figure 9.5e is presented as the fourth input pattern, with 17 nonzero pixels. The feedforward connections compute the inputs to the first three units in F_2. Those are

$$\sum_h \hat{w}_{h1} x_h = 5 \times \tfrac{2}{11} = 0.91,$$

$$\sum_h \hat{w}_{h2} x_h = 9 \times \tfrac{2}{19} = 0.95,$$

and

$$\sum_h \hat{w}_{h3} x_h = 13 \times \tfrac{2}{27} = 0.96,$$

respectively. Therefore, the third unit becomes the winner in the F_2 layer. Computation of the second similarity measure by the feedback connections gives $\frac{13}{17} = 0.76 > \rho = 0.7$. Therefore, this pattern is classified as a pattern from cluster 3. Since Fig. 9.5d is a proper subset of Fig. 9.5e, there is no change to the connection weights for cluster 3 (see property 1 of the ART1 algorithm).

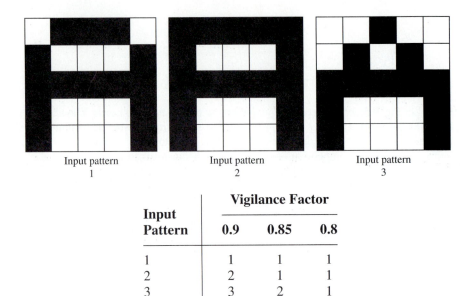

Input pattern 1   Input pattern 2   Input pattern 3

Input Pattern	Vigilance Factor		
	0.9	0.85	0.8
1	1	1	1
2	2	1	1
3	3	2	1

FIGURE 9.6
The effect of the vigilance parameter on cluster formation in ART1.

As can be seen, ART1 basically computes the binary intersection of all patterns in a cluster and uses it as the prototype. A problem observed in the foregoing example is that the first similarity measure can be very close for the different clusters, especially when the number of bits in the input is large. This could present a problem in picking a winner in F_2. Another problem is the sensitivity to the vigilance parameter.

> **Example 9.3.** This example illustrates the effect of the vigilance factor. Shown in Fig. 9.6 are three patterns. The table in the figure shows the clustering of the three patterns with different vigilance factor values. For example, when the vigilance parameter $\rho = 0.8$, all three patterns are classified into one cluster, whereas when $\rho = 0.9$, each pattern forms a separate cluster. This shows that the ART clustering algorithm is very sensitive, probably more than is desirable, to the vigilance factor.

9.3   SELF-ORGANIZING FEATURE MAPS

Maps of sensory surfaces are discovered in many parts of the brain; for example, there are topographic maps of the visual space onto the surface of the visual cortex, tonotopic maps of frequency in the auditory cortex, and maps of the body surface onto the somatosensory cortex [195, 198, 418]. These maps seem to indicate that some aspects of information processing for a sensory modality are related to the physical locations of the cells on a surface. This is referred to as a *topographic representation*.

The common occurrence of the topographic mapping in so many different sensory systems is a strong indication that it serves important information-processing functions. It is not certain how the biological mapping relations are developed in the nervous system [380]. Current belief is that the synaptic connections are probably not completely determined in a biological neural system by genes to achieve the various mappings. Perhaps multiple mechanisms are involved during development. Learning or "conditioning" may be one of the mechanisms for creating such mappings [195, 418]. Once a map is formed, some systems can show considerable plasticity in the maps in response to various environmental stimuli. This may be explainable to some extent by the learning and self-organization mechanism discussed in this section.

Two types of topographic maps are considered. A *topographic map* is a topology-preserving (in other words, neighborhood relation–preserving) map from the input space to the output space. The output space is usually a set of units, arranged either in a one-dimensional line or a two-dimensional plane. The basic idea is that inputs that are close together in the input space according to a metric should be mapped to output units that are close together.

In the first type of topographic map, there are only a small number of continuous input variables, and the metric is defined in the Cartesian coordinate space. The inputs are to be mapped to an output array of units. For example, if the real-valued input variables are (x_1, x_2), the output may be an array of units in a two-dimensional plane. Another example is the case of three real-valued input variables (x_1, x_2, x_3) that are mapped to a two-dimensional array of units, with the three input variables constrained to assume values on a sphere.

In the second type of topographic map the input variables (x_{ij}) are given on an array, which is normally two-dimensional. The map is to transform the activity of the input array to an activity in an output array, which is also normally two-dimensional. For example, the input array may have units turned on in a small neighborhood. This activity is to be transferred to a small neighborhood of units in the output array.

There is also another type of map, the *feature map*, in which similar features, such as orientation and pattern, are mapped to nearby units. The difference is that the output map is organized according to the similarity of features in the input patterns, not their location in the input space. This normally cannot be achieved by one layer of units. We consider next the first type of topographic map.

9.3.1 The Kohonen Map

In the winner-take-all competitive learning network, only connections to the winner are updated and updating of the weights does not rely in any way on the spatial relations among the units in the competition layer. Therefore, as expected, the winner-take-all network cannot develop any spatial organization.

Kohonen demonstrated the formation of a topographic map of the first type by unsupervised self-organization [198, 200]. Units in the output layer start off by responding randomly to the input signal. Kohonen identified two key mechanisms for a network to self-organize spatially.

1. Locate the unit that best responds to the given input. This unit is called the *winning unit*.
2. Modify the connections to the winning unit and connections to units in its neighborhood.

The neighborhood within which units are updated together with the winning unit is called the *winning neighborhood*. The basic idea is to make the winning unit and units in its neighborhood more likely to respond well to inputs similar to the current input. The winning unit (and the winning neighborhood) is selected by applying the criterion in Eq. (9.2). Assume that the unit that responded the best is at the center of the winning neighborhood. The updates to the connection weights to this unit should be larger than those to other units in the winning neighborhood. Actually, the magnitude of updates should gradually taper off from the central winning unit. This can be realized by multiplying with a *neighborhood function* $N_j(\| \mathbf{i} - \mathbf{j} \|)$, where $\| \mathbf{i} - \mathbf{j} \|$ is a metric that indicates the distance from unit $\mathbf{i}$ to the central winning unit $\mathbf{j}$. (Boldface letters are used to denote the units because the index will be multidimensional if the units are arranged in an n-dimensional array.) A typical choice of an isotropic neighborhood function is

$$N_j(\| \mathbf{i} - \mathbf{j} \|) = \exp\left(- \| \mathbf{i} - \mathbf{j} \|^2 / 2\sigma^2(k)\right), \tag{9.23}$$

where $\sigma(k)$ may decay with time index k. That is, as time evolves, the size of the winning neighborhood may shrink. This may be useful in stabilizing the learning result.

In computer simulation the winning neighborhood and neighborhood function can easily be selected. In a network hardware implementation this can be done by modifying the winner-take-all network so that a neighborhood of units wins together. That is, a neighborhood of units yields nonzero outputs, not just a single winner. Then all the units with nonzero output should have their connections updated so that they are more likely to respond well to the same input. There is a simple way to achieve this by modifying the lateral connections of the output layer. In a winner-take-all competition layer, only the self-connection is excitatory, and the lateral connections to other units are all inhibitory. To have a neighborhood "win" together, lateral connections should have the form shown in Fig. 9.7: excitatory to nearby units and

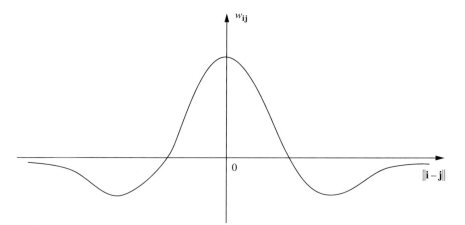

FIGURE 9.7
The center-on and surround-off pattern of lateral connections. The origin is the site of a unit, and the horizontal axis represents the distance away from the unit at the origin. The vertical axis shows the value of the connection weight from the unit at the origin to a unit at the given location.

inhibitory to units that are far away. This is similar to the center-on and surround-off connection patterns seen in a number of brain regions. Kohonen [198, 200] used a network that was *locally connected* for selecting a winning neighborhood; that is, the lateral connections were not complete. The connection weights are shown in Fig. 9.8. Limited local lateral connections may bear more resemblance to a biological neural system. A winning neighborhood is illustrated in Fig. 9.9. The unit that responds best to the input yields the maximum positive output value. The responses in the nearby units are also positive but gradually taper off to zero when moving away from the center, as shown in Fig. 9.9. This implements a desired neighborhood function. As shown in Fig. 9.9*b*, outputs from units 20 to 30 are all nonzero. Note that local

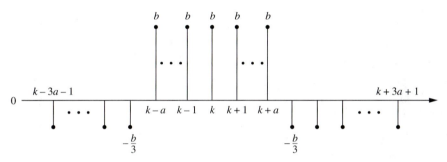

FIGURE 9.8
The local lateral connection weights used by Kohonen to select a winning neighborhood.

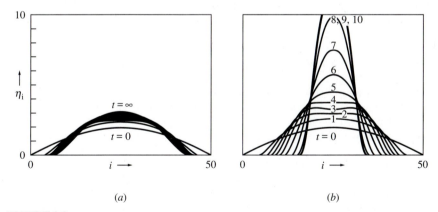

FIGURE 9.9
Development of activity in time over a one-dimensional interconnected array, vs. unit position in the network used by Kohonen to select the maximum units. The lateral connection weights are given in accordance with Fig. 9.8. (*a*) Lateral feedback below a certain critical value ($a = 5$, $b = 0.024$ in Fig. 9.8). (*b*) Lateral feedback exceeding the critical value ($b = 0.039$). (*Source:* T. Kohonen, "Self-Organizing Formation of Topologically Correct Feature Maps," *Biological Cybernetics*, 43: 59–69. © 1982 Springer-Verlag, New York. Reprinted with permissions of the publisher and author.)

lateral connections may cause some problems. If there are peaks at the initial state that are farther apart than the range of the lateral connections, the resulting steady-state response of the network will also have more than one peak, regardless of the height of the peaks at the initial state.

The Kohonen map network first selects the unit whose connection weight vector is closest to the current input vector as the winning unit (by applying Eq. (9.2)). After a winning neighborhood is selected, the connection vectors to the units whose output values are positive are rotated toward the input vector. If the network is arranged in a one-dimensional array, the weight w_{hj} of the connection from input variable x_h to unit j in the output layer is updated as follows:

$$w_{hj}(k+1) = \frac{w_{hj}(k) + \alpha(k)y_j(k)x_h}{\| \mathbf{w}_j(k) + \alpha(k)y_j(k)\mathbf{x} \|}, \tag{9.24}$$

where the $\| \bullet \|$ norm may be either the Euclidean norm or some other convenient norm. The denominator is for normalization. This is the same as in the case of winner-take-all competitive learning. It is necessary for stabilization to make the step size $\alpha(k)$ decay with time. The $y_j(k)$ term plays the role of the neighborhood function. Connections are updated only to units whose outputs $y_j(k)$ are nonzero. The updates are scaled by the value of $y_j(k)$, which has the shape shown in Fig. 9.9b. For a two-dimensional array of output units, the index j should be interpreted as a two-dimensional index, and Fig. 9.9b shows a cross section of $y_j(k)$.

Example 9.4. Consider the following example [198, 200]. The output layer is a rectangular array of units. Each unit is connected to three continuous variables x_1, x_2, x_3, which represent the inputs. All units in the output layer have short-range excitatory and long-range inhibitory lateral connections. The inputs are coordinates of randomly distributed points on the unit sphere. For training, the input vectors are randomly picked on the unit sphere without order. The connection weight vectors are initially set to random unit vectors in three dimensions.

The order of the connection weight vectors is illustrated by a lattice of lines, as shown in Fig. 9.10. Each intersection point in the map represents a connection weight vector of unit length. Two points are connected by a line if the two corresponding units are in the same row or column and are adjacent in the array. Fig. 9.10 shows the development of the connection weight vectors over time. As can be seen, the map becomes organized, gradually, into a rather regular grid. This indicates that connection weight vectors of nearby units become closer together by self-organization.

Example 9.5. Another example is the formation of frequency maps. Figure 9.11 shows a one-dimensional Kohonen map network that receives sinusoidal signals and becomes ordered according to the signal frequency. The signal is passed through a set of resonators or bandpass filters tuned at random to different frequencies. Five connections to each output unit are picked at random from the filter outputs. Therefore, there is no initial correlation or order in the structure or parameters.

Then sinusoidal signals with randomly chosen frequencies are presented to the filters. After a number of training steps, the output array units become sensitized to different frequencies in either ascending or descending order. The results of two experiments are shown in Table 9.1. The numbers in the table indicate those test frequencies to which each output unit becomes most sensitive [198].

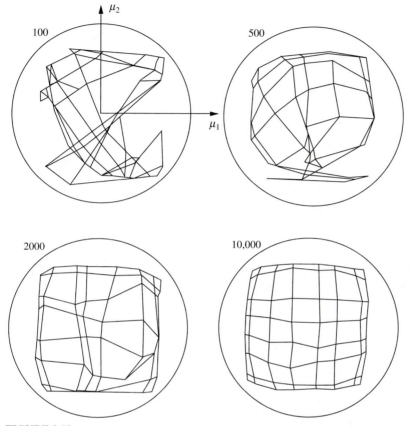

FIGURE 9.10
An example of a Kohonen map. (*a*) The projection of the distribution of the training vectors on a unit sphere to a two-dimensional plane. (*b*)–(*d*) Development of the distribution of the connection vectors over time. The number of training steps is shown in the distribution. Interaction occurs only between nearest neighbors. (*Source:* T. Kohonen, "Self-Organizing Formation of Topologically Correct Feature Maps," *Biological Cybernetics,* 43: 59–69. © 1982 Springer-Verlag, New York. Reprinted with permissions of the publisher and author.)

In these experiments, 20 bandpass filters are used, each of which is second-order with a quality factor $Q = 2.5$ and the center frequency selected at random in the range $[1, 2]$. The training frequencies are selected at random from the range $[0.5, 1]$. There are ten output units. Although this model was a completely fictitious one, it has a striking resemblance to the tonotopic maps in the auditory cortex of mammals [309].

It can be shown that the Kohonen map algorithm is an approximation to gradient descent [316]. Hence, there are the usual problems with local minima and convergence rate. Another question concerns the effects of the shape and size of the center-on surround-off lateral connections on the performance of the algorithm. Analyses of these problems are available only for one-dimensional cases [314, 315, 316]. For some special phenomena of the Kohonen map, see refs. [198, 200].

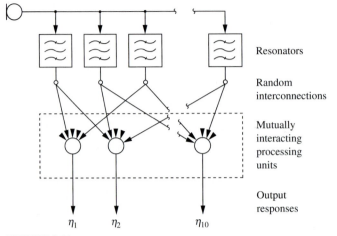

FIGURE 9.11
Illustration of the one-dimensional system used in the self-organized formation of a frequency map. (*Source:* T. Kohonen, "Self-Organizing Formation of Topologically Correct Feature Maps," *Biological Cybernetics,*
43:59–69. © 1982 Springer-Verlag, New York. Reprinted with permissions of the publisher and author.)

TABLE 9.1
Frequency map of two experiments

	1	2	3	4	5	6	7	8	9	10
Experiment 1, 2000 steps	0.55	0.60	0.67	0.70	0.77	0.82	0.83	0.94	0.98	0.83
Experiment 2, 3500 steps	0.99	0.98	0.98	0.97	0.90	0.81	0.73	0.69	0.62	0.59

9.3.2   Analysis of Kohonen Maps

Although the basic principles of the Kohonen map seem simple, precise mathematical analysis of the mapping has been done only for very simple cases. In this subsection, analysis of the Kohonen map for the simplest case, is given [200]. Although
much simplified, it should facilitate the understanding of the basic nature of the self-
organizing process.

The network to be analyzed is shown in Fig. 9.12. It is a one-dimensional array
of n units with a single input. Each unit u_i has a single connection weight w_i from
this input x. The distance between the input x and a weight w_i is computed as $|x - w_i|$.
The winning unit j is chosen such that

$$|x - w_j| = \min_i |x - w_i|. \tag{9.25}$$

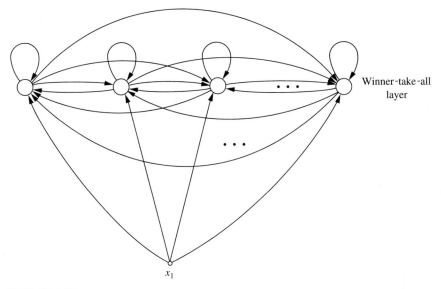

FIGURE 9.12
The simple network used for analyzing the self-organizing process in a Kohonen map. For the sake of simplicity, only one input x_1 has been shown. Other inputs, if present, would be similarly connected to the units in the winner-take-all layer.

For the self-organizing process, let N_j denote a neighborhood of the jth unit u_j whose weights are to be updated. This neighborhood N_j will be defined to consist of the winning unit u_j and its two immediate neighbors u_{j-1} and u_{j+1}. If the winning unit is a boundary unit, u_1 or u_n, then N_j contains only one immediate neighbor of u_j, namely either u_2 or u_{n-1}. The weights are updated as follows:

$$\Delta w_i = \alpha(k)(x - w_i), \quad \text{for } i \in N_j,$$
$$\Delta w_i = 0 \text{ otherwise.}$$

$$(9.26)$$

The analysis is given in two parts. The first part considers the formation of ordered sequences of the weights w_i. The second part investigates the characteristics of the converged weights.

9.3.2.1 ORDERING OF WEIGHTS. Define the following measure of the degree of ordering of the weights:

$$D = \sum_{i=2}^{n} |w_i - w_{i-1}| - |w_n - w_1|.$$

$$(9.27)$$

Obviously, $D \geq 0$. The equality holds only if all the weights form a monotonic sequence, either in an ascending or descending order. D is called the *index of disorder*. Kohonen proved the following ordering theorem.

Theorem 9.1 Ordering theorem [200]. Assume that the winning unit is u_j. If $3 \leq j \leq n - 2$, then D decreases in updating in 14 out of 18 possible cases.

Proof. For $3 \leq j \leq n - 2$, three weights $\{w_{j-1}, w_j, w_{j+1}\}$ are updated. Therefore, only four terms in the summation expression for D are affected. Denote the summation of the four affected terms as

$$S = \sum_{i=j-1}^{j+2} |w_i - w_{i-1}|. \tag{9.28}$$

There are 16 sign combinations of the four terms in S. Eight cases are symmetric with respect to the remaining eight. Therefore, we only consider the eight cases with $w_{j-1} > w_{j-2}$, as listed in Table 9.2.

The change ΔD of the index of disorder D in the eight cases can be found using Eq. (9.26) and (9.28). The signs of ΔD in the eight cases are listed below. When determining the signs, note that the input x is closest to w_j when u_j is the winning unit. ΔD_i, in the following equations, corresponds to the $(i + 1)$st row in Table 9.2:

$$\Delta D_0 = 0$$
$$\Delta D_1 = 2\alpha(k)(x - w_{j+1}) < 0$$
$$\Delta D_2 = 2\alpha(k)(w_{j+1} - w_j) < 0$$
$$\Delta D_3 = 2\alpha(k)(x - w_j) \begin{cases} < 0 & \text{for } x < w_j \\ > 0 & \text{for } x > w_j \end{cases}$$
$$\Delta D_4 = 2\alpha(k)(w_j - w_{j-1}) < 0$$
$$\Delta D_5 = 2\alpha(k)(x - w_{j-1} + w_j - w_{j+1}) < 0$$
$$\Delta D_6 = 2\alpha(k)(w_{j+1} - w_{j-1}) < 0$$
$$\Delta D_7 = 2\alpha(k)(x - w_{j-1}) < 0 \tag{9.29}$$

Since x can be either larger or smaller than w_j in ΔD_3, there are nine possible cases. As can be seen, in the nine cases above, D is unchanged for one case (ΔD_0) and is increased for one case (ΔD_3). In all remaining seven cases D is decreased. The conclusion is similar for the nine symmetric cases. Therefore, out of 18 possible cases, the index of disorder is reduced in 14 cases.

Similar results can be obtained for the boundary cases, when the winning unit u_j is at the two ends, $j = 1, 2, n - 1$, or n. This is left as an exercise.

TABLE 9.2
Eight cases of sign combinations of the four summation terms

Case	$w_{j-1} - w_{j-2}$	$w_j - w_{j-1}$	$w_{j+1} - w_j$	$w_{j+2} - w_{j+1}$
0	> 0	> 0	> 0	> 0
1	> 0	> 0	> 0	< 0
2	> 0	> 0	< 0	> 0
3	> 0	> 0	< 0	< 0
4	> 0	< 0	> 0	> 0
5	> 0	< 0	> 0	< 0
6	> 0	< 0	< 0	> 0
7	> 0	< 0	< 0	< 0

In summary, there are many more cases in which D decreases than cases in which D increases or stays constant. This is the reason for the observed self-ordering in the Kohonen map. However, the ordering theorem does not state anything about the frequency of occurrence of the different cases during the self-ordering process: that depends on the whole history of the updating operations. Only in the beginning, when the weights are randomly assigned, may we assume that the different cases occur with comparable probabilities. When the weights are less ordered, the decreases in D will be frequent. When the ordering starts to build up, the cases in which D stays about the same become more and more frequent, and finally constitute most of the steps. Once all the weights are ordered, there is no case in which D would increase, including the boundary cases. Therefore, we have the following corollary to Theorem 9.1.

> **Corollary 9.1.** If all the weights are ordered, they cannot become disordered in further updating.

A more rigorous proof is desired for the statement that ordering occurs almost surely (i.e., with probability 1). Let $x = x(k) \in \mathbb{R}$ be a random scalar input. Assume that $x(k)$ has a probability density function $p(x)$ over a finite support, and suppose that $x(k_1)$ and $x(k_2)$ are independent for $k_1 \neq k_2$. Then, we have the following theorem.

> **Theorem 9.2** **[200].** With probability 1, the weights $w_i(k)$ become ordered in either ascending or descending order when $k \to \infty$.

> *Proof.* The proof is based on the observation that the self-organizing process in a Kohonen map is a *Markov process* and on the property of the *absorbing region* of a Markov process. In a Markov process the transition probability from an absorbing region into itself is 1. It can be shown [278] that if an absorbing region is reached by some sequence of inputs that has a positive probability, starting from arbitrary initial values and a random sequence of inputs, the region is reached with probability 1 when $k \to \infty$. The absorbing region is now identified with an ordered sequence of weights w_i. Select an interval $[a, b] \subset \mathbb{R}$ such that $p(x) > 0$, $x \in [a, b]$. By repeatedly picking inputs $x \in [a, b]$, it is possible to bring all weights within the interval $[a, b]$ in a finite time.
>
> Note that if u_j is the winning unit, then only three weights w_{j-1}, w_j, and w_{j+1} will change. Therefore, it is possible to choose input x repeatedly such that if w_{i-2}, w_{i-1}, and w_i are disordered, w_{i-1} will be brought between w_{i-2} and w_i. This can be achieved without affecting the relative order of other subsequences. For instance, if $w_{i-1} < w_{i-2} < w_i$, then selection of x from the vicinity of w_i will bring w_{i-1} between w_{i-2} and w_i. Note that w_{i-2} is not changed, because the winning unit is u_i. This sorting can be continued systematically. An overall order will then result in a finite number of steps. Since the input x picked here has positive probability, the theorem is proved. For a detailed proof of this theorem, see refs. [84, 315].

9.3.2.2 CONVERGENCE PHASE. Kohonen paid particular attention to the distribution of the weights as a function of the probability density $p(x)$ of the inputs used for learning. For this purpose, let us consider the asymptotic values of the weights. In a strict sense, asymptotic values are obtained in a mean-squared sense, or almost surely, only if the coefficient $\alpha(k)$ in Eq. (9.26) decreases to zero. We consider a less restricted case here. We analyze the dynamic behavior of the expectancy of the weights $E[w_i]$. It will be shown that these operators converge to unique limits. The variances of the weights can then be made arbitrarily small by a suitable choice of $\alpha(k)$ as $k \to \infty$. Assume that the weights are already ordered. Without loss of generality, further assume that the weights are ordered in ascending order, as illustrated in Fig. 9.13. Let the support of the input probability density function be $[a, b]$. After the weights are ordered, we have $[w_1, w_n] \subset [a, b]$. From the updating rule in Eq. (9.26) and the definition of the neighborhood N_j, it is known that weight w_i is affected only if the input x falls within an interval I_i as follows (assume $n \geq 5$):

$$\text{for } 3 \leq i \leq n - 2: \quad I_i = \left[\frac{w_{i-2} + w_{i-1}}{2}, \frac{w_{i+1} + w_{i+2}}{2} \right]$$

$$\text{for } i = 1: \quad I_i = \left[a, \frac{w_2 + w_3}{2} \right]$$

$$\text{for } i = 2: \quad I_i = \left[a, \frac{w_3 + w_4}{2} \right]$$

$$\text{for } i = n - 1: \quad I_i = \left[\frac{w_{n-3} + w_{n-2}}{2}, b \right]$$

$$\text{for } i = n: \quad I_i = \left[\frac{w_{n-2} + w_{n-1}}{2}, b \right]. \tag{9.30}$$

Consider the weight update Δw_i as an approximation to the derivative $\dot{w}_i = dw_i/dt$. For a given time instant, the mathematical expectation of $\dot{w}_i$ is

$$< \dot{w}_i > \triangleq E[\dot{w}_i] = \alpha(k)(E[x \mid x \in I_i] - w_i)p(x \in I_i), \tag{9.31}$$

where $p(x \in I_i)$ is the probability for x to fall within the interval I_i. $E[x \mid x \in I_i]$ is the center of gravity of I_i and depends on the probability density function $p(x)$ in the interval I_i. A general solution of this equation for arbitrary $p(x)$ is difficult. We first analyze a simplified case by assuming that $p(x)$ is a uniform distribution over $[a, b]$, and zero outside $[a, b]$. In this case, the center of gravity of I_i can be easily found. Equation (9.31) now becomes

$$\text{for } 3 \leq i \leq n - 2: \quad < \dot{w}_i > = \frac{\alpha}{4}(w_{i-2} + w_{i-1} + w_{i+1} + w_{i+2} - 4w_i)p(x \in I_i)$$

$$< \dot{w}_1 > = \frac{\alpha}{4}(2a + w_2 + w_3 - 4w_1)p(x \in I_1)$$

$$< \dot{w}_2 > = \frac{\alpha}{4}(2a + w_3 + w_4 - 4w_2)p(x \in I_2)$$

$$< \dot{w}_{n-1} > = \frac{\alpha}{4}(w_{n-3} + w_{n-2} + 2b - 4w_{n-1})p(x \in I_{n-1})$$

$$< \dot{w}_n > = \frac{\alpha}{4}(w_{n-2} + w_{n-1} + 2b - 4w_n)p(x \in I_n)$$

$$\tag{9.32}$$

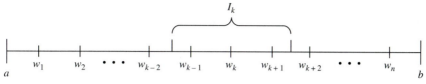

FIGURE 9.13

An example of weights in ascending order. The closed interval $[a, b]$ is the support of the input probability density function $p(x)$.

Starting with arbitrary initial conditions $w_i(0)$, the most probable average trajectories $w_i(t)$ in continuous time t can be obtained from the solution of the equivalent differential equation corresponding to Eq. (9.32),

$$\frac{d\mathbf{w}}{dt} = \mathbf{P}(\mathbf{Fw} + \mathbf{h}),\tag{9.33}$$

where

$$\mathbf{w} = [w_1 \ w_2 \ \cdots \ w_n]^{\mathrm{T}}$$

$$\mathbf{F} = \frac{\alpha}{4}
\begin{bmatrix}
-4 & 1 & 1 & 0 & 0 & 0 & 0 \\
0 & -4 & 1 & 1 & 0 & 0 & 0 \\
1 & 1 & -4 & 1 & 1 & 0 & 0 \\
0 & 1 & 1 & -4 & 1 & 1 & 0 \\
& & & & \ddots & & & \\
& & & & & 0 & 1 & 1 & -4 & 1 & 1 & 0 \\
& & & & & 0 & 0 & 1 & 1 & -4 & 1 & 1 \\
& & & & & 0 & 0 & 0 & 1 & 1 & -4 & 0 \\
& & & & & 0 & 0 & 0 & 0 & 1 & 1 & -4
\end{bmatrix}$$

$$\mathbf{h} = \frac{\alpha}{2}[a \ a \ 0 \ 0 \ \cdots 0 \ b \ b]^{\mathrm{T}}$$

$$\mathbf{P} = \mathrm{diag} \ [p(x \in I_1)p(x \in I_2)\ldots, \ p(x \in I_i)\ldots p(x \in I_n)].\tag{9.34}$$

The first-order linear differential equation in Eq. (9.33) has a fixed point solution. Considering that $\mathbf{P}$ is diagonal without zero diagonal components, a particular solution with $d\mathbf{w}/dt = 0$ is

$$\hat{\mathbf{w}} = -\mathbf{F}^{-1}\mathbf{h}.\tag{9.35}$$

It can be proven that $\mathbf{F}^{-1}$ exists. The general solution of Eq. (9.33) is difficult to attain. It has been shown that convergence to a fixed point is true in general [84, 314]. Kohonen calculated the asymptotic values of the weights for different numbers of units. The results are listed in Table 9.3 and in Fig. 9.14. The support of $p(x)$ is assumed to be in [0, 1]. The following observations are made from Table 9.3 and in Fig. 9.14.

TABLE 9.3
Asymptotic values of the weights, with $[a, b] = [0, 1]$

Number of units (n)	w_1	w_2	w_3	w_4	w_5	w_6	w_7	w_8	w_9	w_{10}
5	0.2	0.3	0.5	0.7	0.8					
6	0.17	0.25	0.43	0.56	0.75	0.83				
7	0.15	0.22	0.37	0.5	0.63	0.78	0.85			
8	0.13	0.19	0.33	0.44	0.56	0.67	0.81	0.87		
9	0.12	0.17	0.29	0.39	0.5	0.61	0.7	0.83	0.88	
10	0.11	0.16	0.27	0.36	0.45	0.55	0.64	0.73	0.84	0.89

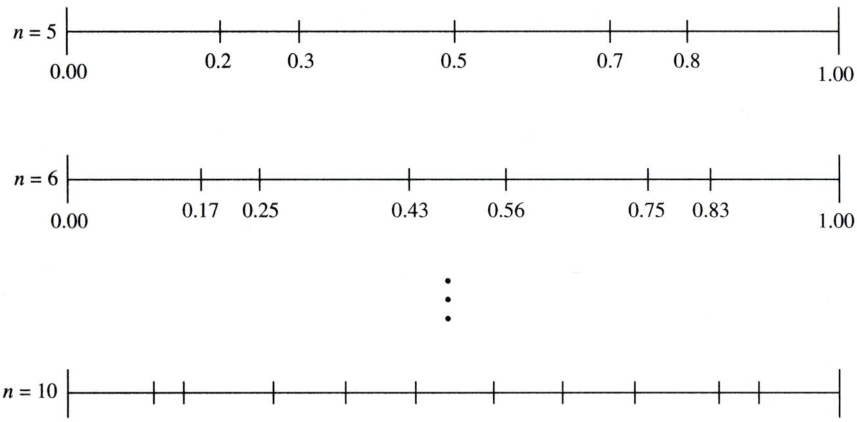

FIGURE 9.14
Asymptotic values of the weights, with $[a, b] = [0, 1]$ for different values of n shown in Table 9.3. The labelings are only shown for the $n = 5$ and $n = 6$ cases to avoid clutter.

1. The weights at the two ends are shifted inwards by approximately $1/n$. This effect decreases as n increases.

2. The weights $\{w_i\}_{i=3}^{n-2}$ are distributed almost evenly.

We may conclude that when n is large, the weights are distributed evenly in $[a, b]$ for uniform $p(x) = $ nonzero constant, $x \in [a, b]$. Therefore, the weights are a true representation of the input density function $p(x)$ when $p(x)$ is uniform.

     The above result may be generalized to a one-dimensional array of units with two-dimensional inputs. The network is similar to Fig. 9.12 but with two inputs x_1, x_2. In this case, the intervals I_i become Voronoi tessellations [277, 303] (see Sections 2.6 and 5.3) of the two-dimensional input space. When the array of units also becomes two-dimensional, the analysis is much harder. It may still be possible to formulate the problem into differential equations, but closed-form solutions of the equations are not available in general.

     Consider next how the weights will be distributed if the density function $p(x)$ is of general form. Again, only the one-dimensional case seems to be amenable to simple analysis. Only the basic principles will be illustrated here. For a more detailed analysis, see [314, 315]. Recall that the key to the self-organization process in the Kohonen map is the updating of units in the winning neighborhood N_j. The size of the winning neighborhood N_j decays with time. When this size is reduced to 1 (i.e., when it contains only the winning unit), there is no "ordering power" left. However, the asymptotic distribution of the weights will be easier to compute in this case. The computation results should be qualitatively consistent with the case of a larger winning neighborhood. Rewrite the system equations when the size of the winning neighborhood is 1.

$$\frac{dw_k}{dt} = \alpha(t)(x(t) - w_k(t)), \qquad u_k \text{ is the winning unit,}$$

$$\frac{dw_i}{dt} = 0, \qquad\qquad\qquad \text{for } i \neq k. \tag{9.36}$$

The support $[a, b]$ of the probability function $p(x)$ is partitioned into intervals within each of which the x's are closest to the weight w_i in the interval. This partition may be considered as a Voronoi tessellation in one dimension with respect to the weights w_i. The separating planes become straight lines orthogonal to the one-dimensional axis. The intervals are

$$I_i = \left[\tfrac{1}{2}(w_{i-1} + w_i), \tfrac{1}{2}(w_i + w_{i+1})\right].$$

The values of the input x are picked with probability $p(x)$. Since at equilibrium the expectation of the right side of Eq. (9.36) must be zero for any nonzero $\alpha(t)$, we have

$$\int_{I_i} p(x)(x(t) - w_i(t))dx = 0. \tag{9.37}$$

A solution to this equation is that the weight w_i at equilibrium coincides with the center of gravity of the interval I_i:

$$w_i(t) = \frac{E[x(t) \mid x(t) \in I_i]}{\int_{I_i} p(x)dx} = \frac{\int_{I_i} p(x)x(t)dx}{\int_{I_i} p(x)dx}. \tag{9.38}$$

Equation (9.38) tells us where the weights may be in equilibrium within an interval. It does not tell us directly how the intervals are distributed in $[a, b]$. It can be shown that in the one-dimensional case the asymptotic local point density of the weights, in the average sense, is of the form $f(p(x))$, where f is some continuous, monotonically increasing function [200, 314]. Ideally, f should be linear. However, for general nonuniform $p(x)$ this is not the case. It has been shown that in one dimension the density of the weights w_j is proportional to $p^{2/3}(x)$ for general nonuniform $p(x)$ [314]. This may be corrected by monitoring the winning frequency of the units. If a unit wins the competition too often, it may be disabled for a while to allow other units to win [155]. However, such an operation is nonlocal. In two dimensions no general expression of the density distribution of weights in terms of the density distribution of the inputs is known.

9.3.2.3 CONVERGENCE RATE.
It is observed from experiments [129, 158] that a map that starts with a topology of complicated tangles may take a long time to

converge. The tangles normally need to be fairly flattened out before the weights can adjust to follow the input probability density. An example of such a tangle in a two-dimensional map is the twist seen in Fig. 9.10.

The analysis of movements of the weight vectors is difficult in two dimensions. Geszti [129] investigated movements of the weights in the convergence process for the one-dimensional case. We know now that a monotonically ordered sequence of weights maintains its order in updating; that fact controls how the junction between two monotonically ordered segments can move. Such a junction can move one unit to the left or right at each update, as illustrated in Fig. 9.15. A junction may be eliminated either when it moves to the edge or when two junctions meet. No new junctions may be created. When all junctions are eliminated, the weights are totally ordered, and the process is considered to have converged. An estimate of the time required for convergence may be obtained based on this fact. For example, the single junction in Fig. 9.15 must move to either end of the array for the process to converge. The junction moves only when the input x is closest to the weight at this junction unit. For uniform input probability, this happens with a probability of $1/n$ with n units. Then, each time the junction moves, it moves one step either to the right or to the left with equal probability. This leads to a *random walk*, and an average order of n^2 steps are required for the junction to move to one end of the array. Therefore, the total time required for convergence is of order n^3. The situation may be improved by making the winning neighborhood highly asymmetric so that the movement of the junction will not be a random walk. The movement is then more likely to be along one direction, and the convergence time can be reduced to an order of n^2.

In two dimensions the dominant problem that slows down convergence is the elimination of twists. It has been found that an anisotropic winning neighborhood in two dimensions will eliminate twists faster and speed up convergence significantly [129].

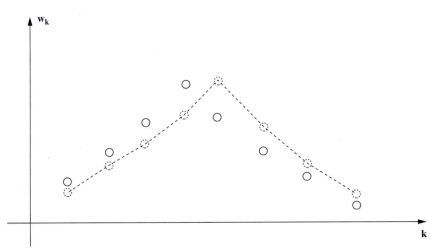

FIGURE 9.15
The movement of a junction between two monotonically ordered segments in a one-dimensional Kohonen map. The dotted circles represent the weights after an update. The junction can move only one step in an update.

9.3.3 Adaptive and Learning Vector Quantization

Samples from a segment of a signal, such as a speech waveform, may be stacked as a vector. Since the size of the vector can be very large, transmission and digital processing of the data is usually done after compression. *Vector quantization* (VQ) is often used for data compression. VQ may be viewed as a data-reducing technique, where all input vectors that fall into a particular cell (such as a Voronoi cell obtained by a spatial tessellation of the input space) are represented by a much smaller *code word* associated with that cell. In pattern classification, for example, the input vector could be a feature vector in multidimensional feature space. Encoding the input vector to a code word, followed by decoding, results in a *quantized* vector, which may be viewed as an approximant to any input vector in the cell associated with the code word. This approximation causes some distortion in representation, but this disadvantage is offset by the considerable amount of savings realized in storage and reduction in the computational complexity of processing the compressed data.

In Section 5.3 it was seen that the Voronoi diagram over a set of points in the Euclidean metric partitions the space in accordance with the *nearest-neighbor* criterion. Therefore, a vector quantizer based on the Voronoi diagram is optimal from the standpoint of encoding distortion. There is a similarity between the ordering of a feature map and the design of the *code book* (which is comprised of the code vectors) in VQ. Kohonen's SOFM procedure computes the Voronoi diagram–based code vectors approximately, using *unsupervised competitive learning* (UCL). Subsequently, Kohonen extended the so-called *adaptive vector quantization* (AVQ) algorithm using his UCL rule to several *learning vector quantization* (LVQ) algorithms that are based on supervised learning rules. The UCL rule will also be encountered in Section 9.4.1 in this chapter.

The AVQ algorithm based on the UCL rule is the simplest. Before this algorithm is applied to several examples, the main steps will be described that need to be programmed to solve the type of problems illustrated in these examples. This algorithm is the neural network version of *adaptive K-means clustering,* used earlier in pattern recognition [205, pp. 16–23]. The neural network being trained has a winner-take-all layer, connected to the input layer of nodes by edges of a directed bipartite graph, as in Fig. 9.12. The number of neurons in the output layer is the number of classes, and the number of neurons in the input layer equals the number of input parameters or the dimension of the input space. The UCL-based AVQ algorithm used in the subsequent Examples is particularly simple, and the following pseudocode describes the three basic steps it shares with other algorithms that use supervised or unsupervised learning; the differences between algorithms occur in the particulars of the rules in these basic steps. For more information about the special features in the other algorithms referred to above, the reader may consult reference [205, pp. 20–28].

UCL-based AVQ algorithm steps.

1. *Initialization:* Assume that there are N training exemplars from p clusters. Let $\mathbf{w}_i(k)$ be the connection weight vector associated with the ith cluster at time index

k, and let $\mathbf{x}(k)$ be a randomly picked input vector at the same time index. Then, $\mathbf{w}_i(0)$ is initialized in some proper way; random selection often suffices. Assuming a much larger number of input vectors $\mathbf{x}_i$ than the number of code book vectors $\mathbf{w}_i$, one may assign the following initialization:

$$\mathbf{w}_i(0) = \mathbf{x}_i, \qquad i = 1, \ldots, p.$$

2. *Competition:* Find the "winning" connection weight vector

$$\mathbf{w}_j(k) = \min_i \| \mathbf{w}_i(k) - \mathbf{x}(k) \|,$$

where $\| \bullet \|$ denotes the L_2 norm. Other norms could also be chosen. The units of the winner-take-all layer have nonmodifiable connections amongst themselves.

3. *Learning:* The connection weights from the inputs to the winning unit j are updated, whereas weight vectors $\mathbf{w}_i$ to other units $i \neq j$ remain unchanged. Thus,

$$\mathbf{w}_j(k + 1) = \mathbf{w}_j(k) + \alpha_k(\mathbf{x}(k) - \mathbf{w}_j(k)),$$
$$\mathbf{w}_i(k + 1) = \mathbf{w}_i(k), \qquad \text{if } i \neq j,$$

where

$$\alpha_k = 0.1\left(1 - \frac{k}{N}\right),$$

and N is the number of training exemplars from the p clusters. In this way, ultimately the connection weight vectors approximate the probability density function of $\mathbf{x}$.

Example 9.6. 2000 training exemplars are obtained from four 2-D Gaussian distributions with the same covariance matrix, $225\mathbf{I}$, and different mean weight vectors: $(0, 40)$, $(40, 40)$, and $(40, 0)$. The random exemplars are shown in Figure 9.16a. Figure 9.16b shows four initial mean weight vectors (clockwise from lower left) at coordinate locations

$(17.4743, -5.433)$,
$(9.4026, 19.6170)$,
$(41.1262, 8.6744)$,
$(45.2741, -21.3541)$,

and the convergence of the UCL-based AVQ trained weights to the corresponding final mean weight vectors of the four Gaussian clusters at coordinate locations

$(0.1011, -1.1966)$,
$(-1.9337, 41.9273)$,
$(41.1992, 41.3609)$,
$(41.4564, 0.8194)$.

Example 9.7. 1500 training exemplars are obtained from three 2-D Gaussian distributions with covariance matrices $225\mathbf{I}$, $144\mathbf{I}$, and $169\mathbf{I}$, and mean weight vectors $(0, 0)$,

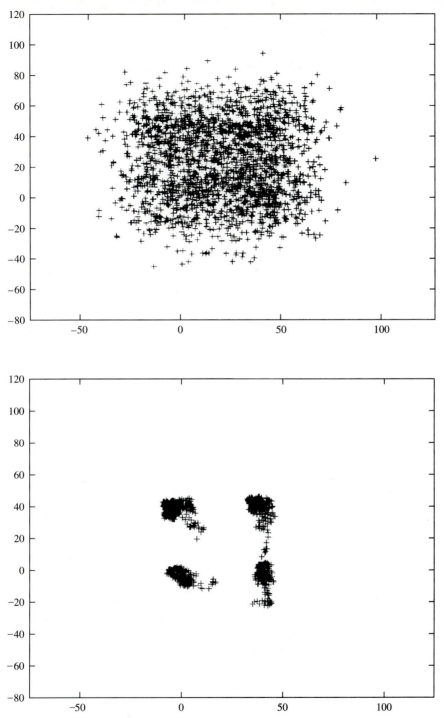

FIGURE 9.16
The exemplars drawn independently from four Gaussian distributions and their clustering. (a) 2000 two-dimensional (2-D) training exemplars from four Gaussian distributions with identical covariance; (b) convergence of UCL-trained weight vectors for the four clusters.

$(0, 40)$, and $(20, 30)$, respectively. The random exemplars are shown in Fig. 9.17*a*. Figure 9.17*b* shows three initial mean weight vectors (clockwise from lower left) at locations

$(0.0493, -3.3102)$,

$(1.0671, 27.4726)$,

$(6.0870, 34.2712)$,

and the convergence of the UCL-based AVQ trained weights to the corresponding final mean weight vectors of the three clusters at

$(-0.6266, -0.35015)$,

$(-2.1571, 41.6648)$,

$(22.6592, 28.7990)$.

Example 9.8. 2000 training exemplars are obtained from four 2-D uniform distributions with the same covariance matrix, $225\mathbf{I}$, and different mean weight vectors: $(0, 0)$, $(0, 12)$, $(12, 0)$, and $(12, 12)$. The random exemplars are shown in Fig. 9.18*a*. Figure 9.18*b* shows four initial mean weight vectors (clockwise from upper right) at coordinate locations

$(5.7532, 13.1798)$,

$(6.9955, -0.3679)$,

$(-5.8407, 9.2506)$,

$(-4.7688, 17.8156)$,

and the convergence of the UCL-based AVQ trained weights to the corresponding final mean weight vectors of the four clusters at coordinate locations

$(13.6022, 10.0867)$,

$(11.1108, -1.3408)$,

$(-0.9573, 1.4664)$,

$(1.3295, 13.5247)$.

The LVQ algorithms that employ supervised learning were proposed by Kohonen for fine-tuning the map after its initial ordering. The class membership of each training exemplar must be known in this case. The basic LVQ suffers from several shortcomings, and variants were developed in response to those drawbacks.[1] The *LVQ2* algorithm, an improved version of *LVQ1*, adjusts the boundaries between categories to keep misclassifications to a minimum by training the interconnection weights in the portion of the structure that is characterized by a complete directed

[1]J.A. Kangas, T.K. Kohonen, and J.T. Laaksonen, "Variants of Self-Organizing Maps," *IEEE Transactions on Neural Networks, 1* (1): 93–99 (March 1990).

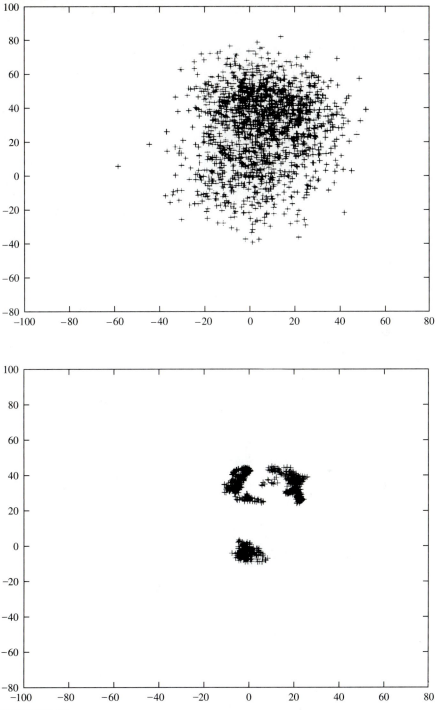

FIGURE 9.17
The exemplars drawn independently from three Gaussian distributions and their clustering.
(*a*) 1500 2-D training exemplars from three Gaussian distributions with distinct covariances;
(*b*) convergence of UCL-trained weight vectors for the three clusters.

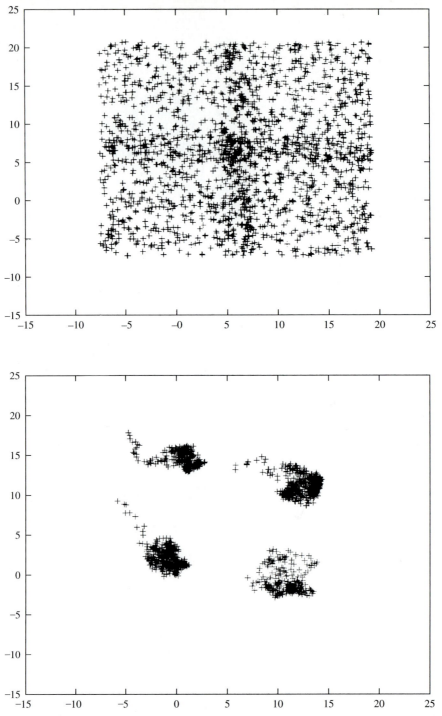

FIGURE 9.18
The exemplars drawn independently from four uniform distributions and their clustering. (*a*) 2000 2-D training exemplars from four uniform distributions with identical covariance; (*b*) convergence of UCL-trained weight vectors for the four clusters.

bipartite graph. To do so, LVQ2 uses competitive learning with the winner-take-all strategy to find the output node closest to the training pattern. If the training pattern's class differs from the output node's class, then LVQ2 finds the next best match. If a node other than the winning node is associated with the correct class, the algorithm moves that next best match closer to the training exemplar and the originally more successful incorrect node(s) away from the exemplar. The process continues until the optimum result is approximated. An algorithm can also update near neighbors of the winning neuron but keep the other losing neurons unchanged.

9.3.4   Two-Dimensional Topographic Maps

The work by Willshaw and von der Malsburg [418] and Amari [16] are examples of topographic maps of the second type. Both the input and the output are either one- or two-dimensional arrays, as shown in Fig. 9.19. Activities in the input array, called the *presynaptic layer,* are to be mapped to activities in the output array, called the *postsynaptic layer.*

There are short-range excitatory and long-range inhibitory lateral connections among units in each array. The connections from the input array to the output array are learned according to the Hebbian rule. Because of the lateral connections within each array, if active units are close together, their local mutual excitation will reinforce each other, leading to localized activation; if units far apart are active, their long-range inhibition will damp or inhibit each other. As a result, units close together tend to be active at the same time. Therefore, locally activated units in the presynaptic layer will be mapped to locally activated units in the postsynaptic layer. These two clusters of active units will increase the positive couplings on the connections between the two sets of units.

It is assumed that the total connection strength from presynaptic units to a postsynaptic unit is constrained not to exceed a constant. This assumption has an important role in the selection and removal of the connections, because when some connection weights are increased, others to the same unit will decrease. A connection with close to zero weight can be removed.

Initially, presynaptic units are randomly connected to the postsynaptic layer with random weights. To drive the learning a few presynaptic units are made active, spontaneously, at random. In addition, it is assumed that connections from presynaptic units are continuously grown to contact the postsynaptic units. These contacts will be removed if not immediately reinforced by the Hebbian rule. Over a sufficient period of learning, small clusters of presynaptic units become exclusively connected to small clusters of postsynaptic units. Weights of the remaining connections become zero. Local minima in this type of map appear as incompatible parts of mapping relations. To prevent this, the map is restricted to develop in one region at the beginning. A continuous map will then be spread out from this region, referred to as the *region of nucleation* in ref. [418].

Another problem is the orientation of the map. For example, a sequence of units 1234 in the presynaptic layer may be mapped to $4'3'2'1'$ or any of the other seven possible orientations. Since no local mechanism can specify the orientation,

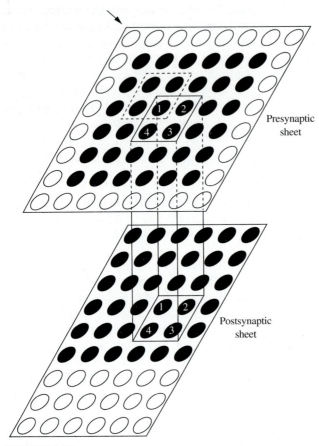

FIGURE 9.19
Topographic map from a presynaptic layer to a postsynaptic layer. The
four numbers in the circle are the polarity markers. (*Source:* D.J. Willshaw and C. von der Malsburg, "How Patterned Neural Connections
Can Be Set Up by Self-Organization," *Proc. Roy. Soc. London B,* 194:
431–445, 1976, Fig. 2. © 1976 The Royal Society, London. Reprinted
by permission of the publisher and authors.)

an initial bias is necessary if a particular orientation is to be achieved. This bias is
provided by *polarity markers* in ref. [418]. Units in a particular small region in the
presynaptic layer are connected with positive weights to a small postsynaptic region
in the required orientation.

Assume that there are M units in the presynaptic array and N units in the postsynaptic array. Let $w_{hj}(t)$ be the time-varying connection weight from presynaptic
unit h to postsynaptic unit j. Let e_{ji} and i_{jr} be the time-varying short-range excitatory
and long-range inhibitory lateral connections from postsynaptic unit j to postsynaptic units i and r, respectively. The state evolution equations of the postsynaptic units
are similar to those in the continuous Hopfield network and are described by

$$\frac{dh_j(t)}{dt} = -\alpha h_j(t) + \sum_{h=1}^{M} x_h(t)w_{hj}(t) + \sum_{i=1}^{N} h_i(t)e_{ij}(t) - \sum_{r=1}^{N} h_r(t)i_{rj}(t)$$

$$j = 1, 2, \ldots, N, \tag{9.39}$$

where $h_j(t)$ is the net input to postsynaptic unit j, and the state $y_j(t)$ of the postsynaptic unit j is given by a linear threshold model [391, 418] different from the standard TLU:

$$y_j(t) = \begin{cases} h_j(t) - \theta_j & \text{if } h_j(t) > \theta_j \\ 0 & \text{otherwise.} \end{cases} \tag{9.40}$$

Then only those connections between strongly active presynaptic and postsynaptic clusters are strengthened, by an amount proportional to the presynaptic activity $x_h(t)$ and the postsynaptic activity $y_j(t)$ according to the Hebbian rule,

$$\Delta w_{hj} = \beta x_h(t) y_j(t). \tag{9.41}$$

The connection weights are normalized to keep the total connection strength to a postsynaptic unit constant, so that

$$\frac{1}{M} \sum_{h=1}^{M} w_{hk} = C, \tag{9.42}$$

where C is a constant. This scaling has two roles. First, it prevents the weights from growing without limit. Second, the scaling forces the connection weights that are not reinforced by learning to decay to small values, therefore enabling them to be removed. Note that this scaling is not a local computation. One possible interpretation is that the total connection strength is limited by the total amount of certain resources available, such as transmitter chemicals or energy.

Willshaw and von der Malsburg used two sheets, each containing 6×6 units, in their simulation. Four units are used as polarity markers. An example of their simulation result is shown in Fig. 9.20. This figure shows a postsynaptic unit at the weighted center of the cluster of the presynaptic units connected to it. Each postsynaptic unit is shown as a point of intersection of lines. The weighted center of the cluster of presynaptic units connected to postsynaptic unit j is computed as $\sum_h w_{hj} \mathbf{x}_h$, where $\mathbf{x}_h$ is the vector associated with the Cartesian coordinates of the presynaptic unit h in the presynaptic array. The line connecting two points indicates that the two postsynaptic units are adjacent in the postsynaptic array. Since the postsynaptic units are plotted at the cluster centers of the presynaptic array, the postsynaptic map so constructed is necessarily smaller than the presynaptic array.

Willshaw and von der Malsburg performed computer simulations of the self-organizing maps. To provide a mathematical analysis, Amari [16] considered one-dimensional topographic maps based on the same principles as in [418]: short-range excitation, long-range inhibition, and Hebbian rule for updating connection weights between presynaptic and postsynaptic layers. However, networks with discrete units were replaced by a continuous field in ref. [16]. Instead of mapping between two arrays of units, a mapping between two continuous fields was considered. This is

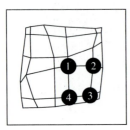

(a)

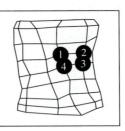

(b)

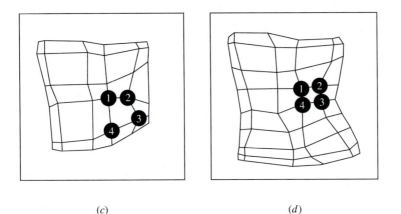

(c)   (d)

FIGURE 9.20

Maps of postsynaptic cluster centers drawn on the presynaptic layer. (*Source:*
D.J. Willshaw and C. von der Malsburg, "How Patterned Neural Connections
Can Be Set Up by Self-Organization," *Proc. Roy. Soc. London B,* 194: 431–445,
1976, Fig. 3. © 1976 The Royal Society, London. Reprinted by permission of the
publisher and authors.)

similar to Amari's neural field theory [14, 15, 190]. This line of investigation is
particularly useful for the understanding of the global properties of undifferentiated
networks. Note that ref. [16] treated only one-dimensional fields. Extension of the
analysis to two dimensions is nontrivial because of the much richer topology in the
two-dimensional case.

Following the argument that the distribution of the weights should reflect the
input probability density in the Kohonen map (Section 9.2.2), it is observed [16]
that if one area of the presynaptic field is activated more often than other areas, the
corresponding cluster in the postsynaptic field will expand. Consider the cluster in
the postsynaptic field connected with the presynaptic area as the representation of
the latter; this expansion corresponds to a finer resolution in the representation of the
more frequently used presynaptic area. This seems to be a reasonable and useful
property of self-organization.

9.3.5 A Multilayer Self-Organizing Feature Map

An example of multilayer self-organizing feature maps is the network by Fukushima [119, 120], which is based on earlier models called the *cognitron* and *neocognitron* [118, 121]. The network has a hierarchical multilayered structure. Each layer actually has two sublayers. One, called the *S*-plane, consists of *S* units, and the other, the *C*-plane, consists of *C* units. The units in the network may have both excitatory and inhibitory connections. The transfer characteristic of an *S* unit is shown in Fig. 9.21. Each *C* unit receives signals from a group of *S* units that have receptive fields of similar characteristics at slightly different positions. The network has forward connections from the input layer to the output layer and backward connections from the output layer to the input layer. The forward signals are for pattern classification and recognition. The backward signals are for selective attention, pattern segmentation, and associative recall.

Figure 9.22 illustrates the signal flow in the network. Layers in the forward paths and backward paths are drawn separately. An input pattern is presented to the lowest stage of the forward paths, called the *input layer*, which is a two-dimensional array of receptor units. The highest stage of the forward paths is called the *recognition layer*. The "grandmother" type of representation is used at the recognition layer; i.e., the presence of an input pattern is represented by the activation of a unique unit *r*. The output of the recognition layer is sent to the lower stages through the backward paths. Finally, the backward paths lead to the *recall layer*, which yields an associative recall of the recognized pattern. The associative recall result will be the recognized pattern with noise and deformation removed. In the recognition-association process, the forward signals gate the flow of the backward signals, and the backward signals either facilitate or inhibit the forward signals. This process is similar to that of

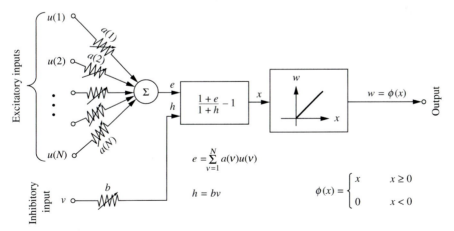

FIGURE 9.21
Transfer characteristics of a unit used in the neocognitron. (*Source:* K. Fukushima, "A Neural Network for Visual Pattern Recognition," *IEEE Computer,* 21(3): 65–76, 1988. © 1988 IEEE. Reprinted with permission of the publisher.)

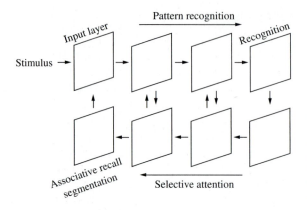

FIGURE 9.22
Signal flow in the Fukushima network. (*Source:* K. Fukushima, "A Neural Network for Visual Pattern Recognition," *IEEE Computer,* 21(3): 65–76, 1988. © 1988 IEEE. Reprinted with permission of the publisher.)

the ART networks [69, 70, 71]. The interaction between bottom-up and top-down propagations may be a key process in biological vision systems.

Figure 9.23 shows the various units and the connection patterns in the network. The letters u and w indicate that the units are in the forward and backward paths, respectively. Three processing layers and the input layer are shown. In each processing layer, only one of each kind of units is shown. Actually, each layer has many such units, arranged in a two-dimensional array. In the figure, a single line indicates a one-to-one connection between the units, and a double-line connection indicates converging or diverging connections. A more detailed connection pattern is shown in Fig. 9.24. If only the feedforward paths are considered, this network has almost

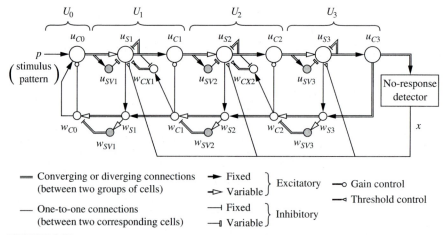

FIGURE 9.23
Connections and units in the layers of the Fukushima network. (*Source:* K. Fukushima, "A Neural Network for Visual Pattern Recognition," *IEEE Computer,* 21(3): 65–76, 1988. © 1988 IEEE. Reprinted with permission of the publisher.)

the same structure and function as the neocognitron [118, 121]. As can be seen in Fig. 9.23, u_S and u_C planes are arranged alternately. The u_S units are for feature extraction. Weights on connections converging to u_S units are learned. Initially, the weights are all set to zero.

In the network, feedforward connections are reinforced before the backward connections. In this way, during the reinforcement of the forward connections, there is no backward signal flow in the network. The forward connections are reinforced in a way similar to the Kohonen self-organizing map. That is, connections to all units in a neighborhood of the unit that has the maximum response are reinforced. This neighborhood can be picked out by short-range excitatory and long-range inhibitory lateral connections in a plane. First, the connections coming from activated units from the previous plane to the unit that has the maximum

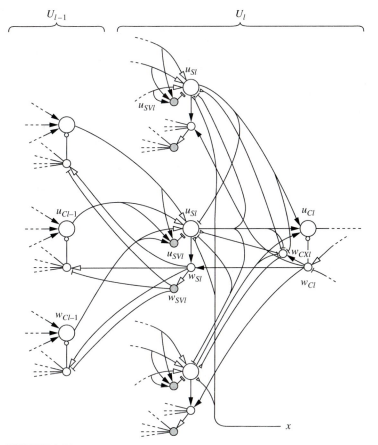

FIGURE 9.24
A detailed illustration of connections between neighboring units in the Fukushima network. (*Source:* K. Fukushima, "A Neural Network for Visual Pattern Recognition," *IEEE Computer,* 21(3): 65–76, 1988. © 1988 IEEE. Reprinted with permission of the publisher.)

response are reinforced. Then the connections in the neighborhood are reinforced in the same way (either by the same amount or by an amount decaying with distance away from the maximum-responding unit). After reinforcement of the forward connections, the backward connections are reinforced by the same amount as their counterparts in the forward connections.

Reinforcement of connections to the maximum-responding unit is illustrated in Fig. 9.25. Only forward connections converging to a u_S unit are shown. The u_S unit has learnable excitatory connections from a group of u_C units of the preceding layer; it also has a learnable connection from a subsidiary inhibitory unit, the u_{SV} unit. The u_{SV} unit has fixed excitatory connections from the same group of u_C units as the u_S units, and it always responds with the average intensity of the outputs of the u_C units. The weights of the learnable connections are set to nearly zero values initially. Suppose this u_S unit has the maximum response among all the u_S units in its neighborhood when a training pattern is presented. Then all the learnable connections, both excitatory and inhibitory, from the activated u_C and u_{SV} units are reinforced. This reinforcement rule is rather simple; it is more of a memorizing rule than a learning rule.

The reinforced connections from the u_C units to the u_S unit actually form a template that *exactly* matches the spatial distribution of the response of the u_C units in the preceding layer. This rule enables the network to recognize the patterns quickly, because they are simply memorized.

An interesting question is, "What happens if the training patterns used are deformed and noisy?" The inhibitory connections are not reinforced as strongly, because the output of the u_{SV} unit is not as large. Then all the u_S units in a neighborhood of the maximally responding u_S unit have their connections reinforced with the same spatial distribution. As a result, all the u_S units in the neighborhood respond to the

u_C

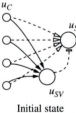 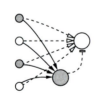

u_S

u_{SV}

| Initial state | Stimulus presentation | After reinforcement |

---> Excitatory ⎫
—▪ Inhibitory ⎬ variable   →→ Excitatory fixed
               ⎭

FIGURE 9.25
Illustration of reinforcement of connections to the maximum-responding unit. Only forward connections converging to a u_S unit are shown: (*a*) before a training pattern is presented; (*b*) presentation of a training pattern; (*c*) after the connections are reinforced. (*Source:* K. Fukushima, "A Neural Network for Visual Pattern Recognition," *IEEE Computer,* 21(3): 65–76, 1988. © 1988 IEEE. Reprinted with permission of the publisher.)

presence of the same feature at different positions in the preceding layer. If an irrelevant feature is present, the nonselective inhibitory signal from u_{SV} is stronger than the direct excitatory signals from the u_C units; thus, the u_S unit will not respond. Once a unit is made to be selective to a feature, it totally loses its plasticity. When a different feature is presented, a unit that maximally responds to the new feature will be selected. If the unit responding maximally to one feature is damaged and ceases to function, then another unit that responds maximally among all the remaining ones will be selected. However, this self-repairing property is effective only if the damage occurs when learning is still allowed.

When the signal reaches the recognition layer, the winner-take-all mechanism ensures that only one unit is activated. The output of this unit is sent back to the lower stages through the backward paths. The backward signals are controlled by gate signals from the forward paths so that they retrace the same routes as the forward signals. The backward signals are sent back only from the single activated unit at the recognition layer that corresponds to the recognized pattern. Therefore, only signal components corresponding to the recognized pattern reach the recall layer.

The output of the recall layer gives a segmentation result, because only components relevant to a single pattern are selected from the stimulus at the input layer because of the way the backward connections are learned. After the forward connections are reinforced, the backward connections from a w_S unit descending to the w_C units in a lower layer are reinforced automatically to have a weight proportional to the forward connections from u_C units to the u_S unit paired with the w_S unit (see Fig. 9.24). Therefore, if an excitatory forward connection is reinforced from a u_C unit to a u_S unit, an excitatory backward connection forms automatically from the corresponding w_S unit to the corresponding w_C unit.

The inhibitory backward connections via the subsidiary unit w_{SV} that corresponds to the u_{SV} unit in the forward path are treated similarly. Corresponding to the fixed forward connections that converge to a u_C unit from a number of u_S units, there are many backward connections diverging from a w_C unit to w_S units. However, not all the w_S units receiving excitatory backward signals should be activated. This is because to activate a u_C unit in the forward path, the activation of one preceding u_S unit is sufficient; usually, only a small number of preceding u_S units are actually activated. To achieve a similar response in the w_S units in the backward paths, a gate signal from the paired u_S unit is required in addition to the backward excitatory signals from the w_C units for a w_S unit to activate. As a result, the backward signals from w_C units to w_S units retrace the same route as the forward signals from u_S units to u_C units (see Figs. 9.23 and 9.24).

Not only do the forward signals gate the backward signals, as just described; the backward signals also facilitate the forward signals. The backward signals supply a gain control signal from each w_C unit in the backward paths to the corresponding u_C unit in the forward paths. When a w_C unit is inactive, the gain between the weighted sum of inputs and the output of the corresponding u_C unit gradually attenuates from its initial value of 1.0 with the passage of time. When the w_C unit is activated, however, the attenuated gain is recovered. In this way, only forward signal paths where there are backward signals in the corresponding backward paths are facilitated. This mechanism plays a role in the selective attention function. When more than one particular pattern is present at the input layer, only the forward paths corresponding to this pattern are facilitated by the backward signals, because only one unit at the recognition layer can be active at a time. The forward paths corresponding to the other patterns gradually die without facilitation by backward signals. In summary, the forward signals control the route the backward signals travel using gate signals, and the backward signals facilitate the forward signals by controlling the gain of the corresponding units in the forward paths.

It is natural to ask how attention can be switched to different patterns. This is achieved by momentarily interrupting the backward signal flow. Once the backward signal is interrupted, the facilitating signals to the forward paths disappear. Then the u_C unit gains that were previously kept high by backward facilitating signals are lowered. The gains of those u_C units that were previously attenuated are recovered by the same signal (not shown in Fig. 9.23) that interrupts the backward signal flow. As a result, signals corresponding to the previous pattern will have difficulty flowing through the forward paths, and a previously inactive unit at the recognition layer usually wins the competition. The backward signals from this unit will further facilitate the forward signal to establish the new recognition and segmentation result firmly.

If a part of the input pattern is missing or corrupted by noise, the feature that should exist there fails to be extracted in the forward paths. The flow of the backward signals will be stopped at that point. In this case, the threshold for extracting that feature will be automatically lowered so that partial or noisy traces of the undetected features will be extracted. The w_{CX} units detect the failure to extract a feature when the units in the backward paths are activated but the corresponding forward units are not (see Figs. 9.23 and 9.24). The signal from the w_{CX} units reduces the effect of inhibition of the u_S units by lowering the threshold of feature extraction of the u_S units. Hence the connection from a w_{CX} unit to a u_S unit is called a *threshold control*. When the threshold is lowered, the u_S unit will respond to vague traces of the feature to which it normally will not respond. Then the backward signals can be further propagated down the layers through the path unlocked by the gate signal from the newly activated unit in the forward path. Therefore, a complete pattern will appear at the recall layer. Noise will be eliminated and missing parts will be filled in. The pattern of the recall layer gives the result of an autoassociative recall.

In some cases no unit at the recognition layer wins the competition, as when the input pattern differs too much from the patterns used in training or when too many patterns are superimposed. At this no-response state, the signal flow in the network stops due to lack of backward signals. Then the no-response detector shown in Fig. 9.23 sends a threshold control signal to all the u_S units in all the layers to lower their threshold for feature detection. The longer the recognition layer is inactive, the lower the thresholds will be reduced. Eventually, one unit at the recognition layer will be activated.

This network is a complicated system with impressive performance. Fukushima reported the simulation result of a three-layer network (not counting the input layer) with about 41,399 units. The input layer is a square array with 19×19 units. The network is able to achieve a certain degree of scale- and shift-invariant recognition. The recognition is also unaffected by deformation and noise to a certain extent. This appreciable tolerance of deformation and noise is achieved by making each layer tolerate a small amount of deformation and noise; a single layer would not be able to accomplish this.

After a sufficient period of unsupervised learning, the network is able to focus its attention selectively to a sequence of patterns in a composite of learned patterns, to segment one pattern from others, and to recognize the patterns separately. Like the ART network, this network is also capable of serial processing, such as in the attention-switching mechanism; in the backward and forward propagation of signals to establish a firm recognition; and in the threshold control signal, which is generated only after the backward signals are stopped or after the no-response state is detected at the recognition layer.

For these tasks, this network also learns very quickly. In the example in ref. [119], each of five training patterns is presented 3, 4, and 4 times for training layers 1, 2, and 3, respectively (the training of higher layers is done only after the preceding layers are trained). Why is this large network able to learn so fast? The answer lies in the way the connections are learned. As described before, it is a simple memorization, and it is totally local in the sense that the connection weights of one unit are affected only by one feature. The locality feature is achieved by a competition mechanism that selects the unit for reinforcement. An interesting question to consider is what happens if the training patterns used are deformed and noisy. Variations of this type of localized, memorization-style learning have been used in other networks, such as those in control applications, and may provide a useful compromise in the designing of large networks for complicated tasks.

9.4 HYBRID LEARNING

The architectures for ART- and SOFM-based ANNs do not contain hidden layers. The networks in this section have a common hidden layer between the input and output layers. The underlying graphs between the input layer and the hidden layer and between the hidden layer and the output layer are complete bipartite graphs. The network differs from the layered networks studied in Chapter 5 in its learning strategies. In fact, as suggested in the section title, both supervised and unsupervised learning are employed. The connection weights of the edges of the lower bipartite graph are determined by a Kohonen type of unsupervised competitive learning, whereas the edge weights of the upper bipartite graph are determined by supervised learning. Lateral connections could be allowed in the hidden and output layers but are taken to be absent in the radial basis function network.

9.4.1 Counterpropagation Network

Hecht-Nielsen [153] developed the *counterpropagation network* (CPN), which learns a near-optimal lookup-table approximation to the mapping being approximated. As stated above, the CPN involves both supervised and unsupervised learning. We first consider a feedforward counterpropagation network, in which case the associated graph is directed from bottom to top. The network learns an approximation to the vector-valued mapping $\mathbf{y} = \mathbf{f}(\mathbf{x})$, where $\mathbf{y}$ is an $m \times 1$ vector and $\mathbf{x}$ is an

$n \times 1$ vector. A feedforward CPN has two layers, as shown in Fig. 9.26. The hidden layer, connected by weights from the layer of inputs, constitutes an unsupervised winner-take-all competitive learning network. The lateral connections, therefore, in the hidden layer are similar to those in the winner-take-all network described in Section 9.1.1. The output layer learns the estimated $\hat{\mathbf{y}}$ value associated with the current input vector $\mathbf{x}$ by the mapping. In Fig. 9.26, for easy illustration, $n = 3$, $m = 2$, and the number N of units in the winner-take-all layer is also 3. In general, n, m, and N can be arbitrary positive integers.

There are two stages in the counterpropagation learning process:

1. *Unsupervised competitive learning*: The unsupervised competitive learning network is allowed to develop its weights *first*.
   a. In the first phase of competitive learning, unit j in the first layer wins the competition at time index k if

$$\| \mathbf{m}_j(k) - \mathbf{x}^i \| \leq \| \mathbf{m}_r(k) - \mathbf{x}^i \| \qquad \text{for } r = 1, 2, \ldots, N, \quad (9.43)$$

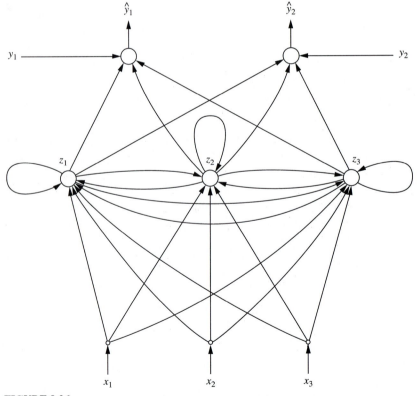

FIGURE 9.26
The feedforward counterpropagation network that learns the approximation of the mapping from $\mathbf{x}$ to $\mathbf{y}$.

where $\mathbf{m}_r(k)$ is the $n \times 1$ weight vector for the connections from the input layer to the rth unit in the first layer. If the weight vectors $\mathbf{m}_r$ are unit vectors, then Eq. (9.43) is equivalent to

$$\mathbf{m}_j^T(k) \cdot \mathbf{x}^i \leq \mathbf{m}_r(k) \cdot \mathbf{x}^i$$

for all r. This competitive learning can be implemented using the winner-take-all network discussed in Section 9.1.1. If we denote the output vector from the first-layer units by $\mathbf{z}$, we have

$$\mathbf{z} = \boldsymbol{\delta}_{jr}, \tag{9.44}$$

where $\boldsymbol{\delta}_{jr}$ is an $(N \times 1)$ vector that denotes that only the winning unit j outputs a 1, and the outputs from all other units are 0.

   b. In the second phase of the competitive learning, the weight vector from the input layer to the winning unit is updated. The update can be carried out using either Eq. (9.5) or Eq. (9.7). After the clusters have stabilized, the weights $\mathbf{m}_r$ are fixed for all r. This is realized by letting $\alpha(k)$ decay to zero in Eq. (9.5) or Eq. (9.7).

2. *Supervised learning of the estimate:* After the unsupervised learning phase is completed, one unit in the first layer is active for a given input vector. The active unit represents the cluster to which the given input vector belongs. Then supervised learning is performed on the connections from the winning unit j to all the units in the second layer.

   a. Denote the connection weights from the winning unit j to all the units in the second layer by $\mathbf{u}_j$. The learning of the weights is governed by the following equation:

$$u_{jr}(k + 1) = u_{jr}(k) + \eta(y_r(k) - u_{jr}(k))z_j(k), \qquad \text{for } r = 1, 2, \ldots, m, \tag{9.45}$$

where the learning rate η satisfies the inequality $0 < \eta < 1$. Multiplication of z_j in the second term indicates that only the connections from the winning unit to the second layer are updated. It can be shown (left as an exercise) that after a sufficient number of updates the weight vector $\mathbf{u}_j$ approaches the average of all the vectors $\mathbf{y}$ corresponding to the cluster represented by the winning unit j. In other words, $\mathbf{u}_j$ approaches the cluster average $\bar{\mathbf{y}}$ of all the vectors $\mathbf{y}$ associated with those input vectors $\mathbf{x}$ that cause unit j to be the winning unit in the first layer.

   b. The output of the second layer is given as

$$\hat{y}_r = \sum_{i=1}^{N} u_{ir}(k)z_i(k). \tag{9.46}$$

Therefore, the output vector $\hat{\mathbf{y}}$ approaches the cluster average $\bar{\mathbf{y}}$ after a sufficient number of updates.

    Note that to realize counterpropagation learning, a control circuit is required that schedules the learning stages in sequence. After learning, the network is equivalent to a nearest-match lookup table approximating the mapping $\mathbf{y} = \mathbf{f}(\mathbf{x})$. The equivalent lookup table is shown in Fig. 9.27. An input $\mathbf{x}$ to the network is compared to the weight vectors $\{\mathbf{m}_r\}_{r=1}^N$. The weight vector $\mathbf{m}_j$ closest to the input vector is chosen. In the network this is realized by having only the jth unit in the winner-take-all layer active. In the lookup table this corresponds to choosing the nearest-match entry j in the first column. Then the second layer outputs the cluster average (approximate) $\bar{\mathbf{y}}_j$. This average is over all the desired outputs associated with inputs that fall in the cluster represented by unit j in the first layer. This corresponds to cross-referencing $\bar{\mathbf{y}}_j$ in the second column from $\mathbf{m}_j$ in the lookup table. If all the learning exemplars are from a compact set $\mathbf{A} \subset \mathbb{R}^n$, and the mapping $\mathbf{y} = \mathbf{f}(\mathbf{x})$ is continuous on $\mathbf{A}$, the accuracy of approximating the mapping will increase as the number of units in the winner-take-all layer increases. In fact, the mean square error can be made as small as desired by choosing a sufficiently large N. Thus, for continuous functions the CPN can function as a universal function approximator. That is, it possesses the same universal approximator capability as multilayer feedforward networks using the backpropagation algorithm. However, a CPN is less useful as a universal approximator than backpropagation learning, because to achieve a desired accuracy the number N of units required in the winner-take-all layer is usually much larger than the number of units required in backpropagation learning.

Counterpropagation networks are often useful for rapidly prototyping a complex system containing mapping networks. This is because counterpropagation learning typically converges orders of magnitude faster to achieve best performance. If all the learning exemplars are from a known compact set $\mathbf{A} \subset \mathbb{R}^n$, the unsupervised learning stage may be shortened by selecting the initial weights $\mathbf{m}_r(0)$ from a uniform probability distribution in $\mathbf{A}$. Counterpropagation networks are also best suited to applications that require an adaptive lookup table structure.

The feedforward CPN just described can be extended to a full counterpropagation network. A full counterpropagation network (Fig. 9.28) learns the mapping in both directions, from $\mathbf{x}$ to $\mathbf{y}$ and from $\mathbf{y}$ to $\mathbf{x}$. It is basically two feedforward counter-

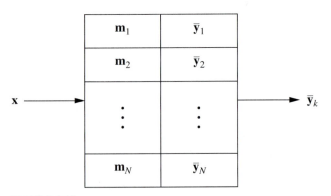

FIGURE 9.27
After learning, a counterpropagation network is equivalent to a nearest-match lookup table.

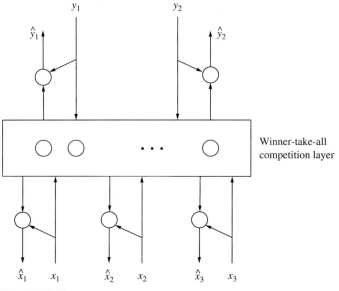

FIGURE 9.28
A full counterpropagation network that learns the approximations of the
mappings in both directions, from **x** to **y** and from **y** to **x**.

propagation networks put together. One network learns the mapping from **x** to **y**, and
the other learns the mapping from **y** to **x**. The two feedforward counterpropagation
networks share the winner-take-all layer.

A variant of the CPN is obtained by allowing more than one unit to win in the
competitive learning layer. This is achieved by changing the lateral inhibitions in
the MAXNET to those having a wider on-center as shown in Fig. 9.8. For further
discussions and open problems in such a variant, see ref. [155].

9.4.2   Regularizing Networks and Radial Basis Functions

The approximation scheme described above belongs to a class of networks with one
layer of hidden units, called *regularizing networks*. In addition to the CPN, other
subsets of regularizing networks include the *Radial Basis Function* (RBF) network
and its generalization, the *Hyper Basis Function* (HBF) network. The basic topology
of the RBF network consists of an input layer, one hidden layer, and an output layer,
so the underlying graphs for the bottom and top halves are complete bipartite graphs.
Additional ramifications in the basic architecture are determined by the particular
learning rules used. With the availability of a large number of hidden layer units,
the network can well approximate a broad class of mappings. There is also considerable flexibility in the choice of the transfer characteristics of the hidden layer
units; the sigmoid type of activation function, used in multilayer feedforward networks trained with backpropagation, does not yield the approximating capabilities of

RBF networks. The RBF networks use Gaussian activation functions in addition to other proven possibilities. Unlike the CPN network, the RBF network uses a learning paradigm that is much more general and versatile than winner-take-all competitive learning.

The theory of RBF networks is still the subject of extensive ongoing research. Therefore, this chapter refrains from making a discursive presentation of this topic; enough information is presented to arouse the reader's curiosity for further investigations into this topic, and some of the problems included at the end of this chapter will serve to educate the reader on the basics as well as scopes of RBF networks.

The radial basis function network was proposed by Broomhead and Lowe [58] and later expanded by many others, e.g., [74, 262]. The theoretical basis for this type of network lies in interpolation theory, which is a well-developed branch of mathematics. The underlying graph of a multiple-input multiple-output RBF network is a node-coalesced concatenation of bipartite graphs $K_{r,p}$ and $K_{p,m}$, where r, p, m denote, respectively, the number of inputs, hidden layer nodes, and outputs, as is shown in Fig. 9.29. Thus, the network provides a map from the space $\mathbb{R}^r$ to $\mathbb{R}^m$. Without sacrificing generality but to achieve brevity of exposition, we restrict our treatment here to the case where $m = 1$. In that case, the mapping realizes as output the function

$$f(\mathbf{x}) = \sum_{i=1}^{p} w_i \psi \left(\| \frac{\mathbf{x} - \mathbf{c}_i}{\sigma_i} \| \right),$$

where $\mathbf{x} \in \mathbb{R}^r$, ψ is the activation function that maps the nonnegative semi-infinite real interval to the real line, the $\mathbf{c}_i$'s are vector-valued parameters called *centroids*, the σ_i's are positive-valued shaping parameters for the activation functions, and the w_i's are the scalar connection weights from the hidden nodes to the output node. The nonlinearity in the output node could be any one of several functions, including a hard-limiter. The norm $\| \cdot \|$ is usually taken to be the L_2-norm, though other norms have also been considered [286]. It has been shown that by setting the σ_i's to be

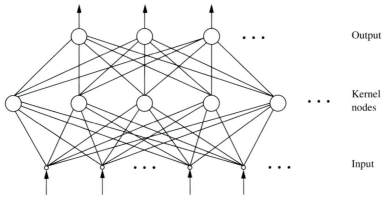

FIGURE 9.29
The radial basis function network with multiple inputs and outputs is shown. The direction of signal flow is from bottom (input) to top (output).

equal and with mild restrictions on the activation functions, the RBF network can provide arbitrarily good approximations, as a function of the size of the hidden layer, to specified functions that are square-integrable (in the L_2-norm case), essentially bounded, and continuous with compact support [286].

Another advantage of the network considered in this section is its ability to generalize well after training. The training methods used, though often quite simple, have produced good results. However, the promise of better performance with more sophisticated training schemes provides a needed challenge for further fruitful research. Other advantages include faster convergence and simple network structure coupled with easier control over network performance. However, more training examples may be required to achieve a performance comparable to that of a multilayer feedforward network trained by backpropagation, when that happens to converge to a good solution.

The activation function, $\psi(\mathbf{x})$, in an RBF network is required to be radially symmetric. This means that

$$\text{if } \| \mathbf{x}_1 \| = \| \mathbf{x}_2 \|, \qquad \text{then } \psi(\| \mathbf{x}_1 \|) = \psi(\| \mathbf{x}_2 \|).$$

The most commonly used function for this purpose has been the r-variate Gaussian function,

$$\psi(x_1, x_2, \ldots, x_r) = \exp(-[(x_1 - c_1)^2 + (x_2 - c_2)^2 + \cdots + (x_r - c_r)^2]),$$

in the real-valued inputs, $x_1, x_2, \ldots, x_r$, with the centroid at coordinate location $(c_1, c_2, \ldots, c_r)$ in the r-*dimensional* real Euclidean space. Note that the kernel within square brackets in the above function is the Euclidean distance between the vectors $\mathbf{x} = (x_1 \ x_2 \ \cdots \ x_r)^{\mathrm{T}}$ and $\mathbf{c} = (c_1 \ c_2 \ \cdots \ c_r)^{\mathrm{T}}$. This function, in addition to being radially symmetric, also has the attractive property of *product separability*, since it can be expressed as a product of r univariate functions. Other popular activation functions include the *thin-plate spline*, defined by

$$\psi(r) = \left(\frac{r}{\eta}\right)^2 \ln\left(\frac{r}{\eta}\right),$$

where η is a positive parameter and r denotes the distance between vectors $\mathbf{x}$ and $\mathbf{c}_i$.

Training is accomplished first at the hidden layer by unsupervised learning and then at the output layer by supervised learning. At the hidden layer, the centroids are calculated by, say, a K-means clustering algorithm. Sometimes a subset of the training exemplars is chosen to define the centroids. In certain cases the number of hidden units equals, initially, the number of exemplars; the centroids are defined by the feature vectors associated with the exemplars, and then the number of hidden units is trimmed as desired. Alternatively, the size of the hidden layer is made to grow to the proper size starting from one hidden unit. The smoothing (shaping) parameters are usually either chosen by trial-and-error adjustments or selected almost arbitrarily subject only to simple guidelines. Some efforts have been expended toward training the shaping parameters as well as determining the number of units and their centroids in the hidden layer [188, 270], but the results are far from complete. Learning in the output layer follows the determination of the parameters in the activation function. Typically, this could be done by the application of the LMS algorithm, described in Chapter 4. After the initial training of the complete network, the network parameters in the hidden layer may be fine-tuned by applying supervised learning to both the hidden and the output layers simultaneously.

The radially symmetric constraint on the activation function is sometimes relaxed to decrease the number of units in the hidden layer and further improve the performance of the network in pattern classification and function approximation tasks. For example, the radially symmetric property of a multivariate Gaussian function may be generalized to the *elliptically* symmetric property by replacing $x_i - c_i$ with $(x_i - c_i)/\beta_i$, for each i, where β_i is a positive real-valued parameter. The Euclidean distance between the pattern vector and the centroid is then said to be replaced by the *Mahalanobis distance*. Simulation results have shown that the performance of networks can often be improved when the radially symmetric constraint is relaxed as in this case.[2]

9.5   SUMMARY AND DISCUSSION

This chapter discusses unsupervised learning and self-organization in recurrent networks. Unsupervised competitive learning and its applications are presented first. Competitive learning networks are useful in categorizing or finding clusters in the input data in an unsupervised manner. The focus in Section 9.1.1 is on the winner-take-all type of competitive networks. It is believed that a more distributed version of competitive learning may be more advantageous. A competitive learning network with a more distributed representation is less well understood and is an interesting topic for research.

The Hamming network as an associative memory is examined in Section 9.1.2. It is based on a winner-take-all competitive network. The Hamming network implements an optimal minimum error classifier and scales more favorably than a Hopfield network.

The stability of the clusters formed by a competitive learning network is not guaranteed. The winning unit may continue to change even when the same set of input vectors is continuously presented. This may be prevented by gradually reducing the learning rate α to zero; however, the network will not be able to learn any new clusters then. Grossberg calls this phenomenon the stability and plasticity dilemma. The dilemma occurs because at times the plasticity must be reinstated (activated) by increasing α so that the network can learn new patterns. At other times, the plasticity must be deactivated to promote stability. In biological neural networks the learning and recognition phases are simultaneously present, whereas in an ANN the two phases are separated, with learning taking place prior to recognition. Adaptive resonant networks are presented in Section 9.2 to deal with this dilemma.

---

[2]J. Park and I.W. Sandberg. Nonlinear approximations using elliptic basis function networks. *Circuits, Systems, and Signal Processing*, 3(1): 99–113, 1994.

The clustering algorithm implemented by the ART1 network is given in Section 9.2.1 in terms of a discrete-time pattern-clustering algorithm, and the ART1 network is discussed in Section 9.2.2. An important contribution of the ART architectures is the demonstration of the feasibility of using several subnetworks to execute, collectively, a *serial-nature algorithm*. This may be the only realistic way for artificial neural networks to accomplish any complicated task and is consonant with the properties of the biological neural network. A later development, ART2, is intended for classification of analog patterns; however, efforts to implement the complete ART2 network may be difficult. Another development, ART3, has been particularly geared toward the simulation of biological synapses.

In the winner-take-all competitive learning network, only connections to the winner are updated. The updating of the weights does not rely in any way on the spatial relations among the units in the competition layer. Therefore, as expected, it cannot develop any spatial organization. Kohonen identified two key mechanisms for a network to self-organize spatially. First, locate the unit that best responds to the given input; this unit is called the winning unit. Second, modify the connection weight to the winning unit and also the connection weights to units in its defined neighborhood. The self-organization behavior of Kohonen maps is discussed in Section 9.3.1. A simplified but insightful analysis of the self-organizing process in a one-dimensional case is given in section 9.3.2. It is shown that the weights in a Kohonen map become ordered with probability 1 as the time index $k \to \infty$. Kohonen paid particular attention to the distribution of the weights as a function of the probability density $p(x)$ of the inputs used for learning. It is shown that for uniform input density distribution, the weights are distributed evenly (except at boundaries). Therefore, the weights are true representatives of the input density function $p(x)$ when $p(x)$ is uniform. However, for general nonuniform $p(x)$, the weight distribution is not linearly proportional to the input probability. It has been shown that in one dimension the density of the weights w_k is proportional to $p^{2/3}(x)$ for general nonuniform $p(x)$. No similar results for the density distribution of weights in terms of the density distribution of the inputs are known in two or higher dimensions. Theoretical analysis yields insights on the convergence process in a Kohonen map. It is found that the choice of an asymmetric neighborhood for updating may significantly improve the convergence speed.

Topographic maps from a presynaptic two-dimensional array to a postsynaptic two-dimensional array are introduced in Section 9.3.3. There are short-range excitatory and long-range inhibitory lateral connections among units in each array. The connections from the input array to the output array are learned according to the Hebbian rule. As a result, locally activated units in the presynaptic layer will be mapped to locally activated units in the postsynaptic layer. A nonlocal scaling plays an important role in the self-organization process in these maps. It limits the total connection strength up to a constant. This enables connections that are not strengthened by learning to die out. One possible interpretation of this scaling is that the total connection strength is limited by the total amount of characterizing resources available, such as transmitter chemicals or energy.

Following the line of thought that the distribution of the weights should reflect the input probability density function in the Kohonen map (Section 9.3.2), it is observed that if one area of the presynaptic field is activated more often than other areas, the corresponding cluster in the postsynaptic field will expand. Consider the cluster in the postsynaptic field connected to the presynaptic area as the representation of the latter. This expansion corresponds to a finer resolution in the representation of the more frequently used presynaptic area. This seems to be a reasonable and useful property of self-organization.

In Section 9.3.4 an example of a multilayered self-organizing feature map, by Fukushima, is presented. This is a complicated network with many different functional units. There are two main signal flow paths: the forward path and the backward path. The network is used to recognize and segment patterns from images of multiple patterns degraded by missing parts, noise, and overlap. The recognition process involves both bottom-up feature extraction and recognition, using the forward path, and top-down object segmentation and attention selection, using the backward path. The forward signals gate the backward signals, and the backward signals facilitate the forward signals. Such cooperation of backward and forward signals is necessary for successful performance of any visual recognition systems.

The main lessons learned from the work by Fukushima and the ART networks are that for a neural network to accomplish complicated tasks, the set of desirable characteristics should include the following:

1. It should be able to perform serial logic computation and processing.
2. There should be several subnetworks working together. In Fukushima's network, the forward part and the backward part are two such subnetworks; so are the two fields in the ART networks.
3. There should be more than one type of unit and more types of connections besides excitatory and inhibitory, such as the gate control signal and gain control function in Fukushima's network and the reset unit in the ART networks.

Designing this type of network is very much like designing digital combinational and sequential logic circuits.

Hybrid learning algorithms, which have both an unsupervised phase and a supervised phase, typified in the counterpropagation network and the radial basis function network, are discussed in Section 9.4. The counterpropagation network applies winner-take-all unsupervised competitive learning in the unsupervised phase. Counterpropagation networks are often useful for rapidly prototyping a complex system containing mapping networks. However, a counterpropagation network is less useful as a universal approximator than multilayer feedforward networks using sigmoidal nonlinearities and backpropagation learning, because to achieve a desired accuracy the number N of units required in the winner-take-all layer is usually much larger than the number of units required in backpropagation learning. The last drawback is alleviated by regularizing networks, typified by the RBF network, which with its many possible generalizations and ramifications creates a fertile arena for research activity. For more on RBF networks, consult Chapter 7 in the recent text by Haykin.[3]

Following are some representative problems. Since the topics falling under the jurisdiction of this chapter are rather extensive, some of the problems also serve as vehicles of description of topics that could not be covered to the depth desired, either to conserve space or to honor the ongoing research currently underway that is likely to provide more definitive results in the near future.

PROBLEMS

9.1. From the description provided in the text, sketch the structure of a Hamming network, showing all possible connections. Suppose that an exemplar is described by the bipolar binary bit pattern

$$(-1\ 1\ 1\ -1\ 1\ -1\ -1\ -1).$$

(a) Calculate the weight vector associated with the exemplar given.

(b) Suppose that an input pattern is

$$(1\ -1\ -1\ 1\ 1\ 1\ -1\ -1).$$

Calculate the inner product (dot product) between the weight vector you found in the preceding part and the above input pattern. With the threshold of each neuron in the lower subnetwork (characterized by the bipartite graph) of the Hamming network set in the standard manner, calculate the output from the particular neuron (unit) in the lower subnetwork to which the inner product you computed is applied.

9.2. Does the Hamming distance between binary vectors satisfy the definition for a metric in a metric space? Justify.

9.3. Given are four clusters in a two-dimensional feature space. Each cluster is characterized by a distribution

$$p_i(x, y) = \exp\left\{-\frac{1}{\sqrt{2\pi\sigma_{ix}\sigma_{iy}}}\left(\frac{(x-m_{ix})^2}{\sigma_{ix}^2} - \frac{(x-m_{ix})(y-m_{iy})}{\sigma_{ix}\sigma_{iy}} + \frac{(y-m_{iy})^2}{\sigma_{iy}^2}\right)\right\},$$
$$i = 1, 2, 3, 4.$$

The means and standard deviations of the cluster are

i	m_{ix}	m_{iy}	σ_{ix}	σ_{iy}
1	0	0	1/2	1/2
2	2	2	1/4	1/2
3	3	4	1/2	1/4
4	4	2	1/4	1/2

The training exemplar set contains $\lfloor p_i(x_k, y_l)/0.2 \rfloor$ exemplars from the ith cluster at each integer point in $[-2, 6] \times [-2, 6]$, i.e., x_k and y_l are integers in $[-2, 6]$, where $\lfloor z \rfloor$

[3]S. Haykin, *Neural Networks: A Comprehensive Foundation*, Macmillan, New York, 1994.

is the integer part of z. Use the training set so obtained to train a competitive learning network. Compare the cluster movement of the learned clusters with a decaying α and nondecaying α. In the decaying-α case, after the learned clusters have stabilized, compare the learned cluster prototype with the actual cluster center (m_{ix}, m_{iy}).

9.4. In comparison with the Hopfield network, the Hamming network has the advantage of larger storage capacity and the ability to process similar patterns, a smaller number of connections, and no spurious output. Carry out an experimental comparison of the Hopfield network and the Hamming network with respect to a suitable data file.

9.5. Prove properties 1 through 8 for the ART1 clustering algorithm.

9.6. Propose an alternative ART1 clustering algorithm and network, in which the Hamming distance provides the single similarity measure and which uses bipolar binary units.

9.7. Generate a data file consisting of four input patterns of 25 pixels each. You may create, for example, square arrays of binary $(0, 1)$ representations of the uppercase letters A and X and one suitable distorted version of each. Use the ART1 algorithm to cluster the input patterns. You may take the value of the vigilance factor to be 0.7. Study what happens to the original clustering if the vigilance factor is changed sequentially to 0.95, 0.9, 0.85, and 0.8.

9.8. In Section 9.3.1, local lateral connections illustrated in Fig. 9.11 were used to select a winning neighborhood. In the example associated with Fig. 9.11, the length of the input array is 50, and the range of lateral interaction is only 16 on each side of a neuron. In other words, each neuron looks only at a maximum of 16 of its neighbors on each side. Is it always true that a unique winning neighborhood containing the unit with the maximum initial value can be found through local interaction in this fashion? Demonstrate your conclusion with computer simulations.

9.9. Formulate and prove the ordering theorem (Theorem 9.1) for $k = 1, 2, \ n - 1$, or n.

9.10. The connection weights from the winner-take-all layer to the second layer are updated using Eq. (9.45) in learning. Show that after a sufficient number of updates the weight vector $\mathbf{u}_i$ approaches the average of all the vectors $\mathbf{y}$ corresponding to the cluster represented by the winning unit i.

9.11. Assume that all the learning exemplars are from a compact set $\mathbf{A} \subset \mathbb{R}^n$ and are sampled from $\mathbf{A}$ by following a uniform probability distribution. In addition, assume that the mapping $\mathbf{y} = \mathbf{f}(\mathbf{x})$ satisfies the condition $\| \mathbf{f}(\mathbf{x} + \Delta\mathbf{x}) - \mathbf{f}(\mathbf{x}) \| \leq c \, \| \Delta\mathbf{x} \|$ in $\mathbf{A}$ for sufficiently small $\| \Delta\mathbf{x} \|$, where c is a positive constant. Show that a counterpropagation network can approximate the function with an arbitrarily small mean-squared error by making N sufficiently large, i.e., by using sufficiently many units in the winner-take-all layer.

9.12. Either prove or disprove the statement that the only product-separable radially symmetric function, based on the L_2-norm, is the multivariate Gaussian function.

9.13. Consider the class of radial basis function networks that is used to compute the function

$$\Psi(\mathbf{x}) = P_B \left[\sum_{i=1}^{M} \alpha_i \phi_i(\mathbf{x}) \right],$$

where α_i's are real-valued weights, $\mathbf{x} \in \mathbb{R}^n$, $\phi_i(\mathbf{x}) = \exp(- \| \mathbf{x} - \mathbf{c}_i \|)$, for $i = 1, 2, \ldots, M$, are fixed basis functions with fixed centers $\mathbf{c}_i$ in the n-dimensional Euclidean space $\mathbb{R}^n$ with the Euclidean norm denoted by $\| \cdot \|$, and

$$P_B[y] = \begin{cases} 1, & \text{if } y \geq 0 \\ 0, & \text{if } y < 0. \end{cases}$$

(a) It is claimed that the VC dimension of the network cannot exceed $M + 1$. Either justify or refute this claim.

(b) If, instead of the set of Gaussian basis functions, another set of functions $(1, \phi_1, \phi_2, \ldots, \phi_M)$ are chosen that are linearly independent, will the VC dimension of the resulting network be the same as in the preceding part? Justify.

9.14. The generic structure of a Voronoi diagram–based neural network, which was studied in Section 5.3, is shown in Fig. P9.14. For the sake of computational simplicity, you may restrict your attention to a real two-dimensional input space, where both the VoD and the DT can be easily and directly visualized. Also, you may focus only on the single-output case. Assume that you have at your disposal a source of fixed external input.

(a) Study the possibility as well as the effect of using the radial basis symmetric Gaussian functions with fixed centers and widths (standard deviations) for the transfer characteristics of the units in the first of the two hidden layers in the generic structure, where the connection weights have already been obtained either from the VoD or the DT over a set of points in the input feature space.

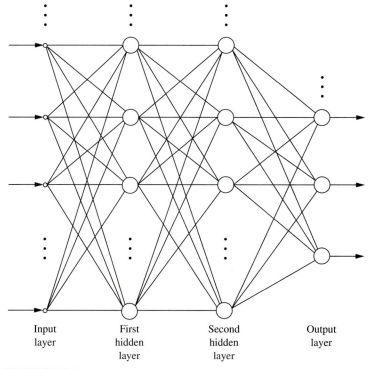

| Input layer | First hidden layer | Second hidden layer | Output layer |

FIGURE P 9.14
The architecture of a VoD (or also DT)-based neural network, showing the direction of variation of the structure. Growth as well as shrinkage is possible, and the dots indicate that possibility. Signal flow is from left to right in the figure.

(*b*) Study the effect of using the VoD in rectilinear metric [218, 290] on the values of the connection weights.

(*c*) Carry out a study of the feasibility of computing suitable bounds for the VC dimension of the generic structure with a specified number of units in each of the hidden layers when hard-limiters are used as nonlinearities in the second hidden layer and either the radial basis functions in the first part or sigmoids are used as nonlinearities in the first hidden layer.

(*d*) It is possible to train for the centers and the widths of the radial basis functions. Discuss what happens to the VC dimension of the original network when the parameters adapt during training.

PART
IV

APPLICATIONS OF NEURAL NETWORKS

N eural networks, inspired by the information-processing strategies of the brain, are proving to be useful in a variety of applications, and their full potential is far from realization. In manufacturing, for example, neural network technology is being increasingly applied or planned for application in complex manufacturing processes that have not been adequately tackled by more conventional technologies. In previous chapters the reader learned how a neural network can be trained to realize complicated nonlinear mappings from the space of inputs to the space of outputs and how it can be designed to serve as an associative memory capable of correct recall when the input is noisy or incomplete. These features equip the neural network very well for modeling, analyzing, forecasting, and optimizing the performance of manufacturing plants. The possibility for exploiting the correlating and generalizing strengths of neural networks in the computer-integrated manufacturing of integrated circuits has been highlighted in a recent survey[1] that underscores the increasing interest being shown by industries and universities to apply neural networks to manufacturing tasks of very great complexities, including process modeling, process optimization, monitoring and control, process diagnosis, and commercial product fabrication. The processes themselves could have diverse origins in civil, chemical, electrical, industrial, materials, mechanical, nuclear, and transportation engineering.

Neural networks have been used extensively in continuous speech recognition and synthesis, image processing and coding, pattern recognition and classification, power load forecasting, interpretation and prediction of financial trends for stock market analysis, manufacturing of composite structures, production of printed circuit boards, process modeling, monitoring and control, reliable and flexible routing of telecommunication networks in the presence of component failure or malfunction, and many other problems occurring in our expanding technological base. The advantages of the neural network in many of these applications are that the network can be updated continuously with new data to optimize its performance at any instant; the network's ability to handle a large number of input variables rapidly; and the network's ability to filter noisy data and interpolate incomplete data.

Though the domain of application of artificial or synthetic neural networks is extensive and expanding, the degree of success has varied with the type of application. This does not close the door to possibilities for improvement but instead challenges us to examine the limitations in our approaches with respect to the choice of structures and learning rules. Therefore, the applications selected for presentation in Chapter 10 are intended for providing the reader with a balanced perspective of the spectacular successes; the diversity of problems in communications, control, and other areas that can be tackled through neurocomputing as opposed to classical computing; and the need for exercising caution when making inferences from performance evaluation over limited data sets. Even though in some cases the original expectations may not have been made with regard to the quality of solutions over unconstrained data sets, one cannot fail to be impressed by the skill with which the principles of neurocomputing in ANNs, studied earlier in the text, were applied. With greater understanding of biological neural networks, it is expected that wider incorporation of their unique features and characteristics in ANNs will extend the capabilities of synthetic neural networks.

---

[1]G.S. May. Manufacturing ICs the neural way. *IEEE Spectrum,* 31 (9): 47–51, September 1994.

CHAPTER 10

NEURAL NETWORK APPROACHES TO SOLVING HARD PROBLEMS

In parallel with the development of theories and architectures for neural networks, the scopes for applications are broadening at a rapid pace. It is impossible for us even to attempt to cover every application. In this chapter several representative applications will be presented where the various types of neural networks discussed in the foregoing chapters have been applied with varying degrees of success. By now, the readers might be in a position to surmise that a neural network is far from being a magic dust that can be sprinkled on every imaginable problem. Not only is there a price to be paid in terms of specialized parallel architecture and learning time; there are types of problems (involving, for example, numerical and symbolic manipulations) for which neural networks are simply not geared, in comparison with digital computers. Neural networks may develop intuitive concepts in such cases [25] but are *inherently ill-suited for implementing rules precisely*, as in the case of rule-based computing. Some of the decision-making tools in the human brain, such as the seats of consciousness, thought, and intuition, do not seem to be within our capability for comprehension in the near future and are dubbed by some to be essentially nonalgorithmic. If the computations required in a task are well understood, and efficient algorithms (such as the discrete Fourier transform computation based on the fast Fourier transform) are known, it is advisable to use those. For such tasks, even setting aside the cost of specialized hardware and learning time, the performance of a neural network could at best be equal, and very likely fall short. On the other hand, if the nature of computations required in a task is not well understood or there are too many exceptions to the rules (as in cognitive and behavioral tasks of perception), or if the known algorithms are too complex and inefficient (as in some constrained optimization problems), neural networks may have a better potential of offering an acceptable solution. Although simulations are important for evaluating and better understanding the scopes as well as limitations of neural networks, the real potential of such networks lies with the specialized, massively parallel hardware designed specifically to implement a given task efficiently.

The application that best demonstrates the simplicity and power of neural networks is probably the ALVINN (Autonomous Land Vehicle in Neural Networks) system, developed by Pomerleau [300, 301]. After training over a two-mile stretch of highway, ALVINN drove the CMU *Navlab* (Carnegie-Mellon University Navigation Laboratory), equipped with video cameras and laser range sensors, for 21.2 miles (34.1 km) at an average speed of 55 mph (88.5 km/h) on a relatively old highway open to normal traffic. ALVINN was not disturbed by passing cars while it was being driven autonomously. What is surprising is the simplicity of the networks and the training techniques used in ALVINN, which will be discussed in detail in Section 10.6. ALVINN nearly doubled the previous world record for autonomous navigation distance held by Dickmanns' group in Germany [93, 94, 95]. This group used a four-dimensional (spatial plus temporal) dynamic prediction-error-feedback approach utilizing high-level spatiotemporal models for autonomous vehicle guidance. In their record run, the test vehicle, *VaMoRs,* was driven autonomously for 12 miles (19.3 km) with speeds up to 65 mph (104.6 km/h) on a newly paved and painted stretch of highway closed to other traffic.

Several other representative applications of neural networks that are either used or close to being used in practice and that yielded better or equal performance over non–neural network approaches are worth mentioning. These include the time series prediction network by Wan [396]; the phonetic typewriter for the Finnish language by Kohonen [199]; the NETtalk neural network, which reads English text, by Sejnowski and Rosenberg [347]; the neural network capable of predicting secondary protein structures by Qian and Sejnowski [305]; the neural networks for recognition of handwritten digits by the AT&T group [215] and by the French ESPCI group [194]; and the silicon retina by Mead's group at Caltech [253].

The examples cited above well illustrate the nature of the neural network approach. The development cost is low, and a working system may be obtained even when the computations required in a task are not well understood (so that explicit programming for every possible situation is not possible). Therefore, when there is not enough understanding of the computation required to solve the problem, a neural network method may be more effective than an explicit programming rule-based approach. As can be expected, when sufficient understanding as well as an efficient algorithm for a task exist, a neural network may not fare as well, in terms of accuracy, time complexity, and space complexity. In some instances claims of the effectiveness of neurocomputing to solve certain problems were overly optimistic. A case in point is the traveling salesperson problem encountered in Chapter 3. The problem of image compression, which is so critical in modern communications, can be tackled with neural networks, but there is scope for very great improvement. Other applications include storage and retrieval of complete patterns from partial or incomplete data and the apparently inexhaustible supply of hard combinatorial problems to which neural network principles can be creatively applied. For instance, the data association problem in multitarget tracking has been the subject of recent investigations by researchers in the neural network area. Though success in all cases cannot be ensured, especially at the outset, the excitement inspired by a new approach, with scope for improvement in many cases, and the existence of a fertile arena for newer applications make the efforts very worthwhile. The following sampling of topics is expected to serve not only as a source of inspiration from successes but also as a prudent reminder of a need for caution. Furthermore, we hope that the reader will become convinced that the materials in the earlier chapters open the door to a panorama of applications.

10.1   THE TRAVELING SALESPERSON PROBLEM

In Chapter 3 the traveling salesperson problem was described. It belongs to the category of problems classified as *NP-complete,* and therefore it is natural to explore techniques that provide good suboptimal solutions in reasonable time. The recurrent neural network structure with a complete-graph topology, presented in Chapter 8, provides one such technique.

Given n vertices, representing n cities, the traveling salesperson problem requires finding a Hamiltonian loop (a closed edge train that is also a circuit or loop, as defined in Chapter 2) of shortest length that has a specified vertex as both the initial vertex and the terminal vertex. It is straightforward to see that there are $n!$ such loops. In an n-city problem there are $2n$ loops of equal length, because each loop has an n-fold degeneracy of the initial city on the tour and a two-fold degeneracy of the city sequence order. Therefore, the number of distinct loops from which the shortest one has to be identified is $n!/2n = (n-1)!/2$.

In the neural network approach to the solution of the problem based on the use of the Hopfield network, it is necessary to determine an energy function that incorporates the constraints. We use a representation scheme that allows the sequence of cities in a Hamiltonian loop to be inferred from the output states and locations of the n activated (ON) neurons in the network. This can be achieved by using an $n \times n$ array of neurons for n cities. The rows of the array correspond to the n cities, and the columns of the array are associated with the positions of the cities in the Hamiltonian loop. This is illustrated in Fig.10.1. A feasible solution, then, is characterized by a *permutation matrix*, which has exactly one nonzero element, namely 1, in each row and each column. Each of the $n!$ permutation matrices may be uniquely associated with a loop from the set of $n!$ loops over the n vertices. The output from a neuron in the kth row and jth column will be denoted by v_{kj}, where the first subscript k denotes the kth city and the second subscript j denotes that this kth city is in the jth position in the tour. The energy function E originally used contained four terms, each multiplied by a constant. Let the distance between the kth and rth cities be d_{kr}. E was chosen

$$E = \frac{A}{2}\sum_k\sum_i\sum_{j \neq i} v_{ki}v_{kj} + \frac{B}{2}\sum_j\sum_k\sum_{r \neq k} v_{kj}v_{rj} + \frac{C}{2}\left(n - \sum_k\sum_i v_{ki}\right)^2$$

$$+ \frac{D}{2}\sum_k\sum_{r \neq k}\sum_j d_{kr}v_{kj}(v_{r(j+1)} + v_{r(j-1)}), \tag{10.1}$$

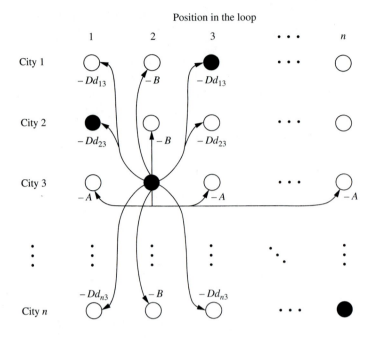

FIGURE 10.1
A neural network for solving the traveling salesperson problem. Connections for only one neuron are shown. Fixed biases are not indicated. The filled circles represent neurons in the ON state, and the blank circles represent neurons in the OFF state. The connection weights are explicitly shown, and the minus sign indicates that these weights are inhibitory. The distance between the ith and jth cities is d_{ij}, and the upper-case letters are selected constants.

where A, B, C, and D are the constants assigned according to the emphasis given on the individual constraints. The first term of E will be zero if and only if each row in the $(n \times n)$ array of neurons (each output belongs to the interval $[0, 1]$) contains no more than one activated neuron, the remaining entries in the row being zero. The second term is zero if and only if each position-in-tour column contains no more than one activated neuron, the remaining entries in the column being zero. The third term is zero if and only if there are n entries, each of value 1, in the entire output matrix. Finally, the fourth term incorporates the requirement of shortest loop. If A, B, and C are sufficiently large, then all the low-energy states of a network described by the energy function E will be associated with a Hamiltonian loop. The total energy of the state will be the length of the Hamiltonian loop, and the states with the shortest paths will be the lowest energy states. The motivation behind the above choice is the analog Hopfield network introduced in Section 8.2.1. In the form of the energy function, shown in Eq. (8.45), for such a network, the last term is omitted in the high-gain limit. The output v_{ki} from a neuron at location (k, i) is related to the net input u_{ki} to this neuron by the scaled tansigmoid function.

$$v_{ki} = \frac{1}{2}\left(1 + \tanh\left(\frac{u_{ki}}{u_0}\right)\right) \triangleq g(u_{ki}). \qquad (10.2)$$

In this equation the parameter u_0 determines the steepness of gain.

Ignoring the constant term, Eq. (10.1) may be expressed in the form

$$E = -\frac{1}{2}\sum_{ki}\sum_{rj} w_{(ki)(rj)}v_{ki}v_{rj} - \sum_{ki} v_{ki}I_{ki}, \qquad (10.3)$$

where I_{ki} is the bias current to the neuron at coordinate location (k, i). On comparing Eqs. (10.1) and (10.3), it is clear that the weight $w_{(ki)(rj)}$ from the output of the neuron at location (r, j) on the plane of the array to the input of the neuron at location (k, i) is given by

$$w_{(ki)(rj)} = -A\delta_{kr}(1 - \delta_{ij}) - B\delta_{ij}(1 - \delta_{kr}) - C - Dd_{kr}(\delta_{j(i+1)} + \delta_{j(i-1)}), \qquad (10.4)$$

where δ_{kr} denotes the *Kronecker delta*, which is 1 when $k = r$ and 0 when $k \neq r$. Also, the input current provides a fixed bias

$$I_{ki} = Cn. \qquad (10.5)$$

As seen from Eq. (10.4), all the connections are inhibitory. These connections are illustrated in Fig. 10.1 (the fixed bias is not shown in the figure).

The choices for the constants A, B, C, D in Eq. (10.1) that provide good solutions are the consequences of compromise between always obtaining legitimate Hamiltonian loops (D small relative to $A, B,$ and C) and weighting the distances heavily (D large relative to $A, B,$ and C). Better results often emerge after replacing the third term in Eq. (10.1) with a sum of two terms as follows:

$$\frac{C}{2}\left(\sum_i\sum_j v_{ij} - n\right)^2 = \frac{H}{2}\sum_i\left(\sum_j v_{ij} - 1\right)^2 + \frac{F}{2}\sum_j\left(\sum_i v_{ij} - 1\right)^2, \qquad (10.6)$$

where H and F are two constants that permit separate weightings of the connection weights for the rows and columns, respectively.

The energy function E that generates the connection weight matrix from the elements defined in Eq. (10.4) and the bias current in Eq. (10.5) may be implemented via the analog Hopfield network. The equations of motion described in Eq. (8.38), for each of the n^2 neurons, may be directly written down from the connection weights and bias currents. For $k = 1, 2, \ldots, n$ and $i = 1, 2, \ldots, n$, these equations of motion are obtained from

$$\tau_{ki}\frac{du_{ki}}{dt} = -\frac{\partial E}{\partial v_{ki}},$$

where τ_{ki} is the time constant; see Eq. (8.40). If a term similar to the third term in Eq. (8.45) were allowed in the energy function, the foregoing equation becomes

$$\tau_{ki}\frac{du_{ki}}{dt} = -u_{ki} - A\sum_{\substack{j \\ j \neq i}} v_{kj} - B\sum_{\substack{r \\ r \neq k}} v_{ri} - C\left(\sum_k\sum_i v_{ki} - n\right)$$

$$- D\sum_r d_{kr}(v_{r(i+1)} + v_{r(i-1)}), \qquad (10.7)$$

where the input u_{ki} to a neuron is defined by the inverse of the *map g*, i.e., the transfer characteristic in Eq. (10.2), which relates the output v_{ki} to that input u_{ki} by

$$v_{ki} = g(u_{ki}),$$

so that

$$u_{ki} = g^{-1}(v_{ki}) = g^{-1}(g(u_{ki})).$$

The existence of the inverse $g^{-1}(\cdot)$ is guaranteed from the monotonic nature of $g(\cdot)$. A good suboptimal solution to the problem often requires several trials with the choices of initial conditions as well as the values of the constants in the energy function.

The equation of motion provides a complete description of the temporal evolution of the state of the circuit, starting from an initial state. The space is the interior of an n^2-dimensional "unipolar" hypercube, $[0, 1]^{n^2}$. In the high-gain limit, the minima occur only at the vertices of this cube. Clearly, the number, $|V|$, of vertices of this cube is

$$|V| = 2^{n^2}.$$

For the n-city traveling salesperson problem the ratio $r(n)$ of the number of valid solutions (from which the minimum value is to be determined) to the number of possible states that are candidates for the minimum is

$$r(n) = \frac{(n-1)!}{2(2^{n^2})}.$$

The ratio $r(n)$ asymptotically approaches zero. This implies that for large n the probability of finding a valid solution among the large number of possible states is low. In fact, it was determined later [181, 419] that the original optimism [164] of applying this method for solving the traveling salesperson problem has to be tempered. Especially, in the formulation of Eq. (10.7), it was shown that as the network size is scaled up, the method does not even produce valid solutions. For further development of the Hopfield-Tank approach see [383]. Another neural network–based approach to the traveling salesperson problem is the elastic net method [102] using the self-organizing networks encountered in Chapter 9.

10.2   MULTITARGET TRACKING

When multiple targets are tracked simultaneously, the major problem is caused by the uncertainty regarding the origin of measurements. A particular measurement could come from any one of a cluster of targets being tracked, from a new target whose existence was unknown previously, or from a false alarm. In any scan the track updating is done for each target by using the measurement indicated by a hypothesis that is considered to be the combination of an *a priori* hypothesis from the previous scan and a hypothesis for data received in the current scan. The number of hypotheses required in data association leads to a very large combinatorial problem. For example, suppose that there are 10 measurements in a cluster of five targets. Each measurement could have come from a new target besides the five targets being tracked, or it could originate from any one of a variety of clutters, therefore causing false alarm. Thus, there are 7 possibilities for one measurement, and the number of hypotheses for all the 10 measurements is 7^{10}. In spite of the fact that all the 7^{10} hypotheses would not be feasible, the cardinality of the set of feasible data association hypotheses could still be very large. Tracking many moving targets simultaneously is a task whose complexity grows out of all proportions to the number of targets [381].

The algorithms devised for multiple-target tracking require the comparison of every incoming measurement or target state report with every candidate track to determine whether or not they might be associated. The effort that must be assigned in these algorithms to solve the correlation problem for n tracks and n reports is proportional to n^2. For large values of n, a combinatorial bottleneck in data association often takes place. Approaches for the tackling of this combinatorial problem range from enumerative techniques using integer programming, cluster analysis, evidential analysis based on the Dempster-Schafer theory, fuzzy logic, and statistical inference to various search procedures in optimization theory. The use of neural networks for the purpose has been proposed [348]. There are pros as well as cons to this approach, which uses the analog Hopfield structure described in Section 8.2.1. Implementation in analog circuitry is a desirable feature, although the choice of energy function was made in an *ad hoc* manner. As in the traveling salesperson problem, suboptimal solutions were generated. However, scope exists for improving on these suboptimal solutions by proper selection of the energy functions. For stimulating such research and to provide the reader with another application of neural networks in attacking a combinatorially hard problem of importance, the results in this area of application are briefly documented as follows [427].

The main task in the tracking of multiple targets in clutter is the computation of the *a posteriori* probabilities, denoted by β_j^t, where β_j^t for $j \neq 0$ is the probability that measurement j originated from target t, and β_0^t is the probability that none of the received measurements were from target t. The neural network–based procedure for computing the *a posteriori* probabilities is similar in many ways to the solution of the traveling salesperson problem described in the preceding section. In the approach proposed, β_j^t is approximated by the output voltage V_j^t of a neuron in an $(m + 1) \times n$ array of neurons, where m is the number of measurements and n is the number of targets. Thus the columns of the array are associated with targets, and the rows correspond to measurements or reports. Two assumptions are made, namely that no two returns can come from the same target and no two targets send the same return. The sum of the elements in each row and column of the array is 1. The *Probabilistic Data Association Filter* (PDAF)[2] used for tracking a single target in clutter performs poorly in the multiple-target scenario, when intersecting trajectories or closely moving targets are present. In such situations the *Joint Probabilistic Data Association Filter* (JPDAF)[2] has been used with some success, especially when the targets are of the nonmaneuvering type. Probabilistic data association is needed because of the uncertainty present in associating targets and clutter with measurements.

---

[2] Y. Bar-Shalom and T.E. Fortmann. *Tracking and Data Association*, Academic Press, Inc., Orlando, FL, 1988.

Let ρ_j^t denote the PDAF counterpart of β_j^t for a JPDAF. The energy function E_{DAP}, proposed in ref. [348] in the data association problem (DAP) for computing the β_j^t's approximately, is as follows. Its form is similar to the energy function in the traveling salesperson problem.

$$E_{DAP} = \frac{A}{2}\sum_{r=0}^{m}\sum_{t=1}^{n}\sum_{\substack{\tau=1\\ \tau\neq t}}^{n} v_r^t v_r^\tau + \frac{B}{2}\sum_{t=1}^{n}\sum_{r=0}^{m}\sum_{\substack{j=0\\ j\neq r}}^{m} v_r^t v_j^t + \frac{C}{2}\sum_{t=1}^{n}\left(\sum_{r=0}^{m} v_r^t - 1\right)^2$$

$$+ \frac{D}{2}\sum_{r=0}^{m}\sum_{t=1}^{n}\left(v_r^t - \rho_r^t\right)^2 + \frac{E}{2}\sum_{r=0}^{m}\sum_{t=1}^{n}\sum_{\substack{\tau=1\\ \tau\neq t}}^{n}\left(v_r^t - \sum_{\substack{j=0\\ j\neq r}}^{m}\rho_j^\tau\right)^2, \tag{10.8}$$

where $A, B, C, D,$ and E are suitable constants. In Eq. (10.8) v_j^t is the output voltage of a neuron in a $(m+1)\times n$ array of neurons and is intended to be an approximation to the *a posteriori* probability β_j^t in the JPDAF. By taking the derivative of E_{DAP} with respect to v_j^t, the dynamic equation describing the state of the jth neuron is obtained in a straightforward fashion. If u_j^t denotes the input to the neuron at location (j, t), its dynamics is described by (denoting the time constant by τ_j^t)

$$\tau_j^t \frac{du_j^t}{dt} = -\frac{\partial E_{DAP}}{\partial v_j^t}.$$

Let $T_{jr}^{t\tau}$ denote the connection strength (weight) between the neurons at locations (r, τ) and (j, t) in the planar array of neurons for $t, \tau = 1, 2, \ldots, n$ and $j, r = 0, 1, \ldots, m$. For the energy function chosen in Eq. (10.8), these connection strengths and the input currents I_j^t, for $t = 1, 2, \ldots, n$ and $j = 0, 1, \ldots, m$, are

$$T_{rj}^{t\tau} = \begin{cases} -(C + D + E(n-1)), & \text{if } t = \tau \text{ and } r = j \text{ (self-feedback)} \\ -A, & \text{if } t \neq \tau \text{ and } r = j \text{ (row connection)} \\ -(B + C), & \text{if } t = \tau \text{ and } r \neq j \text{ (column connection)} \\ 0, & \text{if } t \neq \tau \text{ and } r \neq j \text{ (global connection)}. \end{cases} \tag{10.9}$$

$$I_r^t = C + (D + E)\rho_r^t + E\left(n - 1 - \sum_{\tau=1}^{n}\rho_r^\tau\right). \tag{10.10}$$

Note that only the currents depend on ρ_j^t, which are computed from the measurements that constitute the input data. This is contrary to the traveling salesperson problem, where the connection strengths depend on the input data, which in that case are the intercity distances.

The first two terms of E_{DAP} in Eq. (10.8) are identical to the corresponding terms of the energy function in the traveling salesperson problem. However, these two terms in Eq. (10.8) are based on different assumptions. A dominating v_r^t is assumed to be present in each row and each column. The third term of E_{DAP} is used to constrain the sum of the v_r^t's in each column to unity. The fourth term is small only if v_r^t is close to ρ_j^t. Finally, the fifth term is minimized if v_r^t is not large, unless for each $\tau \neq t$ there is a unique $j \neq r$ such that ρ_j^τ is large. A comprehensive analysis of the effects of the choices of the various components in E_{DAP} is available [427]. In summary, convergence of the neuron outputs to the true data association probabilities cannot be guaranteed.

The attractiveness of analog circuit implementation and the lure of parallel as opposed to sequential computational strategies for calculating the *a posteriori* probabilities suggest investigation into better ways for selecting energy functions and use of other structures and learning rules [173].

10.3 TIME SERIES PREDICTION

Predicting the future has always been one of humanity's desires. Time series measurements are the means for us to characterize and understand a system and to predict its future behavior. If there are underlying deterministic equations, the system's behavior can be determined by solving the equations with the given initial condition. In *time series prediction* these equations and the initial conditions are either unknown or only partially known, so one needs to find out the rules that govern the system evolution and the actual current state of the system. The governing rules may be inferred from the regularities in past time series measurements.

Gershenfeld and Weigend [397] defined three goals for time series analysis: forecasting, modeling, and characterization. *Forecasting* is predicting the short-term evolution of the system. *Modeling* involves finding a description that accurately captures the features of the long-term behavior. The goal of *characterization* is to determine the fundamental properties of the system, such as the degrees of freedom or the amount of randomness. The three goals are related but may not be identical. Models that produce good short-term forecasts may perform poorly on long-term behavior and vice versa. The complexity of model useful for short-term prediction may not be related to the actual complexity of the system, because it may contain the model of short-term noise. Modeling and characterization are the goals of system identification in control and signal processing.

The traditional methods for time series prediction use the moving average (MA), autoregressive (AR), or the combination of the two, the ARMA model, as described below. Let the input time series be $\{x_i\}$ and the time series to be predicted be $\{y_i\}$.

Moving average (MA) model: An mth-order MA model is a finite impulse response (FIR) filter that sums the current and m immediate past values of x_i (after appropriate weighting with constant multipliers, b_j's) to predict y_i.

$$y_i = \sum_{j=0}^{m} b_j x_{i-j}. \tag{10.11}$$

Autoregressive (AR) model: An nth order AR model is an infinite impulse response (IIR) filter that sums the weighted n immediate past values of y_i and the weighted value of the present input to predict the current value of the time series. Thus,

$$y_i = \sum_{j=1}^{n} a_j y_{i-j} + b_0 x_i, \tag{10.12}$$

where x_i is either an input control signal or a driving noise.

Autoregressive and moving average (ARMA) model: An ARMA model is a combination of MA and AR and is given as

$$y_i = \sum_{j=1}^{n} a_j y_{i-j} + \sum_{j=0}^{m} b_j x_{i-j}. \tag{10.13}$$

For detailed analyses of these models, see any text on time series or stochastic process, e.g., [54, 285]. These models are linear and are inadequate for even very simple nonlinear systems.

The fundamental principle in chaotic time series prediction is that such series may be described by a deterministic equation with a small number of parameters. For the predictor, these effective variables, constituting the *attractors* of motion of the system in state space, are combinations of the original variables in the high-dimensional space and may not number to be an integer. The question is how to find out these new variables. Packard et al. [280] showed that it is not necessary to find what combinations produced these variables as long as there are enough past measurements of the time series. Takens [373] proved that there exists a smooth function that will correctly predict the future value of a time series using at most $2n + 1$ past measurements of the same time series, where n is the number of effective variables. However, the form of the smooth prediction function in Takens' theorem is not known. A feedforward neural network that uses tapped delay, as described in Section 5.2.3, is a natural fit for learning this function from time-delayed data. The hope is that a neural network could not only learn the smooth prediction function but also be trained to emulate unexpected short-term regularities in a time series. For more details, see refs. [72, 280].

The Santa Fe Institute organized a competition on time series prediction in 1991 [397]. Six sets of time series were made available to the public through ftp (Internet file transfer protocol) on August 1, 1991, and competition entries were accepted until January 15, 1992. The entries were tested on the last part of the six sets of time series, to which the participants had no access. The time series used in the competition, the programs, the results of analysis, and visualization are available by anonymous ftp at ftp.santafe.edu (for help with ftp, send email to ftp@santafe.edu).

The six sets of time series used are [397]:

1. A clean physical laboratory experiment, consisting of 1,000 points of the fluctuations in a far-infrared laser. This time series is approximately described by three coupled ordinary differential equations.

2. Physiological data from a patient with sleep apnea, consisting of 34,000 points of the heart rate, chest volume, blood oxygen concentration, and EEG. These time series are related, but the underlying relations are not well understood.

3. High-frequency currency exchange rate data, consisting of 10 segments of 3,000 points each of the exchange rate between the Swiss franc and the U.S. dollar. The average time between two quotes is between one and two minutes. If the market is sufficient, this should be a random walk, which is an example of a Markov process.

4. A numerically generated series designed for the competition, consisting of the positions of a driven particle in a four-dimensional nonlinear multiple-well potential (nine degrees of freedom) with a small nonstationary drift in the well depths.

5. Astrophysical data, consisting of 27,704 points in 17 segments of the time variation of the intensity of a variable white dwarf star. The intensity variation arises from a superposition of relatively independent spherical harmonic multiplets. There is significant noise in the observations.

6. J.S. Bach's final (unfinished) fugue from the *The Art of the Fugue*. This series is added after the close of the formal competition.

Neural network approaches produced some of the best short-term predictions. However, methods that reconstruct the state space by time-delay embedding and develop a representation for the geometry in the system's state space yielded better longer-term predictions than neural networks in some cases [339, 397].

Wan [396] provided winning entries for some of the prediction tasks. He used a network whose input and internal connections are all tapped delay lines, as discussed in Section 5.2.3. The same network architecture, called a *spatiotemporal network,* has also been used for nonlinear system identification [29]. Conventional methods for nonlinear system identification have limited success. Neural network approaches are still too preliminary to judge.

10.4 TALKING NETWORK AND PHONETIC TYPEWRITER

The problems of performing text-to-speech and speech-to-text conversions with the help of neural networks are briefly considered below. Additional details with emphasis on speech recognition (speech-to-text conversion) may be found in the monograph by Morgan and Scofield.[3]

10.4.1 Speech Generation

One of the earliest successful applications of the backpropagation algorithm for training multilayer feedforward networks was in a speech generation system called NETtalk, developed by Sejnowski and Rosenberg [347]. NETtalk is a fully connected layered feedforward network with only one hidden layer. It was trained to pronounce written English text. Turning a written English text into speech is a difficult task, because most phonological rules have exceptions that are context-sensitive.

---

[3]D.P. Morgan and C.L. Scofield, *Neural Networks and Speech Processing,* Kluwer Academic Publishers, Boston, MA, 1991.

A commercial product, DECtalk by the Digital Equipment Corporation, produces intelligible speech from a written text. It is a complicated rule-based system with lookup tables and rules to handle exceptions and irregularities. That system was developed over a number of years.

In contrast, NETtalk requires no knowledge of the phonological rules and enumeration of the exceptions. It is a simple network that learns the same function in several hours using exemplars. The input to NETtalk consists of seven consecutive characters from a written text. A line of text is continuously presented at one end of the one-dimensional array of input units. The effect is that of a text line being scanned by a moving window. The desired output is a phoneme code, which is sent to a speech synthesizer that pronounces the letter at the center of the input window. Each of the 26 letters, a space, and two punctuation marks is represented by a unit at the input layer, for a total of 29 units. This is multiplied by 7 to encode 7 character positions in a text. Therefore, a total of 203 input units are used. Only one hidden layer is present. For continuous speech, 80 hidden units are used. 26 output units are needed to represent 23 articulatory features and 3 stress features. Therefore, for continuous speech the network consists of 309 units (including input units) and 18,629 connection weights (including one weight to represent the threshold for each unit).

After roughly 12 hours of CPU time on a DEC VAX, NETtalk reproduced phonemes from the training set with 95% accuracy, and with approximately 80% accuracy on the test set. The network was trained using both the backpropagation algorithm (Section 5.2) and the Boltzmann machine learning algorithm (Section 8.4). Both algorithms produced comparable results; however, the backpropagation algorithm learned faster.

The performance of DECtalk is better than that of NETtalk. DECtalk required many years of research by linguists, whereas NETtalk was simply trained using exemplars. Much improvement of NETtalk's performance may be expected by increasing the window size from 7 characters to provide it with more context information.

10.4.2 Speech Recognition

Kohonen used his self-organizing map, discussed in Section 9.3, for the inverse problem to that addressed by NETtalk: speech recognition. He developed a phonetic typewriter for the Finnish language [199]. The phonetic typewriter takes as input a speech and converts it into written text. Speech recognition in general is a much harder problem than turning text into speech. The spectra of the same phoneme spoken by different speakers may have a lot of variation. Besides, some phonemes, such as vowels, have stationary spectra, whereas plosive phonemes, such as /b/, /d/, and /g/, are recognizable only from the analysis of their transient behavior. There are three dimensions for measuring the difficulty of a speech recognition system: continuous speech vs. discrete words; general purpose vocabulary vs. limited vocabulary; and speaker-independent vs. speaker-specific. Currently, there is no successful speaker-independent, general-purpose continuous speech recognition system in existence. All commercial systems, regardless of the techniques used, make some compromises on at least one of these three dimensions. Kohonen's phonetic typewriter is a speaker-dependent speech recognition system for continuous speech with unlimited vocabulary. It can also be applied for isolated word recognition.

Current state-of-the-art English speech recognition systems are based on the *hidden Markov model* (HMM). The HMM, which is a Markov process, consists of a number of states, the transitions between which depend on the occurrence of some symbol. An output probability distribution characterizes the probability of occurrence of this symbol, and a transition probability describes the likelihood of a transition. The stochastic process that produces the sequence of symbols belonging to a word in the vocabulary is not observable but hidden and is responsible for the modeling of the variations between observed sequences of the same class. Because of the high level of irregularities between phonemes and spelling, speech recognition systems for English consider individual words as the unit for recognition. By contrast, the Finnish language is highly phonetic; i.e., the correspondence between phonemes and spellings is very regular. Therefore, it is possible to decompose the speech recognition problem into two steps: recognition of individual phonemes and translation of phonemes to letters.

Many different approaches to tackling the speech recognition problem using neural networks have been reported, e.g., see refs. [231, 421]. Kohonen's approach is unique in that it is based on the unsupervised topographic mapping network discussed in Section 9.3, and it has been brought to a commercial stage, after verification by extensive tests. Phonemes form a topographic map of the network weights by self-organization. Detection of a phoneme requires the finding of the closest prototype vector. First, a speech signal is sampled every 9.83 ms at 256 evenly distributed points; note that the duration of a complete phoneme is from 40 to 400 ms. A fast Fourier transform (FFT) is performed on the sampled and quantized digital signal. The spectral power values are grouped into 15 spectral channels from 200 Hz to 5 kHz. The outputs from the 15 channels form a 15-dimensional pattern vector. The root-mean-square value of the spectral power of the speech signal represents the signal magnitude, which may be used as an optional component for improvement of the accuracy. Another technique for improving the accuracy is by producing a pattern vector out of two spectra 30 ms apart. Kohonen found that both cases improved the accuracy only slightly, by about 1% to 2%.

Kohonen used a two-dimensional array of 96 units with center-on surround-off lateral connections as in the Kohonen map, discussed in Section 9.3. Each unit receives 15 connections from the 15 spectral channels. The map then self-organizes by following the process described in Section 9.3. After this self-organizing process stabilizes ($\alpha(k) = 0$), it is found that different examples of the same phoneme tend to cluster together on the map. In other words, units close together correspond to the same phoneme. This is shown in Fig. 10.2, where the units, shown as circles, are labeled with the symbols of the Finnish phonemes to which they learned to give best response. Most units give a unique response. Some units respond to two phonemes as labeled in the figure. Recognition of some plosive phonemes, such as /k/, /p/, /t/, from this map is not reliable, and an auxiliary map is used.

Because each pattern vector represents only a segment of signal shorter than a true phoneme, evolution to a stationary phoneme can be observed when pattern vectors are continuously presented to the network. The speech signal of a word gives a trajectory in this map, as shown in Fig. 10.3. Due to speaker and context variations, there are overlapping regions among the different phonemes in the 15-dimensional

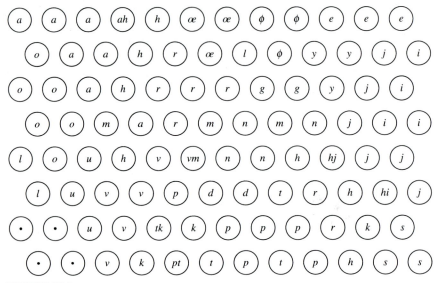

FIGURE 10.2
The phonetic map for the Finnish language formed by self-organization. (*Source:* Reprinted with permission from T. Kohonen, "The Neural Phonetic Typewriter," *IEEE Computer,* 21(3):11–22, 1988. ©1988 IEEE.)

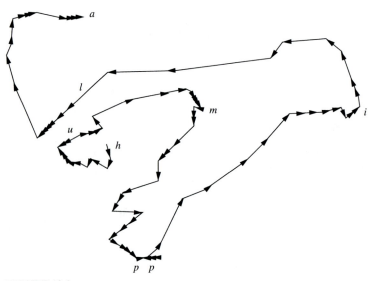

FIGURE 10.3
The trajectory in the phonetic map when the Finnish word *humppila* is uttered. Each arrow represents the movement caused by one pattern vector, corresponding to the spectrum of 9.83 ms of speech signal. (*Source:* Reprinted with permission from T. Kohonen, "The Neural Phonetic Typewriter," *IEEE Computer,* 21(3): 11–22, 1988. ©1988 IEEE.)

pattern space. Therefore, 100% accuracy in phoneme classification cannot be achieved. The Kohonen map is optimal in the sense that a pattern vector is classified to a phoneme from which it has the minimum distance. This is because after learning, the classification of the pattern space realized by a Kohonen map is a Voronoi tessellation.

Even if spectrum classification were error-free, we still cannot have 100% reliability in identifying phonemes, because of their context sensitivity; i.e., phonemes are affected by their neighbors. To capture the context sensitivity of the phonemes requires a much longer segment of speech, and hence, a much larger network. Instead, a rule-based symbolic postprocessing step was applied. Hybrid integration of symbolic processing and neural networks combines the strength of both worlds, and has been shown to be a good strategy in dealing with hard problems. This will be illustrated again in Section 10.5, which covers the use of neural networks for autonomous land vehicle navigation.

Kohonen developed a program that automatically constructed the grammatical transformation rules for determining the context-sensitive phonemes using speech samples and their correct reference transcriptions. A typical number for the rules is anywhere between 15,000 to 20,000. A hash-coding (hashing) technique was used to search for matching rules in real time. The performance of the phonetic typewriter was extensively tested. With symbolic postprocessing, 92% to 97% accuracy was achieved for continuous speech with unlimited vocabulary, depending on the speaker and the difficulty of the text. Enrollment of a new speaker requires a dictation of 100 words and less than 10 minutes of unsupervised learning time. Accuracy for isolated word recognition with a 1000-word vocabulary reached 96% to 98%. The complete system was implemented on a PC using a coprocessor board with digital signal processing (DSP) chips, which simulate the neural network computations. The architecture of the coprocessor board is shown in Fig. 10.4. Self-organization took

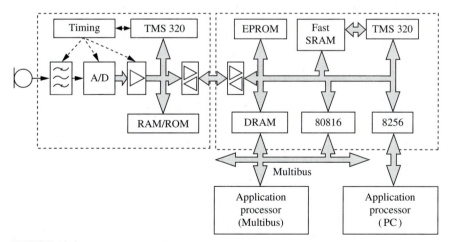

FIGURE 10.4
The architecture of the coprocessor board for the phonetic typewriter. (*Source:* Reprinted with permission from T. Kohonen, "The Neural Phonetic Typewriter," *IEEE Computer,* 21(3):11–22, 1988. ©1988 IEEE.)

less than 10 minutes on this system, and recognition was in real time. Note that the technology used in this system is close to 10 years old now. Special neural network hardware may be used for even faster speed.

10.5 AUTONOMOUS VEHICLE NAVIGATION

Vision-based autonomous vehicle and robot guidance have proven difficult for algorithm-based computer vision methods, mainly because of the diversity of unexpected cases that must be explicitly dealt with in the algorithms and the real-time constraint.

Pomerleau [300, 301] successfully demonstrated the potential of neural networks for overcoming these difficulties. His ALVINN (Autonomous Land Vehicle in Neural Networks) set a world record for autonomous navigation distance. After training on a two-mile stretch of highway, it drove the CMU *Navlab,* equipped with video cameras and laser range sensors, for 21.2 miles with an average speed of 55 mph on a relatively old highway open to normal traffic. ALVINN was not disturbed by passing cars while it was being driven autonomously. *ALVINN nearly doubled the previous distance world record for autonomous navigation.* What is surprising is the simplicity of the networks and the training techniques used in ALVINN, which consists of several networks, each trained for a specific road situation:

Single-lane paved road
Single-lane dirt road
Two-lane neighborhood street
Multilane highway

A monocular color video input is sufficient for all of these situations; therefore, no depth perception is used in guiding the vehicle. Not using stereo vision saves a significant amount of time, because matching of correspondence points in a stereo pair of images is computationally expensive. Laser rangefinder and laser reflectance inputs are also tested. The laser reflectance input resembles a black-and-white video image and can be handled in the same way as a video image. Reflectance input is advantageous over video input, because it appears the same regardless of the lighting conditions. This allows ALVINN to be trained in daylight and tested in darkness. Laser rangefinder input is useful for obstacle avoidance. However, a laser range image needs to be processed differently, because its image pixel values represent distance instead of lightness. We will focus the discussion on video image input.

A network in ALVINN for each situation consists of *a single hidden layer of only four units,* an output layer of 30 units and a 30 × 32 retina for the 960 possible input variables. The retina is fully connected to the hidden layer, and the hidden layer is fully connected to the output layer, as shown in Fig. 10.5 for two representative nodes (out of a total of 960). The graph of the feedforward network is a node-coalesced cascade of directed versions of bipartite graphs $K_{960,4}$ and $K_{4,30}$. Pomerleau tried networks with more layers and more hidden units but did not observe significant performance improvement over this simple network [301]. Because of the real-time constraint of the task, a simple network is definitely preferred. The

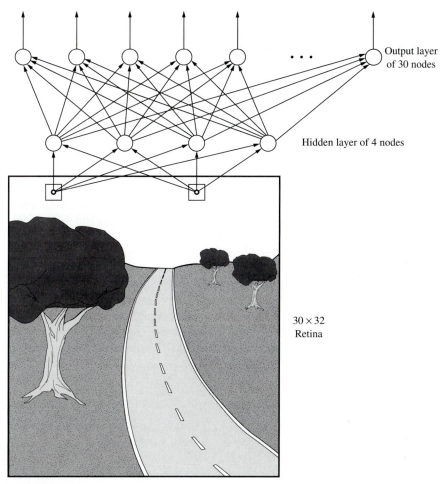

FIGURE 10.5
The graph of a network in ALVINN. It is a node-coalesced cascade of two directed bipartite graphs. (*Source:* After D. A. Pomerleau, "Neural Network Perception for Mobile Robot Guidance," Ph. D. thesis, School of Computer Science, Carnegie-Mellon University, 1992.)

image on the retina is a low-resolution version of a color video image with 480×512 pixels. A 16×16 neighborhood in the video image is randomly sampled and averaged to produce a single pixel on the retina. The outputs from the three channels of a color video image—namely, red (R), green (G), and blue (B)—are combined to produce a single image on the retina according to the equation

$$p = \frac{B}{255} + \frac{B}{R + G + B} \qquad (10.14)$$

where p is the brightness of the combined image. This combination is based on empirical observation. What is interesting is that it approximates the learning result if one chooses to add another layer to learn the preprocessing from video image to the retina [301]. The darkest 5% of the pixels on the retina are assigned the minimum activation level of -1, and the brightest 5% are assigned the maximum activation level of 1. The remaining 90% of the pixels are assigned activation values proportional to their brightness relative to the two extremes.

The 30 output units are arranged in a one-dimensional array for controlling the steering wheel. The steering direction is represented by a Gaussian activation pattern in the output layer, as illustrated in Fig. 10.6. The distributed pattern representation of the output proves to be useful in evaluating the reliability of the network output. If the vehicle under the guidance of one network (e.g., for single-lane paved road) transits into a new situation (e.g., multilane highway) the network will be confused. There is a high likelihood that the output pattern will significantly deviate from a Gaussian pattern. This signals the ALVINN to pick another network to guide the vehicle.

Each network is trained using the backpropagation algorithm with a technique Pomerleau called *training-on-the-fly;* i.e., the network is trained by observing a person driving. A sequence of training pairs, consisting of input images and the person's response, is obtained during a drive. Training can be performed at the same time. There are several potential problems with the training-on-the-fly approach. They are all due to the low level of diversity or, in other words, the high level of similarity, in the training data. For example, the network needs to learn how to recover from

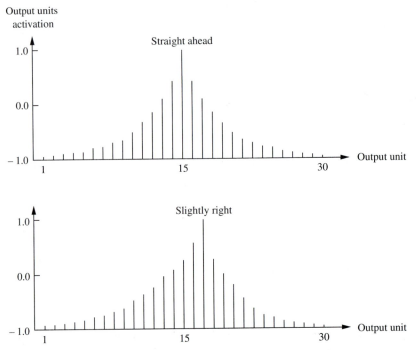

FIGURE 10.6
The representation of two steering directions in the output layer from the plot of output unit activation value versus the output unit. (*Source:* After D. A. Pomerleau, "Neural Network Perception for Mobile Robot Guidance," Ph. D. thesis, School of Computer Science, Carnegie-Mellon University, 1992.)

various mistakes. A sequence of consistently similar training data will also cause the network to overlearn the current situation and forget about what it might have learned about other situations. Diversity in the training data is necessary for valid generalization. Pomerleau used several techniques to solve these problems. First, the input images and the steering directions are geometrically transformed as if the vehicle had been in different positions relative to the road. Second, structured noise is added to the input images to simulate different situations on the road, such as passing cars, guardrails, and trees. New training pairs are formed using a new image with added structure noise and the same steering direction as the noise-free image. These techniques greatly increase the diversity of the training data, thus leading to good generalization of learning.

After each network is trained for a specific situation, how is the system going to decide when to use which network? Pomerleau proposed two techniques for selecting a network: output appearance and input reconstruction. Output appearance measures the deviation of the shape of the output response from the Gaussian shape. Although not always true, there is a high level of correlation between the Gaussian shape of the output response and the applicability of the network to the current situation. Input reconstruction feeds the output response back through the connections and the hidden layer to reconstruct an input image. The difference between the real input image and the reconstructed image provides another indication of the applicability of the network to the current situation. These two techniques can then be used to guide the choice of the right network for the current situation.

Due to the fact that neural networks are not good at remembering maps and planning the route, a symbolic component is added to the system for these functions. The symbolic component is also responsible for generating structured noises and transformations to increase the diversity of the training data and for coordinating all the components in the system.

10.6 HANDWRITTEN DIGIT RECOGNITION

Automatic recognition of handwritten characters is one of the benchmark problems in pattern recognition research. Two efforts are discussed in this section. One is based on the backpropagation algorithm of Section 5.2; the other is based on the idea of growth algorithms in Section 7.1.

Members of a group at AT&T Bell Laboratories have been working in the area of neural networks for many years. One of their projects involves the development of a neural network recognizer for handwritten digits [65, 215, 330]. A feedforward layered network with three hidden layers [215] is used as shown in Fig. 10.7. One of the key features in this network is the integration of constraints on the connection weights that reduce the number of free parameters to enhance the probability of valid generalization by the network, as discussed in Section 6.2. The constraint is derived from the observation that for shift- and rotation-invariant feature detection, all the receptive fields should perform the same function regardless of their position on the retina. Therefore, corresponding connections to units with different receptive fields are forced to be the same.

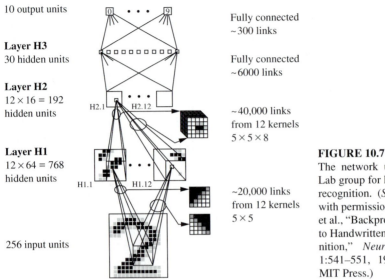

10 output units

Fully connected
~300 links

Layer H3
30 hidden units

Fully connected
~6000 links

Layer H2
12 × 16 = 192
hidden units

H2.1   H2.12

~40,000 links
from 12 kernels
5 × 5 × 8

Layer H1
12 × 64 = 768
hidden units

H1.1   H1.12

~20,000 links
from 12 kernels
5 × 5

256 input units

FIGURE 10.7
The network used by the Bell Lab group for handwritten digits recognition. (*Source:* Reprinted with permission from Y. Le Cun, et al., "Backpropagation Applied to Handwritten Zip Code Recognition," *Neural Computation,* 1:541–551, 1989. ©1989 The MIT Press.)

The data used for training and testing were obtained from digitized handwritten ZIP codes supplied by the U.S. Post Office. Locating the ZIP code and separating each digit are very difficult tasks. The segmentation task was addressed at a later stage in the work. The Bell Labs group first used manually segmented and normalized numerals that fit within a 16 × 16 retina. All pixel values in the retina image are normalized to within the range $[-1, 1]$. A total of 9,298 exemplars are used, of which 7,291 are required to train the network and the remaining 2,007 serve as test exemplars. Some of the ZIP codes and the segmented and normalized numerals are shown in Fig. 10.8. An important feature of this database is that both the training set and the test set contain many ambiguous and unclassifiable exemplars.

The output layer consists of ten units, each representing a numeral. The three hidden layers are denoted by H1, H2, and H3, respectively. The first hidden layer, H1, consists of 12 groups of 64 units arranged as 12 independent 8 × 8 feature maps. The 12 feature maps will be designated as H1.1, H1.2,..., H1.12. Each unit in a feature map takes input from a 5 × 5 neighborhood on the input retina (except at the boundary of the retina). A unit in H1 whose connections extend past the boundaries of the retina takes its input from a virtual background whose state equals a constant. For units in H1 that are one unit apart, their receptive fields in the retina are two pixels apart. Thus, the input image is undersampled, and some position information is eliminated. A similar 2-to-1 undersampling occurs as one goes from H1 to H2. The rationale is that although high resolution may be needed to detect a feature, its exact position need not be determined with equally high precision.

The constraint that corresponding connections to units with different receptive fields should be the same is enforced on the connections from the retina to H1. That is, each of the 64 units in H1.1 uses the same set of 25 weights. Therefore, each feature map in effect performs a nonlinear undersampled convolution with a 5×5 kernel.

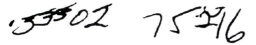

FIGURE 10.8

Examples of ZIP code image, and segmented and normalized numerals from the testing set. (*Source:* Reprinted with permission from Y. Le Cun, et al., "Backpropagation Applied to Handwritten Zip Code Recognition," *Neural Computation,* 1:541–551, 1989. ©1989 The MIT Press.)

Units in different feature maps (e.g., H1.1 and H1.7) share different sets of weights. This allows each feature map to be trained to pick up a different feature. Units are free to adjust their own thresholds. Thus, H1 layer consists of $8 \times 8 \times 12 = 768$ units and $768 \times 25 + 768 = 19,968$ connections and thresholds. However, there are only 1,068 free parameters (25 connection weights times 12 plus 768 thresholds).

The H2 layer also consists of 12 feature maps, each arranged in a 4×4 array. Denote these feature maps as H2.1, H2.2, ..., H2.12. Each unit in H2 combines local information from 8 of the 12 feature maps in H1. Its receptive field is composed of eight 5×5 neighborhoods at identical locations in the eight H1-layer feature maps. Thus, a unit in H2 has 200 connections from H1 plus a threshold. Once again, all units in a given map are constrained to have the same weight vector. In total, layer H2 contains $12 \times 4 \times 4 = 192$ units and $192 \times 201 = 38,592$ connections and thresholds. However, the number of free parameters is only $12 \times 200 + 192 = 2,592$. Layer H2 is fully connected to the third hidden layer, H3, which has 30 units. The number of connection weights and thresholds from H2 to H3 is $30 \times 192 + 30 = 5,790$. Layer H3 is then fully connected to the output layer, which has 10 units. This adds another 310 connection weights and thresholds. In summary, the network has 1,256 units, 64,660 connections, and 9,790 independent parameters.

The network was trained using the backpropagation algorithm. The transfer characteristic used for each unit was a scaled hyperbolic tangent. The target values for the output units were chosen within the quasilinear range of the sigmoid. As pointed out in Section 5.2, this prevents the weights from growing too large. It was found that training can be extremely slow if some weights are too small. Before training, the weights were randomly initialized following a uniform distribution. After each pass through the training set, the performance was measured both on the training set and the test set. The network was trained for 23 passes through the training set (167,693 pattern presentations). After training, the percentage of misclassified patterns was 0.14% on the training set (10 mistakes) and 5.0% on the test set (102 mistakes). The convergence was extremely quick, showing that the backpropagation algorithm can be used on fairly large tasks. This speed was partly due to the high redundancy of real data.

In a realistic application, the percentage of patterns that must be rejected to reach a given level of accuracy is of greater interest. If the difference between the activation levels of two mostly active units is below a threshold, the network is considered to be confused and the pattern is rejected. It was found that 12.1% of the test patterns were rejected for the network to achieve a 1% classification error on the remaining test set. More recently, using a network similar to the one just described with 100,000 connections and 2,600 independent parameters, the Bell Labs group achieved a 9% rejection ratio for 1% classification error. *These performance data are believed to be the best for automatic recognition of handwritten digits.*

It is worth mentioning that networks with more free parameters lead in general to worse performance. Based on their simulation success, the Bell Labs group implemented a neural network with 136,000 connections for recognition of handwritten digits using a mixed analog/digital neural network chip [330].

The aforementioned network takes as input only manually segmented and normalized images. More recently, the Bell Labs group developed methods that integrated segmentation and recognition together. A recognition-based segmenter is reported in ref. [246]; it is a hybrid of connected-components analysis, vertical cuts, and a neural network recognizer. Connected components that are single digits are handled by connected-components analysis. Connected components that are combined or dissected digits are handled by the vertical-cut segmenter. The four main stages of processing are preprocessing, in which noise is removed and the digits are deslanted; connected-components analysis segmentation and recognition; vertical-cut-point estimation and segmentation; and direct lookup. The system was trained and tested on approximately 10,000 images of five- and nine-digit ZIP code fields taken from real mail.

Another new method is the shortest-path segmentation method [65], which combines dynamic programming and a neural network recognizer for segmenting and recognizing character strings. This method was applied to two problems: recognition of handwritten ZIP codes and recognition of handwritten words. For the ZIP codes the method was used to segment the images automatically during training. The dynamic programming stage both performs the segmentation and provides inputs and desired outputs to the neural network. For handwritten word recognition, the shortest path segmentation method was combined with a "space displacement neural network" approach, in which a single-character recognition network is extended over the entire word image and the shortest-path segmentation technique is then used to rank-order a given lexicon. The technique can also be extended to generate K rank-ordered candidates by finding the K shortest paths.

A growth network approach was also applied to the task of handwritten digits recognition by the French ESPCI group [194]. A Stepnet algorithm, which is very similar to the divide-and-conquer algorithm in Section 7.1, was applied to construct a network for the task. The basic idea of Stepnet is the same as in other growth algorithms. It decomposes the problem into simpler subproblems, which can be solved by linear separators. The network constructed is also similar to the divide-and-conquer algorithm with one hidden layer. One output unit, which can be implemented by an AND gate, is used for each digit from 0 to 9.

Instead of letting the network learn to extract features from the segmented and normalized 16×16 raw image, as the Bell Labs group did [215], the ESPCI group applied handcrafted feature extraction. They applied edge detection and line thinning first. Afterwards, the image was scanned by a 5×5 window to detect horizontal, vertical, and two-diagonal-direction line segments. The four features are represented on four 8×8 feature maps. The four feature maps are then used as inputs to the neural network. More complicated features, such as curved segments, stop points, and line intersections, are not extracted.

A network is then constructed from the training set by applying the Stepnet divide-and-conquer algorithm. The final network constructed has a single hidden layer with 45 units. The output layer has 10 units, which compute AND functions of inputs from the layer below. The input retina has $4 \times 8 \times 8 + 1 = 257$ units. The total number of independent parameters is $256 \times 45 + 45 = 11,565$. Although the number of independent parameters is larger than that for the network in Fig. 10.7, the network itself is significantly smaller. An advantage of this size reduction is easier implementation in hardware, compared with the Bell Labs network. Classification performance similar to that of the Bell Labs approach was achieved. This work shows that growth algorithms are applicable in complex real-world classification problems.

The members of the Bell Labs group also extended their work to the task of verification of signatures written on a touch-sensitive pad using a "Siamese" time delay neural network [57]. The network consists of two identical subnetworks joined at their output. During training, the network learns to measure the similarity between pairs of signatures. When the network is used for verification, only one-half of the Siamese network is evaluated. The output of this half-network is the feature vector for the input signature. Verification consists of comparing this feature vector with a stored feature vector for the signer. Signatures closer than a chosen threshold to this stored representation are accepted; all other signatures are rejected as forgeries.

Related applications include face recognition and two- and three-dimensional object recognition. A multimodular neural network was developed for character and face recognition [364]. Methods to integrate various neural networks into a unique pattern recognition system were developed [364]. Within this system it is possible to realize feature extraction and recognition in successive modules, which are cooperatively trained. Neural network approaches to practical two- and three-dimensional object recognition have been reported.

10.7 IMAGE COMPRESSION BY A MULTILAYER FEEDFORWARD STRUCTURE TRAINED THROUGH BACKPROPAGATION

Image compression is crucial in the transformation of multimedia information through communication channels that have inherent limitations of capacity. An image, when compressed, saves storage space, reduces the data rate of transmission, and can lower processing cost. Compression is realized through data reduction by retention of essential information to which the sensory organs are more sensitive. The *compression ratio*, defined as the ratio of the data rates before and after compression, varies from one application to another. In facsimile and television a compression ratio of 5 is considered to be satisfactory for recovery without significant deterioration of image quality. A much higher compression ratio is necessary in commercial uses of video telephones, where the data rate may be 50 megabits per second (Mb/sec) and the data rate after compression is required to be about 64 kilobits per second (kb/sec). In such cases the quality of the received image is usually very poor, as evidenced by the "jerkiness" associated with motion in images at the receiving end. Many image-compression schemes have been developed. For example, compression algorithms and their implementation in application-specific integrated circuits (ASICs) based on the use of a particular transform, the *discrete cosine transform* (DCT), are discussed in ref. [88]. Other image coding techniques, based on sub-band coding, pyramidal decompositions and wavelets, and hybrid coding (spatial and temporal coding for sequences of image frames), have been described in [389, 168]. Since the objective of achieving the highest compression ratio and lowest transmission rate constrained by a preset measure of picture quality is far from being achieved, a neural network approach [363], in spite of its drawbacks with respect to the multilayer feedforward network, is considered here for two reasons. First, as in other applications, neural networks serve to provide a novel approach to solving classical problems; second, it is possible that other models or structures might provide better results—a possibility that might stimulate further research.

Consider the graph of a feedforward network in Fig. 10.9. It has an input layer, a hidden layer, and an output layer. The numbers of nodes r in the input and output layers are the same, but the number of nodes p in the hidden layer is much less. Consider this as an image compression channel. The number of pixels in the image to be compressed is r, and the number to be transmitted is p. Therefore, the compression ratio is r/p. The pixel values of the exemplar images could be ordered after row-by-row scan (other alternatives exist) of the images in order to define the input vectors. To obtain perfect reconstruction at the receiving end from the transmitted compressed data, the target vector at the output associated with a particular input vector is made identical to this input vector. During the training phase by backpropagation, the transfer characteristics of the hidden and output units are required to be not only continuous but also differentiable. After training and before transmission, the graph of the network is changed to that in Fig. 10.10 by replacing the hidden

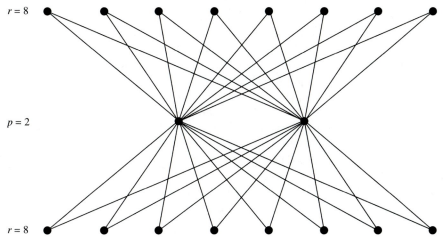

FIGURE 10.9
A layered graph formed as a node-coalesced cascade of $K_{r,p}$ and $K_{p,r}$, where $r \gg p$.

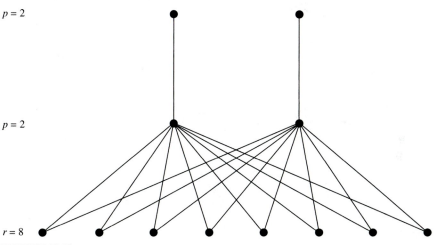

FIGURE 10.10
A layered graph formed as a node-coalesced concatenation of $K_{r,p}$, an identity graph between two
layers each having p nodes, and (not shown here) $K_{p,r}$, where $r \gg p$.

layer with the *identity graph*, shown in the same figure. This identity graph is generated by superposing one layer of p nodes directly above another layer of p nodes
with one edge present between each node in the bottom layer to the node directly
on top of it in the layer above. There are no other edges in the identity graph except
for these p edges. A unit weight is assigned to each of these p edges, so the network
associated with the identity graph not only realizes the identity mapping from each
vector at the input space to exactly the same vector at the output space (a property

inherent also in the network associated with the graph in Fig. 10.9 during the training phase) but does so with direct connections between each lower-layer node to the corresponding upper-layer node. Subsequently, the transfer characteristics of the units associated with the nodes of $K_{p,p}$ are changed to hard-limiters, and the trained network associated with the graph in Fig. 10.10 is spliced to yield two networks. The graph characterizing the network at the transmitting end is $K_{r,p}$, whereas the characterizing graph of the network at the receiving end is $K_{p,r}$.

The scheme just described was tested with a chosen network, whose interconnection weights were trained with a set of letters from the English alphabet. Specifically, the training data consisted of digitized representations of characters A, B, C, D, E, F, G. Each character was represented as a 7×5 binary matrix, as shown in Fig. 10.11. The compression ratio required is $\frac{35}{8}$. Therefore, there are 35 inputs, and the hidden layer has 8 units. The output layer in Fig. 10.9 for this problem has 35 nodes, corresponding to 35 units in the output layer of the network. The MATLAB Neural Network Toolbox, to which the reader is referred, was used.

In the training phase the following choices were made before the backpropagation algorithm was applied. The activation function chosen for each of the units in the hidden layer and the output layer was *logsig,* as defined in MATLAB. The delta learning rule was applied with a learning rate of 0.01, and subsequently a momentum and adaptive learning rate technique, in accordance with the paradigm *trainbpx* in the MATLAB Toolbox, was also applied. The goal for the sum-of-squares error was set at 0.5. Starting with random initial weights, the paradigm *trainbp* in the MATLAB Toolbox, which uses a fixed learning rate, was applied in training over 13,808 epochs and produced a final error of 0.499958, which is less than the preset maximum value of 0.5.

In the test phase the trained network was divided into two subnetworks as just described. The subnetwork at the transmitting end consisted of 35 nodes at the input layer and 8 units in the output layer, whereas the subnetwork at the receiving end contained 8 nodes at the input layer and 35 units in the output layer. The activation functions of units at the output layers of both subnetworks were changed to *hardlim with bias* as defined in MATLAB. The first subnetwork compresses the 7×5 binary image of a given character (35 bits) into an 8-bit binary sequence, which is the compressed data transmitted through a communication channel to the receiving end, where the second subnetwork converts the 8-bit binary sequence to a 35-bit sequence for mapping into a 7×5 binary image. Fig. 10.11 shows the results of testing with the same set of exemplars that were used in the training of the two-layer network whose graph is given in Fig. 10.9. These particular results were obtained after training with a learning rate in the combined momentum and adaptive learning rate mode of operation. The mean squared error and the learning rate are plotted in Fig. 10.12 as a function of the number of epochs. Reconstruction of the exemplars is seen to be satisfactory. A compromise between accuracy of reconstruction and computational cost is usually necessary. Note the increased amplitude of oscillatory behavior and the sudden jump in the learning rate, caused, most likely, by a somewhat flat error surface. The results of generalization when the data compressed is noisy are shown in Fig. 10.13. Varying degrees of noise were simulated by revers-

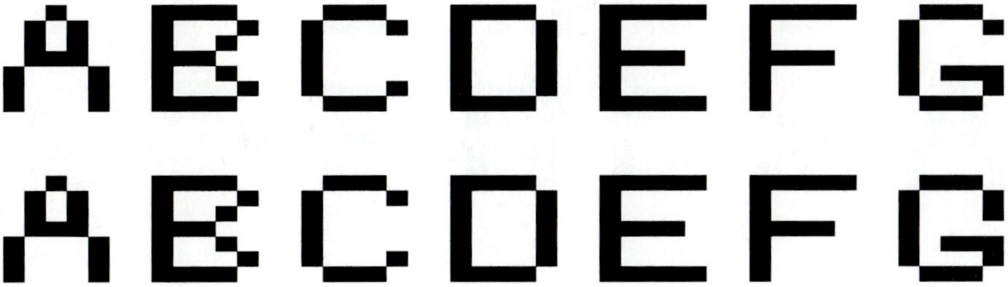

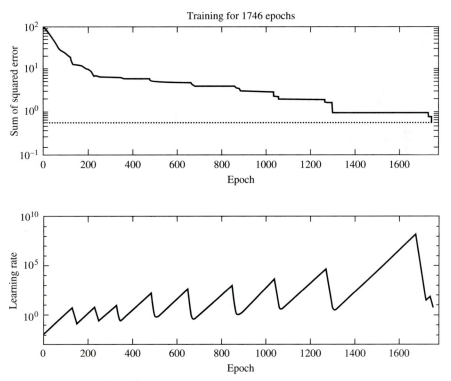

FIGURE 10.11
The set of exemplars used during the training phase of the network for data compression is shown in the top row. The corresponding results in the testing phase, which followed the training phase, are shown in the bottom row.

ing at random certain percentages of bits in the binary representation of the training exemplars. As expected, the accuracy of reconstruction deteriorated with increasing levels of noise. Other letters, such as H, I, J, K, L, M, N, were not recovered, as shown in Fig. 10.14. This is consistent with the fact that test exemplars and training exemplars did not share a common underlying probability distribution, which is one of the requirements in distribution-free learning, discussed in Chapter 6.

FIGURE 10.12
Mean sum of squared error and learning rate in the adaptive mode of operation during the training phase versus the number of epochs.

FIGURE 10.13
Reconstruction from compressed noisy data. The letters on the top row of each set are noisy test samples of the training exemplars, and the corresponding ones on the bottom are the results of recovery from the compressed data with varying degrees of noise. (*a*) 10% flipped bits; (*b*) 20% flipped bits; (*c*) 30% flipped bits; (*d*) 40% flipped bits.

HIJKLMN
FECFCEF

FIGURE 10.14

The letters at the top are test samples, and the corresponding ones at the bottom are the results of recovery from compressed data.

10.8   CHARACTER RETRIEVAL USING THE DISCRETE HOPFIELD NETWORK

The ability of the Hopfield network, referred to sometimes as a *crossbar associative network* (CAN), to store patterns is illustrated next, as well as its limitations. Though the upper bound for estimates of memory capacity in such a completely-connected N-neuron network could be as high as $N/2 \ln N$, the actual realized capacity is much less. In addition to the exemplars stored by training, there could also be *spurious states,* which may be responsible for errors in the recall phase. The approach for training used here is the one suggested in the Neural Network Toolbox associated with MATLAB based on [224]. See *solvehop* in the MATLAB *Neural Network Toolbox User's Guide*.

The exemplars, which are binary representations of all characters from A to T, are shown in Fig. 10.15. Each character is represented in that figure by a 14×10 binary matrix, with 0 and 1 values associated with, respectively, white and black pixels. Therefore, 140 neurons are required in the CAN to store the images. Starting with an initial output vector, the network, whose topology is characterized by K_n with self-loops added at each node, iterates until a stable output vector, which constitutes a memory, is reached. Each neuron has a *satlin with bias* (see MATLAB) type of nonlinearity. The *solvehop* program provides the designer with interconnection weights and biases responsible for stable output vectors as given by the matrix of target vectors associated with the exemplar images. It is recognized that spurious stable vectors, which are undesirable, may also be created.

FIGURE 10.15

The binary representations chosen for each of the twenty exemplars.

Two experiments were carried out in the test phase. In the first experiment noise was added to the binary representations of A, B, C, D, E, and F by reversing each bit with probability 0.2. Fig. 10.16 has in the first column six of the original exemplars. In column 2 of Fig. 10.16 are the corresponding noisy images, and columns 3 to 10 contain the images after every three iterations starting from the corresponding noisy versions in the second column. After 24 iterations, the original binary images are recovered from their noisy versions. In the second experiment the binary representations of the subset of six exemplars just considered were contaminated by reversing each bit with probability 0.3. The recovered images after every five iterations are displayed in columns 3 through ten in Fig. 10.17. Again, column 2 contains the noisy version from which iteration begins, and the noise-free exemplars are shown in the first column. Even after 40 iterations, the recovered images in the last column are not all identical to the corresponding ones in the first column. Note that the type of nonlinearity does not lead to binary-valued recovered images; gray levels, corresponding to output values between 0 and 1, are noticeable. Finally, the performance of the trained network was tested on incomplete exemplars. The ability to recall correctly in this case depended on the degree to which the patterns were incomplete and the similarity of these incomplete patterns to any subset of the original patterns.

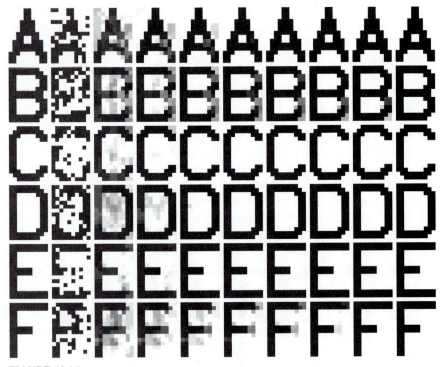

FIGURE 10.16
Recovery of original images in column 1 from their noisy versions in column 2 after 24 iterations in a Hopfield net in the first experiment. The results after every three iterations are shown in columns 3 through 10.

FIGURE 10.17

Recovery of original images in column 1 from their noisy versions in column 2 after 40 iterations in a Hopfield net in the second experiment. The results after every five iterations are shown in columns 3 through 10.

10.9 VISUAL PROCESSING NETWORKS

Vision is known to be a very difficult and computationally extremely expensive task for serial computers. It is estimated that about a third of the human cerebral cortex is devoted to the visual functions of perception of depth, shape, motion, color and recognition, etc. [196]. From this observation it seems that for an autonomous intelligent system to achieve real-time vision, a good strategy is to equip it with a large amount of dedicated specialized vision hardware. There are many powerful digital vision systems in the market. Carver Mead at Caltech proposed a different approach [253]. His group is building a very compact, analog special-purpose vision system and other sensory processors using current VLSI technology. These "smart sensors" incorporate significant signal-processing capabilities in the sensors and the associated circuits in order to reduce the transmission bandwidth and the computational load in subsequent stages. This paradigm is emerging as a possible competitor to the general-purpose digital vision machines [196].

The best-known design from Mead's group is the *silicon retina,* illustrated in Fig. 10.18 [253, 254, 356]. The silicon retina computes the spatial and temporal derivatives of the image projected on its phototransistor array. It has a straightforward structural relationship to a primate retina. The major divisions of a primate

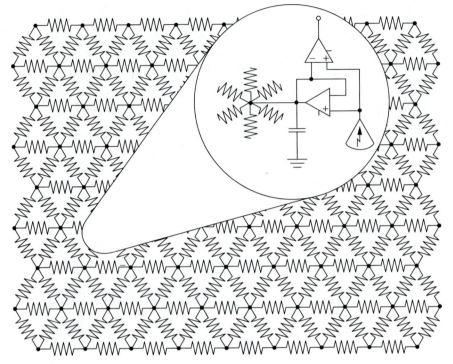

FIGURE 10.18
Simplified diagram of the silicon retina showing the resistive network. A single pixel element is illustrated in the circular window. (*Source:* Carver Mead, *Analog VLSI and Neural Systems* (p. 234), ©1989 by Addison-Wesley Publishing Company Inc. Reprinted by permission of the publisher.)

retina are shown in Fig. 10.19. Light is transduced into an electrical potential by the *photoreceptors* (R) at the top. The primary signal pathway is from the photoreceptors through the *triad synapses* (at the end of the photoreceptors) to the *bipolar cells,* then to the retinal *ganglion cells* (G), which provide the output of the retina. There are two types of bipolar cells: the *invaginating* bipolar cells (IB) and the *flat* bipolar cells (FB), as illustrated in Fig. 10.19. The primary signal pathway intersects two layers of neurons and synapses between the photoreceptors and the ganglion cells. Just below the photoreceptors are the *horizontal cells* (H), forming the *outer-plexiform* layer. Below this layer and above the ganglion cells is the *inner-plexiform* layer, consisting of *amacrine cells* (A). The cells connecting the two plexiform layers are called the *interplexiform cells* (IP). The triad synapse is at the point of contact among the photoreceptor, the horizontal cells, and the bipolar cells. The resistive network in Fig. 10.18 corresponds to the horizontal cell layer. The primary signal pathway proceeds from the photoreceptor and the circuit representing the bipolar cell, shown in the circular window in Fig. 10.18. The image signal is processed in parallel at each node of the network. The hexagonal resistive network is uniform with a common resistance value R. The resistive elements in the network are realized by exploiting the current-voltage relationship of a small transistor circuit [253]. When the volt-

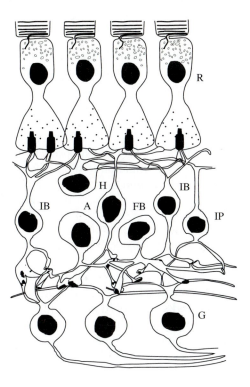

FIGURE 10.19
Cross-section of a primate retina. (*Source:* Reprinted with permission from M.A.C. Maher, et al., "Implementing Neural-Architectures Using Analog VLSI Circuits," *IEEE Trans. Circuits and Systems, 36:* 643–652, 1989. ©1989 IEEE. Adapted from J.E. Dowling, *The Retina: An Approachable Part of the Brain,* Belknap Press of Harvard University Press, Cambridge, MA, 1987.)

age across the element is within its linear range—a couple of hundred millivolts—it functions like a constant resistance whose value can be controlled over five orders of magnitude.

A key feature of the photoreceptor circuit is its automatic gain control function so that its output voltage is logarithmic over four to five orders of magnitude of the incoming light intensity. This is analogous to the cone photoreceptors of the vertebrate retina. This wide operating range is much greater than those of video camera–based vision systems. The high degree of independence of a perceived image from the absolute illumination level is crucial for a vision system to function in the real world. It is worth pointing out that the silicon retina consumes power less than 1 mW, most of which is used in the photoconversion stage.

The network performs the following computations:

1. The photoreceptors take the logarithm of the incoming light intensity.
2. The signal from a photoreceptor is connected to a resistive network node by a transconductance of value G. The signals spread in the resistive network of horizontal cells and are spatially and temporally averaged. Spatial averaging is achieved by the resistive network, and temporal averaging is achieved by the capacitor in the circuit.
3. The output from a bipolar cell is proportional to the difference between the photoreceptor signal and the horizontal cell signal at the corresponding node in the resistive network.

Let the output voltage of the photoreceptor at node k be u_k, and let the voltage at the same node in the resistive network be $\bar{u}_k$. Neglecting the temporal smoothing by the capacitance, the current fed into the network at node k is $i_k = G(\bar{u}_k - u_k)$. In steady state, the current going into the node must equal the current exiting the node. Therefore, we have

$$\sum_{m=1}^{6} \frac{u_k - u_{k_m}}{R} = i_k,$$ (10.15)

where u_{k_m}, $m = 1, 2, \ldots, 6$ are the steady-state voltages at the six neighboring nodes of node k. This is in fact a simple finite-difference approximation to the Laplacian operator ∇^2 at node k. That is, Eq. (10.15) is an approximation to

$$Ri(x, y) = \nabla^2 u(x, y) = RG(\bar{u}(x, y) - u(x, y)).$$ (10.16)

Therefore, the current at each node at steady state yields a spatially high-pass filtered version of the logarithmically compressed image density. Similarly, temporal differentiation is achieved by using the capacitive elements from the nodes to the ground. A question with an interconnected network such as the silicon retina is whether there will be oscillation. The criteria for robust stability in a class of lateral inhibition networks coupled through resistive networks are proved in ref. [422]. For detailed circuit design considerations, see ref. [253].

An important principle illustrated by the silicon retina is the massive sharing of connections. It is observed that the biological retina, like many other areas of the brain, minimizes wiring by arranging the signal representation such that as many connections as possible can be shared. The resistive network is the ultimate example of sharing connections. By including a pixel's own input in the average, the weighted average over a neighborhood for every position in the image can be computed using the same shared structure. This uniform structure may work well for the retina because it is reasonable to assume that the functions at different locations in the retina should be fundamentally the same, at least in some area. This same argument was the reason for sharing weights in the handwritten digit recognition network by the Bell Labs group, discussed in Section 10.6. Sharing connections and using only local connections to propagate information, as in the silicon retina, reduce the total number of connections and facilitate implementation using VLSI technology. Reducing the number of connections also improves a network's ability to generalize. However, it should also be noted that when connections are highly shared, a network's functional capacity is greatly reduced, which is why generalization may be improved.

Mead's group also designed a visual motion detection network [253]. The network consists of an array of the photoreceptors used in the silicon retina and analog computation elements to extract the velocity information from a uniformly moving image. The fact that single units in the early visual system have small receptive fields causes the well-known *aperture problem* in visual motion detection, illustrated in Fig. 10.20. In the figure a small circle represents the receptive field of a unit. Motions of the object that have the same perpendicular component in a small circle (i.e., those whose tips fall on the constraint line) are indistinguishable to the corresponding unit. However, a unique velocity can be determined when there are two nonparallel constraint lines, because there is only one common velocity. When all constraint

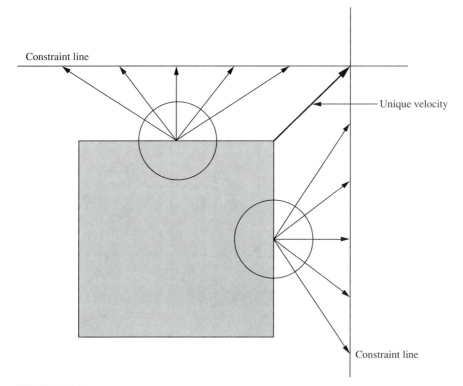

Constraint line

Unique velocity

Constraint line

FIGURE 10.20
Illustration of the aperture problem. The small circles represent local motion detectors, which can only measure the motion components perpendicular to the moving edges of the object. The correct motion is the common vector between the two sets of local motions bounded by the constraint lines.

lines are parallel or nearly parallel, an illusion will be created. An example is the pole in front of a barber shop. The stripes on the pole have a horizontal velocity, but our visual system interprets a vertical velocity. Tanner and Mead [253, Ch. 14, pp. 229–255] designed the constraint-solving circuit illustrated in Fig. 10.21. The circuit contains a set of global connections that distributes a best guess of velocity to all the individual constraint-generating sites. Each site performs a computation to check whether the global velocity satisfies its constraint. If there is an error, circuitry within the local site supplies a *force* that tends to move the global velocity towards satisfying the local constraint. Collectively, the global velocity that receives the strongest support will provide the final answer. The global velocity components are represented as voltages on the global connections. The correcting forces are currents that charge or discharge the global connections.

An alternative network for computing visual motion is given in ref. [25]. The network is illustrated in Fig. 10.22. The output layer, labeled MT, has an $(m \times n)$ array of units. The $m = n$ case was discussed in ref. [25]; this will be called the *generic array*. A unit in the ith row and jth column of the array will be associated with the label (D_i, S_j) for $i = 1, 2, \ldots, m$ and $j = 1, 2, \ldots, n$. The unit at location

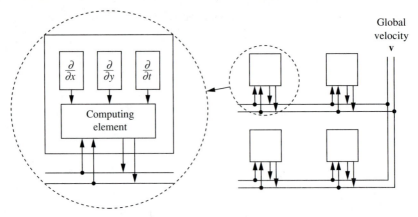

FIGURE 10.21
Block diagram of the constraint-solving circuit cell and array. (*Source:* Carver Mead, *Analog VLSI and Neural Systems* (p. 259), ©1989 by Addison-Wesley Publishing Company Inc. Reprinted by permission of the publisher.)

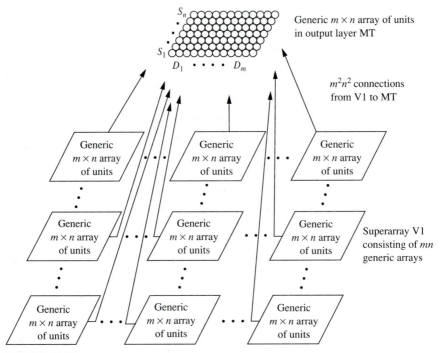

FIGURE 10.22
A network for computing visual motion. The layer MT has an $(m \times n)$ array of units. The superarray V1 has an $(m \times n)$ array of subarrays, where each subarray has $(m \times n)$ units. (After J.A. Anderson, et al., "Experiments with Representation in Neural Networks: Object Motion, Speech and Arithmetic," in *Synergetics of Cognition* (p. 54–69), edited by H. Haken and M. Stadler, Springer, Berlin, 1990.)

442

(D_i, S_j) is most sensitive to a local velocity with direction D_i and speed S_j. The input layer, labeled V1, is a superarray consisting of $(m \times n)$ copies of the $(m \times n)$ generic array. Each array in V1 has a receptive field located at different positions in the image. Each unit responds to a local velocity vector with a given direction and speed. A unit labeled (D_i, S_j) in an array in V1 will be active if the corresponding velocity associated with this unit satisfies the local constraint line. Each unit labeled (D_i, S_j) in each of the mn arrays in the input layer V1 is connected to the unit labeled (D_i, S_j) in layer MT. Thus, there are $m^2 n^2$ connections between the units in V1 and the units in MT. Sereno [349] used the Widrow-Hoff learning rule, which was studied in Chapter 4, to train the connection weights of the one-layer (the input layer is not counted as a layer) feedforward network introduced in ref. [25] to compute the global velocity. The same rule may, naturally, be applied to train the $m^2 n^2$ connections when $m \neq n$. Unlike the networks by Mead's group, this network is only simulated. The global velocity may also be computed in an alternative way without training. If all units in V1 are connected to the corresponding units in MT with equal and positive weights, the unit in MT that receives the strongest support gives the global velocity. The unit receiving the strongest support may be identified by lateral inhibitive connections in MT such as in the winner-take-all network of Section 9.1.

Many other specialized visual processing VLSI networks have been reported, including improved motion detection networks using correlation and spatiotemporal energy models, as well as specialized networks for surface interpolation based on regularization, for detecting discontinuities, for stereo vision, and for computing the first and second image moments [145, 171, 196].

These specialized analog networks produced impressive performance. They are optimally suited to analog sensory data, because no sampling is required, eliminating any temporal aliasing problems. In addition, their robustness to imprecision or errors in the circuits, high processing speed, low power consumption, and small size make analog sensors better alternatives to digital vision systems in many applications. The main shortcomings of analog sensors are their inflexibility and low precision compared with their digital counterparts. However, precision is not of top concern in most vision applications; the capability to process visual information in real time is the overriding requirement. Research along this direction shows that solving a hard problem by integrating solutions of decomposed smaller subtasks, using many special-purpose networks tuned for these subtasks, is a promising strategy.

10.10 CONCLUSION AND DISCUSSION

This chapter presents several representative applications of neural networks to problems that have proven difficult for conventional non–neural network methods. Some other important applications where neural networks have shown promise are briefly mentioned. The domain of applications of both feedforward and feedback neural network structures is rapidly expanding, as is evident from two recent books.[4,5]

---

[4] A.F. Murray, ed. *Applications of Neural Networks,* Kluwer Academic Publishers, Boston, MA. 1995.
[5] G.F. Page, J.B. Gomm, and D. Williams, eds. *Application of Neural Networks to Modeling and Control,* Chapman & Hall, London and New York, 1993.

Feedforward networks have been applied to the prediction of the secondary structure of proteins [45, 305]. A 62% accuracy was achieved on a test set, compared to about 53% for the best available non–neural network alternative. A neural network approach is currently the method of choice for this application.

It has been demonstrated that neural networks, both multilayer feedforward and recurrent, can be used for the identification and control of nonlinear dynamical systems [223, 271]. Narendra's group proposed a dynamic backpropagation method for application of neural networks in control [271]. Their method is based on combining the gradient methods in optimization and control theory with the backpropagation methods in neural networks to obtain the gradient of a performance index of nonlinear dynamic systems. Though the method applies to any interconnection of linear dynamical systems and multilayer neural networks, considerable computational costs are incurred even for low-order dynamical systems. In addition, the step size of the gradient method has to be kept small in order to guarantee stability, and generating stable adaptive algorithms has been difficult. Dynamic systems with feedback are very versatile, and unlike in pattern classification, feedback is almost indispensable in control. Moreover, nonlinear dynamical systems are required in many applications. Feedback may be incorporated into a neural network by use of a tapped delay line to create delayed versions of the output. Similarly, delayed versions of the input may be generated by feeding the input sequence through another tapped delay line. The tapped outputs from the two delay lines are then used as inputs to a neural network to realize a nonlinear discrete autoregressive system. The training problem of the recurrent structure becomes, naturally, more complicated. Besides recurrent backpropagation, described in Chapter 8, other variants for training recurrent neural networks include *truncated backpropagation*, which is an approximation to recurrent backpropagation, and *real-time recurrent learning* [416], which is very similar to dynamic backpropagation. Simulation results showed that identification and adaptive control using neural networks are practically feasible. Even before the emergence of the backpropagation method and popularization of a variety of training methods for neural network structures that incorporate feedback, the Madaline was used in the early 1960s at Stanford University to balance a broomstick, based on principles in adaptive control. During the last decade such engineering efforts have been extended to the eye-hand coordination of robot arms moving in response to feedback from camera images [154].

The neocognitron, described in Section 9.3, has been reported to identify handwritten characters with very high accuracy regardless of scaling, translation, rotation, and some small distortion. Neural networks have also been successfully applied to the tasks of scheduling airline flights; processing loan applications; allocating documents in multiprocessor information-retrieval systems; automatic target recognition [322]; classification of radar clutter [151] (this is useful in the tracking of multiple targets in clutter by facilitating the computation-intensive task of data association; the task may also be done with Hopfield nets, as discussed in the text or with Boltzmann machines [173]); computational vision for industrial automated inspection; medical diagnosis; forecasting of weather, solar flares, etc.; power allocation and scheduling; plus a host of other applications in business, defense, commerce, health care, and other industries.

Neural network approaches have produced the best results to date in autonomous navigation, prediction of secondary protein structures, handwritten digit recognition, and some short-term time series prediction tasks. One of the common effective strategies in applying neural networks to solving hard problems is the hybrid integration of symbolic processing and neural networks to combine the strengths of both worlds. Another good strategy is the decomposition of a hard problem so that as much as is possible can be solved with special-purpose hardware. This is because neural network algorithms and models are not inherently suited for implementation on general-purpose computers.

An appreciable number of massively parallel hardware implementations of neural networks have been built that yield performance significantly superior to that attainable on powerful mainframe serial computers. For example, a 576-neuron wafer-scale complementary metal-oxide-semiconductor (CMOS) digital VLSI circuit was designed to solve the 16-city traveling salesperson problem in less than a tenth of a second [245]. Actually, the neural chips built by those authors are also capable of implementing learning algorithms using backpropagation, where a high degree of precision in the interconnection weights is desirable. The silicon retina, built on an analog VLSI chip, and its variants also show many advantages over their digital counterparts. There has been an impressive activity in neural-chip development ever since the first commercial chip was introduced in the U.S. market in 1989 by Syntonic Systems of Beaverton, Oregon [344]. This chip used a modified version of ART-1 theory.

It is not clear currently, because of conflicting claims, whether the digital VLSI or analog VLSI technology has an overall superiority in the hardware implementation of neural networks. It is fair to assert that digital circuits are preferable for high-resolution weight representation, whereas analog components are most appropriate for learning algorithms with high fault tolerance and requiring only moderate precision [113]. The demands and requirements of particular applications also dictate the choice of a particular technology. In some cases the learning process may be slow but fast decisions are to be made (credit card fraud detection, for example). Here learning may be off-chip but decision making is on-chip. In other cases, such as real-time speaker-independent voice recognition systems, both learning and decision making are to happen fast. Some chips combine both analog and digital processing. It is likely that most artificial neural systems will have massively hard-wired front ends consistent with biological neural systems, which derive their emergent collective computational power from an analog mode of operation. The limitations of accuracy in electronic implementations of analog circuitry can be overcome by allowing the connection weights to be digitally controlled for higher resolution performance. Thus, speed as well as accuracy is attainable with the simultaneous deployment of both analog and digital technologies. In spite of tremendous progress during the last decade, a considerable distance has to be traversed before the full capabilities at the materials, devices, architecture, algorithm, and systems levels are realized for simulating the distinctive features and functions of a biological neural network.

Optical implementations of neural networks may provide an alternative because of their capability in realizing high connectivity and massive parallelism, even though optical computers have low dynamic range [110]. However, analog

VLSI technology proponents are hoping to overcome the limitations of the number of connections on the chip through wafer-scale implementation. Similar to the silicon retina, it is conceivable that someday a "silicon brain" might be developed. With *ultralarge-scale integration* (ULSI) becoming a reality, it remains to be seen whether such an achievement is feasible through analog ULSI or digital CMOS ULSI. For further information on the status of neural network hardware the reader is referred to the May 1993 Special Issue on the subject, published in the *IEEE Transactions on Neural Networks*.

We do not provide a problem section for this chapter. As an exercise or project, the readers may attempt to duplicate some of the examples discussed in this chapter. The examples may be scaled down if time is insufficient. The readers may also apply neural networks to other problems in their area of interest.

REFERENCES

[1] Y.S. Abu-Mostafa. Complexity in neural systems. In C. Mead, *Analog VLSI and Neural Systems,* Addison-Wesley, Reading, MA, 1989.

[2] Y.S. Abu-Mostafa and D. Psaltis. Optical neural computers. *Scientific American,* 256:88–95, March, 1987.

[3] W. Ackermann. Zum Hilbertschen Aufbau der reelen Zahlen. *Math. Ann.,* 99:113–118, 1928.

[4] D.H. Ackley, G.E. Hinton, and T.J. Sejnowski. A learning algorithm for Boltzmann machines. *Cognitive Science,* 9:147–169, 1985.

[5] D.H. Ackley and M.S. Littman. Generalization and scaling in reinforcement learning. In D.S. Touretzky, editor, *Advances in Neural Information Processing Systems II,* pp. 550–557, Morgan Kaufmann, San Mateo, CA, 1990.

[6] L.F. Agnati, B. Bjelke, and K. Fuxe. Volume transmission in the brain. *American Scientist,* 80:362–373, 1992.

[7] S.C. Ahalt, P.K. Chen, C.T. Chou, and T.P. Jung. Implementation of a vector quantization codebook design technique based on a competitive learning artificial neural network. *J. Supercomputing,* 5:307–330, 1992.

[8] A. Aho, J.E. Hopcroft, and J.D. Ullman. *Design and Analysis of Computer Algorithms.* Addison-Wesley, Reading, MA, 1974.

[9] J.S. Albus. *Brains, Behavior, and Robotics.* BYTE Books, Peterborough, NH, 1981.

[10] L.B. Almeida. Backpropagation in perceptrons with feedback. In R. Eckmiller and C. von der Malsburg, editors, *Neural Computers,* pp. 199–208, Springer-Verlag, Berlin/Heidelberg, 1988.

[11] L.B. Almeida. Backpropagation in non-feedforward networks. In I. Aleksander, editor, *Neural Computing Architecture,* pp. 74–91, North Oxford Academic, London, 1989.

[12] J. Alspector and R.B. Allen. A neuromorphic VLSI learning system. In P. Losleben, editor, *Advanced Research in VLSI,* pp. 313–349, MIT Press, Cambridge, MA, 1987.

[13] J. Alspector, R.B. Allen, V. Hu, and S. Satyanarayana. Stochastic learning networks and their electronic implementation. In D.Z. Anderson, editor, *Neural Information Processing Systems, Denver, 1987,* pp. 9–21, American Institute of Physics, New York, 1988.

[14] S. Amari. A method of statistical neurodynamics. *Kybernetik,* 14:201–215, 1974.

[15] S. Amari. Dynamics of pattern formation in lateral-inhibition type of neural fields. *Biol. Cybern.,* 27:77–87, 1977.

[16] S. Amari. Topographic organization of nerve fields. *Bull. Math. Biology,* 42:339–364, 1980.

[17] D.J. Amit. *Modeling Brain Function.* Springer-Verlag, Berlin/Heidelberg, 1989.

[18] D. Amit, H. Gutfreund, and H. Sompolinsky. Spin-glass models of neural networks. *Phys. Review A,* 32:1007–1018, 1985.

[19] D. Amit, H. Gutfreund, and H. Sompolinsky. Storing infinite number of patterns in a spin-glass model of neural networks. *Phys. Review Letters,* 55:1530–1533, 1985.

[20] D. Amit, H. Gutfreund, and H. Sompolinsky. Information storage in neural networks with low levels of activity. *Phys. Review A,* 35:2293–2303, 1987.

[21] D.Z. Anderson. Coherent optical eigenstate memory. *Optics Letters,* 11:56–58, 1986.

[22] J.A. Anderson. A memory model using spatial correlation functions. *Kybernetik,* 5:113–119, 1968.

[23] J.A. Anderson. A simple neural network generating an interactive memory. *Math. Biosciences,* 14:197–220, 1972.

[24] J.A. Anderson, A. Pellionisz, and E. Rosenfeld. Introduction to ART2. In *Neurocomputing 2*, pp. 147–150, MIT Press, Cambridge, MA, 1990.

[25] J.A. Anderson, M.L. Rossen, S.R. Vicuso, and M.E. Sereno. Experiments with representation in neural networks: object motion, speech and arithmetic. In H. Haken and M. Stadler, editors, *Synergetics of Cognition*, pp. 54–69, Springer-Verlag, Berlin, 1990. (Also in *Neurocomputing 2*, J.A. Anderson, A. Pellionisz, and E. Rosenfeld, editors, pp. 701–716, MIT Press, Cambridge, MA, 1990.)

[26] A. Andes, B. Widrow, M. Lehr, and E. Wan. MRIII: A robust algorithm for training analog neural networks. In *Proc. Intl. Joint Conf. on Neural Networks, Washington, DC, 1990*, volume 1, pp. 533–536, The IEEE, Inc., Piscataway, NJ, 1990.

[27] M. Anthony and N. Biggs. *Computational Learning Theory: An Introduction*. Cambridge University Press, Cambridge (UK), 1992.

[28] A.F. Atiya. Learning on a general network. In D.Z. Anderson, editor, *Neural Information Processing Systems*, pp. 22–30, American Institute of Physics, New York, 1988.

[29] A. Atiya and A. Parlos. Nonlinear system identification using spatiotemporal neural networks. In *Proc. Intl. Joint Conf. on Neural Networks, Baltimore, MD, 1992*, vol. 2, pp. 504–509, The IEEE, Inc., Piscataway, NJ, 1992.

[30] A.G. Barto and P. Anandan. Pattern-recognizing stochastic learning automata. *IEEE Trans. Systems, Man, and Cybernetics*, 15:360–375, 1985.

[31] A.G. Barto, R.S. Sutton, and C.W. Anderson. Neuronlike adaptive elements that can solve difficult learning control problems. *IEEE Trans. Systems, Man, and Cybernetics*, 13:834–846, 1983.

[32] J. Battle, F. Harary, and Y. Kodama. Every planar graph with nine points has a non-planar complement. *Bull. Amer. Math. Soc.*, 68:569–571, 1962.

[33] E.B. Baum. A proposal for more powerful learning algorithms. *Neural Computation*, 1:201–207, 1989.

[34] E.B. Baum. The perceptron algorithm is fast for nonmalicious distributions. *Neural Computation*, 2:248–260, 1990.

[35] E.B. Baum and D. Haussler. What size net gives valid generalization? *Neural Computation*, 1:151–160, 1989.

[36] S. Becker and Y. Le Cun. Improving the convergence of the backpropagation learning with second-order methods. In G. Hinton, D. Touretzky, and T. Sejnowski, editors, *Proc. 1988 Connectionist Models Summer School, Pittsburgh*, pp. 29–37, Morgan Kaufmann, San Mateo, CA, 1989.

[37] L.W. Beineke. The decomposition of complete graphs into planar subgraphs. In F. Harary, editor, *Graph Theory and Theoretical Physics*, chap. 4, Academic Press, New York, 1967.

[38] L.W. Beineke, F. Harary, and J.W. Moon. On the thickness of complete bipartite graph. *Proc. Cambridge Philosophical Soc.*, 60:1–5, 1964.

[39] M. Bellmore and G.L. Nemhauser. The traveling salesman problem: a survey. *Operations Res.*, 16:538–558, 1968.

[40] C. Berge and A. Ghouila-Houri. *Programming, Games and Transportation Networks*. Wiley, New York, 1965.

[41] E. Bienenstock and C. von der Malsburg. A neural network for invariant pattern recognition. *Europhysics Letters*, 4:121–126, 1987.

[42] G. Bilbro, T.K. Miller, W.E. Snyder, D.E. van den Bout, and M. White. Optimization by mean field annealing. In D.S. Touretzky, editor, *Advances in Neural Information Processing Systems (Denver 1988)*, pp. 91–98, Morgan Kaufmann, San Mateo, CA, 1989.

[43] A. Blum and R.L. Rivest. Training a 3-node neural network is NP-complete. *Neural Networks*, 5:117–128, 1992.

[44] A. Blumer, A. Ehrenfeucht, D. Haussler, and M.K. Warmuth. Learnability and the Vapnik-Chervonenkis dimension. *J. Assoc. Comput. Mach.*, 36:929–965, 1989.

[45] H. Bohr, J. Bohr, S. Brunak, R. Cotterill, B. Lautrup, L. Norskov, O. Olsen, and S. Petersen. Protein secondary structure and homology by neural networks: the α-helices in rhodopsin. *FEBS (Federation of European Biochemical Societies) Letters*, 241:223–338, 1988.

[46] N.K. Bose. Bibliography on layout design problem. *IEEE Circuits and Systems Magazine*, 7(4):6–8, August 1974.

[47] N.K. Bose. *Applied Multidimensional Systems Theory*. Van Nostrand Reinhold, New York, 1982.

[48] N.K. Bose. *Digital Filters*. Elsevier Science North-Holland, New York, 1985.

[49] N.K. Bose. Learning before and after Wiener. In P. Masani and V. Mandrekar, editors, *The Norbert Wiener Centenary Congress, East Lansing, MI,* American Mathematical Society, Providence, RI, 1995.

[50] N.K. Bose, R. Feick, and F.K. Sun. General solution to the spanning tree enumeration problem in multigraph wheels. *The IEEE Trans. Circuit Theory,* 20:6970, 1973.

[51] N.K. Bose and A.K. Garga. Neural network design using Voronoi diagrams: preliminaries. In *Proc. Intl. Joint Conf. on Neural Networks, Baltimore, MD, June 1992,* vol. 3, pp. 127–132, The IEEE, Inc., Piscataway, NJ, 1992.

[52] N.K. Bose and A.K. Garga. Neural network design using Voronoi diagrams. *IEEE Transactions on Neural Networks,* 4(5):778–787, September 1993.

[53] N.K. Bose and K.A. Prabhu. Thickness of graphs with degree-constrained vertices. *IEEE Transactions Circuits and Systems,* 24:184–190, 1975.

[54] G.E.P. Box and G.M. Jenkins. *Time Series Analysis: Forecasting and Control,* rev. edn. Holden-Day, San Francisco, 1976.

[55] R.P. Brent. Fast training algorithms for multilayer neural nets. *IEEE Transactions on Neural Networks,* 2(3):346–354, May 1991.

[56] M.A. Breuer. *Design Automation of Digital Systems,* vol. 1. Prentice-Hall, Englewood Cliffs, NJ, 1972.

[57] J. Bromley, J.W. Bentz, L. Bottou, I. Guyon, K.Y. LeCun, C. Moore, E. Sackinger, and R. Shah. Signature verification using a "Siamese" time delay neural network. *Intl. J. Pattern Recognition and Artificial Intelligence,* 7:669–688, 1993.

[58] D.S. Broomhead and D. Lowe. Multivariable functional interpolation and adaptive networks. *Complex Systems,* 2:321–355, 1988.

[59] J. Bruck. On the convergence properties of the Hopfield model. *Proc. IEEE,* 78:1579–1585, 1990.

[60] J. Bruck and J.W. Goodman. A generalized convergence theorem for neural networks. *IEEE Trans. Inform. Theory,* 34:1089–1092, 1988.

[61] J. Bruck and V.P. Roychowdhury. On the number of spurious memories in the Hopfield model. *IEEE Trans. Inform. Theory,* 36:393–397, 1990.

[62] A.E. Bryson and Y.C. Ho. *Applied Optimal Control.* Blaisdell, New York, 1969.

[63] T.H. Bullock, R. Orkand, and A. Grinnell. *Introduction to Nervous Systems.* W.H. Freeman, San Francisco, CA, 1977.

[64] J. Bumann and K. Schulten. Storing sequences of biased patterns in neural networks with stochastic dynamics. In R. Eckmiller and C. von der Malsburg, editors, *Neural Computers (Neuss 1987),* pp. 231–243, Springer-Verlag, Berlin/Heidelberg, 1988.

[65] C.J. Burges, J.I. Ben, J.S. Denker, Y. LeCun, and C.R. Nohl. Off-line recognition of handwritten postal words using neural networks. *Intl. J. Pattern Recognition and Artificial Intelligence,* 7: 689–704, 1993.

[66] B.J. Cain. An improved probabilistic neural network and its performance relative to other models. In *Applications of Artificial Neural Networks, Proc. SPIE,* vol. 1294, pp. 354–365, 1990.

[67] A. Canning and E. Gardner. Partially connected models of neural networks. *Journal of Physics A,* 21:3275–3284, 1988.

[68] G.A. Carpenter and S. Grossberg. Neural dynamics of category learning and recognition: attention, memory consolidation, and amnesia. In J. Davis, R. Newburgh, and E. Wegman, editors, *Brain Structure, Learning, and Memory,* AAAS Symposium Series, 1985, Westview Press, Boulder, CO, 1988.

[69] G.A. Carpenter and S. Grossberg. A massively parallel architecture for a self-organizing neural pattern recognition machine. *Computer Vision, Graphics and Image Processing,* 37:54–115, 1987.

[70] G.A. Carpenter and S. Grossberg. ART2: self-organizing of stable category recognition codes for analog input patterns. *Applied Optics,* 26:4919–4930, 1987.

[71] G.A. Carpenter and S. Grossberg. The ART of adaptive pattern recognition by self-organizing neural network. *IEEE Computer,* pp. 77–88, March 1988.

[72] M. Casdagli, M. Eubank, J.D. Farmer, and J. Gibson. State space reconstruction in the presence of noise. *Physica D,* 51:52–98, 1991.

[73] A. Cayley. A theorem on trees. *Quarterly J. Math.,* 23:376–378, 1889.

[74] S. Chen, S.F. Cowan, and P.M. Grant. Orthogonal least squares learning algorithm for radial basis function networks. *IEEE Trans. Neural Networks,* 2:302–309, 1991.

[75] D. Cheriton and R.E. Tarjan. Finding minimum spanning trees. *SIAM J. Comput.*, 5:724–742, Dec. 1976.

[76] N. Christofides. *Graph Theory: An Algorithmic Approach.* Academic Press, New York, 1975.

[77] L.O. Chua and T. Roska. The CNN paradigm. *IEEE Trans. Circuits and Systems I—Fundamental Theory and Applications,* 40:147–156, 1993.

[78] L.O. Chua, T. Roska, and P.L. Venetianer. The CNN is universal as the Turing machine. *IEEE Trans. Circuits and Systems I—Fundamental Theory and Applications,* 40:289–291, 1993.

[79] L.O. Chua and L. Yang. Cellular neural networks: theory. *IEEE Trans. Circuits and Systems,* 35:1257–1272, 1988.

[80] L.O. Chua and L. Yang. Cellular neural networks: applications. *IEEE Trans. Circuits and Systems,* 35:1273–1290, 1988.

[81] M.A. Cohen and S. Grossburg. Absolute stability of global pattern formation and parallel memory storage by competitive neural networks. *IEEE Trans. Syst., Man, and Cybernetics,* 13:815–826, 1983.

[82] S.A. Cook. On the complexity of theorem-proving procedures. In *Proc. Third Annual ACM Symposium on the Theory of Computing, Shaker Heights, OH,* pp. 151–158, Association for Computing Machinery, New York, 1971.

[83] A. Coolen and F. Fujik. A learning mechanism for invariant pattern recognition in neural networks. *Neural Networks,* 2:495–506, 1989.

[84] M. Cottrell and J.C. Fort. A stochastic model of retinotopy: a self-organizing process. *Biol. Cybern.,* 53:405–411, 1986.

[85] R. Courant and H. Robbins. *What Is Mathematics?* Oxford University Press, New York, 1941.

[86] T. Cover. Geometrical and statistical properties of systems of linear inequalities with applications to pattern recognition. *IEEE Trans. Electronic Computers,* 14:326–334, 1965.

[87] G. Cybenko. Approximation by superpositions of a sigmoidal function. *Mathematics of Control, Signals, and Systems,* 2:304–314, 1989.

[88] N. Demassieux and F. Jutand. A real-time discrete cosine tranform chip. *Digital Signal Processing,* 1:6–14, 1991.

[89] J. Denker. Neural networks refinements and extensions. In J. Denker, editor, *Neural Networks for Computing,* pp. 121–128, American Institute of Physics, New York, 1986.

[90] J. Denker, D. Schwartz, B. Wittner, S. Solla, R. Howard, L. Jackel, and J. Hopfield. Large automatic learning, rule extraction, and generalization. *Complex Systems,* 1:877–922, 1987.

[91] B. Derrida, E. Gardner, and A. Zippelius. An exactly soluble asymmetric neural network model. *Europhysics Letters,* 4:167–173, 1987.

[92] S. Deutsch and A. Deutsch. *Understanding the Nervous System.* IEEE Press, New York, 1993.

[93] E.D. Dickmanns. Visual dynamic scene understanding exploiting high-level spatio-temporal models. In *Proc. 10th Intl. Conf. Pattern Recognition, Atlantic City, NJ, June 16–21, 1990.* vol. 2, pp. 373–378, IEEE Computer Society Press, Washington, DC, 1990.

[94] E.D. Dickmanns. A general dynamic vision architecture for UGV and UAV. *Applied Intelligence,* 2:251–270, 1992.

[95] E.D. Dickmanns, B. Mysliwetz, and T. Christians. An integrated spatio-temporal approach to automatic visual guidance of autonomous vehicles. *IEEE Trans. Systems, Man, and Cybernetics,* 20:1273–1284, 1990.

[96] S. Diederich and M. Opper. Learning of correlated patterns by local learning rules. *Phys. Review Lett.,* 58:949–953, 1987.

[97] E.W. Dijkstra. A note on two problems in connection with graphs. *Numerische Math.,* 1:269–271, 1959.

[98] V. Dotsenko. Neural networks: translation-rotation, and scale-invariant pattern recognition. *J. Phys. A: Math. Gen.,* 21:783–787, 1988.

[99] J.E. Dowling. *The Retina: An Approachable Part of the Brain.* Belknap Press of Harvard University Press, Cambridge, MA, 1987.

[100] D.Z. Du and F.K. Hwang. An approach for proving lower bounds: solution of Gilbert-Pollak's conjecture on Steiner trees. In *Proc. 31st Symposium on Foundations of Computer Science,* pp. 76–85, IEEE Computer Society Press, Los Alamitos, CA, 1990.

[101] R. Durbin and D.E. Rumelhart. Product units: a computationally powerful and biologically plausible extension to the backpropagation networks. *Neural Computation,* 1:133–142, 1989.

[102] R. Durbin and D. Willshaw. An analog approach to the traveling salesman problem using the elastic net method. *Nature,* 326: 689–691, 1987.

[103] D.A. Durfee and F.S. Shoucair. Comparison of floating gate neural network memory cells in standard VLSI CMOS technology. *IEEE Trans. Neural Networks,* 3:347–353, 1992.

[104] R.A. Dwyer. Higher-dimensional Voronoi diagrams in linear expected time. In *Discrete and Computational Geometry,* vol. 6, pp. 343–367, Springer-Verlag, New York, 1991.

[105] H. Edelsbrunner. *Algorithms in Combinatorial Geometry.* Springer-Verlag, New York, 1987.

[106] E. Edelson. Conduits for cell/cell communication. *MOSAIC, National Science Foundation,* 21(2):48–56, March 1990.

[107] S.E. Fahlman. Fast-learning variations on backpropagation: an empirical study. In G. Hinton, D. Touretzky, and T. Sejnowski, editors, *Proc. 1988 Connectionist Models Summer School, Pittsburgh,* pp. 38–51, Morgan Kaufmann, San Mateo, CA, 1989.

[108] D.C. Farden. Tracking properties of adaptive signal processing algorithms. *IEEE Trans. Acoust., Speech and Signal Processing,* ASSP-29:439–446, 1981.

[109] N.H. Farhat. Optoelectronic analogs of self-programming neural nets: architectures and methods for implementing fast stochastic learning by simulated annealing. *Applied Optics,* 26:5093–5103, 1987.

[110] N.H. Farhat. Optoelectronic neural networks and learning machines. *IEEE Magazine on Circuits and Devices,* 5:32–41, 1989.

[111] I. Fary. On straight line representations of planar graphs. *Acta Sci. Math. (Szeged),* 11:229–233, 1948.

[112] J.A. Feldman and D.H. Ballard. Connectionist models and their properties. *Cognitive Science,* 6:205–254, 1982.

[113] S.Y. Foo, A.R. Anderson, and Y. Takefuji. Analog components for the VLSI of neural networks. *IEEE Magazine on Circuits and Devices,* 6:18–26, 1990.

[114] R.L. Francis. A note on the optimum location of new machines in existing plant layouts. *J. Industrial Engineering,* 14:57–59, 1963.

[115] R.L. Francis, L.F. McGinnis, Jr., and J.A. White. *Facility Layout and Location, An Analytical Approach,* 2nd edn., Prentice Hall, Englewood Cliffs, NJ, 1992.

[116] M. Frean. The upstart algorithm: a method for constructing and training feedforward networks. *Neural Computation,* 2:198–209, 1990.

[117] K Fukunaga. *Introduction to Statistical Pattern Recognition.* Academic Press, New York, 1972.

[118] K. Fukushima. Neocognitron: a self-organizing neural network model for a mechanism of pattern recognition unaffected by shift in position. *Biological Cybernetics,* 36:193–202, 1980.

[119] K. Fukushima. A neural network for visual pattern recognition. *IEEE Computer,* 21(3):65–75, March 1988.

[120] K. Fukushima. Analysis of the process of visual pattern recognition by the neocognitron. *Neural Networks,* 2:413–420, 1989.

[121] K. Fukushima, S. Miyake, and T. Ito. Neocognitron: a neural network model for a mechanism of visual pattern recognition. *IEEE Trans. Systems, Man, and Cybernetics,* 13:826–834, 1983.

[122] K. Funahashi. On the approximate realization of continuous mappings by neural networks. *Neural Networks,* 2:183–192, 1989.

[123] S.I. Gallant. Perceptron-based learning algorithms. *IEEE Trans. Neural Networks,* 1:179–191, 1990.

[124] M.R. Garey and D. Johnson. *Computers and Intractability: A Guide to the Theory of NP-Completeness.* W.H. Freeman, San Francisco, CA, 1979.

[125] M.R. Garey and D.S. Johnson. The rectilinear Steiner tree problem is NP-complete. *SIAM J. Appl. Math.,* 32(4), June 1977.

[126] A.K. Garga and N.K. Bose. A neural network approach to the construction of Delaunay tessellation of points in $\mathbb{R}^n$. *IEEE Trans. Circuits and Systems, Part I,* 41:611–613, 1994.

[127] A.K. Garga and N.K. Bose. Structure training of neural networks. In *Proc. IEEE Intl. Conf. Neural Networks,* IEEE World Congress on Computational Intelligence, Orlando, FL, June 26 to July 2, 1994, vol. 1, pp. 239–244, The IEEE, Inc., Piscataway, NJ, 1994.

[128] M.S. Gazzaniga. Organization of the human brain. *Science, AAAS,* 245:947–952, Sept. 1, 1989.

[129] T. Geszti. *Physical models of neural networks.* World Scientific, Singapore, 1990.

[130] A. Gibbons and W. Rytter. *Efficient Parallel Algorithms.* Cambridge University Press, Cambridge, Great Britain, 1988.

[131] E.N. Gilbert and H.O. Pollak. Steiner minimal trees. *SIAM J. Appl. Math.,* 16:1–29, 1968.

[132] C.L. Giles and T. Maxwell. Learning, invariance, and generalization in high-order neural networks. *Applied Optics,* 26:4972–4978, 1987.

[133] F. Giroso and T. Poggio. Representation properties of networks; Kolmogorov's theorem is irrelevant. *Neural Computation,* 1:465–469, 1989.

[134] D. Goldfarb and M.J. Todd. Chapter 2: Linear programming. In G.L. Nemhauser, A.H. G.R. Kan, and M.J. Todd, editors, *Optimization,* pp. 73–170, North-Holland, Amsterdam, 1989.

[135] M. Golea and M. Marchand. A growth algorithm for neural network decision trees. *Europhys. Letters,* 12:205–210, 1990.

[136] S.W. Golomb. *Shift Register Sequences.* Aegean Park Press, Laguna Hills, CA, 1982.

[137] H.P. Graf, L.D. Jackel, R.E. Howard, B. Straughn, J.S. Denker, W. Hubbard, D.M. Tennant, and D. Schwartz. VLSI implementation of a neural network memory with several hundreds of neurons. In J.S. Denker, editor, *Neural Networks for Computing (Snowbird 1986),* pp. 182–187, American Institute of Physics, New York, 1986.

[138] S. Grossberg. Adaptive pattern classification and universal recoding: I. Parallel development and coding of neural feature detectors. *Biological Cybernetics,* 23:121–134, 1976.

[139] S. Grossberg. Adaptive pattern classification and universal recoding: II. Feedback, expectation, olfaction, illusions. *Biological Cybernetics,* 23:187–202, 1976.

[140] S. Grossberg. Competitive learning: from interactive activation to adaptive resonance. *Cognitive Science,* 11:23–63, 1987.

[141] B. Gruenbaum and G.C. Shephard. *Tilings and Patterns.* W.H. Freeman and Co., New York, 1986.

[142] A. Guez, V. Protopopsecu, and J. Barhen. On the stability, storage capacity, and design of nonlinear continuous neural networks. *IEEE Trans. Systems, Man, and Cybernetics,* 18:80–87, 1988.

[143] K. Gutzmann. Combinatorial optimization using a continuous state Boltzmann machine. In *IEEE First Intl. Conf. Neural Networks,* vol. III, pp. 721–734, San Diego, 1987.

[144] R.K. Guy. Latest results on crossing number. In *Recent Trends in Graph Theory,* pp. 143–156. Springer-Verlag, New York, 1971.

[145] J.M. Hakkarainen, J.J. Little, H. Lee, and J.L. Wyatt. Interaction of algorithm and implementation for analog VLSI stereo vision. In B.P. Mathur and C. Koch, editors, *Visual Information Processing: From Neurons to Chips, Proc. SPIE,* vol. 1473, pp. 173–184, 1991.

[146] P.L. Hammer and S. Rudeanu. *Boolean Methods in Operations Research and Related Areas.* Springer-Verlag, New York, 1968.

[147] H. Hammerstrom. Working with neural networks. *IEEE Spectrum,* 41:46–53, 1993.

[148] M. Hanan. On Steiner's problem with rectilinear distance. *SIAM J. Appl. Math.,* 14(2):255–265, 1966.

[149] F. Harary. *Graph Theory.* Addison-Wesley, Reading, MA, 1969.

[150] J.G. Harris, C. Koch, E. Staats, and J. Luo. Analog hardware for detecting discontinuities in early vision. *Intl. J. Computer Vision,* 4:211–223, 1990.

[151] S. Haykin and C. Deng. Classification of radar clutter using neural networks. *IEEE Trans. Neural Networks,* 2:589–600, 1991.

[152] D.O. Hebb. *Organization of Behavior.* Wiley, New York, 1949.

[153] R. Hecht-Nielsen. Nearest matched filter classification of spatiotemporal patterns. *Applied Optics,* 26:1892–1899, 1987.

[154] R. Hecht-Nielsen. Neurocomputing: picking the human brain. *IEEE Spectrum,* 25:36–42, 1988.

[155] R. Hecht-Nielsen. *Neurocomputing.* Addison-Wesley, Reading, MA, 1990.

[156] M. Held and R. Karp. A dynamic programming approach to sequencing problems. *J. SIAM,* 10:196–210, 1962.

[157] M. Held and R.M. Karp. The traveling-salesman problem and minimum spanning trees: part 2. In *Mathematical Programming,* vol. 1, pp. 6–25. North-Holland, Amsterdam, 1971.

[158] J. Hertz, A. Krogh, and R.G. Palmer. *Introduction to the Theory of Neural Computation.* Addison-Wesley, Reading, MA, 1991.

[159] M.W. Hirsch. Convergent activation dynamics in continuous time network. *Neural Networks,* 2:331–349, 1989.

[160] A.L. Hodgkin and A.F. Huxley. A quantitative description of membrane current and its application to conduction and excitation in nerve. *J. Physiology, London,* 117:500–544, 1952.

[161] M. Holler, S. Tam, H. Castro, and R. Benson. An electrically trainable artificial neural network (ETANN) with 10240 "floating gate" synapses. In *Proc. IEEE Intl. Joint Conf. Neural Networks, Washington, DC, 18–22 June 1989,* vol. 2, pp. 191–196, The IEEE, Inc., Piscataway, NJ, 1989.

[162] J.J. Hopfield. Neural networks and physical systems with emergent collective computational abilities. *Proc. Natl. Acad. Sci. USA,* 79:2554–2558, 1982.

[163] J.J. Hopfield. Neurons with graded response have collective computational properties like those of two-state neurons. *Proc. Natl. Acad. Sci. USA,* 81:3088–3092, 1984.

[164] J.J. Hopfield and D.W. Tank. Neural computations of decisions in optimization problems. *Biological Cybernetics,* 52:141–152, 1985.

[165] J.J. Hopfield and D.W. Tank. Computing with neural circuits: a model. *Science,* 233:625–633, 1986.

[166] K. Hornik, M. Stinchombe, and H. White. Multilayer feedforward network are univeral approximators. *Neural Networks,* 2:359–366, 1989.

[167] K.D. Hsu and D. Psaltis. Experimental demonstration of optical neural computers. In D.Z. Anderson, editor, *Neural Information Processing Systems, Denver, 1987,* pp. 377–386, American Institute of Physics, New York, 1987.

[168] C.L. Huang. Contour image sequence compression through motion analysis and hybrid coding method. *Multidimensional Systems and Signal Processing,* 3:241–266, 1992.

[169] S.C. Huang and Y.F. Huang. Bounds on the number of hidden neurons in multilayer perceptrons. *IEEE Trans. Neural Networks,* 2:47–55, 1991.

[170] D.H. Hubel and T.N. Wiesel. Brain mechanisms of vision. *Scientific American,* 241:150–162, September, 1979.

[171] J. Hutchinson, C. Koch, J. Luo, and C. Mead. Computing motion using analog and binary resistive networks. *IEEE Computer,* 21:52–63, 1988.

[172] F.K. Hwang. On Steiner minimal trees with rectilinear distance. *SIAM J. Appl. Math.,* 30:104–114, 1976.

[173] R. Iltis and R.A. Ting. Calculating association probablities using parallel Boltzmann machines. *IEEE Trans. Neural Networks,* 4(2):221–233, March 1989.

[174] B. Irie and S. Miyake. Capabilities of three-layered perceptrons. In *IEEE Conf. Neural Networks, San Diego, 1988,* vol. 1, pp. 641–648, The IEEE, Inc., Piscataway, NJ, 1988.

[175] R.A. Jacobs. Increased rate of convergence through learning rate adaptation. *Neural Networks,* 1:295–307, 1988.

[176] E. Jen, editor, *1989 Lectures in Complex Systems.* Addison-Wesley, Redwood City, CA, 1990.

[177] H.F. Jensen. An upper bound for the rectilinear crossing number of the complete graph. *J. Combinatorial Theory,* 10B:212–216, 1971.

[178] E.M. Johansson, F.U. Dowla, and D.M. Goodman. Backpropagation learning for multilayer feedforward neural networks using the conjugate gradient method. *Intl. J. Neural Systems,* 2(4):291–301, 1992.

[179] J.S. Judd. *Neural Network Design and the Complexity of Learning.* MIT Press, Cambridge, MA, 1990. The book is based on the author's Ph.D. thesis in 1988.

[180] B.L. Kalman and S.C. Kwasny. A superior error function for training neural networks. In *Proc. Intl. Joint Conf. Neural Networks, Washington, DC, 1991.* pp. 49–52, The IEEE, Inc., Piscataway, NJ, 1991.

[181] B. Kamgar-Parsi and B. Kamgar-Parsi. Hopfield model and optimization problems. In H. Wechsler, editor, *Neural Networks for Perception,* Academic Press, San Diego, CA, 1992.

[182] Y. Kamp and M. Hasler. *Recursive Neural Networks for Associative Memory.* Wiley, Chichester, England, 1990.

[183] I. Kanter and H. Sompolinsky. Associative recall of memory without errors. *Phys. Review A,* 35:380–392, 1987.

[184] N. Karmarkar. A new polynomial time algorithm for linear programming. *Combinatorica,* 4:373–395, 1984.

[185] D.G. Kelly. Stability in contractive nonlinear neural networks. *IEEE Trans. Biomed. Eng.,* 37:231–242, 1990.

[186] A. Kerschenbaum and R. Van Slyke. Computing minimum spanning trees efficiently. In *Proc. 25th Ann. Conf. ACM,* pp. 518–527, 1972.

[187] L.G. Khachian. A polynomial algorithm in linear programming. *Soviet Math. Doklady,* 20:191–194, 1984.

[188] R.M. Kil. Parameter estimation of a network with kernel functions of bounds and locality. In *Science of Artificial Neural Networks II, Proc. SPIE,* vol. 1966, pp. 284–295, 1993.

[189] S. Kirkpatrick, C.D. Gelatt Jr., and M.P. Vecchi. Optimization by simulated annealing. *Science,* 220:671–680, 1983.

[190] K. Kishimoto and S. Amari. Existence and stability of local excitations in neural fields. *J. Math. Biol.,* 7:303–318, 1979.

[191] D. Kleinfeld. Sequential state generation by model neural networks. *Proc. Natl. Acad. Sci., USA,* 83:9469–9473, 1986.

[192] D. Kleinfeld. and H. Sompolinsky. Associative network models for central pattern generators. In C. Koch and I. Segev, editors, *Methods in Neuronal Modeling: From Synapses to Networks,* MIT Press, Cambridge, MA, 1989.

[193] D.J. Kleitman. The crossing number of $K_{5,n}$. *J. Combinatorial Theory,* 9:315–332, 1970.

[194] S. Knerr, L. Personnaz, and G. Dreyfus. Handwritten digit recognition by neural networks with single-layer training. *IEEE Trans. Neural Networks,* 3:962–968, 1992.

[195] E.I. Knudsen, S. du Lac, and S.D. Esterly. Computational maps in the brain. *Annual Rev. Neuroscience,* 10:41–65, 1987.

[196] C. Koch. Implementing early vision algorithms in analog networks: an overview. In H.G. Schuster, editor, *Applications of Neural Networks,* VCH, Weinheim, Germany, 1992.

[197] T. Kohonen. Correlation matrix memories. *IEEE Trans. Computers,* 21:353–358, 1972.

[198] T. Kohonen. Self-organized formation of topologically correct feature maps. *Biological Cybernetics,* 43:59–69, 1982.

[199] T. Kohonen. The neural phonetic typewriter. *IEEE Computer,* 21:11–22, March 1988. (Also in J. Anderson, A. Pellionisz, and E. Rosenfeld, editors, *Neurocomputing 2,* pp. 653–668, MIT Press, Cambridge, MA, 1990.)

[200] T. Kohonen. *Self-Organization and Associative Memory,* 3rd edn., Springer-Verlag, Berlin, 1989.

[201] A.N.K. Kolmogorov. On the representation of continuous functions of many variables by superposition of continuous functons of one variable and addition. *Dokl. Akad. Nauk SSSR,* 114:953–956, 1957.

[202] B. Kosko. Adaptive bidirectional associative memories. *Applied Optics,* 26:4947–4860, 1987.

[203] B. Kosko. Bidirectional associative memories. *IEEE Trans. Systems, Man, and Cybernetics,* 18: 49–60, 1988.

[204] B. Kosko. *Neural Networks and Fuzzy Systems.* Prentice Hall, Englewood Cliffs, NJ, 1992.

[205] B. Kosko, editor, *Neural Networks for Signal Processing,* Prentice-Hall, Englewood Cliffs, NJ, 1992.

[206] R. Kree and A. Zippelius. Recognition of topological features of graphs and images in neural networks. *J. Phys. A: Math. Gen.,* 21:813–818, 1988.

[207] J. Kruskal, Jr. On the shortest spanning subtree of a graph and the traveling salesman problem. *Bell Syst. Tech. J.,* pp. 48–50, 1956.

[208] H.W. Kuhn. The Hungarian method for the assignment problem. *Naval Research Logistics Quarterly,* 2:83-97, 1955.

[209] H.W. Kuhn. "Steiner's" problem revisited. In G.B. Dantzig and B.C. Eaves, editors, *Studies in Mathematics, 10, Studies in Optimization,* pp. 52–70. The Mathemetical Association of America, 1975.

[210] S. Kullback. *Information Theory and Statistics.* Wiley, New York, 1959.

[211] K.J. Lang and M.J. Witbrock. Learning to tell two spirals apart. In G. Hinton, D. Touretzky, and T. Sejnowski, editors, *Proc. 1988 Connectionist Models Summer School, Pittsburgh,* pp. 52–59, Morgan Kaufmann, San Mateo, CA. 1989.

[212] C.G. Langton. *Artificial life: Proc. Interdisc. Workshop on the Synthesis and Simulation of Living Systems, 1987, Los Alamos, New Mexico.* Addison-Wesley, Redwood City, CA, 1989.

[213] C.G. Langton. *Artificial Life II: Proc. Interdisc. Workshop on the Synthesis and Simulation of Living Systems, 1990, Los Alamos, New Mexico.* Addison-Wesley, Redwood City, CA, 1992.

[214] Y. Le Cun. Une procedure d'apprentissage pour réseau à seuil assymétrique. In *In Cognitiva 85: À la Frontière de l'Intelligence Artificielle des Sciences de la Connaissance des Neurosciences*, pp. 599–604, CESTA, Paris, 1985.

[215] Y. Le Cun, B. Boser, J. Denker, D. Henderson, R. Howard, W. Hubbard, and L. Jackel. Backpropagation applied to handwritten ZIP code recognition. *Neural Computation*, 1:541–551, 1989.

[216] Y. Le Cun, S. Denker J, and S.A. Solla. Optimal brain damage. In D. Touretzky, editor, *Advances in Neural Information Processing Systems 2*, pp. 598–605, Morgan Kaufmann, San Mateo, CA, 1990.

[217] B.W. Lee, B.J. Sheu, and H. Yang. Analog floating-gate synapses for general-purpose VLSI neural computation. *IEEE Trans. Circuits and Systems*, 38:654–658, 1991.

[218] D.T. Lee and C. K Wong. Voronoi diagrams in $l_1(l_{inf})$ metrics with 2-dimensional storage applications. *SIAM J. Computing*, 9:200–211, 1980.

[219] J.H. Lee, N.K. Bose, and F.K. Hwang. Use of Steiner's problem in suboptimal routing in rectilinear metric. *IEEE Trans. CAS*, 23(7):470–476, July 1976.

[220] T.C. Lee and A.M. Peterson. Adaptive vector quantization using a self-development neural network. *IEEE J. Selected Areas in Communications*, 8:1458–1471, 1990.

[221] Tsu-Chang Lee. *Structure Level Adaptation for Artificial Neural Networks*. Kluwer Academic Publishers, Boston, MA, 1991.

[222] M. Lesho, V. Lin, A. Pinkus, and S. Schocken. Multilayer feedforward networks with a nonpolynomial activation function can approximate any function. *Neural Networks*, 6:861–867, 1993.

[223] A.U. Levin and K.S. Narendra. Control of nonlinear dynamical systems using neural networks: controllability and stabilization. *IEEE Trans. on Neural Networks*, 4:192–206, 1993.

[224] J.H. Li and A.N. Michel. Analysis and synthesis of a class of neural networks: linear systems operating on a closed hypercube. *IEEE Trans. Circuits and Systems*, 36:1405–1422, 1989.

[225] P. Liang. Problem decomposition and subgoaling in artificial neural networks. *Proc. IEEE Conf. Syst., Man, and Cybernetics, Nov. 4–7, 1990, Los Angeles, CA*, pp. 178–181, The IEEE, Piscataway, NJ, 1990.

[226] P. Liang. Design of artificial neural networks based on the principle of divide-and-conquer. In *Proc. IEEE Intl. Symp. on Circuits and Systems, Singapore, June, 1991*, pp. 1319–1322, The IEEE Press, Piscataway, NJ, 1991.

[227] P. Liang and N. Jamali. Artificial neural networks with quasi-polynomial synapses and product synpatic contacts. *Biol. Cybern.*, 70:163–175, 1993.

[228] R. Linsker. From basic network principles to neural architecture. In *Proc. Natl. Acad. Sci., USA*, vol. 83, pp. 7508–7512, 8390–8394, 8779–8783, 1986.

[229] R. Linsker. Self-organization in a percpetual network. *IEEE Computer*, pp. 105-117, March 1988.

[230] R.P. Lippmann. An introduction to computing with neural nets. IEEE ASSP Magazine, pp. 4–22, April 1987.

[231] R.P. Lippmann. Review of neural networks for speech recognition. *Neural Computation*, 1:1–38, 1989.

[232] J.D.C. Little, K.G. Murty, D.W. Sweeney, and C. Karel. An algorithm for the traveling salesman problem. *J. Oper. Res.*, 11:972–989, Nov. 1963.

[233] W.A. Little and G.L. Shaw. A statistical theory of short and long term memory. *Behavioral Biology*, 14:115–133, 1975.

[234] W.A. Little and G.L. Shaw. Analytical study of the memory storage capacity of a neural network. *Mathematical Biosciences*, 39:281–290, 1978.

[235] H. Loberman and A. Weinberger. Formal procedures for connecting terminals with a minimum total wire length. *J. ACM*, 4:428–437, October 1957.

[236] A.L. Loeb. *Space Structures*. Addison-Wesley, Reading, MA, 1976.

[237] G.E. Loeb. The functional replacement of the middle ear. *Scientific American*, vol. 252, no. 2: 104–111, February, 1985.

[238] J.B. Lont and W. Guggenbuhl. Analog CMOS implementation of a multilayer perceptron with nonlinear synapses. *IEEE Trans. Neural Networks*, 3:457–465, 1992.

[239] G.G. Lorentz. The 13th problem of Hilbert. In *Proc. Symposia in Pure Math*, vol. 28, pp. 419–429. American Mathematical Society, 1976.

[240] C. Lund and M. Yannakakis. On the hardness of approximating minimization problems. In *Proc. 25th ACM Symposium on the Theory of Computing*, pp. 286–293, 1993.

[241] R.J. Macgregor. *Neural and Brain Modeling*. Academic Press, London, 1987.

[242] D.J.C. MacKay and K.D. Miller. Analysis of Linsker's application of Hebbian rules to linear networks. *Network: Computation in Neural Systems,* 1:257–297, 1990.

[243] B.B. Mandelbrot. *The Fractal Geometry of Nature*. Freeman, San Francisco, 1982.

[244] M. Marchand, M. Golea, and P. Rujan. A convergence theorem for sequential learning in two-layer perceptrons. *Europhys. Letters,* 11:487–492, 1990.

[245] A. Masaki, Y. Hirai, and M. Yamada. Neural networks in CMOS: a case study. *IEEE Magazine on Circuits and Devices,* 6:13–17, 1990.

[246] O. Matan, H.S. Baird, J. Bromley, C.J.C. Burges, J.S. Denker, L.D. Jackel, Y. Le Cun, E.P.D. Pednault, W.D. Satterfield, C.E. Stenard, and T.J. Thompson. Reading handwritten digits—a ZIP code recognition system. *IEEE Computer,* 25:59–63, July 1992.

[247] K. Matsuoka. Stability conditions for nonlinear continuous neural networks with asymmetric connection weights. *Neural Networks,* 5:495–500, 1992.

[248] H. Maturana and F. Varela. *Autopoiesis and Cognition*. D. Reidel Publishing Company, Dordrecht, Holland, 1980.

[249] J. Mayer. Decomposition de trois graphes planaires. *J. Combinatorial Theory,* 13:71, 1972.

[250] W.S. McCulloch and W.A. Pitts. A logical calculus of the ideas immanent in neural nets. *Bull. Math. Biophysics,* 5:115–133, 1943.

[251] R.J. McEliece, E.C. Posner, E.R. Rodemich, and S.S. Venkatesh. The capacity of the Hopfield associative memory. *IEEE Trans. Inform. Theory,* 33:461–482, 1987.

[252] T. McKenna, J. Davis, and S.F. Zornetzer, editors. *Single Neuron Computation*. Academic Press, San Diego, CA, 1992.

[253] C. Mead. *Analog VLSI and Neural Systems*. Addison-Wesley, Reading, MA, 1989.

[254] C.A. Mead and M.A. Mahowald. A silicon model of early visual processing. *Neural Networks,* 1:91–97, 1988.

[255] Z.A. Melzak. On the problem of Steiner. *Canadian Math. Bull.,* 4:143-148, 1961.

[256] N. Metropolis, A.W. Rosenbluth, M.N. Rosenbluth, A.H. Tellor, and E. Tellor. Equation of state calculations for fast computing machines. *J. of Chem. Phys.,* 21:1087–1092, 1953.

[257] M. Mezard and J. Nadal. Learning in feedforward layered networks: the tiling algorithm. *J. Phys. A,* 22:2191–2203, 1990.

[258] D.A. Miller and S.W. Zucker. Efficient simplex-like methods for equilibria of nonsymmetric analog networks. *Neural Computation,* 4:167–190, 1992.

[259] W.T. Miller III, F.H. Glantz, and L.G. Kraft III. CMAC: an associative neural network alternative to backpropagation. *Proc. IEEE,* 78(10):1561–1567, October 1991.

[260] M. Minsky. *Computation: Finite and Infinite Machines*. Prentice-Hall, Englewood Cliffs, N.J., 1967.

[261] M.L. Minsky and S.A. Papert. *Perceptron*. Expanded edn. MIT Press, Cambridge, MA, 1988 (first published in 1969).

[262] J. Moody and C.J. Darken. Fast learning in networks of locally-tuned processing units. *Neural Computation,* 1:281–294, 1989.

[263] B. Moore. ART 1 and pattern clustering. In G. Hinton, D. Touretzky, and T. Sejnowski, editors, *Proc. 1988 Connectionist Models Summer School, Pittsburgh,* pp. 174–185, Morgan Kaufmann, San Mateo, CA, 1988.

[264] N. Morgan. Big dumb neural nets: a working brute force approach to speech recognition. In *Proc. IEEE World Congress on Computational Intelligence, Orlando, Florida, June 1994,* vol. 7, pp. 4462–4465, IEEE Computer Society Press, Los Alamitos, CA, 1994.

[265] D.J. Mortana and L. Davis. Training feedforward networks using genetic algorithms. In *Proceedings of 11th Intl. Joint Conf. on Artificial Intelligence (IJCAI), Detroit, MI, 1989,* pp. 762–767, Morgan Kaufmann, San Mateo, CA, 1989.

[266] B. Mueller and J. Reinhardt. *Neural Networks*. Springer-Verlag, Berlin/Heidelberg, 1990.

[267] J. Munkres. Algorithm for the assignment and transportation problems. *J. SIAM,* 5:32–38, 1957.

[268] S. Muroga and I. Toda. Lower bound of the number of threshold functions. *IEEE Trans. Electronic Computers,* EC-15:805, 1966.

[269] O.J. Murphy. Nearest-neighbor pattern classification perceptrons. *Proc. IEEE,* 78:1595–1598, Oct. 1990.

[270] M.T. Musavi, W. Ahmed, K.H. Chan, K.B. Faris, and D.M. Hummels. On the training of radial basis function classifiers. *Neural Networks,* 5:595–603, 1992.

[271] K.S. Karendra and K. Parthasarathy. Identification and control of dynamical systems using neural networks. *IEEE Trans. Neural Networks,* 1(1):4–27, March 1990.

[272] B.K. Natarajan. *Machine Learning.* Morgan Kaufmann, San Mateo, CA, 1991.

[273] N.J. Nilsson. *The Mathematical Foundations of Learning Machines.* Morgan Kaufmann, San Mateo, CA, 1965.

[274] T. Nitta. An analysis on decision boundaries in the complex-backpropagation network. In *Proc. IEEE World Congress on Computational Intelligence,* vol. 2, pp. 934–939, Orlando, FL, June 1994, IEEE Computer Society Press, Los Alamitos, CA, 1994.

[275] S.J. Nowlan and G.E. Hinton. Simplifying neural networks by soft weight-sharing. *Neural Computation,* 4:473–493, 1992.

[276] E. Oja. Neural networks, principal components, and subspaces. *Intl. J. Neural Systems,* 1:61–68, 1989.

[277] A. Okabe, B. Boots, and K. Sugihara. *Spatial Tessellations: Concepts and Applications of Voronoi Diagrams.* Wiley, New York, N.Y., 1992.

[278] S. Orey. *Lecture Notes on Limit Theorems for Markov Chain Transition Probablities.* Van Nostrand Reinhold, London, 1971.

[279] A. Owens. On the biplanar crossing number. *IEEE Trans. Circuit Theory,* 18:277–280, March 1971.

[280] N.H. Packard, J.P. Crutchfield, J.D. Farmer, and R.S. Shaw. Geometry from a time series. *Phys. Rev. Letters,* 45:712–716, 1980.

[281] F.P. Palermo. A network minimization problem. *IBM J.,* pp. 335–337, Oct. 1961.

[282] G. Palm. On associative memory. *Biol. Cybernetics,* 36:19–31, 1980.

[283] Yok-Han Pao. *Adaptive Pattern Recognition and Neural Networks.* Addison-Wesley, Reading, MA, 1989.

[284] C.H. Papadimitriou and K. Steiglitz. *Combinatorial Optimization: Algorithms and Complexity.* Prentice-Hall, Englewood Cliffs, NJ, 1982.

[285] A. Papoulis. *Probability, Random Variables, and Stochastic Processes,* 3rd edn. McGraw-Hill, New York, 1991.

[286] J. Park and I.W. Sandberg. Universal approximation using radial-basis-function networks. *Neural Computation,* 3:246–257, 1991.

[287] D.B. Parker. Learning logic. *Technical Report TR-47,* Center for Computational Research in Economics and Management Sciences, MIT, 1985.

[288] D.B. Parker. Optimal algorithms for adaptive networks: second-order backpropagation, second-order direct propagation, and second-order Hebbian learning. In *Proc. First IEEE Intl. Conf. Neural Networks,* San Diego, 1987, pp. 593–600, The IEEE Inc. Piscataway, NJ, 1987.

[289] B.A. Pearlmutter. Learning state space trajectories in recurrent neural networks. *Neural Computation,* 1:263–269, 1989.

[290] M. Pechanec and N.K. Bose. Recursive construction and analysis of planar Voronoi diagram in l_1 metric. *Proceedings of Conference on Information Sciences and Systems,* The Johns Hopkins University, Baltimore, MD, March 1995.

[291] R. Penrose. *The Emperor's New Mind.* Oxford University Press, Oxford, 1989.

[292] L. Personnaz, I. Guyon, and G. Dreyfus. Collective computation properties of neural networks: new learning mechanisms. *Phys. Rev. A,* 34:4217–4228, 1986.

[293] C. Peterson and J.R. Anderson. A mean field theory learning algorithm for neural networks. *Complex Systems,* 1:995–1019, 1987.

[294] C. Peterson, J.D. Keeler, and E. Hartman. An optoelectronic architecture for multilayer learning in a single photorefractive crystal. *Neural Computation,* 2:25–34, 1990.

[295] C. Peterson and B. Soderberg. A new method for mapping optimization problem onto neural networks. *Intl. J. Neural Systems,* 1:3–22, 1989.

[296] J.C. Picard and H.D. Ratliff. Minimum cuts and related problems. *Networks,* 5:357–370, 1974.

[297] F.J. Pineda. Generalization of back-propagation to recurrent neural networks. *Phys. Rev. Letters,* 59:2229–2232, 1987.

[298] F.J. Pineda. Dynamics and architecture for neural computation. *J. Complexity,* 4:216–245, 1988.

[299] F.J. Pineda. Recurrent back-propagation and the dynamical approach to adaptive neural computation. *Neural Computation,* 1:161–172, 1989.

[300] D.A. Pomerleau. ALVINN: an autonomous land vehicle in a neural network. In D. Touretzky, editor, *Advances in Neural Information Processing Systems I,* pp. 305–313. Morgan Kaufmann, San Mateo, CA, 1989.

[301] D.A. Pomerleau. *Neural Network Perception for Mobile Robot Guidance.* Ph.D. thesis, School of Computer Science, Carnegie-Mellon University, 1992. Also published by Kluwer Academic Publishers, Boston, MA, 1993.

[302] M.B. Pour-El and I. Richards. The wave equation with computable initial data such that its unique solution is not computable. *Adv. Math.,* 39:215–239, 1981.

[303] F.P. Preparata and M.I. Shamos. *Computational Geometry.* Springer-Verlag, Berlin, 1985.

[304] R.C. Prim. Shortest connection networks and some generalizations. *Bell Syst. Tech. J.,* 36:428–437, 1957.

[305] N. Qian and T.J. Sejnowski. Predicting the secondary structure of globular proteins using neural network models. *J. of Molecular Biol.,* 202:865–884, 1988.

[306] P. Raghavan. Learning in threshold networks. In *Proc. First Workshop on Computational Learning Theory,* pp. 19–27. Morgan Kaufmann, San Mateo, CA, 1988.

[307] U. Ramacher and U. Rueckert, editors. *VLSI Design of Neural Networks.* Kluwer Academic Publisher, Norwell, MA, 1991.

[308] C.R. Rao and S.K. Mitra. *Generalized Inverse of Matrices and Its Applications.* Wiley, New York, 1971.

[309] R.A. Reale and T.J. Imig. Tonotopic organization in auditory cortex of cat. *J. Comp. Neurol.,* 192:265–291, 1980.

[310] C.N. Reeke, Jr., O. Sporns, and G.M. Edelman. Synthetic neural modeling: The "Darwin" series of recognition automata. *Proc. IEEE,* 78:1498–1530, 1990.

[311] E.M. Reingold, J. Nievergelt, and N. Deo. *Combinatorial Algorithms.* Prentice-Hall, Englewood Cliffs, NJ, 1977.

[312] A. Renyi. *Probability Theory.* North-Holland, Amsterdam, 1962.

[313] U. Riedel, R. Kuhn, and J.L. van Hemmen. Temporal sequences and chaos in neural nets. *Phys. Rev. A,* 38:1105–1108, 1988.

[314] H. Ritter and K. Schulten. On the stationary state of Kohonen's self-organizing sensory mapping. *Biol. Cybernetics,* 54:99–106, 1986.

[315] H. Ritter and K. Schulten. Convergence properties of Kohonen's topology conserving maps: fluctuations, stability, and dimension selection. *Biol. Cybernetics,* 60:59–71, 1988.

[316] H. Ritter and K. Schulten. Kohonen's self-organizing maps: exploring their computational capablilities. In *Proc. IEEE Intl. Conf. Neural Networks, San Diego, 1988,* vol. 1, pp. 109–116, The IEEE, Inc., Piscataway NJ, 1988.

[317] A.J. Robinson and F. Fallside. Static and dynamic error propagation networks with applications to speech coding. In D.Z. Anderson, editor, *Neural Information Processing Systems,* pp. 632–641, American Institute of Physics, New York, 1988.

[318] R. Rohwer. The moving targets training algorithm. In D.S. Touretzky, editor, *Neural Information Processing Systems II,* pp. 558–565, Denver, 1989.

[319] R. Rohwer and B. Forrest. Training time-dependence in neural networks. In *IEEE First Intl. Conf. Neural Networks, San Diego, 1987,* vol. II, pp. 701-708, The IEEE Inc., Piscataway NJ, 1987.

[320] F. Rosenblatt. On the convergence of reinforcement procedures in simple perceptrons. *Technical Report VG1196-G-4,* Cornell Aeronautical Laboratory, February 1960.

[321] F. Rosenblatt. *Principles of Neurodynamics.* Spartan, New York, 1962.

[322] M.W. Roth. Survey of neural network technology for automatic target recognition. *IEEE Trans. Neural Networks,* 1(1):28–43, March 1990.

[323] J. Rubner and K. Schulten. Development of feature detectors by self-organization. *Biol. Cybern.,* 62:193–199, 1990.

[324] D.E. Rumelhart, G.E. Hinton, and R.J. Williams. Learning internal representations by error propagation. In D.E. Rumelhart and J.L. McClelland, editors, *Parallel Distributed Processing,* vol. 1, pp. 318–362. MIT Press, Cambridge, MA, 1986.

[325] D.E. Rumelhart, G.E. Hinton, and R.J. Williams. Learning representations by back-propagating errors. *Nature,* 323:533–536, 1986.

[326] D.E. Rumelhart and D. Zipser. Feature discovery by competitive learning. *Cognitive Science,* 9:75–112, 1985.

[327] R.L. Russo, P.H. Oden, and P.K. Wolff. A heuristic procedure for the partitioning and mapping of computer logic graphs. *IEEE Trans. Computers,* 20:1455–1462, 1971.

[328] R.L. Russo, and P.K. Wolff. A computer-based design approach to partitioning and mapping of computer logic graphs. *Proc. IEEE,* 60:28–34, January 1972.

[329] S. Saarinen, R. Bramley, and G. Cybenko. Ill-conditioning in neural network training problems. *SIAM J. Sci. Comput.,* 14(3):693–714, May 1993.

[330] E. Sackinger, B.E. Boser, J. Bromley, Y. Le Cun, and L.D. Jackel. Application of the ANNA neural network chip to high-speed character recognition. *IEEE Trans. Neural Networks,* 3:498–505, 1992.

[331] H. Sakoe. Neural networks applied to speech recognition. *IEICE Trans. on Fundamentals of Electronics Communications and Computer Sciences,* 75:546–551, 1992.

[332] F.M.A. Salam. New artificial neural net models: basic theory and characteristics. In *Proc. IEEE Intl. Symp. on Circuits and Systems, New Orleans, LA, May 1990,* pp. 200–203, The IEEE, Inc., Piscataway, NJ, 1990.

[333] F.M.A. Salam, M.R. Choi, and Y. Wang. Artificial neural nets in MOS silicon VLSI/LSI. In I.K. Sethi and A.K. Jain, editors, *Artificial Neural Networks and Statistical Pattern Recognition,* pp. 243–270. Elsevier Science Publishers, 1991.

[334] F.M.A. Salam and Y. Wang. A real-time experiment using a 50-neuron CMOS analog silicon chip with on-chip digital learning. *IEEE Trans. Neural Networks,* 2:461–464, 1991.

[335] F.M.A. Salam, Y. Wang, and M.R. Choi. On the analysis and design of neural nets. *IEEE Trans. Circuits and Systems,* 38:337–342, 1991.

[336] I.W. Sandberg. Structure theorems for nonlinear systems. *Multidimensional Systems and Signal Processing,* 2:267–286, 1991.

[337] T.D. Sanger. Optimal unsupervised learning in a single-layer feedforward neural network. *Neural Networks,* 2:459–473, 1989.

[338] T.D. Sanger. An optimality principle for unsupervised learning. In D.S. Touretzky, editor, *Advances in Neural Information Processing Systems,* pp. 11–19. Morgan Kaufmann, San Mateo, CA, 1989.

[339] T. Sauer. Time series prediction using delay coordinates embedding. In A.S. Weigend and N.A. Gershenfeld, editors, *Time Series Prediction: Forecasting the Future and Understanding the Past,* pp. 175–193. Addison-Wesley, Reading, MA, 1993.

[340] H. Sawai, Y. Minami, M. Miyatake, A. Waibel, and K. Shikano. Connectionist approaches to large vocabulary continuous speech recognition. *IEICE Trans. on Communications, Electronics, Information and Systems,* 74:1834–1844, 1991.

[341] J. Schürmann. Multifont word recognition system with application to postal address reading. *Proc. Intl. Joint Conf. on Pattern Recognition,* pp. 658–662, 1976.

[342] J. Schürmann. *Polynomklassifikatoren für die Zeichenerkennung.* Oldenbourg-Verlag, München, 1977.

[343] D. Schwartz, V. Samalam, S. Solla, and J. Denker. Exhaustive learning. *Neural Computation,* 2:371–382, 1990.

[344] T.J. Schwartz. A neural chips survey. *AI Expert,* pp. 34–38, 1990.

[345] T.J. Sejnowski. Open questions about computation in cerebral cortex. In J. McClelland and D. Rumelhart, editors, *Parallel Distributed Processing,* MIT Press, 1986.

[346] T.J. Sejnowski, P.K. Kienker, and G. Hinton. Learning symmetry groups with hidden units: beyond the perceptron. *Physica,* 22D:260–275, 1986.

[347] T.J. Sejnowski and C.R. Rosenberg. Parallel networks that learn to pronounce English text. *Complex Systems,* 1:145–168, 1987.

[348] D. Sengupta and R. Iltis. Neural solution to the multitarget tracking data association problem. *IEEE Tran. Aerospace and Electronics Systems,* 25:96–108, 1989.

[349] M.E. Sereno. *Neural Computation of Pattern Motion: Modeling Stages of Motion Analysis in the Primate Visual Cortex.* MIT Press, Cambridge, MA., 1993.

[350] S. Seshu and M.B. Reed. *Linear Graphs and Electrical Networks.* Addison-Wesley, Reading, MA, 1961.

[351] I.K. Sethi. Entropy nets: from decision trees to neural networks. *Proc. IEEE,* 78:1605–1613, 1990.

[352] G.M. Shepherd. *Neurobiology.* Oxford University Press, New York, 1983.

[353] D. Sherrington. Complexity due to disorder and frustration. In E. Jen, editor, *1989 Lectures in Complex Systems,* Addison-Wesley, Redwood City, CA, 1990.

[354] P.Y. Simard, M.B. Ottaway, and D.H. Ballard. Analysis of recurrent backpropagation. In D. Touretzky, G. Hinton, and T. Sejnowski, editors, *Proc. 1988 Connectionist Models Summer School, Pittsburgh,* pp. 103–112, Morgan Kaufmann, San Mateo, CA, 1988.

[355] J.A. Sirat and J.P. Nadal. Neural trees: a new tool for classification. *Network,* 1:423–438, 1990.

[356] M.A. Sivilotti, M.A. Mahowald, and C.A. Mead. Real-time visual computations using analog CMOS processing arrays. In P. Losleben, editor, *Advanced Research in VLSI: Proc. 1987 Stanford Conf.* pp. 295–312. MIT Press, Cambridge, MA, 1987. Reprinted in J.A. Anderson and E. Rosenfeld, editors, *Neurocomputing: Foundations of Research,* MIT Press, Cambridge, MA, 1988, pp. 703–711.

[357] C.A. Skarda and W.J. Freeman. How brains make chaos in order to make sense of world. *Behavioral and Brain Sciences,* 10:161–195, 1987.

[358] J.M. Smith, D.T. Lee, and J.S. Liebman. An $O(n \log n)$ heuristic for the rectilinear Steiner minimal tree problem. *Eng. Optimization,* 4:179–192, 1980.

[359] W.D. Smith and P.W. Shor. Steiner tree problems. *Algorithmica,* 7:329–332, 1992.

[360] H. Sompolinsky. The theory of neural networks: the Hebb rules and beyond. In J.L. van Hemmen and I. Morgenstern, editors, *Heidelberg Colloquium on Glassy Dynamics (1986),* pp. 485–527. Springer-Verlag, Berlin, 1987.

[361] H. Sompolinsky, A. Crisanti, and H.J. Sommers. Chaos in random neural networks. *Phys. Rev. Letters,* 61:259–262, 1988.

[362] H. Sompolinsky and I. Kanter. Temporal association in asymmetric neural networks. *Phys. Rev. Letters,* 57:2861–2864, 1986.

[363] M. Sonehara, M. Kawato, S. Miyake, and K. Nakane. Image data compression using a neural network model. In *Intl. Joint Conf. Neural Networks, Washington, DC, 1989.* vol. II, pp. 35–42, The IEEE Inc., Piscataway, NJ, 1989.

[364] F.F. Soulie, E. Viennet, and B. Lamy. Multi-modular neural network architectures: applications in optical character and human face recognition. *Intl. J. Pattern Recognition and Artificial Intelligence,* 7:721–755, 1993.

[365] D.F. Specht. Probabilistic neural networks and the polynomial Adaline as a complementary techniques for classification. *IEEE Trans. Neural Networks,* 1(1):111–121, March 1990.

[366] D.F. Specht. A general regression neural network. *IEEE Trans. Neural Networks,* 2(6):568–576, November 1991.

[367] D.A. Sprecher. On the structure of continuous functions of several variables. *Trans. Amer. Math. Soc.,* 115:340–355, March 1965.

[368] D.L. Standley and B.K. Horn. Analog CMOS IC for object position and orientation. In B.P. Mathur and C. Koch, editors, *Visual Information Processing: From Neurons to Chips, Proc. SPIE,* vol. 1473, pp. 194–201, 1991.

[369] D.L. Stein. Disordered systems: mostly spin glasses. In D. L Stein, editor, *Lectures in the Sciences of Complexity,* Addison-Wesley, Redwood City, CA, 1989.

[370] D.L. Stein, editor, *Lectures in the Sciences of Complexity.* Addison-Wesley, Redwood City, CA, 1989.

[371] K. Steinbuch. Die Lernmatrix. *Kybernetik (Biol. Cybernetics),* 1:36–45, 1961.

[372] H. Steinhaus. *Mathematical Snapshots.* Oxford University Press, New York, 1960.

[373] F. Takens. Detecting strange attractors in turbulence. In D.A. Rand and L.S. Young, editors, *Dynamical Systems and Turbulence, Lecture Notes in Mathematics,* vol. 898. Springer-Verlag, Berlin, 1981.

[374] D.W. Tank and J.J. Hopfield. Neural computation by time compression. *Proc. Natl. Acad. Sci., USA,* 84:1896–1900, 1987.

[375] A.J. Ticknor and H. Barrett. Optical implementation of Boltzmann machines. *Optical Engineering,* 26:16–21, 1987.

[376] H. Tomabechi and H. Kitano. Beyond PDP: the frequency modulation neural network. In *Proceedings of 11th Intl. Joint Conf. on Artificial Intelligence (IJCAI)*, pp. 186–192, 1989.

[377] G.T. Toussaint, guest editor. Special issue on computational geometry. *Proc. IEEE*, 80, September 1992.

[378] H.C. Tuckwell. *Stochastic Processes in the Neurosciences*. CBMS-NSF Regional Conference Series in Applied Mathematics, Society for Industrial and Applied Mathematics (SIAM), Philadelphia, PA, 1989.

[379] W.T. Tutte. On the non-biplanar character of the complete 9-graph. *Canadian Math. Bulletin*, 6:319–330, 1963.

[380] S.B. Udin and J.W. Fawcett. Formation of topographic maps. *Ann. Rev. Neuroscience*, 11:289–327, 1988.

[381] J.K. Uhlmann. Algorithms for multiple-target tracking. *Amer. Scientist*, 80:128–141, 1992.

[382] L.G. Valiant. A theory of the learnable. *Comm. ACM*, 27:1134–1142, 1984.

[383] D.E. van den Bout and T.K. Miller. Improving the Hopfield-Tank neural network through normalization and annealing. *Biological Cybernetics*, 62:129–139, 1989.

[384] J.L. van Hemman and R. Kuhn. Nonlinear neural networks. *Phys. Rev. Letters*, 57:913–916, 1986.

[385] V.N. Vapnik. *Estimation of Dependences Based on Empirical Data*. Springer-Verlag, Berlin, 1982.

[386] V.N. Vapnik and A.Y. Chervonenkis. On the uniform convergence of relative frequencies of events to their probabilities. *Theory of Probability and Its Applications*, 16:264–280, 1971.

[387] S.S. Venkatesh. Computation and learning in the context of neural network capacity. In H. Wechsler, editor, *Neural Networks for Perception*, vol. 2, pp. 173–207. Academic Press, 1992.

[388] A. Vergis, K. Steiglitz, and B. Dickinson. The complexity of analog computation. *Math. and Comp. in Simulation*, 28:91–113, 1986.

[389] M. Vetterli and K.M. Uz. Multiresolution coding techniques for digital television. *Multidimensional Systems and Signal Processing*, 3:161–187, 1992.

[390] T.P. Vogl, J.K. Mangis, A.K. Rigler, W.T. Zink, and D.L. Alkon. Accelerating the convergence of the backpropagation method. *Biol. Cybernetics*, 59:257–263, 1988.

[391] C. von der Malsburg. Self-organization of orientation sensitive cells in the striate cortex. *Kybernetik*, 14:85–100, 1973.

[392] C. von der Malsburg and W. Schneider. A neural cocktail-party processor. *Biol. Cybernetics*, 54:29–40, 1986.

[393] K. Wagner and D. Psaltis. Multiplayer optical learning networks. *Applied Optics*, 26:5061–5076, 1987.

[394] A. Waibel. Modular construction of time delay neural networks for speech recognition. *Neural Computation*, 1:39–46, 1989.

[395] J.A. Waldvogel. The bird's eye view. *American Scientist*, pp. 342–353, July-August 1990.

[396] E.A. Wan. Time series prediction using a connectionist network with internal delay lines. In A.S. Weigend and N.A. Gershenfeld, editors, *Time Series Prediction: Forecasting the Future and Understanding the Past*, pp. 195–217. Addison-Wesley, Reading, MA, 1993.

[397] A.S. Weigend and N.A. Gershenfeld. *Time Series Prediction: Forecasting the Future and Understanding the Past*, Addison-Wesley, Reading, MA, 1993.

[398] A.S. Weigend and D.E. Rumelhart. The effective dimension of the space of hidden units. In *Proc. IEEE Intl. Joint Conf. Neural Networks, Singapore, 18–21 Nov. 1991*, vol. 3, pp. 2069–2074, The IEEE Inc., Piscataway, NJ, 1991.

[399] A.S. Weigend, D.E. Rumelhart, and B.A. Huberman. Generalization by weight-elimination applied to currency exchange rate prediction. In *Proc. IEEE Intl. Joint Conf. Neural Networks, Seattle, WA, 8–14 July 1991*, vol. 1, pp. 837–841, The IEEE Inc., Piscataway, NJ, 1991.

[400] G. Weisbuch and F. Fogelman-Soulié. Scaling laws for attractors of Hopfield networks. *Journal de Physique Lettres (Paris)*, 46:623–630, 1985.

[401] E. Weiszfeld. Sur le point pour lequel la somme des distances de *n* points donnés est minimum. *Tohoku Math. J.*, 43:355–386, 1937.

[402] P.J. Werbos. *Beyond Regression: New Tools for Prediction and Analysis in the Behavioral Sciences*. Ph.D. thesis, Harvard University, 1974.

[403] P.J. Werbos. Generalization of backpropagation with application to a recurrent gas market model. *Neural Networks,* 1:339–356, 1988.

[404] P.J. Werbos. *The Roots of Backpropagation.* John Wiley and Sons, Inc., New York, 1994.

[405] H. White, editor. *Artificial Neural Networks: Approximation and Learning Theory.* Blackwell Publishers, Cambridge, MA, 1992.

[406] D. Whitley and T. Hanson. Optimizing neural networks using faster, more accurate genetic search. In J.D. Schaffer, editor, *Proc. 3rd Intl. Conf. Genetic Algorithms,* pp. 391–396, Morgan Kaufmann, San Mateo, CA, 1989.

[407] V.K.M. Whitney. Algorithm 422: minimal spanning tree. *Comm. ACM,* 15:273, April 1972.

[408] B. Widrow. Adaline and Madaline: plenary speech. In *Proc. 1st IEEE Intl. Conf. Neural Networks, San Diego, 1987,* pp. 143–158, The IEEE Inc., Piscataway, NJ, 1987.

[409] B. Widrow and M.A. Lehr. Thirty years of adaptive neural networks: Perceptron, Madaline and backprogagation. *Proc. IEEE,* 78:1415–1442, 1990.

[410] B. Widrow, J.M. McCool, M.G. Larimore, and C.R. Johnson Jr. Stationary and nonstationary learning characteristics of the LMS adaptive filter. *Proc. IEEE,* 64:1151–1162, 1976.

[411] B. Widrow and S.D. Stearns. *Adaptive Signal Processing.* Prentice-Hall, Englewood Cliffs, NJ, 1985.

[412] N. Wiener. *Cybernetics.* MIT Press, Cambridge, MA, 1948.

[413] R.J. Williams. On the use of backpropagation in associative reinforcement learning. In *Proc. IEEE Intl. Conf. on Neural Networks, San Diego, 1988,* vol. 1, pp. 263–270, The IEEE Inc, Piscataway, NJ, 1988.

[414] R.J. Williams. Simple statistical gradient-following algorithms for connectionist reinforcement learning. *Machine Learning,* 8:229–256, 1992.

[415] R.J. Williams and D. Zipser. Experimental analysis of the real-time recurrent learning algorithm. *Connection Science,* 1:87–111, 1989.

[416] R.J. Williams and D. Zipser. A learning algorithm for continually learning fully recurrent neural networks. *Neural Computation,* 1:270–280, 1989.

[417] D.J. Willshaw, O.P. Buneman, and H.C. Longuet-Higgins. Non-holographic associative memory. *Nature,* 222:960–962, 1969.

[418] D.J. Willshaw and C. von der Malsburg. How patterned neural connections can be set up by self-organization. *Proc. Royal Soc. London B,* 194:431–445, 1976.

[419] G.V. Wilson and G.S. Pawley. On the stability of the travelling salesman problem algorithm of Hopfield and Tank. *Biological Cybernetics,* 57:63–70, 1988.

[420] T. Winograd and F. Flores. *Understanding Computers and Cognition.* Ablex Publishing Corporation, Norwood, NJ, 1986.

[421] J.X. Wu and C. Chan. Isolated word recognition by neural network models with cross-correlation coefficients for speech dynamics. *IEEE Trans. Pattern Analysis and Machine Intelligence,* 15:1174–1185, 1993.

[422] J.L. Wyatt and D.L. Standley. Criteria for robust stability in a class of lateral inhibition networks coupled through resistive grids. *Neural Computation,* 1:58–67, 1989.

[423] A.C. Yao. An $O(|E| \log \log |V|)$ algorithm for finding minimum spanning trees. *Inf. Proc. Lett.,* 4:21–23, Sept. 1975.

[424] H.F. Yin and P. Liang. A connectionist expert system combining production system and associative memory. *Intl. J. Pattern Recognition and Artificial Intelligence,* 5:523–544, 1991.

[425] A.L. Yuille, D.M. Kammen, and D.S. Cohen. Quadrature and the development of orientation selective cortical cells by Hebb rules. *Biol. Cybernetics,* 61:183–194, 1989.

[426] M. Zak. Terminal attractors in neural networks. *Neural Networks,* 2:259–274, 1989.

[427] B. Zhou and N.K. Bose. A comprehensive analysis of "neural solution to the multitarget tracking data association problem." *IEEE Trans, Aerospace and Electronics Systems,* 29:260–263, 1993.

[428] J.M. Zurada. *Introduction to Artificial Neural Systems.* West Publishing Company, St. Paul, MN, 1992.

A

BASICS OF GRADIENT-BASED OPTIMIZATION METHODS

This appendix provides some of the basics of gradient-based optimization methods, which are frequently used in neural network algorithms. It is self-contained and is for readers who want to review some introductory material in unconstrained and, to a lesser degree, constrained optimization theory. The references at the end are for perusal of the subject matter in greater depth if occasion demands.

Gradient-based, minimum-seeking algorithms are based on the following first-order necessary condition, from introductory calculus, for an interior point of a set to be an *extreme point,* i.e., either a minimum or a maximum point:

Theorem A.1. Let Ω be an open subset of $\mathbb{R}^n$, and f be a function with continuous first-order derivatives in Ω (i.e., $f \in C^1$). If $\mathbf{x}^* \in \Omega$ is an extreme point of f, then $\nabla f(\mathbf{x}^*) = \mathbf{0}$, where $\nabla f(\mathbf{x}^*)$ is a column vector obtained from evaluation of the gradient vector,

$$\nabla f(\mathbf{x}) = \left[\frac{\partial f}{\partial x_1} \; \frac{\partial f}{\partial x_2} \; \cdots \; \frac{\partial f}{\partial x_n} \right]^{\mathrm{T}}$$

at $\mathbf{x}^*$.

This condition holds not only at local and global extrema but also at *saddle points.* For the point $\mathbf{x}^*$ to be a global minimum, the value of f at $\mathbf{x}^*$ must be less than its value at all the local minima in the set, including those on the boundary. Modification of Theorem A.1 to include minimum or maximum points on the boundary of Ω is straightforward and is left as an exercise.

The first-order condition in Theorem A.1 is true for both minimum and maximum points. A function f will be defined to belong to C^n if it has continuous nth-order derivatives. A sufficient condition for a minimum point is given as follows, using the *Hessian matrix,* $\mathbf{H}(\mathbf{x})$, defined as

$$(\mathbf{H}(\mathbf{x}))_{ij} = (\nabla^2 f(\mathbf{x}))_{ij} = \frac{\partial^2 f(\mathbf{x})}{\partial x_i \partial x_j}.$$

Theorem A.2. Let $f \in C^2$ in Ω and $\mathbf{x}^* \in \Omega$. If $\nabla f(\mathbf{x}^*) = \mathbf{0}$ and the Hessian matrix $\mathbf{H}(\mathbf{x}^*)$ is positive-definite, then $\mathbf{x}^* \in \Omega$ is a strict minimum point of f.

The proof of Theorem A.2 is straightforward and is left as an exercise.

A.1   THE GRADIENT DESCENT METHOD

The backpropagation algorithm and the Hopfield network update rule are gradient descent–type methods that seek out the points where the gradient is zero, based on Theorem A.1. The basic idea is very simple. At each iteration, one chooses a point along the direction in which the function decreases the fastest, i.e., along the direction of the negative of the gradient. The standard gradient method is defined by the iteration

$$\mathbf{x}_{k+1} = \mathbf{x}_k - \alpha_k \nabla f(\mathbf{x}_k), \tag{A.1}$$

where $\alpha_k > 0$ is the step size. In the optimal case, this step size should be chosen such that $f(\mathbf{x}_{k+1})$ is a minimum of $f(\mathbf{x})$ along the negative direction of the gradient. The point $\mathbf{x}_{k+1}$ can be found by searching along a line in this direction.

Commonly used stopping criteria for the gradient descent algorithm are

$$|f(\mathbf{x}_{k+1}) - f(\mathbf{x}_k)| < \epsilon \tag{A.2}$$

and

$$|\mathbf{x}_{k+1} - \mathbf{x}_k| < \delta. \tag{A.3}$$

A combination of these two criteria may be necessary to avoid the *flat-plateau problem* for the criterion in Eq. (A.2) alone, as shown in Fig. A.1, and the *steep-slope problem* for the criterion in Eq. (A.3) alone, as shown in Fig. A2.

A fundamental difficulty with a gradient descent–type algorithm is that it may stop at any local minimum. However, when the function $f(\mathbf{x})$ is quadratic, there is only one extremum. In that case, when the algorithm converges, it will be at a global minimum or global maximum. This is the case with the perceptron algorithm. Since a nonquadratic function can be approximated locally by a quadratic function using the Hessian matrix, we present the following analysis of the gradient descent method for quadratic functions.

Assume

$$f(\mathbf{x}) = \tfrac{1}{2}\mathbf{x}^T\mathbf{Q}\mathbf{x} - \mathbf{x}^T\mathbf{b} + c, \tag{A.4}$$

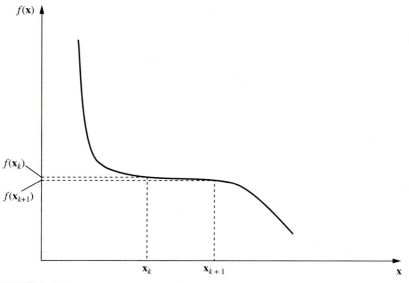

FIGURE A.1
The flat-plateau problem for the stopping criterion in Eq. (A.2). The gradient descent algorithm will stop at $\mathbf{x}_{k+1}$, although it is not at a minimum point.

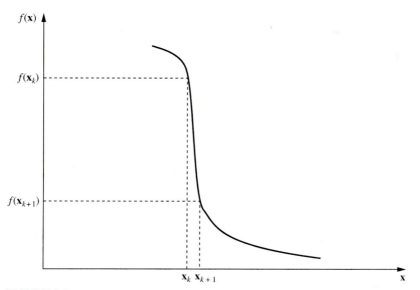

FIGURE A.2
The steep-slope problem for the stopping criterion in Eq. (A.3). The gradient descent algorithm will stop at $\mathbf{x}_{k+1}$, although it is not at a minimum point.

where $\mathbf{Q}$ is a positive-definite, real symmetric $n \times n$ matrix, $\mathbf{b}$ is an $(n \times 1)$ real-valued vector, and c is a real-valued scalar. The unique minimum point $\mathbf{x}^*$ of f can be found by setting the gradient to zero. Since $\nabla f(\mathbf{x}) = \mathbf{Qx} - \mathbf{b}$, this leads to the equation,

$$\mathbf{Qx}^* = \mathbf{b}. \tag{A.5}$$

Therefore, the iteration update in the gradient descent method for a quadratic cost function is

$$\mathbf{x}_{k+1} = \mathbf{x}_k - \alpha_k(\mathbf{Qx}_k - \mathbf{b}). \tag{A.6}$$

The value of the step size α_k that minimizes $f(\mathbf{x}_{k+1})$ can be found by setting

$$\frac{df(\mathbf{x}_k - \alpha_k(\mathbf{Qx}_k - \mathbf{b}))}{d\alpha_k} = 0, \tag{A.7}$$

yielding

$$\alpha_k = \frac{(\mathbf{Qx}_k - \mathbf{b})^{\mathrm{T}}(\mathbf{Qx}_k - \mathbf{b})}{(\mathbf{Qx}_k - \mathbf{b})^{\mathrm{T}}\mathbf{Q}(\mathbf{Qx}_k - \mathbf{b})}. \tag{A.8}$$

With the step size α_k chosen as in Eq. (A.8), we have the following important result on the convergence rate of the gradient descent method.

Theorem A.3. For any $\mathbf{x}_0 \in \mathbb{R}^n$, the gradient descent method with α_k chosen as in Eq. (A.8) converges to the unique minimum point $\mathbf{x}^*$ of a quadratic function f. Moreover, the following inequality holds at every iteration k:

$$E(\mathbf{x}_{k+1}) \le \left(\frac{r-1}{r+1}\right)^2 E(\mathbf{x}_k) \tag{A.9}$$

where $E(\mathbf{x}) = \frac{1}{2}(\mathbf{x} - \mathbf{x}^*)^{\mathrm{T}}\mathbf{Q}(\mathbf{x} - \mathbf{x}^*)$, and r is the *condition number* of the matrix $\mathbf{Q}$, defined as the ratio of the largest and the smallest eigenvalues, i.e., $r = A/a$ where A and a are, respectively, the largest and smallest eigenvalues of $\mathbf{Q}$.

Theorem A.3 can be proved based on the observation that if $\mathbf{x}^{*\mathrm{T}}\mathbf{x}^* = c$, then $E(\mathbf{x}) = f(\mathbf{x}) + \frac{1}{2}\mathbf{x}^{*\mathrm{T}}\mathbf{Qx}^*$ and on the following lemma.

Lemma A.1. For a positive-definite symmetric $n \times n$ matrix $\mathbf{Q}$, the inequality

$$\frac{(\mathbf{x}^{\mathrm{T}}\mathbf{x})^2}{(\mathbf{x}^{\mathrm{T}}\mathbf{Qx})(\mathbf{x}^{\mathrm{T}}\mathbf{Q}^{-1}\mathbf{x})} \ge \frac{4aA}{(a+A)^2} \tag{A.10}$$

holds for any n-dimensional vector $\mathbf{x}$ where a and A are as defined in Theorem A.3.

Theorem A.3 shows that when α_k is optimally chosen, the gradient descent method for a quadratic function converges linearly and the convergence rate is approximately determined by the condition number r. It slows down as r increases. A larger r means that the contours of f become more eccentric. This implies that a single dominating eigenvalue (interpreted to be one that is either significantly larger or significantly smaller than the other eigenvalues) will slow down the gradient descent method. It should be noted that when α_k is not chosen as in Eq. (A.8), the convergence rate will be slower than that given in Theorem A.3.

Theorem A.3 can be extended to a nonquadratic function $f(\mathbf{x})$ by approximating f in the neighborhood of a minimum point $\mathbf{x}^*$ by a quadratic function with $\mathbf{Q}$ equal to the Hessian matrix $\mathbf{H}(\mathbf{x}^*)$ of f.

A.2 NEWTON'S METHOD

Newton's method locally approximates the function f by a quadratic function and minimizes the approximated quadratic function exactly at each iteration. At iteration k, the function f is approximated by the truncated Taylor series

$$f(\mathbf{x}) \approx f(\mathbf{x}_k) + (\nabla f(\mathbf{x}_k))^{\mathrm{T}}(\mathbf{x} - \mathbf{x}_k) + \tfrac{1}{2}(\mathbf{x} - \mathbf{x}_k)^{\mathrm{T}}\mathbf{H}(\mathbf{x}_k)(\mathbf{x} - \mathbf{x}_k). \quad (A.11)$$

This quadratic function is minimized at

$$\mathbf{x}_{k+1} = \mathbf{x}_k - \mathbf{H}^{-1}(\mathbf{x}_k)\nabla f(\mathbf{x}_k). \quad (A.12)$$

Eq. (A.12) occurs in the standard Newton's method. By Theorem A.2, the Hessian matrix is positive-definite at a minimum; therefore, its inverse exists.

The following theorem shows that Newton's method has second-order convergence if the initial point $\mathbf{x}_0$ is sufficiently close to a minimum point.

Theorem A.4. Let $f \in \mathbb{C}^3$ be a function in $\mathbb{R}^n$, and assume that the Hessian matrix is positive-definite at a minimum point $\mathbf{x}^*$. Then, if the initial point $\mathbf{x}_0$ is sufficiently close to $\mathbf{x}^*$, Newton's method converges to $\mathbf{x}^*$, and the order of convergence is at least 2.

Second-order convergence means that $|\mathbf{x}_{k+1} - \mathbf{x}^*| \le \beta |\mathbf{x}_k - \mathbf{x}^*|^2$ where $\beta > 0$ and $\mathbf{x}_k$ is assumed to satisfy $\beta |\mathbf{x}_k - \mathbf{x}^*| < 1$. Although the second-order convergence of Newton's method compares favorably to the linear convergence of the gradient descent method, Newton's method does not guarantee decrease in f at points far away from a minimum. To correct this problem, a modified Newton's method has been introduced. In this modification,

$$\mathbf{d}_k = -(\epsilon_k \mathbf{I} + \mathbf{H}(\mathbf{x}_k))^{-1}\nabla f(\mathbf{x}_k), \qquad \mathbf{x}_{k+1} = \mathbf{x}_k - \alpha_k \mathbf{d}_k, \quad (A.13)$$

where ϵ_k is the smallest nonnegative constant that makes the eigenvalues of $(\epsilon_k \mathbf{I} + \mathbf{H}(\mathbf{x}_k))$ greater than or equal to a predetermined constant $\delta > 0$. When $\alpha_k = 1$ and $\epsilon_k = 0$, the modified Newton's method reduces to the standard Newton's method. Again, $\alpha_k \ge 0$ is the step size. It is used to prevent an increase in the function f when the standard Newton's method is applied to a nonquadratic function. At points far away from the minimum of a nonquadratic function, $\mathbf{H}(\mathbf{x}_k)$ may not be positive-definite. The parameter $\epsilon_k \ge 0$ is introduced to make $(\epsilon_k \mathbf{I} + \mathbf{H}(\mathbf{x}_k))$ positive-definite so that a decrease in f is guaranteed for small α_k. The fact that increasing ϵ_k guarantees a decrease in f becomes clear in the extreme case when ϵ_k is very large, because the algorithm then approximates the gradient descent method.

Evaluation of the inverse of the Hessian matrix is costly when the dimension of the problem becomes large. A class of methods uses approximations to the true inverse of the Hessian matrix to avoid the direct computation of the inverse. The basic idea is to construct improved approximations of this inverse using the information gathered in the descent process. The analysis of convergence of such methods is more difficult. Interested readers are referred to the references at the end of this appendix. The next section introduces the conjugate gradient method, which avoids inversion of the Hessian matrix.

A.3   THE CONJUGATE GRADIENT METHOD

The second-order convergence obtained in the method described in the preceding section is useful when accurate, reasonably fast answers are required. Since the task of computing the inverse of the Hessian matrix can be computation-intensive, attempts have been made to dispense with that requirement.

The conjugate gradient method provides faster convergence for quadratic functions than the gradient descent method, while avoiding computation of the inverse of the Hessian matrix. In the case of quadratic functions, exact answers are obtainable without calculating second-order derivatives, as discussed next.

Given a symmetric matrix $\mathbf{Q}$, two vectors $\mathbf{d}_1$ and $\mathbf{d}_2$ are said to be *conjugate* with respect to $\mathbf{Q}$ if $\mathbf{d}_1^T\mathbf{Q}\mathbf{d}_2 = 0$. An important result is that when the matrix $\mathbf{Q}$ is positive-definite, a set of nonzero conjugate vectors is also linearly independent. The conjugate gradient algorithm for a quadratic problem is defined as follows:

1. Let $\mathbf{d}_0 = -\nabla f(\mathbf{x}_0) = \mathbf{b} - \mathbf{Q}\mathbf{x}_0$, where $\mathbf{x}_0 \in \mathbb{R}^n$ is an arbitrary starting point.
2. For $k = 0, 1, \ldots, n - 1$, define $\nabla f(\mathbf{x}_k) = \mathbf{Q}\mathbf{x}_k - \mathbf{b}$, and do

a.
$$\mathbf{x}_{k+1} = \mathbf{x}_k + \alpha_k\mathbf{d}_k, \qquad \text{where } \alpha_k = -\frac{(\nabla f(\mathbf{x}_k))^T\mathbf{d}_k}{\mathbf{d}_k^T\mathbf{Q}\mathbf{d}_k} \qquad (\text{A.14})$$

b.
$$\mathbf{d}_{k+1} = -\nabla f(\mathbf{x}_{k+1}) + \beta_k\mathbf{d}_k, \qquad \text{where } \beta_k = \frac{(\nabla f(\mathbf{x}_k))^T\mathbf{Q}\mathbf{d}_k}{\mathbf{d}_k^T\mathbf{Q}\mathbf{d}_k}. \qquad (\text{A.15})$$

The reader may wish to verify that the vectors $\mathbf{d}_0, \mathbf{d}_1, \ldots, \mathbf{d}_{n-1}$ generated by this algorithm are conjugate with respect to $\mathbf{Q}$.

The next theorem holds for the conjugate gradient algorithm if the function to be minimized is a quadratic one.

> **Theorem A.5.** The conjugate gradient algorithm in Eqs. (A.14) and (A.15) converges to the unique minimum of a quadratic function after n steps; i.e., $\mathbf{x}_n = \mathbf{x}^*$ where $\mathbf{x}^*$ satisfies $\mathbf{Q}\mathbf{x}^* = \mathbf{b}$.

The proof is based on the fact that the set of conjugate vectors $\mathbf{d}_0, \mathbf{d}_1, \ldots, \mathbf{d}_{n-1}$ are linearly independent and the solution $\mathbf{x}^*$ can be expressed as a linear combination of the set of conjugate vectors.

A direct extension of the conjugate gradient algorithm for quadratic problems to nonquadratic problems is through approximation of the function locally by a quadratic using the Hessian matrix $\mathbf{H}(\mathbf{x}_k)$ at each step in place of the $\mathbf{Q}$ matrix for the quadratic function. The *extended conjugate gradient algorithm* is as follows:

Extended conjugate gradient algorithm.

1. Compute $\mathbf{d}_0 = -\nabla f(\mathbf{x}_0)$ where $\mathbf{x}_0 \in \mathbb{R}^n$ is an arbitrary starting point.
2. For $k = 0, 1, \ldots, n - 1$, do

$$\mathbf{x}_{k+1} = \mathbf{x}_k + \alpha_k \mathbf{d}_k, \qquad \text{where } \alpha_k = -\frac{(\nabla f(\mathbf{x}_k))^{\mathrm{T}} \mathbf{d}_k}{\mathbf{d}_k^{\mathrm{T}} \mathbf{H}(\mathbf{x}_k) \mathbf{d}_k} \qquad \text{(A.16)}$$

$$\mathbf{d}_{k+1} = -\nabla f(\mathbf{x}_{k+1}) + \beta_k \mathbf{d}_k, \qquad \text{where } \beta_k = \frac{(\nabla f(\mathbf{x}_k))^{\mathrm{T}} \mathbf{H}(\mathbf{x}_k)}{\mathbf{d}_k^{\mathrm{T}} \mathbf{H}(\mathbf{x}_k) \mathbf{d}_k} \qquad \text{(A.17)}$$

3. Replace $\mathbf{x}_0$ by $\mathbf{x}_n$ and go back to step 1.

Stopping criteria, as discussed in connection with the gradient descent method, may be applied. This algorithm still uses the Hessian matrix, although computation of the inverse Hessian matrix is avoided. Algorithms exist that do not use the Hessian matrix at all, and interested readers are referred to the bibliography at the end of this appendix.

A.4 CONSTRAINED OPTIMIZATION

The discussions so far are for unconstrained optimization problems. A constrained optimization problem is stated as

$$
\begin{array}{lll}
\text{minimize} & f(\mathbf{x}) & \\
\text{subject to} & h_1(\mathbf{x}) = 0 & g_1(\mathbf{x}) \leq 0 \\
& h_2(\mathbf{x}) = 0 & g_2(\mathbf{x}) \leq 0 \qquad \text{(A.18)} \\
& \vdots & \vdots \\
& h_p(\mathbf{x}) = 0 & g_q(\mathbf{x}) \leq 0
\end{array}
$$

where $p \leq n$ and $\mathbf{x} \in \Omega \subset \mathbb{R}^n$. The functions $h_i(\mathbf{x})$ and $g_j(\mathbf{x})$ are called the *functional constraints,* and $\mathbf{x} \in \Omega$ is called the *set constraint.* All functions are normally assumed to be in $\mathbb{C}^2$. The functional constraints may be denoted by two vector functions $\mathbf{h}(\mathbf{x}) = \mathbf{0}$ and $\mathbf{g}(\mathbf{x}) \leq \mathbf{0}$.

A point $\mathbf{x}^*$ is said to be a *regular point* of the functional constraints if it satisfies $\mathbf{h}(\mathbf{x}^*) = \mathbf{0}$ and $\mathbf{g}(\mathbf{x}^*) \leq \mathbf{0}$ and the gradient vectors $\nabla h_i(\mathbf{x}^*), \nabla g_j(\mathbf{x}^*), 1 \leq i \leq p, j \in J = \{j \mid g_j(\mathbf{x}^*) = 0\}$, are linearly independent.

The conditions for a point to be a minimum point of the constrained optimization problem are given below without proof. The first one is a necessary condition known as the *Kuhn-Tucker condition.*

Theorem A.6. If $\mathbf{x}^*$ is a minimum point for the problem in Eq. (A.18) and is also a regular point of the constraints, then there exists a vector $\boldsymbol{\lambda} \in \mathbb{R}^p$ and vector $\boldsymbol{\gamma} \in \mathbb{R}^q$ where $\boldsymbol{\gamma} \geq \mathbf{0}$ such that

$$[\nabla f(\mathbf{x}^*)]^{\mathrm{T}} + \boldsymbol{\lambda}^{\mathrm{T}} \nabla \mathbf{h}(\mathbf{x}^*) + \boldsymbol{\gamma}^{\mathrm{T}} \nabla \mathbf{g}(\mathbf{x}^*) = \mathbf{0} \qquad \text{(A.19)}$$

$$\boldsymbol{\gamma}^{\mathrm{T}} \mathbf{g}(\mathbf{x}^*) = \mathbf{0}. \qquad \text{(A.20)}$$

Note that the gradient of a vector function is a matrix; e.g., $(\nabla \mathbf{h}(\mathbf{x}))_{ij} = \partial h_i(\mathbf{x})/\partial x_j$.

In the following second-order sufficient condition, we use the notation $\mathbf{H}_{h_i}(\mathbf{x})$ to denote the Hessian matrix for the function $h_i(\mathbf{x})$.

Theorem A.7. Assume $f, \mathbf{h}, \mathbf{g} \in C^2$. If a point $\mathbf{x}^*$ satisfies the constraints $\mathbf{h}(\mathbf{x}^*) = \mathbf{0}$ and $\mathbf{g}(\mathbf{x}^*) \leq \mathbf{0}$, then there exist $\boldsymbol{\lambda} \in \mathbb{R}^p$ and $\boldsymbol{\gamma} \in \mathbb{R}^q$ where $\boldsymbol{\gamma} \geq \mathbf{0}$ such that

$$[\nabla f(\mathbf{x}^*)]^T + \boldsymbol{\lambda}^T \nabla \mathbf{h}(\mathbf{x}^*) + \boldsymbol{\gamma}^T \nabla \mathbf{g}(\mathbf{x}^*) = \mathbf{0} \tag{A.21}$$

$$\boldsymbol{\gamma}^T \mathbf{g}(\mathbf{x}^*) = 0, \tag{A.22}$$

and the Hessian matrix

$$\mathbf{H}(\mathbf{x}^*) = \mathbf{H}_f(\mathbf{x}^*) + \sum_{i=1}^{p} \lambda_i \mathbf{H}_{h_i}(\mathbf{x}^*) + \sum_{j=1}^{q} \gamma_j \mathbf{H}_{g_j}(\mathbf{x}^*) \tag{A.23}$$

is positive-definite on the subspace

$$S = \{\mathbf{y} \mid \nabla \mathbf{h}(\mathbf{x}^*)\mathbf{y} = 0 \quad \text{and} \quad \mathbf{y}^T \nabla g_j(\mathbf{x}^*) = 0 \quad \text{for all} \quad j \in J\} \tag{A.24}$$

where $J = \{j \mid g_j(\mathbf{x}^*) = 0, \gamma_j > 0\}$.

These conditions tell us that the basic idea of seeking the point with zero gradient still applies as in the unconstrained optimization case, except that it should be for a new function formed from the function being optimized and the constraints. In the simplest case with only equality constraints, this combined function is called the Lagrangian of the problem and is defined as

$$L(\mathbf{x}, \boldsymbol{\lambda}) = f(\mathbf{x}) + \boldsymbol{\lambda}^T \mathbf{h}(\mathbf{x}) \tag{A.25}$$

Constrained optimization methods are more involved and are not as widely used in neural network studies, because constraints are usually enforced by the network's structures. Therefore, a condensed introduction to constrained optimization methods will not be presented here, because it would be difficult to digest. Interested readers are referred to the sources listed in the following bibliography.

BIBLIOGRAPHY

P.R. Adby and M.A.H. Dempster. *Introduction to Optimization Methods*. Halsted Press, New York, 1974.

L. Cooper and D. Steinberg. *Introduction to Methods of Optimization*. Saunders, Philadelphia, 1970.

R.W. Daniels. *An Introduction to Numerical Methods and Optimization Techniques*. North-Holland, New York, 1978.

Karl-Heinz Elster, editor. *Modern Mathematical Methods of Optimization*. VCH, New York, 1993.

R. Fletcher. *Practical Methods of Optimization*. 2nd ed. Wiley, New York, 1987.

J.E. Dennis Jr. and R.B. Schnabel. *Numerical Methods for Unconstrained Optimization and Nonlinear Equations*. Prentice-Hall, Englewood Cliffs, NJ, 1983.

D.G. Luenberger. *Linear and Nonlinear Programming*. Addison-Wesley, Reading, MA, 1984.

D.G. Luenberger. *Optimization by Vector Space Methods*. Wiley, New York, 1969.

E. Polak. *Computational Methods in Optimization: A Unified Approach*. Academic Press, New York, 1971.

INDEX

DISCARD